GLOBAL STRATEGIC MANAGEMENT

PHILIPPE LASSERRE

GLOBAL STRATEGIC MANAGEMENT

THIRD EDITION

palgrave
macmillan

First edition 2002
Second edition 2007
Third edition published 2012 by
PALGRAVE MACMILLAN

Palgrave Macmillan in the UK is an imprint of Macmillan Publishers Limited, registered in England, company number 785998, of Houndmills, Basingstoke, Hampshire RG21 6XS.

Palgrave Macmillan in the US is a division of St Martin's Press LLC, 175 Fifth Avenue, New York, NY 10010.

Palgrave Macmillan is the global academic imprint of the above companies and has companies and representatives throughout the world.

ISBN-13: 978-0-230-29381-6

This book is printed on paper suitable for recycling and made from fully managed and sustained forest sources. Logging, pulping and manufacturing processes are expected to conform to the environmental regulations of the country of origin.

A catalogue record for this book is available from the British Library.

A catalog record for this book is available from the Library of Congress.

10 9 8 7 6 5 4 3 2 1
21 20 19 18 17 16 15 14 13 12

Printed and bound in China

To Michelle

During the preparation of this third edition my wife, Michelle, left our world. I want to thank her for all the support she gave me despite her suffering and I want to dedicate this book to her.

Heureux qui comme Ulysse a fait un beau voyage (J. DU BELLAY)

ABOUT THE AUTHOR

Philippe Lasserre is Emeritus Professor of Strategy and Asian Business at INSEAD.

He obtained his masters degree from ESSEC (Paris) and his PhD from the University of Texas at Austin. Since 1975, he has been involved in teaching, research, and consulting in strategic management and international business. He is the author of various articles on strategy, business in Asia and joint ventures and he has co-authored *Strategies for Asia Pacific* (Palgrave Macmillan: 1995, 1999, 2006) and *Strategy and Management in Asia Pacific* (McGraw-Hill: 1999). He has been a visiting professor in various universities in Singapore, at the China European Business School in Beijing and Shanghai, at the University of Texas in Dallas, at Curtin University in Perth, and finally at Thunderbird University in Glendale Arizona. He currently lives in France.

BRIEF CONTENTS

Part I THE PROCESS OF GLOBALIZATION 1

Chapter 1 Globalization of markets and competition 2
2 Designing a global strategy 26
3 Designing a global organization 71
4 Global strategic alliances 104
5 Global mergers and acquisitions 149
6 Assessing countries' attractiveness 174
7 Entry strategies 206

II MANAGING GLOBALLY 227

8 Global marketing 228
9 Global operations 249
10 Global innovation 284
11 Cross-cultural management 310
12 Global human resource management 335
13 Global financial management 363

III BROAD ISSUES IN GLOBALIZATION 399

14 Emerging global players 400
15 The social responsibility of the global firm 420
16 Global trends 456

Glossary 489
Index of subjects 505
Index of names 509
Index of companies and organizations 513

LONG CONTENTS

	List of figures	xviii
	List of tables	xxiii
	List of Mini-Cases	xxvi
	List of examples	xxvii
	Mini-cases and examples grids	xxviii
	List of abbreviations	xxxi
	Tour of the book	xxxii
	Publisher's acknowledgements	xxxiv
	Introduction to the third edition	xxxix
	How can this book be used?	xli
	Appendix I.1 List of potential case studies to be used to support the book	xlii
	Notes	xlv
	References and further reading	xlv
Part I	**THE PROCESS OF GLOBALIZATION**	1
Chapter 1	**Globalization of markets and competition**	2
	The phenomenon of globalization	2
	What are the factors that push for globalization?	4
	The benefits of globalization	7
	The factors that work against globalization: the localization push	12
	The benefits of localization	15
	Global/multi-local mapping	16
	Globalization: the macro picture	17
	Summary and key points	20
	Appendix 1.1 Positioning a business on the global/multi-local mapping	21
	Learning assignments	22
	Key words	23
	Web resources	23
	Notes	24
	References and further reading	24

Chapter 2 Designing a global strategy 26
A company business strategy 29
Framework for a global strategy 32
Global strategies and the small and medium-sized enterprise (SME) 51
Summary and key points 59
Appendix 2.1 Measuring corporate globalization 62
Appendix 2.2 Selected government support programs 66
Learning assignments 67
Key words 67
Web resources 67
Notes 68
References and further reading 69

Chapter 3 Designing a global organization 71
Structure, processes and culture 72
The global functional model 77
The geographical model 80
The single matrix model 82
The multi-business global product division model 84
The multi-business geographical model 86
The multi-business matrix model 87
Hybrid structural models 91
The transnational model 92
Regional organizational structures 94
Summary and key points 99
Appendix 3.1 Types of organizational design 100
Learning assignments 101
Key words 101
Web resources 102
Notes 102
References and further reading 102

Chapter 4 Global strategic alliances 104
Strategic alliances: typology and framework 105
Global alliances 106
Understanding the strategic context and spelling out the strategic value of an alliance 112
Partner analysis 115
Negotiation and design 122
Implementation 128
Global multilateral alliances 132
Alliance constellation management 133
Local joint ventures 134

	Partner selection	136
	Joint venture decay and failure	139
	Criteria for successful alliances	141
	Summary and key points	144
	Learning assignments	146
	Key words	146
	Web resources	147
	Notes	147
	References and further reading	147
Chapter 5	**Global mergers and acquisitions**	149
	The rationale for cross-border M&A's	150
	Cross-border acquisitions performance	154
	Deciding on the M&A	155
	Integrating the companies: the integration phase	159
	Integrating the companies: the transition phase	162
	Integrating the companies: the consolidation phase	165
	Summary and key points	168
	Learning assignments	171
	Key words	171
	Web resources	171
	Notes	171
	References and further reading	172
Chapter 6	**Assessing countries' attractiveness**	174
	Why is a country attractive?	174
	Market, resources and industry opportunities	177
	Assessing market opportunities	178
	Assessing resource opportunities	183
	Competitive context	187
	Country risk analysis	190
	Putting it all together	192
	Summary and key points	198
	Appendix 6.1 Comparison of Brazil and Mexico, household expenditures and appliances	202
	Learning assignments	203
	Key words	203
	Web resources	204
	Notes	204
	References and further reading	205
Chapter 7	**Entry strategies**	206
	Why enter? Defining strategic objectives for a country presence	207
	When to enter? First mover, follower or acquirer?	208

Entry modes: how to enter? 210
Entering a country through wholly-owned subsidiaries 211
Entering a country through acquisitions 212
Entering a country through joint ventures 214
Entering a country through arm's-length agreements: licensing, franchising, agents and distributors 215
Entering a country through a representative, technical or procurement office 216
Entry modes seen as 'real options' 217
Comparing entry modes 217
Choosing an entry mode 218
Summary and key points 220
Learning assignments 224
Key words 224
Web resources 224
Notes 224
References and further reading 225

Part II MANAGING GLOBALLY 227

Chapter 8 Global marketing 228
Customer behavior, convergence and global segmentation 228
Product standardization 230
Global branding 231
Advertising 234
Global solution selling 239
Global marketing positioning 242
Summary and key points 243
Learning assignments 246
Key words 246
Web resources 247
Notes 247
References and further reading 247

Chapter 9 Global operations 249
The globalization of value chains: offshore production and outsourcing 251
Selecting operational sites 253
Global manufacturing networks 253
Global sourcing 258
Global logistics 261
The global management of infrastructure projects 263
Internet and global operations 266
Summary and key points 275

Learning assignments 281
Key words 281
Web resources 281
Notes 282
References and further reading 282

Chapter 10 Global innovation 284
The international product life cycle model 284
Globalization of R&D: benefits and constraints 288
Design of global R&D networks 289
Management of global R&D networks 290
International transfer of technology 293
Global knowledge management 295
Summary and key points 302
Learning assignments 306
Key words 307
Web resources 307
Notes 307
References and further reading 307

Chapter 11 Cross-cultural management 310
Failures in cross-cultural interaction 310
The different facets of culture 311
National cultural differences 312
The impact of cultures on global management 320
Summary and key points 329
Learning assignments 332
Key words 332
Web resources 332
Notes 332
References and further reading 333

Chapter 12 Global human resource management 335
Assignment of personnel: the global human resource wheel 337
Expatriate management 339
Localization 348
Skills development 352
Summary and key points 356
Learning assignments 359
Key words 359
Web resources 359
Notes 360
References and further reading 360

Chapter 13 Global financial management 363
Hedging against currency fluctuations 364
Project finance 367
Global capital structure 369
Trade finance 373
Summary and key points 376
Appendix 13.1 Hedging exposure to currency risk: a case study 379
Appendix 13.2 A pulp mill project in Indonesia 386
Appendix 13.3 Development banks providing project equity funding 390
Appendix 13.4 Official export credit agencies for OECD member countries 394
Learning assignments 396
Key words 397
Web resources 397
Notes 398
References and further reading 398

PART III BROAD ISSUES IN GLOBALIZATION

Chapter 14 Emerging global players 400
Emerging countries and their development 400
Emerging countries and their institutional and business environments 404
Emerging countries and global firms 405
Summary and key points 414
Appendix 14.1 A profile of the BRICS (2009) 415
Learning assignments 417
Key words 417
Web resources 418
Notes 418
References and further reading 418

Chapter 15 The social responsibility of the global firm 420
Corporate social responsibility 421
An ongoing debate 421
Global companies and business ethics 423
Global companies and sustainable development 429
Global corporations and human dignity 434
Global corporations and global citizenship 439
Social responsibility and global firms: an on-going challenge 443
Summary and key points 445
Appendix 15.1 The OECD Guidelines for Multinational Enterprises 448
Appendix 15.2 Major business ethics codes 449
Appendix 15.3 Main nongovernment organizations involved in corporate social responsibility 450

	Learning assignments	451
	Key words	452
	Web resources	452
	Notes	452
	References and further reading	454
Chapter 16	**Global trends**	456
	Global challenges	457
	Future scenarios	471
	The future of global corporations	474
	Summary and key points	478
	Appendix 16.1 A simplified methodology for elaborating scenarios	481
	Learning assignments	484
	Key words	484
	Web resources	485
	Notes	485
	References and further reading	486
	Glossary	489
	Index of subjects	505
	Index of names	509
	Index of companies and organizations	513

LIST OF FIGURES

1.1	International transportation and communication costs, 1920–90	5
1.2	Globalization push factors	7
1.3	A multinational competitive configuration	10
1.4	A global competitive configuration	11
1.5	Historically globalization took place in three steps	12
1.6	Localization push factors	15
1.7	Global/multi-local mapping: different industries have different competitive requirements	16
1.8	Global/multi-local mapping for the financial sector: different segments have different competitive requirements	17
2.1	Business, corporate and global strategy	28
2.2	The purpose of strategy	29
2.3	SONY's global development	31
2.4	Global strategy framework	32
2.5	Mapping of global ambition	35
2.6	Mapping of the tire industry	36
2.7	The evolution of Whirlpool globalization (GRI)	37
2.8	Generic value chain	40
2.9	Typical globalization of the value chain	41
2.10	A generic global distribution of activities in the value chain	42
2.11	Sources of competitive advantage	43
2.12	The Transfer, Adapt, Create model applied to the globalization of mass retailing	46
2.13	The global/multi-local mapping and global structures	50
2.14	National strategies: capital allocation filter	57
2.15	Essilor's business process	58
2.16	Perspective of market development	59
2.A1	A graphical representation of the Global Revenue Index (GRI)	64
3.1	Philips and Matsushita: global organizational designs and their evolution	76
3.2	The global functional organizational design	78
3.3	The geographical organizational design	80

3.4 The single matrix organizational design 83
3.5 The multi-business global product division organizational design 85
3.6 Multi-business geographical organizational design 86
3.7 Multi-business matrix organizational design 88
3.8 The evolution of global organizational models 91
3.9 Convergence of global organizational designs 93
3.10 Profiles of regional headquarters in global firms 94
3.11 Organizational structure of regional headquarters 97
3.12 ACER's organizational model 98
4.1 Various types of international alliances 106
4.2 Framework for the analysis of strategic alliances 108
4.3 Organization of the Cross Company Teams and Global Alliance Committee in the Renault–Nissan Alliance 109
4.4 The Nissan Revival Plan and the Cross Functional Teams 110
4.5 New organization of the Renault–Nissan Alliance 111
4.6 Renault alliances and global acquisition network 112
4.7 Value creation and extraction in alliances 114
4.8 Fit analysis in strategic alliances 115
4.9 Assessing the strategic fit based on the criticality of the alliance for partners 116
4.10 Strategic fit against partners' strategic agendas 118
4.11 Method for assessing capabilities fit 119
4.12 Capabilities fit in the case of Renault and Nissan 120
4.13 Organizational designs in alliances 122
4.14 Typical items in a joint venture agreement 124
4.15 Alliance stages and alliance managers' skills 127
4.16 Communications flows in alliances 128
4.17 The 'death valley' spiral 129
4.18 Types of alliance constellations 132
4.19 Partner choices in country-based joint ventures 136
4.20 Joint venture decay 140
5.1 Trends in global mergers and acquisitions, 1990–2010 150
5.2 The pre-acquisition and post-acquisition processes in global M&As 155
5.3 Cash flow-based valuation for M&As 159
5.4 Contingent integration modes 161
6.1 General investment framework 175
6.2 Framework for country market, resources and industry attractiveness assessment 177
6.3 Relationship between GDP per capita and Internet users per 100 people, 2009 179
6.4 Relationship between GDP per capita and the production of cement per capita, 2010 180

6.5 The 'middle-class effect' 180
6.6 The 'middle-class effect' in China 181
6.7 Market segmentations 182
6.8 Cost of labor and level of education in service industry 186
6.9 Overall quality of infrastructure 187
6.10 Framework for country risk analysis 191
6.11 Variability of economic growth, Argentina versus Brazil, 1970–2009 192
6.12 Political and economic risks in selected countries 193
6.13 Foreign direct investment and country risks 194
6.14 Overall risk profile and average yearly growth in household appliances, Mexico and Brazil, 2005–2009 203
7.1 Entry modes 210
7.2 Factors influencing entry modes 211
7.3 Mapping of entry modes choices 219
8.1 Western versus Asian hierarchy of needs 229
8.2 Customer segmentation 230
8.3 Global product standardization types 231
8.4 Global brand positioning 233
8.5 A financial global account management network servicing a leading European manufacturer 239
8.6 Global solution selling: an international bid for a power plant in China 240
8.7 Capabilities required for global solution selling 241
8.8 Sales and distribution 241
8.9 Various global marketing positions 242
9.1 The global operations network 249
9.2 Forms of offshoring 251
9.3 Strategic roles of international factories and their evolution 254
9.4 Different models of internationalization of services 257
9.5 Different global sourcing designs 258
9.6 Michelin's European flow of products 262
9.7 Airbus logistics 263
9.8 Players in an international infrastructure project 264
9.9 Players in the Internet space 268
9.10 Reach versus richness trade-off 269
10.1 The international product life cycle 285
10.2 Nestlé global R&D architecture 286
10.3 Global resources leveraging for HDD technology at ST Microelectronic 287
10.4 Evolution over time of global R&D activities 289
10.5 Global R&D projects 292

10.6	Knowledge creation, sharing and 'melding' in global firms	297
11.1	The three layers of culture	311
11.2	Country clusters	316
11.3	Framework for negotiation with reference to international contracts	321
11.4	Negotiation attributes and cultural differences	323
12.1	Global human resource issues	335
12.2	The global human resource wheel	338
12.3	Human resource wheels	338
12.4	The changing nature of international staffing	339
12.5	The expatriate challenges	340
12.6	Expatriates' acculturation: the 'four Fs'	341
12.7	The primary ingredients of individual managerial behavior required for success in expatriate assignments in Asia	343
12.8	Indices of cost of living and wage level in the world (base 100 in New York)	344
12.9	Expatriate tenure	346
12.10	Human resources practices supporting expatriation	347
12.11	Global management development in a global oil company	354
13.1	Key issues in global financial management	363
13.2	Variation of major currencies against the US$, 1990 to 2010, yearly average	364
13.3	Documentary credit in international trade	374
13.A1	The option hedge for the US champagne distributor	384
13.A2	The forward and option hedges for the US champagne distributor	385
13.A3	Projected cash flows for LouisianaPaper project	387
13.A4	The Indonesia project is still more attractive in spite of higher inflation	388
13.A5	The Indonesia project NPV goes down just below the Singaporean project, which is free of political and tax risks	389
13.A6	The Indonesian project is better than the Singaporean one if there is no terrorist attack or if there is only a 10% chance of terrorist attack with no tax increase	390
14.1	GDP growth rates: emerging countries vs. the world (average 2000–2009)	401
14.2	Capital formation	403
14.3	Foreign trade and investments	404
14.4	The three segments in emerging markets	406
14.5	Advantages and disadvantages of offshoring and offsourcing in the various elements of the value chain	408
14.6	The strategic development of emerging markets champions	409
14.7	Competitive dynamic of emerging countries champions	409
15.1	Social responsibility issues and the global firm	420
15.2	The global ethical web	422

15.3 Corruption and development 426
15.4 Industrial CO_2 emissions, 1998, metric tons per capita 431
15.5 CO_2, temperature and sea level projections 431
15.6 Spot prices for CO_2 (EUA in Euros) 432
15.7 Eco-investment components 433
16.1 Global challenges and the global corporation 457
16.2 The global income gap, GDP per capita OECD/ low income, 1980–2010 461
16.3 Total primary energy demand in Million Tons of Oil Equivalent (MTOE) 464
16.4 Global temperatures and concentration of greenhouse gases (GHG) 1854–1994 465
16.5 Deforestation change in forest area between 1990 and 2010 466
16.6 Portfolio of processes 475
16.7 A new organizational model 475
16.A1 Decision tree of independent variables 483
16.A2 Example of simple causal paths for price setting in the oil industry 483

LIST OF TABLES

1.1	Globalization data	3
1.2	Illustrations of the shortening of product life cycles	6
1.3	The societal effects of globalization	18
2.1	Distribution of world market by region in selected industries in 2005 (percentage of US$ value)	34
2.2	Distribution of markets and revenues in tires (2010)	34
2.3	Global positioning	39
2.4	Capabilities leading to competitive advantage	43
2.5	Sources of competitive advantage of global companies	45
2.6	Building global sustainable advantage	45
2.7	Organizational designs for global strategies	48
2.8	SMEs' economic weight in Europe, USA and Asia Pacific	51
2.9	SMEs' internationalization forms and frequencies	52
2.10	Typology of international SMEs	52
2.11	Obstacles to internationalization as perceived by SMEs	53
2.12	HSBC distribution of net income and profit	56
2.A1	Ranking of global firms according to their TNIs (2010)	63
2.A2	Goodyear: calculation of the Global Revenue Index (GRI)	65
3.1	Philips's global organizational design until the late 1980s	73
3.2	Matsushita's global organizational design until the late 1980s	75
3.3	Characteristics of the global functional organizational design	79
3.4	Characteristics of geographical organizational design	81
3.5	Characteristics of the single matrix organizational design	83
3.6	Characteristics of the multi-business global product division organizational design	85
3.7	Characteristics of the multi-business geographical organizational design	87
3.8	Characteristics of the multi-business matrix organizational design	89
4.1	Main strategic objectives pursued in various types of alliance	113
4.2	Receptivity in learning	132
4.3	Types of local partners for market entry joint ventures	137

4.4	Eight criteria for successful alliances	141
5.1	Cross-border megamergers above US$20 billion, 2008–2011	151
5.2	List of acquisitions made by Mittal Steel prior to 2006	153
5.3	Value creation in M&As	156
5.4	Failures in the integration process	159
5.5	An example of a linear framework for integration	160
6.1	A selection of models and sources of countries' assessment	176
6.2	Macro indicators used in international market assessments	179
6.3	Characteristics of demand according to country life cycle clusters	183
6.4	Capital endowment of natural resources (2005)	184
6.5	Porter's industry analysis and international business entry	188
6.6	Major types of incentive for foreign investments	190
6.7	Cluster characteristics, Asia Pacific	195
6.8	Ease of doing business rankings for Poland, the Czech Republic and Hungary	198
7.1	Entry strategy objectives	209
7.2	Advantages and disadvantages of being a first mover	210
7.3	Types of local partners for country-based joint ventures	213
7.4	Comparing various entry modes	218
8.1	Customer needs and value curves	229
8.2	Top 10 global brands ranking (2011)	232
8.3	Examples of corporations using global and local brands	232
8.4	Major global advertising agencies, 2010	235
9.1	Index of offshoring in 2005	250
9.2	Criteria for facilities' location	252
9.3	Strategic roles of global factories	255
9.4	Phases in international infrastructure projects	265
9.5	Global use of the Internet	266
9.6	Effects of the Internet on globalization	271
9.7	Organizational requirements for e-business	273
10.1	R&D capabilities	285
10.2	Performance evaluation criteria	291
10.3	Classification of technology	294
10.4	Opportunities and constraints for knowledge management in global companies	295
10.5	Tools and approaches used for knowledge management in the metanational corporation	297
10.6	Intellectual property rights and their infringement	298
10.7	Protection of intellectual property rights	299
11.1	Trompenaars' six value orientations	314
11.2	Differences in economic cultures	318

11.3	Types of multicultural team	320
11.4	Impact of culture on negotiating behavior: a comparison of US and Japanese responses	324
11.5	Chinese business negotiating styles	325
11.6	Business practice differences	326
13.1	Summary statistics of monthly returns for some stock markets, 1999–2010, correlation coefficients	369
13.2	Country distribution of domestic and foreign listed companies for various stock exchanges, 2010	371
13.3	Types of international bond	372
13.A1	Comparison of currency option costs for four exchange rates	383
14.1	Difference between traditional middle-class strategies and bottom of the pyramid strategies	405
14.2	Some examples of emerging countries global champions	410
14.3	Analysis for possible PANELSOL expansion	412
15.1	Corruption indices	424
15.2	A checklist of anti-corruption measures	428
15.3	List of environmental issues linked to industrial and agricultural activities	430
15.4	Human rights principles for companies: a checklist	438
15.5	Global Compact and the Ten Principles	442
16.1	World population, from 2010 to 2100	460
16.2	Regional agreements	462
16.3	Global risks	468
16.4	Four global scenarios	471
16.5	Management competencies for new roles	476
16.6	Data relating to Pulau Vicente	478

LIST OF MINI-CASES

Mobile Telephony Services	19
HSBC: The World's Local Bank	55
Essilor: A Global Player	57
ACER: Global Organizational Evolution	97
Danone vs. Wahaha: Conflicts in a Joint Venture in China	142
The Acquisition of Harbin Brewery	166
Fastkomfort: Assessing Countries in Eastern Europe	195
Lubricador SA	219
HSBC Global/Local Advertising	242
eBay and Skype: Failed Synergies in the Internet Space	274
Global Giants' R&D Networks	299
Working Across Cultures: The Engineering Consultants' Clashes	327
Global Managers	354
Aguaciudad in the Philippines	375
PANELSOL Ltd	411
BYD (Build Your Dream)	413
Shell and Cosan	445
The Pandemic Threat	477

LIST OF EXAMPLES

Elevator industry	9
SONY Corporation	29
White goods industry	36
Gemplus	55
Philips	72
Matsushita	74
Apple	79
International Service Systems	81
Citigroup	84
3M	85
SABMiller	87
BASF	88
DaimlerChrysler–Mitsubishi, and Renault–Nissan	105
The Renault–Nissan Alliance	108
DaimlerChrysler	151
Air France KLM	152
Lenovo and IBM	152
SONY/Columbia Studios	152
ArcelorMittal	153
South African Brewery	154
Carrefour	206
Citibank	238
Li and Fung	258
Freemarkets Online and Ariba	260
Michelin	261
Enron	265
Yahoo!	271
Nestlé	286
ST Microelectronic	287
Hewlett Packard (HP)	291
Helvetica Chemical	336
Asea Brown Boveri (ABB)	351
Saurer	407
Unilever	407
General Electric	407
Soccer balls (Sialkot and Reebok)	435
Nike	436
Unocal and Total of France	437
AMD	440
HP and i-community	440
Bayer	440
Carrefour	440
DaimlerChrysler	441
IndoMedia	444
The Millennium Project	473

MINI-CASES AND EXAMPLES GRIDS

The following grid demonstrates the geographical reach of the Mini-Cases and the examples which have been highlighted in the third edition. The companies featured in these cases and examples have been chosen because they are 'transnational' and have their origins in a diverse range of countries, from China to the Philippines, and the USA to Brazil.

Mini-Cases

Chapter	Title of Mini-Case	Worldwide	Europe	Asia/ Middle East	Americas	Asia Pacific	Africa	Oceania
1	Mobile telephony services	X						
2	HSBC: The World's Local Bank		X	X	X	X	X	
2	Essilor: a global player		X	X	X	X	X	
3	ACER: Global Organizational Evolution	X	X	X	X	X		
4	Danone vs. Wahaha: Conflicts in a Joint Venture in China		X			X		
5	The Acquisition of Harbin Brewery				X	X	X	X
6	Fastkomfort: Assessing Countries in Eastern Europe		X					
7	Lubricador SA		X			X		
8	HSBC Global/Local Advertising	X						
9	eBay and Skype: Failed Synergies in the Internet Space		X		X			
10	Global Giants' R&D Networks		X	X	X	X		
11	Working Across Cultures: The Engineering Consultants' Clashes		X		X	X		X
12	Global Managers		X		X	X		
13	Aguaciudad in the Philippines		X			X		
14	PANELSOL Ltd		X	X	X	X		
14	BYD (Build Your Dream)		X	X	X	X		
15	Shell and Cosan		X		X			
16	The Pandemic Threat							X

Examples

Chapter	Company/industries in example	Worldwide	Europe	Asia/ Middle East	Americas	Asia Pacific	Africa	Oceania
1	Elevator industry	X	X	X				
2	SONY Corporation		X		X	X		
2	White goods industry		X		X	X		
2	Gemplus		X		X	X		
3	Philips		X		X			
3	Matsushita		X		X	X		X
3	Apple	X			X			
3	International Service Systems		X		X	X		
3	Citigroup	X		X	X	X		
3	3M	X						
3	SABMiller	X	X		X	X	X	
3	BASF	X	X	X	X	X	X	X
4	DaimlerChrysler–Mitsubishi, and Renault–Nissan		X			X		
4	The Renault–Nissan Alliance		X			X		
5	DaimlerChrysler		X		X	X		
5	Air France KLM		X		X	X		
5	Lenovo and IBM							
5	SONY/Columbia Studios				X	X		X
5	ArcelorMittal		X	X	X			
5	South African Brewery		X		X	X	X	
7	Carrefour		X			X		
8	Citibank	X	X		X	X		
9	Li and Fung		X		X	X	X	

Examples *cont.*									
Chapter	**Company/industries in example**	**Worldwide**	**Europe**	**Asia/ Middle East**	**Americas**	**Asia Pacific**	**Africa**	**Oceania**
9	Freemarkets Online and Ariba	X						
9	Michelin		X		X	X		
9	Enron			X				
9	Yahoo!		X		X			
10	Nestlé		X		X	X	X	
10	ST Microelectronic	X	X					
10	Hewlett Packard (HP)				X	X		
12	Helvetica Chemical		X		X			
12	Colgate-Palmolive	X			X			
12	Asea Brown Boveri (ABB)				X	X		
14	Saurer		X			X		
14	Unilever				X			
14	General Electric			X				
15	Soccer balls (Sialkot and Reebok)			X				
15	Nike				X	X		
15	Unocal and Total of France		X		X	X		
15	AMD	X						
15	HPI			X				
15	Bayer						X	
15	Carrefour				X			
15	DaimlerChrysler				X			
15	IndoMedia					X		
16	The Millennium Project	X						

LIST OF ABBREVIATIONS

APV	Adjusted Present Value
ASEAN	Association of South East Asian Nations
ASP	Application Service Providers
B2B	Business to Business
BOT	Build Operate and Transfer
BPI	Bribe Payers Index
CEO	Chief Executive Officer
CIA	Central Intelligence Agency
CIF	Cost Insurance Freight
CPI	Corruption Perception Index
EDI	Electronic Data Interchange
EIU	Economist Intelligence Unit
FDI	Foreign Direct Investment
FOB	Free on Board
GATT	General Agreement on Trade and Tariffs
GBU	Global Business Unit
GCI	Global Capability Index
GDP	Gross Domestic Product
GDP/Cap	Gross Domestic Product per capita
GNP	Gross National Product
GNP/Cap	Gross National Product per capita
GRI	Global Revenue Index
HRM	Human Resource Management
IFI	International Financial Institution
II	Internalization Index
ILO	International Labour Organization
IMD	International Institute for Management Development
IMF	International Monetary Fund
IPR	Intellectual Property Rights
IRR	Internal Rate of Return
JIT	Just in Time
JV	Joint Venture
LIBOR	London Inter-Bank Offered Rate
M&A	Mergers and Acquisitions
MNC	Multinational Corporation
NAFTA	North American Free Trade Agreement
NPV	Net Present Value
NYSE	New York Stock Exchange
OECD	Organisation for Economic Cooperation and Development
OEM	Original Equipment Manufacturing
PCN	Parent Country National
PPP	Purchasing Power Parity
R and D or R&D	Research and Development
RFQ	Request for Quotation
RHQ	Regional Headquarters
ROI	Return on Investment
ROW	Rest of World
SBU	Strategic Business Unit
SME	Small and Medium-sized Enterprise
SRI	Socially Responsible Investing
TCN	Third Country National
TI	Transparency International
TNC	Transnational Corporation
TNI	Transnational Index
UN	United Nations
UNCTAD	United Nations Centre for Trade and Development
WACC	Weighted Average Cost of Capital
WTO	World Trade Organisation

TOUR OF THE BOOK

1 CHAPTER INTRODUCTION AND LEARNING OBJECTIVES | These are a guide through the material in each chapter and allow progress to be checked.

chapter

1 GLOBALIZATION OF MARKETS AND COMPETITION

Introduction

Chapter 1 defines what globalization means for a business enterprise. It differentiates globalization from the traditional process of setting up subsidiaries abroad and makes a distinction between a *multinational company* and a *global company*. Based on the example of the Otis Elevator Company, it looks at how a company having multiple international subsidiaries can move toward a global competitive configuration through which its international activities can be strongly coordinated and integrated across borders. This transition from a multinational to a global position was driven by various social, political, economic and technological factors that are described in the chapter. The benefits of globalization are described, as well as the constraints. Some factors are still pushing toward a local approach to management, on a country-by-country basis, and the factors inducing this localization are analyzed.

Finally, global/multi-local mapping is presented as a tool to position industries, companies and businesses according to the relative importance of global versus local approaches. The chapter ends by introducing some of the societal issues associated with globalization.

Learning objectives

At the end of the chapter you will be able to:

- define globalization, understand what a global firm is, and how it differs from a multinational company
- identify the forces pushing toward globalization
- identify the forces pushing for localization
- position an industry or a business on the global/multi-local map
- discuss the benefits and pitfalls of globalization.

The phenomenon of globalization

Over the past 30 years international trade and investment have grown much faster than the world economy as a whole. Firms have multiplied their presence outside their country of origin, employing more and more people and selling and buying technology internationally. (See Table 1.1). More and more products are sold in similar stores, with similar features and carry a common brand across the globe. Factories that were prosperous in the Western

2 MINI-CASES | Chapters contain case studies to help you apply key concepts in global strategy to the real world of business. The case studies are largely based on diverse 'transnational' companies originating from, for example, China, the Philippines, Latin America, Europe and the USA and which operate across the world.

1 GLOBALIZATION OF MARKETS AND COMPETITION

MINI-CASE

Mobile Telephony Services

Mobile telephony expanded rapidly during the two decades of the 1990s and 2000s. By 2011 there were around 5.2 billion mobile subscribers in the world (77% of the world's population).

According to the International Telecommunication Union (ITC), the distribution of customers is as follows: Asia Pacific: 2.649 billion, Americas: 880 million, Europe: 741 million, rest of the world: 979 million.

The industry is divided broadly into two major sub-industries: a) mobile equipment manufacturers: phones and docking stations, for example; and 2) mobile services operators.

Around the world, mobile services are operated mainly by local telephone companies with their own national brands. Some operators such as Vodaphone (UK) or Orange (France) have developed their presence internationally by acquiring or participating in the capital of local operators.

Most consumers use pre-paid services for the use of mobile phones. Various packages of pre-paid services as well as additional add-ons (Internet access, mobile banking, email, games...) are offered by the operators according to the characteristics of their markets. Customers are divided between personal accounts (roughly 65 to 90%, according to the country) and corporate accounts (from 10 to 35%). Some of the corporate accounts are multinational firms that want to benefit from a 'global' offer.

Mobile operators purchase their own network equipment and control its installation. They also procure large quantities of handsets that they include in their pre-paid contracts at discounted prices.

The key activities of mobile phone operators are:

- Procurement of network hardware and software: suppliers are multinational firms such as Nokia, Erikson and Alcatel-Lucent. There are two major standards used in the world: Global Standard Mobile with around 80% penetration and CDMA (15%). Japan and Korea use a standard of their own.
- Procurement of handsets. The major manufacturers of handsets are Nokia (23% global market share), Samsung (16%), LG (7.5%), BlackBerry (3%) and Apple (4.6%).
- Network installation and maintenance carried out by equipment suppliers plus local infrastructure companies under the control of the service provider.
- Software developments for new applications and services. From 2008 to 2011 around 300,000 applications for mobile phones and smartphones have been developed in the world. The main applications are games, news and social networking.
- Marketing and brand management. Products are marketed under a variety of local brands. Multinational players try to use their global brand (such as Orange), although advertising is country specific.
- Sales and distribution are organized differently from country to country.
- Billing is done according to local standards.
- Regulation with local authorities. Operators have to comply with local regulations.
- Finance and control. Treasury is managed centrally while day-to-day transactions are the duties of local managers.

3 FIGURES AND TABLES | The book makes full use of figures and tables, some classic and others new, to illustrate the theory.

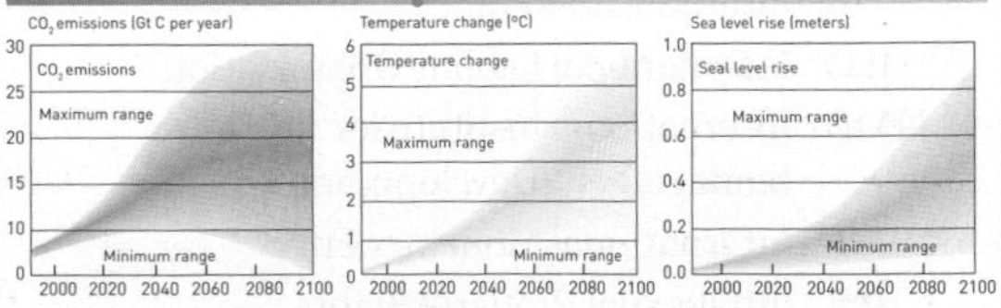

Figure 15.5 CO_2, temperature and sea level projections

Source: Intergovernmental Panel on Climate Change (2001) reproduced in *United Nation Framework Convention on Climate Change: The First Ten Years*, Bonn, Germany, Climate Change Secretariat, 2004, UNFCC, 2004 p. 22

4 IN-CHAPTER EXAMPLES | Examples are scattered throughout the text to consistently reinforce how the theory is put into practice. Longer examples are highlighted and exemplify global strategy at work in companies such as SONY, Gemplus, Apple and Carrefour.

Globalization at the level of the firm

EXAMPLE

To illustrate the phenomenon of globalization let us take the example of the elevator industry in Europe in the late 1960s as represented in Figure 1.3.

In each country of Europe, different firms fought for a share of the elevator market. Competitors were either local companies or subsidiaries of large multinational companies like Otis or Schindler. Each competitor designed, marketed, manufactured, installed and serviced elevators for their respective markets. The subsidiaries of the multinationals had all the activities of the value chain (marketing, design, production, installation and service) under their control. The French subsidiary of Otis designed elevators for the French market, manufactured them in French factories, sold them with a French sales force and maintained them with a French

5 SUMMARY AND KEY POINTS | These provide an abbreviated version of the main concepts and theories, useful for revision and checking understanding of the key points.

Summary and key points

1 Companies

A global company:

- can be defined as a company that operates in the main markets of the world in an integrated and coordinated way
- carries out one activity (e.g. manufacturing) or a component of the activity (e.g. manufacturing one sub-part only) of the value chain in one country, which serves the company's worldwide market.

A multinational company:

- operates in many markets of the world with little or no integration or coordination among

6 LEARNING ASSIGNMENTS | You can test your understanding of the chapter by undertaking these assignments, which also encourage further thought.

7 KEY WORDS | These appear at the end of each chapter and can be used as checklists for revision.

8 WEB RESOURCES | Useful web resources are included for students who want to go a little further.

Learning assignments

1 In 2010, the distribution of sales and people of AXA, the insurance company, is shown below:

	Europe	NAFTA	Asia	Rest of World
Revenue (billion €)	49,600	10,300	9400	12,800
Personnel	75,000	17,000	15,000	19,000

Assuming that the figures are representative of the situation in 2010, what is AXA's position on a GCI/GRI mapping?

2 In your opinion, for which industries could the UK, Italy and Australia be 'key' countries?

3 What could be the benefits of positioning oneself as a standardized global niche differentiator (see Table 2.3, p. 39)? What kind of competitive advantages does it require?

4 What are the capabilities needed to be a broad adaptive cost leader?

5 What are the ways to sustain competitive advantage?

6 What types of competitive advantage does being a first mover provide?

7 Can you sketch the mapping of the value chain for:

(a) A consulting firm

(b) An airline

(c) A trading firm

(d) A corporate and investment bank?

8 For each of the entities in Question 7 (a)–(d), can you represent a possible global distribution of their value chain, as illustrated in Figure 2.8 (p. 40)?

Key words

- Business strategy
- Corporate strategy
- Cost leadership
- Differentiation
- Global business strategy
- Global Capability Index
- Global corporate strategy
- Global positioning
- Global Revenue Index
- Value chain
- Value curve
- Value proposition

Web resources

<http://www.businessweek.com/globalbiz/index.html>
Business Week – Global business.

9 REFERENCES AND FURTHER READING | These sections identify key texts for further research and include books and journal articles.

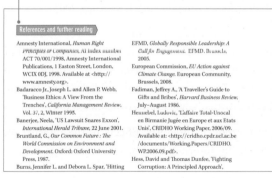

References and further reading

Amnesty International, *Human Right Principles of Companies*, AI Index number ACT 70/001/1998, Amnesty International Publications, 1 Easton Street, London, WCIX 0DJ, 1998. Available at <http://www.amnesty.org>.

Badaracco Jr., Joseph L. and Allen P. Webb, 'Business Ethics: A View From the Trenches', *California Management Review*, Vol. 37, 2, Winter 1995.

Banerjee, Neela, 'US Lawsuit Snares Exxon', *International Herald Tribune*, 22 June 2001.

Bruntland, G., *Our Common Future : The World Commission on Environment and Development*. Oxford: Oxford University Press, 1987.

Burns, Jennifer L. and Debora L. Spar, 'Hitting

EFMD, *Globally Responsible Leadership: A Call for Engagement*. EFMD. Brussels, 2005.

European Commission, *EU Action against Climate Change*. European Community, Brussels, 2008.

Fadiman, Jeffrey A., 'A Traveller's Guide to Gifts and Bribes', *Harvard Business Review*, July–August 1986.

Hennebel, Ludovic, 'L'affaire Total-Unocal en Birmanie Jugée en Europe et aux Etats Unis', CRIDHO Working Paper, 2006/09. Available at: <http://cridho.cpdr.ucl.ac.be/documents/Working.Papers/CRIDHO.WP.2006.09.pdf>.

Hess, David and Thomas Dunfee, 'Fighting Corruption: A Principled Approach',

10 COMPANION WEBSITE | www.palgrave.com/business/lasserre3e

Visit the companion website for a range of teaching and learning resources including:

For lecturers

- PowerPoint presentations for each chapter
- A lecturer manual containing guideline answers to Mini-Case questions; teaching notes; and answers to learning assignments
- A testbank of multiple choice and essay questions

For students

- Learning assignments
- Chapter-by-chapter links to suggested long case studies
- A searchable glossary of key terms
- A list of acronyms
- Web links and resources
- Multiple choice questions for revision

PUBLISHER'S ACKNOWLEDGEMENTS

The author and publishers are grateful to the following for permission to reproduce figures, tables and extracts of text:

The Academy of Management for permission to reproduce Figure 11.2, 'Country Clusters' from Ronen, S. and O. Shenkar, 'Clustering Countries on Attitudinal Dimensions: A Review and Synthesis', *Academy of Management Review*, 10(3), 1985, pp. 435–54.

Amnesty International Publications, for permission to reproduce Table 15.4 'Human rights principles for companies: a checklist', extracted from *Human Right Principles or Companies*, AI index number ACT 70/001/1998, Amnesty International Publications, <http://www.amnesty.org>.

A.T. Kearney for permission to reprint Figure 6.8, 'Cost of labour and level of education in services', from A.T. Kearney Global Services Location Index, 2007. Copyright © A.T. Kearney, 2007.

Booz & Company for permission to reproduce Table 5.5, 'An example of a linear framework for integration'. Adapted and reprinted with permission from 'Post-Merger Integration: What Makes Mergers Work?' by Albert J. Viscio, John R. Harbison, Amy Asin and Richard P. Vitaro from the Fourth Quarter 1999 issue of strategy+business magazine, published by Booz & Company. Copyright © 1999. All rights reserved. <http://www.strategy-business.com>

Business Strategy Review for permission to reproduce Table 9.6, 'Effects of the Internet on globalization' from Yip, G., 'Global Strategy in the Internet Era', Business Strategy Review 11(4), 2000, p. 6.

The Caux Round Table for permission to use Table 15.2, 'A checklist of anti-corruption measures' from the Caux Round Table Global Dialogue, September 2000, Singapore.

Essilor International for permission to use the two adapted figures in the Chapter 2 Mini-Case: 'Essilor's business process' on p. 58 (available at: *<http://www.essilor.com/en/Group/International/Pages/Organization.aspx>*) and 'Perspective of market development' on p. 59, taken from 'Perspective of market development, Presentation to Essilor shareholders of first half of 2011; ESTIN & CO for ESSILOR INTERNATIONAL, ESSILOR INTERNATIONAL © 2011 (available at: <http://www.essilor.com/en/shareholders/Reports/Essilor_Slides_H12011Results.pdf>).

Graham Hankison and Philippa Cowking for permission to adapt Figure 8.4, 'Global brand positioning', from Hankinson, G., and P. Cowking, *The Reality of Global Brands*. London: McGraw Hill, 1996.

HarperCollins for permission to use material from Ghoshal and Bartlett, *The Individualized Corporation: A Fundamentally New Approach to Management* in Figure 16.6, 'Portfolio of processes', Figure 16.7, 'A new organizational model', and Table 16.5, 'Management competencies for new roles'.

HSBC PLC for permission to reproduce material in the Mini-Case 'HSBC: The World's Local Bank' in Chapter 2, pp. 55–7 Data is taken from the *HSBC Annual Report 2010* available at <http://www.hsbc.com/1/2/investor-relations> and from the *Group Strategy, Investor Day* document of 11 May 2011, p.15. The figure entitled 'National strategies: capital allocation filter' can be found at: <http://www.hsbc.com/1/content/assets/investor_relations/strategy_day/2011/110511_strategy_day_gulliver.pdf>.

Harvard Business School for permission to reproduce the following figures in the book: Table 4.4, 'Eight criteria for successful alliances', from Moss Kanter, R., 'Collaborative Advantage', *Harvard Business Review*, July–August 1994, pp. 96–108, Harvard Business Press. Copyright © 2001, Harvard Business Publishing; Figure 9.3, 'Strategic roles of international factories and their evolution', and Table 9.3, 'Strategic roles of global factories', reprinted with permission from 'Making the Most of Foreign Factories' by Kasra Ferdows, *Harvard Business Review*, March 1997. Copyright © 1997 Harvard Business Publishing; Figure 10.3, 'Global resources leveraging for HDD technology at ST Microelectronic' and Figure 10.6, 'Knowledge creation, sharing and 'melding' in global firms', both from *From Global to Metanational: How Companies Win in the Knowledge Economy* by Yves L. Doz, Jose Santos, and Peter J. Williamson, Harvard Business Press, 2001. Copyright © 2001 Harvard Business Publishing; all rights reserved.

Hellmut Schütte and Palgrave Macmillan for permission to reproduce Figure 8.1, 'Western versus Asian hierarchy of needs', from Schutte, H., and D. Ciarlante, *Consumer Behaviour in Asia*, published 1998.

IDLO for permission to reproduce Table 11.4, 'Impact of culture on negotiating behaviour: a comparison of US and Japanese responses', from Sunshine, R.B., *Negotiating for International Development*, International Development Law Institute, Dordrecht: Martinus Nijhoff, 1990.

INSEAD for permission to reprint Figure 4.11 'Method for assessing capabilities fit', adapted from Krishna, L.N. and Francesca Gee, 'General Electric and SNECMA', INSEAD Case Study 04/94-3450, 1994; material in the Mini-Case entitled 'Global Managers' in Chapter 12, pp. 354–5 adapted from Henri Claude de Bettignies: 'Evaluation', INSEAD Euro Asia Centre Case. With Permission.

John Wiley and Sons for permission to use the figure 'Three Layers of Culture' from Laurent, A., *The cross-cultural puzzle of international human resource management*, 1986, and Figure 4.15,

'Alliance stages and alliance managers' skills' from Spekeman, Robert E. and Lynn A. Isabella, *Alliance Competence: Maximising the Value of Your Partnerships*. New York, 2000.

Lester Lloyd-Reason and Terry Mughan for permission to reproduce Table 2.10, 'Typology of international SMEs' from Lloyd-Reason, L. and T. Mughan (2003), 'Competing effectively in international markets: identifying need, sharing best practice and adding value to the Eastern Region through skills and knowledge transfer', *Final Report for the East of England Development Agency*, available at: <http://eastofenglandobservatory.org.uk>

The Millennium Report for permission to reproduce 'Global State of the Future in 2011 – The World Score Card' in Chapter 16, on p. 474 from *The Millennium Report 2011*, United Nations.

Nissan for permission to reproduce Figure 4.4, 'The Nissan Revival Plan and the Cross Functional Teams', from Nissan Motor Facts File, 2000; and Figure 4.5, 'New organization of the Renault–Nissan Alliance', available at: <http://www.renault.com/fr/groupe/l-alliance-renault-nissan/pages/fonctionnement-et-structure.aspx>.

Oanda.com for permission to reproduce Figure 13.2, 'Variation of major currencies against the US$, 1990–2010, yearly average'.

OECD for permission to reproduce the following tables and figures:

Table 2.11, 'Obstacles to internationalization as perceived by SMEs' (Figure 1, p. 46 from OECD (2008), *Removing Barriers to SME Access to International Markets*, OECD Publishing, <http://dx.doi.org/10.1787/9789264045866-en)>;

Table 9.1, 'Index of offshoring in 2005', based on data from Figure L.7.1. and Figure L.7.2., from OECD (2010), Measuring Globalisation: OECD Economic Globalisation Indicators 2010, OECD Publishing, <http://dx.doi.org/10.1787/9789264084360-en>.

Figure 16.4, 'Global temperatures and concentration of greenhouse gases (GHG), 1854–1994', reproduced from 'Meeting of the OECD Council at Ministerial Level 2001: Key Information'. <http://www.oecd.org/dataoecd/47/22/1869800.pdf>

We would also like to thank OECD for permission to adapt the following:

Figure 9.4, 'Different models of internationalization of services', based on Chart 2 from Lindner, A., B. Cave, L. Deloumeaux and J. Magdeleine, 'Trade in Goods and Services: Statistical Trends and Measurement Challenges', Statistics Brief, October 2001, No.1, <www.oecd.org/std/statisticsbrief>;

Appendix 2.2 'Selected government support programs', based on Annex 1.2 from OECD (2008), *Removing Barriers to SME Access to International Markets*, OECD Publishing, <http://dx.doi.org/10.1787/9789264045866-en>.

Pearson Education for permission to reproduce Table 11.3, 'Types of multicultural team', from Schneider and Barsoux, Managing Across Cultures, 2nd Edition 2003, p. 218.

Random House for permission to use material from Ghoshal and Bartlett, *The Individualized Corporation: A Fundamentally New Approach to Management* in Figure 16.6, 'Portfolio of processes', Figure 16.7, 'A new organizational model', and Table 16.5, 'Management competencies for new roles'.

Tony Fang, author of *Chinese Business Negotiating Style* (Thousand Oaks: Sage Publications) for permission to reproduce Table 11.5, 'Chinese business negotiating styles'.

Transparency International for permission to include Table 15.1, 'Corruption indices', reprinted from the Corruption Perceptions Index and the Bribe Payers Index, Copyright © 2011 Transparency International: the global coalition against corruption. Used with permission. For more information, visit <http://www.transparency.org>.

The UN for permission to reproduce Figure 15.5, 'CO_2, temperature and sea level projections' from *The United Nations Framework Convention on Climate Change: The First Ten Years*, Bonn, Germany Climate Change Secretariat, 2004, UNFCC, 2004, p. 22.

UNCTAD for permission to reproduce Table 1.1 'Globalization data' from the *UNCTAD World Investment Report 2011*; the table 'Ranking of Global firms according to their TNIs (2010)' on p. 63 in Appendix 2.1 from World Investment Report 2011, Annex table 29: 'The world's top 100 non-financial TNCs'; and Table 6.6, 'Major types of incentives for foreign investments', from *Incentives and Foreign Direct Investment: United Nations Conference on Trade and Development*. Geneva: United Nations Publications, 1996.

The World Economic Forum for permission to use Figure 6.9, 'Overall quality of infrastructure' from the *Global Competitiveness Report* (2010–11); and the table entitled 'An example of an uncertain scenario on p. 484 of Chapter 16, from 'China and the World: Scenarios to 2025'. World Economic Forum: <https://members.weforum.org/pdf/Asia/China_Scen.pdf>

INTRODUCTION TO THE THIRD EDITION

Since the second edition of this book published in 2007, the globalization of the economy has seen its momentum challenged by two financial crises. Starting in the USA, the so-called 'subprime' crisis has obliged governments around the world to engage in Neo-Keynesian policies in order to consolidate the stumbling global financial system. More recently the 'Eurozone' crisis has called into question one of the most ambitious international cooperations and has seen populations asking for more protectionism. In the Middle East, dictatorial regimes have been ousted by the revolutionary 'Arab Spring' and the newly formed governments are trying to find a way between global exchange and Islamic tradition. During these difficult times, emerging countries from Asia, Latin America and Africa have increasingly asserted their newly found economic and financial power and demanded a bigger participation in world governance. The tsunami that struck Fukushima in Japan in March 2011 creating a nuclear accident has convinced many nations to reconsider their energy policy. Despite all of this, globalization, even though criticized, is still active. Firms are moving to the new emerging economies in order to capture the consumption appetite of the growing middle classes. It is still relevant and important to put together all aspects of global strategic management.

This third edition is still about global firms and global management. Its objective remains to help undergraduate and graduate students, as well as company executives, to understand the main issues that companies and their managers confront when they 'go global' or 'manage globally', and to cope with these issues. Data have been updated and several new cases and examples added. At the end of each chapter there are now one or two new 'Mini-Cases' that students may discuss in class.

The book has been designed to support courses on strategic management in global firms, equivalent to a series of course notes to be read in preparation for a class or to compound and expand upon class content afterwards. Students can be assigned work on a case study for each of the topics covered in the book. The textbook can also be used as a guide for managers and executives.

There are a number of excellent textbooks on international business already available[1] so how does this book compare with others?

First, the focus of the book is on **firms and their employees**. It addresses the strategic and management issues that global companies confront when they operate across borders. From strategic analysis, formulation to implementation in the various business functions, the book reviews the main aspects of operating globally. Macroeconomic and political factors that traditional international business textbooks cover, such as international trade and investment flows, the problems of economic development in emerging countries, the analysis of international and regional institutions such as the World Trade Organisation (WTO), the United Nations (UN), the World Banks and other development banks, the European Union (EU), the North American Free Trade Agreement (NAFTA), the Association of South East Asian Nations (ASEAN) and the like, and the geopolitical analysis of diplomacy and defence are not discussed. It is assumed that students interested in those topics will read specialized books on the subjects or attend courses taught by economists or political scientists.

Second, the book takes the view that **the traditional international business paradigm based on the study of foreign investments in 'foreign' countries by 'home' country firms is no longer valid for studying global firms**. The home-host country traditional paradigm establishes a hierarchy among countries' business locations. As it will be argued and shown in the examples and cases in this book, global firms progressively abandon their original nationality to manage a network of firms in an integrated and coordinated way out of 'centers' that are no longer necessarily located in their country of origin. Scholars like Chris Bartlett, Sumantra Ghoshal, Yves Doz and C.K. Prahalad, and more recently Peter Williamson and José dos Santos,[2] have studied this evolution in business activity and they created the terms 'transnational' or 'metanational' to describe these new types of corporations. Later, George Yip analyzed what he called 'Total Global Strategy'[3] and this book was inspired largely by their theoretical and empirical work. Obviously, classic issues such as entry strategies or expatriate management will not be forgotten, but the overall tone of the book looks at how, ultimately, international or multinational firms become global and are managed globally.

Third, the book aims to **describe and analyze the key strategic and managerial challenges for firms**, but does not pretend to be exhaustive or encyclopaedic. As Michel Montaigne said, it is better *'d'avoir une tête bien faite qu'une tête bien pleine'* (to have a well-rounded brain rather than a full one). Since the book aims at providing present or future international managers with the strategic and managerial tools needed for operating globally a lot of theoretical developments have been deliberately omitted. Transaction costs theory, locational theory and agency theory, for instance, despite their scientific pertinence, have been left out because their treatment would require more space than is available here. The quotation of a multitude of articles published in academic journals and collections of papers in the field of international business such as the *Journal of International Studies*, the *Strategic Management Journal* or the *Academy of Management Journal* has been strictly limited. Those who want to know more are invited to look at the lists of 'References and further reading' at the end of each chapter as well as the works quoted during the text.

Fourth, it appeared important to illustrate the points made in the text with **several new examples and Mini-Cases** that have been inserted in the chapters. These examples and Mini-Cases deal with 'transnational' firms from various places of origin such as China, the Philippines, Latin America, Europe and the USA, which now operate across the world.

Finally, the book borrows considerably from the work done by professors or ex-professors at the **European Institute of Business Administration (INSEAD)**, and has favoured their works rather than others. This has been a deliberate choice, given the long-standing involvement of the author in the intellectual life of this institution and the quality of the research undertaken there.

How can this book be used?

This book can be used in three ways:

- As a stand-alone textbook for a course based on lectures and exercises. At the end of each chapter there are questions that can serve as learning assignments to prepare for such lectures, or to follow them.
- As background reading for a course based on case studies. To that end, the book's Appendix below lists potential cases that the author has used to support each chapter of the book. Those cases are available in international clearing houses such the Harvard Business School Clearing House or the European Case Clearing House. There are also some excellent casebooks available.[4]
- As a reference book, particularly in executive programmes or for individual readers who want to get acquainted with global strategic management without being burdened by too much theory and background reading.

Appendix I.1 List of potential case studies to be used to support the book

(HBS = Harvard Business School, Cambridge, Massachusetts, USA; IMD = International Institute for Management Development, Lausanne, Switzerland; INSEAD = Institut Européen d'Administration des Affaires, Fontainebleau-Singapore; Ivey= Richard Ivey School of Business, Toronto, Canada; Thunderbird = Thunderbird School of Global Management, Glendale, Arizona, USA)

CHAPTER	CASES	REFERENCE
1 Globalization of markets and competition	• The Global Oil Industry and Latin America	INSEAD, 2011
	• AXA and the Non-Life Insurance Industry in Europe in 2010	INSEAD, 2011
	• The Global Tire Industry and Michelin in 2004	INSEAD, 2005
	• Mass Retailing in Asia: The Markets	INSEAD, 2005
	• Note on the Global Hotel Industry	Ivey, 2008
	• The Global Oil and Gas Industry, 2010	Thunderbird, 2011
2 Designing a global strategy	• Globalization of Komatsu: digging out of trouble	INSEAD, 2010
	• Forging a Global Bank (A)	INSEAD, 2010
	• Baidu and Google in China's Internet Search Market: Pathways to Globalization and Localization	INSEAD, 2009
	• Lessons From Breakthrough Strategic Moves Over the Last Century	INSEAD, 2009
	• Cemex: Building a Global Latina	INSEAD, 2008
	• Cemex: Cementing a Global Strategy	INSEAD, 2007
	• Grolsch: Growing Globally	HBS, 2011
	• L'Oreal And The Globalization Of American Beauty	HBS, 2011
	• McKinsey and the Globalization Of Consultancy	HBS, 2010
	• Teva Pharmaceutical Industries, Ltd.	HBS, 2009
	• CEMEX (A): Building the Global Framework (1985–2004)	Thunderbird, 2007
	• LG Electronics: Global Strategy in Emerging Markets	Thunderbird, 2007
3 Designing a global organization	• The Rogue Trader	INSEAD, 2011
	• Philips versus Matsushita: The Competitive Battle Continues	HBS, 2009
	• Novartis Pharma: The Business Unit Model	HBS, 2003
	• Have You Restructured For Global Success?	Ivey, 2011
	• Renewing GE	Ivey, 2011
4 Global strategic alliances	• Renewing the Fujitsu–AMD Joint Venture (part A)	INSEAD, 2009
	• The TNT/WFP Partnership, 'Moving the World' Five Years On	INSEAD, 2009
	• Essilor Korea (part A)	INSEAD, 2009
	• Hyundai Card and GE Money: Re-branding decisions in a successful joint venture	INSEAD, 2008
	• GM's Asian Alliances: Fifteen Years After	INSEAD, 2005
	• Fiat–Chrysler Alliance: Launching the Cinquecento in North America	HBS, 2011
	• CIBC Mellon: Managing a Cross-Border Joint Venture	Ivey, 2010
5 Global mergers and acquisitions	• The Takeover of Arcelor by Mittal Steel: Change in a Mature Global Industry (part A)	INSEAD, 2010
	• The Acquisition of Abbey (A)(B)(C)	INSEAD, 2009
	• The Acquisition of Alliance & Leicester and Bradford & Bingley (part E)	INSEAD, 2008
	• Cap Gemini Ernst & Young (A) Two Views	INSEAD, 2004
	• InBev and Anheuser-Busch	Thunderbird, 2010

CHAPTER	CASES	REFERENCE
6 Assessing countries' attractiveness	• Concise Profiles series : Brazil, India, China, Hong Kong, Indonesia, Japan, Malaysia, Philippines, Singapore, South Korea, Taiwan, Thailand, Vietnam • A World of Risk and a Road Map to Understand It 'The 4 Quadrants' • Sherritt Goes to Cuba (A): Political Risk in Uncharted Territory	INSEAD, 2011 INSEAD, 2006 HBS, 2011
7 Entry strategies	• INTEL in Costa Rica: A Success Story? • Whirlpool in China : Entering the World's Largest Market • eBay's Strategy in China: Alliance or Acquisition	INSEAD, 2005 INSEAD, 2001 HBS, 2007
8 Global marketing	• Google Street View in France (A): Building Buzz for a New Product Launch • GE Healthcare (A): Innovating for Emerging Markets (A), (B) • Wipro: Building a Global B-2-B Brand • Pfizer and the Distribution of Pharmaceuticals in Europe in 2009 • L'Oréal: Global Brand, Local Knowledge, • Schneider Electric Global Account Management	INSEAD, 2011 INSEAD, 2011 INSEAD, 2009 INSEAD, 2009 HBS, 2011 IMD, 2003
9 Global operations	• Semiconductor Manufacturing International Company in 2011 • Wal-Mart China: Sustainable Operations Strategy • Lego Group: An Outsourcing Journey • Genpact Inc. – Business Process Outsourcing to India • Coloplast A/S – Organizational Challenges in Offshoring	HBS, 2011 HBS, 2009 Ivey, 2009 Ivey, 2009 Ivey, 2008
10 Global innovation	• Teva Pharmaceuticals: Global Integration Rank Xerox: The Global Transfer of Best Practices (A), (B),5c) • Siemens AG: Global Development Strategy • Siemens ShareNet: Building a Knowledge Network • Leo Burnett Co. Ltd.: Virtual Team Management	INSEAD, 2003 INSEAD, 2002 HBS, 2002 HBS, 2002 Ivey, 2003
11 Cross-cultural management	• Polygon Hotel in Dubai: Challenges of Cross-Cultural Negotiations • Leading Across Cultures at Michelin (part A) • Negotiating in China • Negotiation in China: How Universal?	INSEAD, 2011 INSEAD, 2009 Ivey, 2011 University of Hong Kong, 2011
12 Global human resource management	• From Jaguar to Bluebird – Mark Chan returns home after his expatriate assignment (A)(B • Andreas Weber's reward for success in an international assignment – a return to an uncertain future (A)(B) • Albert 'Jack' Stanley in Nigeria (A) • Solvay Group: International Mobility and Managing Expatriates • From Regional Star to Global Leader • Global Talent Management at Novartis • Finance Leadership in Novartis Consumer Health Businesses • People Management Fiasco in Honda Motorcycles and Scooters India Ltd.	INSEAD, 2003 INSEAD, 2003 HBS, 2011 HBS, 2011 HBS, 2009 HBS, 2008 HBS, 2006 University of Hong Kong, 2006
13 Global financial management	• Arcelor Mittal Takeover • Arcelor: Undervaluation: Threat or Opportunity? • Clariant–BTP Acquisition Acquisition Wave in the Fine Chemicals Industry (A) • DCF vs. Real Options: How Best to Value Online Financial Companies (with an Application to Egg) • Subprime Meltdown: American Housing and Global Financial Turmoil • International Finance • Foreign Exchange Hedging Strategies at General Motors: Transactional and Translational Exposures • Teaching Project Finances	INSEAD, 2009 INSEAD, 2009 INSEAD, 2006 INSEAD, 2001 HBS, 2008 HBS, 2006 HBS, 2006 Ivey, 2011

CHAPTER	CASES	REFERENCE
14 Emerging global players	• Olam International	INSEAD, 2011
	• Marcopolo: The Making of Global Latina	INSEAD, 2011
	• A Middle Eastern Enfant Terrible Goes Global	INSEAD, 2010
	• The DIFI Conquest of Emerging Markets (A): Polish and Czech Strategies 'Will they call...?'	INSEAD, 2009
	• DIFI in Russia (B): Learning from Past Experiences? Building an ambitious future?	INSEAD, 2009
	• Building a Global Latina (part A)	INSEAD, 2011
	• Recipes for Success in China: KFC's Radical Approach to China	INSEAD, 2011
	• Haier: Taking a Chinese Company Global in 2011	HBS, 2011
	• Renewing GE: The Africa Project (B)	HBS, 2011
	• L'Oréal: Expansion in China	HBS, 2006
	• Carlsberg in Emerging Markets	Ivey, 2011
	• Bundy Asia Pacific–China Strategy	Ivey, 2008
15 The social responsibility of the global firm	• Tibotec: Partnership with HIV/AIDS Alliance in Uganda: Working Together for Development	INSEAD, 2011
	• Technology Choice under Carbon Regulation	INSEAD, 2010
	• The Pfizer Freiburg Energy Initiative (A)	INSEAD, 2010
	• A Global Leader's Guide to Managing Business Conduct	HBS, 2011
	• Kitchen Best: Ethics when Doing Cross-Boundary Business in Southern China	HBS, 2011
	• IKEA's Global Sourcing Challenge	HBS, 2011
	• Indian Rugs and Child Labor (A)	HBS, 2006
16 Global trends	• A Projection of Global Prospects: The World Bank Study Imagines the Year 2030 and Implications for the Future of Capitalism	HBS, 2011

You can find the cases on the following websites:
Harvard Business School cases: <http://hbsp.harvard.edu/>
IMD Cases: <http://www.imd.org/research/information/tofind/cases.cfm>
INSEAD cases: <http://www.insead.edu/facultyresearch/research/order_cases.cfm>
Ivey Business School Cases: <https://www.iveycases.com>
Thunderbird School of Global Management cases:
<http://www.thunderbird.edu/knowledge_network/case_series/>
In addition the following sites distribute cases:
The European Case Clearing House (ECCH): <http://www.ecch.com/educators/>
Indian School of Business: <http://www.isb.edu/ctlc/Cases.Shtml>
Darden School of Business: <https://store.darden.virginia.edu/>
The Asian Business Case Centre: <http://www.asiacase.com/nanyangCase.asp>
You may also find interesting video clips on You Tube (see for instance <http://www.youtube.com/watch?v=9M5wWSA5vQQ>)

Notes

1 Peng (2009), Tallman (2009), Hill (2007), Inkpen and Ramaswamy (2006).
2 Bartlett and Ghoshal (2002), Bartlett and Doz (1990), Doz and Prahalad (1987), Doz, Santos and Williamson (2002).
3 Yip (1995).
4 De La Torre, Doz and Devinney (2000), Bartlett and Ghoshal (2000).

References and further reading

Ariño, Africa, Pankaj Ghemawat and Joan E. Ricart, *Creating Value through International Strategy*. Basingstoke: Palgrave Macmillan, 2004.

Bartlett, Christopher A. and Sumantra Ghoshal, *Managing Across Borders: The Transnational Solution*. 2nd edn. Boston, MA: Harvard Business School Press, 2002.

Bartlett, Christopher A., Yves L. Doz, and Gunnar Hedlund, *Managing the Global Firm*. Abingdon: Routledge, 1990.

Bartlett, Christopher A., Sumantra Ghoshal and Julian Birkinshaw, *Transnational Management: Text, Cases, and Readings in Cross-Border Management*. 4th edn. New York, NY: McGraw-Hill, 2004.

De la Torre, José, Yves L. Doz and Timothy Devinney, *Managing the Global Corporation: Case Studies in Strategy and Management*. 2nd edn. Boston, MA: McGraw-Hill, 2000.

Doz, Yves L. and C. K. Prahalad, *The Multinational Mission: Balancing Local Demands and Global Vision*. New York, NY: Free Press, 1987, London: Macmillan, 1987

Doz, Yves L., Jose Santos and Peter J. Williamson, *From Global to Metanational: How Companies Win in the Knowledge Economy*. Boston, MA: Harvard Business School Press, 2002.

Dunning, John H. and Sarianna M. Lundan, *Multinational Enterprises and the Global Economy*. 2nd edn. Cheltenham: Edward Elgar, 2008.

Hill, Charles W. L., *International Business: Competing in the Global Marketplace*. 6th edn. Boston, MA: McGraw-Hill, 2007.

Hitt, Michael A. R. Duane Ireland and Robert E. Hoskisson, *Strategic Management: Competitiveness and Globalization: Concepts and Cases*. 9th edn. Mason, OH: Thomson South-Western, 2011.

Inkpen, Andrew and Kannan Ramaswamy, *Global Strategy: Creating and Sustaining Advantage Across Borders*. New York, NY: Oxford University Press, 2006.

Kamel, Mellahi, Jedrzeil Frynas and Paul Finlay, *Global Strategic Management*. New York, NY: Oxford University Press, 2009.

Morrisson, Janet, *International Business*. Basingstoke: Palgrave Macmillan, 2009.

Peng, Mike W. *Global Strategy*. 2nd edn. Mason, OH: South-Western College Publishing, 2009.

Rugman, Alan M., *The Oxford Handbook of International Business*. 2nd edn. Oxford: Oxford University Press, 2009.

Tallman, Stephen, *Global Strategy: Global Dimensions of Strategy*. Chichester: Wiley, 2009.

Verbeke, Alain, *International Business Strategy: Rethinking the Foundations of Global Corporate Success*. Cambridge: Cambridge University Press, 2009.

Yip, George S., *Total Global Strategy: Managing for Worldwide Competitive Advantage*. Englewood Chiffs, NJ: Prentice Hall, 1995.

part

I THE PROCESS OF GLOBALIZATION

Part I, The Process of Globalization, looks at *why* and *how* a firm globalizes

Chapter 1 **Globalization of markets and competition** | Chapter 1 defines what 'globalization' means for a business enterprise, differentiates it from the traditional process of extending internationally and makes a distinction between a multinational and a global company. It also looks at the factors that have driven globalization as well as the localization factors restraining it. It ends by proposing a mapping of industries and firms according to the extent to which they are exposed to globalization or localization drivers.

Chapter 2 **Designing a global strategy** | Chapter 2 analyzes the different components of a global strategy. It includes the formulation of objectives, the choice of countries and regions, the competitive positioning of the products and services, the design of and the investment in a global business system to create and sustain global competitive advantages and the choice of a global organization.

Chapter 3 **Designing a global organization** | Chapter 3 describes the advantages and disadvantages of various forms of global organizational designs, from pure geographical to global and matrix models. It ends by presenting the transnational organizational culture that is considered necessary to support the structure, processes and system of the global organization.

Chapter 4 **Global strategic alliances** | Chapter 4 looks at strategic alliances as a recent and important means of reaching a global position. A framework for the analysis of global strategic alliances and recommendations for their implementation are given in this chapter.

Chapter 5 **Global mergers and acquisitions** | Chapter 5 focuses on mergers and acquisitions (M & As) as means of achieving globalization. It offers an analysis of the various phases of global M & As, from the pre-acquisition phase, to valuation and post-acquisition.

Chapter 6 **Assessing countries' attractiveness** | Chapter 6 looks at the first step in the decision to develop a presence in a country, and the analysis of opportunities and risks. It covers such aspects as country risk analysis, industry and competition analysis, market opportunities and host government policies.

Chapter 7 **Entry strategies** | Chapter 7 discusses the various decision choices in entering a country. It considers the timing of entry and the various forms of entry, ranging from wholly owned subsidiaries to joint ventures and licensing, each form being analyzed in terms of its advantages and disadvantages.

chapter

1 GLOBALIZATION OF MARKETS AND COMPETITION

Introduction

Chapter 1 defines what globalization means for a business enterprise. It differentiates globalization from the traditional process of setting up subsidiaries abroad and makes a distinction between a *multinational company* and a *global company*. Based on the example of the Otis Elevator Company, it looks at how a company having multiple international subsidiaries can move toward a global competitive configuration through which its international activities can be strongly coordinated and integrated across borders. This transition from a multinational to a global position was driven by various social, political, economic and technological factors that are described in the chapter. The benefits of globalization are described, as well as the constraints. Some factors are still pushing toward a local approach to management, on a country-by-country basis, and the factors inducing this localization are analyzed.

Finally, global/multi-local mapping is presented as a tool to position industries, companies and businesses according to the relative importance of global versus local approaches. The chapter ends by introducing some of the societal issues associated with globalization.

Learning objectives

At the end of the chapter you will be able to:

- define globalization, understand what a global firm is, and how it differs from a multinational company
- identify the forces pushing toward globalization
- identify the forces pushing for localization
- position an industry or a business on the global/multi-local map
- discuss the benefits and pitfalls of globalization.

The phenomenon of globalization

Over the past 30 years international trade and investment have grown much faster than the world economy as a whole. Firms have multiplied their presence outside their country of origin, employing more and more people and selling and buying technology internationally. (See Table 1.1). More and more products are sold in similar stores, with similar features and carry a common brand across the globe. Factories that were prosperous in the Western world have been closed and transferred to low-cost countries. The English language is now considered as the lingua franca for major business transactions. Televised broadcasts of events taking place in one place on earth are visible in real time everywhere. This is what is commonly named 'globalization'.

Table 1.1: Globalization data

US$ at 2010 prices ($billion)	**1982**	**1990**	**2010**	**Average growth rate 1982–2010**
World GDP	10,899	22,206	62,909	6.5%
Trade (export of goods and services)	2247	4382	18,713	7.9%
Foreign direct investment (inward stock)	647	2081	19,141	12.9%
Cross border M&A	25	99	339	9.8%
Sales of foreign affiliates*	2741	5101	32,960	9.3%
Employment of foreign affiliates (1000s)*	19,537	21,470	62,218	4.2%
Export of foreign affiliates*	647	1498	6239	8.4%
Royalties	9	29	191	11.5%
Daily foreign exchange transactions	30		4000	19.1%

* This refers to affiliates of multinational companies defined as firms having more than 50% equity in wholly owned enterprises abroad or at least 10% equity in joint ventures.

Source: UNCTAD, *World Investment Report 2011*.

In today's business world, managers, politicians, journalists and academics commonly use the concepts of 'globalization', 'global industries', 'global competition', 'global strategies' and 'global corporations'. More and more companies are confronted with the need to globalize or die. While these concepts are widely used, their exact meaning is often not properly understood. For some people, globalization means to expand the company's presence abroad, for others it means standardizing a product and selling it to the world, for yet others it denotes an approach to management in which decision-making is centralized at corporate headquarters. There are many reasons for this confusion; one is due to the fact that the concept of globalization is relatively new. Before the 1970s hardly anyone talked about globalization; the most frequently used terminology, when referring to companies operating in various parts of the world, was 'international', 'multinational' or occasionally 'trans¬national'. International and multinational companies have been around for many years. Even if we ignore the East India Company, which started in the early seventeenth century, modern corporations like Unilever, Nestlé and Procter & Gamble were operating all over the world at the end of the nineteenth century. They are known as multinational companies, but nobody would have called them global. The global concept appeared in the early 1970s and progressively invaded boardrooms, classrooms and editorial offices. What is the exact meaning of globalization? What forces generated it? And what are the consequences for firms?

There is no well-established definition of globalization. Here we will propose as a definition: 'The process by which people, products, information and money can move freely across borders'. As a consequence, markets may tend to converge, providing room for standardization of products, and production centres can be located at economical and convenient places around the world. This implies, as we will see, a more centralized management of firms. We will look first at the macro-economic, technological and political factors that have generated such a global environment and then look at how firms have changed their operations to take advantages of the new opportunities offered by these factors.

SOME GLOBAL DEFINITIONS

Globalization: The process by which people, products, information and money can move freely across borders

Global industries are industries in which, in order to survive, competitors need to operate in the key world markets in an integrated and coordinated way. Industries like aerospace, computers, telecommunication equipment, appliances, power generation, large industrial projects, insurance and re-insurance and corporate data transmission are examples. In these sectors it is difficult to sustain competition if you do not cover the whole world (or nearly) as a market, and if you do not integrate operations to make them cost- and time-effective.

Global companies are the companies that operate in the main markets of the world in an integrated and coordinated way. Companies like Coca Cola, Asea Brown Bovery, Sony and Citibank are global companies.

Globalizing is the phenomenon of the transition of industries whose competitive structure changes progressively from multinational to global. Industries such as telecommunications, processed food, personal care and retail are in the process of globalization.

Global integration and coordination are the organizational structure and management processes by which various activities scattered across the world are made interdependent. As examples, global manufacturing integration implies the specialization of factories and the cross-shipment of parts between different production sites; global product development requires the coordination of various research centres and marketing teams; global account management demands that different country subsidiaries provide a service according to a plan negotiated centrally, and so on.

What are the factors that push for globalization?

Political factors: liberalization of trade and investments

Globalization became a reality at the beginning of the 1970s because of the convergence of several political, technological, social and competitive factors.[1]

The main political factor has been the development of *free trade* among nations. Two main organizations have been the source of trade liberalization: the General Agreement on Tariffs and Trade (GATT) (now replaced by the World Trade Organization, WTO) and the European

Union (EU), to which we may add the progressive opening of emerging nations to foreign investments.

The GATT, which was founded in 1946 by 23 nations, initiated a series of negotiations, called 'rounds', aimed at reducing tariff concessions to create liberalization of trade. The GATT became the WTO in 1995. The Kennedy Round in the mid-1960s, the Tokyo Round in the early 1970s and the Uruguay round in the late 1980s created an environment that fostered international trade: during the period following the Kennedy Round the average weighted tariff rate among GATT members decreased by 34% and after the Tokyo round by 60%.

The European Economic Community (EEC) was established on 25 March 1957 by the Treaty of Rome, signed by Belgium, France, Italy, Germany, Luxembourg and the Netherlands, with the aim of creating a common market and economic and political integration among the six member states. As a result, goods, people and financial flows could move freely across countries. During the 1970s, the EEC was enlarged with the entry of the United Kingdom, Ireland and Denmark, followed by Spain, Portugal and Greece in the 1980s and by Sweden, Austria and Finland in the 1990s. Companies like Otis could take advantage of European integration to create their own integrated trading network.

Finally, in parallel with what was happening in the industrialized countries, developing nations progressively adopted more positive attitudes toward foreign direct investment (FDI). At first, investment laws were designed to attract foreign investors in order to induce them to produce locally, but over the years the legislation has evolved toward a more open stance, favouring cross-border investments. Between 1991 and 2004 the number of regulatory changes favourable to FDI totalled 2006 worldwide while unfavourable changes numbered just 150.

Technological factors: transport, communication and economies of scale

Another set of 'push factors' for globalization is related to *technological progress*, which lowered the cost of transport and communication as well as the unit cost of production through economies of scale or the localization of productive capacities and sourcing in low-cost economies.

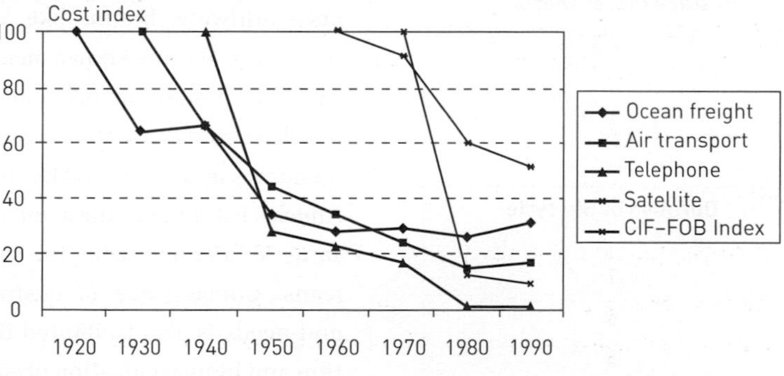

Figure 1.1 International transportation and communication costs, 1920–90

Source: World Bank, *World Development Report*, 1995.

Air, rail and road transport and the use of containers in maritime transport have reduced the cost of shipping goods from country to country as well as, in the case of air transport, favoring the travel of managers. The development of telecommunications has reduced the cost of information exchange between business units scattered around the globe. Between 1950 and 1990, the transportation costs of air transport, ocean freight and transatlantic phone calls decreased by some 56%, 14% and 29%, respectively. For satellite charges, there was an approximate decrease of 90% between 1970 and 1990 (Figure 1.1).

Progress in manufacturing technology gave a tremendous impetus to the need to concentrate production in world-class factories benefiting from huge economies of scale, thus encouraging the rationalization and integration of production systems.

Beside manufacturing concentration, companies have been able to source components or services from low-cost countries, either by setting up their own operations or by purchasing locally.

Table 1.2 Illustrations of the shortening of product life cycles

General product category	Time of invention to commercial exploitation (years)
Electric motor	65
TV	52
Vacuum tube	33
Zip-fastener	30
X-ray tube	18
Frozen foods	15
Nuclear reactors	10
Radar	5
Solar batteries	3

Appliance category	Average length of introductory stage (no. of years)
Period 1922–42	12.5
Period 1945–64	7
Period 1965–79	2

Intel microprocessor products	Duration of life cycle
286	7
386	6
486	5
Pentium	5

Sources: Baker and Hart (1999, p. 115); Michaels, Olshaysky and Qualls (1981, pp. 77–8); Michel, Salle and Valla (1996, p.178).

Another source of economies of scale comes from the need to quickly amortize research and development (R&D) expenditures. Companies are confronted with a dual pressure: R&D budgets are increasing and product life cycles (PLCs) are reducing (Table 1.2). Companies need to launch products and services at the same time in all major markets in order to be able to recoup their investments.

Social factors: convergence of consumer needs

International air transport and the diffusion of lifestyles by movies and TV series have increased the brand awareness of consumers worldwide. Brands like Sony, Nike, Levi or Coca Cola are known nearly everywhere. Kenichi Ohmae,[2] in his book 'Triad Power', has discussed the 'Californization of society' – teenagers in Sao Paolo, Mumbai, Milan or Los Angeles listening to the same music, using the same MP3 and wearing the same pair of blue jeans. Convergence of customer behaviour and needs is also facilitated by the urbanization and industrialization of societies. The less cultural and the more technical the product, the more likely it is to be standardized and appeal to masses of consumers in all countries: DVDs, PCs, mobile phones or elevators, cranes and robots are products for which national differences do not matter much.

Competitive factors

The 1960s saw the emergence of Japanese competitors in markets that traditionally had been dominated by American or European competitors. Japanese firms, and later Korean firms, adopted a global approach at the very beginning of their international expansion. One of the reasons is that they did not have many national subsidiaries and their international expansion was occurring at the time of the opening of trade barriers. Right at the beginning they designed products for the world market, creating *global brands* such as 'Sony' or 'Panasonic', and their efficient production system gave them a cost advantage in electronics and automotive parts. Competitors had to adopt a similar strategic stance if they wished to survive.

Another competitive force that pushed companies to globalize is the *globalization of customers*. During the 1970s, Citibank created a Global Account Management Unit to service those corporate customers who had international subsidiaries. Figure 1.2 summarizes these 'push factors' in favour of globalization.

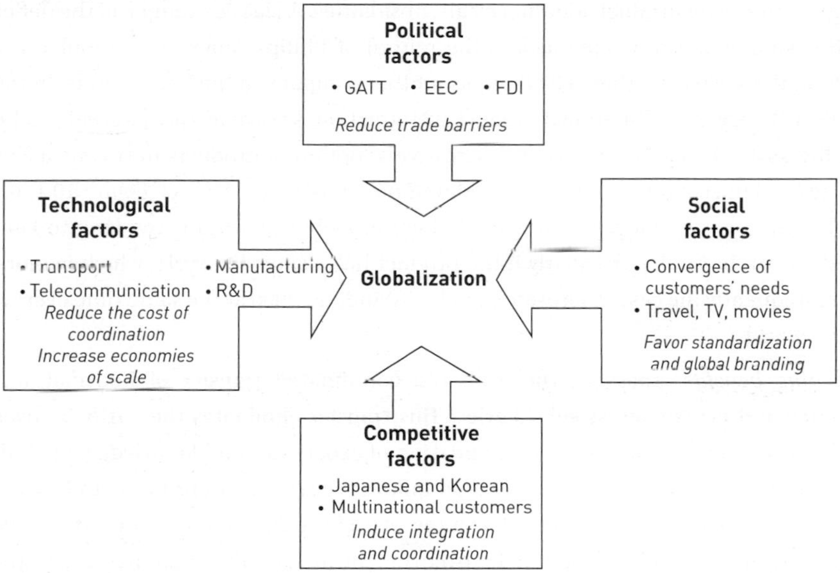

Figure 1.2 Globalization push factors

The benefits of globalization

The benefits of globalization can be assessed from two points of view: the business and competitive point of view and the macro socio-economic point of view. In this chapter we will focus on the business and competitive benefits. A more general discussion on the socio-economic benefits and costs of globalization will be included later in the chapter, while this part focuses on the benefits to a corporation of adopting a global strategy.

The business and competitive benefits can be grouped into four categories: cost, learning, timing and arbitrage.

(1) ***Cost benefits.*** These come, on the one hand, from economies of scale in product/process standardization as well as increased bargaining powers over suppliers of raw materials, components, equipment and services and, on the other hand, from the ability to organize a logistic and sourcing network based on location factors. Examples of economies of scale through standardization are numerous; in the example mentioned earlier, Otis was able to lower the cost of elevators in Europe by 30% after introducing a pan-European manufacturing system.

(2) ***Timing benefits.*** These are due to the coordinated approach to product launching in the early stage of the product life cycle. In a multinational setting, each subsidiary is more or less free to adopt products for its own market. This is sometimes called 'the shopping caddy' approach to product adoption. Such an approach generates inefficiencies in the management of the product life cycle since the optimal volume is obtained only after a lengthy process of product adoption by all subsidiaries. A classic example of the deficiency of the 'shopping caddy' approach is the refusal of Philips America to adopt the video system, the V2000, developed by Philips's mother company in the Netherlands. In the late 1960s a theory of multinational product introduction, known as the 'international product life cycle' theory, postulated a progressive adoption of products over time according to the level of economic and scientific development of countries (see Figure 10.1, p. 285). Such a theory is no longer valid when industries globalize: waiting too long to launch a product can be fatal, particularly if the product has a short life cycle, which is more and more frequently the case. Microsoft launched Windows 2000 at the same time everywhere in the world.

(3) ***Learning benefits.*** These accrue from the coordinated transfer of information, best practice and people across subsidiaries. This transfer eliminates the costly 'reinvention of the wheel' and facilitates the accumulation of experience and knowledge. In Thailand, Unilever formulated and implemented an innovative strategy to produce and market ice creams. The Thai experience served as a template for other countries in the Asia Pacific region, giving to the company a first-mover advantage. This example illustrates the benefits that can be gained from a coordinated transfer of best practice.

(4) ***Arbitrage benefits.*** These come from the advantages that a company managed globally can gain in using resources in one country for the benefit of another country subsidiary. These advantages can be direct competitive advantages or indirect cost advantages. A competitive advantage can be gained by playing a 'global chess game': for instance, engaging in a price war in one country in order to mobilize the resources of competitors in that country, depriving them of cash flow which could be used elsewhere. This strategy was

used by Goodyear, the US tyre giant, when in the early 1970s, Michelin from France moved into North America. Goodyear, which had a small market share in Europe, engaged in a price war that Michelin was obliged to counter by lowering its prices, and de facto reducing its financing scope for its American expansion. Another type of arbitrage comes from differential cost elements such as taxes, interest and possibly risk reduction through the pooling of currencies.

Those four benefits are real but achieving them is subject to certain conditions, and their adoption has to be measured against the real competitive advantage they provide to the firms adopting them.

The benefits in cost reduction obtained by economies of scale are contingent upon the market responsiveness to standardization and whether customers are price sensitive. If, on the contrary, customers are not responsive and prefer tailored products and services to standardization, a global approach is less appropriate. A similar reasoning applies to the benefits of timing. As for purchasing power, it may be limited for culturally sensitive services such as advertising.

The benefits of learning are positive if the experience gained in one country is applicable to another. If it is not the case, there is a *timing deficit*: the time it takes to realize that you have made a mistake, plus the time to learn about the new environment. At Disneyland Paris®, two years were lost because the transfer of knowledge from Florida and California did not help the European operation.

The benefits of arbitrage can be offset by the cost of managing the arbitrage and the legal barriers that may exist in order to prevent such arbitrage. In the case of tax arbitrage, governments are very careful to make sure that global companies do not abuse their arbitrage power.

Despite those limitations, more and more companies recognize the competitive benefits of globalization. However, you should be aware there are still some factors that work against globalization and this is what we will consider after the following example of globalization.

Globalization at the level of the firm

EXAMPLE

To illustrate the phenomenon of globalization let us take the example of the elevator industry in Europe in the late 1960s as represented in Figure 1.3.

In each country of Europe, different firms fought for a share of the elevator market. Competitors were either local companies or subsidiaries of large multinational companies like Otis or Schindler. Each competitor designed, marketed, manufactured, installed and serviced elevators for their respective markets. The subsidiaries of the multinationals had all the activities of the value chain (marketing, design, production, installation and service) under their control. The French subsidiary of Otis designed elevators for the French market, manufactured them in French factories, sold them with a French sales force and maintained them with a French after-sales organization; the management was essentially French. In Germany, Otis designed, manufactured, sold, installed and serviced elevators for the German market; and so on in nearly every major country. In smaller countries products or components were exported from major countries' subsidiaries. The operations were *self-contained* in each country and the results were evaluated on a *country-by-country* basis. Such a situation had prevailed since the 1880s. It corresponds to what was referred to as a multinational or multi-domestic world, in which multinational companies like Otis were competing in separate domestic markets around the world.

By the end of the 1960s several key elements played a role in changing this competitive structure. One national manager at Otis perceived that the European business context was changing. First, the Treaty of Rome in 1957 had created the European Economic Community (EEC), at that time called the Common Market. This meant that tariff barriers across Europe were coming down; it became possible to produce components in one country and export them to other countries. This allowed companies to concentrate on the production of components in one specialized factory and to have a network of specialized factories across Europe, each of them making one product category or one component. Components would be cross-shipped for ultimate installation in the various client countries.

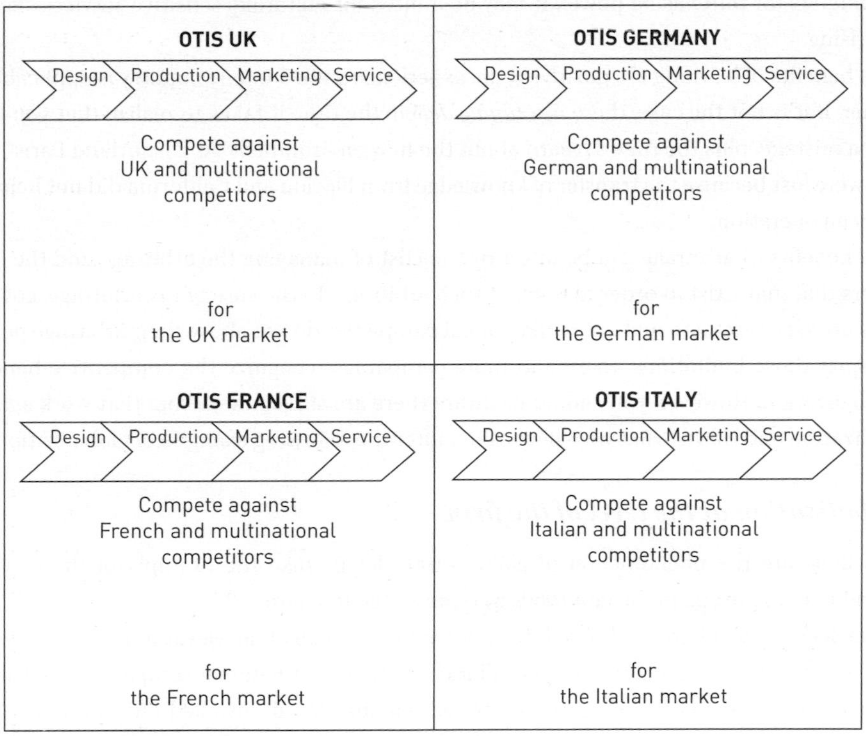

Figure 1.3 A multinational competitive configuration

The benefits of such a system were obvious – by concentrating production the company could benefit from economies of scale and some cost savings could be passed to the customer in the form of price reductions, leading to higher market share. Products could be designed for the whole market (standardized): instead of having country segmentation you would have pan-European segmentation based on use, i.e. high-rise buildings, low-rise buildings, and so on.

This would be possible only if customers in Europe – architects, engineers, real-estate developers, housing departments, etc. – had a common view about what an elevator should be like. Despite the differences in housing organization across countries, elevators were essentially technical products with very little cultural content and therefore able to be standardized. Only selling methods would vary from country to country. The Otis manager perceived this as an opportunity to gain market share in Europe and engaged in the pan-European strategy depicted in Figure 1.4 in which design centres and factories were specialized and inter-dependent.

From a management point of view this was a radical change: national managers were no longer responsible for the whole value chain as before, but only for part of it. They were obliged to coordinate with other countries and they were dependent on a coordinating organization called the European headquarters. This led to a very successful outcome. By 1975, Otis had captured 40% of the European market, containing Japanese penetration, and competitors if they wanted to survive were obliged to adopt a similar strategy. This concept was further expanded and today Otis is organized by product lines on a worldwide basis. There are still country subsidiaries, which take care of installation, maintenance, public relations and personnel, but otherwise product development and manufacturing is coordinated globally by product lines. From being a 'multinational', Otis has become a 'global' company.

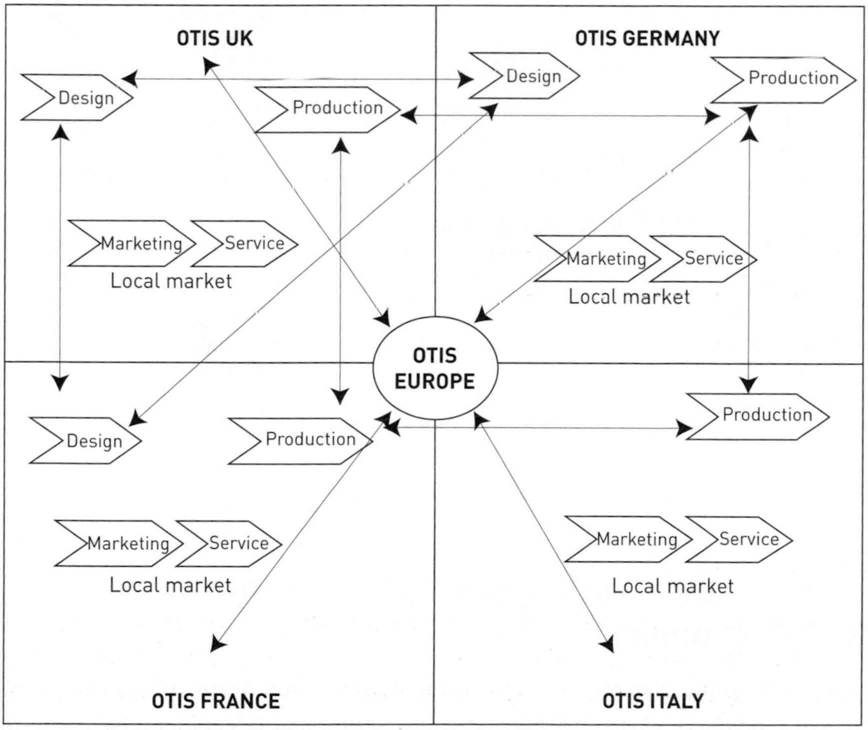

Figure 1.4 A global competitive configuration

This phenomenon of an *active coordinated and integrated presence* in the main regions of the world is what 'global company' means. It is important to observe that this change gave Otis a competitive advantage and competitors were obliged to adopt a similar approach in order to survive. Globalization is neither a consultant's fad nor a management buzzword; it is a competitive imperative in an increasing number of industries.

Historically the evolution of globalization from an enterprise point of view can be best described as in Figure 1.5. It has evolved in three steps: (1) international trade: export and sourcing, (2) multinational investments: setting up value-adding activities in different countries and (3) integration and coordination of activities across regions and countries.

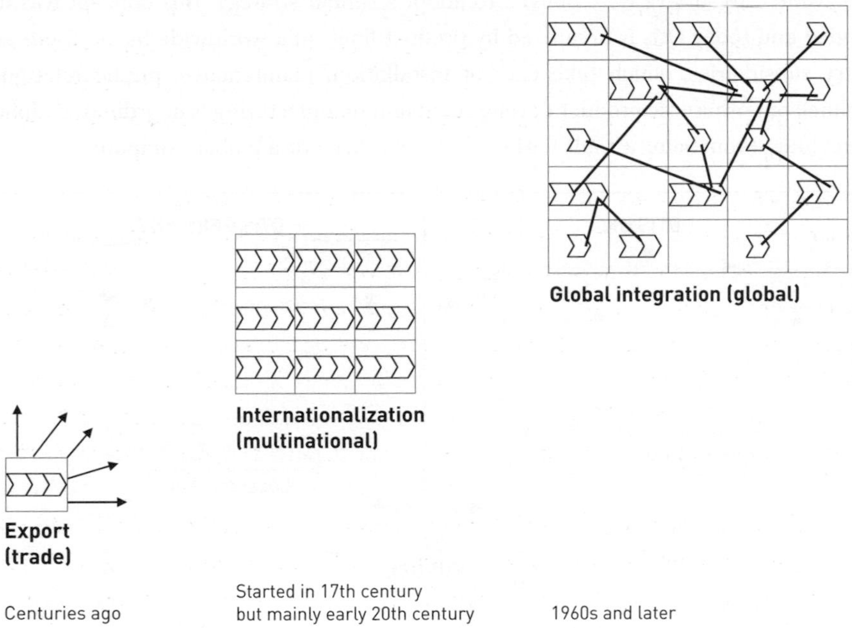

Figure 1.5: Historically globalization took place in three steps

The factors that work against globalization: the localization push

As mentioned earlier, globalization is associated with some degree of standardization of products and practices plus a high level of coordination and integration of activities in the company's value chain. Factors that defeat standardization, coordination and integration are working against globalization. We can group those factors into four main categories: cultural, commercial, technical and legal.

(1) ***Cultural factors: attitudes, tastes, behavior and social codes***
When the consumption of a product or a service is linked to traditions and national or religious values, global standardization is not effective. Some products – for instance, Kretek (tobacco and clove) cigarettes in Indonesia, or the Pachinko (pinball) game in Japan – are unique to one society and their globalization is nearly impossible, although it could be argued that with innovative marketing it may be possible. Examples are the arrival of 'Beaujolais nouveau' wine, typically a Burgundy and Parisian bistro event before the 1970s, now available in Tokyo, Paris or New York on the same day, and Halloween trick or treating, a typical US festivity, is now celebrated in Europe. This shows that even some highly cultural goods and customs can be appreciated by customers all over the world, but it remains that tastes in food and drink, social interactions in sales negotiations, attitudes toward hygiene, cosmetics or gifts vary from culture to culture, thus hampering a global product design or approach. In the Asia-Pacific region, for instance, personal relationship building rather than legal contracts is the normal way to conduct business. Time and effort are required to build these personal ties, which in a US context would be considered a waste of time.

(2) ***Commercial factors: distribution, customization and responsiveness***
In some sectors, distribution networks and practices differ from country to country and as a consequence the ways of managing the network, motivating dealers and distributors, pricing and negotiation are hardly amenable to global coordination. For instance, the marketing and distribution of pharmaceutical products differ according to the country's health system. In some countries, like Japan, doctors sell medicine, while in other countries pharmacists are selling to patients who get a refund (or not) from their insurance company, while in yet other cases pharmaceutical products are delivered free of charge to the patient.

Responsiveness to customers' demands as well as customization are other factors which almost by definition defeat standardization. Private savings or current accounts for individuals, loans to small and medium-size enterprises (SMEs), mortgages, consulting activities and individual architectural designs are services for which a local presence and a fast reaction to customers' requirements are needed for competitive success. Although some practices, processes or methodologies can be standardized on a worldwide basis (consultants, engineering, architects or auditors, for example), it remains that specific customer requests have to be taken into consideration, thus limiting globalization.

(3) ***Technical factors: standards, spatial presence, transportation and language***
Technical standards in electrical, civil, chemical or mechanical engineering can create a burden for global companies. Scale economies and cost benefits of global integration and standardization cannot be exploited fully when technical standards vary greatly. In certain cases, standards can be changed without major modification – as, for instance, in

consumer electronics, where creating video multi-standard products with PAL for some European countries, SECAM for France and the Middle East, and NTSC for the USA does not represent a major hurdle for global manufacturing. In other instances, standards are not that easy to accommodate and require specific local production lines, as is mainly the case for beer, for instance.

Some industries need to occupy a physical space in order to create and distribute their products and services: retail banking, retailing, hotels, local telephones services, hospitals, entertainment and car dealers are examples of industries where the services have to be produced locally. In those industries there are still some advantages in globalizing certain functions such as back office functions (accounting, data processing, global sourcing, transfer of best practice, etc.) but the location constraint still limits globalization benefits. In the future, e-commerce is likely to reduce spatial constraints considerably, particularly when it comes to virtual services such as banking or movies on demand. E-commerce with physical products can also eliminate the spatial constraint as far as the customer interface is concerned but is still hampered by logistical constraints. The example of Amazon.com demonstrates that it is possible for a customer in Paris or in Rio de Janeiro to order a book through Amazon, but the same customer will have to bear shipping costs that will eliminate the basic cost advantage of the e-bookstore. This is the reason why Amazon is looking for local partnerships outside the United States, thus moving toward a more multinational business design.

The impediments of transportation are significant if the cost of transport cancels out the benefits of concentration of production. Bulk commodities like cement or basic chemicals are more economically produced in local plants rather than in global centralized units, despite the scale economies that could be gained: the cost and the risks of transport cancel out the benefits of centralized production. Similarly, when production systems are not scale-intensive and small production units can achieve similar costs to large plants – in plastic moulding, for instance – there are no major benefits in building a global production system.

Finally, languages can add constraints to global approaches. These constraints can be significant when it comes to services to individual customers: training services, personal banking and personal telecommunication or retailing are possible examples. However, there are two major trends that can reduce language constraints. English has become more and more a 'global language' and industries such as graduate business training or high-level consultancy can use English without the need for translation.

(4) *Legal factors: regulation and national security issues*

Governments impose regulatory constraints that often work against globalization, either because they limit the free flow of personnel (regulation on work permits), cash (exchange control, tax), goods (customs duties, quotas), data (censorship, the Internet and EDI control), or because they impose localization constraints (local content policies, local ownership and joint venture policies).

Over the years, thanks to the GATT and now the WTO and also multilateral agreements (European Union (EU), ASEAN, NAFTA, etc.) and International Monetary Fund (IMF) requests, government legislation is leaning toward more open legislative contexts that favor globalization. However, some constraints still exist. Some sectors such as telecommunications, media, banking and insurance are still tightly controlled and some countries (such as China and India) or regional blocks (the EU), still impose local content requirements.

Finally, governments are much concerned with national security and will prevent foreigners gaining too much control of their defence or strategic sector industries. In the defence sector, for instance, where R&D costs are huge and economies of scale significant, globalization would be fully justified, but is in fact limited because of national security constraints. Figure 1.6 summarizes the localization push.

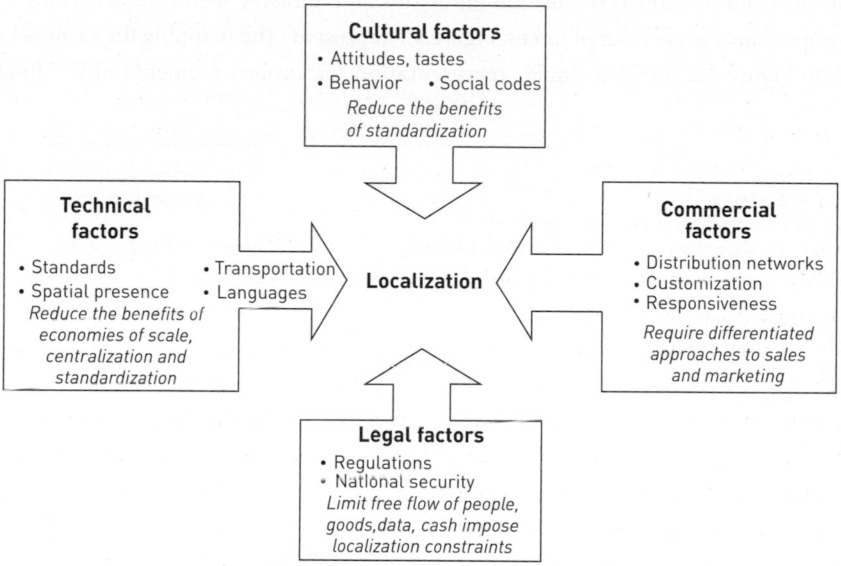

Figure 1.6 Localization push factors

The benefits of localization

The benefits of localization, instead of a global integrated and coordinated approach, are essentially customer-oriented benefits that give firms an increased market power and ultimately an increased market share. The benefits of localization are flexibility, proximity and quick response time.

- **Proximity** is the capability to be close to the market, to understand the customer's *value curve*.
- **Flexibility** is the capability to adapt to consumer demand in the various dimensions of the marketing mix: product/service design, distribution, branding, pricing and services. Ultimately, flexibility leads to *customization*.

- **Quick response time** is the ability to respond at once to specific customers' *demands.*

Proximity, flexibility and quick response time are very much related to each other: proximity provides the basis for flexibility and flexibility provides the basis for a quick response. All three give a competitive advantage when local cultural, technical, commercial and legal contexts vary so much from country to country.

Global/multi-local mapping

The two sets of forces – globalization and localization – are shaping the competitive structure of industries and inducing companies to configure their worldwide business systems with the right mix of coordination, integration or decentralization. Global/multi-local mapping is a tool that has been developed to position industries and industry segments according to the relative importance of each set of forces. Figure 1.7 represents the mapping for various industries, while Figure 1.8 shows a similar representation for various segments of the financial sector.

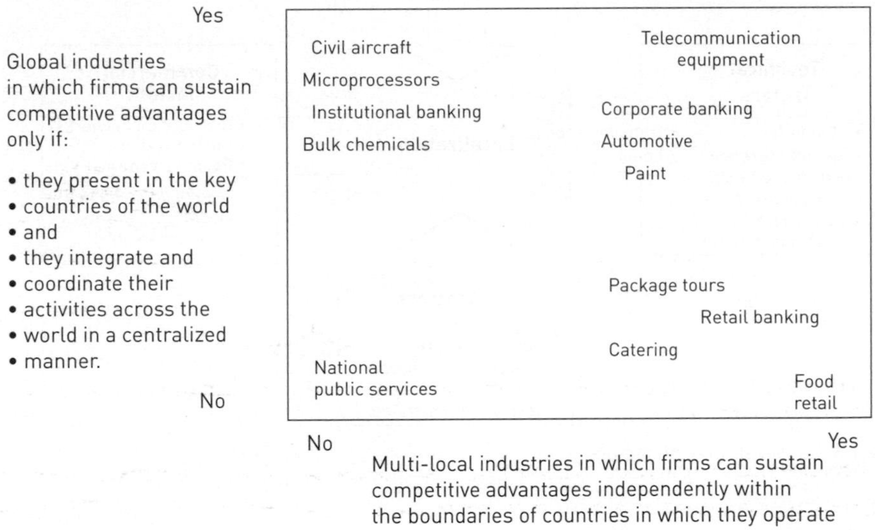

Figure 1.7 Global/multi-local mapping: different industries have different competitive requirements

The mapping in Figures 1.7 and 1.8 reveals that industries and segments can be broadly positioned into three types of competitive situations:

- **Type I:** *Global forces* dominate and firms in those industries can sustain competitive advantage by operating across the world in a coordinated way. There are few advantages to pushing for local adaptation of products, services and approaches. What matters is efficiency, speed, arbitrage and learning. These industries are global, as in the case of the microchip, bulk chemical or civil aircraft industries.
- **Type II:** *Local forces* dominate and flexibility, proximity and quick response are determining capabilities for competitive advantage. Firms can operate independently in different

countries; their approaches are different from country to country. Food retailing, consumer banking or voice telephony fall in this category.

- **Type III:** In these industries there is a *mix of global and local forces at play* and competitiveness cannot be achieved without achieving the benefits of global coordination and, at the same time, the benefits of flexibility, proximity and quick response time. This positioning is increasingly becoming the dominant competitive battleground for a vast majority of sectors.

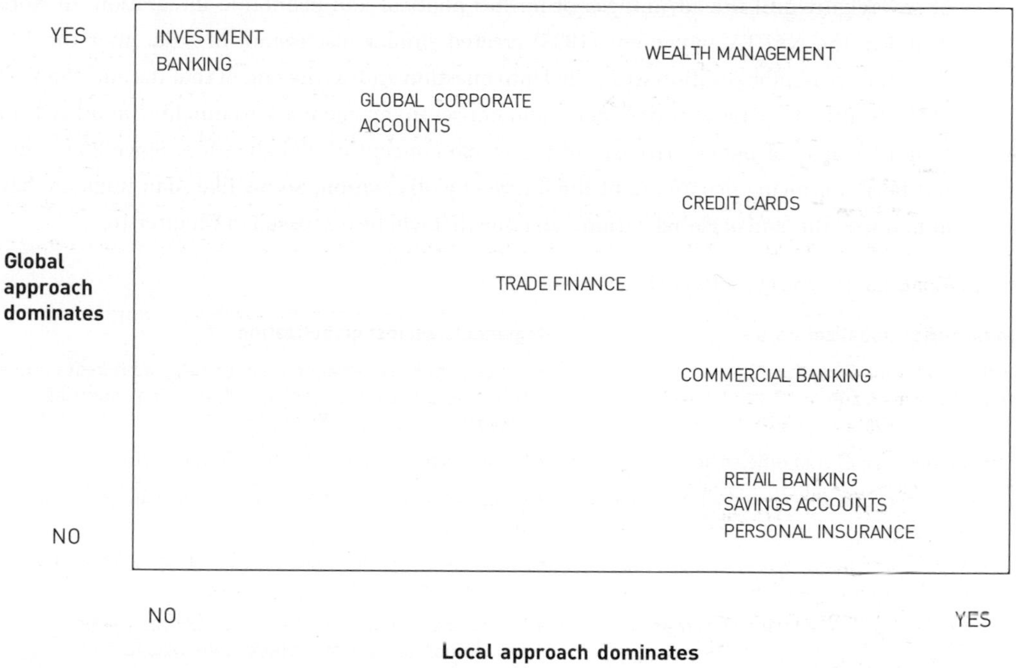

Figure 1.8 Global/multi-local mapping for the financial sector: different segments have different competitive requirements

Global/multi-local mapping can be used for assessing a situation at a point in time or to anticipate evolution over time. It can also serve as mapping for the various activities of the value chain. As will be seen in Chapters 2 and 3, a good understanding of industry positioning will help the formulation of business and national strategies, as well as the implementation of an effective organizational design.

In Appendix 1.1 there is a questionnaire that will help managers to position their business using the Global/multi-local mapping tool.

Globalization: the macro picture

In 1817, David Ricardo in his *Theory of Comparative Advantage*[3] showed that it was beneficial to nations to specialize and trade goods in which they had a *comparative advantage*. This laid the foundation of trade theory, which itself is the underlying foundation of globalization: in a perfect global setting where goods, people, data and money flow freely, companies can adopt an integrated and coordinated approach to their operations and the competitive battlefield would be the world. Since Ricardo's time, partisans and adversaries of free trade have exchanged heated debates about the pro and cons of globalization for society. Table 1.3 summarizes those arguments.

This debate gained political visibility during the 1990s. In Europe, the Treaty of Maastricht (signed in 1992) adopted the euro as a single currency, generating a heated debate on the loss of sovereignty and the advantages of further political and economic integration. In North America, the NAFTA agreement (1995) created similar discussion. In Asia, after the 1997 financial crisis, globalization was called into question and, at the end of that decade, the WTO at the Seattle ministerial conference could not set up an agenda for launching another trade round because of public criticism of the whole concept of globalization. Since 2001, there has been a growing debate about the future of globalization. Some, like Alan Rugman, have announced the 'end of globalization',[4] an issue that will be discussed in Chapter 16.

Table 1.3 The societal effects of globalization

Arguments in favour of globalization	Arguments against globalization
• Creates overall wealth for all nations because specialization increases trade	• Imposes massive strain on labour force both in developed countries (job destruction) and developing countries (sweatshops, child labor)
• Reduces inflation because of cost efficiencies	• Standardizes customer tastes. Reduces diversity
• Benefits customers because of price reduction owing to cost efficiencies	• Induces concentration of power in a few global corporations
	• Introduces a 'jungle' leading to the domination of the strongest multinational
• Better allocation of natural, financial and human resources	• Harms the environment because of unrestrained exploitation of natural resources such as forests
• Reduces corruption because of free market trade	• Reduces capacity for nations to protect their national interests, cultures and values

Source: Ricardo (1967).

Despite all this political turmoil, some analysts think that the world is becoming progressively more integrated. According to the consulting firm McKinsey,[5] by 1997, truly global markets represented approximately US$6 trillion out of a total world output of US$28 trillion (21%). The firm anticipates that by 2030 the proportion of global markets will amount to US$73 trillion out of US$91 trillion (80%). However, as will be seen in Chapter 16, this forecast may be challenged.

Pragmatically, companies adopt a competitive positioning which tends to foster further globalization. The development of information technologies, the fluidity of capital markets, the creation of megamergers in the telecoms, computer, oil, pharmaceutical, power and car industries demonstrate that business firms are increasingly behaving as if they were already living in a global world.

MINI-CASE

Mobile Telephony Services

Mobile telephony expanded rapidly during the two decades of the 1990s and 2000s. By 2011 there were around 5.2 billion mobile subscribers in the world (77% of the world's population).

According to the International Telecommunication Union (ITC), the distribution of customers is as follows: Asia Pacific: 2.649 billion, Americas: 880 million, Europe: 741 million, rest of the world: 979 million.

The industry is divided broadly into two major sub-industries: a) mobile equipment manufacturers: phones and docking stations, for example; and 2) mobile services operators.

Around the world, mobile services are operated mainly by local telephone companies with their own national brands. Some operators such as Vodaphone (UK) or Orange (France) have developed their presence internationally by acquiring or participating in the capital of local operators.

Most consumers use pre-paid services for the use of mobile phones. Various packages of pre-paid services as well as additional add-ons (Internet access, mobile banking, email, games...) are offered by the operators according to the characteristics of their markets. Customers are divided between personal accounts (roughly 65 to 90%, according to the country) and corporate accounts (from 10 to 35%). Some of the corporate accounts are multinational firms that want to benefit from a 'global' offer.

Mobile operators purchase their own network equipment and control its installation. They also procure large quantities of handsets that they include in their pre-paid contracts at discounted prices.

The key activities of mobile phone operators are:

- Procurement of network hardware and software: suppliers are multinational firms such as Nokia, Erikson and Alcatel-Lucent. There are two major standards used in the world: Global Standard Mobile with around 80% penetration and CDMA (15%). Japan and Korea use a standard of their own.
- Procurement of handsets. The major manufacturers of handsets are Nokia (23% global market share), Samsung (16%), LG (7.5%), BlackBerry (3%) and Apple (4.6%).
- Network installation and maintenance carried out by equipment suppliers plus local infrastructure companies under the control of the service provider.
- Software developments for new applications and services. From 2008 to 2011 around 300,000 applications for mobile phones and smartphones have been developed in the world. The main applications are games, news and social networking.
- Marketing and brand management. Products are marketed under a variety of local brands. Multinational players try to use their global brand (such as Orange), although advertising is country specific.
- Sales and distribution are organized differently from country to country.
- Billing is done according to local standards.
- Regulation with local authorities. Operators have to comply with local regulations.
- Finance and control. Treasury is managed centrally while day-to-day transactions are the duties of local managers.

MINI-CASE

- Human Resources. Employment regulations are specific to countries' legislation while human resource policies are decided by the Corporate Office.
- Strategy, Mergers and Acquisitions, Alliances belong to the corporate domain.

Questions:

1) Using your knowledge, the data provided and global/multi-local mapping can you decide whether mobile telephony is a global industry?
2) Now do the analysis for each of the activities listed above.

Summary and key points

1 Companies

A global company:

- can be defined as a company that operates in the main markets of the world in an integrated and coordinated way
- carries out one activity (e.g. manufacturing) or a component of the activity (e.g. manufacturing one sub-part only) of the value chain in one country, which serves the company's worldwide market.

A multinational company:

- operates in many markets of the world with little or no integration or coordination among operations.

2 Globalization:

- Is the phenomenon of the progressive transition of industries from a multinational to a global competitive structure
- Four factors are pushing companies to globalize:
  - *Political*: reduces trade barriers
  - *Technological*: reduces the cost of coordination and increases economies of scale
  - *Social*: encourages standardization and global branding
  - *Competitive*: induces integration and coordination
- Going global has four competitive benefits:
  - *Cost*: economies of scale and increased bargaining powers
  - *Timing*: reaches the optimal production volume and increases the reach of a product with a short product life cycle
  - *Learning*: facilitates best practices to be adopted across subsidiaries through the experience effect and the transfer of knowledge
  - *Arbitrage*: is derived when a global company uses resources in one country for the benefit of a subsidiary in another country.

3 Localization

- Four driving forces reduce the need to globalize:
  - *Cultural:* reduces the benefits of standardization

  - *Commercial:* requires differentiated approaches to sales and marketing
  - *Technical*: reduces the benefits of economies of scale, centralization and standardization
  - *Legal*: limits free flow of resources and imposes localization constraints
- Being local has three benefits:
  - *Proximity*
  - *Flexibility*
  - *Quick response time.*

4 Global /multi-local mapping

is used to identify the competitive requirements of an industry or a business segment and can assist companies in formulating business and national strategies.

Appendix 1.1 Positioning a business on the global /multi-local mapping

Assign a score for each question from 1 to 3

		1	*2*	*3*	
To what extent customers have similar demands for functionality and design across countries	Very different				Very similar
To what extent products or services have a high proportion of standard components across countries	Low proportion of standard components				High proportion of standard components
To what extent customers (or distributors) are themselves operating in different countries and are buying centrally your products or services	Buying locally				Buying centrally
To what extent significant economies of scale in your industry are important for the cost of the product (i.e. business needs very high volume to obtain low cost)	Low economies of scale				High economies of scale
To what extent the speed of introducing new products worldwide is important for competitiveness	Speed is not that important				Speed is very important
To what extent the sales of your product or service are based on technical factors or alternatively on cultural factors	Highly cultural				Highly technical
To what extent experience gained in other countries by a 'sister' subsidiary can be successful if applied in other countries	No great benefits				Yes, highly beneficial
To what extent competitors in your industry operate in a 'standardized' way across countries and are successful in doing so	Competitors are localizing				Competitors are successful in standardized approaches
To what extent pricing can be different from country to country without introducing dysfunctionality	Pricing has to be coherent across borders				Pricing can be very different
To what extent distribution channel management differs from country to country	Not so different				Yes, very different

		1	2	3	
To what extent business regulations and contexts differ from country to country requiring a high degree of local practices	Not too different				Highly different
To what extent products or services require a high degree of interaction with customers (customization)	Low customization				High customization
To what extent transportation costs are high compared to the product costs	Not so high				Very high
To what extent customer interface is critical for success	Not critical				Very critical

Questions 1 to 8 represent the importance of global forces while questions 9 to 14 represent the importance of local forces. It is then possible to map a business by a simple mathematical operation as in the following figure. Add your totals for each score to the box below to find out if your business is suited to a global or local approach.

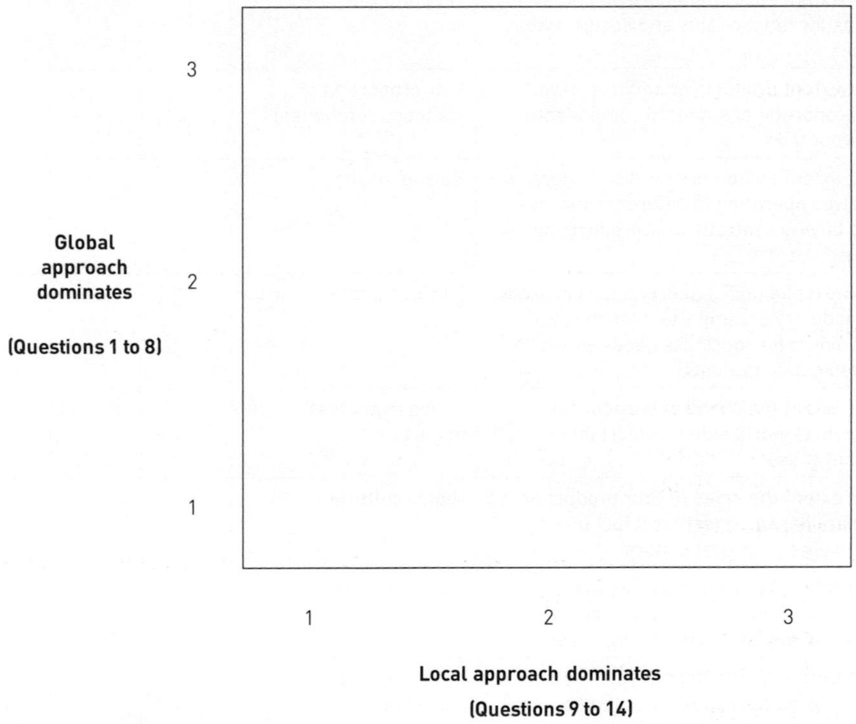

Learning assignments

1 Among the enterprises that you know, can you identify one that can be classed a global company? Why?

2 Why, in Figure 1.8, are savings accounts positioned low on global approaches and high on local approach while investment banking is high on global approach and low on local approach?

3 In Figure 1.7, food retailing is positioned as a local business, with a very low globalization score. However, in the press, companies like Tesco, Wal-Mart and Carrefour are classed as 'global retailers'. Explain this discrepancy.

4 What are the social factors that have been pushing for globalization and which have been pushing against?

5 What are the benefits of having a local approach?

6 When the Otis Elevator Company introduced the change described at the beginning of the chapter, there was a lot of resistance from the various heads of the European subsidiaries. Why? What arguments do you think the people hostile to globalization used?

7 Can Apple be classed as a global firm? Why?

Key words

- Arbitrage benefits
- Comparative advantage
- Global companies
- Global industries
- Global/multi-local mapping
- Globalization
- International product life cycle
- Multinational companies

Web resources

<http://knowledge.insead.edu/home.cfm >
A link to the database of INSEAD Knowledge under the category of Globalization.

<http://www.businessweek.com/mediacenter/>
Business Week – Globalization.

<http://www.mckinseyquarterly.com/>
McKinsey Quarterly – Globalization.

<http://www.nato.int>
Provides information on North Atlantic Treaty Organization (NATO), including its 19 member countries, its organization and values.

<http://www.wto.org/>
Provides information about the WTO.

<http://www.imf.org/>
Provides statistics and papers from the International Monetary Fund (IMF).

<http://data.worldbank.org/>
World Bank data online.

<http://www.unctad.org/>
UNCTAD data, particularly the World Investment Report section.

<**http://www.oecd.org/**>
OECD resources.

<**http://epp.eurostat.ec.europa.eu/**>
European Union data.

Visit the companion website at **http://www.palgrave.com/business/lasserre3e** for a multitude of weblinks and resources, self-test questions for revision and a searchable glossary.

Notes

1 George Yip (1992) gives four globalization drivers: cost, market, competition and government. These are similar to those presented here.
2 Ohmae (1985).
3 Ricardo (1967).
4 Rugman (2000).
5 Lowell and Fraser (1999, pp. 68–81).

References and further reading

Books and articles

Baker, Michael and Susan Hart, *Product Strategy and Management*. London: Prentice-Hall, 1999.

Bartlett, Christopher A. and Sumantra Ghoshal, *Managing Across Borders: The Transnational Solution*. Boston, MA: Harvard Business School Press, 1989.

Fraser, Jane N. and Jeremy Oppenheim, 'What's New about Globalization?', *McKinsey Quarterly*, 2, 1997, pp. 168–79.

Harvard Business School Global Strategies: Insights from the World's Leading Thinkers. Boston, MA: Harvard Business School Press, 1900. (This book contains a collection of *Harvard Business Review (HBR)* articles.)

Humes, Samuel, *Managing the Multinational: Confronting the Global–Local Dilemma*. London: Prentice-Hall, 1993.

International Bank for Reconstruction and Development, *Global Economic Prospects, Managing the New Wave of Globalization*, The World Bank, Washington, 2007

Lowell, L. Bryan and Jane N. Fraser, 'Getting to Global', *McKinsey Quarterly*, 4, 1999, pp. 68–81.

Michaels, R.E., R.Z. Olshaysky and W. Qualls, 'Shortening of the PLC – An Empirical Test', *Journal of Marketing*, 4, 1981.

Michel, D., R. Salle and J. Valla, *Marketing industriel*, Paris: Economica, 1996, *from Nouvel Economiste*, 1026.

Micklethwait, John and Adrian Wooldridge, *A Future Perfect: The Challenges – and the Promise – of Globalization*. London: Heinemann, 2000.

Mirza, Hafiz (ed.), *Global Competitive Strategies in World Economy: Multilateralism, Regionalization and the Transnational Firm*, New Horizons in International Business. London: Edward Elgar, 1998.

Ohmae, Kenichi, *Becoming a Triad Power*. New York: McKinsey & Co., 1985.

Porter, Michael E. (ed.), *Competition in Global Industries*. Boston, MA: Harvard Business School Press, 1986.

Porter, Michael E., *The Competitive Advantage of Nations*. New York: Free Press, 1998.

Prahalad, C.K. and Yves L. Doz, *The Multinational Mission: Balancing Local Demands and Global Vision*, 1st edn. New York: Free Press, 1987.

Rangan, Subramanian and Robert Z. Lawrence, *A Prism on Globalization*. Washington, DC: Brookings Institution, 1999.

Ricardo, David, *The Principles of Political Economy and Taxation*. Homewood, IL: Irwin, 1967.

Rugman Alan, *The End of Globalization: A New and Radical Analysis of Globalization and What it Means for Business*. London: Random House, 2000.

Yip, George, *Total Global Strategy: Managing for World Wide Competitive Advantage*. Englewood Cliffs, NJ: Prentice-Hall, 1992.

Journals

BUSINESS

Business week

Fortune

Economist

International Management

Financial Times

SEMI-ACADEMIC

Multinational Business

Harvard Business Review

California Management Review

Columbia Journal of World Business

Sloan Management Review

European Management Journal

ACADEMIC

Journal of International Business Studies

Strategic Management Journal

International Human Resources Management

chapter

2 DESIGNING A GLOBAL STRATEGY

Introduction

The globalization of industries discussed in Chapter 1 was led by some precursor companies that identified early on the opportunities of designing and implementing global strategies. In this chapter, based on the experience of leading global companies, a framework for the formulation of global strategies is proposed.

The chapter starts by defining what *business strategy* is about and how it applies to *global companies*. It gives an example of how SONY Corporation has developed its global strategy. The framework for the strategy consists of:

- ***Global ambition***: stating the long-term objectives of the corporation as well as the relative importance of regions in its global footprint.
- ***Global positioning***: choice of countries, customer segments and value proposition
- *Global business system*: investments in resources, assets and competence to create a global value chain and global capabilities either directly or through alliances and acquisitions
- ***Global organization***: global structure, processes, coordination and human resources (HR) management.

This chapter details all these elements and provides some tools:

- The ***Global Revenue Index*** and the ***Global Capabilities Index***, measuring the extent to which a company can be considered as a global player, a regional player or simply a global exporter or a global sourcer
- The classification of countries according to their ***strategic importance*** (key countries, emerging countries, platform countries, marketing countries)
- The definition of ***global positioning*** according to the scope of markets, value proposition and of competitive approach based on cost leadership or differentiation
- ***Business system*** design
- ***Competitive advantages*** analysis
- ***Sustainability*** of competitive advantages.

It then describes three stages in the process of globalization: export, multinational and global.

The chapter ends by sketching the various forms of organizational structures found among multinational and global firms.

Learning objectives

At the end of this chapter you will be able to:

- identify a global strategy by breaking down all its elements
- contribute meaningfully to the formulation of a global strategy
- describe a global business system
- identify the sources of competitive advantages in a given company.

ORIGIN, CONTENT, PURPOSE AND DRIVERS OF STRATEGY

Strategy (from the Greek, *stratos*: an army and *agein*: to lead) has traditionally been a military art. The ancient Chinese military theorist, Sun Tzu (circa 500 BC) stated that 'the supreme art of war is to subdue the enemy without fighting'.

Strategy as an art of war was transferred into a business context in the early 1960s. This does not mean that there was no 'strategy' behind business decisions earlier; but there were no formal theories of business strategy.

There are several schools of thought about what business strategy is, but all schools recognize that business strategy has to do with *choice* and *investments*. A business strategy will generally cover the following:

- **Ambition**: Choice of *long-term objectives* for the business
- **Positioning**: Choice of products and customer *segments* and of a *value proposition* to customers
- **Capabilities building**: Choice of investments in order to create a business system able to *deliver value competitively*
- **Organization**: Choice of *people*, *structure*, *processes and systems*.

The concept of strategy may apply at various levels in a corporation (See Figure 2.1). The most frequent distinctions are:

- **Business strategy** (also called *competitive strategy*) applies at the level of a business operating in a particular industry segment. It defines the way the business wants and is able to compete in its segment.

If the market in which the firm operates is global, its business strategy will be a **global business strategy** that defines its long-term objectives for the world market; selects its value proposition for the world market; builds, integrates and coordinates its business system to gain and sustain a global competitive advantage and puts in place an organization to manage its operations worldwide.

- **Corporate strategy** applies at the level of a company engaged in different business segments: the multi-business corporation. It essentially defines the portfolio of businesses in which the corporation wants to operate and the resource allocation pattern among those businesses.

If the corporation operates globally, the corporate strategy will be a **global corporate strategy** which will integrate the various global strategies of the different businesses in the corporate portfolio.

Purpose and Drivers of Strategy

The purpose of business strategy is to build and sustain a competitive business system in selected markets leading to economic value creation. Economic value is created when the revenues generated by the business is equal or larger than the total cost of doing business. (See Figure 2.2.)

Economic value is driven by two major forces:

- the macro structural characteristics of the industry in which the company operates (Porter, 1980)
- the ability to build and sustain competitive advantages (Porter, 1985)

Hence the key choices of strategy are first to decide where the company will compete and second to invest in capabilities leading to competitive advantages.

	Business strategy **Competing in one industry**	**Corporate strategy** **Competing in several industries and/or industry segments**	**Global strategy** **Competing in several countries**
Ambition	• Business definition • Mission/vision • Long-term objectives	• Business definition • Mission/vision • Long-term objectives • Relative importance of businesses	• Business definition • Mission/vision • Long-term objectives • Relative importance of regions and countries
Positioning	• Which customer segments? • Which countries? • Our value proposition?	• Which businesses? • Degree of integration • Our competitive principles • (Differentiation/costs)	• Which regions/countries? • Degree of integration • Our competitive principles (global/local)
Capabilities building	• Business system design • Key investments • Acquisition, mergers, joint ventures, alliances?	• Resource allocation among businesses • Mergers, acquisitions, alliances • New entries/exit	• Resource allocation among regions/countries • Designing global value chain • Mergers acquisitions, alliances • New entries/exit
Organization	• HRM development • Structure • Processes • Policies • Values and culture	• Corporate internal governance • Corporate HRM • Structure • Policies • Values and culture	• Corporate internal governance • HRM policies • Global structure • Degree of autonomy of subsidiaries • Integration and co-ordination among subsidiaries • Values and culture

Figure 2.1 Business, corporate and global strategy

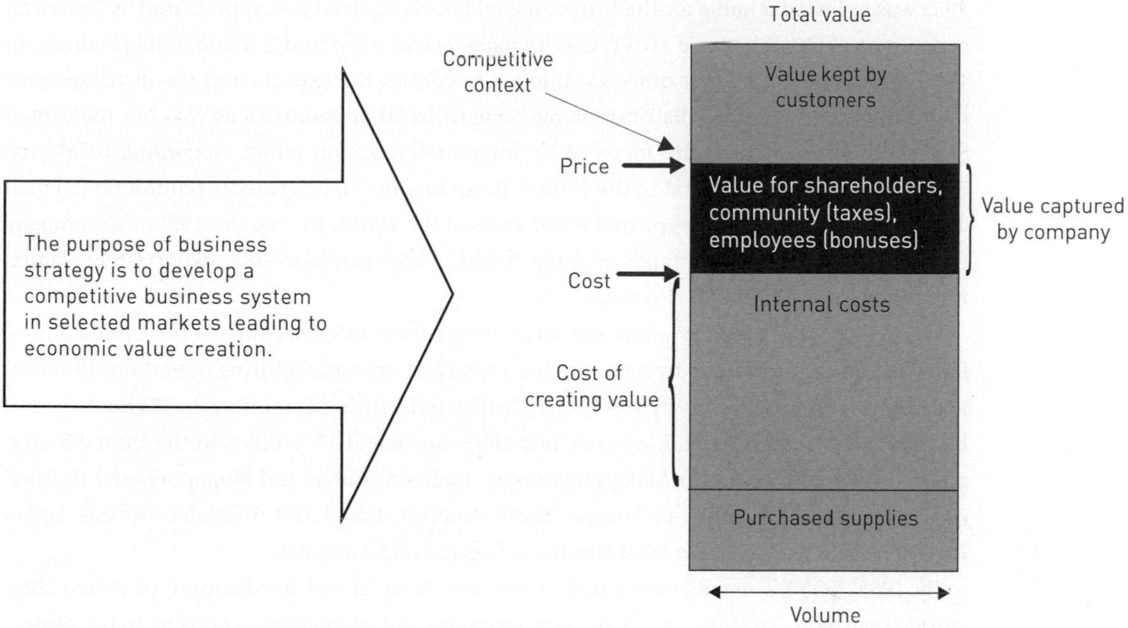

Figure 2.2 The purpose of strategy (adapted from Besanko *et al.*, 2007)

A company business strategy

A company business strategy is a set of *fundamental choices* which defines its long-term objectives, its value proposition to the market, how it intends to build and sustain a competitive business system and how it organizes itself (see box opposite for a more detailed definition of strategy).

A business strategy is global when a company competes in the key markets of the world and when the business system is made of integrated and coordinated activities across borders.

The Sony Corporation case presented below illustrates how a global strategy has been developed over time.

EXAMPLE

SONY Corporation globalization[1]

Foundation and expansion

In 1953, Akio Morita, the co-founder of Tokyo Tsushin Kogyo KK (TTKKK), a company making tape recorders and magnetic tape, visited the United States. Morita bought a licence for a new electronic component, the transistor, from Bell Laboratories. The purchase of this licence allowed TTKKK engineers to develop a transistorized radio in 1955 and a pocket-sized radio in 1957.

During his trip to the United States, Morita realized the importance of the American market. He decided that his company needed to market its products outside Japan, and firstly in the most important market of the world, the US market. One of the first decisions taken in

1953 was to invent a name for the firm that could be recognized and appreciated by American consumers. TTKKK became SONY, and its name became the brand name of its products. In 1960, SONY opened its first office in America to control the exports and the distribution of its products. It concluded distribution agreements in other countries as well but the United States initially remained the focus of its internationalization effort. According to Morita, SONY needed to succeed first in the United States in order to increase its reputation in Japan and then to spread into Europe and other parts of the world. During the 1960s the company exported radios, magnetic tapes and black and white television sets; exports represented more than 50 per cent of its revenues.

In 1971, the first overseas plant, manufacturing colour TVs, was built in the United States, followed during the decade by a progressive expansion of manufacturing operations in America, Europe and Asia Pacific. By 1990, SONY had manufacturing operations in 17 countries and by 2000, 43 subsidiaries outside Japan, including movie and TV studios in the United States, component manufacture in Malaysia, Taiwan, Thailand, Korea and Singapore, and finished product assembly factories in Europe, North America, Brazil and Australia. Outside Japan, R&D centres were located in West Germany, England and Australia.

By 1988, SONY's management had coined the term 'global localization' to define their world operations. The intention was to balance sales and production according to the respective weight of North America, Asia and Europe. Three regional headquarters – in New York, Cologne and Singapore – were set up in the mid-1980s to coordinate the activities in North America, Europe and Asia (outside Japan). *Product groups* are in charge of developing products and setting up global strategies while *regional groups* are in charge of developing markets. Both products and regions work in a coordinated fashion.

By 2011, 20 per cent of SONY's revenues were generated in North America, 48 per cent in Asia, 21 per cent in Europe and 11 per cent in the rest of the world.

Analysis of SONY's global strategy

Looking at the example of SONY, you can see some key characteristics of the strategy developed by the company:

- First was the decision taken very early by Morita that the Japanese market was not the right battlefield for the consumer electronics business; for him, the world market was the right battlefield. SONY had the *ambition* to become a global player in the key world markets. Based upon this initial ambition, SONY implemented a *strategy* that ultimately gave a significant market presence in the key regions of the world.
- Second, even if the world was the right competitive arena, some markets like the United States in the 1960s were considered as *key markets*, to be developed as a priority.
- Third, Morita was thinking not only in terms of market conquests but was looking at the *interactive positive effects* of success in one market, the United States, on other markets in Japan and in Europe. This interactive thinking, linking together markets all over the world is characteristic of global thinking: the world is not a collection of markets but a set of *interacting markets*.

- Fourth, *localization* of marketing, manufacturing and later on R&D activities was put in place in order to achieve a balance between sales and production on a worldwide basis. Production centres were designed for serving the world and their location selected according to the comparative advantages of each country. Production centres in Asia were built to produce low-cost components, while factories in the United States and Europe were built in order to be close to consumers. SONY built up an *integrated network* of production and, later on, research centres, worldwide.
- Fifth, as early as 1953, SONY realized that to succeed in the world market it was necessary to have a *global name*: hence 'SONY', that can be understood everywhere and that can become a very important competitive asset. At the end of the 1990s SONY was among the brands that were the most recognized in the world.
- Sixth, attached to its global image, SONY's value proposition to customers across the world was to offer innovative, miniaturized audio and video products that enhanced customer satisfaction thanks to their functionality and quality. Such differentiated *global positioning* was consistent in all markets.
- Seventh, in 1972, the Head of SONY America was an American whose salary was higher than the equivalent SONY executives. Foreigners were brought on to the main board in 1989. In order to support its global strategy Morita developed a *global management* team.
- Eighth, the globalization process was *progressive* and spread over time, as shown in Figure 2.3.

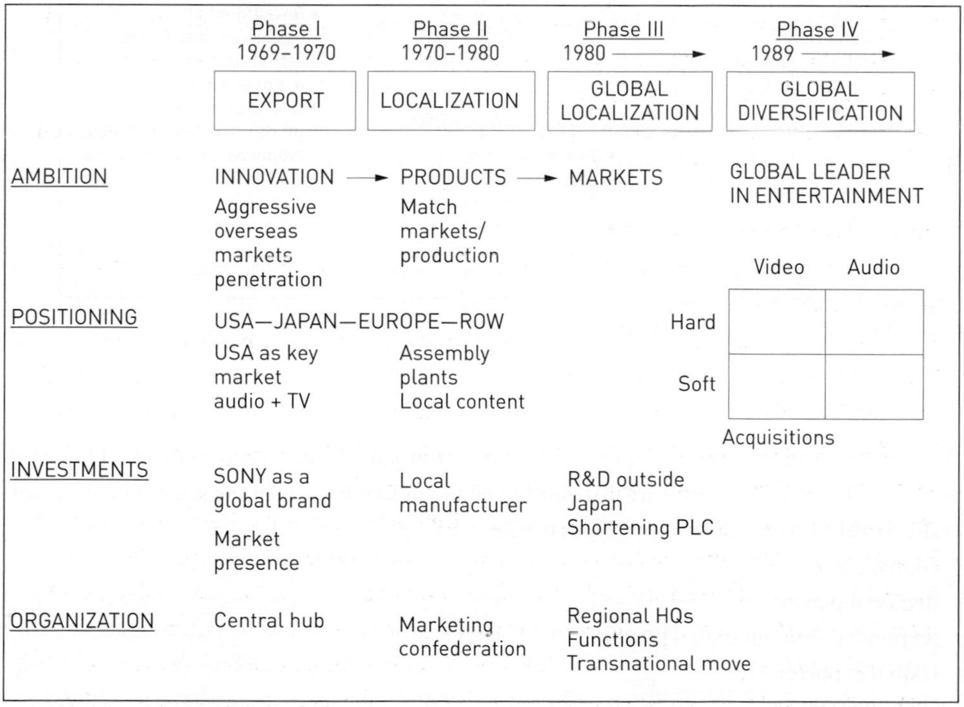

Figure 2.3 SONY's global development

Based on SONY's example it is now possible to describe more formally the components of a global strategy.

Framework for global strategy

A global strategy is made up of four major components (see Figure 2.4):

- A global strategic *ambition*
- A global strategic *positioning*
- A global *business system*
- A global *organization.*

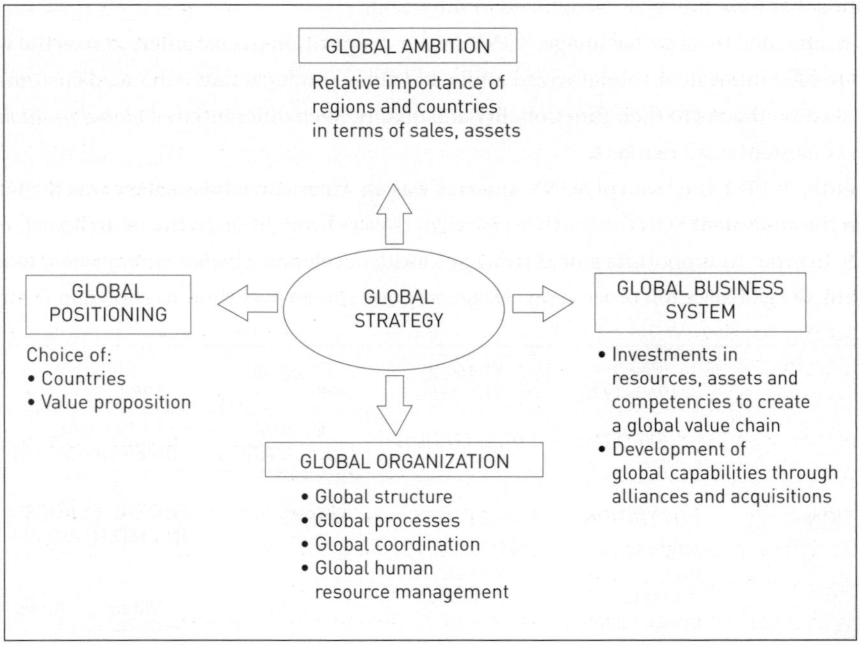

Figure 2.4 Global strategy framework

Global ambition

The global strategic ambition expresses the role a company wants to play in the world marketplace and how it views the future distribution of its sales and assets in the key regional clusters of the world. You can identify five types of role:

- Global player
- Regional player
- Regional dominant global player
- Global exporter
- Global operator.

A company whose ambition is to be a **global player** aspires to establish a *sustainable competitive position in the key markets of the world* and to build an integrated business system of designs spread over those key markets. SONY would qualify for such a description of its role, as would Unilever, Ericsson, Nokia, Alcatel, Motorola, Shell, Xerox, Canon, Procter & Gamble and Citibank.

A **regional player** defines its role as capturing a *strong competitive advantage in one of the key regions of the world* – North America, Europe or Asia – and being a marginal or relatively weak competitor in the other parts. Peugeot or Fiat in automobiles, NEC or Barclays would be examples of such an ambition.[2]

A **global exporter** is a company whose role is to *sell across the key markets of the world* products manufactured or services operated in its home country and that builds foreign operations only to support the export drive. The major aerospace or defence companies like Boeing, Airbus and Raytheon can be classified in this category despite the fact that they have some supporting assets (maintenance, sales offices, etc.) outside their home region.

A **global sourcer** is a company that procures a large fraction of its product components from factories[3] located outside its base market and which concentrates its sales in its *domestic market.* In such a case the ambition would hardly qualify as global: however, many managerial issues of integration and coordination of activities, both in-house factories or long-term subcontracting, would be quite similar to those that a global company would have to face.

In order to assess the degree of global ambition exhibited by companies, we will look at their distribution of sales, assets and personnel.

In 2005, the world economy produced US$42,000 billion of goods and services, 31 per cent in North America, 26 per cent in Asia and 32 per cent in Western Europe, the rest being spread over Africa, South America, the Middle East and Eastern Europe.

In certain industries the distribution of markets can differ from the distribution of GDP, and growth differentials will make the future distribution of world markets different from what it is today. Table 2.1 gives a distribution of world markets by regions.

A pure, global company would ideally exhibit three major characteristics:

- First, it would have a distribution of its sales proportional to the distribution of markets in its industry. For instance Sony's distribution of sales, with 28 per cent in North America, 23 per cent in Europe and 39 per cent in Asia replicates very closely the 23, 36, and 38 per cent distribution of consumer electronic industry markets.
- Second, it would have a distribution of its assets and workforce proportional to the distribution of markets in its industry.
- Third, it would manage its activities in an integrated and coordinated way across the globe.

Obviously, this may not apply to all industries since no industry has the same degree of pressure towards globalization, as has been discussed in Chapter 1. In a global industry like the tire industry, in which market distribution is 26 per cent in North America, 31 per cent in Europe, 30 per cent in Asia and 13 per cent in the rest of the world, the distribution of revenues of the four major players differs substantially from the industry distribution as shown in Table 2.2.

Table 2.1 Distribution of world market by region in selected industries in 2005 (percentage of US$ value)

Industry	Europe (%)	North America (%)	Asia Pacific (%)	Rest of the World (%)
Advertising	19	57	23	1
Clothing & footwear	32	27	25	15
Computer hardware	27	27	39	7
Construction materials	18	9	63	10
Consumer electronics	30	23	38	9
Cosmetics	37	22	27	14
Data processing services	29	52	14	9
Electrical appliances	28	27	34	10
Electrical equipment	23	20	42	15
Environmental services	31	39	23	7
Health care equipment	34	46	18	2
Home furniture	44	22	18	15
Insurance	34	38	25	3
Mobile phones	30	25	42	3
Paint & coatings	26	27	35	12
Pharmaceuticals	28	48	18	6
Retailing	32	30	23	15
Specialist chemicals	45	39	11	4
GDP billion US$ (2005)	12,900	13,500	10,700	4400
GDP % (2005)	31	32	26	11

Source: Various compilations by author.

Table 2.2 Distribution of markets and revenues in tires (2010)

Company	North America (%)	Europe (%)	Asia (%)	Rest of the World (%)
Industry	26	31	30	13
Bridgestone	36	12	42	10
Goodyear	43	34	11	12
Michelin	34	43	← 23 →	
Pirelli	16	40	10	34
Continental	19	60	16	5

Source: Companies' annual reports.

The globalization indices

For evaluating the extent to which a company has followed a global ambition, there are two useful globalization indices. Appendix 2.1 gives a technical explanation of the measurement of those indices.

- The **Transnational Index** (TNI), used by the United Nations Conference on Trade and Development (UNCTAD), which is a composite ratio of the proportion of activities made outside the home country of a multinational firm. For instance in the tire industry, assuming that Europe is the 'home' region of European suppliers, Continental's TNI would be 40, much lower than Michelin (TNI=66), Pirelli (TNI=60), Goodyear (TNI=57) or Bridgestone (TNI=58), because of its higher concentration of activities in Europe.
- The **Global Revenue Index** and the **Global Capability Index.**

The Global Revenue Index (GRI) represents a company's distribution of sales in the major world regions as a percentage of the industry distribution of demand in the same regions.[4] If in an industry the world market is divided in the proportion of 30% in North America; 30% in Europe , 30% in Asia and 10% in the rest of the world, the GRI will compare the actual distribution of sales of a company in those four major regions with sales distribution for the industry as a whole. A company with a low GRI is more concentrated in one region while a company with a high GRI will have a distribution of sales close to the industry.

The Global Capability Index (GCI) represents in a similar way the distribution of *assets* or *personnel.* Companies which rely heavily on external sourcing will have a low GCI score. This is because the company cannot deploy resources and capabilities at will but relies on external parties to supply the capability. This reliance on external parties also means that the company can face potential problems such as product/service unavailability, time delays in delivery, or price pressure from the overseas suppliers.

By combining the GCI and the GRI in one chart, we obtain a mapping of the *global ambition of players* (Figure 2.5).

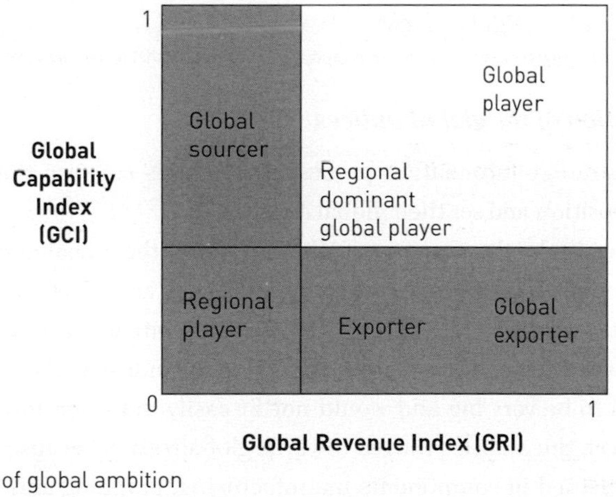

Figure 2.5 Mapping of global ambition

A company low in both GRI and GCI would be a **regional player**, a company low in GRI and high in GCI would be a **global operator**, a company low in GCI and high in GRI would be a **global exporter**, while a company high in both dimensions would be a **Global player** and a company with an average score in both dimensions would be a **Regional dominant global**

player. Figure 2.6 shows the mapping of the five leading companies in the tire industry. The tire industry is considered as a global industry and all four players are in the **global player** quadrant.

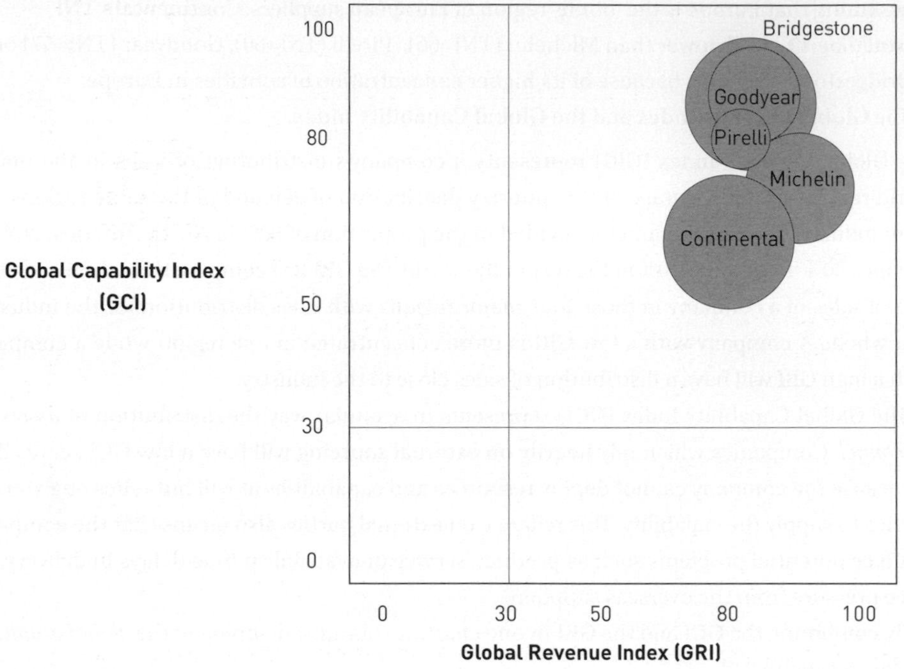

Figure 2.6 Mapping of the tire industry

(The size of the bubbles is proportional to total sales 2010)

Sources: www.bridgestone.com, www.conti-online.com, www.goodyear.com, www.michelin.com, www.pirelli.com

EXAMPLE

A dynamic utilization of the global indices

As part of the strategy formulation process, companies can use the global indices to analyze their position and set their global ambition.

To illustrate, we will take the example of Whirlpool and the global appliance industry. In 1980 Whirlpool was essentially a regional operator. Its sales and assets were concentrated in the United States. Its GRI was 0.35 and its GCI 0.40. The white goods industry (refrigerators, washers, cookers) was at that time primarily a regional industry. For instance, American refrigerators tended to be very big and would not fit easily in European or Japanese homes. Progressively, however, the industry moved towards globalization because of the huge economies of scale to be gained in components manufacturing, branding and R&D. The Swedish company, Electrolux, moved aggressively in Europe to become a pan-European company and invested in the United States and Asia to become a global player. The Whirlpool management realized that its future would be at stake if it did not follow a globalization path. The first step of this process was an alliance with the Philips appliance business, which was transformed into a straight acquisition. From a single regional player, Whirlpool moved into the position of a dual regional player with a strong delocalization of its factories, particularly in Latin America. Then, in the early 1990s, Whirlpool realized that the Asia Pacific region was going to represent 40 per cent of world sales for refrigerators, washers and cookers. It set up its ambition to gain a significant position in Asia. By the year 2010, Whirlpool had become a global player (see Figure 2.7).

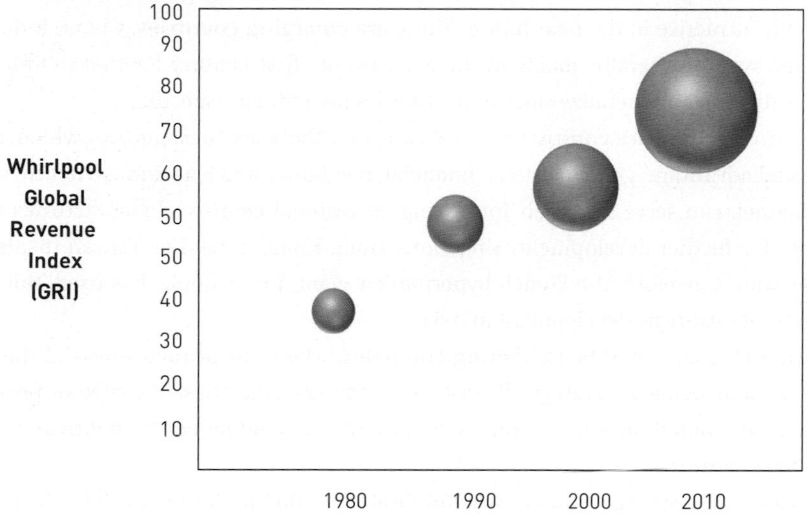

Figure 2.7 The evolution of Whirlpool globalization (GRI). Bubbles are proportional to sales.

Source: www.whirlpool.com

Global positioning

Global positioning consists of two types of choices:

- First, the *choice of countries* in which the company wants to compete and the role that those countries have to play in the global country portfolio.
- Second, the definition of the various *value propositions* for the product or services of the company, corresponding to the type of segments and countries in which the company wants to compete.

Choice of countries

Depending on the industry, countries differ in the opportunities they offer to companies for their strategic development. Some countries, given their size, growth or the quality of their human, natural or locational resources, are critical for companies' long-term competitiveness. Those countries are classed as **key countries.** Not to be present in these countries is a serious handicap for companies who want to be global players. As mentioned earlier, Europe, North America and Asia are the three regional clusters that a global player would consider, but within those clusters some countries are more important than others, and should be given priority. In Asia, for instance, in the automotive sector, Japan, Korea and, in the future, China can be considered as key. In Europe, Germany and, to a certain extent, the United Kingdom or France are also key countries.[5] In the pulp and paper industry, in which natural resources are a key component of competitive advantage, countries like Indonesia can be considered as key, while California (Silicon Valley) would be key for Internet players.

The second category of countries is countries that exhibit a high growth rate, making them strategically attractive in the near future. These are **emerging countries**. China, India, Brazil and Poland would generally qualify in the early twenty-first century for that definition but, again, it is difficult to generalize since opportunities are industry-specific.

The **platform countries** constitute a third category. These are the countries which, because of locational advantage, good logistical, financial, regulatory and legal infrastructure or qualified personnel, can serve as a 'hub' for setting up regional centres, global factories that are 'platforms' for further development. Singapore, Hong Kong, Ireland or Taiwan display these characteristics. Carrefour, the French hypermarket giant, for example, has used Taiwan as a platform for its strategic development in Asia.

A fourth category would be **marketing countries**, where the attractiveness of the market is good, without being as strategically critical as the key countries. The type of presence in such countries should be assessed on its own merits, depending on the political, economic and business context.

Countries with a strong resource base but limited market prospects would be classified as **sourcing countries**; for instance, Malaysia for rubber or Saudi Arabia for petroleum.

Typically, a global company will control a portfolio of operations in these different categories of country. The benefit of such categorization is to establish *priorities* in investments and to guide *entry strategies* (a topic that will be discussed in Chapter 7).

Value proposition

The value proposition is the definition of a customer's *value attributes* that the company is offering to the market. It implies:

- Choice of value attributes
- Choice of customer segments
- Choice of degree of world standardization of the product/service offering.

Value attributes are the elements of the products or services that customers value when making their purchasing decision. Those include the product design, functionality, performance, quality, customization and price, as well as the related service, the brand, the availability and other features. The set of those attributes for a particular group of customers and a particular product or service is the customer's **value curve**.

Professor Michael Porter, from the Harvard Business School, has identified two 'generic' strategies corresponding to two types of value attributes:[6]

- A proposition based on value-enhancing attributes such as performance, quality, service, customization. Porter calls this type of value attribute *differentiated.*

- A proposition based on price for standardized products or services. Porter calls this type *cost leadership*.

The same typology can apply to global positioning: the company can either position itself as a **global differentiator** or a **global cost leader**.

Customer segments are the groups of customers that have *similar value curves*. Those customer groups can be identified by income level, geographical location, age, socio-psychometric attributes in consumer goods and service industries or by industry, size and purchasing behaviour in business-to-business (B2B) industries. The strategic choice at this level will be to decide whether the company concentrates its segmentation on one or two customer groups, a positioning that Michael Porter qualifies as *focused*, or whether it attempts to embrace many or all customer segments, a positioning qualified as *broad*.

The third component of a value proposition is the choice between a standardized versus an adaptive-value proposition across countries. If you adopt a similar or standardized value attribute to the same type of customer segments across the globe, the approach will be qualified as *standard*; if you try to differentiate value attributes and segments according to the country or regions, the approach will be qualified as *adaptive*.

Then the company's value proposition will consist of trying to identify the customer groups it wants to serve (focused or broad), the type of value attribute it wants to offer (cost versus differentiation) to those customers, and whether it is homogeneous or not across countries (standardized versus adaptive). Coca Cola, Swatch or SONY, for instance, have a standard value proposition across the globe and serve similar segments. Unilever and Procter & Gamble adjust their value proposition and their segmentation in different countries.

The combination of those three choices will lead to eight different positionings, which are illustrated in Table 2.3 below with some examples.

Table 2.3 Global positioning

Global niche players				Broad global players			
Standard differentiated	**Cost leader**	**Adaptive differentiated**	**Cost leader**	**Standard differentiated**	**Cost leader**	**Adaptive differentiated**	**Cost leader**
Standardized niche differentiator	Low-cost standardized niche	Differentiated niche adapter	Low-cost niche adapter	Broad standardized differentiator	Broad standardized cost	Broad adaptive differentiator	Broad adaptive cost leader
Example: Swatch, Intel	**Example:** Acer	**Example:** McDonald's	**Example:** Carrefour	**Example:** SONY	**Example:** Matsushita	**Example:** Unilever, P&G, Philips	**Example:** Electrolux

The strategic choice of a value proposition dictates the type of capabilities that are needed to compete globally, and therefore the type of business system in which the company needs to invest.

Global business system

The third element of a global strategy consists of deploying a business system across countries in order to transfer and reinforce the company's competitive advantages as well as building new ones. We will define first what a business system is and describe the components of a global business system and second how global firms recreate, reinforce and transfer their competitive advantages

Global business system and its components

A *business system* is the configuration of the various activities that a firm carries out internally or externally through alliances in order to design, produce and deliver the value to customers and ultimately to capture value for itself. Professor Michael Porter has named a company business system as a '*value chain*'.[7] Global business system design consists of breaking down the company value chain into elements that are spread and integrated across the world. Each company has a different value chain according to the type of industry in which it operates and the degree of vertical integration it has adopted.

However, three major generic components of a value chain can be distinguished:

- *Innovative activities*: R&D, knowledge, creation, design
- *Productive activities*: procurement, manufacturing, back office, operations, logistics
- *Customer relationship activities*: marketing, sales, distribution, customer services.

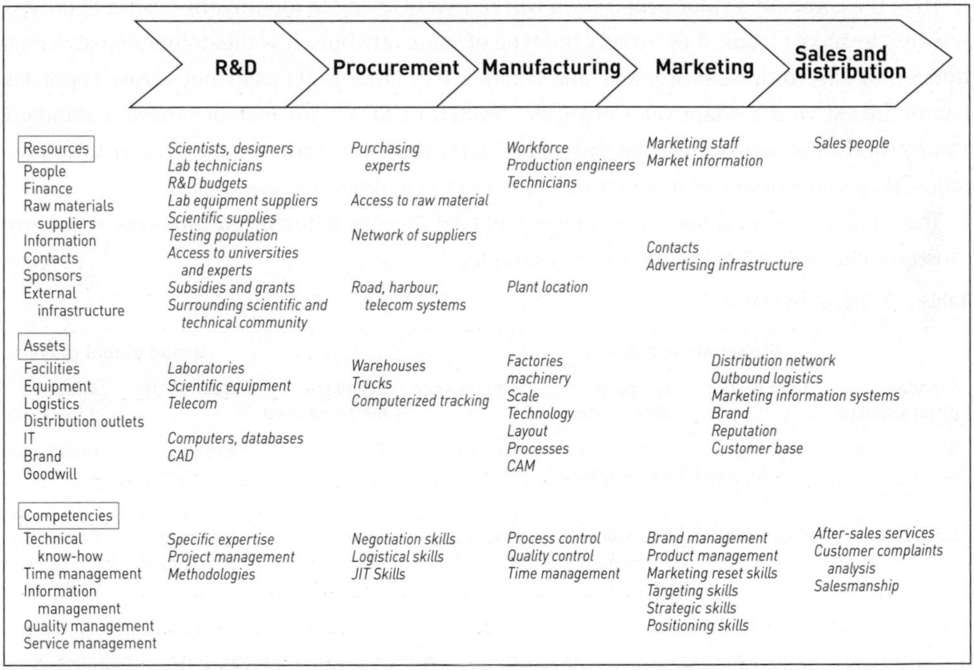

Figure 2.8 Generic value chain

In each of these activities, the company deploys resources, assets and competencies. Figure 2.8 represents a generic value chain, showing the key resources assets and competencies that are typically found in each activity.

During the process of globalization, companies progressively split their value chain by spreading their activities across the world. The typical path of globalization of the value chain is described in Figure 2.9. The first stage is the *export stage* in which the only elements of the value chain which are set up in foreign countries are the sales, and even then not through direct investment but through local distributors, agents or licensing. The only possible direct investment at this stage, if the size of the market justifies it, is the creation of a representative office in one country or a regional office for a group of countries. Those representative offices are set up to seize opportunities, identify agents, distributors and partners, organize the trade flow and prepare future substantial investments.

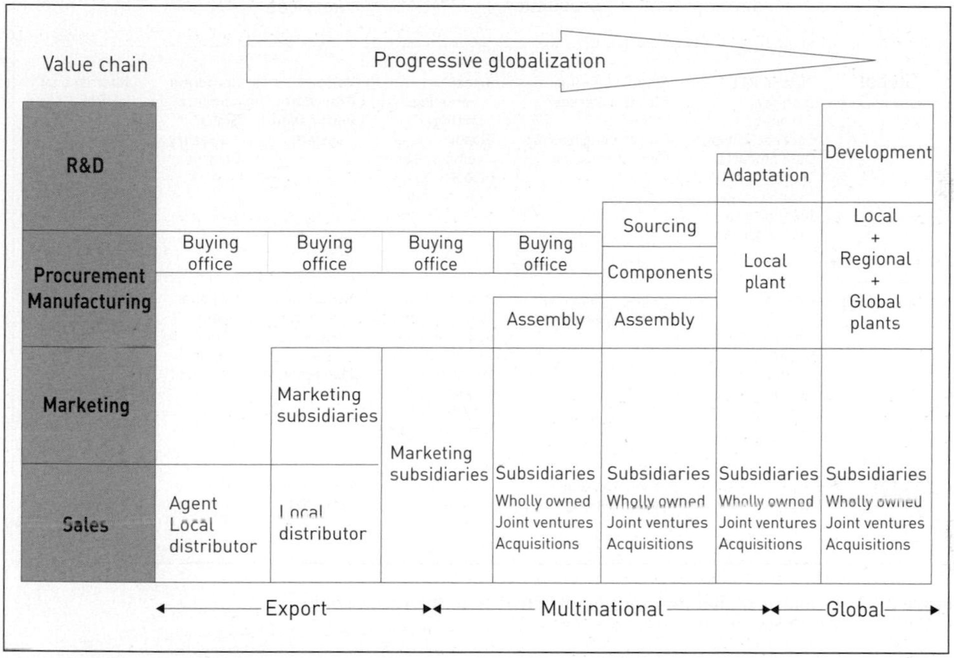

Figure 2.9 Typical globalization of the value chain

The second stage is to invest in *marketing subsidiaries* to actively manage the marketing mix. Those subsidiaries are staffed with expatriates plus local recruits and their role is to coordinate the activities of the distributors, organize the promotion, set up logistics and service centres and, in some cases, some operational facilities, such as testing laboratories or assembling operations to support the sales effort. Those marketing subsidiaries may eventually take over the local distributors. When the market justifies or when local governments require a localization of value adding activities, companies invest in manufacturing or operational facilities for the service sectors. Some R&D facilities may be localized as well, in order to adapt products or services to local conditions. These foreign investments are made either as wholly owned subsidiaries or joint ventures or acquisitions of local firms. At this stage, as the number of those investments increases, the company is a multinational, managing a portfolio of relatively independent worldwide subsidiaries.

During the final stage of globalization, multinational companies feel the competitive need to integrate and coordinate their worldwide operations to take advantage of economies of scale, transfer of know-how and resource optimization. This leads to an interlocking set of value chain activities which falls broadly into three categories: the activities which have a global role to serve the whole world (*global activities*, such as global research centres, or global plants), those which have a regional role (*regional activities*) and those which are purely local (*local activities*). Figure 2.10 shows how these three categories interact.

	Research & development	Sourcing production	Marketing	Customer services	Finances	HRM
Global	Central R&D Technical strategy Core technology Core products Technology conferences Technological intelligence	Global factories Global materials flow Process engineering Central sourcing	Global marketing strategy Global communication Global positioning	Policies Procedures Information system	Corporate finance Global treasury Control	International HRM
Regional	Regional products development Regional intelligence Regional seminars	Regional factories Regional sourcing	Regional intelligence Regional product Management Regional accounts Regional bidding	Regional customer support Logistics Maintenance	Regional debt financing Regional control	Regional careers Training
Local	Local laboratories	Local production Local sourcing	Distribution Promotion Sales	After-sales services	Local borrowing	Local careers Training

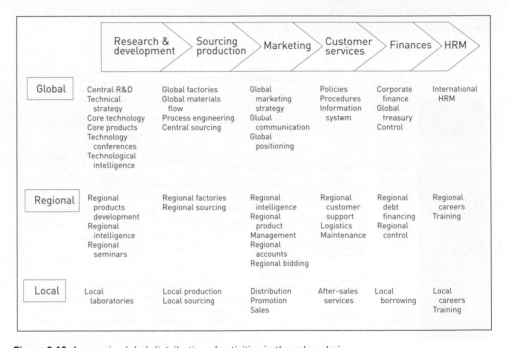

Figure 2.10 A generic global distribution of activities in the value chain

Competitive advantages

Competitive advantages are capabilities that are difficult to replicate or imitate and are non-tradable. Traditionally, there are three types of capability that lead to competitive advantages (Porter 1985):

- Capabilities leading to an increase in customer value through performance, quality and brand services: a *differentiated* value proposition
- Capabilities leading to a lower cost base, such as low-cost labour, low-cost sourcing, economies of scale in production, efficiency: a *cost leadership* value proposition.

In addition other types of competitive advantage have been identified:

- Capabilities leading to being ahead of the competition in developing new products or services: an *innovative advantage*[9]

Table 2.4 Capabilities leading to competitive advantage

Differentiation: Capabilities leading to enhanced customer value	**Cost leadership: Capabilities leading to low-cost position**	**Innovative advantage: Capabilities leading to being ahead in developing new products or services**	**Time-based advantage: in adapting more quickly to change and delivering value to customer**
• Superior technology • Superior quality • Innovative design • Better functionality • Customization • Better related services • One-stop shopping • Solution selling • Brand image • Responsive distribution • Customer relationships • Customer services • Financing	• Low-cost raw material • Low-cost labour • Economies of scale • Economies of scope • Cumulative volume • Customer base • Network externalities • Efficient process technology • Time management • Productivity management	• Creating new market spaces • Finding new solutions • Developing radical change in value chain management • Creating new business designs • Developing Blue Ocean strategies	• Faster R and D • Faster logistics • Quick response time

	R & D	Procurement	Manufacturing	Marketing Sales and distribution	General management
Resources based	Higher quality scientists and technologists Better database Higher amount of funding for R&D More creative designers	Better suppliers Larger supplier base Cheaper sources of supplies Higher quality supplies	Better location and infrastructure Higher qualification of workforce Lower labor costs	Good quality channel partners Superior strategic and marketing intelligence Higher quality marketing and sales personnel	Higher quality managerial personnel Cheaper captial cost Strong "sponsors" Privileged access to licenses from authorities
Assets based	Superior existing products line Patents More efficient CAD	More effective warehousing and inventories management Electronic data purchasing Economies of scale due to high volume of purchase	Economies of scale due to volume Better quality/cost processes More advanced CAM Proprietary equipment	Well-established brand/reputation Density and scope of distribution	Better electronic data management and transmission network
Competencies based	Proprietary scientific/technological know-how Superior product development Superior research techniques Faster product development	More effective supply chain management (Just in Time) More effective supplier relationship management	Better quality plant management Better process management Better time management	Superior product and brand management Superior customer relationship management	Better financial management Better human resource management Superiority in strategizing More effective, timely, responsive organizational mechanisms 'better' corporate culture

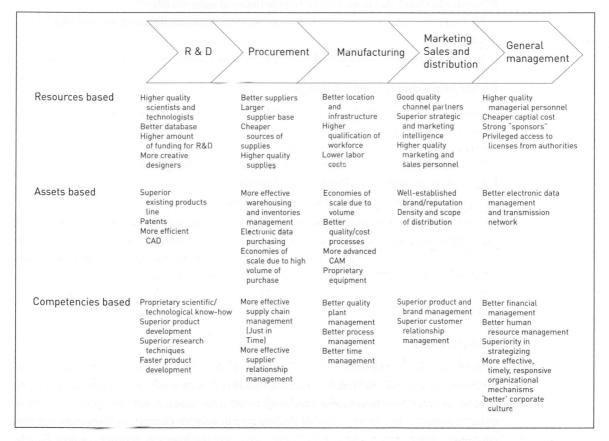

Figure 2.11 Sources of competitive advantage

- Capabilities in adapting more quickly to change and delivering value to customer leading to *time-based advantage*.[10]

These capabilities are shown in Table 2.4.

Those competitive advantages find their sources in the proprietary ownership or access to valuable resources, assets or competencies. These sources of competitive advantage are described in Figure 2.11.

Sustainability of competitive advantage

Competitive advantage, in order to be valuable, needs to be long-lasting. From an economic point of view, a competitive advantage is similar to a monopoly that the company creates for itself and which gives the company a *profit advantage* (an economic rent). This happens only if this monopoly is not immediately destroyed by imitation.

There are four ways of achieving sustainability:

- Customer loyalty due to a strong brand or a unique customer value
- Positive feedback due to accumulated experience or network effect[11]
- Pre-emption of key resources such as location, key personnel, distribution networks, patents etc.
- Imitation barriers such as inimitable competencies or costly capabilities to copy or replicate.

Global firms' competitive advantages

For global firms, the central issue is to be able to utilize their existing advantages in multiple-country leverages in order to compete successfully with local players and other global competitors. This can be done in two ways:

- By being among the first competitors to enter a given market: *first-mover advantages.*
- By exploiting capabilities already built up in other countries in order to displace and dominate existing competitors: *leveraging advantages.*

The determining factors in doing so are linked to the ability to transfer existing competitive capabilities from one country to another, to adapt some capabilities to local conditions and also to create new ones fitted to local markets. This ability to transfer, adapt and create will be discussed later on in the chapter. Table 2.5 describes the typical sources of competitive advantages of global firms and Table 2.6 shows how such global firms typically achieve sustainability.

Global chess

In addition to leveraging their intrinsic competitive advantages, global companies possess the ability to play a global 'chess game', meaning that they can *cross-subsidize* from one country to another in order to compete more effectively. A company uses its cash flow in one country in order to subsidize the development of the business in another country, or loses money in one country in order to gain a higher profit compensating the losses in another country. Finally, tax arbitrage through transfer pricing mechanisms allows global companies to optimize their overall return given the constraints imposed by the various regulatory authorities.

Table 2.5 Sources of competitive advantage of global companies

Manufacturing	Services
Access to a globally scarce resource Access to natural resources: agribusiness, mining, etc. Access to low-cost labor: labor-intensive industry Access to supply network **Critical mass built at home** Efficient manufacturing system size **'Network' effect** Specialized network of production sites **Established product performance, quality** **Competences built over time** Technology management **Image, brands and reputation** **'Piggybacking'** Associated with the international development of another firm or industry	Access to a globally scarce resource Access to financial resources: banking, insurance Access to qualified human resources: designers, entertainers, etc. Access to information: consulting activities **Critical mass built at home** Credit cards, courier services, airlines, transport **'Network' effect** Consulting, engineering, financial services, brokerage, buying services, shipping agency, news agencies, hotel chains **Competences built over time** Consulting, engineering, hospital management, legal, education, etc. **Image, brands and reputation** Hotel, fast foods, distribution, training, etc. **'Piggybacking'** Associated with the international development of another firm or industry Some consulting activities, banking, engineering, hotels

An example of the global 'chess game' was provided in the 1970s, when Michelin of France entered North America with the radial tire technology that American tire producers did not control on a large scale. In order to delay Michelin's entry and to make it more painful, Goodyear engaged in a price war in Europe where it had a relatively small market share, to oblige Michelin, the market leader in Europe, also to lower its prices and therefore to be deprived of a source of cash flow that could have been used to finance its expansion in the United States. Another example of cross-subsidization is provided by Citibank and its Global Account Management Programme. A global marketing plan is negotiated by the Citibank parent

Table 2.6 Building global sustainable advantage

Mode of building advantages	Type of sustainability			
	Customer loyalty	**Network externalities**	**Accumulated volume**	**Pre-emption**
First mover	Introduce new concept or product Create new brand	Create standard in key countries right at the beginning of the product life cycle	Build volume rapidly Use experience effect from global operations to be a cost leader	Capture locations, distribution, available talents, partners, etc.
Leverage	Use global brand Leverage R&D to innovate and differentiate	Use existing global customer base to expand globally		

account manager with the corporate client for its financial needs worldwide. Citibank may give 'sweetener' financing for a project in Argentina, for instance, but as a *quid pro quo* will get a large share of a securitization in Hong Kong. In such a case, 'Argentina' subsidizes Hong Kong for the overall benefit of the company.

The transferability of capabilities in multinational and global firms: the Transfer, Adapt, Create model

Obviously one of the central issues when firms globalize is to know which capabilities can be easily transferred internationally to new territories without any change (*Transfer*), which capabilities can be transferred with some adaptation to local conditions (*Adapt*) and which ones have to be created from scratch when entering new countries (*Create*).

Figure 2.12 gives an example of the application of the *Transfer, Adapt, Create* model in the case of mass retailers such as Wal-Mart, Tesco or Carrefour. For instance, in supply chain management, electronic data processing can be transferred without change. Nearly all competencies that form the basis of the companies' competitive strengths need to be adapted to take into consideration the behavior of local consumers, suppliers and employees. Physical assets cannot be transferred and need to be created on the spot, and even intangible assets like brands, even if global brands are used, need to be recreated in the localities because they are not known to consumers.

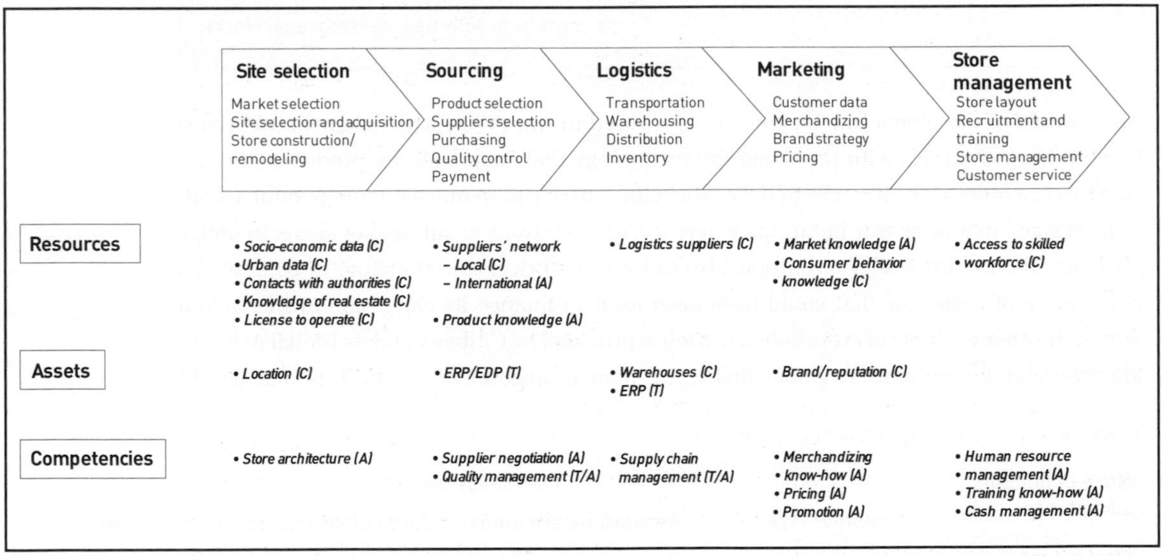

Figure 2.12: The Transfer, Adapt, Create model applied to the globalization of mass retailing

For each component of the value chain the capabilities that can be transferred (T), adapted (A) or created (C) are identified.

The role of partnership and strategic alliances in building global capabilities

In the process of globalization, companies may usually need to acquire and complement their capabilities by setting up *partnerships*. Although we will discuss global strategic partnership in Chapter 4, it is useful, at this stage, to note that partnerships are very often critical for achieving a global presence and building global competitive advantages, even for the most alliance-allergic firms, such as Michelin of France, which tried to build a global presence by itself, was forced to make an acquisition in the United States (Uniroyal) and several joint ventures in Asia (Japan, Korea, Thailand). Strategic alliances for globalization can take several forms:

- *Global alliances*, the role of which is to pool complementing capabilities to reach world markets, or to achieve a critical mass in R&D. The most common examples of world market partnerships are the airline alliances such as Star or One-World, or Concert in the telecoms sector between BT and AT&T. R&D global alliances are frequent in aerospace, life sciences, electronic defence industries or oil exploration.
- *Partnerships for market entry*, joint ventures, franchises or licensing, the role of which is to comply with local government requirements (as has been the case in China) or to facilitate entry or minimize risks in a particular country.
- *Acquisitions* that, from an ownership point of view, are not partnerships, since one party takes over the other, but from a management point of view can be equated to an alliance since different national and corporate cultures have to be combined. Acquisitions may have either a global or a local scope.

Global organization

The final element of a global strategy is the design of an *organizational architecture* which is able to support and implement the global ambition, global positioning and global business system already described. In Chapter 3, we will discuss in more depth the various types of global organizations and the issues associated with their implementation. Here, we will limit our comments to the key elements of choices that may be considered during the strategy formulation process.

Alongside the global development path described in Figure 2.9, Stopford and Wells (1972), Heenan and Perlmutter (1979), Prahalad and Doz (1987) and Bartlett and Ghoshal (2000) have identified different types of structures, systems and cultures in the management of global firms.[12] These are summarized in Table 2.7.

These different organizational choices have been mapped by Bartlett and Ghoshal in a grid that positions the various types of global structures according to the competitive requirements of global integration and local responsiveness, as in Figure 2.13.

The choice of an adequate organizational model is contingent upon the following factors:

- The nature of the *competitive context in the industry*. As discussed in Chapter 1, the more 'global' is the industry, the more integrated and coordinated the activities and the more the organizational structure should reflect this integration. The world functional, the global business structure or the matrix structure fulfill this requirement.
- The *strategic positioning* adopted by the firm. A standardized positioning using cost leadership as a competitive advantage will require a tightly integrated organization such as the centralized hub or the global business structure.

Table 2.7 Organizational designs for global strategies

Phases of global development	*Structure*	*Process*	*Culture*
Early export	Export department Within marketing and sales All activities at home Distributors, agents in foreign countries Export managers travel Possible foreign representative offices	Domestic process plus: International database (market research) International financing Instruments (trade financing)	Domestic corporate culture dominates Pioneering phase Export managers as missionary
Large export and early multinational subsidiaries	International division as distinct from domestic activities Subsidiaries report to International Division on a country-by-country basis	Specific planning and control processes for international operations International careers distinct from domestic ones	Ethnocentric culture Expatriate domination High degree of operational autonomy in subsidiaries
Full multinational	Geographical structure The world is organized by region National subsidiaries report to regional headquarters which report to corporate headquarters The company is a confederation of national units	Localization Multiple processes fitted to national requirements Only a few central policies Careers essentially national except for a few international managers	Pluricentric Except for a few international managers, each national entity reflects its national culture International diversity prevails
Global	Integrated structures Two types: (A) Global-functional structure: each key function is managed centrally	Global standardization Common processes and standard procedures across borders Activities coordinated centrally Synergies systematized Careers international	Global mind Strong corporate values Common themes Corporate culture Corporate culture prevails above any national culture including culture of the mother company

Table 2.7 Organizational designs for global strategies (continued)

Phases of global development	*Structure*	*Process*	*Culture*
Global (continued)	(B) Single matrix structure: dual line of reporting, geographical and functional	Dual information process: Global and local but working in integrated manner Transfer of people and knowledge A large number of policies to define responsibilities and avoid conflicts	Negotiating culture Ability to solve conflicts Requires strong corporate values
	(C) Transnational network Not really a structure but more a way of managing global companies in such a way that efficiency, responsiveness and innovation are optimized	Multidimensional information system: transfer of people and knowledge	Team mind Culture of sharing, transfer and cooperation
Multi-business	The business diversity adds another dimension of complexity in the organization of global operations		
Global product When the company is at the same time multi-country and diversified	Three types of structures, processes and culture may apply depending on prevailing competitive context of the industry: (A) Multi-business geographical structure The company is organized by region/countries which are in charge of managing multiple products' businesses in each country Each country is in charge of formulating the appropriate strategy for each business line and is responsible for profits. Business managers support national policies but do not have profit responsibilities (B) Global business structure Each business is integrated centrally The country subsidiaries are implementors of centrally formulated strategies and policies Profit responsibilities are assigned to global business managers who manage their global business according to competitive conditions (C) Multi-business matrix structure Dual-line business/geography Profit responsibilities are in the hands of both business managers and national managers		

Source: Adapted from Stopford and Wells (1972), Prahalad and Doz (1987), Bartlett and Ghoshal (2000), Heenan and Perlmutter (1979).

Global strategies and the multi-business firm

In the previous sections of this chapter we developed a framework for the formulation of global strategies made up of four elements: ambition, positioning, investment and organization. This framework applies when a company operates in a homogeneous industry environment. If the company is multi-business, and controls a portfolio of different business sectors, the framework applies at the level of each business but not directly at the level of the total corporation. As is often the case, in a given corporation, some businesses are more global than others and the rules of competition differ from business to business. For instance, in the telecommunication industry, voice telephony and mobile telephony are essentially local or national businesses, while corporate data is a global business. France Telecom's stated strategic ambition is to be a national player in France, a European player for mobile and a global player for corporate data.

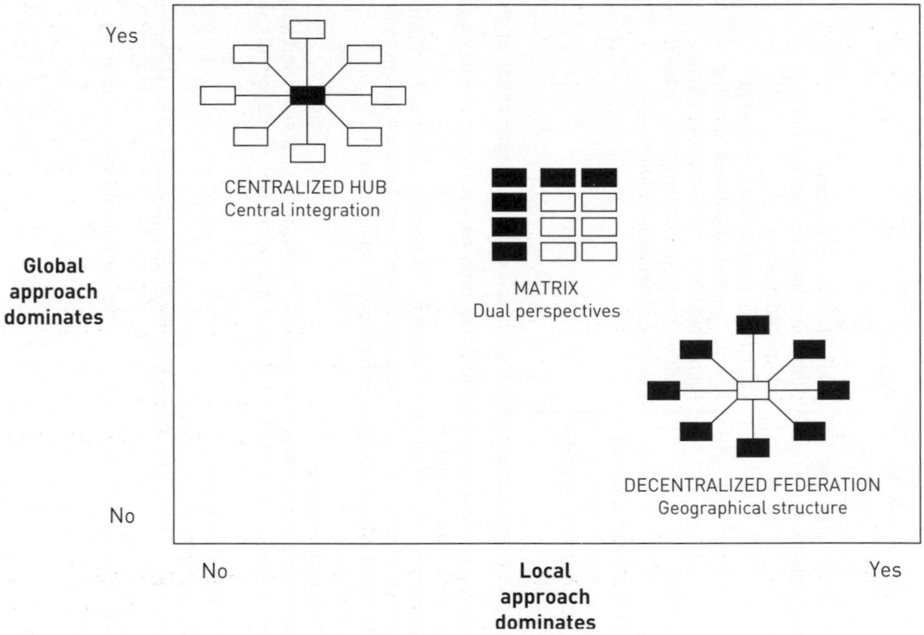

Figure 2.13 The global/multi-local mapping and global structures
Source: Author's own creation, adapted from Bartlett and Ghoshal (1989) Figures 3.1, 3.2, 3.3 pp. 50–52.

However, the global corporate strategy of a multi-business corporation is more than the mathematical sum of the global strategies of each business it controls.[13] It may be defined in terms of the four elements described earlier, but with a modified content:

- *Corporate global ambition*: Overall strategic direction assigned to the group for its globalization. Does the corporation want to be a global player in all businesses it controls or does it assign different global profiles to different businesses? What is the overall mission for the group?
- *Corporate global positioning*: Which businesses does the corporation want to be in? Does the corporation view its business portfolio as homogeneous in terms of competitive

positioning? Does it want to be a cost leader across the board? Does it want the businesses to share a common global brand?

- *Global business system*: To what extent do business units share resources, assets and competencies in order to optimize synergies? What are the corporate priorities in resource allocation among businesses?
- *Global organization*: Is the global structure organized according to a geographical design, a global business design or a matrix design? What is the role of the corporate headquarters in the strategic and operational control of the business units? Does the corporation set up regional headquarters to coordinate activities at regional level? What kind of human resource management (HRM) has the corporation put in place? Are the key managerial functions managed globally for all businesses or at business level or at regional level?

All those questions boil down to the key consideration: What is the *value added of corporate activities* in fostering the global competitiveness of the business units?

In Chapter 3 we will give more details on that issue and some examples will be presented with the analysis of Asea Brown Boveri (ABB).

Global strategies and the small and medium-sized enterprise (SME)

Small and medium-sized enterprises (SMEs) represent a large proportion of economic activities in the world (Table 2.8). However their participation in international trade and investment remains limited. According to the European network for SME survey research on a sample of 7745 small and medium-sized enterprises in Europe, their main global activities are sourcing and exporting. Only 3% reported to have set up subsidiaries and 3% to have entered into some form of joint venture (Table 2.9).

Table 2.8 SMEs' economic weight in Europe, USA and Asia Pacific

Region/Country	Definition of SMEs	Number of SMEs over total (%)	SMEs' employment over total (%)	SMEs' value added or turnover over total (%)
EUROPE 27	Fewer than 250 employees	99.8%	66.6%	60%
USA	Fewer than 500 employees	99.9%	59.8%	38.3%
ASIA PACIFIC	Varies from fewer than 100 employees to fewer than 300	From 94.4% Malaysia to 99.99% Indonesia	From 40.4% Malaysia to 99% Indonesia	From 26% Malaysia to 63% Indonesia

Sources: Eurostats, 2008, US Census Bureau, 2008, ESCAP, 2009.

Does the framework presented here apply to SMEs as well as large multinational and global enterprises? The answer to that question is 'yes and no'. 'No', because of SMEs' limited resource base; SMEs are not generally able to create global capabilities by deploying assets,

Table 2.9 SMEs' internationalization forms and frequencies

Type of internationalization	Percentage of total SMEs
Foreign supplier (importing only)	30%
Exporting only	18%
Collaboration, primarily with foreign SMEs	3%
Subsidiary, branch or joint venture abroad	3%
Note: The above percentages cannot be totaled, since individual companies may figure in several categories.	

Source: European Commission, Observatory of European SMEs, 2003/4, p.14.

resources and competencies in the 20–30 countries that represent 90 per cent of world demand. 'Yes', because if these companies are competing in sectors that are confronted with global competition and new market opportunities are located outside their national boundaries, they also need to 'think global'.

Obviously their global strategic design will probably not be as comprehensive and complex as the one that has been developed here, but the ambition, position, investment and organization framework may be a useful tool for organizing their thinking.

Different types of SMEs and their globalization potential

Not all SMEs are candidates for global expansion. A large proportion, estimated at around 40 per cent of SMEs, are involved in activities that are not related to international sourcing, exporting or producing. These are the traditional local services, small shops or artisans. A small proportion, estimated at around 5 to 10 per cent, are strategically affected by globalization either because their products or services are challenged by global competitors, or they contribute to global value chains of bigger multinational companies, or their innovative products need to be deployed globally for economic or competitive reasons. These would include high-tech entrepreneurial firms, sub-contractors, or niche players in advanced services or luxury products. The remaining 50 per cent could be involved or are marginally involved in international activities but a number of barriers deter them.

Based on a survey done in the East of England with 1200 SMEs[14] a typology of international SMEs was developed at different stages of internationalization (Table 2.10)

Table 2.10 Typology of international SMEs

The Curious	Only marginal consideration of export activities
The Frustrated	Have experienced international activities but do not push very hard
The Tentative	Limited experience but are still limited because of a lack of market intelligence
The Enthusiastic	Considerable experience of international activity but still are limited by their resources
The Successful	High experience and skills

Source: Lloyd-Reason and Mughan, quoted in OECD, *Removing Barriers to SME*, 2008, pp.20–21.

Recent surveys suggest that the overall trend of globalization for large multinational companies has created opportunities for SMEs to participate in the global value chains of those large global players.[15] One such opportunity is known as 'piggybacking' where large firms help their smaller sub-contractors or suppliers to set operations close to their own foreign investments. Another form of involvement in the global value chain is the generalization of outsourcing by large firms who want to concentrate on their core competencies and open opportunities for external suppliers to provide the goods and services that were previously produced internally.

Most SMEs will perceive themselves as 'global exporters', relying on local distributors and agents for the sales and marketing of their products. Some more daring companies will set up representative offices in key countries in order to support their marketing efforts and control and coordinate their distributors. The most resourceful will establish operational subsidiaries either directly or through partnerships of resources to 'globalize'.

In all cases, they will have to address the question of their competitive positioning and the deployment of capabilities to capture the market opportunities. In any case SMEs will have to overcome the barriers to internationalization and find ways to enhance their global capabilities.

Barriers to internationalization for SMEs

Table 2.11 provides a list of the barriers to internationalization for SMEs.

As can be seen from the table, those barriers belong to two categories: one category is related to financial issues and the other to the ability to deal with a foreign environment. In fact SMEs have to deal with two sorts of liabilities when they engage in international/global business: the liability of size and the liability of foreignness. Both liabilities end up with a problem of resources, whether financial, human or bargaining power.

Table 2.11 Obstacles to internationalization as perceived by SMEs

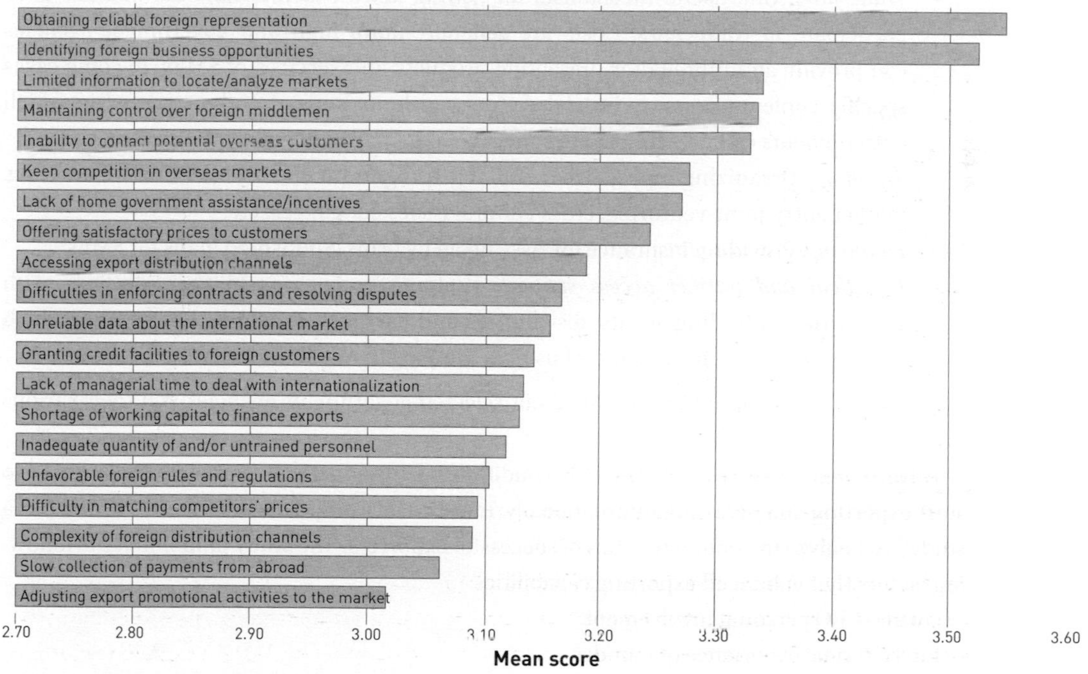

Source: Figure 1, p.46 from OECD (2008), *Removing Barriers to SME Access to International Markets*, OECD Publishing, <http://dx.doi.org/10.1787/9789264045866-en>

Overcoming the barriers

Two majors sources of initiative may help SMEs to overcome the barriers to internationalization: first government-led initiatives and second company-led initiatives.

- Government-led initiatives. Many governments and international organizations, conscious of the difficulties that many SMEs face, have tried to implement specific programs. In 1997 the OECD clustered government support initiatives into four categories: 1) Financial help programs, 2) Business environment facilitators, 3) Capabilities enhancement programs and 4) Assistance in information gathering.[16] Below is a list of the kinds of action that government can implement in order to foster global capabilities of SMEs.
  - *Information gathering and distribution.* Most governments, thanks to their diplomatic networks, have access to a myriad of information about business opportunities and risks in many countries. Factual and legal information can be made available on-line, special reports on countries and industries made available. Tailor-made, customized studies can be proposed at affordable costs.
  - *Advice and consulting.* When an entrepreneur is considering exporting or investing in a particular region, a specialized government agency can provide consultancy and advisory services about various alternatives, potential partners, market access and legal issues that can help the company to evaluate the costs and benefits as well as the specific risks.
  - *Trade fairs.* One useful mechanism for getting known in international markets is to participate in trade fairs. Costs are generally quite high and government agencies can provide an umbrella for presenting products and services of SMEs. In some cases specific conferences on industrial sectors can be organized and sponsored in which entrepreneurs can present papers about their company and products.
  - *Training.* Organizing specialized training programs on international marketing, market entry, joint-venturing, cross-cultural issues, languages, etc.
  - *Financing.* Providing insurance for risks taken by firms. Sponsored loans for SMEs.
  - *Logistical and market access supports.* Helping companies in their dealings with authorities, in finding agents, distributors and partners. Providing offices from which entrepreneurs can initiate their business. Helping in negotiations.

Appendix 2.2 gives some information about selected government agencies and their various programs.

Government support is not the only condition for small and medium-sized businesses to start exporting and investing internationally. In 2004 the European Community carried out a study[17] to analyze the characteristics of successful exporters. The study pinpointed the following factors that enhanced exporting capabilities:

- Owner/CEO personal involvement
- International experience of founder
- Consistency and persistence.

In addition, the study pinpointed the significant benefits of the Internet for SMEs in their internationalization process, both in term of information gathering and e-market opportunities.

EXAMPLE

Gemplus

In the late 1980s, the French company Gemplus, one of the first companies to enter the market for smartcards immediately after its formation in Marseille in the South of France, created a subsidiary in Germany, a joint venture company in Singapore and a marketing company in the United States. This strategy reflected the nature of the industry: the technology of the smartcard is pervasive; it has numerous applications in banking, telecommunications, transport and Internet transactions; it has the potential to become global. National boundaries do not provide strong entry barriers, but national legislations and established infrastructures make national presence a competitive requirement. Network externalities, customer base and first-to-enter are competitive weapons in this industry. Gemplus, a medium-sized technology firm, realized this competitive imperative and, right at the beginning, devoted a large proportion of its limited resources to global expansion.

MINI-CASE 1

HSBC: The World's Local Bank

The Hong Kong and Shanghai Banking Corporation was created in Shanghai in 1865. Its primary business was to finance trading with China. Up to the Second World War, it rapidly expanded in the Asia Pacific region: Japan, Malaysia, the Philippines and Thailand, with a limited presence in the USA and Europe. After 1950, the bank embarked on a series of acquisitions in Europe (UK, France), the Middle East, Latin America (Mexico, Argentina, Brazil) and the USA. It is listed on the New York, London, Paris and Hong Kong stock exchanges. The bank moved its corporate headquarters from Hong Kong to London in 1993. Its network comprises 7500 offices in 87 countries. In 1999 it adopted the name of HSBC and positioned the bank as the 'world's local bank', defining itself as a global bank with strong local presence and knowledge.

It serves four customer groups: Global Private Banking and Markets; Commercial Banking; Retail Banking; and Personal Financial Services, hence managing a combination of global and local businesses.

- HSBC Global Banking and Markets provides tailored financial solutions to 4200 clients worldwide: government, corporate and institutional clients. It is managed as a global business from offices in around 60 countries. Clients are served by teams that bring together relationship managers and product specialists. Its services include investment banking, trade finance, asset management, leveraged acquisition, project finance, foreign exchange as well as research services. Its focus is on emerging markets, particularly in Asia, that are expected to contribute 46 per cent to growth in revenue.
- HSBC Commercial Banking provides financing needs to over 3.2 million local corporations and small and medium-sized companies across the globe. Its services include trade finance, cash management, loans, investments, insurance, foreign exchange and assistance in international investment. The business is managed locally with strong connections to specialists from other businesses.

MINI-CASE 1

- HSBC Retail Banking (also named HSBC Premier Family Services) serves around 92 million clients in 61 countries with current and savings accounts, insurance, credit cards, investments and private loans and all kinds of family related financial needs. It is managed locally.
- HSBC Private Banking offers banking, investment and private fiduciary services to wealthy customers (high net worth clients). It operates locally in 91 offices with strong connections to other HSBC businesses.

The bank operates in four regions: Europe (2821 Offices), Asia Pacific (1830 offices), Middle East and Africa (302 offices) and the Americas (3821 offices).

A distribution of net income and profit before tax are given in Table 2.12.

Table 2.12 HSBC distribution of net income and profit

Percentages (2010)	Global banking and markets	Commercial banking	Retail banking	Private banking	Others	Total
Operating income (net)						**54,000 Million US$**
Europe	14%	6.35%	11.2%	3.3%	**-0.3%**	**34%**
Asia/Middle East-Africa	11%	8%	13%	1%	**3%**	**36%**
Americas	8%	7%	13%	1%	**1%**	**29%**
Total operating income	33%	21%	37%	5%	**3%**	**100%**
Profit and losses before taxes						**19,000 Million US$**
Europe	14.2%	6.3%	6.8%	3.2%	**-8.4%**	**22%**
Asia/Middle East-Africa	22.9%	17.6%	21.6%	1.5%	**2.2%**	**66%**
Americas	13.2%	7.9%	-9.7%	0.6%	**-0.1%**	**12%**
Total profit and losses before taxes	**50%**	**32%**	**19%**	**5%**	**-6%**	**100%**

Source: HSBC Annual Report 2010 available at <http://www.hsbc.com/1/2/investor-relations>

In his presentation of the 2010 annual report, the Group Chief Executive, Stuart Gulliver, indicated that the strategy to be the world's leading international bank was based upon *'a) leveraging the HSBC brand and the network of businesses which covers the world's most relevant geographies; b) competing as a universal bank across the full financial services spectrum only where the bank has scale and can achieve appropriate returns; c) enhancing efficiency by taking full advantage of local, regional and global economies of scale, in particular by adopting a common systems architecture wherever possible and d) maintaining capital strength and a strong liquidity'*.

As indicated, the global strategy is based on a presence in the most relevant countries. Capital allocation for national strategies is based on two dimensions. The first dimension is called development and connectivity: it measures the potential for development as well as the international connections of the country (for instance Germany and Eastern Europe).

MINI-CASE 1

The second dimension is the potential for value creation through growth, profitability, efficiency and liquidity. These two dimensions: connectivity/development and wealth creation provide a framework for capital allocation as represented in Figure 2.14:

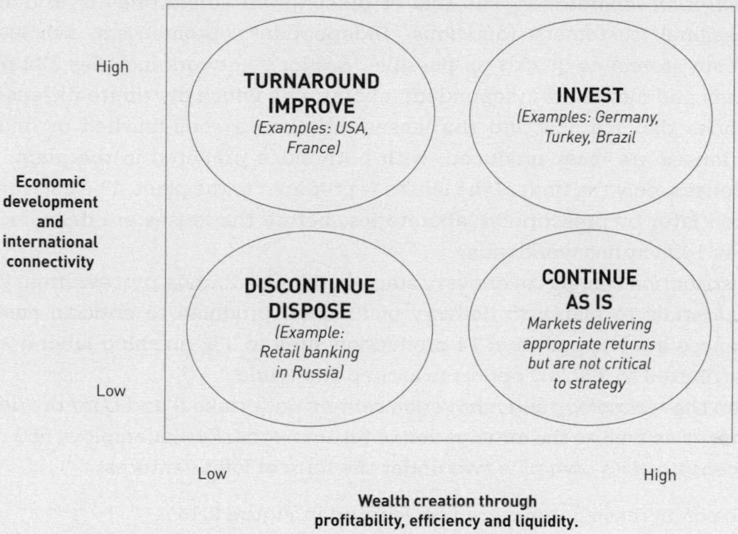

Figure 2.14 National strategies: capital allocation filter

Source: Group Strategy, Investor Day, 11 May 2011, available at <http://www.hsbc.com/1/2/investor-relations>

Questions:

1) Classify HSBC's four businesses: global/local. What are the implications for strategic decision-making?
2) Which parts of their business system do HSBC want to keep global? Why?
3) What are the pros and cons of the capital allocation process shown in Figure 2.14?

MINI-CASE 2

ESSILOR: A Global Player

Essilor is the result of the merger in 1972 of two French ophthalmological companies: Essel, a specialist in corrective glass lenses and Silor, specialist in plastic lenses. The products were exported through a network of local distributors but, in 1979, the company embarked on a global strategy with the opening of its first international factory in the Philippines and the progressive acquisition of local distributors. Global development has been made through a mixture of greenfield investments, acquisitions and alliances. Between 2008 and 2010 it acquired or allied with 83 companies in the world.

By 2011 Essilor was the number one player for corrective optical lenses with a global market share of around 28 per cent. Its turnover in 2010 was 3.9 billion euros with a profit of 490 million euros. It has 42,700 employees worldwide.

MINI-CASE 2

The Essilor business process of corrective lenses is based on five entities:

- The *retail optical shops* (opticians) providing customer contact, with ophthalmologists determining the type of lens required. Essilor relies on 300,000 independent optical shops around the world
- The *prescription laboratories*. The role of prescription laboratories is to deliver lenses to professional customers (opticians, independent optometrists, wholesalers and optical chain stores) as quickly as possible. Essilor's network includes 332 prescription laboratories and numerous independent laboratories which distribute its lenses.
- The *factories* that manufacture the lenses either in a semi-finished or finished form. Finished lenses are mass produced, with both sides prepared in the plant. For semi-finished lenses, only the front of the lenses is prepared in the plant. The back and coatings are applied later by prescription laboratories, before the lenses are delivered to stores. Essilor has 14 factories worldwide.
- The *12 distribution centers* cover every stage in the distribution process: from the delivery of raw materials to plants to delivery of finished products to optician customers. At Essilor, lenses are shipped from 14 production sites to 332 finishing laboratories, before being distributed to 300,000 opticians around the world.
- In addition *the technology and innovation centers* undertake R and D for the development of new lenses as well as the anticipation of future needs. Essilor employs 550 researchers in three centers of its own plus two under the form of joint ventures.

The linkages of all these entities are represented in Figure 2.15.

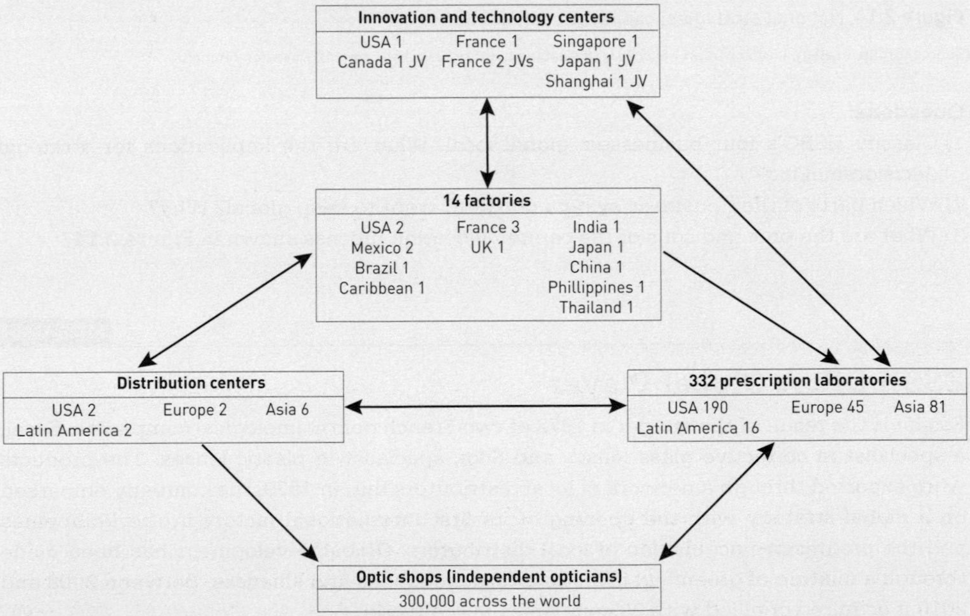

Figure 2.15 Essilor's business process

Source: Perspective of market development, Presentation to Essilor shareholders of first half 2011, ESTIN & Co for ESSILOR INTERATIONAL, ESSILOR INTERNATIONAL © 2011. Available at: <http://www.essilor.com/en/Group/International/Pages/Organization.aspx>

MINI-CASE 2

Essilor's strategy is based on four pillars:

- Innovation in products, services and marketing as well as the quality of its relationships with opticians all over the world.
- The growth and development of middle markets in emerging countries. The Figure 2.16 represents the company's views about the perspective of market development.
- The pursuit of acquisitions and partnerships.
- Offer check-ups and supply lenses in order to develop markets where access to optical care is difficult.

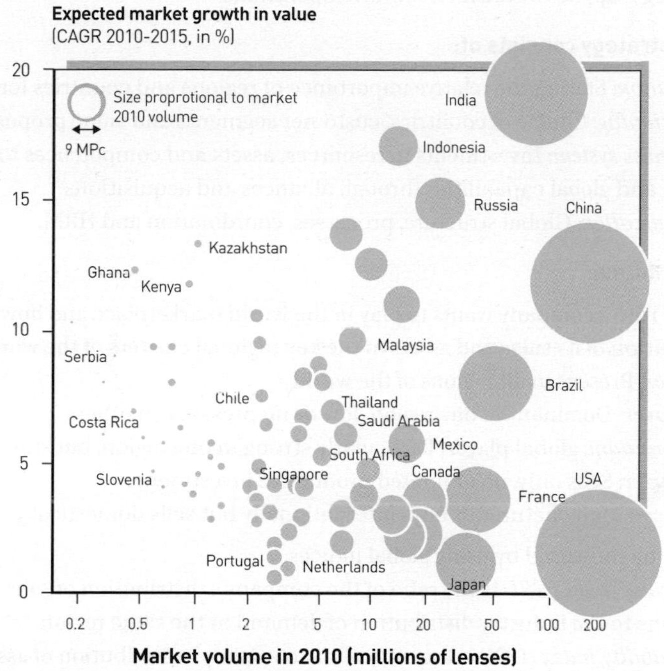

Figure 2.16 Perspective of market development

Source: Perspective of market development, Presentation to Essilor shareholders of first half 2011, ESTIN & Co for ESSILOR INTERNATIONAL, ESSILOR INTERNATIONAL © 2011. Available at: <http://www.essilor.com/en/Group/International/Pages/Organization.aspx>

Questions:

1) Based on the description of the business system and Figure 2.15, what are the strategic and organizational challenges for Essilor's global management?
2) In chart 2.16 it appears that the most potentially attractive markets are in emerging countries. Do you think that the Essilor's strategic pillars are in line with the market prospects?
3) What issues would be involved in developing the business in China, India, Indonesia and Russia?

Summary and key points

1 A company business strategy is a set of *fundamental choices* which define its long-term *objectives*, its *value proposition* to the market, how it intends to build and sustain a competitive *business system* and how it *organizes* itself

2 There are different level of strategy:

- *Business Strategy*: applies at the level of an industry
- *Corporate strategy*: applies at the level of a multi-business corporation
- *Global strategy*: applies at the level of world operations

3 A global strategy consists of:

- *Global ambition*: Stating the relative importance of regions and countries for a company
- *Global positioning*: Choice of countries, customer segments and value proposition
- *Global business system*: Investments in resources, assets and competences to create a global value chain and global capabilities through alliances and acquisitions
- *Global organization*: Global structure, processes, coordination and HRM.

4 Global ambition:

Expresses the role a company wants to play in the world marketplace and how it views the future distribution of its sales and assets in the key regional clusters of the world:

- *Global player*: Present in all regions of the world
- *Regional player*: Dominant in one region, low or no presence in others
- *Regional dominant*: global player: Particularly strong in one region, but still active in others
- *Global exporter*: Sells only, no or limited productive investments
- *Global sourcer*: Manufactures or buys internationally but sells domestically.

Ambition can be measured by using global indices:

- *Global Revenue Index (GRI)* is the ratio of the company's distribution of sales in the major world regions to the industry distribution of demand in the same region.
- *Global Capability Index (GCI)* is the ratio of the company's distribution of assets or personnel in the major world regions to the industry distribution in the same region.

5 Global positioning involves *choice of countries* and *value proposition*:

- *Choice of countries*: There are five types of country where global positioning occurs:
  - *Key countries*: Countries critical for the long-term competitiveness of the company because of their size, growth or available resources
  - *Emerging countries*: Countries that exhibit high growth rate for a particular industry
  - *Platform countries*: Countries which can serve as a 'hub' for setting up regional centres, global factories that are 'platforms' for further development
  - *Marketing countries*: Countries with attractive markets without being as strategically critical as the key countries
  - *Sourcing countries*: Countries with a strong resource base but limited market prospects.
- *Value proposition*: choice of value attributes, customer segments, degree of standardization.
  - *Value attributes* are the elements of the products/services that customers value when making their purchasing decision

- The *customer segments* are the particular groups of customers who request similar value attributes (value curve)
- Degree of world standardization of products/services:
  - A *standardized value proposition* adopts a similar or standard value attribute to the same type of customer segment across the world
  - An *adaptive value proposition* tailors the value proposition to different regions.
- The choices of global positioning depend on the company's decisions on the:
- *Scope* of targeted customer segments (broad/focused player)
- *Approach* of making a value proposition in different countries (standardized/adaptive)
- Choice of *generic strategies* adopted (differentiation or cost leadership).

6 Global business system:

A global business system distributes the company value chain across the world. It involves the building and developing of capabilities to compete successfully in the global market space.

- *Value chain*: there are three major generic components of a value chain: *Innovative* activities, *productive* activities, *customer relationship* activities
- *Capabilities*: there are three types of capabilities: differentiation, cost leadership and innovation. Capabilities that are unique to a company and non-replicable by competitors constitute a company's *competitive advantage.*

7 Competitive advantages: proprietary ownership or access to valuable assets, resources or competencies. Competitive advantages are sustainable if they provide:

- *Customer loyalty*: Can be built on brand or where there are high switching costs involved
- *Positive feedback* such as network externalities and experience effects
- *Pre-emption of key resources*: such as location or key personnel, or
- *Barriers to imitation*: appropriation by one company of key capabilities that competitors will find difficult to access or to replicate.

Modes of building competitive advantage:

- *First-mover advantages*: Being among the first competitors to enter a given market
- *Leveraging advantages*: Exploiting capabilities already built in other countries.

8 Evolution of firms in the globalization process

There are three stages of progress:

- *Export*
  - Sales is the only element in the value chain which is set up in foreign countries
  - As the company progresses through the export stage, it invests in marketing subsidiaries to actively manage the marketing mix;
- *Multinational*

  The company manages a portfolio of relatively independent worldwide wholly owned subsidiaries or joint ventures
- *Global*

  A global company integrates and coordinates its worldwide operations to take advantage of economies of scale, transfer of know-how and resource optimization; this leads to an interlocked set of value chain activities which falls broadly into three categories: global, regional and local.

9 The transferability of capabilities:

In the process of globalization, capabilities need to be identified that can be: easily transferred internationally into new territories without any change (*transfer*); or transferred with some adaptation to local conditions (*adapt*); and which have to be created from scratch when entering new countries (*create*).

10 Partnerships:

Companies usually need to acquire and complement their capabilities by setting up partnerships; global strategic partnerships are often critical for achieving a global presence and building global competitive advantage.

Forms of strategic alliances include:

- Global alliances to pool complementing capabilities to reach world markets or achieve a critical mass in R&D
- Local partnerships – joint ventures, franchises or licensing for market entry
- Acquisitions.

11 Global organization (see Chapter 3):

Organization *choice* is dependent on the phases of global development:

- Early export
- Early multinational subsidiaries
- Full multinational
- Global
- Global multi-business.

Three types of global organization can be distinguished:

- Centralized hub
- Decentralized federation
- Matrix.

Organizational *dimensions* cover:

- Structure
- System/processes
- Culture.

12 Small and medium-sized enterprises (SMEs):

Only a small proportion are engaged in global operations. Their international exposure is essentially export or sourcing. Only 5 per cent to 10 per cent of SMEs are really international.

Appendix 2.1 Measuring corporate globalization

According to the definition given in this textbook, corporate globalization includes two major dimensions: first the presence of a company in the key markets of the world and second an integrated and coordinated management of activities across the world. It is extremely difficult to measure the second dimension since no indicator is available to assess the degree of coordination and integration; only a qualitative analysis can evaluate it. Measurements concentrate on the first dimension: the extent to which a company is deployed across the world.

There are two main approaches for that:

- Measures assessing the proportion of activities outside the country of origin of a particular company. This method is the one adopted by UNCTAD in its yearly World Investment Report
- Measures assessing the extent to which a particular company has deployed its activities in the key markets of the world in the same proportion as the weight of those markets. This method is the one proposed in this chapter with the Global Revenue Index (GRI) and the Global Capabilities Index (GCI). A similar approach is adopted by Alan Rugman when he considers that a company is global when its sales are distributed across the three major regions of the world (Europe, North America, Asia) in such a way that two regions do not represent more than 70 per cent.

The UNCTAD Transnational Index (TNI) and Internationalization Index (II)

UNCTAD publishes every year in its World Investment reports a ranking of firms according to their Transnational Index (TNI). The TNI is calculated as the average of three ratios: foreign sales to total sales, foreign assets to total assets and foreign employment to total employment. It has also included in recent reports the Internationalization Index (II) that is calculated as the ratio of the number of foreign affiliates to the total number of affiliates.

Table 2.A1 lists the TNI and II of some selected global firms and its components.

Table 2.A1 Ranking of global firms according to their TNIs (2010) (Figures on sales and assets are in million US$)

Foreign assets	TNI [b]	Corporation	Home economy	Industry [c]	Assets		Sales		Employment		TNI [b] (per cent)
					Foreign	Total	Foreign	Total	Foreign [d]	Total	
17	1	Nestlé SA	Switzerland	Food, beverages and tobacco	113,574	1,118,818	103,154	105,209	271,605	281,000	96.8
40	2	Anglo American plc	United Kingdom	Mining & quarrying	62,238	66,656	25,772	27,960	92,000	100,000	92.5
18	3	Anheuser-Busch InBevNV	Belgium	Food, beverages and tobacco	108,440	114,342	32,193	36,297	104,126	114,313	91.5
97	4	Pernod-Ricard SA	France	Food, beverages and tobacco	31,070	33,264	8821	9821	15,796	18,453	89.6
59	5	Nokia OYJ	Finland	Electrical & electronic equipment	44,140	52,276	55,729	56,220	112,586	132,427	89.5
86	6	Linde AG	Germany	Chemicals	32,731	35,927	15,432	17,044	41,262	48,430	88.9
85	7	WPP PLC	United Kingdom	Business services	33,074	38,111	12,737	14,417	91,767	101,387	88.5
35	8	Xstrata PLC	Switzerland	Mining & quarrying	66,430	69,709	22,902	30,499	36,436	38,561	88.3
54	9	Unilever PLC	Netherlands/ United Kingdom	Diversified	49,637	55,007	54,003	58,625	136,000	165,000	88.3
77	10	Schneider Electric SA	France	Electricity, gas and water	36,876	41,490	23,580	25,934	102,490	123,482	87.6
14	11	ArcelorMittal	Luxembourg	Metal and metal products	124,392	130,904	71,290	78,025	198,896	262,832	87.4
95	12	Barrick Gold Corporation	Canada	Gold mining	31,190	33,322	10,498	10,924	14,271	20,000	87.0
66	13	Philips Electronics NV	Netherlands	Electrical & electronic equipment	39,573	43,117	32,587	33,668	84,388	119,001	86.5
50	14	Lafarge SA	France	Non-metallic mineral products	52,784	56,780	18,534	21,416	60,052	75,677	86.3
4	15	Vodafone Group Plc	United Kingdom	Telecommunications	224,449	242,417	63,069	71,315	65,729	8499	86.1

Foreign assets	TNI [b]	Corporation	Home economy	Industry [c]	Assets Foreign	Assets Total	Sales Foreign	Sales Total	Employment Foreign [d]	Employment Total	TNI [b] (Per cent)
70	16	SABMiller PLC	United Kingdom	Food, beverages and tobacco	38,750	39,108	22,917	28,311	54,590	70,131	86.0
84	17	Liberty Global Inc	United States	Telecommunications	33,250	33,329	8876	9017	11,774	20,000	85.7
3	18	BP plc	United Kingdom	Petroleum expl./ref/ distr.	243,950	272,262	234,313	297,107	65,926	79,700	83.7
68 .	19	AstraZeneca PLC	United Kingdom	Pharmaceuticals	38,956	56,127	31,317	33,269	53,309	61,700	83.3
79	25	CemexS. AB. de C.V.	Mexico	Non-metallic mineral products	36,416	41,684	10,771	14,107	34,900	46,533	79.6
64	26	Schlumberger Ltd	United States	Other consumer services	41,761	51,767	21,139	27,447	87,124	108,000	79.5
11	27	Telefonica SA	Spain	Telecommunications	140,882	173,403	54,409	80,446	232,114	269,047	78.4
61	28	BG Group plc	United Kingdom	Electricity, gas and water	43,437	50,299	13,393	17,166	4212	6172	77.5
2	29	Royal Dutch Shell plc	Netherlands/ United Kingdom	Petroleum expl./ref/ distr.	271,672	322,560	230,697	36,8056	82,000	97,000	77.1
7	30	Total SA	France	Petroleum expl./ref/ distr.	175,001	192,034	143,047	18,6061	57,686	92,855	76.7

Source: UNCTAD, Annex Tables from World Investment Report 2011, Annex table 29: The world´s top 100 non-financial TNCs. Available at <http://www.unctad.org/WIR>

The Global Revenue Index (GRI) and the Global Capabilities Index (GCI)

These indices attempt to evaluate the extent to which a company's distribution of sales and capabilities reflect the industry distribution of markets. For instance, if in an industry such as the tire industry the world markets are distributed as North America (29 per cent), Europe (28 per cent), Asia Pacific (30 per cent) and the Rest of the World (13 per cent), we could argue that a perfect global firm would have its sales and assets distributed in the same proportion: ideally both the industry and the firm would be distributed along the diagonal of Figure 2.A1. In fact most nearly all firms are not located along the diagonal because their sales are somewhat more important in one region than in another one. For example, Goodyear sales are distributed as North America

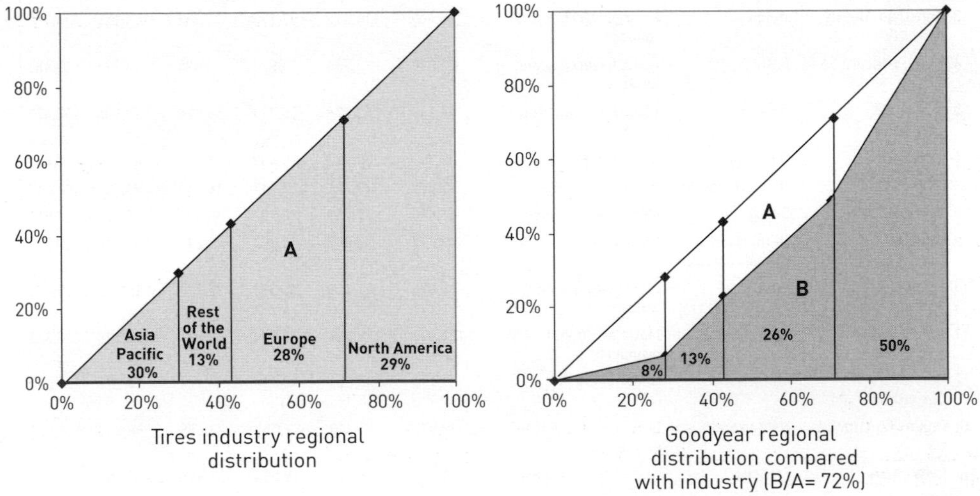

Figure 2.A1 A graphical representation of the Global Revenue Index (GRI)

(50%), Europe (26%), Asia Pacific (8%) and the Rest of the World (16%) along the lower line in figure 2.A1. The two indices described below represent the ratio between area B (Goodyear distribution) and area A (industry distribution).

The **Global Revenue Index** (GRI) is calculated by taking the ratio of the company distribution of sales in the major world regions to the industry distribution of demand in the same regions. It is calculated with the formula:

$$\text{GRI} = \sum_{1}^{n} [Ix_n(cumRX_n + cumRX_{(n-1)})]$$

Where:

n is the number of regions taken into consideration.

In practice $n = 4$, since there are four major clusters: North America, Europe, Asia and the Rest of the World

Ixn is the industry demand in the region as a proportion of world demand, cumRX_n is the cumulative proportion of sales achieved by the company in region n in ascending order; for instance, since Goodyear sales are 26 per cent in Europe, 50 per cent in North America, 8 per cent in Asia and 13 per cent in the rest of the world, Goodyear's cumulative proportion (cum*RX*) is 8 per cent for Asia, 16 percent the rest of the world, 50 per cent for Europe, 100 per cent for North America.

The calculation of Goodyear's GRI is shown in Table 2.A2.

A company whose sales distribution matches the exact distribution of its industry market would have a GRI of 100 per cent.

A company that concentrates its sales in one region and sells nothing elsewhere would obtain a GRI corresponding to the percentage of demand in this region. For instance, if Goodyear's sales were entirely concentrated in North America, Goodyear's GRI would have been 29 per cent.

GRI is by definition used for measuring how *global* a company is. For firms engaged in an industry which is local in nature, the GRI will favor the firms that are in countries/regions with the biggest consumption for that industry. For example, in the restaurant business, which is local in nature, US restaurants would have had a higher GRI than that of Asian restaurants during the Asian Crisis simply because US people visited restaurants more often than Asians during that period. In this case, the higher GRI of the US restaurants should not be interpreted as the US restaurants being more global than their Asian counterparts, as the majority of both the US and Asian restaurants are local players.

Table 2.A2 Goodyear: calculation of the Global Revenue Index (GRI)

Distribution of sales	Asia (%)	Rest of the World (%)	Europe (%)	North America (%)
Industry	30	13	31	26
Goodyear *RX*	11	12	34	43
cum*RX*	11	23	57	100
cumRX_n	0	11	23	57
cum*RX*+cumRX_n	11	34	80	157
Ix *(cumRX+cumRX_n)	3.3	4.42	24.80	40.82

Then Goodyear's GRI (%) = 3.3 + 4.42 + 24.00 + 40.82 = 73.34
Similar calculations will derive the following results for the other players:
Michelin GRI = 65
Bridgestone GRI = 79
Pirelli GRI = 58

Also, for companies which implement globalization by competing in small markets (e.g. South America, Eastern Europe), the GRI does not reflect the extent of global sales the company has. This is owing to the fact that the companies' sales are in world markets that the other major global players in the industry have not yet fully explored. For example, ACER, the Taiwanese PC company, had a relatively low GRI at the early stage of its globalization strategy where it began to capture the South American markets. Nonetheless, the low GRI score correctly reflects the fact that the company did not closely resemble the industry's demand pattern. This type of company will further expand to the major world markets after establishing itself in smaller foreign markets. Once established in the major world markets, it will have a higher GRI.

The Global Capability Index (GCI) is calculated in a similar way, but instead of taking the distribution of sales, you take the distribution of assets for capital-intensive industries or else of *personnel*. The 'capability' described here is in-house capability, not capability that a firm can acquire through external sourcing like outsourcing, sub-contracting or strategic alliances with overseas companies in which the firm has no ownership in the alliance partner(s) and/or alliance venture. For strategic alliances in which a firm has ownership interest, you can theoretically include in the GCI calculation the proportional amount of assets which the company owns or has control over. When gathering data for the calculation of GCI, care should be taken, and an attempt should be made to account for off-balance sheet assets such as asset finance by sales and leaseback arrangements.

Companies which rely heavily on external sourcing will have a low GCI score. This is because the company cannot deploy resources and capabilities at will but relies on external parties to supply the capability. This reliance on external parties also means that the company can face potential problems such as product/service unavailability, time delays in delivery, or price pressure from the overseas suppliers.

Appendix 2.2 Selected government support programs

Country	Program	Objectives of Program	Focus	Finance	Environment	Capability	Access
Australia	NEDP	Assist SME in exporting	E				X
	EMDG	Grants program to encourage exports	E	X			
Canada	EXPORT help	Access to experts to assist exporters	E			X	X
	SME Financial program	Finance or guarantee financing for capital investments	E	X			X
European Union	Euro Info Center	Provide market information	E/I/F				X
France	FASEP	Guarantee against economic risks for FDI	F			X	
	Partnership France	Piggybacking scheme	F				
Germany	Worldwide Active	Overall support	E/I	X	X	X	X
Japan	JERO Programs	All kinds of support	E/I/F	X	X	X	X
UK	Passport to Export	Program to enhance capabilities	E			X	
USA	SBA	Provide loans and information	E	X			X
	Passport to Export	Develop trading capabilities				X	

(E) Export, (I) Import, (F) Foreign investments and cooperation
Source: Based on Annex 1.2. from OECD, *Removing Barriers to SME Access to International Markets*, OECD Publishing, 2008

Learning assignments

1 In 2010, the distribution of sales and people of AXA, the insurance company, is shown below:

	Europe	NAFTA	Asia	Rest of World
Revenue (billion €)	49,600	10,300	9400	12,800
Personnel	75,000	17,000	15,000	19,000

Assuming that the figures are representative of the situation in 2010, what is AXA's position on a GCI/GRI mapping?

2 In your opinion, for which industries could the UK, Italy and Australia be 'key' countries?

3 What could be the benefits of positioning oneself as a standardized global niche differentiator (see Table 2.3, p. 39)? What kind of competitive advantages does it require?

4 What are the capabilities needed to be a broad adaptive cost leader?

5 What are the ways to sustain competitive advantage?

6 What types of competitive advantage does being a first mover provide?

7 Can you sketch the mapping of the value chain for:
(a) A consulting firm
(b) An airline
(c) A trading firm
(d) A corporate and investment bank?

8 For each of the entities in Question 7 (a)–(d), can you represent a possible global distribution of their value chain, as illustrated in Figure 2.8 (p. 40)?

Key words

- Business strategy
- Corporate strategy
- Cost leadership
- Differentiation
- Global business strategy
- Global Capability Index
- Global corporate strategy
- Global positioning
- Global Revenue Index
- Value chain
- Value curve
- Value proposition

Web resources

<http://www.businessweek.com/globalbiz/index.html>
Business Week – Global business.

<http://www.forbes.com/forbesglobal/>
Forbes Global Magazine online, with a section on companies and strategies.

<http://harvardbusinessonline.hbsp.harvard.edu/>
Harvard cases and *Harvard Business Review* reprints.

<http://www.mckinseyquarterly.com/>
McKinsey consulting business review.

<http://www.ey.com/Home>
Ernst & Young Consulting.

<http://www.atkearney.com/>
A.T. Kearney consulting.

<http://www.bcg.com/expertise_impact/publications/default.aspx>
BCG Consulting .

Visit the companion website at **http://www.palgrave.com/business/lasserre3e** for a multitude of weblinks and resources, self-test questions for revision and a searchable glossary.

Notes

1 This section is based on the Harvard Business School case study 9-391-071, written by Thomas W. Malnight under the supervision of Michael Yoshino.

2 Note that the distinction between a global player and a regional player is more a function of the relative importance of each major region of the world in the company's portfolio than the published ambition of the company in its external communications. Many companies assert that they are 'global', although their accounts reflect a strong concentration of their sales in one region. However, this situation may change if there is a real strategic ambition to become a real global player supported by the appropriate investments. Renault, for instance, a traditional European player, has acquired controlling positions in Nissan and Samsung automobiles, transforming the company into a European, Asian and also North American player thanks to Nissan's operations in the United States.

3 Global sourcing applies also to some service sectors; for instance, a software company setting up a programming operation in India but limiting its sales to one country would be a global operator. Similarly, a domestic mass retailer that had purchasing offices across the world and long-term contracts would also be a global operator.

4 A similar calculation could be done by taking the major countries, but it becomes more complicated. However, it is perfectly possible to apply a similar methodology by taking the ten major world markets, for instance, or applying it at the level of a region (the distribution of sales in Asia Pacific, for instance, among the key countries of the region).

5 The European case presents the particularity of being a set of countries, but also a common market, with a free movement of people, capital and goods and having endorsed a single currency (the Euro). In theory, Europe, from the point of view of global players, could be considered as a 'country' and therefore the concept of key countries should not apply. However, cultural, structural and political differences have led global companies to carefully assess each national context in making their global positioning and investment decisions. In the future, Europe will probably be like the United States,

where foreign investors will compare the relative strategic importance of California versus Texas or Washington State.

6 Porter (1980).

7 The concept of the value chain was developed by Porter (1985, 1986).

8 A more elaborate treatment can be found in Porter (1985, 1986).

9 Doz and Mikko (2008) and Kim and Mauborgne (2005).

10 Stalk (1988).

11 *Network effects* exist when the customer base of a product or service is such that it induces other product or service providers to adopt it in their own value proposition, which in turn induces new customers to buy the original product or service. This *virtuous circle* creates a positive loop that reinforces the company's competitive position. The classic example of network effects is Windows versus Macintosh operating systems. Windows being an open system induces various PC makers to make Windows-based machines that in turn induce software makers to produce Windows-based software. Customers, having more Windows software, bought Windows-based machines.

12 Stopford, Wells (1972); Prahalad and Doz (1987); Bartlett and Ghoshal (2000).

13 Goold, Campbell and Alexander (1994).

14 Lloyd-Reason and Mughan (2003).

15 OECD (2007).

16 OECD (2008).

17 European Commission (2004).

References and further reading

Bartlett, Christopher A. and Sumantra Ghoshal, *Managing Across Borders: The Transnational Solution*. Boston, MA: Harvard Business School Press, 1989.

Bartlett, Christopher A. and Sumantra Ghoshal, 'Going Global: Lessons from Late Movers', *Harvard Business Review*, March–April 2000, pp. 132–42.

Besanko David, David Dranove, Mark Shanley and Scott Schaefer, *The Economics of Strategy*. New York: John Wiley, 2007.

Davidson, William H., *Global Strategic Management*. New York: John Wiley, 1982.

Doremus, Paul N., Louis W. Pauly, Simon Reich and William W. Keller, *The Myth of the Global Corporation*. Princeton: Princeton University Press, 1999.

Doz, Yves L. and C.K. Prahalad, *The Multinational Mission*. New York: Free Press, 1987.

Doz Yves L. and Kosone Mikko, *Fast Strategy: How Strategic Agility Will Help You to Stay Ahead of the Game*. Philadelphia, PA: Pearson Education, Wharton School Publishing, 2008.

European Commission, *Internationalisation of SMEs*. Office for Official Publications of the European Communities, Luxembourg, 2004.

Faulkner David O. and Andrew Campbell, *The Oxford Handbook of Strategy, I and II*. Oxford: Oxford University Press, 2003.

Ghemawat Pankaj, *Redefining Global Strategy, Crossing Borders in a World Where Differences Still Matter*. Boston, MA: Harvard Business School Press, 2007.

Goold, Michael, Andrew Campbell and Marcus Alexander, *Corporate-Level Strategy*. New York: John Wiley, 1994.

Hamel, Gary and C.K. Prahalad, 'Do You Really Have a Global Strategy?' *Harvard Business Review*, July–August 1985, pp. 139–48.

Heenan, David and Howard Perlmutter, *Multinational Organization Development*. Boston, MA: Addison-Wesley, 1979.

Kim Chan W. and Renée Mauborgne, *Blue Ocean Strategy: How to Create Uncontested Market Space and Make the Competition Irrelevant*. Boston, MA: Harvard Business School Press, 2005.

Lloyd-Reason, Lester and Terry Mughan, 'Competing effectively in international markets: identifying need, sharing best practice and adding value to the Eastern Region through skills and knowledge transfer', Final Report for the East of England Development Agency, 2003, <http://eastofenglandobservatory.org.uk>

Mellaahi Kamel, J. George Frynas and Paul Finlay, *Global Strategic Management*. Oxford: Oxford University Press, 2005.

OECD, *Enhancing The Role of SMEs in Global Value Chains*. OECD Background Report, Paris: OECD, 2007.

OECD, *Removing Barriers to SME Access to International Markets*. Paris: OECD Publishing, 2008, <http://dx.doi.org/10.1787/9789264045866-en>

Ohmae, Kenichi, *Becoming a Triad Power*. New York: McKinsey & Co., 1985.

Porter, Michael E., *Competitive Strategy: Techniques for Analyzing Industries and Competitors*. New York: Free Press, 1980.

Porter, Michael E., *Competitive Advantage. Creating and Sustaining Superior Performance*. New York: Free Press, 1985.

Porter, Michael E., *Competition in Global Industries*. Boston, MA: Harvard Business School Press, 1986.

Prahalad, C.K. and Yves L. Doz, *The Multinational Mission: Balancing Local Demands and Global Vision*, 1st edn. New York: Free Press, 1987.

Rennie, Michael W., 'Global Competitiveness: Born Global', *McKinsey Quarterly*, 4, 1993, pp. 45–52.

Rugman M. Alan, *The Regional Multinationals: MNEs and Global Strategic Management*, Cambridge, UK: Cambridge University Press, 2005.

Russ, M. and J.K. Jones, 'International Virtual Industry Clusters and SMEs: Early Process Policy Recommendations', in Knut I. Westeren (ed.), *Aspects of the Knowledge Economy: Innovation, Learning and Clusters*. Cheltenham: Edward Elgar Publishing, forthcoming.

Russ, M. and J.K. Jones, 'Industry Clusters, SMEs and Public Policy', *International Journal of Management and Business*, 2(2), forthcoming.

Stalk, Georges, 'Time – The next source of Competitive Advantage', *Harvard Business Review*, July–August 1988.

Stopford, John and Louis Wells, *Strategy and Structure of Multinational Enterprises*. New York: Basic Books, 1972.

UNCTAD, *Integrating Developing Countries SMEs into Global Value Chains*. New York: United Nations, 2010.

Verdin, Paul and Nick Van Heck, *From Local Champions to Global Masters: A Strategic Perspective on Managing Internationalization*. London: Palgrave Macmillan, 2001.

Yip, George, *Total Global Strategy: Managing for Worldwide Competitive Advantage*. Englewood Cliffs, NJ: Prentice-Hall, 1992.

chapter

3 DESIGNING A GLOBAL ORGANIZATION

Introduction

In Chapter 2 various models of organizational designs were introduced. It has been argued that those designs were contingent upon the nature of the global industry context as well as the strategic positioning and business system selected by corporations. In practice, whatever the type of design chosen, companies engaged in global business have to cope with a dual requirement:

- They need to efficiently introduce and leverage their competitive advantages across borders; consequently their organizational design demands a certain degree of *coordination and centralization*
- They need to adapt to local conditions; consequently their organizational design demands a certain degree of *decentralization* and local autonomy.

Organizational design reflects the way companies put this dual demand into action through the implementation of three interlocking elements:

- *Organizational structure:* how roles, responsibilities and power are assigned.
- *Organizational processes:* how decisions are made, resource allocation commitments decided, policies enacted and rewards, sanctions and control exercised. Organizational processes include information processes, decision-making processes, planning and control processes and performance evaluation processes.
- *Organizational culture:* the shared values and the dominant logic[1] of doing business; the 'dos' and 'don'ts' and what kind of behaviour is rewarded or sanctioned.

This chapter discusses the various organizational designs used by corporations in their international, multinational and global operations. Based on the work of prior research, three generic organizational models are identified:

- *Global hub:* a worldwide functional or global product structure
- *Confederation:* a multinational geographical structure
- *Multidimensional:* a matrix or transnational structure.

A variety of structures is derived from these three generic models. These are described and illustrated in turn, showing their advantages and disadvantages. It can be argued that there is no single best structure and that the adoption of a particular structure is contingent upon the competitive imperative. The chapter ends by advocating that global firms should develop a culture and management process of the 'transnational' model and by discussing the roles of Regional Headquarters (RHQs).

Learning objectives

At the end of the chapter you will be able to:

- identify the benefits and issues for each organizational type
- participate in a meaningful way in designing an appropriate organization in the context of a particular global firm
- understand the characteristics of the transnational model and be able to introduce its features in a particular firm.

Structure, processes and culture

The configuration and evolution of structure, processes and culture in different globalization settings can be best illustrated by the example of two companies which operate in a similar industrial environment: NV Philips and Matsushita.[2]

EXAMPLE

Philips: evolution of a global organization

Founded in 1882 in Eindhoven, Holland, as a producer of light bulbs, Philips rapidly expanded into geographical internationalization as well as product diversification. As early as 1899 it started to export its products, and by 1912 it had established subsidiaries in the United States, Canada and France. Philips's product line expanded to electronic vacuum tubes, radios, X-rays and later on to electrical appliances, TVs, videos, electronic components, medical equipment and telephony. By the year 2000, Philips was a US$30 billion company involved in 150 countries with nine major product lines. Philips's global organizational design was based on the predominance of national subsidiaries called National Organizations (NOs). Each NO built its own technical and marketing activities in order to adapt products to local conditions. Countries initiated product development – as, for instance, in Canada where the first color TV was created. Although 14 product divisions in Eindhoven were theoretically in charge of product development and global marketing, national subsidiaries had the real power of making strategic decisions, since they controlled the assets and reported directly to the Board. Except for a few high-flyers, most executive careers at Philips were built within NOs. This organizational design was the 'administrative heritage'[3] of Philips's early expansion in international markets at a time when political, economic and technological forces were in favour of strategic adaptation and responsiveness to local country-specific conditions; Philips's design was representative of a multi-business geographical model. Table 3.1 gives a summary of the traditional Philips global organizational system.

Starting in the early 1980s, this global geographically oriented organization was challenged by the forces of globalization and the emergence of strong Japanese competitors. The ability of Philips to bring products rapidly to market and to produce them at competitive costs forced top management to reconsider the organization. During the 1980s and 1990s four different chairmen embarked on reorganization with the aim of moving away from the geographical decentralized confederation in favour of a more globally efficient network of operations. The restructuring was not without resistance and led to a drastic reduction in headcount and to the disposal of several business lines. In 1990 Philips posted a loss of $2.5 billion. Tom Timmer, appointed chairman in 1990, and later Cor Boonstra, who replaced him in 1996, rationalized the global structure by shifting the power from the national reorganization toward global business units.

Table 3.1 Philips's global organizational design until the late 1980s

Organizational dimensions	Need for local adaptation	Need for global leverage and efficiency
Structure		
Design	Geographical Units (NOs)	Product Divisions (PDs)
Power	NOs control assets Marketing Product adaptation Production	Research direction supervises eight separate laboratories located in Europe and the United States
Responsibilities	Responsible for profit and return on assets	PDs formally responsible for product development and global marketing
Reporting	NOs report to the Board	
Processes		
Planning	Mainly made within NOs	An International Council established in the mid-1950s to organize meetings with the principal managers of the NOs and the Board. Frequent visits to foreign affiliates by senior corporate management
Decision-making	Senior management Committees of each NO ensure that Product Groups' directions fit with national strategies	PDs organize cross-functional coordination PDs set directions for product marketing
Careers	Mostly within NOs except for top managers	Top managers (the elite group) have career built through successive foreign tours of duty
Culture	Strong technological and commercial competencies embodied in national culture	Strong technological and commercial culture corporate-wide

Source: Author's own table based on information in Bartlett (1992).

Matsushita: evolution of a global organization

Matsushita, founded in 1918 by Konosuke Matsushita, was, after the Second World War, the dominant Japanese player in the appliances and later consumer electronics industries. Benefiting from a 40 per cent market share in Japan, Matsushita embarked on an internationalization strategy in 1953 with the opening of its American subsidiary, Matsushita Electric Corporation of America. Over the years, the company controlled more than 200 subsidiaries outside Japan. These subsidiaries are divided into two broad categories: wholly owned single-product plants reporting directly to the product divisions in Japan; and sales, marketing and assembling subsidiaries producing and selling product lines for local markets reporting to Matsushita Electric Trading Company (METC), a legal entity supervising overseas operations. The 36 central product divisions headquartered in Japan had a strong control over the first category of operations, while METC subsidiaries were tightly controlled by the Japanese headquarters through the assignment of Japanese expatriates to key positions in local subsidiaries. These Japanese expatriates maintained strong relationships with corporate senior executives, and corporate managers frequently visited local operations. Matsushita's organizational design was representative of a 'global hub' form of organization. See Table 3.2 for details of Matsushita's global organizational design until the late 1980s.

In the mid-1980s a newly appointed President launched a programme named 'Operation Localization', with the objective of putting in place localization of personnel, technology, material and capital. Local nationals were appointed to key positions, procurement of components with local suppliers was progressively implemented and products could be adapted to meet local requirements. METC became the sole coordinator of all foreign operations, and regional headquarters were set up in North America, Europe and South East Asia. In spite of all these efforts, the product divisions still played a dominant role in company strategy and few senior foreign managers occupied a central position.

Philips and Matsushita: the search for global organizational fit

The two examples just described illustrate quite well the search for 'fit' between the strategic requirements imposed upon global companies and their organizational responses. This evolutionary search is represented in Figure 3.1.

The vertical axis of Figure 3.1 measures the requirements for efficiency and leverage demanded by the industrial competitive context while the horizontal axis measures the requirement for local adaptation and responsiveness; this represents the global/multi-local mapping introduced in Chapter 1. Philips's organizational design up until the 1980s is positioned in the lower right-hand corner as a decentralized confederation: the corporate headquarters in the centre are linked to the various national subsidiaries on a one-to-one basis with very little integration across subsidiaries. Each national subsidiary is shown tinted to indicate that the locus of strategic decision-making is in their hands. Matsushita's design, on the other hand, is located in the upper left-hand corner as an integrated global organization with the locus of power in the centre.

Table 3.2 Matsushita's global organizational design until the late 1980s

Organizational dimensions	*Need for local adaptation*	*Need for global leverage and efficiency*
Structure		
Design	Marketing and local production subsidiaries (overseas companies) reporting to METC	Product Companies (PCs) Reporting to PDs in Japan
Power	Overseas companies in charge of marketing and local production when needed Planning of sales and profit determined centrally by METC	PDs in Japan responsible for product development (R&D), global production and sourcing
Responsibilities	Local marketing	PDs responsible for product development, global manufacturing and marketing
	Responsible for return on sales	Responsible for return on assets
Reporting	Subsidiaries report to METC	Subsidiaries report to PDs
Processes		
Planning	Mainly made at headquarters between METC and Product Divisions (PDs)	PDs prepare global product strategies
Decision-making	Autonomy of local managers to achieve targets	PDs organize cross-functional coordination PDs set directions for product marketing
Careers	Main functions in the hands of expatriates	Expatriate managers sent to transfer products and process technologies and provide headquarters with market information
	Expatriate managers maintain relationships with 'mentors'	Expatriate managers maintain relationships with 'mentors' at headquarters
Culture		Matsushita philosophy: 'The Seven Spirits of Matsushita' developed by the company's founder is spread throughout the world by expatriate managers

Source: Author's own creation based on information in Harvard Business School case study 9-392-156, written by Robert Lightfoot under the supervision of Christopher Bartlett (1992).

Both designs are the result of the historical development of the firm – their 'administrative heritage' – from the time when their international expansion started. Philips created subsidiaries abroad early in the twentieth century at a time when technological, economic and, later on, political barriers (the First and Second World Wars) forced each subsidiary to operate independently. Matsushita, which globalized its operations after the Second World War during a period of increasing trade liberalization and technological development in transport and communication, could adopt a more centralized approach which favored efficiency and transfer of product and manufacturing technologies across borders. Because the industrial context of the 1960s and 1970s was favourable to a global integrated approach, Matsushita's organization was more appropriate than Philips's. As, for instance, in the case of the VCR technology, Philips's corporate headquarters was not able to persuade Philips North America, the US subsidiary, to adopt the V2000 system developed by Philips laboratories. Instead, Philips North America adopted the competitive VHS system. The successive reorganizations undertaken by various chairmen was an attempt to become more integrated. Those efforts are represented graphically by the West–East arrow in Figure 3.1. Matsushita, whose integrated design proved successful in the 1960s, 1970s and 1980s, felt on the other hand that an increased variety in market characteristics and sourcing opportunities demanded a more localized approach. This is represented by the South–North arrow in Figure 3.1. Both companies have tried to build on their strengths and compensate for their weaknesses by building an organizational design which simultaneously satisfies the requirements for global efficiency/leverage and local responsiveness.

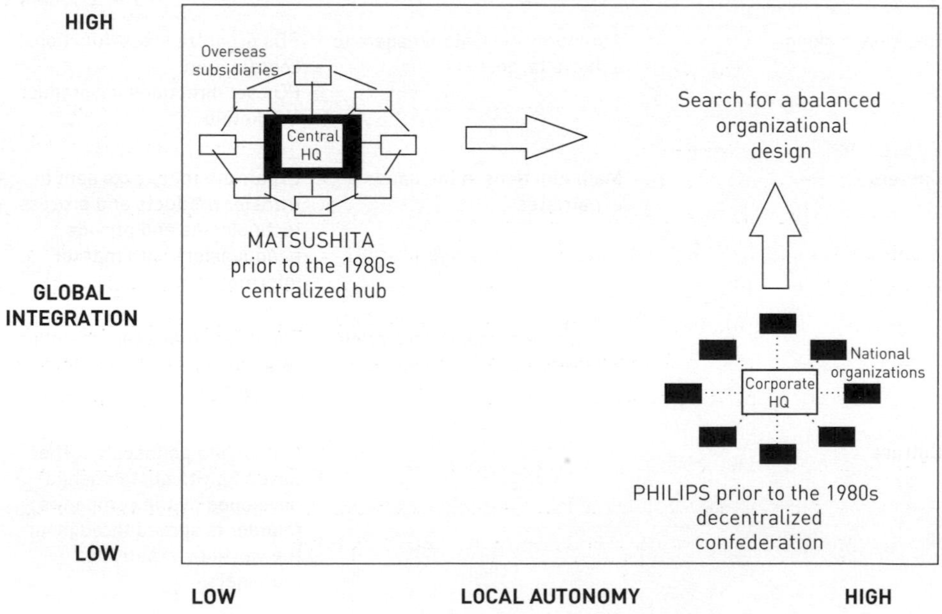

Figure 3.1 Philips and Matsushita: global organizational designs and their evolution

Source: Author's own creation based on information in Bartlett (1992).

By the mid-1980s both companies had undertaken some change in order to develop competencies in the dimension in which they were less strong. Philips attempted to gain efficiency and leverage while keeping its strong national responsiveness, while Matsushita attempted to gain local responsiveness while preserving their strong global efficiency capabilities. Both companies tried to become 'multidimensional' in their organization.

In 2008 Matsushita changed its name to Panasonic and during the first decade of the twenty-first century has changed its organizational design twice in order to reflect the new reality. In 2011 Panasonic is organized around three business sectors (Consumers, Components and Devices, and Solutions) regrouping 14 business domains and 556 companies as well as five regional headquarters.

Similarly, Philips has evolved from a pure geographical structure to an organization based in 2011 on three business sectors (Healthcare, Lifestyle, Lighting), grouping operations in 100 countries.

The organizational evolution of these two giants, Philips and Matsushita, is a good illustration of the constraints that globalization puts on companies and the type of responses that are sought to solve the constraints of efficiency, leverage and responsiveness.

Since the 1990s, customer-based organizations have gained in popularity among companies as part of their positioning and value proposition to customers. This strong customer focus has prompted some companies (e.g. Reuters and SingTel) to restructure their organization and form departments which are based on *customer groups*. By having designated staff specializing in customer groups, customer needs and responsiveness can be better catered for.

With increased customer convenience and responsiveness, however, comes the trade-off of reduced technical competence among staff of the service provider. Since each person is now serving a customer group, their knowledge is spread across the wide range of products which are being offered to that particular customer group. It could be argued that customers may not be expecting flawless technical advice (e.g. details of printer specification) or may not be able to discern that ineffective 'expert' advice is due to a lack of knowledge or underlying uncertainty surrounding the advice (e.g. a bank's investment advice given to customers). The remaining part of this chapter will be devoted to describing and analyzing different organizational models: the global functional model, the single and multi-business geographical models, the global product division model, the single and multi-business matrix models and the transnational model.

These models will be presented according to the respective contribution of the three dimensions of organizational design (structure, processes and culture) to the three value creation activities: innovation, operational efficiency and marketing impact.

The global functional model

The global functional design is based upon the worldwide centralization of decision-making, coordination and control at the level of the key functional activities such as R&D, operations and marketing. All strategic decisions and operational policies are made at headquarters level. Country subsidiaries are local legal entities; the heads of country subsidiaries have responsibilities with the regard to the laws of the countries in which they operate, but in practice all the key business decisions relative to products, production, operations and marketing are activated from headquarters. The functional managers within the subsidiaries take their instruction from the corporate vice-president or director in charge of their function. The only autonomous decisions are those related to the practical implementation of policies, such as sales management, or those with a strong local legal content, such as tax reporting or personnel management.

This organizational model fits companies or business units of multi-business corporations operating in single business environments with strong demand for global integration and coordination.

The global functional organizational design is represented in Figure 3.2 and its characteristics described in Table 3.3. An example of global functional design is provided below.

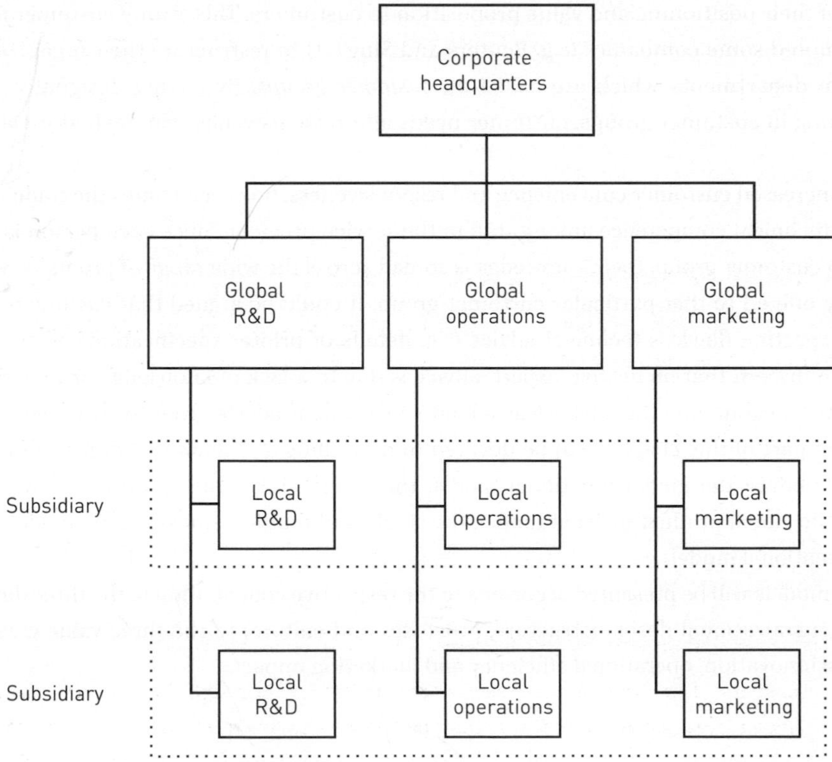

Figure 3.2 The global functional organizational design

Table 3.3 Characteristics of the global functional organizational design

Organizational	Innovation	Efficiency of operations	Marketing impact dimension
Structure Central functional executive exercises global power and responsibilities	• Central R&D function • If various research centers, research policies are centrally led • Subsidiaries' R&D managers report to central R&D • Sales function quite autonomous	• Central operational function such as vice-president manufacturing • Subsidiaries' operational managers report to central vice-president operations	• Central marketing function • Subsidiaries' marketing managers report to central marketing vice-president • Country managers in charge of local interface with government and legal matters
Processes	• R&D strategy and budgets decided centrally • Control and reporting centrally organized • R&D worldwide policies • Global standardized product development	• Global supply chain management • Global factories and operational centers • Central policies	• Key marketing policies set globally • Global advertising • Global pricing • Global sales policies • Some local adaptation of sales practices depending upon authorization by center • Countries are nominally profit centers but without much power to influence profit
Culture	• Careers are managed globally • High level of transfer of personnel • Expatriates are key transferors of technology • Strong product/technology identity	• Careers managed globally • High level of transfer of personnel • Expatriates are key transferors of best practice • Strong technology identity	• Marketing careers are managed globally • High level of transfer of personnel • Expatriates are key transferors of best practice • Strong brand identity

EXAMPLE

Global functional organizational design at Apple

Created by Steve Jobs and Steve Wozniak in 1976, Apple Computer Inc, the creator of Macintosh, iPod, iPhone and iPad is by 2011 one of the largest corporations in the world, with products marketed around the world. Its organizational structure is based on the functional model. The main functions headed by a senior executive are: Software, Industrial Design, Operations, Software Engineering, Product Marketing, Global Communication, Internet Services, Mac Hardware Engineering, iPhone Software Design , and Legal and Finance.

International subsidiaries are essentially for marketing and selling products and sourcing components and devices.

Advantages of the global functional organizational design

The key advantages of this model are the efficiencies obtained through the coherence of decisions and policies, leading to the optimization, concentration and specialization of resources, which in turn produces economies of scale, avoids duplication of effort and favors rapid transfer of know-how from headquarters to the subsidiaries. The benefits of those efficiencies are best obtained when products are standardized and economies of scale and rapid transfer of central know-how are key determinants of competitive advantage – examples are commodities businesses such oil or basic chemicals, or industries in which manufacturing or operational systems demand size optimization and complex supply chain logistics, such as the car industry.

Disadvantages of the global functional organizational design

The disadvantages of this model are more visible when either the competitive context is fragmented into several segments, calling for distinct capabilities, or when the markets and local business environments are significantly different. In such cases a standardized, undifferentiated approach leads to inflexibility, local disfunctionalities and market rejection. Internally, it fosters bureaucracy and discourages initiative.

The geographical model

The geographical organizational design, unlike the global functional design, is based on the worldwide decentralization of decision-making, coordination and control at the level of the subsidiaries. In such a model, central functions or product management roles are sometimes non-existent or, when they do exist, play an advisory, stimulating or coordinating role without much executive power. The relationships between the subsidiaries and the central functional directors or product managers are sometimes referred to as 'dotted-lines' relationships, to signify that there are no hierarchical links. Functional managers within business units report to the national manager, who in turn reports either directly to the chief executive or to a central senior manager in charge of international operations. In many cases, intermediary executive powers are given to regional executives located at regional headquarters in the key regions of the world. National managers develop strategies and adapt or select products which fit with their local environment. Policies are set up locally. In many cases, national or regional managers sit on the corporate executive committee. As in the case of Philips prior to the 1980s, the global strengths of the business come from its basic technological capabilities (products in particular) and from the global management of key expatriates who rotate from country to country.

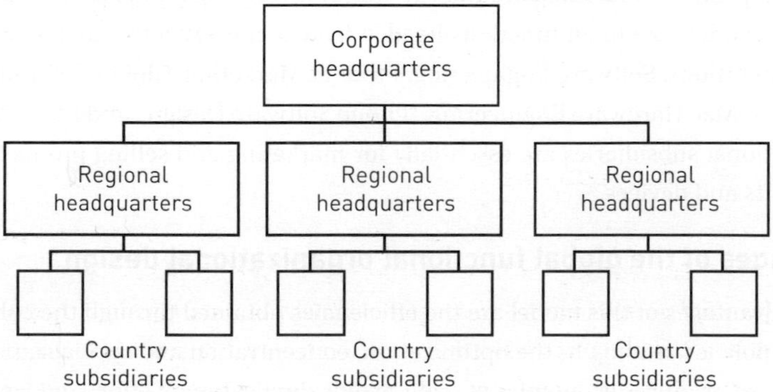

Figure 3.3 The geographical organizational design

The geographical organizational design is represented in Figure 3.3 and its characteristics described in Table 3.4. The example below provides an illustration of a geographical organization.

Table 3.4 Characteristics of geographical organizational design

Organizational dimension	Innovation	Efficiency of operations	Marketing impact
Structure National or regional subsidiaries have strategic and operational responsibilities	• R&D centers are distributed • Central R&D center focuses on fundamental research • Central R&D center and product managers propose innovation but have no power to impose • Local companies have power to adapt products locally or have the discretion to choose from the corporate product portfolio the products they want to commercialize in their territory	• Self-contained operations at the level of countries/regions • Scale efficiency obtained with country volume	• Local brands and promotion • Local pricing • Local distribution and maintenance
Processes	• Very little attempt to share and transfer best practices • Reliance on subsidiaries' self-interest • Regular information about corporate programs through conferences and forums, but subsidiaries are free to decide what kind of innovation they adopt	• Arms-length transactions among subsidiaries and between central factories and subsidiaries • Transfer pricing issues • Very often information systems are not compatible	• Marketing policies: subsidiaries' management has a high degree of discretion in implementation • Countries are profit and investment centers
Culture	• Pride in locally adapted products • Careers essentially local • Local identity • Autonomy	• Careers essentially local • Local identity • Autonomy	• Careers essentially local • Local identity • Entrepreneurship • Autonomy

International Service Systems A/S (ISS)

EXAMPLE

Headquartered in Denmark, the ISS group specializes in cleaning services. It employs around 520,000 employees in local companies spread across over 50 countries. The group is organized around four major regional divisions: Asia Pacific, Europe, Latin America and North America. Poul Andreassen, who was the key architect of this organizational design, thought that the 'most profitable way to provide services is through small stand-alone companies led by a local manager who is encouraged to think of the business as his or her own'.

He intentionally erected a barrier around the operational units which he called 'the Chinese Wall' to keep out top management.[4] The company still relied on independent operations in 2011. As stated in their website 'The cornerstone of ISS is our multi-local approach with strong entrepreneurial leadership teams working at a high level of independence in each of our 50 country organizations. This is emphasised by strong local incentives and freedom to perform according to local market conditions'.[5] The role of the corporate center is to provide financial and marketing expertise to the various countries.

Source: Ghoshal (1993).

Advantages of the geographical organizational design

The main advantage of this model is its flexibility and ability to incorporate local specificity into the company's competitive approach. Products tailored to consumer demands, advertising campaigns reflecting local culture, and investment practices fitting with national policies enable companies to make more appealing value propositions. The ability to adapt and change competitive parameters without involving lengthy negotiations with the corporate center gives geographically structured companies a better chance to capture rising opportunities, or react rapidly to changing local conditions. Those advantages are more significant when customers' tastes and needs differ significantly across countries, for economic, cultural, social or political reasons and when scale economies can be attached easily within national boundaries. Traditionally foods, cosmetics, personal services and government-regulated industries are those in which geographical design has worked well.

Disadvantages of the geographical organizational design

Disadvantages arise when local autonomy creates too much duplication, erodes economies of scale or slows down the transfer of innovation. When customers become global and require a 'global' pricing or service, geographically structured companies may lose their competitiveness if they do not introduce some element of global coordination. As seen in Chapter 1, the overall competitive context in many industries has been pushing in favour of globalization, and geographically managed companies like Philips have been disadvantaged.

The single matrix model

The single matrix model is an organizational design in which both functions and geography are given equal power and responsibilities. In such a case the R&D global vice-president would be responsible for the global R&D budget and would have some authority over the career of scientists and designers, but national managers would have some authority over the allocation of resources, local laboratories and the career of scientists or designers. A similar dual responsibility would apply for operations and marketing. The end result of this design is a shared executive power which puts middle managers in a situation of having 'dual bosses'. This design is very often used by professional firms such as engineering companies, advertising or consultancy firms.

The objective of such a design is to solve the requirements of efficiency, leverage and responsiveness through a dual structure. It aims to develop a culture of 'thinking globally, acting locally' by institutionalizing the tensions arising from the two competitive imperatives.

The single matrix organizational design is represented in Figure 3.4 and its characteristics described in Table 3.5. An example of a single matrix structure is provided below.

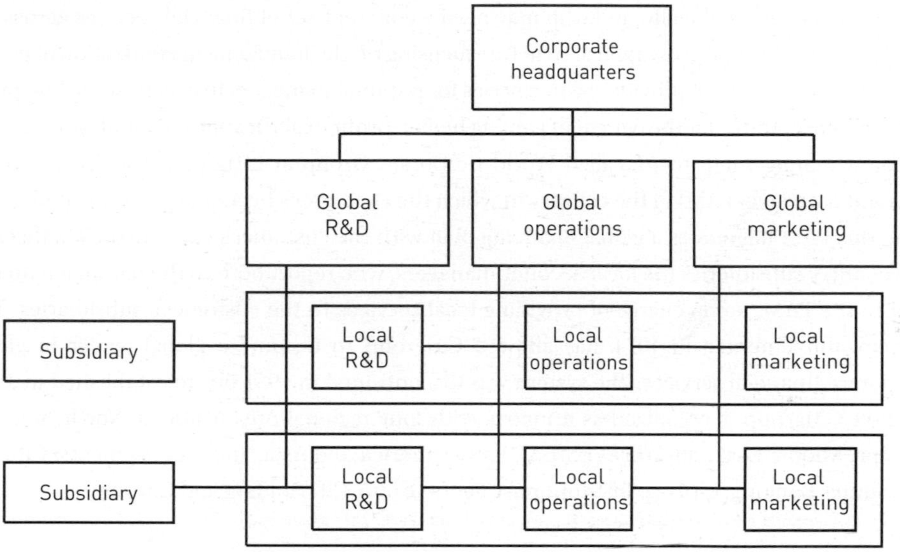

Figure 3.4 The single matrix organizational design

Table 3.5 Characteristics of the single matrix organizational design

Organizational	Innovation	Efficiency of operations	Marketing impact dimension
Structure Both functions and countries are given equal power and responsibilities	• Central R&D responsible for product innovation • Local subsidiaries responsible for product adaptation	• Central operations responsible for global operations and optimization • Local subsidiaries responsible for local results	• Central marketing responsible for global marketing strategies • Local subsidiaries responsible for local marketing strategies
Processes	• Global research strategic plan and budget drawn up by global vice-president • Local budgets at subsidiaries level • Conferences for transfer of best practice	• Strategic investment in global factories or operational centers by global vice-president • Global best practice • Local operational responsibilities	• Global marketing plan • Local marketing plans • Reconciliation through strategic planning meetings
Culture	• 'Think global, act local' • Dual identity • Negotiation	• Local operating procedures • 'Think global, act local' • Dual identity • Negotiation	• 'Think global, act local' • Dual identity • Negotiation

EXAMPLE

Citigroup Matrix Management

Known in the past as Citibank, Citigroup (Citi) is a banking institution operating all over the world. Citibank was traditionally structured along a multi-business geographical reporting line. One of its activities, the management of global accounts, was very easily managed according to the single matrix design. Global accounts are the large corporate customers who themselves operate globally, and who may need a coherent set of financial services across the world. The traditional geographical structure focusing on the individual maximization of profits at country level did not provide the incentives for national managers to accept some low-profit deals in one country for the benefit of gaining higher-profit deals in another country. The global account management team, called World Corporate Group at Citigroup, appoints a parent account manager (PAM) in the country in which the customer's headquarters is located. Every year, this PAM negotiates a global financing plan with the customer's chief financial officer. In the country subsidiaries the local account managers, who report both to the national manager and to the PAM, are in charge of providing local services to the customer's subsidiaries. This system, implemented in 1974, has allowed Citigroup to become a global leader in global corporate financial services. The system was discontinued in 1981 but re-established in 1985. In 2011 Citigroup is organized as a matrix with four regional organizations: North America, Europe, Middle East and Africa (EMEA), Latin America and Asia, and four segments: Citicorp Consumer Banking, Citicorp Institutional Clients Group, Citi Holding and Corporate.

Sources: Malnight and Yoshino (1995) for Global Account and Citi website for 2011 organization.

The advantages and disadvantages of this model will be discussed together with the multi-business matrix model presented below.

The multi-business global product division mode

When a company has diversified into several business activities to become a multi-business corporation, it has the choice of three different organizational models to manage its global operations. Either it organizes itself along the *product dimension* or along the *geographical dimension* or with a *matrix*. The first organizational model is known as the multi-business global product division organization, which is represented in Figure 3.5 and its characteristics described in Table 3.6. The example of 3M below illustrates a multi-business global product division organization.

In this model, the company is divided into *business divisions*, each in charge of a product or service line. Each division chief executive is responsible for the global performance of its business and, as such, formulates its global strategy and puts in place the organizational design which best fits its competitive context. In some cases divisions act independently from each other and subsidiaries of one division in one country frequently do not interact at all with subsidiaries of another division. Within the division, the organizational design can be one of the three kinds described earlier: global functional, geographical or matrix.

If the competitive contexts of the division differ, one division can be organized geographically, for instance, and another use the global functional model. National subsidiary managers report to division heads. In this model, the divisional global headquarters of one business can be located in one country while the headquarters of another division are based in another country and the corporate headquarters in another one. The corporate headquarters' role is limited to overall strategic planning, financial control and executive career management.

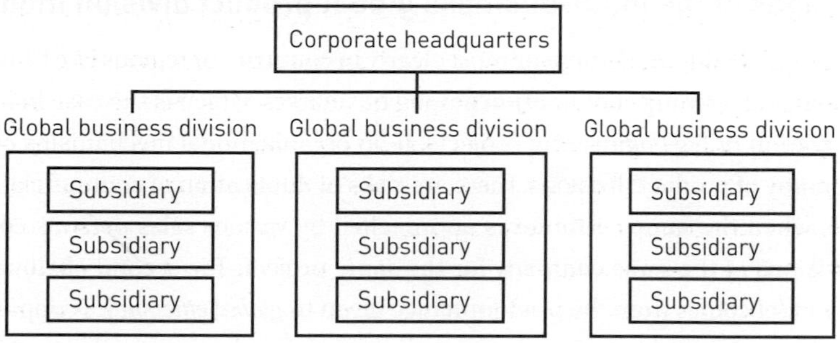

Figure 3.5 The multi-business global product division organizational design

Table 3.6 Characteristics of the multi-business global product division organizational design

Organizational	Innovation	Efficiency of operations	Marketing impact dimension
Structure Global strategic and operational power and responsibilities given to separate product divisions	R&D initiated by product divisions Encourages global standardization	Encourages coordination of activities within divisions Strong efficiency and scale economies within divisions Poor coordination among divisions	Each division develops its own marketing approach Marketing adapted to industry contexts
Processes	Within divisions	Within divisions	Within divisions
Culture	Careers and identity within divisions	Careers and identity within divisions	Careers and identity within divisions

When potential synergies exist between divisions, the corporate headquarters play a more active role and provide some corporate support to subsidiaries such as training, logistics, legal matters and financing, either directly or through regional corporate headquarters.

3M

EXAMPLE

3M is a diversified technology company with a global presence employing 82,000 people in 2011 and operating in more than 65 countries. 3M manages its operations in six operating business segments: Industrial and Transportation; Healthcare; Display and Graphics; Consumer and Office; Safety, Security and Protection Services; and Electro and Communications. These segments have worldwide responsibility for virtually all 3M product lines. Historically 3M was managed on a geographical basis; over time it has moved progressively to a multi-business global structure.

Advantages of the multi-business global product division model

This model gives the global company the flexibility to adapt its structure to the competitive context of each business. By giving division executives the strategic responsibility for their business, this design provides the organizational mechanisms for global efficiency and coordination. This model tends to be favored by the vast majority of multi-business corporations.

Disadvantages of the multi-business global product division model

The disadvantages of this model appear most clearly in countries or regions like China, or when customers demand a strong coordination among businesses, which is the case in information system integration or big engineering projects. If no organizational mechanisms compensate for the autonomy of product divisions, there are risks of duplication of commercial effort – as, for instance, when the same customer is approached by various sales persons coming from different divisions of the same company for the same project. The second obvious disadvantage of this model comes from the predominance given to *global efficiency* as opposed to *local responsiveness.*

The multi-business geographical model

In the multi-business geographical organizational design, country subsidiaries are given full strategic and operational responsibilities for all product lines in their territory. In this design, the central global functions and product divisions have a 'support' or 'dotted-line' role. National or regional units are profit centers and act autonomously. The multi-business geographical organizational design is represented in Figure 3.6 and its characteristics described in Table 3.7. The example below illustrates the multi-business organizational design.

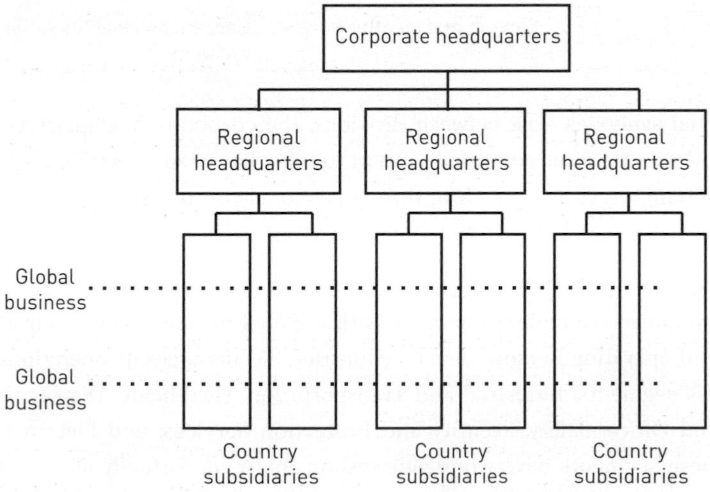

Figure 3.6 Multi-business geographical organizational design

Table 3.7 Characteristics of the multi-business geographical organizational design

Organizational dimension	Innovation	Efficiency of operations	Marketing impact
Structure National or regional subsidiaries have strategic and operational responsibilities Global products or functions have a 'support' role	• Adaptation of products to local conditions • Optimization of product lines at country level	• Adaptation of products to local conditions • Optimization of product lines at country level	• Full localization of marketing mix conditions • Optimization of marketing activities at country level
Processes	• Country-specific	• Country-specific	• Country-specific
Culture	• National identity • Careers within countries	• National identity • Careers within countries	• National identity • Careers within countries

EXAMPLE

SABMiller

SABMiller is one of the largest brewers in the world. It is the result of the acquisition and merger of South African Breweries and Miller (USA). In 2011, it operated in 70 countries with 70,000 employees. It markets 200 brands, some of which are global premium brands such Millers, some of which are purely local. The group is organized in six regions: South Africa, North America, Africa, Asia, Europe and Latin America.

Advantages of the multi-business geographical model

The main advantages of this design are its *flexibility* and *adaptiveness* to local conditions. It encourages the optimization of the product and investment portfolio at country level, fitting with local tastes and regulatory conditions.

Disadvantages of the multi-business geographical model

Sub-optimization of resource allocation and delays in new product introduction are the main pitfalls of this model. In industries in which the pressures for globalization are high, this model leads to inefficiency and loss of competitive advantage. Over the past 20 years, this model has progressively been abandoned by many large global corporations and replaced either by the global product division or by the multi-business matrix (described below).

The multi-business matrix model

As in the single matrix model, this design emphasizes dual (and sometimes triple) responsibilities. In the case of multi-business companies, the responsibilities are shared between the product divisions and the geographical units.

The multi-business matrix organizational design is represented in Figure 3.7 and its characteristics described in Table 3.8. The example below illustrates the multi-business matrix organizational design.

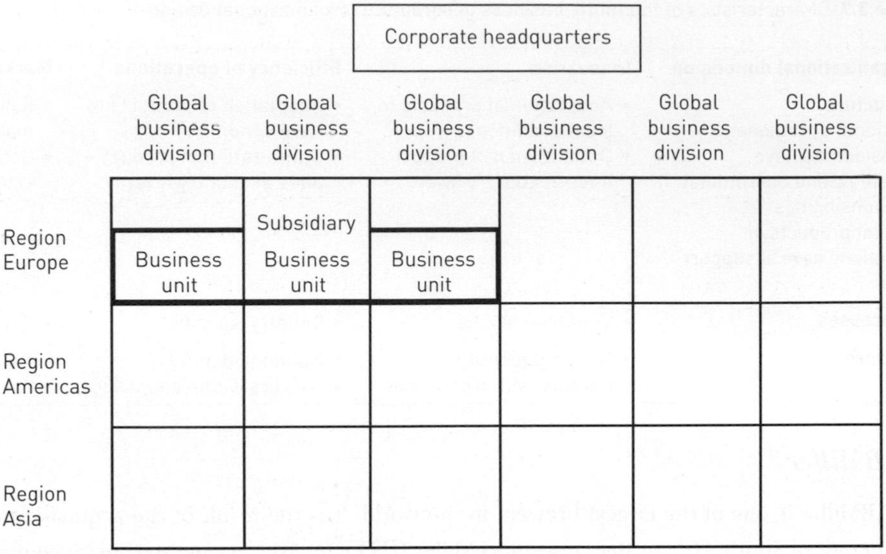

Figure 3.7 Multi-business matrix organizational design

EXAMPLE

BASF

The BASF Group is one of the world's largest chemical corporations, with 385 manufacturing facilities scattered throughout 20 countries and customers in over 170 countries. In 2010, the company's sales reached 64 billion Euros with pre-tax profits of 8 billion Euros. The group's activities are divided into six segments containing 72 Global Business Units (GBUs). The segments are: Chemicals, Plastics, Performance Products, Functional Solutions, Agricultural Solutions, Oil and Gas. These products are organizationally balanced by four regional divisions: Europe, North America, Asia Pacific and South America/Africa/Middle East, with nine competence centers ranging from engineering and maintenance, research centers to global logistics. In addition, three central divisions, five corporate departments and ten competence centers provide management with strategic, financial and legal support. This provided BASF with a three-dimensional matrix. In the 1980s, most important business decisions were still taken in the Ludwigshafen headquarters; organizations with regional responsibilities remained sited in Germany, for the most part staffed by Germans. As part of a new globalization drive, the BASF Group made a major effort to decentralize its international business, moving many of the company's operations and decision-making capabilities and key region-sensitive activities, such as marketing, as well as certain administrative functions into three principal geographical areas: Europe, NAFTA and Asia. In accordance with BASF's long-term strategy, manufacturing capabilities in each region were targeted to receive major investments, with the eventual aim of increasing locally manufactured content to 70 per cent and above. Decision-making was to be non-confrontational; where possible, executives sought to forge a consensus through compromise, with the overall aim of maintaining the long-term health and profits of the BASF Group as a whole. In fact, the ability to compromise represented a crucial career skill within BASF culture; without it, few executives could hope to advance![6]

Source: Crawford and Schütte (2000), BASF Corporate information (2011).

Table 3.8 Characteristics of the multi-business matrix organizational design

Organizational dimension	Innovation	Efficiency of operations	Marketing impact
Structure Strategic and operational responsibilities shared by product and geographical units	• Global product divisions lead global product development • National management adapt products and services locally	• Global factories and operational units • Local factories • Integration of supply chain	• Global marketing 'guidance' • Local integration of product portfolio
Processes Dual systems Free flow of information Multidimensional databases	• Dual strategic plans • Shared information systems • Transfer of 'best practices'	• Dual strategic plans • Shared information systems • Transfer of 'best practices'	• Dual strategic plans • Shared information systems • Transfer of 'best practices'
Culture 'Think global, act local'	• Sharing and negotiating culture	• Negotiating	• Optimization

Advantages of the multi-business matrix organizational design

As Percy Barnevick, a former chairman of Asea Brown Boveri, puts it, 'Matrix management is like breathing, whether you like it or not you are obliged to do it'. The multi-dimensional matrix design is supposed to internalize the pressures for global efficiency, leverage and local responsiveness, as well as achieving synergies among businesses. The mechanism is twofold: at the business level, the global dimension is represented by the executive in charge of the worldwide product division, while the local dimension is in the hands of the business units in the countries. The synergies among businesses are achieved at the region or country level by the regional or national manager. Take, for example, the case of a power-generation firm selling a large project to a public utility in Venezuela through international bids. The national sales people will be in contact with the customer at the pre-bidding stage, discussing specifications and bidding modalities. To make an effective proposition, several divisions have to be involved: one for turbines, one for generators, one for transformation and one for regulation. A *bidding task force* will be gathered by the Venezuelan national manager in order to coordinate the bids of the various divisions. Assuming that the company wins the contract, the national manager will be credited with the sales and the profit on these sales, while each product division will be credited with the sales and the profits for their respective product offering. The project manager in Venezuela will effectively report to the national manager as well as to the different divisions, managing the tensions between the various 'bosses'. By forcing the project managers to make the necessary trade-off between the product divisions and national management, the matrix structure is intended to optimize the dual requirements of global efficiency and local responsiveness.

Disadvantages of the multi-business matrix organizational design

Matrix organizations are complex and may lead to power struggles that cancel out their expected benefits. There are five main pitfalls of matrix structures:

- *Role ambiguity.* Middle managers operating in matrix structures are frequently placed in situations where their 'dual bosses' put pressure on them to achieve conflicting objectives. While, theoretically, the matrix organization is designed to force those managers to 'solve' these conflicts, in reality it does not. Managers will follow whatever instructions they consider come from the 'most powerful boss'. The matrix becomes an illusion.
- *Dilution of responsibilities.* In order to make a matrix work properly, numerous conflict resolution mechanisms have to be put in place, particularly committees, meetings and task forces. Decisions take a long time and, at the end of the day, it is very difficult to untangle who is responsible for what. In case of failure or mistake, it is always possible to find excuses for decisions made by an anonymous unaccountable committee.
- *Cost inefficiencies.* Coordination costs of matrix structures – such as travel, communication, time spent in meetings and delays in making decisions – tend to rise very rapidly without compensation in competitive benefits.
- *Turf battles.* By design, matrix structures encourage product divisions and national managers to assert their power, leading to numerous territorial conflicts. The worst scenario is when customers themselves become involved in the conflict, receiving different value propositions, for instance, from different organizational units.
- *Costs of compromise.* The main danger of the dual tension resolution implied in the matrix design is the danger of compromise. In order to satisfy their 'two bosses', managers may adopt middle-of-the-road solutions, ultimately leading to mediocre decisions. To take an example of such an outcome, let us consider a lubricant company: the sales people in Japan ask for 11 different sizes of cans to serve the motorist market. The global product division has decided that five sizes of can are sufficient to cover the market needs and that it is more cost effective to focus on those five types of can. Here is a typical conflict between global efficiency (five sizes) and local responsiveness (the Japanese market demands 11 sizes). A matrix structure may encourage the local lubricant manager to 'compromise' and propose seven sizes: a decision that will not satisfy the Japanese customer, and will increase costs.

These pitfalls have encouraged many corporations to abandon this type of structural design and return to a simpler product or geographical organization structure. However, this does not overcome the fact that in a global company, the tensions between efficiency, leverage and responsiveness are constant, like 'breathing'. If the matrix structure that is supposed to achieve a symbiotic reconciliation between various competitive requirements does not fulfill this reconciliation, how can it be achieved?

Some companies have implemented *hybrid structures* by which the global product dimension coexists with a regional geographical structure but without forming a matrix, but the vast majority of global firms came to realize that structural answers were not sufficient and whatever the design, the global efficiency and innovation/local responsiveness requirements could be achieved only by a cultural approach. The theory of this approach is provided by the *transnational* model.

Hybrid structural models

Managers in such a structure follow a *single line of reporting*. Global products divisions act as suppliers of innovation, products and components to geographical units in charge of marketing, local production and product adaptation, if needed. There are two types of hybrid model:

- The traditional international division model described briefly in Chapter 2;
- Complex dual structures.

The international divisions model

The international divisions model has been described as the first organizational structure adopted by firms at an early stage of internationalization.[7] In this model, there is a clear distinction between the home-country business units managed by divisional executives in charge of product development, manufacturing and home marketing plus exports and the international subsidiaries which, under the leadership of an international division executive, develop their countries' strategic development. The overseas subsidiaries possess a high degree of autonomy, but are dependent upon the home-country divisions for products and technical support. To the extent that international sales represent a small proportion of total sales and transactions between home divisions, and country subsidiaries are limited, this model fulfills the requirements of global efficiency and local responsiveness.[8] When international sales increase and represent a significant proportion of total turnover, the company begins to feel the need to integrate all activities in a global structure, either geographical, divisional or matrix. In their seminal work, John Stopford and Louis Wells have described this evolution as represented in Figure 3.8.

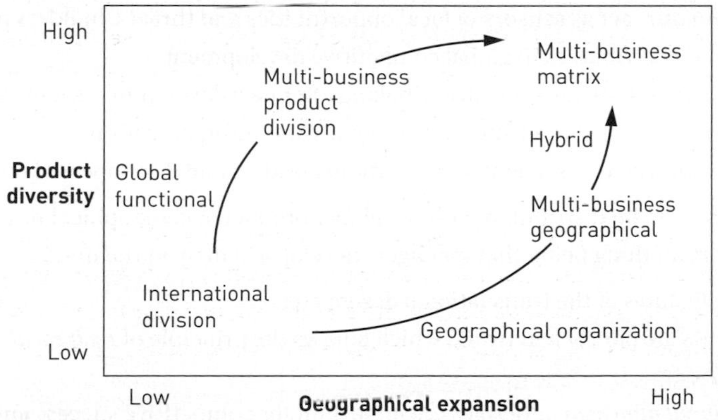

Figure 3.8 The evolution of global organizational models
Source: Adapted from Stopford and Wells (1972).

Complex dual structural models

As mentioned earlier, the logic of dual models is to create within the global organization a mix of different designs. For instance, Citibank built an organization in which a global product division design (consumer banking and corporate banking), a geographical design (country subsidiaries) and a single matrix design for global account management co-exist. Another example is provided by 3M in Europe, which has adopted a global product division design in the form of European Business Centres (EBCs), which would be pan-European product line organizations reporting to the US main product divisions in charge of R&D, manufacturing and technical services to customers. The geographical dimension is represented by regional subsidiaries, which are in charge of the operational results within the countries.[9] The ACER group had in the past similarly divided its global operations in two categories, SBUs which essentially develop products and manufacturing components in world-class factories, and Regional Business Units (RBUs), which are locally based and in charge of assembling, marketing and sales (see the Mini-Case at the end of the chapter). The dual complex designs offer the flexibility to take care of the many specifics of contexts and businesses without locking managers into the straitjacket of a unique organizational design. The obvious pitfalls of these designs are their complexity, which requires from managers a culture similar to that advocated by the 'transnational' model.

The transnational model

Contrary to the other models presented earlier, the transnational organizational design model does not focus on organizational structure but on *management processes and culture.*[10] The transnational design does not prescribe any particular organizational structure, but recognizes that a global organization is made up of four types of differentiated managerial roles:

- *Global business managers* act as strategists, architects of assets distribution and competencies leveraging and coordinators of global activities
- *National managers* act as sensors of local opportunities and threats, builders of national resources and contributors to global competitive development
- *Functional managers* act as specialists, looking after new developments and making sure that best practices are shared and transferred across the organization
- *Corporate managers* act as overall organizational leaders and developers of talent.

These four roles can be distributed within a global product, a geographical or a matrix structure, the important thing being that managers develop a 'matrix in the mind'.

The seven key features of the transnational design are:

- Business units are part of a network, which follows the principle of *reciprocal dependencies.*
- *A non-dominant dimension.* All roles are important for competitive success and therefore no dimension, global, functional or geographical, predominates.

- A clearly defined and tightly controlled set of *operating systems*, and in particular of a transparent and multidimensional information system.
- Good *interpersonal relationships.*
- *Inter-unit decision forums* with active participation of global and functional managers in subsidiaries' boards.
- Strong *corporate values.*
- A culture of *sharing and willingness to collaborate.*

Since the transnational model does not rely on a formal organizational structure it is difficult to find companies that officially represent their organization under the form of a transnational model. However a variety of companies insert in their human resource and coordinating practices a lot of the features of this type of global design. As an example the Acer group mention that its organization is based upon *'the promotion of the spirit of teamwork to enhance company's overall competitiveness, and encourage closer communication between front-end and back-end management teams for better mutual understanding'.*[11]

Since 1990, global corporations have come to understand that the search for an ideal structure is in vain, and that what matters more is the way managers behave. Most of them have now invested in the development of attitudes, skills and behaviour in line with the 'transnational' model (see Figure 3.9).

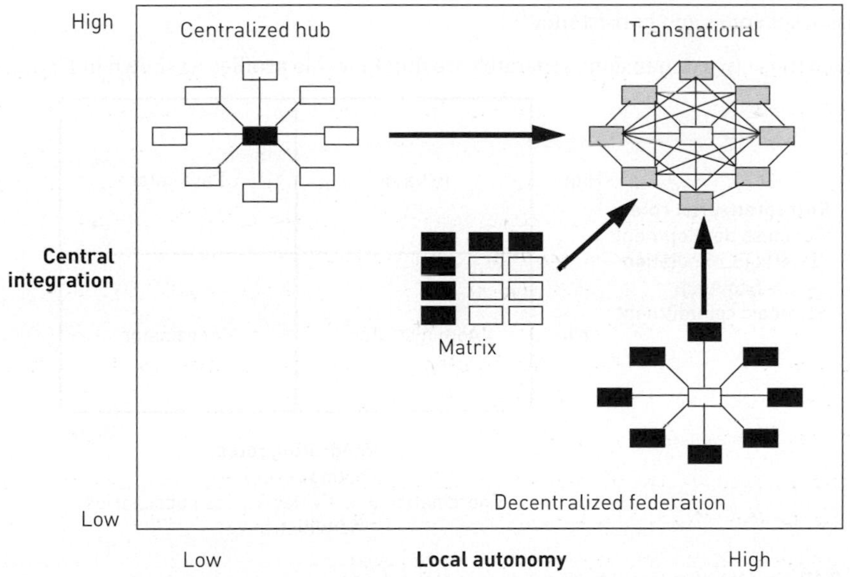

Figure 3.9 Convergence of global organizational designs

Source: Adapted from Bartlett and Ghoshal (1989).

Regional organizational structures

Many multinational corporations have established regional headquarters (RHQs) in order to support and control their global expansion. The motivation to set up a regional headquarters is a recognition that there are significant regional differences and that those differences are too complex, too diverse, too large and too far away to be handled from corporate headquarters.[12] In essence the establishment of a regional headquarters is an intermediary organizational device between a pure global approach directed from the corporate headquarters and a fully decentralized structure based on national subsidiaries' autonomy. The classic locations for regional headquarters have been Brussels or Geneva for Europe, Hong Kong or Singapore for Asia and Miami for Central and South America. Africa has been traditionally integrated with Europe. However, some companies may choose different locations according to their business characteristics.

Regional headquarters have two main roles:

- Entrepreneurial enhancing roles: such as looking for new opportunities (scouting), strategy development and implementation, strategic stimulation, intelligence gathering, new business development, and more generally signalling strategic commitment of the company to local governments and to the business divisions.
- Integrating roles, administrative roles more directly involved with local operations: pooling resources for greater efficiency and effectiveness; benchmarking and spreading best practices; coordinating activities across borders and business divisions. The aim here is to achieve synergies and consistency.[13]

If we take those two dimensions separately we find four role profiles as shown in Figure 3.10.

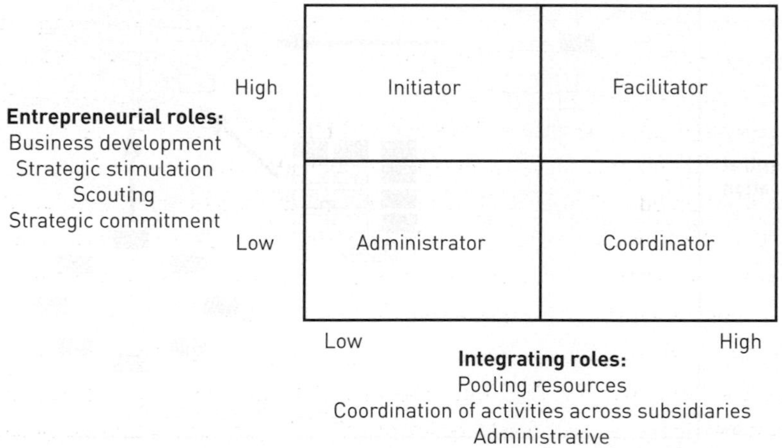

Figure 3.10 Profiles of regional headquarters in global firms
Source: (Lasserre, 1996).

The first of these profiles, the *administrator*, is for RHQs limiting themselves to clerical activities such as taxation, legal services or finance. There are no or very few entrepreneurial functions, which are either directly governed from the corporate center or left to the local subsidiaries.

The second profile, the *coordinator*, would describe an RHQ whose function is essentially to integrate and coordinate activities, to manage some central operations such as logistics, sourcing, training and making sure that synergies across subsidiaries are taking place.

The third profile, the *initiator*, would consist of an RHQ in charge of only strategic development, information gathering and initiating deals.

Finally, the *facilitator* profile would describe an RHQ that fulfills both entrepreneurial and integrating roles.

Over time these roles may change. It would not be unusual for a company that wants to enter a region to start with a regional office that concentrates on entrepreneurial and strategic developments and as such would present an *initiator* profile. Over time it may need to become a *facilitator* in order not only to stimulate strategic development but also to provide support and synergies to the operations.

When the businesses are well established in the region, the role of the RHQ may lessen to that of a *coordinator* or even an *administrator*.

Such a development is not always the case and in some companies the role of the RHQ increases instead of decreasing.[14]

Schütte[15] has identified three types of regional headquarters (Figure 3.11):

(1) ***The global RHQ*** is characterized by a strong alliance of its staff with the corporate headquarters. Global RHQs tend to be in charge of a limited number of global businesses and report to a senior manager who is responsible for these businesses on a worldwide basis. The RHQ can therefore be considered as an extension of the corporate HQ, staffed primarily by managers dispatched from HQ, who see themselves as enforcers and controllers. It will undertake the coordination of functional activities such as finance and human resource management, and can represent headquarters in board meetings of the subsidiaries and during discussions with governments. It will, however, be less involved in synergy development between different businesses. It will also be relatively weak in representing regional concerns at headquarters. The advantage of the global RHQ lies in its simplicity: the organization is streamlined and focused. There are problems associated with the global RHQ. The main issue is that as an agent of corporate headquarters, the regional office downgrades the role of regional and national managers to implementers. This can lead to demotivation, and the loss of local initiative and reduced feedback from the region.

(2) ***The multi-domestic RHQ*** operates in a geographical environment which is perceived to be different from other parts of the world. The staff of the RHQ feels strongly committed to the region and obliged to fight for the region or defend it against pressures for globalization originating from HQ. The multi-domestic RHQ acts as a representative body of the operating units in the region and of their concerns. It therefore relies heavily on consensus between them and on their support. Its main purpose is to amplify the views of these local subsidiaries, which individually are too small to carry much weight at HQ. The advantage of this particular RHQ model lies in the devotion of the managers to the cause of the region. Ideally, the staff working in a multi-domestic RHQ will include managers from the region or at least

expatriates with a long track record in the region. Strong advocacy of regional concerns may lead to a view of the world which is too one-sided and therefore not in the overall interest of the multinational corporation (MNC). The multi-domestic RHQ is a suitable model for an MNC needing to build a closer network in a region and win more recognition at HQ. It may be ideal for MNCs in which a region is not yet fully positioned on the mental map of the world or is still considered peripheral. The structure has the potential of creating a strong organizational unit in the corporation.

(3) ***The transnational RHQ*** is a structure in which there is a recognition of the need for global integration but at the same time the characteristics of the region distinguish it from other regions and that an appropriate approach is required. For practical reasons the transnational RHQ has to have an organizational structure which allows both the global and local forces to exert influence on decision-making at the regional level. The matrix organization offers such a structure, with geographical concerns represented by sub-regions or countries and business concerns by product divisions or SBUs. The advantages of the transnational RHQ operating through a matrix organization are obvious. It serves as a regional forum where conflicting interests can be brought together for negotiation and solution. Over time, this experience leads to better understanding and a common spirit within the region. Synergies are possible between the businesses and the countries as well as across businesses and countries. When sufficient delegation takes place at HQ, the transnational RHQ emerges as a powerful organizational unit where decisions for the region are made without recourse to HQ. However, as mentioned earlier, the experience with matrix organizations in general is not wholly satisfactory. A second drawback of the transnational RHQ relates to the tendency to create a large, if not overblown, regional organization in order to accommodate all interested parties. In the extreme case an existing matrix at HQ level is simply replicated in the region, an arrangement which will not be well received in times of lean management and de-layering. Bearing in mind its advantages and disadvantages, the transnational RHQ emerges as a suitable model for large, experienced and diversified MNCs with mature regional managers. Through its flexible structure, it allows a multitude of perspectives, and maintains the balance between global and local needs without allowing one to dominate the other.

As indicated earlier, the organizational structure of RHQs may evolve over time according to the different roles assigned to them.

An alternative to regional headquarters: the Gateway–Hub structure

Proposed by C.K. Prahalad and Hrishi Battacharya[16] the Gateway–Hub model consists of a global company selecting ten gateway countries in the developed world (USA, Japan, Germany, UK, France, Italy, Spain, Canada, Australia, Netherlands) and ten in the emerging world (China, India, Brazil, Mexico, Russia, South Korea, Indonesia, Turkey, South Africa, Thailand). Those gateways would have authority over most management decisions and serve as hubs for developing and coordinating activities in surrounding countries.

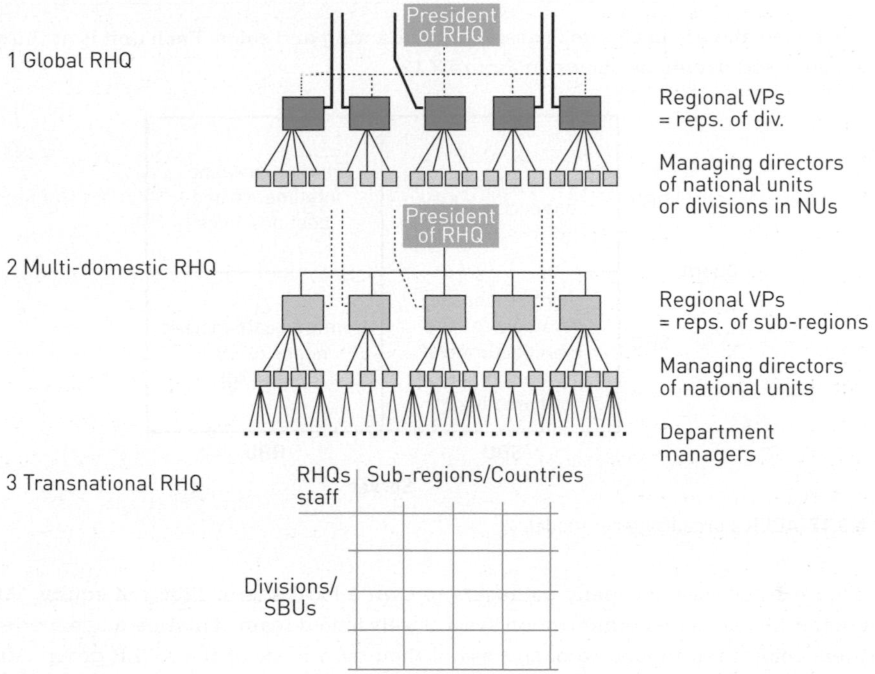

Figure 3.11 Organizational structure of regional headquarters (from Lasserre and Schütte, 2006)

MINI-CASE

ACER: Global Organizational Evolution

The ACER group, created in Taiwan in 1976, is in 2011 the Number 2 PC and notebook company in the world. With revenue of around 20 Billion US$ it employs 8000 people worldwide. Since its creation Acer has seen its global organization evolving to follow the management philosophy of its founder Stan Shih, as well as the industry's evolution.

The global organization has evolved in the following stages:

- **Stage 1: Initial Steps in Globalization: 1976–1990.**
  As early as 1979 Acer (known at the time as Multitech) started to export personal computers combining OEM contracts and sales under its own brand. To manage its operations American executives were recruited but were difficult to control. They acted quite autonomously and took sometimes inadequate initiatives. A European office was opened in Germany to coordinate distributors and do market research. In emerging countries such as Thailand, Indonesia, Brazil, Chile, Argentina, South Africa, Mexico and India, ACER initiated a series of joint ventures. By 1990 it became obvious that the international operations needed to be reorganized.
- **Stage 2: Creating a Multinational Organization: 1990–2000**
  Stan Shih organized the global operations according to the client–server principle. The business units are divided into two broad categories: the SBUs, which essentially develop products and manufacture components in world-class factories, and the RBUs, which are

MINI-CASE

locally based and are in charge of assembly, marketing and sales. Each unit is at the same time client and server, as shown in Figure 3.12.

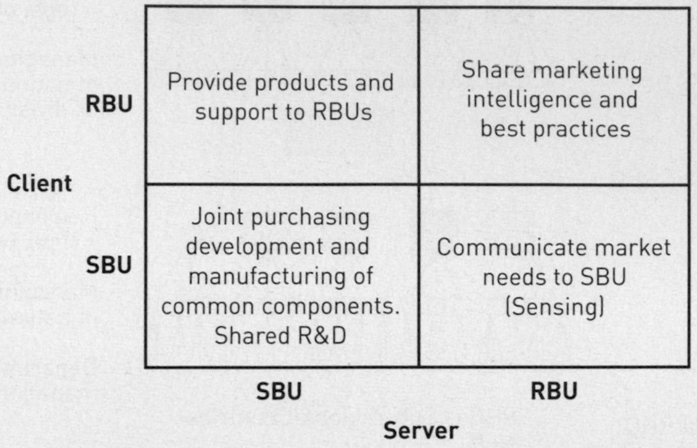

Figure 3.12 ACER's organizational model

Stan Shih wanted local company managers to own a local shareholding of equity. 'At the heart of the client – server organization lies a closely linked team of mature and experienced managers committed to long-term success of their own piece of the ACER group. Mutual understanding and trust, communication and consensus are the cornerstone of ACER management' (see note 11).

- **Stage 3: The Early 2000s**
  In December 2000, J.T. Wang was appointed as the president of ACER responsible for turning around ACER PCs worldwide. At the time, the ACER group employed around 37,000 people in 232 enterprises in 41 countries supporting a network of distributors in 100 countries. In 2001 the bursting of the Internet bubble precipitated a decline in PC sales. Wang initiated a profound restructuring. He introduced a more centrally integrated approach based on three global principles: One Global Company, One Global Brand, and One Global Team.
  - The principle of **One Global Company** led to the de-listing of all locally listed international subsidiaries and the repurchase back of all minority shares by ACER Inc. The group was reorganized at first into three divisions that ultimately were reduced to two after the spin-off of one of them:
    - *ACER Brand Operation (ABO)* whose responsibility was to design, market and distribute products across the world.
    - *The Design, Manufacturing and Service Division (DSM)* in charge of R&D, manufacturing and service of all IT products. DSM was spun off in 2001.
    - The third organizational leg was the *Holding and Investment Business* that was in charge of all, taking care of ACER's holdings in various businesses.
  - The principle of **One Global Brand** stated that only the ACER brand could be used for IT products.
  - The principle of **One Global Team** required that all managers abandon their parochialisms.

MINI-CASE

- **Stage 4: Beyond 2010**
  In 2007 ACER bought Gateway and Packard Bell and became the number 2 world provider of notebooks. It relies now on four global brands: ACER, Gateway, Packard Bell and E Machines. By 2011 the ACER organization was still based on the principle of One Global Team sharing strong corporate values. Operations are divided into:
  - Regional operations: Europe/Middle East/Africa (EMEA), Pan America, Taiwan, China, Asia Pacific
  - Global operations: PCs Global, Smart handheld Business, Channels, Marketing, E-Enabling Services
  - Global functions: Finance, Human Resources, Legal, General Affairs.

Three key principles underlie ACER's new management to ensure successful decision-making:

- To promote the spirit of teamwork to enhance the company's overall competitiveness, and encourage closer communication between management teams
- To simplify operational systems and processes to boost effectiveness and speed
- To strengthen corporate governance and enhance company sustainability.[17]

Questions:

1) What were the major hurdles to ACER becoming a global company? How did it overcome them?
2) During its initial phase of global development, ACER relied on OEM, alliances and acquisitions, and had a decentralized management. Why? What are the pros and cons?
3) What do you think are the advantages and disadvantages of the client–server principle for global competitiveness?
4) What were the reasons behind ACER's strategic and organizational changes in 2001? Analyze the advantages and disadvantages of such changes.

Summary and key points

1 A global business organization should balance the following dual requirements:

- efficiently maintain *competitive advantages* across borders
- adapt to *local conditions.*

2 Organizational designs.

- There are three main models of organizational design:
  - *Global hub:* a worldwide functional or global product structure
  - *Confederation:* a multinational geographical structure
  - *Multidimensional:* a matrix or transnational structure.
- There are three key elements of organizational design:
  - *Organizational structure:* assignment of roles, responsibilities and power
  - *Organizational processes:* decision-making, resource allocation, rewards and appraisal systems, planning and control
  - *Organizational culture:* shared values, reward system.

- Types of *organizational design* (or model): (see the summary of the common types of model in the table in Appendix 3.1 on p. 103).
- The *Transnational* model
  - *is different from* the other organizational designs as it focuses on management processes and culture instead of organizational structures
  - possesses seven main features:
    - a network of business units
    - a non-dominant dimension
    - a clearly defined and tightly controlled set of information systems
    - good interpersonal relationships
    - inter-unit decision forums
    - strong corporate values
    - a willingness to share and collaborate.
- Most global companies have now realized that the search for an ideal structure is futile and have invested in the development of *attitudes*, *skills* and *behaviour* which are in line with the transnational model.
- Many multinational corporations have established regional headquarters (RHQs) in order to support and control their global expansion.

  There are two major roles for regional headquarters: entrepreneurial and integrating, leading to four types of RHQs:
  - Initiator: high on entrepreneurial role/low on integrating
  - Coordinator: high on integrating role/low on entrepreneurial
  - Facilitator: high on both dimensions

Appendix 3.1 Types of organizational design

	Global functional model	Geographical model	Single matrix model	Multi-business global product division model	Multi-business geographical model	Multi-business matrix model	International divisions model	Dual complex structure model
Organizational structure	Centralized decision-making, coordination and control	Decentralized decision-making, coordination and control	Both functions and geography are given equal power and responsibilities	Each business division is responsible for a product or a service Within the division, organizational design can be matrix or global functional or geographical	Country subsidiaries have full strategic and operational responsibilities for all products in their territories	Emphasizes dual or triple responsibilities which are shared between product divisions and geographical units	Overseas subsidiaries have high autonomy but rely upon home country division for products and technical support	A mix of different designs with global product division and geographical subsidiaries
Supporting line(s)	Functional manager reports to vice-president or director in charge of their functions	Functional manager reports to local national manager	Middle-managers typically have two bosses	Country subsidiary managers report to division heads	Central global functions and product divisions have a 'dotted-line' role	Same as single matrix model	Division executives manage home country businesses and international division executives manage international subsidiaries	Reporting line is complex and depends on the choice of organizational design

	Global functional model	Geographical model	Single matrix model	Multi-business global product division model	Multi-business geographical model	Multi-business matrix model	International divisions model	Dual complex structure model
Advantages	Efficiencies Economies of scale Rapid transfer of know-how	Flexibility Can incorporate local needs Can quickly adapt to market conditions	Global efficiencies Local responsiveness	Flexibility Global efficiencies Global coordination	Flexibility Adaptive to local conditions Optimization of product and investment portfolio at country level	Refer to the single matrix model	Global efficiencies Local responsiveness	Flexibility
Disadvantages	Inflexibility Local disfunctionalities Market rejection Bureaucracy Discourages initiatives	Diseconomies of scale Duplication Lack of global coordination means poor at serving global customers	Potential power struggles Role ambiguity Dilution of responsibilities Cost inefficiencies Turf battles Costs of compromise	Duplication of commercial effort Lack of local responsiveness	Sub-optimization of resources allocation Delay in new product introduction Inefficiencies and loss of competitive advantage for industries which require globalization	Refer to the single matrix model	Inflexibility Market rejection	Complexity
Potential application	Single business environment with strong demand for global integration and coordination	Businesses where customer tastes or needs differ significantly across countries	Professional firms such as consulting or engineering	Vast majority of multi-business corporations with relatively high product diversity and significant geographical expansion	Becoming less popular with large global corporations	Decreasing popularity	Other models will be used when international sales become a significant amount of turnover	Companies with sophisticated and diverse offerings

- Administrator: low on both dimensions

- An RHQ's organization reflects the corporate design: Global, Multi-Local or Transnational.

Learning assignments

1 Why have Philips and Matsushita changed their organizational design over time?

2 What are the benefits of having a geographical organization?

3 What are the typical difficulties in implementing a matrix organization?

4 What are the characteristics of the transnational model?

5 To what extent does the transnational model differ from the other organizational model?

Key words

- 'Dotted-lines' relationship
- Global hub
- International divisions
- Matrix
- Organizational culture
- Organizational processes
- Organizational structure
- Transnational
- Regional headquarters

Web resources

<http://www.boozallen.com/insights>
Booz Allen consulting: see the section on Ideas and Insights: strategy and organization.

<http://www.bcg.com/expertise_impact/publications/default.aspx>
BCG Consulting.

<http://www.euromonitor.com/>
Provides industries data.

Visit the companion website at **http://www.palgrave.com/business/lasserre3e** for a multitude of weblinks and resources, self-test questions for revision and a searchable glossary.

Notes

1 Prahalad (1986).
2 This example is derived from Bartlett (1992, 1999).
3 The concept of 'administrative heritage' was developed in Bartlett and Ghoshal (1989).
4 This quotation is taken from Ackenhusen (1993a).
5 Crawford and Schütte (2000).
6 Quoted in Kets de Vries (1994).
7 Stopford and Wells (1972).
8 Stopford and Wells (1972).
9 Ackenhusen (1994b).
10 Developed by Bartlett and Ghoshal (1989). See also Bartlett and Ghoshal (1990, 1992).
11 See 'Acer appoints Jim Wong as Corporate President', April 2011, at <http://www.acer-group.com> [accessed 30 September 2011].
12 Lasserre and Schütte (2006), ch. 9.
13 Lasserre (1996).
14 Guey-Huey, Yu and Seetoo (2010).
15 Schütte (1998).
16 Prahalad and Battacharya (2008).
17 Clyde-Smith and Williamson (1997); Shih, Wang and Yeung, (2006); Yeung (2004); Acer (2001); and Acer Annual Reports, 2008 and 2010.

References and further reading

Ackenhusen, Mary, 'BS-International Service System A/S', INSEAD Case Study 11/93/4220, 1993a.

Ackenhusen, Mary, 'The 3M Company: Integrating Europe', INSEAD Case Study 06/94/4317, 1993b.

Bartlett, Christopher A., 'MNCs: Get Off the Reorganization Merry-Go-Round', *Harvard Business Review*, March–April 1983, pp. 138–46.

Bartlett, Christopher A, '"Philips and Matsushita": A Portrait of Two Evolving Companies', Harvard Business School, Case Study 9-392-156, 1992.

Bartlett, Christopher A., '"Philips vs Matsushita": Preparing for a New Round', Harvard Business School Case Study 9-399-102, 1999.

Bartlett, Christopher A. and Sumantra Ghoshal, *Managing Across Borders: The Transnational Solution*. Boston, MA: Harvard Business School Press, 1989.

Bartlett, Christopher A. and Sumantra Ghoshal, 'Matrix Management: Not a Structure, a Frame of Mind', *Harvard Business Review*, July–August 1990, pp. 138–45.

Bartlett, Christopher A. and Sumantra Ghoshal, 'What Is a Global Manager?' *Harvard Business Review*, September–October 1992, pp. 124–32.

Centre for Asian Business Cases, 'Acer: The Reorganization'. Hong Kong, 2001.

Clyde-Smith, Deborah and Peter Williamson, 'The ACER Group: Building an Asian Multinational', INSEAD Euro Asia Centre Case Study 01/98-4712, 1997.

Crawford, Robert and Hellmut Schütte, 'BASF: Working the Matrix in Asia', INSEAD Euro Asia Centre Case Study 04/2999-4845, 2000.

Davis, Stanley M., *Managing and Organizing Multinational Corporations*. Oxford: Pergamon Press, 1979.

Flamant, Anne-Claire, Sumie Fujimura and Pierre Willes, 'Renault and Nissan: A Marriage of Reason', INSEAD Case Study 10/2001-4928, 2000.

Franko, Larry, *The European Multinationals*. New York: Harper & Row, 1976.

Ghoshal, Sumantra, 'BS-International Service System A/S', INSEAD Case Study 11/93/4220, 1993.

Guey-Huey Li, Chwo-Ming Yu and Dah-Hsian Seetoo, 'Toward a Theory of Regional Organization', *Management International Review*, 50, 2010, pp. 5–33.

Kennedy, Robert E., Cynthia A. Montgomery, Lisa Cladderton and Harold Hogan, 'Tyco International (A)', Harvard Business School Case 9-798-061 (1998).

Kets de Vries, Manfred, 'Percy Barnevick and ABB', INSEAD Case Study 05/94/4308, 1994.

Lasserre, Philippe, 'Regional Headquarters: The Spearhead for Asia Pacific Markets', *Long Range Planning*, 1996, (29) 30–37.

Lasserre, Philippe and Hellmut Schütte, *Strategies for Asia Pacific*. Basingstoke: Palgrave Macmillan, 2006.

Malnight, Thomas W. and Michael Y. Yoshino, 'Citibank: Global Customer Management', Harvard Business School Case Study 9-395-142, 1995.

Prahalad, C.K., 'The Dominant Logic', *Strategic Management Journal*, 7(6), 1986, pp. 485–501.

Prahalad, C.K. and Hrishi Battacharya, 'Twenty Hubs and No HQ', *Strategy and Business*, Issue 50, Spring 2008.

Pucik, Vladimir, Noel M. Tichy and Carole K. Barnett, *Globalizing Management: Creating and Leading the Cooperative Organization*. New York: John Wiley, 1992.

Schütte, Hellmut, 'Between Headquarters and Subsidiaries: The RHQ Solution', in J. Birkinshaw and N. Hood (eds.), *Multinational Corporate Evolution and Subsidiaries Development*. Basingstoke: Macmillan Press, 1998.

Shih, Stan, J.T. Wang and Arthur Yeung, 'Building Global Competitiveness in a Turbulent Environment: Acer's Journey of Transformation', 2005, in William H. Mobley and Elizabeth Weldon (eds.), *Advances in Global Leadership*. Bingley: Emerald Group Publishing, 2005, pp. 201–217.

Stopford, John and Louis Wells, *Strategy and Structure of Multinational Enterprises*. New York: Basic Books, 1972.

Yeung, Arthur, Baoyi Pu and Judy Qu, 'Acer: Competitive Advantage through Global Integration', *CEIBS Business Review*, August 2010.

chapter

4 GLOBAL STRATEGIC ALLIANCES

Introduction

While Chapters 1–3 looked at globalization of industries, firms and organizational structure, Chapters 4 and Chapter 5 look at two main vehicles through which firms have globalized over the past 30 years: *global strategic alliances* and *global mergers* and *acquisitions* (M&As).

With increased pressures for globalization, technological developments and compression of time to market, companies have increasingly searched outside their internal boundaries to build or reinforce their global competitive capabilities. Since 1980 there has been a dramatic increase in international strategic alliances, mergers and acquisitions.

In this chapter we will look at the strategic and managerial issues involved in global strategic alliances, while in Chapter 5 we will study more particularly global M&As.

Strategic alliances are not recent phenomena, but their pace of growth and the variety of their forms has been increasing. In the new economy, alliances are the normal way of doing business. We will first define what a strategic alliance is, discuss the various potential types of alliances and study the aspects of forming, analyzing, negotiating and implementing global strategic alliances.

An **alliance** is the sharing of capabilities between two or more firms with a view to enhancing their competitive advantages and/or creating new business without losing their respective strategic autonomy. A *global alliance* is one in which the object is either to develop a *global market presence* (**global reach alliance**) or to enhance the *worldwide competitive capabilities* of the firm (**global leverage alliance**).

There are various types of alliance: some of them have a global scope, with the perspective of enhancing the competitive presence of the partners across the world; some have a more local focus, the global firm wishing to penetrate a given country by setting up local joint ventures.

A framework for studying the various steps of alliance formation and implementation has four main steps:

- Understanding the *strategic context* and spelling out the *strategic value* of an alliance
- Analysis of *partner(s)*: strategic fit, capabilities fit, cultural fit and organizational fit
- Negotiation and design of the alliance *structure*
- *Implementation*: integration, cooperation and evolution.

At the end of the chapter we shall present some criteria for successful alliances.

Learning objectives

- At the end of the chapter you will be able to:
- formulate a global alliance strategy
- analyze the various fits among partners
- structure an alliance negotiation
- anticipate potential issues in alliance management and to set up the proper mechanisms to solve them.

EXAMPLE

A short story of two partnerships: DaimlerChrysler–Mitsubishi Motors and Renault–Nissan

In 2000 an agreement was signed between DaimlerChrysler (DCX), the US–German automobile group, and Mitsubishi Motors, according to which DCX would acquire 34 per cent of Mitsubishi and would collaborate in the design, production and marketing of vehicles. Mitsubishi was suffering losses and quality problems. DCX sent some senior executives to manage the troubled company and increased its stake to 37 per cent. Still the situation did not improve and there were still some conflicting views about the way to solve the problems. By 2004 Andreas Renshler from DCX was named chief executive of Mistsubishi; however, by 2005 DCX walked away from the alliance.

In 1999 an agreement was signed between Renault of France and Nissan of Japan. Under the agreement Renault would inject 4.6 billion Euros to bail out Nissan and would take a 36.8 per cent stake in Nissan. The alliance was managed by Carlos Ghosn, a Lebanese Brazilian-born executive from Renault. After two years Nissan's turnaround was completed and the alliance is still active.

Those two examples show two different alliance paths, one apparently successful and one unsuccessful. Both of them started with a similar view to foster globalization and to improve operations. In the case of Renault–Nissan, as will be discussed later, the alignment of objectives between partners and the mutual trust that was built up over time were a source of a fruitful partnership. In the case of Daewoo–GM in the late 1980s, lack of alignment of objectives and trust led to the dissolution of the venture.

Strategic alliances: typology and framework

An alliance can be defined as the *sharing of capabilities between two or more firms* with a view to enhancing their competitive advantages and/or creating new business without losing their respective strategic autonomy. What makes an alliance *'strategic'* is that the sharing of capabilities, such as R&D, manufacturing or marketing affects the long-term competitiveness of the firms involved and implies a relatively long-term commitment of resources by partners.

According to economists, a joint effort involving the contribution of separate firms can be organized either through a *market contract*, such as a buyer–supplier contract, or through the *merger of capabilities* under a single management control, as in the case of a merger, an acquisition or an internal development. An alliance is somewhere in between, when either full control is not feasible, for legal or practical reasons, or when a contract is difficult to draw up because of the uncertainties involved and none of the parties involved has the ability to develop the needed capability internally. As a consequence, a strategic alliance has been sometimes defined as 'a governance structure involving an incomplete contract between separate firms and in which *each partner has limited control*'.[1] An alliance is an incomplete contract to the extent that 'it cannot specify fully what each party should do under *every conceivable condition*' and, therefore, requires that both parties engage in some form of trusting, open-ended relationship in which decision-making is shared in order to allocate resources and distribute the outcome of the joint activity according to the prevailing business conditions.

International business and the pressure for globalization often make alliances necessary. Four types of alliance can be distinguished, which depend on the scope (global or local) and the object (market access or capabilities enhancing), as in Figure 4.1.

A *local* alliance would be one in which either the object is for a foreign company to penetrate a local market (*alliance for market entry*) or to have access to a set of resources available in a particular country (resource-based *country alliance*). A *global* alliance would be one in which the object would be either to develop a global market presence (*global reach alliance*) or to enhance the worldwide competitive capabilities of the firms (*global leverage alliance*).

Scope \ Object	Market	Capabilities
Global	**Global reach alliances** (Geographically complementing partnerships)	**Global leverage alliances** (R&D partnerships joint manufacturing)
Local	**Alliances for country market entry** (Traditional joint ventures in emerging markets)	**Alliances for country resources access** (Joint ventures in resource-rich countries)

Figure 4.1 Various types of international alliances

Global alliances

Global alliances are much more complex and subtle in their strategic and economic scope than traditional local alliances, which will be analyzed later in this chapter.

Doz and Hamel (1998) distinguish three broad types of strategic alliance:

- *Coalitions* (what Doz and Hamel call 'co-option') are alliances of competitors, distributors and suppliers in the same industry putting together their capabilities with a view to spanning world markets (the search for 'global reach') or to establish a common standard. Airline alliances such as ONEWORLD, SKYTEAM or STAR represent good examples of such a coalition.

- *Co-specializations* are alliances of firms that join their respective unique but complementary capabilities to create a business or develop new products or technology. What characterizes this type of alliance is that each partner contributes to a unique asset, resource or competency. Combined together, the capabilities of partners create the needed capabilities for business development. Airbus and GE-SNECMA in the aerospace industry are examples of such alliances.
- The primary purpose of *learning alliances* is to serve as a vehicle for know-how transfer between partners. A classic example is the alliance formed between Toyota and General Motors (GM), called the NUMMI project, where the fundamental purpose for GM was to learn 'lean' manufacturing processes and for Toyota to learn how to operate in a highly unionized North American environment.

Global strategic alliances differ from country-based joint ventures in five main aspects:

- First, they differ not only in their geographical scope – local versus global – but also in the complexity of their *strategic objectives*. While in the case of country-based joint ventures the objectives are straightforward; these are less obvious in the case of strategic alliances. Very often market objectives are combined with technological learning or strategic options. Hidden agendas are more often present in strategic alliances than in joint ventures.
- Country-based joint ventures are based on a simple complementary scheme – market access against technology transfer – while strategic alliances have a more complicated *strategic architecture*. Often there is a mixture of complementary capabilities, consolidation of certain activities as well as technology transfer from both sides.
- The *valuation* of strategic alliances is more difficult than for joint ventures since they frequently involve contributions in intangible assets and know-how, and in most situations they take place in new and volatile products or processes.
- In joint ventures the value is created by the venture and distributed to the partner under the form of dividends or transfer pricing. In a strategic alliance value is created not only in the alliance but also outside the alliance through the *applied learning* that partners can utilize in other products of their own.
- Finally, partners in strategic alliances are frequently also *competitors*; this is less often the case in country-based joint ventures.

Framework for analysis

The study of strategic alliances can be divided into four major steps, as shown in Figure 4.2:

- Understanding the strategic context and spelling out the strategic value of an alliance
- Partners' analysis
- Negotiation and design
- Implementation.

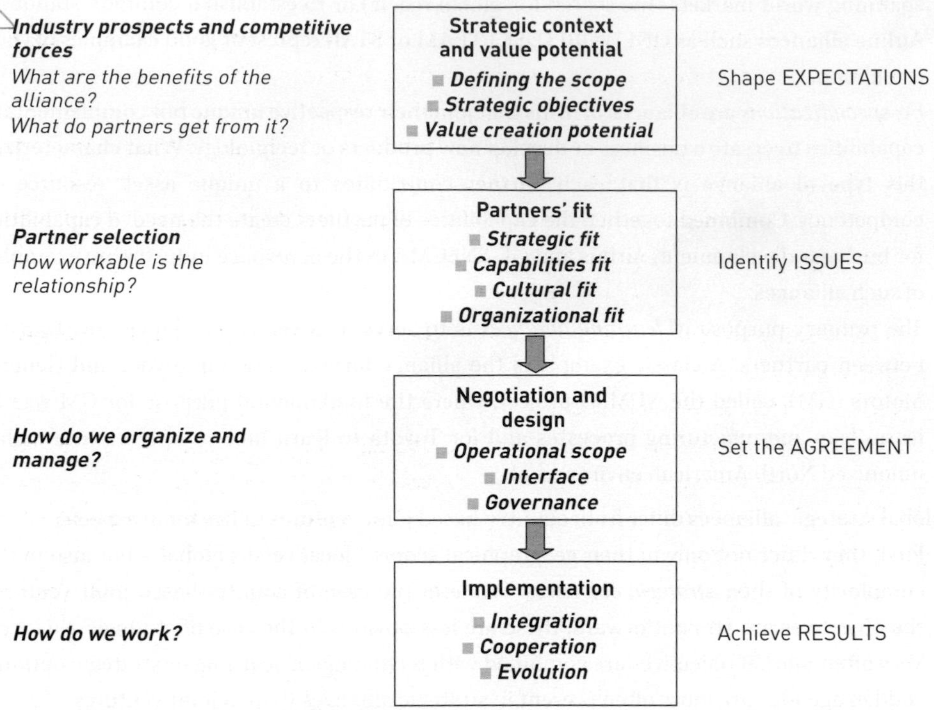

Figure 4.2 Framework for the analysis of strategic alliances

In order to discuss in detail these different steps, we will take the example of the long-lasting strategic alliance between the Japanese company Nissan, and the French company Renault.

EXAMPLE

The Renault–Nissan alliance[2]

With the globalization and consolidation of the automotive industry, the only means for ensuring long-term sustainability is by forming a larger group to leverage market power. For Renault, a European player, alliance was essential for long-term sustainable growth and expansion. Finding a partner in Asia was therefore a critical mission for Renault. For a financially troubled company like Nissan, finding a partner was the only means of survival in the increasingly competitive global auto industry. In 1998, Nissan's debts were estimated at US$21 billion or 2.5 times equity.

After a period of fact-finding and joint valuation of potential synergies, on 27th March 1999 Mr. Louis Schweitzer, CEO of Renault and Mr. Yoshikazu Hanawa, CEO of Nissan Motor Co. announced that they had signed an agreement for a total partnership 'which will create the fourth [largest] automobile manufacturer in the world, while providing growth and profitability to the two partners'.

The agreement was as follows:

- Renault will invest Y605b ($5.1b) to acquire 36.8 per cent of the shares of Nissan Motor Co. and an option to acquire an additional 8 per cent in the future.
- Nissan will have the possibility of becoming a shareholder of Renault.
- Mr. Carlos Ghosn who was formerly executive vice president of Renault will become the new COO of Nissan and join its board of directors.
- Mr. Yoshikazu Hanawa, CEO of Nissan Motor Co., was offered to join the board of directors of Renault.

Carlos Ghosn initiated the Nissan Revival Plan.

- Ghosn made three commitments and if any of those could not be achieved he would resign as well as the Executive committee:
  - Return to profitability for FY2000
  - Achieve consolidated operating profit of 4.5 per cent of sales by FY2002
  - Reduce net debt from 1.4 trillion yen to less than 700 billion yen by FY2002.
- A Global Alliance Committee (GAC) was created as governing body of the alliance to promote joint strategy and synergies between the two companies
- Eleven cross company teams (CCTs) and nine cross-functional teams (CFTs) were to organize synergies (see Figure 4.3).

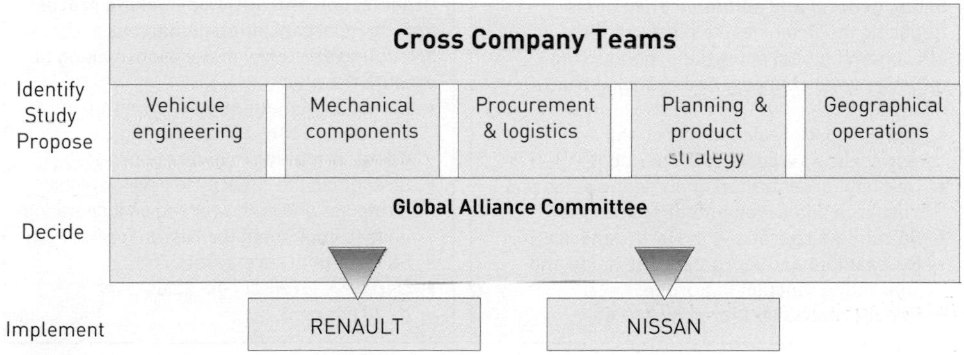

Figure 4.3: Organization of the Cross Company Teams and Global Alliance Committee in the Renault–Nissan Alliance.

The CFTs and CCTs generated over 2000 new ideas (see Figure 4.4).

A year and a half later in 2000 Nissan returned to profitability and the Nissan Revival Plan objectives were fully achieved by 2001, one year ahead of schedule.

Since then the alliance has evolved and is organized according to the structure described in Figure 4.5.

In 2010 the global sales amounted to 6.3 million vehicles and represented 9 per cent of the worldwide market. While the two companies are still operating independently their strategic orientation and the organization of synergies is supervized by a joint management company, Renault–Nissan BV.

Business development
Shifting resources from cost reduction into product developments, Nissan plans to market new products and develop its automobile business.
- Introduce 22 new products globally from FY2000 through FY2002.
- Increase consolidated capital expenditures by 25 per cent (equivalent to approximately 5 percent of consolidated net sales).

Purchasing
Reducing procurement costs by promoting concentrated and global purchasing, and halving the number of suppliers.
- Purchasing costs, which account for fully 60 per cent of Nissan's total costs, will be reduced by 20 per cent over three years, from FY2000 through FY2002.

Manufacturing
Reducing excess domestic production capacity to achieve optimum production efficiency and enhanced cost competitiveness on a global level.
- Terminate manufacturing of vehicles and powertrains in five plants.
  * Five plants: Three assembly plants – Murayama, Nissan Shatai Kyoto, and Aichi Kikai Minato
  Two powertrain operations: Kurihama Plant and Kyusyu Engine Shop
- Improve productivity and the operating rate of the remaining plants.

Research and development
Concentrating its resources and using them effectively by selecting the areas of research and development that is the core competence of the company and sharing with Renault in research and development.

Financial cost
Concentrating on the core automotive business and reducing debt by selling non-core assets.
- Sales of shareholdings.

Sales, general and administrative costs
Reducing inefficiencies: to increase the efficiency of global operations, conducting organizational changes, and reducing the headcount.
- Reduce cost of sales, general and administrative costs by 20 per cent
- Overhaul organization of domestic sales and research and development operations
- Streamline operations in North America
- Re-examine and reorganize the sales and marketing function in Europe
- Reduce global workforce by 21,000.

Organization and decision-making process
Making its organization global and promoting efficiency of decision-making to execute the plan.
- Establish Management Committee in Europe and the USA as strategic decision-making organizations
- Strengthen the capacity to develop global strategies and empower regional operating units to implement the Nissan Revival Plan
- Sales of non-core assets
- Decrease inventory-to-sales level by 30 per cent.

Figure 4.4 The Nissan Revival Plan and the Cross Functional Teams

Source: Nissan Motor Facts File, 2000.

The main synergies are:

- Renault–Nissan Purchasing Organization (RNPO) that sources 75 per cent of the Alliance 2006 worldwide purchases
- Common platforms are being developed
- Cross-manufacturing operation
- Common distribution in Europe
- Common information systems
- Exchange of best practices, especially in the manufacturing sector
- Joint development in the hybrid and fuel-efficient vehicles.

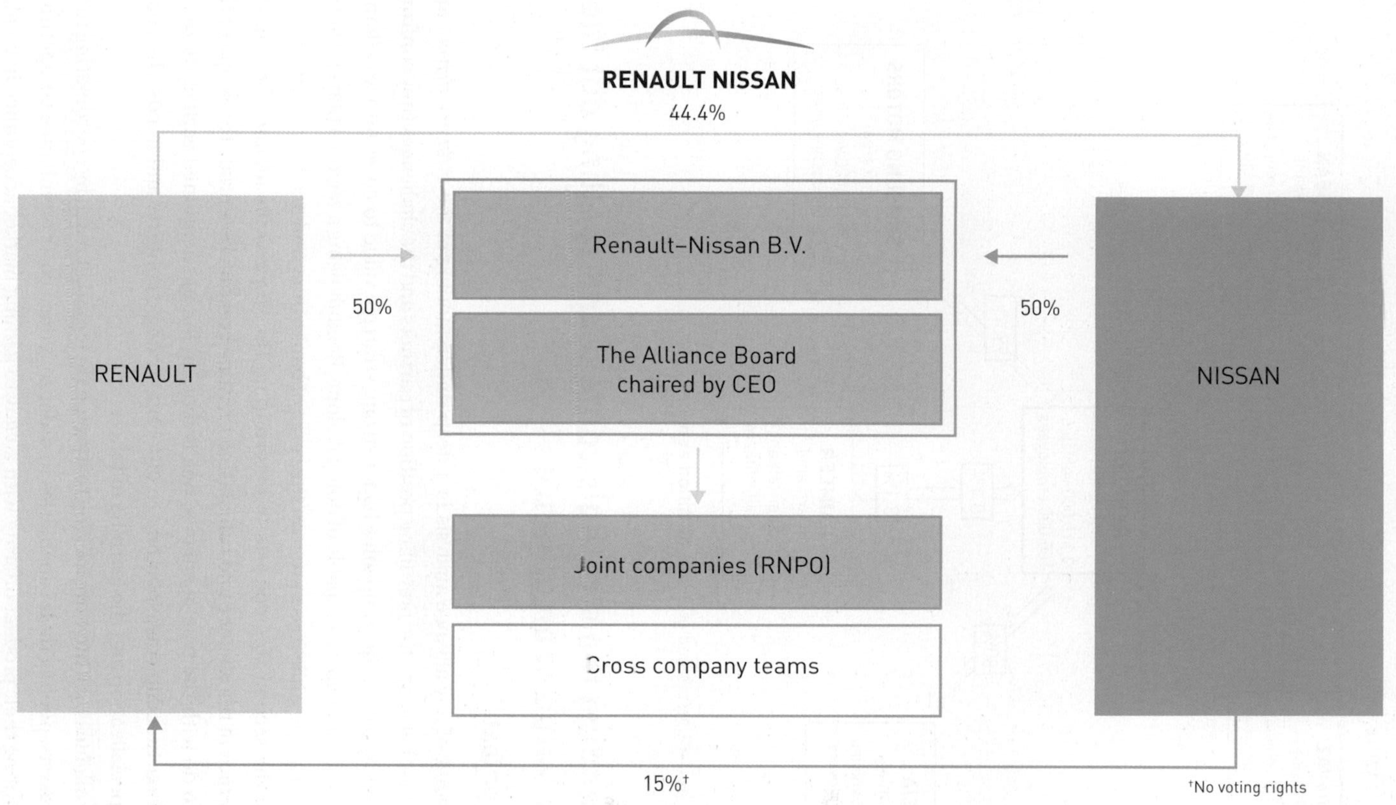

Figure 4.5 New organization of the Renault–Nissan Alliance

Source: Renault website: <http://www.renault.com/fr/groupe/l-alliance-renault-nissan/>

By 2011, Renault was engaged in a network of alliances and acquisitions producing around 8 million cars (Figure 4.6).

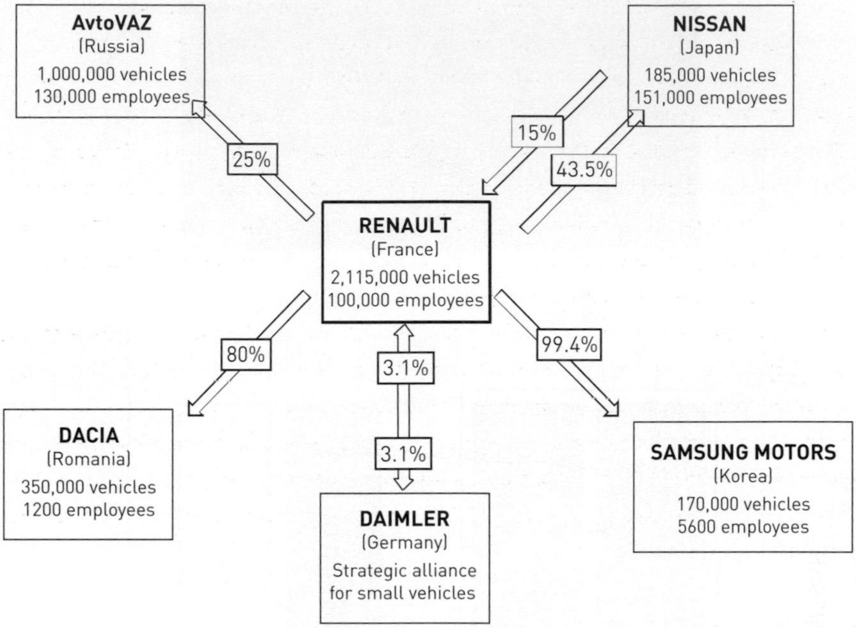

Figure 4.6 Renault alliances and global acquisition network

Understanding the strategic context and spelling out the strategic value of an alliance

Strategic context

The starting point of any alliance analysis is a deep understanding of the *industry drivers* and *competitive forces* that shape the prevailing position of partners and the challenges they confront. For Renault and Nissan, both companies had a strong strategic value to enter into an alliance market and neither of them was capable of doing it alone. Renault being a regional player wanted to reach a global scope while Nissan was on the verge of bankruptcy and needed a partner.

From there the second step consists in determining the *scope of the alliance*, setting the strategic *objectives* of the alliance and calculating its value creation potential. The scope of the alliance has to do with the type of alliance one is looking for. As mentioned earlier, there are three types of partnership corresponding to different strategic contexts and needs: the coalition, the co-specialization and the learning alliance.

In *coalition* alliances, partners are looking to develop their market reach by coordinating their geographical assets, pooling their capabilities in order to reduce costs or enhance competitiveness, or integrating their product offering with a view to gaining market acceptance in a battle for standard. SONY and Philips, for instance, have been co-allied for the development of the

DVD; in the past there was an alliance between IBM, Apple and Motorola. The strategic scope of the alliance is to create a *bigger and stronger competitive player* in the global marketplace. The essence of the alliance is 'size'. The Renault–Nissan case falls into this category.

Co-specialization alliances have a different scope: most of the time they aim at creating new products or at increasing competitiveness through the assembly of relatively independent capabilities. The benefits of co-specialization alliances are exactly the same as the benefits of specialization of business units in an integrated company. Each party will concentrate on what it is good at, and as a consequence will deliver a product, a service or a component with the best concentration of resources and skills. The GE–SNECMA alliance mentioned at the beginning of the chapter falls into this category. Each party focuses on what it is good at and there is no attempt to extract joint learning.

The primary purpose of *learning alliances* is to set the mechanisms in place to transfer valuable competencies through a symmetric exchange of technological know-how. Learning alliances are also designed for co-learning in the sense that partners develop new competencies together. Strategic objectives are subordinated to the respective business strategies of the partners involved. The starting point, then, is for each partner to define what the contribution of the alliance is to its own strategy. Table 4.1 describes the main strategic objectives pursued in various types of alliances.

Table 4.1 Main strategic objectives pursued in various types of alliance

	Coalitions	Co-specialization	Learning
Positioning	• Market reach • Enhance competitiveness through cost reduction or pooling of capabilities • Establish standards • Reporting	• Create new business • Develop new products • Enhance competitiveness through specialization • Complement strengths • Product line	Access to technology
Capabilities			
Resources	• Financing • Sharing risks	• Complementarities of resources • Risk sharing	• Research and marketing personnel • Financing
Assets	• Distribution • Manufacturing • Customer services • Code sharing (Airlines)	• Complementarities of assets	• Access to key tangible and intangible assets
Competencies	• Market knowledge	• Complementarities of know-how	• Technology • Know-how
Economic value	• Economies of scale • Economies of scope • Increased revenues • Increased customer responsiveness • Increased quality	• Maximization of asset utilization by each partner • Faster time to market • Product development (new revenue streams)	• Skills development

Value potential

The *value potential* of the alliance is calculated on the basis of the potential benefits it brings to the alliance partner(s) involved. In theory, it is a straightforward calculation done in two steps (see Figure 4.7):

- **Step one:** value *created* by the *alliance*
- **Step two:** value *captured* by each *partner*.

The value created by the alliance is driven by four factors:

- Revenues generated by the alliance through volume of sales
- Revenues generated by the alliance through the ability to command a high-differentiated price
- Future revenues or costs benefits coming from joint R&D products or processes
- Cost benefits resulting from economies of scale and scope.

The value captured by partners comes from:

- Distribution of the alliance profits when the alliance is structured as an autonomous economic entity
- Profit generated by the sales of intermediary products, components or services to the alliance
- Profits derived from products or processes developed thanks to the alliance – increased revenues or costs reduction coming from the alliance because of increased market reach or economies of scale or scope
- Profits coming from other products whose sales are boosted because of the alliance.

However, whatever the type of alliance, the value created is more difficult to assess than for the traditional joint venture for market entry or natural-resource access. According to Doz and Hamel (1998), the reasons for these problems are:

- Partners bring hard to value non-traded resources, assets or competencies
- The relative contribution is often hard to assess
- Most of the time, much of the value accrues outside the alliance
- The relative value to each partner may shift over time
- Partners may not declare what real value they seek from the alliance:[3]

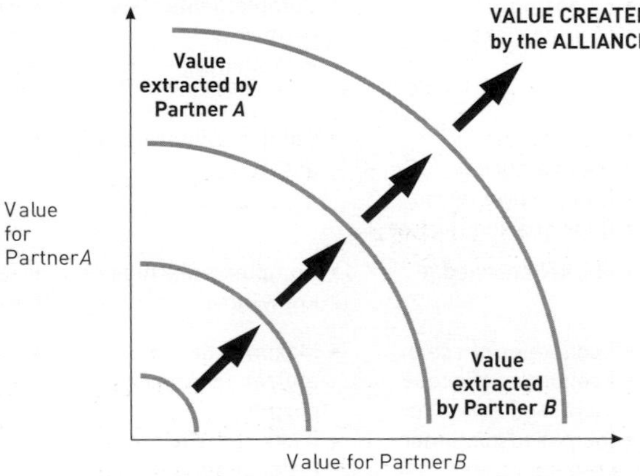

Figure 4.7 Value creation and extraction in alliances

Despite these difficulties, it is advisable to try to measure the value expected from the alliance since it will serve as a yardstick to assess its success or failure.

In the case of Renault–Nissan, the value of the alliance came from the synergies generated by common purchasing, common platforms, joint development and cross manufacturing.

Partner analysis

Partner analysis consists of determining the extent to which the relationship with the proposed partner is viable and valuable. It consists of four assessments (Figure 4.8):

- Strategic fit
- Capabilities fit
- Cultural fit.
- Organizational fit

STRATEGIC FIT
• Are the respective objectives compatible?
• For how long?
CAPABILITIES FIT
• Are the partners willing and able to contribute to the critical resources, assets and competencies needed for competitive success?
CULTURAL FIT
• Can we understand each other?
• Can we communicate?
• Do we share the same business logic?
ORGANIZATIONAL FIT
• Are the decision-making and control mechanisms used by partners conducive to good communication and effective monitoring of the joint venture?

Figure 4.8 Fit analysis in strategic alliances

Strategic fit

The purpose of strategic fit analysis is to assess the degree of *compatibility* among the partners, given their respective explicit or implicit strategic objectives. When stated objectives are explicit the analysis is simple, but when there are implicit objectives (a hidden agenda) behind the stated objectives, the analysis requires an in-depth study of the partner's strategic context – their competitive position and managerial power structure – to unravel the 'real' expectations of the other party. An analysis of strategic fit implies the following assessments:

- *Criticality* of the alliance for the partners
- The relative *competitive* position of partners
- The compatibility in *strategic* agendas.

Answering two very simple questions will evaluate the criticality of the alliance for each partner:

- How important is the alliance for the partners?
- Do they need an alliance to achieve their objectives?

The answers to these two questions can be represented into two different matrixes, as in Figure 4.9, where we can assess the degree of commitment expected from partners to the alliance.

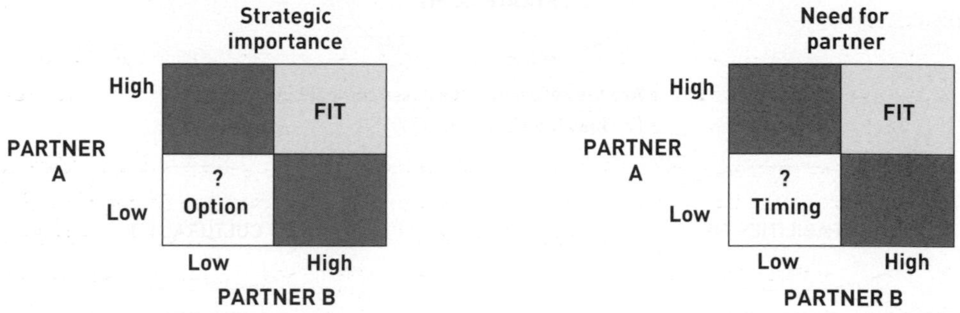

Figure 4.9 Assessing the strategic fit based on the criticality of the alliance for partners

The importance of the alliance for partners is determined on the basis of the contextual analysis done earlier. If both partners have a strong strategic stake in the business, you can expect a high commitment that is favourable to a good fit. If the strategic importance is unbalanced (it is important for one partner but not for the other), there will be a divergence in commitment and the fit will be more questionable. When both partners have a low strategic stake, you may not expect a high degree of commitment from both partners, which by itself represents a fit, but not a favourable one for the future of the alliance. We may wonder, under such conditions, why they should even consider a strategic partnership. The answer to that question can be found in the theory of real options:[4] partners may consider the alliance as a *forward option* for a future decision. In such a case, the degree of commitment may be positive although there is a question mark over what will happen when the option has to be called in or forfeited.

In the case of Renault and Nissan, both partners had a strong motivation to enter into an alliance, Renault for a global presence and Nissan for survival.

The ability to 'go it alone' depends on the existing resources – *assets and competencies* that each partner possesses at the time – and the degree of time pressure put on them. Again, when both parties do not have the necessary capability to venture alone, there is a strong incentive for and commitment to the alliance provided that the capability fit is favourable, as we shall see. Otherwise, an unbalanced situation will create the condition for a misfit. When the two partners can 'go it alone', the only condition under which the commitment would be favourable is when time pressure obliges them to share the tasks in order to accelerate their business entry. Renault had developed strong capabilities in car design and in efficient supply chain while Nissan was excellent in engineering and quality management. The car models were somewhat complementing each other and in terms of geographical presence Renault was strong in Europe and Nissan in Asia and the USA.

The *relative competitive* position of partners is a second important parameter to investigate when assessing a strategic fit. Doz and Hamel (1998, Chapter 4) have developed a typology of competitive positions and postulated their mutual degree of fitness depending upon the type of alliance.

They class competitors in three broad categories: *leaders* (dominant firm in the industry), *challengers* (second-tier firms in the industry) and *laggards* (firms which need to catch up). They conclude that alliances among leaders are plagued with problems.

Renault and Nissan are in the situation of two challengers pooling their specialized capabilities to obtain a synergistic effect. Nissan, after a revival, could be tempted to play the father figure in the partnership, given its already established business, but will probably refrain from it, due to the difficulty in untangling the existing synergies. Again, at this level the fit was favorable.

The last part of strategic assessment is the confrontation of the strategic agendas and their resulting expectations. There are four kinds of strategic agenda:

- *Venturing* agendas
- *Extractive* agendas
- *Sharing* agendas
- *Options* agendas.

In *venturing* agendas partners have a deliberate desire to engage in collaboration to create a business. Their prime motivation is to see the alliance grow and flourish, and they get their reward from the continuation of a successful partnership.

Extractive agendas have a different logic: the objective is to 'learn' or to 'acquire' capabilities from the partner or from the alliance. The prospects of a fit in such a case are short-term: as long as they get the necessary capabilities they stick to the alliance; as soon as the learning or acquisition cycle is achieved, the strategic value of the alliance vanishes.

Sharing agendas are limited ones, their prime objective being to maximize efficiency in certain elements of the value chain through economies of scale and scope. Airline alliances are of that nature: they share flight codes, lounges, frequent flyers programmes and sometimes aircraft maintenance.

Options agendas, as noted earlier, are based on the desire for partners to 'look and see' without committing vast amounts of resources, and using the alliance as an experimental platform for monitoring the business. As in any option, such an agenda has a time limit, at the end of which partners have to make up their mind: break the alliance and continue alone or continue and expand the alliance.

Figure 4.10 gives a graphical representation of those various types of strategic agendas and their combinations.

Both Renault and Nissan were on the venturing agenda: first, because of the importance of belonging to the league of global players, the difficulty of competing against giants like Toyota and the need to invest in new developments such as the hybrid car. An extractive approach by Renault or Nissan was banned by design and replaced by a collaborative one since, as part of the agreement, transfer of best practice was organized and a common platform set up. The scenario of Nissan taking advantage of relative initial competitive position and later on dropping the alliance was an unlikely one. Once partners are engaged in development they have to stick to it, given the huge financial commitment; a retreat by one partner would imply that either it loses its investment or it has duplicated the R&D on its own premises to be able to handle the project alone.

	Venturing agenda: Create and grow business	Extractive agenda: Get capabilities from partner	Sharing agenda: Economies of scale and scope	Option agenda: 'Look and see'
Venturing agenda: Create and grow business	Fit long-term	Problematic fit	Problematic fit	Possible fit
Extractive agenda: Get capabilities from partner	Problematic fit	Fit short-term	Possible short-term fit	Problematic fit
Sharing agenda: Economies of scale and scope	Problematic fit	Possible short-term fit	Fit	Possible short-term fit
Option agenda: 'Look and see'	Possible fit	Problematic fit	Possible short-term fit	Fit short-term

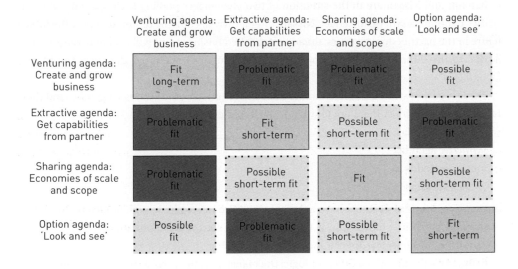

Figure 4.10 Strategic fit against partners' strategic agendas

Capabilities fit

The objective of a capabilities fit analysis is to assess the extent to which partners are capable of contributing to the necessary *competitive capabilities* of the business.

The framework for the analysis of capabilities fit is straightforward; it consists, first, in determining the required resources, assets and competencies needed in the value chain of the business as described in Chapter 2 (Figure 2.11). Then, for each partner, the specific contribution to each element of the value chain is drawn, based on exposed or supposed resource assets and competencies. The last phase of the analysis determines the potential gap to be filled by joint investment and an evaluation is made of whether the mutual contributions plus the additional investments make the future alliance effective.

This logical analysis is depicted in Figure 4.11 and an illustration of the Renault–Nissan case is presented in Figure 4.12. It shows that the complementarities of the contributions were a good fit in this alliance.

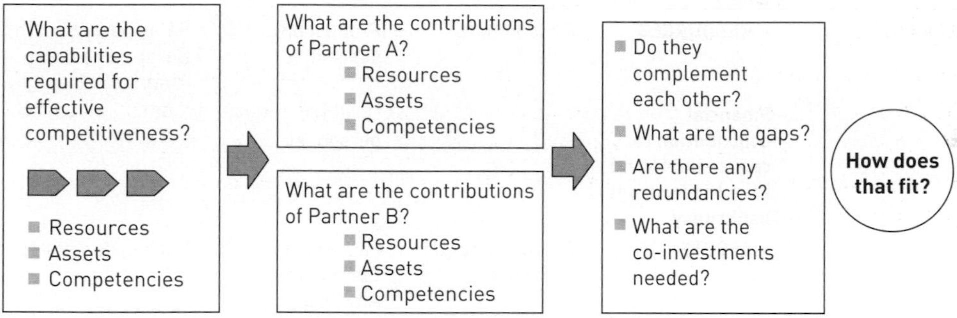

Figure 4.11 Method for assessing capabilities fit

Cultural fit

Three types of cultural differences can be distinguished in global alliances – corporate, industrial and national – each of them likely to create a gap that may affect the future functioning of the partnership. The role of cultural fit analysis is to understand the nature of the differences, to anticipate their possible consequences in the functioning of the alliance and to take action in order to prevent negative effects.

In organizations such as companies, culture is the set of beliefs – values, assumptions and causal models – that influences the way individuals in that organization think and behave. As mentioned earlier, three types of difference in organizational cultures can be identified:

- Differences in *corporate cultures*
- Differences in *industry cultures*
- Differences in *national cultures.*

Corporate culture differences come from the *history* of the company (start-up versus well-established firm), its *ownership* structure (family-owned versus public company versus government-owned), its *managerial* style, (entrepreneurial versus bureaucratic), as well as the personality of its leaders. Good or bad past experiences with strategies and alliances have a strong influence on corporate cultures.

	What is needed?	**TECHNOLOGY**	**PRODUCTION**	**MARKETING**
	• RESOURCES	Financing Researchers	Production specialists Qualified personnel	Contacts with customers Sales people
	• ASSETS	Research center	Factories	Car dealers
	• COMPETENCIES	Car design Hybrid technology Engineering Engines	Quality management Supply chain management	Salesmanship
	Who contributes to what?			
RENAULT	**• RESOURCES**	Researchers	Production specialists	Sales personnel in Europe and Latin America
	Financial contribution to reduce debts and save Nissan from bankrupcy		Qualified personnel	
	• ASSETS	Research center in France	Factories in Europe, Latin America	Europe dealership
	• COMPETENCIES	Monovan Car design Small engines	Supply chain management	European salesmanship
NISSAN	**• RESOURCES**	Researchers	Production specialists Qualified personnel	Sales personnel all over the world
	• ASSETS	Research centers in Japan	Factories in Asia, Europe, USA	Dealership network in Asia, USA, some in Europe
	• COMPETENCIES	SUV Engineering Large engines Hybrid technology	Quality management	Salesmanship in the US and Asia

Figure 4.12 Capabilities fit in the case of Renault and Nissan

Industry cultures are the norms that are derived from the type of business in which firms are engaged: fast-moving consumer goods (FMCG) companies share a marketing mindset that would not fit particularly with a specialist chemical company, for instance.

National or ethnic cultures are the product of the history, educational systems, religions and social codes that each nation has woven over the centuries. In Chapter 11, we will analyze national cultures in more detail, but as far as alliances are concerned, we will take for granted the fact that firms are influenced by the national culture of their country of origin and the citizenship of their key executives.

All three differences can be present in global alliances, and usually at least two of them: the corporate and the national cultural differences. Those differences may impact the alliance management in five main ways:

- On the *definition of objectives* of the alliance: growth versus profit, short-term versus long-term are the major trade-offs that cultural differences may exacerbate
- On the way of *competing and doing business*: price competition versus differentiation
- On the way partners *communicate*: formal versus informal, hierarchical versus horizontal, degree of openness, emphasis on interpersonal communications
- On *financing and re-investing*: distribution of dividend versus reinvestment of profits, and debt policy
- On *human resources management* (HRM): criteria for recruiting, degree of autonomy and criteria for performance evaluation.

Organizational fit

Organizational fit is strongly correlated with cultural fit. The objective is to assess whether the partners' organizational structure *systems* and *procedures* differ significantly to the extent that the organization of the work between partners within the alliance is affected.

- The main dimensions included in organizational fit analysis are:
- The degree of decentralization of decision-making
- The degree of *documentation* of policies and rules
- The *accounting* and *reporting* methods and systems
- The degree of *formalization* of decision-making
- The kind of *incentives* used to motivate personnel.

In the case of Renault and Nissan, the cultural fit was not a priori ideal. On the three dimensions of culture – corporate, industry and national – only the industrial culture suggested a positive fit, since both entities were very focused on the development and manufacturing of cars. In this industry, norms and working methodologies are very much the same across the globe and both companies had had a limited collaboration before. Corporate cultures were highly contrasted: Reanult was originally a state-owned enterprise with a recent revitalization, and Nissan a public company, part of a large *Keiretzu* with a strong conservative attitude. They might have feared that the motivation, the management style and the various organizational mechanisms would all conflict However both companies had a tradition of lifetime employment and a strong bureaucratic background. For the national culture, France and Japan are contrasting countries on many levels: individualism vs. group orientation, seniority vs. performance, bottom-up decision-making vs. top-down, etc. It might have been feared that national pride and other cultural idiosyncrasies would disturb a potential relationship, particularly since Renault was a priori not perceived as a strong global player by the Japanese. This did not happen, for several reasons. First, the strong strategic stake made the partners more reasonable with regard to their national pride. Second, Carlos Gjosn and his team have demonstrated a lot of respect for the Japanese staff and have involved them in all decisions of the Nissan

Revival Plan through the CCTs and CFTs. Third, the governance structure was built so that interactions were organized jointly in the respective joint teams. Finally, English was adopted as a working language. That prevented either party having a natural linguistic dominance.

Negotiation and design

Operational scope

One of the first essentials is to agree on the *organizational design* and the *operational content* of the alliance. When deciding on the organizational design, the parties have to choose between two approaches according to the degree of operational capabilities they want to give to the alliance structure. They can choose between four generic types of alliance design, depending on whether the structure has full operating capabilities or acts as a broker and also whether it is a coalition, a co-specialization or a learning alliance (Figure 4.13).

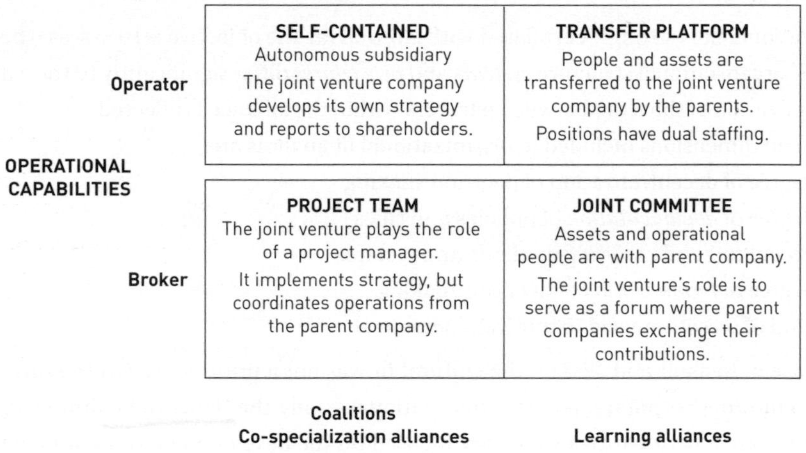

Figure 4.13 Organizational designs in alliances

In broker designs, the alliance structure acts as an intermediary between the two (or more) partners which keep their own operational capabilities (resources, assets and competencies). Broker structures can be either in the form of a project management or coordination structure, or alternatively can consist in a series of joint committees. When the alliance is a coalition or a co-specialization, the alliance structure is generally similar to a project team or a coordination structure. Renault–Nissan adopted this design. The partners formed an independent legal entity named Renault–Nissan BV incorporated in Holland, in which each company owned 50 per cent. The role of this joint venture would be to coordinate activities between the two parties. Each company worked on its own R&D, manufacturing and servicing on the basis of a strategic plan decided upfront. This structure owns no assets and the people working in this structure are essentially relationship managers. Figure 4.13 gives a schematic representation of the organization of the existing alliance structure.

In the case of learning alliances, broker designs will consist generally of joint committees. For instance, in the case of the Alza–Ciba-Geigy alliance for advanced drug delivery systems, the design of the partnership was based on the regular meeting of three committees: an audit committee, a joint research board and a series of joint research conferences.[5]

The operator alliance structure owns and operates its own operational capabilities, which are transferred to it by the parent companies, or the alliance builds and develops with the capital injected by the parents. Again, an operator design can take two different forms: self-contained or transfer platform.

In *self-contained* designs, the alliance structure creates economic value by itself and distributes it to the parent shareholders, as in any company. An example of a highly successful alliance of this type can be found with Fuji Xerox, which develops products, manufactures them and markets them with a high degree of autonomy from the parents.

Transfer platform designs are structures in which the joint venture controls its own resources, assets and competencies and therefore is fully responsible for creating the value. But in such designs, partners allocate engineers and staff to the joint venture with the view of 'learning' from the other partner and from the alliance. A good example is the NUMMI 50/50 joint venture between Toyota and General Motors. General Motors has allocated a factory at Freemont, California, and transferred 2,500 workers plus around 25 engineers to the joint venture. Toyota brings managers and specialists in 'lean' manufacturing systems. NUMMI can be considered as a transfer platform for Toyota to learn how to operate in an American unionized environment, while GM learns how to implement 'lean' manufacturing systems.

Interface and governance

Deciding on the interface and governance for the alliance is probably the most difficult part of the negotiation between partners. Six domains have to be agreed:

- The *legal structure* and the *decision-making* mechanisms
- The degree of *task integration*
- The appointment of *executives*
- The distribution of *value*
- The *reporting* and *communication* processes
- The *conflict resolution* mechanisms.

As far as the legal structure is concerned, the majority of alliances will be created under the form of a joint venture company, in which the respective equity shares will be clearly defined and valuations of contributions and results isolated from the parent companies' own accounts. In joint ventures, executive power is granted to a Board of Directors where each partner has seats corresponding to their equity share. Boards appoint operating executives, who in turn are responsible for producing results with the collaboration of personnel directly recruited by them or 'transferred' by the parent companies. Minority partners may negotiate some 'concurrence' clauses for certain key decisions that give them the right of veto (see below). The articles of association will determine the various elements of the agreement. Figure 4.14 shows the various items that would typically be negotiated and included in a joint venture.

Joint ventures are not the only legal form that alliances can take. Four other types of legal mechanisms that are commonly found in global alliances are:

(1) ***Equity participation by one partner in the capital of the other,*** as in the case of Renault–Nissan (Renault took 37 per cent equity of the capital of Nissan), or in the case of Ciba-Geigy in the capital of Alza. This type of legal structure is very close to an acquisition, but, in reality, as long as the equity partner does not get full control of the operation, it is still considered as an alliance.

(2) ***Joint equity participation,*** in which one partner takes a shareholding in the other partner's capital. This kind of agreement has to be complemented by contractual arrangements that define the scope of the joint activities and their respective valuations. This was the case with the now-defunct alliance between Renault and Volvo. In that case, the joint equity was supposed to be the prelude to a merger that was ultimately refused by Volvo's shareholders.

(3) ***Long-term contract agreements,*** such as distribution agreements or manufacturing agreements. Cisco, for instance, manufactures 75 per cent of its products with external suppliers with whom it has long-term relationships.

(4) ***R&D joint projects.***

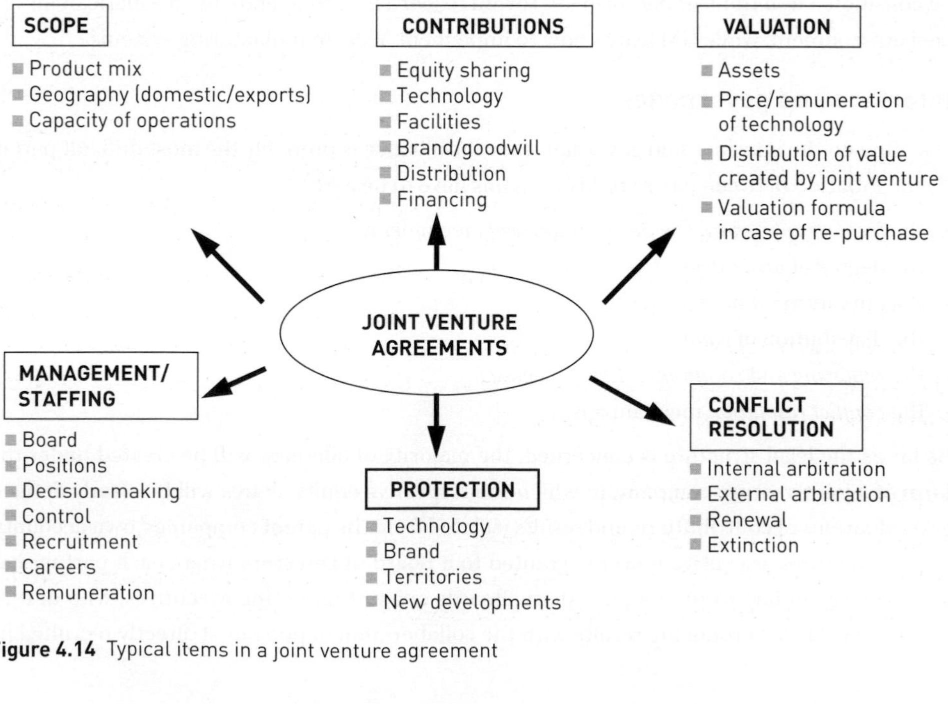

Figure 4.14 Typical items in a joint venture agreement

Legal structure and decision-making mechanism

When negotiating an alliance agreement, the majority of executives insists on having 'control', meaning that they want to obtain the majority shareholding in a joint venture. Many academic studies have found that this is one of the requirements stated by most managers surveyed. However, research has also found that 'control' is not correlated with 'success'.[6] In fact, a legal majority control is only a fraction of the total control over a company or a set of operations. First, there is the possibility for a minority partner to activate 'concurrence' clauses that may limit the power of the majority and ultimately block decisions. You can perceive intuitively that control is real if, and only if, a person or a group of persons is able positively and negatively to influence behaviour. A majority shareholding does not guarantee that. Some authors have even argued that a 50/50 joint venture arrangement is even better than a majority arrangement because it forces partners to make all the necessary effort to make the alliance work.[7] In the case of Renault–Nissan the alliance is organized on two levels: first, at the shareholding level there is a cross shareholding, Renault owning 44.3 per cent of Nissan and Nissan owning 15 per cent of Renault, and second, at the decision-making level with the creation of a strategic management 50/50 joint venture, Renault–Nissan BV deciding on major strategic choices. This hybrid organization is infrequent but may be a blueprint for future global alliances.

The degree of task integration

Task integration defines which activities are carried out by the alliance, which ones are carried out separately, and the extent to which activities carried out by each partner need to be integrated. For instance, when the task is to jointly develop a new product, R&D departments often need to be merged, at least partially, while if the alliance is only a sharing of distribution networks, the amount of interdependency between the two networks may be limited. Integration requires coordination and joint work and therefore is likely to demand *complex management approaches*. Alternatively, if integration is limited, each party fulfills its obligations separately, making coordination straightforward and simple. Limited integration is possible if tasks are defined precisely up-front and the joint output is obtained by 'assembling' the separate outputs together with limited interactions. This is a 'plug-in' operation. This is the model that Renault and Nissan adopted. The synergies are structured only for a certain number of tasks and except for the procurement of components most of the other interactions are organized according to a mode of technology transfer. When the task complexity is such that clear separation of job distribution is not possible, then a self-contained joint venture in which teams are temporarily merged is the best solution. Otherwise, coordination of interdependencies could prove to be a hurdle.

Appointment of executives

Whom to appoint as the alliance leader is often a major issue for the success of the venture, as well as a subject of contention between partners when they negotiate the agreement. Two key issues arise: the amount of parents' transfers and the skills of alliance managers.

Parents' transfer refers to the allocation of managers and staff from each parent to the venture, as opposed to the independent staffing of the alliance structure. When the alliance is a co-specialization or one of reciprocal learning, partners' transfer is expected to be high since the whole purpose is to activate the unique capabilities of partners. Alternatively, when the alliance is a coalition or co-learning (both partners want to learn from the alliance but not necessarily from each other), people transfer is less of an issue.

In the case of transfer, the problem arises of the distribution of *functions and roles*. One technique, known as the 'shadow' organization, consists of putting a manager from one partner in charge of a function with a manager from the other partner as his or her deputy. This technique seems appealing because of its apparent fairness, but it is not necessarily effective, since it reinforces a 'them and us' attitude and leads to a long decision-making process or many conflictual situations. In the case of Renault and Nissan, Carlos Ghosn and 20 Renault managers were transferred to Nissan in order to participate in the Nissan Revival Plan.In addition, French personnel were temporarily detached to the CCTs or the CFTs.

The second important consideration is to select managers with the appropriate skills to manage the alliance. An interesting work by Robert Spekeman and Lynn Isabella has identified different roles and skills of alliance managers; Figure 4.15 gives a summary of their findings. Other authors have stressed the critical importance of the managerial, communication and negotiation skills of managers in the alliance.[8]

Distribution of value

As mentioned earlier, an *alliance creates value* and this value has to be distributed to the partners according to an agreed scheme. Owing to the fact that valuation is complex, alliance negotiators often have difficulty in finding a 'fair' mechanism taking into consideration all the elements that contribute to value. The simplest form is the distribution of profits in a joint venture. This works only if the entire profit is created by the joint venture without any significant input apart from the initial capital from the partners. When profit is dependent on inputs provided by the parents, there is a high risk of *transfer pricing disputes.* In the case of Renault–Nissan there was no issue of value transfer since each company generates its own revenues and profits. As cross-shareholders, each company benefits from the profits generated by the other in proportion to their ownership.

In a revenue-sharing scheme each partner receives the revenues generated by the alliance proportionately to their share of work. Then it is up to each partner to manage its costs and to generate profit. This method implies that there is an up-front agreement on work-sharing. If that is the case, the partners are already familiar with the technology involved and have a pretty good awareness of the relative importance of the work to be completed by each party. An example of this type can be found in the case of GE–SNECMA, a long-lasting alliance in the aero-engine industry.[9] Corrective mechanisms were included in case a work discrepancy appeared during the implementation of the alliance.

Stage: anticipating	Alliance manager role: Visionary
Searching for partners Planning an alliance	• Serve as driving force behind the alliance's creation • Paint picture of the possibilities that forming an alliance might create • Initiate contact with potential partners • Understand company's strategic intent and recognize similarity of intent in potential partner companies
Stage: Engaging	**Alliance manager role: Strategic sponsor**
Evaluating partners Identifying value creation opportunities	• Have authority to commit resources and key personnel to the alliance • Define and promote the dream on which the alliance is based • Actively promote and sell the alliance internally • Help the company identify synergies and imagine possibilities • Create an atmosphere of high energy, personal compatibility and strategic complementarity
Stage: Valuing	**Alliance manager role: Advocate**
Building business plans Negotiating	• Spend a significant amount of time convincing others within the company of the value of the alliance • Take responsibility for developing support for the alliance • Constantly push the dream forward • Rally the right people at the right time • Make things happen 'deep' in the company • Act as champion for the alliance
Stage: Investing	**Alliance manager role: Facilitator**
Demonstrating commitment Leveraging synergies	• Encourage open, honest and straightforward communication among all parties to the alliance • Facilitate effective 'no-blame reviews' • Interact with diplomacy, tact and objectivity • Create bridges between diverse parties with different interests • Resolve conflicts • Exhibit sensitivity to the needs of all parties
Stage: Co-ordinating	**Alliance manager role: Networking**
Creating teams Aligning work processes across partners	• Rely on frequent contacts to expedite alliance business • Know whom to ask for help and when to ask • Put the right people together • Access resources quickly and efficiently through others • Create links between the partner companies' internal networks • Put in face-to-face time in order to cultivate trust in key relationships
Stage: Stabilizing	**Alliance manager role: Manager**
Consolidating Managing	• Shoulder responsibilities for sustaining the alliance • Ensure that the alliance follows its prescribed path • Maintain relationships critical to alliance success • Communicate frequently with all partners • Maintain the alliance's momentum • Actively develop future alliance managers

Figure 4.15 Alliance stages and alliance managers' skills

Source: Spekeman and Isabella (2000).

Reporting and communication processes

Alliance agreements should provide *communication platforms* so that partners remain informed about the development of the venture. Academic research has stressed the importance of communication in the success of alliances.[10] The legal forum for communication is the Board of Directors in a joint venture, but this is not enough. Communication needs to be organized horizontally and vertically among partners and *within* partners, as shown in Figure 4.16.

In the case of Reanult–Nissan, communication is mediated within the CFTs and CCTs under the responsibility of Renault–Nissan BV.

Conflict resolution mechanisms

Friction and conflict is almost inevitable. As will be seen later, disenchantment, frustration and conflict of interests may surface rapidly after the deal is consummated (the 'death valley' problem illustrated by Figure 4.17) or during the life of the alliance.

All contracts include legal provision for conflict management between shareholders in joint ventures by *arbitrage clauses*. The real problem is not these legal mechanisms – which in many cases are employed when the two parties have more or less already decided to terminate their agreements – but the difficulty of creating the *internal mechanisms* for solving problems. In the case of Renault–Nissan, for instance, potential disagreements are dealt with by the joint strategic organization Renault–Nissan BV.

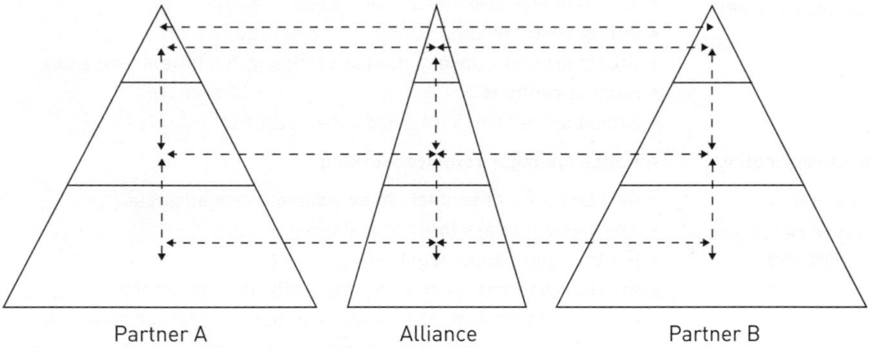

Figure 4.16 Communications flows in alliances

Source: Author's own creation based on information from Doz and Hamel (1998, p. 190).

Implementation

The last stage in alliance management, but not the least, is the implementation stage. Two different aspects of implementation have been identified as critical: integration and cooperation; and learning.

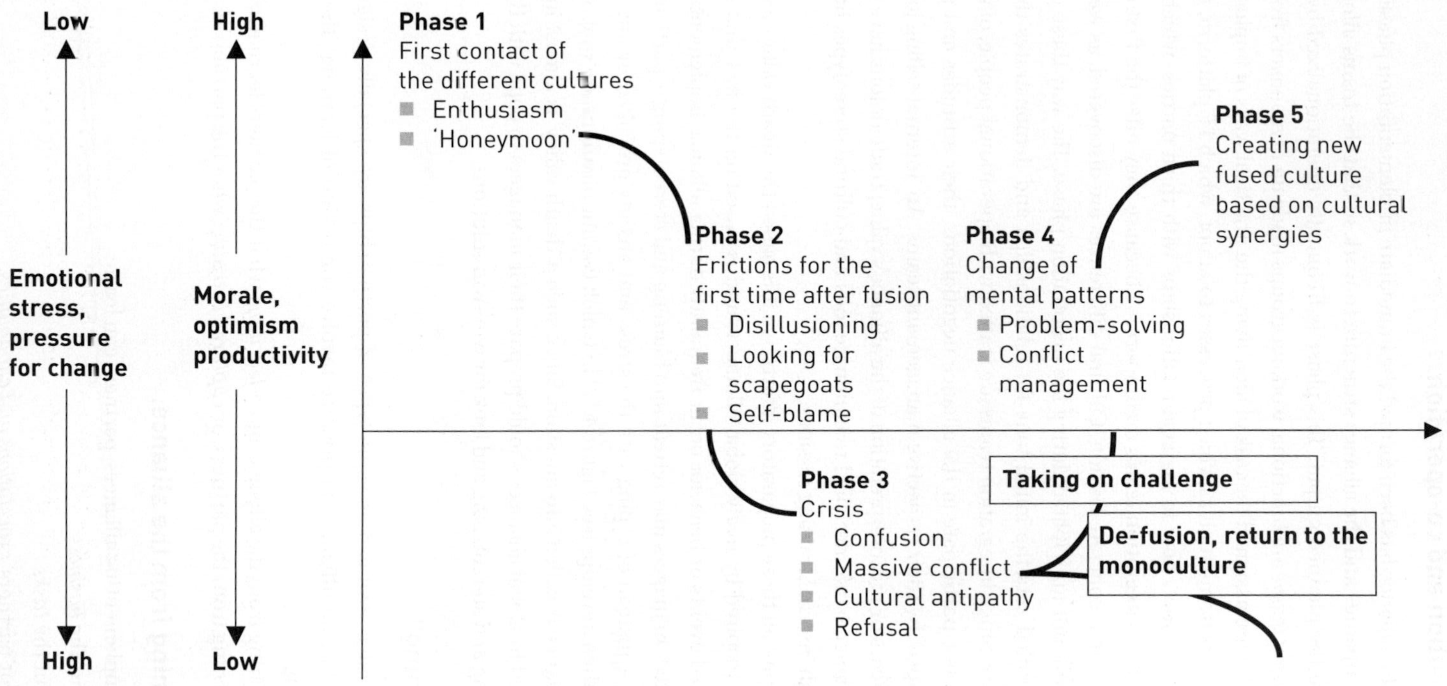

Figure 4.17 The 'death valley' spiral

Integration and co-operation

Once the alliance has been formed the immediate implementation phase is to put the respective companies and the alliance structure to work so that the teams allocated to the alliance achieve the planned output. This phase is frequently operationalized by 'integration teams'. *Integration teams* are functional working groups made up of managers from the different partners who are assigned the task of identifying the practical ways of implementing the alliance. This covers items such as which processes to adopt, which IT platform, the kind of measurements to adopt, how to manage relationships with third parties, which accounting system to use, etc. Integration teams are important because they offer the first opportunity to work together in a concrete fashion. Cultural differences are discovered, as well as practical issues that were not anticipated during the negotiation phase. The way these unanticipated issues are handled sets the initial tone for relationships and demonstrates the actual mindset of partners. Since integration teams are staffed with operational people, of whom a large majority did not participate in the alliance negotiations, their attitudes and perspectives have to be 'shaped' by their respective management teams. An 'internal selling job' is often needed to erode fears or misinterpretation of the alliance's value; trade unions have to be convinced that the alliance is not designed to eliminate jobs and cultural stereotypes have to be challenged through internal training sessions.

Despite all these preparatory efforts, what is called the 'death valley' issue often arises. This model inspired by many global alliances, and is based on the fact that surprises and unanticipated events or behavior occur frequently during alliance implementation. If not properly prepared, managers may retreat into blaming and stereotyping – particularly cultural stereotyping – instead of coping with the stress and anxiety provoked by any 'surprises'. A vicious spiral then develops (see Figure 4.17) in which communications are shut off and the viability of the alliance is called into question. Since such a 'death valley' is almost inevitable, companies engaged in global alliances should prepare their managers to cope with the situation, to avoid blaming and stereotyping and look for win–win solutions.

Learning[11]

As we have seen earlier, some types of partnerships are specially designed as learning alliances, but all alliances in practice involve some kind of learning. There are two forms of learning:

- Learning from the alliance, or *co-learning*: what the partners learn *within the alliance*
- Learning from the partners, or *captured learning*: what the partners learn f*rom each other.*

Learning from the alliance.

- In implementing alliances, partners can learn:
- About the *business*
- About the *tasks*
- About partners' *expectations and capabilities.*

Partners discover jointly the characteristics and trends of markets, the industry and its competitive drivers. This kind of learning is normal in any venture, whether joint or not. The specific issue in the case of a partnership is to put in place the organizational mechanisms for such learning to take place and to be *distributed* to partners. This is done by setting up and using common databases, and possibly with the advent of E-business platforms to integrate the joint venture database to the partner's Intranet software. In addition, the alliance structure should organize reflective and analytical forums for joint planning, seminars, conferences and review sessions.

Partners should also be able to redefine their mutual contributions and work processes in the light of new events and changes in business context. Functional committees and operational reviews can make such mutual adjustments. In the case of Renault–Nissan the CCTs are in charge of the respective contributions of partners and agreements on platforms, joint research, common productions and the like.

Over time, partners' expectations may change and imbalances in the value distribution may appear. This kind of change is obviously one of the most difficult to handle since change in expectations may undermine the initial alliance's foundations. A constant observation of change in a partner's internal context, such as a new CEO, modification of strategic direction, analyst opinions, and so on, helps to predict the likelihood of a shift in expectations. One potential issue in the case of Renault and Nissan would be that one partner becomes highly successful commercially and financially while the other lags behind. That may create over time an imbalance leading to a reconsideration of the alliance.

Learning from the partner

In 1986 Reich and Mankin published an explosive article named 'Joint Ventures with Japan Give Away Our Future'. In a more moderate rein, Doz, Hamel and Prahalad argued in 1989 that Western partners could use alliances to regain competitiveness against Japanese competitors. They gave as an example the case of Thompson Multimedia, which gained expertise in the design and manufacturing of VCRs thanks to its alliance with JVC.

In both cases, the arguments were based on 'learning from the partner' in an alliance context. In practice a 'learning from the partner' approach implies two key capabilities: clarity of objectives and organizational receptivity.

Clarity of objectives implies that the company engaged in an alliance for learning should identify clearly what it wants to learn and set up a learning agenda defining the learning sequence. All capabilities cannot be learned at once. Thomson embarked on a step-by-step approach to learning first the assembly of VCR components, and then the ability to design and manufacture next-generation products such as handheld mini video cameras.

Receptivity is the second type of learning capability. It consists of the various internal organization mechanisms that companies engaged in alliances may use to accumulate, retain and transfer knowledge. Table 4.2 gives a list of such weak and strong learning mechanisms.

Table 4.2 Receptivity in learning

Weak learning capabilities	Strong learning capabilities
• No systematic collection of information	• Organized intelligence
• No sharing of information	• Networked internal information exchange
• 'Not invented here' attitudes	• 'Why' attitude, curiosity, search for benchmarking ar outside best practices
• No 'organizational memory'	• Planned approach to skill acquisition
• Pressure to achieve only operational/ financial results	• Internal training
• Recruitment of people based only on technical professional skills	• Allocation of time and budgets to 'learn' • Recruitment of people based on 'social' as well as professional skills

Global multilateral alliances[12]

Most of the discussions in this chapter have been centered around dyadic alliances involving only two partners. In practice, global companies are often engaged in a multiplicity of alliances, some of them domestic, but the vast majority with 'foreign' partners.

Each product division of multi-business corporations is engaged in *multiple alliances*, so that if you were to count the total number of strategic partnerships for the whole corporation, you might find several hundred, as in the case of IBM, Motorola or Siemens.

Gomez-Casseres has classed these alliances as 'constellations' in which partners are cooperating in one business segment but possibly competing in another.

Doz and Hamel identify three types of constellations (see Figure 4.18).

- Alliance *networks*
- Alliance *portfolios*
- Alliance *webs*.

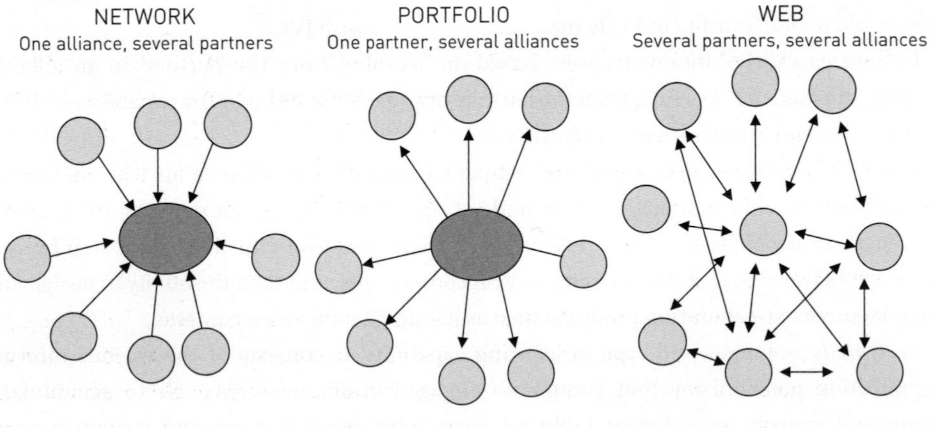

Figure 4.18 Types of alliance constellations

Source: Adapted from Doz and Hamel (1998).

Alliance networks are those to which partners contribute to increase reach, adopt a common standard or promote a new technology. VISA (credit card), SWIFT (banking), STAR (airlines) are alliances of this nature. As in a club, several partners contribute and benefit from the alliance provided they subscribe to the rules and discipline of the network. It is a 'one alliance, multiple partners' design.

Alliance portfolios are those where a company enters into a partnership with multiple companies, with different products, technologies or markets. The company deals with its partner as a portfolio, or on a one-to-one basis. There is no interaction among partners, only between partners and the 'core' party. This is a 'one partner, several alliances' design. Corning Glass is a good example.

Alliance webs are constellations in which partners contribute and benefit interdependently, a 'several partners, several alliances' design. Airbus, during the last 20 years of its existence, functioned as a 'global web'. In an alliance web, you can find some characteristics of alliance networks (a common platform) or of alliance portfolios (one company in the web may have a central nuclear position, as Aerospatiale did for Airbus) but the relationships among partners are more equal and interdependent than in alliance portfolios and even more so than in alliance networks.

Constellations of global partners put a high degree of constraint on companies, because of their complexity and diversity. Managerial challenges can arise at two levels:

- At the *alliance* level: how to make it work?
- At the *partners'* level: how to cope with multiple alliances, and in each alliance how to manage the relationships with other parties?

Alliance constellation management

Depending upon the type of alliance, the managerial challenges vary. In an alliance network you will typically find two kinds of issues: first, alliance *creation and mobilization* and second, alliance *governance and maintenance*.

(1) ***Alliance creation and mobilization.*** Both alliance creation and mobilization depend on core companies or on an outsider (this can be a government body or a new technology developer). Someone has to take the initiative to identify the benefits of those alliances and to 'sell' them to multiple partners. When the benefits of the alliance are obvious, as in the case of airline alliances, the task may be relatively easy, although the key element in that case is to make sure that alliance members are sufficiently compatible among themselves.

(2) ***Alliance governance and maintenance.*** As Lorenzoni and Baden-Fuller (1997) suggest, alliance networks must establish a center or a 'network manager', whose role is to make sure the partners contribute fairly to the partnership and respect the common rules. Alliance managers also serve as an information exchange and clearing house for mutual transaction. The VISA organization serves as an example of such 'network management'.

In an alliance portfolio, the main managerial issues are partner *selection* and *attraction* as well as partnership *leverage* and *relationships.*

(1) ***Partner selection and attraction.*** In an alliance portfolio, the prime objective for the 'nodal' firm (the portfolio manager) is to utilize a multiplicity of co-specialized, co-allied and learning alliances in order to foster its global competitive capabilities.

In selecting partners, the 'nodal' firm will look at firms bringing the necessary complementary capabilities but which are not likely to take advantage of the alliance in order to build their own competing capabilities. Corning, for instance, in its alliances with Siemens to develop, manufacture and sell optic fibers for communication, selected a partner that was not interested in building a competitive position in the design and production of fibers, but only in their utilization.

(2) ***Managing partner leverage and relationship.*** The 'nodal' firm will make sure that the 'relevant' capabilities are obtained from the alliance, but also that it contributes positively and significantly to the partner's expectations. By keeping partnership as a one-to-one relationship, the 'nodal' firm builds a set of *converging capabilities* that are not shared by the whole constellation of partners.

In alliance webs, in contrast, the task of the 'nodal' firm is to build an interdependent set of mutual relationships to which each participant contributes but gains from all the others. Pixtech, for instance, has built a web of partners for the development of Field Emission Display (FED) technology for flat panel displays to be used in a variety of applications.

Partners entering the alliance have to demonstrate their commitment by opening their R&D labs (the LED-related technology) to other partners. Each party has to host meetings in its own facilities for alliance members to exchange their research progress. Reciprocal patent licensing is also involved in this type of alliance.

Local joint ventures

Local alliances under the form of *joint venture* companies have been traditional vehicles for market entry since 1945 in countries that aimed to bring value-adding productive activities to their economy, protecting their natural resources and also promoting the strategic development of national firms. Japan in the 1950s, Korea, China, Indonesia and India in the 1960s are among the countries that have systematically encouraged the formation of international joint ventures between foreign investors and local firms. Although in these countries the legal requirement for joint venture has been somewhat relaxed, a joint venture mindset subsists. The logic of these joint ventures is simple: it consists of an exchange of a market or resources for technology. Foreign investors are invited to bring their products, processes and management technologies alongside their capital in exchange for an entry into the domestic market or an access to key natural resources. The value created by these local alliances is straightforward: the value for the foreign partner is an increase in market penetration and a set of profits coming from various sources – dividends, transfer prices, management fees. The value for the local partner is an increase in know-how, a flow of dividends and other indirect cash flow such as rental fees, local procurement, and so on.

A joint venture is an ambiguous concept, since it embraces several forms of partnership. In this chapter, we shall consider joint ventures as *equity participations in separate legal entities* in which two or more partners invest tangible and intangible capital. Some countries, like China, have set up the concept of 'contractual joint ventures' that are a hybrid form of equity and project partnership agreement, but these are relatively limited and in practice the implications of their management are very similar to equity joint ventures. In emerging markets, joint ventures have been the main form of foreign direct investment (FDI). In 1996, joint ventures represented around 77 per cent of all FDI in Korea, 72 per cent in China, 52 per cent in Latin America and 54 per cent in Eastern Europe.

Three major forces seem to drive foreign investors to enter joint ventures: administrative, capabilities, risks.

Administrative requirements

Some governments want their own people to benefit from industrialization; they often push foreign investors to ally with local firms before granting access to markets or resources. This concern is strongest in countries with import-substitution policies: governments in Indonesia, Malaysia, China, India and Russia, and in the past Japan or Korea, have been most successful in imposing partnerships on foreign investors. Countries such as China, which endorsed wholly owned foreign ventures in March 1992, still encourage Western companies to choose joint ventures. However, since the early 1990s governments have been more flexible and have accepted, in some cases, 100 per cent foreign ownership. In strategically sensitive sectors like media, telecoms, defence or legal professions (including in industrialized countries), foreign investment is banned or the foreign investor is obliged to share ownership with local firms. Foreign equity participation has sometimes also to be shared in order to encourage the country's own citizens to participate in industrial development. Such was the case in Malaysia with the New Economic Policy (NEP) that forced local Malay (*Bumiputra*) equity participation in foreign projects.

Finally, some foreign firms choose to enter into joint ventures to win contracts for important government infrastructure projects. In countries such as Singapore, which has no protectionist regulations, the government has a policy of positive discrimination towards foreign contractors with local joint ventures.

Capabilities requirements

The need for a foreign company to access critical resources, assets and competencies has also favored joint ventures. In most cases, foreign partners look for a local firm with capabilities in distribution, sales, local market knowledge, local production expertise or, more importantly, contacts with decision-makers and business networks. Managerial and human resources are often the most critical resources provided by a local joint venture partner.

Successful multinational companies with experience and resources will be less inclined to tie up with a local partner for that reason: they assume that the market will adjust to them, so they do not need to adjust to the local market. Companies with strong international brands entering newly developing markets may need less local support than late entrants with unknown brands.

Risk hedging

Foreign firms may seek to reduce risk, especially when financial investment is high, or the return on investment (ROI) uncertain. They usually have one of three motivations:

- *Complexity* of a project
- *Uncertain market acceptance* of a product or service
- Country risk in terms of *macroeconomic* and *political stability*.

Partner selection

The type of partner to be selected is a function of the strategic dimensions mentioned earlier. As illustrated in Figure 4.19, there are various partner-choice combinations; Table 4.3 shows the various types of partner available.

When there is no legal obligation to partnership and the foreign investor has the resource and capabilities to operate alone, the best choice is not to enter into a joint venture unless risks and low opportunities push the company to search for a partner. When there is a legal obligation and the company possesses the resources and capabilities, the choice would be to search for a 'non-active' or 'sleeping partner', such as an investment company or some firms that are willing to let the foreign firm take command of the venture. If there is no legal pressure for joint venture and the company needs a partner because it lacks capabilities, it would look for a potential acquisition. If the government requires joint ventures, the choice would be more delicate. Since the foreign party will look for an active partner who can bring the needed capabilities, the assessment of strategic capabilities and cultural fit is critical.

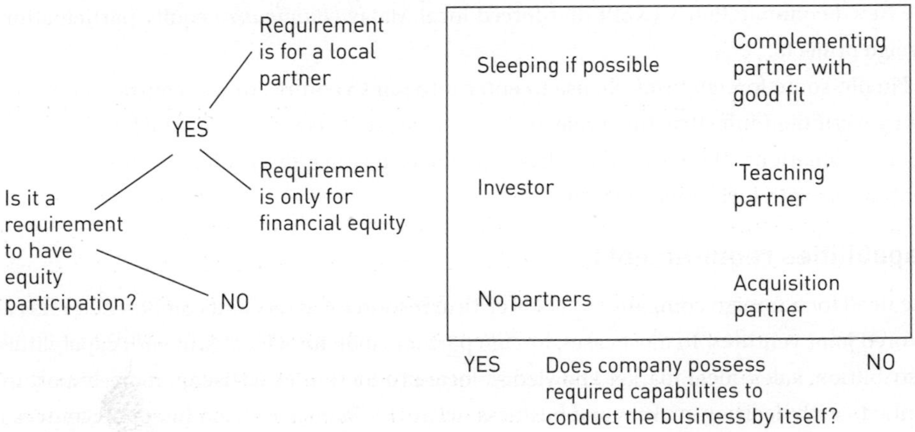

Figure 4.19 Partner choices in country-based joint ventures

Table 4.3 Types of local partners for market entry joint ventures

Partners contributing to operational capabilities	Partners contributing to non-operational resources
• Partner in the *same industry*: brings full capabilities	• *Diversifier*: brings business reputation and country knowledge and looks to enter into a new business
• *Supplier*: secures supplies	• *Investor*: brings finance, looks for return
• *Distributor*: secures market coverage	• *Central or local government*: looks for development and jobs and brings authority
• *Customer*: secures market	• *Political partner*: brings contacts and looks for remuneration
Advantages: Enhances competitive capabilities and speeds up entry	*Advantages*: Speeds up entry, brings knowledge, contacts
Disadvantages: risks of copying and reinforcing/creating a local competitor	*Disadvantages*: Does not provide operational capabilities. Political risks exposure when the partner is a government body or a political partner

In any case the selection of a potential partner has crucial, long-term consequences. It is important to find a partner with *compatible objectives*, and with whom it is possible to communicate and build a stable, lasting partnership; the foreign firm's success will depend on the partner's capabilities and willingness to cooperate, and the climate of mutual trust. Often, firms conduct far too little *advance planning*. In Asia Pacific, for instance, where joint venture had been a predominant entry mode, Western foreign firms conducted little or no screening and, in many cases, ended up choosing a long-term local agent or distributor without searching for alternatives.

To investigate potential partners thoroughly, foreign firms should:

- Require *information*
- Interview in depth the *owner*, top *managers* and *operating staff* in manufacturing and sales
- Ask for *financial data* (although these may be of limited value)
- Interview the local firm's other *joint venture partners*, *bankers*, *suppliers*, *customers* and *competitors*, as well as diplomats and established foreign investors.

Selection criteria

As already described earlier for global alliances, the assessment of fit is an important selection criterion (see Figure 4.8).

(1) ***A strategic fit*** exists when the two partners have *compatible long-term objectives*. They will pool some of their resources to reach goals that they cannot attain alone. Assessing strategic fit involves analyzing the partners' implicit or explicit motives for joining forces, as well as the benefits they expect to gain. In joint ventures for market entry, you typically find three main types of agenda behind the strategic objectives for engaging in joint ventures:

- *The venturing agenda*, in which the two partners want to develop the potential of a given market by creating a new business activity. In this case, the primary intention is to join forces rather than to take advantage of the other partner.

- The *extractive agenda*, in which one partner wants to acquire a key resource, asset or competence from the other. Local partners typically seek product or process technology, hardware and software from foreign joint ventures; they may also want to gain access to international markets. Foreign partners often use joint ventures to build relationships and win market access, or to make up-front profits through high transfer pricing on equipment, components or management services; sometimes they are interested in access to raw materials or low-cost labor rather than in promoting the business of the joint venture itself.
- The *opportunistic agenda*, in which the local partner may want to capitalize on *citizenship* and *political contacts*, or seek a *financial return*. The foreign partner may be complying with regulations, or want to enter into a short-term 'deal'.

A classic example of conflicting goals would be a foreign partner who wants to acquire marketing expertise and a local partner looking for technological expertise.

The degree of commitment to the joint venture is particularly important: the moment of truth comes when unexpected problems arise in day-to-day operations. Even if individual managers assigned to a joint venture are committed, the two parents may give it relatively low priority. When a cooperative agreement is purely opportunistic, commitment is problematic; this is why many opportunistic partnerships end in failure.

(2) A good ***capabilities fit*** means that both partners must be able to contribute to the resources and competencies needed; they must *identify and solve potential gaps* in contribution. The same methodology assessment of capabilities fit as developed earlier applies for joint venture for market entry. What is particularly significant in emerging countries is the fact that due to poor information a good capability fit analysis is difficult. A classic mistake is to overestimate your partner's contribution to the joint venture. Problems also arise when initial resources, assets and competencies become insufficient to sustain competitiveness over time. New funding will be needed; profits will have to be reinvested into the business. A short-term orientation, opportunism or simply the inconsistency of one or both partners may aggravate a potential resource gap.

Valuing contributions that do not have a market price, because they are either not traded or intangible, can cause conflict. Intangibles and technology are often the most valuable contributions brought to a joint venture, and can become a key element in the negotiation.

(3) ***Cultural dissimilarity*** emanating from corporate, industry or national and ethnic differences is always present in international joint ventures, and can create many problems and conflicts when it comes to the practical operations of the venture. As already indicated, cultural differences often lead to a difficult period of adaptation called the **'death valley'**, that requires patience and flexibility on the part of managers. It is therefore important that prior to engaging in an agreement a *cultural fit assessment* be made by trying to answer questions such as: Can we understand each other? Do we speak the same business language? Do we share a common logic? Can we communicate with each other?

(4) Finally the result of an ***organizational fit*** analysis in a joint venture for market entry reveals profound differences in management practices. Most often in emerging countries a local entrepreneurial firm with no procedures may have trouble cooperating with a big, bureaucratic multinational corporation. Organizational fit is hard to achieve when it comes to integrating the local joint venture into the parent company's network of subsidiaries.

Staffing joint ventures

Joint ventures require managers with *political* and *cultural skills* as well as technical competencies. Foreign managers unprepared for cultural complexity will not handle critical situations properly and will jeopardize their parent company's ability to learn. The most important task of managers assigned to joint ventures, particularly when the strategic intent is to extract knowledge from the local environment, is to synthesize and transmit *learning experiences* to each relevant department in their parent company. It would be a mistake to assign managers lacking clout or prestige to a foreign joint venture; the local partner may interpret this as a lack of commitment to the partnership. The worst attitude is to consider such postings as a form of exile for undesirable personnel.

When recruiting local employees, identity and loyalty are critical. Do they feel that they belong to their parent company, or to the joint venture? Most of the time, the local partner will recruit local staff; foreign partners should carefully monitor hiring to ensure that the new employees are loyal to the joint venture, not just to the local partner.

Control

Joint ventures are controlled by a Board of Directors consisting largely of executives, as well as a few non-executive directors; these are usually local personalities who can play a useful role as go-betweens in cases of conflict with the local partners. Western companies tend to prefer having a majority stake in a joint venture, although there is no evidence that this allows them to exert real control. When a firm controls more than 70 per cent of capital, the joint venture can be considered a 'quasi-acquisition', in which case the majority partner is in command. Below 70 per cent, this is not necessarily the case. Several studies have failed to demonstrate significant correlation between shareholding and control: some companies that are in charge of key operational functions can be in control even with a minority stake.

Joint venture decay and failure

It is common for joint ventures to experience a rapid deterioration immediately after start-up as the partners find out more about each other and make efforts to adapt. After this 'death valley' period, relative stability follows, which can last three to six years; after that, mutual interest suddenly drops. The resulting crisis can lead to a split, and this phenomenon, known as joint venture decay, happens when both partners feel that they have acquired whatever advantage they sought from their association; at this moment the impetus for further collaboration can vanish. If both partners want to avert a divorce, they must revitalize their association by *increasing the range* or *broadening the scope* of its activities (Figure 4.20).

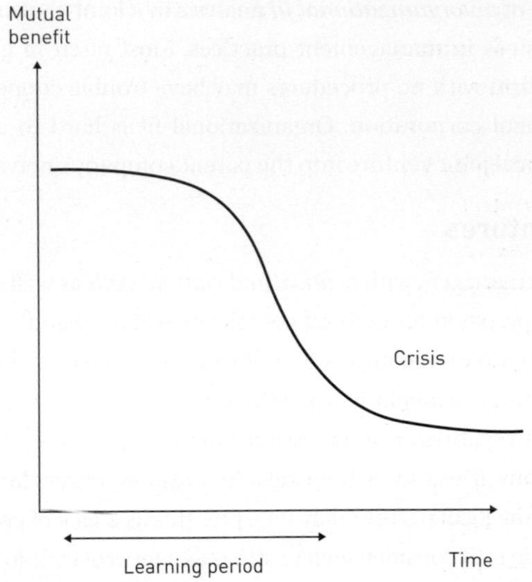

Figure 4.20 Joint venture decay

The experience of foreign companies in joint ventures has not always been a happy one. Empirical evidence on international joint ventures indicates that at most 40–50 per cent end up producing the expected return. Most companies have become disillusioned because of unforeseen problems in setting up and operating their partnerships. There are five main causes of failure or difficulty:

(1) The ***absence of strategic vision.*** When a joint venture is launched hastily, or for purely defensive or opportunistic reasons, the foreign firm often fails to evaluate the intentions and capabilities of the local partner. A classic error in an industrial partnership is to choose a distributor whose corporate culture is likely to be inappropriate to a slow cash-flow cycle, and who will probably privilege a few rapid cash-flow deals instead of investing for the long term.

(2) ***Believing without seeing.*** The art of appearances can be highly refined in some countries and many a foreign investor has been led into mistaking elaborate ceremony for a real commitment.

(3) Failing to understand the local partner's *strategic logic.* In most cases, a thorough investigation would reveal the real intent – for example, to achieve vertical integration to appropriate technology, or simply to enter into an opportunistic deal.

(4) ***Haste in negotiation.*** The desire to conclude a deal rapidly often leads the negotiators to concentrate on financial or legal clauses and neglect *technological* or *operational* issues. In Asian countries, for instance, the contractual stage must be preceded by an *overall planning session* for the project, during which the partners will agree on objectives and strategies. This implies a minimum investment in understanding the partner's logic. It is a good idea

to advance step by step: a licensing contract, for example, can be a good way of testing the capacities of the other party before making a longer-term commitment.

(5) ***Insufficiently prepared staff and lack of organizational support.*** Unprepared expatriate managers who fail to understand their partner's and employees' logic can exacerbate tensions, and damage the reputation of both the joint venture and the foreign parent. Local partners in emerging countries are often highly respected businessmen, and when they suffer what they see as inappropriate treatment at the hands of unsophisticated foreign staff, they quickly become disillusioned. Besides, the joint venture is often poorly served by headquarters (delays in technical assistance, delivery of poorly adapted products, exorbitant transfer pricing, exaggerated administrative rules or constraints that ignore local conditions).

Table 4.4 Eight criteria for successful alliances

• Individual excellence	– Have something to contribute
	– Both partners are strong
	– Have positive intent
• Importance	– Fits strategy of both partners
	– Long-term view
• Interdependence	– Partners need each other
	– Complementary capabilities
	– Nobody can 'go it alone'
• Investment	– Partner shows commitment
	– Investment/reinvestment
• Information	– Reasonable, open communication
	– Sharing of operational information
• Integration	– Shared operating procedures
	– Numerous connections
	– Teachers/learners
• Institutionalization	– Clear responsibilities
	– Clear decision processes
• Integrity	– No abuse
	– Willingness to enhance trust

Source: Moss Kanter (1994).

These five causes of failure are often inter-related, contributing to a *vicious circle of misunderstanding* which can degenerate into open conflict and end in frustration, loss of market share and sometimes legal action. Studies on joint ventures have shown that good cultural and strategic fit, leading to trust between partners, are the crucial factors for success. Foreign enterprises that seriously consider setting up through joint ventures should devote enough resources and effort to carefully preparing and monitoring the selection of a partner and management of the venture as well as management of the continuous flow of communication with their local partners.

Criteria for successful alliances

In this chapter we have tried to describe and analyze the various issues relevant to the management of strategic alliances. In the business world today two observations can be made: first, more and more cross-border alliances are needed as a result of globalization and with the advent of the 'new economy' (see Chapter 14) and second, most of the alliances fail to achieve their expected results. Probably two reasons can explain this poor record. First, a 'control' mindset – executives have difficulty shedding the hierarchical model of management inherited from vertically integrated business activities. Partnership requires a set of skills and mindsets on the part of the manager involved giving them the capacity to work in a network.[13] The second reason relates to the difficulty in building trust between organizations coming from different cultures: mistrust is probably the one single factor that explains partnership failure.[14] Building trust requires competencies that are not necessarily those taught in engineering and business schools; it requires the mastery of techniques belonging to social sciences such as 'negotiation analysis', the art of 'signaling' and the practice of 'credible commitment'.

Rosabeth Moss Kanter (1994) summarized the factors that can be found in successful alliances. Table 4.4 reproduces a valuable checklist for use when considering the design and implementation of particular global strategic alliances.

MINI-CASE

Danone vs. Wahaha: Conflicts in a Joint Venture in China

The Danone–Wahaha joint venture was formed in February 1996 by the French Danone Group (51 per cent of shares directly or indirectly) and the Hangzhou Wahaha Food Group (49 per cent of the shares). At the time the Wahaha Group was a state-owned enterprise owned by the Hangzhou city government but in 1999 was converted into a collectively owned corporation controlled by Mr Zong with 60 per cent shareholdings. By 2000 the group had become the biggest company in the beverage industry in China with total sales of 5.4 billion RMB and total assets of 4.4 billion RMB and more than 40 subsidiaries covering more than 16 provinces.

By 1998, beside the Wahaha venture, Danone had four other joint ventures in China: Guangzhou Milk, Dongxihu Beer, Taoshan Ltd and Shenzhen Danone Health. China represented 4.3 per cent of global sales. By 2006 China represented €1.4 billion turnover (11.6 per cent of global sales), making it the 3rd-largest market in the Danone portfolio.

The joint venture agreement stated that the Wahaha trademark would be transferred to the joint venture and that Mr Zong would be the chairman and chief executive. Over the year Danone and Wahaha formed 39 other joint ventures across the country which in 2006 achieved a turnover of €2 billion. In parallel to the joint venture activities, Zong and his family created companies registered outside China that were not part of any Danone–Wahaha joint ventures but were using the Wahaha trademark to sell competitive products and the same sales staff as were working in the Danone–Wahaha joint ventures. At the end of 2006 Danone discovered this parallel network and consequently asked that those companies be integrated into the Danone–Wahaha network.

After six months of negotiations a formal agreement was reached according to which Danone would acquire 51 per cent of all parallel non-joint-venture companies but finally Zong rejected the terms of the agreement, arguing that it was a manoeuvre by Danone to acquire Wahaha at a low price. Kelly Zong, Mr Zong's daughter, who had a US green

MINI-CASE

card, registered Ever Maple Company in the USA for the sales of the non-joint-venture products. Danone threatened Zong with court action for not respecting the terms of the original agreement, particularly with the use of the Wahaha trademark transferred initially to the joint venture.

According to DANONE: 'The negotiations proposed by Danone did not make any progress. Under such conditions, Danone was forced to proceed with legal action'. (Danone's answer to Dickinson's article quoted in the reference below).

Wahaha said in a statement, 'We will respond actively to the lawsuits filed by Danone in Stockholm and the United States, and we plan to launch a countersuit demanding compensation of two billion, three billion or five billion Euros. We have conclusive evidence that Danone has broken the law. Wahaha is not against the opening-up policy of China, or cooperation with others, or cooperation with foreign investors. However, we want the cooperation to be equal, mutually beneficial, complementary, and mutually respectful with equal interest' (*China Daily*, 4 July 2007).

The trademark issue

The main legal issue was related to the ownership of the trademark. When the joint venture was formed, the trademark was Wahaha's contribution to the joint venture, and it agreed not to use the trademark for any independent business activity. However, this trademark transfer was rejected by China's Trademark Office on the ground that it belonged to the state, the original owner of the Wahaha Group.

The two partners then decided to get around the decision and to enter into an exclusive license agreement for the trademark to be used by the joint venture. They only registered with the Trademark Office an abbreviated license for fear that the full license would be denied. This was accepted by the Trademark Office, which never saw the full license. Technically the trademark was never legally transferred to the joint venture, just the exclusive license.

Dispute, arbitration and lawsuits

The dispute became public when press articles and web postings were implying that Danone was behaving like the foreign powers that invaded China in the nineteenth century. Zong said: 'Danone may damage the economic safety of China and monopolize the Chinese market'. Demonstrations from employees and suppliers took place in support of Zong. Wahaha complained that Danone was free to expand its operations in China by acquiring competitive companies like Robust but it did not allow Wahaha to do the same. It also claimed that the trademark could be used by non-joint-venture companies. As a result both parties resorted to arbitration and litigation.

In July 2008, the Swedish arbitration tribunal rejected Danone's claim that any goods produced by Wahaha must be sold through the venture.

On July 30 2008, The Hangzhou Intermediate People's Court decided to reject Danone's appeal. Thus, the ownership of the Wahaha trademark was denied to the joint venture. According to Chinese Law, this court ruling is the final decision and cannot be appealed.

MINI-CASE

After the last appeals in Stockholm failed, Danone announced at the end of 2009 that through an 'amicable' agreement with Mr Zong it would sell its 51 per cent share to the Wahaha Group. In 2010 Danone also announced that it would sell its stake in Hui yuan Juice in the water business. However, in 2011, Danone is still present in China in the water business, milk products, baby foods and medical nutrition. China represents 4 per cent of its global turnover, a lower proportion than in 2006.

Questions:

1) What type of joint venture is Danone–Wahaha?
2) What is your assessment on the way the deal was negotiated and implemented? What were Danone's mistakes?
3) What do you conclude from the outcome?

This mini-case is based on: a) Steven M. Dickinson, From China Economic Review (Steven M. Dickinson is a partner at the Shanghai office of Harris & Moure PLLC); b) *China Daily* "Danone's non-contract spirit may get it routed", August 10, 2000; c) Jianyong Lu *et al.*, "Danone v Wahaha (A): Who is Having the Last Laugh?, ARRC Case no. 308-244-1, 200; d) "Danone & Wahaha: A Bittersweet Partnership", IMD Case Studies, IMD-3-1949, 2008; e) Pierre Pichére, "Danone crée ses parts de Marché en Chine", Melchior website: http://www.melchior.fr; and f) Wahaha website: Companies News: Wahaha and Danone Gaming on Emotions, Reasoning and Laws', http://en.wahaha.com.cn/news/company/2008/08/22/wahaha962.html

In 2000 the exchange rates were 1$ = 8.2 Rmb and 1.08 €;in 2006 the rates were 1$ = 7.97 Rmb and 0.84 €

Summary and key points

1 An *alliance*:

- is the sharing of capabilities
- between two or several firms
- with the view of enhancing their competitive advantages and/or creating new business
- without losing their respective strategic autonomy.

2 A *strategic alliance*:

- affects the long-term competitiveness of partners and implies a long-term commitment from them.

3 Types of strategic alliance depend on the scope (global/local) and object (market access or capabilities-enhancing).

4 There are three broad types of global strategic alliance:

- *Coalition*
- *Co-specialization*
- *Learning alliance.*

5 There are four major steps for analysis of strategic alliances:

- Understanding the *strategic context* and spelling out the *strategic value* of an alliance
- Analysis of *partner(s)*
- *Negotiation* and *design*
- *Implementation.*

6 Global multilateral alliances:

- can potentially create constellations in which partners cooperate in one business segment but could possibly compete in another.
- There are three types of alliance constellations and each has their own managerial challenges:
  - *Alliance networks*
  - *Alliance portfolios*
  - *Alliance webs.*

7 Local joint ventures:

- are mainly used for market entry or resources access and driven by three forces:
  - Administrative requirement
  - Capabilities
  - Risk.
- Partner selection depends on a combination of legal requirements and internal capabilities the firm possesses.

  Partner categories:
    - Sleeping
    - Complementing
    - Investor
    - 'Teaching'
    - Acquisition

  Partner types:
    - Supplier
    - Customer/distributor
    - Competitor
    - Diversifier
    - Investor
    - Government
- Partner evaluation: uses the same criteria used in assessing alliance partners: strategic fit, capability fit, cultural fit and organizational fit.
- Failures/problems: there are five main reasons why joint ventures fail:
  - Absence of strategic vision
  - 'Believing without seeing'
  - Failure to understand local partner's strategic logic
  - Haste in negotiation
  - Insufficiently prepared staff or lack of organizational support.

8 The eight criteria for successful global alliances are:

- Individual excellence
- Importance
- Interdependence
- Investment
- Information

- Integration
- Institutionalization
- Integrity.

Learning assignments

1. The text distinguishes between alliances and coalitions, co-specialization and learning. To which category do you think the One World Alliance, in which American Airlines, British Airways and Cathay Pacific participate, belongs? What do such partners look for?
2. What are the sources of value creation in an alliance?
3. What are the criteria to be assessed in order to determine the strategic fit between partners?
4. What is an extractive agenda in an alliance?
5. What impact may cultural differences between partners have on global alliances?
6. What are the six domains that need to be negotiated in relation to the interface and governance of an alliance?
7. Compare joint venture decay with the 'death valley' spiral.
8. What would be the problems associated with selecting a partner in the same industry for a new entrant in a country? What would be the benefits?
9. What are the implications of linking up with a political partner?
10. What risks does a new entrant face when partnering with a distributor?
11. Do you see major differenecs between global strategic alliances and joint ventures for market entry?
12. What are the criteria for successful alliances?

Key words

- Alliance
- Capabilities fit
- Coalition alliance
- Constellations
- Co-specializations
- Cultural fit
- 'Death valley'
- Extractive agenda
- Joint ventures
- Joint venture for market entry
- Joint venture decay
- Learning alliances
- Options agenda
- Organizational fit
- Political partner
- Sharing agenda
- Strategic fit
- Venturing agenda

Web resources

<http://www.strategic-alliances.org/>
Association of Strategic Alliance Professionals.

<http://www.mckinseyquarterly.com/>
McKinsey Quarterly – see the section on alliances.

Visit the companion website at **http://www.palgrave.com/business/lasserre3e** for a multitude of weblinks and resources, self-test questions for revision and a searchable glossary.

Notes

1 Gomez-Casseres (1995), ch. 1.
2 Many publications report on the success of the Renault–Nissan Alliance. The Renault website provides a history and the principles of the alliance at <http://www.renault.com/en/groupe/l-alliance-renault-nissan/pages/l-alliance-renault-nissan.aspx>. See also Ghosn, Carlos (2002) pp. 37–44.
3 Doz and Hamel (1998), p.66.
4 Kogut (1991) pp. 19–33; Williamson (1999), pp. 117–26.
5 Akadar, Adil, Enst and Vaish (1997).
6 Geringer and Hebert (1989) pp. 235–54.
7 Bleeke and Ernst (1991), pp. 127–35.
8 Spekeman and Isabella (2000), ch. 8; Yoshino and Rangan (1995), ch. 8.
9 Krishna and Gee (1994).
10 See, for instance, Harrigan (1986) and also Dent (1999).
11 This section is largely based on Doz and Hamel (1998), ch. 7.
12 This section is largely based on Doz and Hamel (1998) ch. 8. See also Gomez-Casseres (1995).
13 Gomez-Casseres (1995), ch. 9.
14 Ariño, de la Torre and Smith Ring (2001), pp. 109–31.

References and further reading

Akadar, Adhwin, Asif Adil, David Ernst and Paresh Vaish, 'Emerging market alliances: Must they be win-lose?', *McKinsey Quarterly*, 4, (1997), pp.120–37.

Ariño, Africa, José de la Torre and Peter Smith Ring, 'Relational Quality: Managing Trust in Corporate Alliances', *California Management Review*, 44(1), 2001, pp. 109–31.

Bleeke, J.A. and David Ernst, 'The Way to Win in Cross Borders Alliances', *Harvard Business Review*, November–December 1991, pp. 127–35.

Cunningham, Mark, under the supervision of R. Angelmar and Yves L. Doz, 'Alza Ciba Geigy Advanced Drug Delivery Systems', INSEAD Case Study 2/94-4243, 1994.

Dent, Stephen M., *Partnering Intelligence: Creating Value for Your Business by Building Smart Alliances*. Palo Alto, CA: Davies-Black Publishing, 1999.

Doz, Yves L. and Gary Hamel, *Alliance Advantage*. Boston, MA: Harvard Business School Press, 1998.

Ernst, David and Tammy Halevy, 'When to Think Alliance', *McKinsey Quarterly*, 4, 2000, pp. 47–55.

Friedheim, Cyrus F., 'The Battle of the Alliances', *Management Review*, September 1999, pp. 46–51.

Geringer. J.M. and Louis Hebert, 'Control and Performance of International Joint Ventures', *Journal of International Business Studies*, Summer 1989, pp. 235–54.

Ghosn, Carlos, 'Saving the Business without Losing the Company', *Harvard Business Review*, January 2002, pp. 37–44.

Gomez-Casseres, Benjamin, *The Alliance Revolution: An Entrepreneurial Approach to Globalization*. Cambridge, MA: Harvard University Press, 1995.

Hamel, Gary, C.K. Prahalad and Yves L. Doz, 'Collaborate with Your Competitors, and Win', *Harvard Business Review*, January–February 1989, pp. 133–39.

Harrigan, Kathryn, *Managing for Joint Venture Success*. Lanham, MD: Lexington Books, 1986.

Inkpen, Andrew C., 'Learning and Knowledge Acquisition through Strategic Alliances', *The Academy of Management Executive*, November 1998, pp. 69–80.

Inkpen, Andrew and Jerry Ross, 'Why Do Some Strategic Alliances Persist Beyond Their Useful Life?', *California Management Review*, 44(1), 2001, pp. 132–54.

Kogut, Bruce, 'Joint Ventures and the Option to Expand and Acquire', *Management Science*, 137(1), 1991, pp. 19–33.

Krishna, L.N. and Francesca Gee, 'General Electric and SNECMA', INSEAD Case Study 04/94-3450, 1994.

Krishna, L.N. and Francesca Gee, 'General Electric and SNECMA', INSEAD Case Study 11/98-3450, 1998.

Lorenzoni, G. and C. Baden-Fuller, 'Creating a Strategic Center to Manage a Web of Alliances', *California Management Review*, 37(3), 1997, pp. 1–18.

Mauri, Alfredo, 'Influence of MNC Network Configuration Patterns on the Volatility of Firm Performance: An Empirical Investigation', *Management International Review*, 49(6), December 2009, pp. 691–707.

Moss Kanter, Rosabeth, 'Collaborative Advantage', *Harvard Business Review*, July–August 1994, pp. 96–108.

Reich, R.D. and E. Mankin, 'Joint Ventures with Japan Give Away Our Future', *Harvard Business Review*, March–April 1986, pp. 78–86.

Solberg, Carl Arthur and François Durrieu, 'Access to Networks and Commitment to Internationalisation as Precursors to Marketing Strategies in International Markets', *Management International Review*, 46(1), 2006, pp. 57–83.

Spekeman, Robert E. and Lynn A. Isabella, *Alliance Competence: Maximizing the Value of Your Partnerships*. New York: John Wiley, 2000.

Tolstoy, Daniel, 'Knowledge combination in networks: evidence from the international venturing of four small biotech firms', *International Entrepreneurship and Management Journal*, 6(2), June 2010, pp. 183–202.

Williamson, Peter, 'Strategy as Options for the Future', *Sloan Management Review*, Spring 1999, pp. 117–26.

Yoshino, M.Y. and U. Rangan, Strategic *Alliances: An Entrepreneurial Approach to Globalization*. Boston, MA: Harvard Business School Press, 1995.

chapter

5 GLOBAL MERGERS AND ACQUISITIONS

Introduction

This chapter focuses on the strategic and managerial issues involved with global mergers and acquisitions (M&As). Global M&As have grown at an accelerated pace since 1990. M&As are instruments used by companies to increase their global reach and competitiveness. Even in the Asia Pacific region, traditionally allergic to M&As, the financial crisis that struck the region in 1997 opened the door.

In this chapter we will look at the two phases of M&As: the *pre-acquisition* phase and the *post-acquisition* phase. The pre-acquisition phase deals with the decision-making process: how companies decide, give a value and negotiate the deal. The post-acquisition phase refers to the managerial processes involved in the integration of the merged companies. This phase is considered by consultants and academics to be the most important source of success or failure.

The critical elements of the pre-acquisition phase are to determine the *strategic and financial* value of the proposed merger or acquisition. The strategic value relates to the increased competitive advantage that firms gain in these deals: whether it increases their global market presence or improves their costs or quality. A merger or an acquisition is justified if, and only if, the value of the new merged or combined entity is bigger than the sum of the value of the independent entities prior to the merger. The financial value of the deal is calculated on the basis of a detailed evaluation of the *future cash flow*. The data needed to calculate cash flow and to identify potential future problems are collected through a due diligence process, and several valuation models are examined in the chapter.

The post-acquisition phase consists of two main sequential steps: *transition management* and *strategic consolidation,* leading to the integration of the merged companies. The transition phase is often critical since it sets the *emotional and organizational* context of the integration. It involves a series of actions aiming at establishing confidence and credibility and focusing people's attention on the achievement of practical results.

The consolidation phase aims at establishing an ongoing working relationship between the two entities. We shall discuss three integration modes related to the operational interdependencies required between the two companies in order to achieve synergies, and the organizational autonomy that the acquired company requires owing to differences in market and environmental conditions. The three modes examined are: preservation, absorption and symbiosis.

Learning objectives

At the end of this chapter you will be able to:

- identify the critical elements of value creation in an acquisition plan and implement integration
- understand the various phases of integration
- explain the different modes of integration.

The rationale for cross-border M&As

Cross-border M&As grew in prominence during the 1990s, mostly fueled by the globalization of markets and competition. The Internet bubble in the early 2000s and the subprime crisis in 2008 slowed down the trend (see Figure 5.1). In the oil and gas, telecommunication and pharmaceutical industries[1] there was the emergence of 'megamergers' (Table 5.1). Three particular events accelerated the movement: the Single European Market (SEM), followed by the advent of the Euro; the 1997 Asian crisis; and the use of the shareholder value model of corporate governance. The SEM and the euro created the economic conditions for consolidation of European companies, the Asian crisis gave an opportunity to Western corporations to buy Asian assets and finally the shareholder value model forced companies to de-diversify but also to concentrate on *core activities*. The example of Aventis illustrates this last point. Aventis was the result of the merger of the life-sciences activities of Rhône Poulenc Rorer (France and United States) and Hoechst (Germany). Before merging, Hoechst and Rhône Poulenc spun off their chemical businesses. The strategic rationale for M&As is not that different from those we described in Chapter 4 for global alliances.

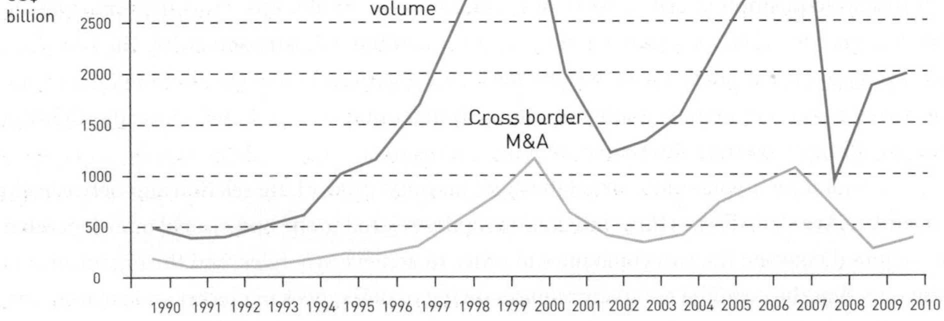

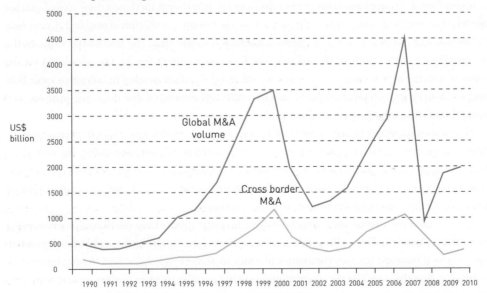

Figure 5.1 Trends in global mergers and acquisitions, 1990–2010 .

Sources: Thomson Financial and UNCTAD, World Investment Reports

There are three main value-creation objectives behind cross-border M&As:

- *Consolidation*: search for scale economies – BP/Amoco/Arco; Aventis
- *Global reach*: extension of international markets – Daimler Benz/Chrysler; Whirlpool/Philips; Vodaphone/Mannesman
- *Competencies acquisitions or options in related or new technologies* – Sony/Columbia; Vivendi/Universal Studios. This will include vertical integration and diversification.

Table 5.1 Cross-border megamergers above US$20 billion, 2008–2011

Acquirer	Target or merged company	Countries' acquirer/target	Industry	Price/deal completed value (US$ billion)
Sanovi Adventis	Genzyme	France/USA	Pharmaceutical	21
Vinipel	Weather Investor	Netherlands/Italy	Telecom	22
International Power	GDF Suez Energy	UK/Belgium	Gas	25
Roche	Genentech	Switzerland/USA	Pharmaceutical	46
InBev	Anheuser Busch	Belgium/USA	Beer	52

Source: Cross-border megamergers above US$20 billion, 2008–2011, Thomson One Banker, <http://banker.thomsonib.com>

Before engaging in a discussion about global M&As, we need to consider some case examples; some of them are relatively recent, some of them less so but with a better understanding of their internal mechanisms.

EXAMPLES

DaimlerChrysler

In May, 1998, Daimler Benz, the German manufacturer of Mercedes-Benz luxury cars, and Chrysler Corp., the American maker of minivans and Jeeps announced a US$36 billion 'merger of equals'. The two companies saw that by combining they would have a better chance of growing in each other's home markets as well as in Asia.The main expected synergy was a cost cutting of US$3 billion annually due to a reduction in purchasing costs of US$1.4 billion and the rest coming from a reduction in fixed costs, R and D rationalization, optimization of production capacities and sales networks.

A few months after the signing of the deal, it was evident the public view of DaimlerChrysler as a 'merger of equals' had begun to crack. Cultural differences between the Germans and the Americans have proven difficult to overcome: the Germans and Americans simply did business differently and the large gap in pay scales created an undercurrent of tension. Most US senior executives retired shortly after the merger and several highly regarded engineers and manufacturing executives defected. The stock price declined rapidly after the merger. In February 2001 the company announced 35,000 job cuts, plant closures and a new product strategy as part of an effort to reduce costs.

After a few year of turmoll the merger started to produce some positive results in 2003 but in 2007 Daimler decided to sell Chysler. The company was sold partially to Cerberus, an investment fund which managed it. The remainder of Chrysler was sold to Fiat which took the majority control in July 2011.

Air France KLM

In September 2003 Air France and KLM announced that they would merge in 2004 to create Air France KLM, the largest global airline in terms of revenue. In practice, Air France obtained management control of KLM but only 49 per cent of the voting rights. The two companies maintained their legal and commercial identity but a series of synergistic moves were rapidly implemented: joint catering contracts, common purchasing, common airport lounges, routes rationalization, joint frequent flyer program. The total cost saving over five years is estimated at 500 million Euros. Cultural differences did not create many issues since the two companies preserve the control over their own operations. Only a small number of areas are combined.

Lenovo and IBM

In December 2004 the Chinese PC manufacturer announced that it would buy the personal computer arm of IBM for $1.25 billion. The IBM PC business was losing money but was three times bigger in sales and global scope than Lenovo. IBM was present in 160 countries while Lenovo was essentially a Chinese player. While this deal made sense from a business point of view, there were concerns about potential cultural clashes. In fact, Lenovo appointed an American chief executive and replaced him within a year by another American, William Amelio, from Dell. Lenovo moved its corporate headquarters to the US and made English the official language of the company.

SONY/Columbia Studios[2]

In 1989, SONY put up $3.4 billion for the purchase of Columbia Pictures in the United States. Akio Morita, SONY's Chairman, spelled out the strategic logic of the deal when he declared that since SONY was the largest video hardware company, he wanted to have a video software company. The synergies were to be found in the complementarity of VCR manufacturing and film-making. Beside the political and somewhat anti-Japanese feelings that this deal generated, the integration of Columbia Studios into SONY's empire was plagued with many problems. SONY was confronted with big cultural clashes due not only to US–Japanese differences, but also and above all by the huge gap between running a hardware manufacturing company and a film studio. In 1994, SONY took a $2.7 billion write-off attributed to loss of goodwill in Columbia Studios. Although today Columbia is still part of SONY's empire, it took the company at least a decade and substantial cash outflows to digest this acquisition.

ArcelorMittal

Mittal Steel was founded in 1989 by Lakshmi Mittal out of the Indian steel business created by his father, Mohan Mittal. Legally registered in Rotterdam, Netherlands, the group grew very early in its history by acquisition in India and outside India. Most of the acquisitions have been with companies facing difficult times. In 2004 it was present in 18 countries in North America, Europe and Asia. Its turnover in 2004 was US$22 billion. Mittal acquisitions are shown in the following table:

Table 5.2 List of acquisitions made by Mittal Steel prior to 2006

1989	Iron Steel Company	Trinidad and Tobago
1997	Thyssen Duisburg	Germany
1998	Inland Steel	USA
1999	Unimetal	France
2001	Annaba	Algeria
2001	Sidex	Romania
2003	BH Steel	Bosnia
2003	Nova Hut	Czech Republic
2003	Balkan Steel	Macedonia
2004	PHS	Poland
2004	ISCOR	South Africa
2005	ISG	USA
2005	Hunan Valin	China
2005	Kryvorizhstal	Ukraine
2005	3 Stelco subsidiaries	Canada

Source: North West India Steel Heritage Project Website: <http://nwisteelheritagemuseum.org/arcelormittal-history.htm>

In 2006 Mittal launched a hostile takeover bid for 18.6 billion Euros on the second largest global steel maker Arcelor from France and the Benelux countries. Arcelor's shareholders resisted the bid and mobilized the French and Belgian political establishment to criticize the deal on nationalistic arguments. Arcelor management engineered a 'white knight' deal with a Russian company. Finally, after a lot of turmoil, Mittal improved its offer to 26.5 billion Euros and was proud to announce in June 2006: 'Creating the world's largest steel company, Mittal Steel and Arcelor reach an agreement to combine the two companies in a merger of equals'. This acquisition was a significant step for Mittal that until then had been focusing on buying relatively small, ailing firms. The main issue was to integrate an already global firm that was not in distress. An integration team was put in place with the objective to achieve the first integration phase within six months. Progress of 25 integration teams was monitored on a weekly basis. The work was divided on a 50–50 per cent basis and supervised by a 10- to 12-people 'integration office'. Synergies to be achieved were valued at 1.6 billion Euros and the objective was achieved by December 2008. In an interview one of the post-merger managers indicated: 'The key qualities of an integration office are to have a thorough understanding of the business, a cultural openness, the capacity to understand people and to see how they can fit together'.

The new company named ArcelorMittal continued expansion by acquisitions in steel and mining operations until the 2009 downturn.

In 2010 ArcelorMittal had revenue of 78 billion Euros, a net income of 2.9 billion Euros and a presence in 60 countries.

South African Brewery globalization by acquisitions

South African Brewery (SAB) was created in 1895. From the early days to the 1960s, the company stayed in its country of origin. In 1974 its first move to internationalize was to set up breweries in the neighbouring countries of Rhodesia, Bostwana, Angola and Lesotho. The development out of Africa was in 1993 with a major acquisition of Hungary's largest brewery. In 1994 SAB formed a joint venture with China Resource Enterprise in Dalian under the name of China Resource Snow Breweries. This joint venture has been the most successful foreign investment in the beer industry in China thanks to a series of acquisitions during the decade 2000–2010:

- 2001: Acquisition of Sichuan Blue Sword Brewery
- 2004: Acquisition of Lion Nathan
- 2009: Acquisition of breweries in Anhui, Lioning, Zhejiang, Shandong
- 2011: Acquisition of three breweries in Heilongjiang, Jiangsu and Henan.

SAB also expanded in the USA in 2002 with the acquisition of Miller and became the second largest brewer in the world, changing its name to SABMiller.

SABMiller expanded in Eastern Europe through acquistions in Poland, the Czech Republic, Italy, Romania, Russia and Slovakia as well as in the Netherlands. It has also acquired breweries in Latin America.

By 2011 SABMiller was operating in 60 countries.

Cross-border acquisitions performance

The six examples above show how difficult it is in the evaluation of M&As to disentangle what is due to international aspects and what is due to good or bad management practices. Several studies have tried to assess the value created by M&As; some have analyzed M&A deals and their results without differentiating between domestic acquisitions and international ones. Overall, those studies have shown that between 45–75 per cent of acquisitions failed to deliver the value that was expected by their initiators.[3] John Kitching,[4] looking at cross-border acquisitions in Europe, found that overall 25 per cent were straight failures and 25 per cent were not worth doing, giving a success score of 50 per cent, while a McKinsey team found a 57 per cent rate of success in their own study of cross-border M&As.[5] The conclusion that can be derived is that international M&As are no worse than domestic ones. One of the reasons for this is that most cross-border acquisitions are horizontal (i.e. in core business) and all the studies found that horizontal acquisitions tended to be more successful than others. The McKinsey studies found that in their sample cross-border acquisitions were essentially done in core businesses, while this was less the case in domestic ones. Since no research has tried to compare performances of horizontal international and horizontal domestic M&As, it is difficult to disentangle what the specific success/failure factors of international acquisitions are. The intuitive conclusion that can be drawn is that, on top of all other management factors, *cultural differences* can be a specific challenge in cross-border deals, as the SONY case demonstrates.

Academics and consultants who have analyzed M&As generally come to the same conclusions.[6] Success or failure comes from two key issues:

The quality of the *pre-acquisition process*: how companies make the M&A decision, give it a value and negotiate the deal

The quality of the *post-acquisition process*: how the integration is managed. This process is considered the most important source of success or failure.

In the remainder of this chapter we will concentrate on the process through which cross-border acquisitions are planned, decided (pre-acquisition) and implemented (post-acquisition), as illustrated in Figure 5.2.

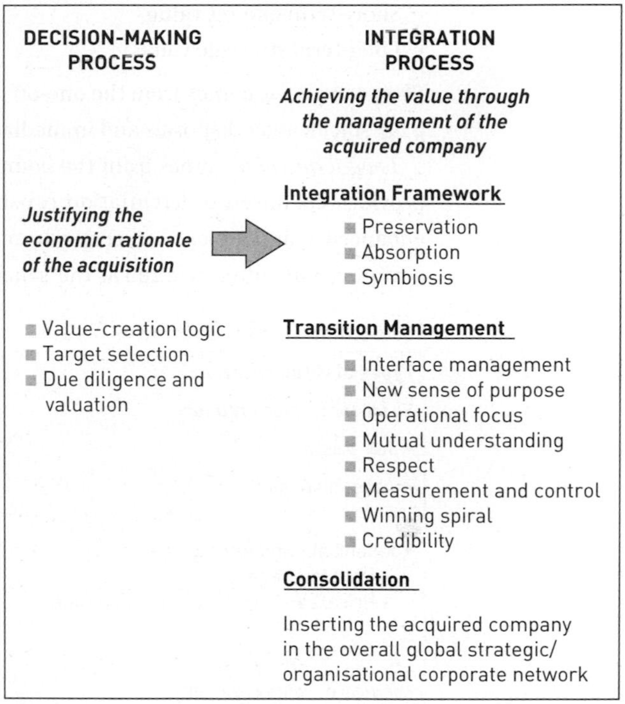

Figure 5.2 The pre-acquisition and post-acquisition processes in global M&As

Source: Author's own creation based on information from Haspeslagh and Jemison (1991).

Deciding on the M&A

Value creation

Theoretically M&As contribute to enhancing the economic value of the companies involved. The economics of M&As are simple: a merger or an acquisition is justified if, and only if, the value of the new merged or combined entity is bigger than the *sum of the value of the independent entities prior to the merger.*

From a strategic point of view, M&As can create the following types of value:

- *Consolidation* of companies operating in the same business area – horizontal M&A: ArcelorMittal belongs to this category
- *Global reach* – extension to international markets: SABMiller
- *Vertical integration* – merging of businesses which are suppliers or buyers of each other's products. For example, in the mid-1900s Toyo Ink, a Japanese printing ink company acquired Francolor, a French producer of organic pigments
- *Diversification* – companies operating in different business domains – the SONY/Columbia deal
- *Options* or the acquisition of a firm in a *new technology* or market to monitor its evolution: for instance the acquisition by the Swiss pharmaceutical group Ciba-Geigy in the early 1980s of the Californian company Alza in order to get access to advanced drug delivery systems technologies.

International M&As usually belong to the first or second type, but the rush toward the 'new economy' (see Chapter 14) has triggered the development of diversification and options M&As.

Whatever the type of M&A, value is created through two modalities:

- Short-term one-off value
- Long-term strategic value.

Short-term value comes from the one-off post-merger realization of cash benefits coming from a tax shield, asset disposals and immediate cost savings or debts leverage.

Long-term value comes from the competitive advantage gained from the merger: either it provides enhanced differentiation capabilities, a larger market, new growth opportunities, enhanced competencies or cost advantages through economies of scale or scope. These advantages are often referred as the 'synergistic' effects of a merger (see Table 5.3).

Table 5.3 Value creation in M&As

Types of value creation	Benefits
Short-term value creation	
• Tax shield	• Diminution of tax bill (cost benefits)
• Asset disposals	• Lower capital invested (higher return, lower cost):
• Financial engineering: – Debt leverage – Price/earnings (P/E) ratio leverage	• Lower cost of capital (assuming cost of debts lower than cost of equity) • Total market value increased after the merger (assuming a P/E differential between buyer and seller and a positive market reaction)
Long-term value creation	
• Pooling and sharing resources and assets – Joint purchasing – Manufacturing rationalization – Joint distribution and logistics – Common IT and central services – Common treasury	Economies of scale and scope (cost benefits)
• Enlarged market – Geography – Products	• Growth potential enhanced • Richer value proposition (higher reach and possibly higher differentiation) • Higher differentiation
• Transfer of competencies – Technology – Best practices	• Processes more effective • Innovation (higher differentiation and lower costs)

Due diligence and valuation

Due diligence and **valuation** are among the main handicaps to global acquisitions, particularly in emerging markets. There are three main reasons for this. First, marketing and strategic information are often less accurate and reliable, or at least less accessible, than in the home country of the buyer. Second, political or nationalistic attitudes may hamper fair assessment. Third, accounting standards are not necessarily in line with international standards. In Korea, for instance, *chaebols* ('conglomerates') do not usually consolidate their accounts, and do not eliminate inter-company transactions within the same group: this can lead to inflated revenues. In South East Asia accounting ledgers are kept for tax purposes and the figures have very little relevance for asset valuation. Major adjustments have to be made:

- *Inventories* may be overvalued
- *Employees' retirement benefits* may not appear or may be underfunded and provisions have to be made for future liabilities
- In certain cases *accruals* are ignored and have to be restated
- *Real estate* has to be valued at market prices, and necessary tax adjustments have to be made
- *Hidden liabilities* such as legal actions may be uncovered.

These adjustments are the most frequent. In the event of the acquisition of a company that is part of a conglomerate, adjustments for any cross-subsidiary transfers which may have distorted announced profitability may have to be made, and checks made as to whether any licenses, distributors or contractual arrangements are still in place after the acquisition. If such contractual assets had originally been granted to the mother company, adequate transfers have to be included in the acquisition agreement. More time and effort is required to validate data than normal: detailed interviews with customers, suppliers and bankers all have to be part of due diligence.

Economic **valuation** is necessary in order for a potential buyer to decide at what price it is willing to conclude the deal – or, in the case of a merger, the relative proportions of shares to be exchanged.

Three main methods are used for such valuations:[7]

Asset-based valuation

This method determines the *actual value of assets minus liabilities*, using a replacement price for physical assets and adjusting for inventories or debtors' book value. Intangible assets and goodwill are estimated using comparable value for similar businesses or using formulas such as dollars per customer. If the company's assets are predominantly physical, this approach may give a fair estimation of its value. When, on the other hand, the company's profitability relies on intangible resources and capabilities such as employees' commitment, knowledge and competencies, this method fails to give a good economic price.

Market-based valuation

This approach relies on *direct market valuation* if the company is listed on a stock exchange or otherwise on market equivalent valuation. When using stock exchange market value, the transaction will require that the bidder puts a premium on the deal. Premiums are based on an anticipation of value added from the merger, either short- or long-term through *synergies*. Research has found that premiums 30–100 per cent over market value are not unusual in cross-border acquisitions.[8] In order to calculate how much premium the company is ready to accept, you are forced to turn to a cash-flow method of valuation since the future profit coming from the merger will accrue over the years and no other method is available to calculate a premium. Stock market prices may not always reflect the economic reality of a firm in countries where stock exchanges are not efficient owing to lack of liquidity, partial listing, lack of proper regulations or insider trading.

When the target company is not listed on the stock market, you can use market equivalent measurements such as P/E ratio, price/cash-flow ratio or price/revenues ratio calculated from similar deals or comparable companies listed on the stock exchange. Such a measurement is crude, and should be used only as a reference since no deal and no company, even in the same industry, is exactly the same. In addition, particular deals may have been done on the basis of unsound calculations and there is no reason to replicate them.

Cash-flow-based valuation

Economic theory would say that this is the only valid method, apart from the actual market price put on the stock market when the market is efficient.[9]

With this method, the value of a firm's equity is equal to the *net present value of future cash flows discounted with the weighted average cost of capital (WACC) minus debts.* In practice, this method implies:

- A calculation of *future cash flows*: revenues – cash costs – increase in required working capital – future investments – taxes
- A determination of the WACC, taking into account the risks of the deal; the WACC is the weighted average of the cost of equity and cost of debts.

In order to calculate future cash flows, it is necessary to forecast revenues based on demand, price and market share assumptions as well as costs over a period that reflects a sound strategic horizon. As mentioned earlier, this can represent a big challenge in cross-border acquisitions in emerging countries or emerging industries where forecasting is more a matter of guesswork than hard computation. Another issue that can arise is the estimation of the WACC: WACC could be risk adjusted to take into consideration different risk profiles in different countries.[10] Another method is to adjust the cash flows for potential risks (see Chapter 13 for more details).

Two kinds of future cash flows need to be valued in M&As:

- *The future cash flow* of the merging or of the acquired company calculated as if the company continued its activities without the merger. This is the **stand-alone value**. Normally, if the company is listed on the stock market its market capitalization should reflect its stand-alone value, otherwise forecasting and discounting are needed.
- The *future value of the added value* brought in short-term and long-term by the merger of the two companies (see Table 5.3). This is the **synergies value**.

These two streams of cash flow give a present value that reflects the **bargaining range** of the price negotiation. Below the stand-alone value no seller would sell (unless as a finesale or because of extreme non-economic pressure) since she/he could achieve this value without being acquired. Above the stand-alone plus synergies value, the buyer company should not buy since, if the calculation is correct, it transfers the value to the seller and does not get anything for itself (Figure 5.3).

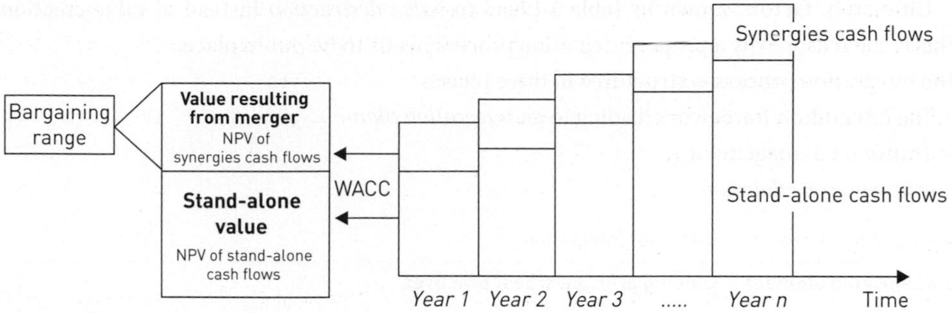

Figure 5.3 Cash-flow-based valuation for M&As

Integrating the companies: the integration phase

The *integration* phase starts once deals have been negotiated and the acquisition or the merger decided. All researchers consider this phase of M&A as the most important, and the major source of failure when not handled properly. Table 5.4 summarizes the main sources of failures and their effects.

Table 5.4 Failures in the integration process

Source of failure in integration process	Effects
Lack of strategic direction	Actions and decisions not understood Resistance to change Uncoordinated decisions
Lack of integration plan	Improvisation Time lost Anxiety not reduced Slow response to events
Leadership vacuum	Anxiety not reduced Bureaucratic hassles Political fights
Determinism (stubborn implementation of the integration plan)	Trying to impose 'pre-fabricated' solutions Arrogant behavior from acquirers' employees Discouragement of front-line staff
Lack of communication	Anxiety not reduced Fears and rumors
Cultural mishandling	Stereotyped clashes, 'them and us' syndrome Politicking Retreat
Lack of operational focus	Too much talk, no action Lack of concrete results No 'quick wins'
Loss of key management talent	Less productive work force Negative signaling to internal and external stakeholders
Wrong synergies	Loss of efficiency Dysfunctional operations
Waste of financial resources, lack of buy-in	No motivation, passivity Politicking

Sources: Haspeslagh and Jemison (1991); Mitchell and Holmes (1996); Viscio *et al.* (1999); Habeck, Kröger and Träm (2000).

Ultimately, factors shown in Table 5.4 lead to *value destruction* instead of value creation. This is the reason why a proper integration process needs to be put in place.

The integration process is structured in three phases:

- The integration framework leading to an *integration plan*
- *Transition* management
- Strategic *consolidation*.

Table 5.5 An example of a linear framework for integration

Post-merger integration element	Guiding principles/best practices
Vision	• Agree on strategic intent and let it guide vision for merger integration • Work to get both sides of the deal to buy into vision and intent • Explicitly identify critical sources of expected value
Architecture for change	• Begin planning early and create detailed plans • Set the right pace; work with a sense of urgency • First attack opportunities that combine the lowest risk with the highest reward
Architecture for the new company	• Focus on relentless identification of sources of value (revenues, cost, etc.) • Incorporate strengths of both companies • Restructure the organization to maximize value • Handle personnel issues swiftly
Leadership	• Choose new leadership quickly • Pick the right people and dedicated resources for the integration process • Show fairness and objectivity by using data to make decisions and by including people from both companies in the decision-making process • Set credible milestones and maintain pressure for progress by providing incentives to reach targets • Keep focus of the integration team on economic value creation • Address cultural issues directly with an explicit plan • Communicate clearly, early, honestly and often; use a decisive tone; do not forget those outside the two companies

Source: Booz Allen in Viscio *et al.* (1999).

Integration framework

An integration *framework* is needed as road map for implementing a merger. Since the post-merger phase is a period of intense anxiety and uncertainty for the employees, suppliers and distributors of the companies involved, it is important that a framework guides the management of the process. Various frameworks have been offered by academics and consultants and they belong to two broad categories:

- *Linear frameworks* that are step-by-step or checklist approaches to integration that apply to all M&As. Table 5.5 illustrates one such framework.
- *Contingent frameworks* that differentiate integration processes according to environmental

and strategic factors. This type of framework does not assume a unique approach to integration. We present here the contingent framework developed by Philippe Haspeslagh and William Jemison (1991).

In their contingent framework, Haspeslagh and Jemison identified three modes of integration, depending on:

- The degree of *required operational interdependencies* between the two companies that are needed to achieve synergies. For instance, the rationalization of manufacturing or the transfer of competencies between companies.
- The degree of *required organizational autonomy* that the acquired company would need because of the difference in market and environment conditions with the acquirer; for instance, an acquisition in a different business or country.

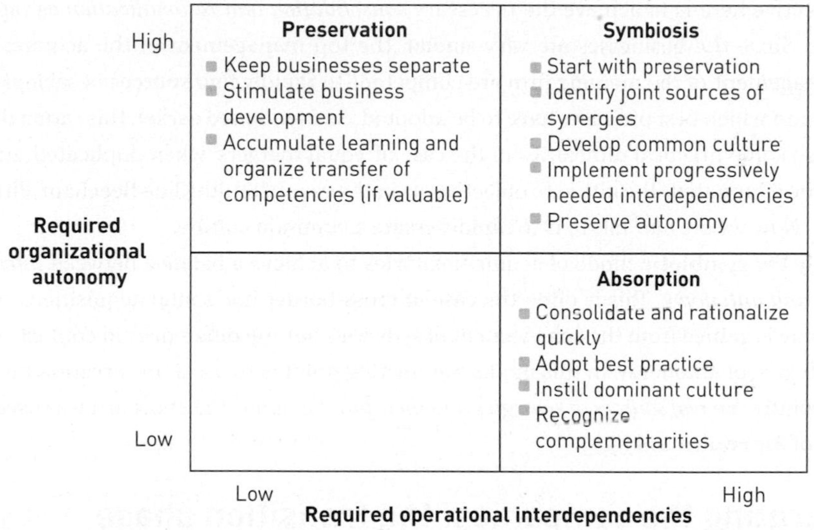

Figure 5.4 Contingent integration modes
Source: Adapted from Haspeslagh and Jemison (1991).

The three integration modes that Haspeslagh and Jemison identified are (see Figure 5.4):

- The *preservation* mode of integration
- The *absorption* mode of integration
- The *symbiotic* mode of integration.

The **preservation** mode fits with situations in which very few operational synergies can be gained and the business context calls for a large autonomy of decision-making, as in the case of diversification or option acquisitions. Since no benefits for interdependencies are to be expected and no major value can be brought in by forcing integration of processes, assets and decision-making, the key objective is first to 'preserve' the identity and autonomy of the acquired company, keeping in place, as far as possible, the existing management and learning progressively the 'rules of the game' of the business. The source of value here essentially comes from an *enlargement of markets* and products as well from the *transfer of resources or new competencies*. In this mode, you should not try to expedite the transfer of new competencies until you have understood their logic and their impact on the organization and culture of the recipient company. Transfer of resources comes essentially from the injection of capital or stimulation of business development by giving access to logistical, IT or distribution facilities to the acquired company. Transfer of people has to be done more for learning than for controlling purposes in such cases. The danger of this mode of integration is that of being confronted by a 'weak' management team in the acquired company that behaves opportunistically in siphoning off the resources of the acquirer. This was the case in the mid-1980s when the UK Midland Bank acquired a Californian financial company.[11]

The **absorption** mode of acquisitions takes place when value is to be expected from the realization of operational synergies in companies operating in similar business contexts. The objective here is to achieve the necessary *consolidation and rationalization* as rapidly as possible. Since the businesses are very similar, the top management of the acquirer or the top management of the merging firm are competent to rapidly find sources of savings and to understand which best practices have to be adopted. As mentioned earlier, this rationalization may raise some practical difficulties in the case of 'equal mergers' when duplicated functions have to be eliminated. The ultimate objective, as in the case of SmithKline Beecham, illustrates that the 'Now we are one' motto is to rapidly create a common culture.

Finally the **symbiotic** mode of acquisitions tries to achieve a balance between *interdependencies and autonomy*. This is often the case in cross-border horizontal acquisitions where a lot of value is gained from the achievement of synergies but the differences in contexts require a high degree of autonomy. In this mode, the starting point is to use a preservation mode and to find jointly the *real sources of synergies and their practicalities*. The approach was used in the merger of Air France and KLM.

Integrating the companies: the transition phase

Whatever the mode of integration is, there is a critical phase in any merger and acquisition, the *transition* phase. Just after a merger or an acquisition, the various stakeholders of the acquired or the merged firms are in a state of shock, or at least of anxiety, and the operations may suffer from the uncertainties surrounding the pre-acquisition phase. In Asia Pacific, for instance, during the late 1990s, Western firms made a lot of acquisitions of financially strapped companies: the situation required a fast turnaround. The transition period is the one during which the acquirer or the merging partners establish their *credibility* and demonstrate their ability to *manage the new concern*.

Eight main issues need to be solved at this stage:

- The appointment of an executive team capable of *leading the integration process* and managing the interface between the two companies
- The expression of a new *sense of purpose*, demonstrating to stakeholders that the acquisition or the merger was well planned

- The focus on *concrete operational results* that motivate employees and distract them from sterile rumors
- The development of a *mutual understanding*, bridging or palliating the cultural gap
- The showing of *respect for the acquired company personnel*, avoiding arrogant behaviour and preventing the 'brain drain' of valuable employees
- The installation of *measurement tools* to measure and control progress
- The creation of a *'winning spiral'* that reinforces a sense of success and achievement
- The demonstration of *credibility* that reassures stakeholders and reduces anxiety.

Appointment of an executive team and interface management

In the case of a merger, the critical issue is to install a management team that is capable of understanding the cultures of the two parties and *transforming* them *into a new culture*. Most of the time this change will be demonstrated by a new logo that may or may not combine the two names of the founding companies: Aventis in the case of Rhône Poulenc-Hoechst, or SmithKlineBeecham. People problems (who is in charge?) need to be sorted out before the beginning of the transition phase, at least for the key roles, to avoid confusion. The projected merger between SKB and Glaxo Wellcome could not be carried through because of disagreements over the designation of the CEO of the new entity. This problem did not arise when SmithKline and Beecham merged.

In acquisitions, the critical issue is to trade off the need to *control* and the need to *preserve the key contacts and knowledge* of the previous management team. There is also the need to make sure that the appointed management team will be an efficient interface between the acquired company and the foreign acquirer. The best way to achieve an efficient interface is to appoint, as managing director, an executive or a team of executives having the capabilities to understand the cultures of both the seller and the buyer organization, and to serve as a bridge between the newly acquired entity and the new owners.

New sense of purpose

Anxiety and resistance reduction can best be achieved if new management communicates credible goals, demonstrating to stakeholders that the merger or the acquisition was well planned, thus reassuring them of a determination to lead the company to success. *Systematic and structured communication campaigns* need to be organized. Through meetings with managers and employees, publications or social events, the new management can disseminate the main messages: what are the objectives, what main direction is the company going to take?

Operational focus

Focusing the attention on *concrete operational details* and *performance targets* has two major advantages. First, it is likely to erase the uncertainty created by the takeover by demonstrating that the company is back in business. As in the case of alliances discussed in Chapter 4, one of the most powerful methods is to create *integration teams*. Task forces are appointed made up of personnel from the acquirer and acquired companies for each of the key operational activities (accounting, purchasing, quality, etc.); the working party is asked to discuss and propose concrete solutions to operational aspects: what kind of software to use for inventory controls, what method to adopt in order to recover ongoing receivables, how to deal with distributors, what the possibilities are of cost reduction in logistics, etc. The advantage of such an approach is that it gives people a tangible sense of participation in the integration process. It also helps to develop mutual understanding among the employees of both the buyer and seller organizations.

Such teams can also rapidly correct any intrinsic weaknesses of the acquired organization. Rapid turnaround is vital, and this is a means of establishing confidence and of demonstrating the visible benefits of the acquisition. Effectiveness is more important than optimized efficiency: a quick minor gain is more important at this stage than a slow major one. This is the reason why the use of integration teams to put in place practical solutions to practical problems is so useful. The involvement of technical and administrative or commercial middle management is critical here, because their technical expertise, if properly combined, can bring quick results.

Mutual understanding and respect

Cross-cultural issues are likely to arise, and especially in cross-border mergers. The ability of the two entities to understand each other is critical for the success of any integration. The objective at the transition phase is not so much to merge the two cultures as to create a climate of *mutual understanding*. The kind of culture that will surface from the merger is contingent upon the mode of acquisition. A preservation mode will not attempt to blend the two cultures but on the contrary will keep them separate, while absorption would seek to create a common culture.[12] Mutual understanding is enhanced when the acquiring company staff and executives show respect for the employees of the acquired company and adopt an attitude sensitive to cultural differences and avoid behaving like the 'conquerors' of a besieged city. The risks are high if the acquirers come and impose their viewpoints, their methodologies and work processes, as if the merged company's practices were not worth considering. Acquirers should instill a climate of mutual understanding by studying carefully the existing practices of the acquired company, and seeking opinions from the employees before introducing change.

Measurement and control

Talking with facts and figures helps communication, allows a measure of improvement and reduces the risk of 'cultural excuses'. The cultural excuses are used in the event of difficulties or disagreements, and are based on impressionistic or stereotypical judgements. The collection of marketing, operational and financial hard facts and figures is a necessary condition for an efficient and productive dialogue. In the case of the merger between SmithKline and Beecham, a specific methodology was introduced in the integration team to guide the process and to measure its progress.

Winning spiral

The search for tangible immediate performance improvement should also be on the agenda of the transition-period management. 'Quick wins' usually derive from the joint efforts of the integration teams, as illustrated in the case of Renault–Nissan (see chapter 4). Rapid performance improvements in quality, costs and market success give people a sense of achievement and enhance their confidence in the whole acquisition process.

Credibility

Confidence is not likely to be established if the various stakeholders do not perceive that what the new owners say, and do, is credible. Credibility relies essentially on the *quality of the people* who are put in place to run the company, and the perception of their real power within the mother organization. It is essential that managers appointed to run the acquired company work closely with the back-up of central headquarters to make sure that the acquisition is well supported by the center, and that sufficient resources are devoted to making it work.

Integrating the companies: the consolidation phase

The consolidation phase is the one that sees the final integration of the two companies and the definition of the respective strategic roles of the *merged company*. In the case of a merger, it consists in creating and finalizing a new organizational structure in which the ex-merging firms dissolve themselves into the new design. SmithKline and Beecham, with the program of a 'Simply Better' way and a strategic definition of the vision of the new company under the umbrella of 'global healthcare', achieved this phase after one year.

In the case of a cross-border acquisition, the consolidation phase consists of providing the acquired company with a *strategic identity* and making sure that it has a specific role in the overall regional or global strategy of the acquirer. Employees, governments and the local community may see the acquisition generally as a foreign intrusion, reminiscent of the old colonial days. During the transition phase described earlier, the purpose was to give confidence to the various stakeholders about the will and capabilities of the acquirer to contribute to the development of the firm. At the consolidation phase, there is a need to confirm that the acquisition is not only a trading of assets or a good bargain, but also a real *strategic move* in which the acquired firm has a role to play. This gives employees a sense of direction and self-esteem. The acquired firm's employees must not feel that they are pawns, but strategic partners, that they are part of a strategic vision and that their contribution is essential in achieving it. One of the best methods is to give the firm some responsibilities in leading strategic initiatives in terms of business or product developments. In the case of Lenovo's acquisition of the computer arm of IBM, IBM was given the strategic leadership for the global development of PCs.

The second challenging task is to be able to make the acquired company part of the family by plugging it into the existing network of *knowledge* and *competencies*. This is achieved through secondment of personnel to other subsidiaries, participation in conferences and seminars, and by teamwork in various operational areas where transfer of competencies can produce value-added results. Control has to be exercised without stifling entrepreneurial benefits. The ideal situation is to rely on most of the existing senior and middle-management talent already existing in the acquired company and to support it with adequate training and reward. An important consideration is the practice of 'fair process' that gains the loyalty and commitment of managers.[13] Fair process is a management practice based on combining those integration principles advantageous to achieving both efficiency and local entrepreneurship. This has also the tremendous benefit of buying in the loyalty of the employees, and the goodwill of governments and local communities. In this way the acquirer is neither an intruder nor an invader, but an *insider*.

MINI-CASE

The Acquisition of Harbin Brewery

On May 2004 Anheuser-Busch, the giant US beer company, announced that it controlled 36 per cent of Harbin Brewery, the fourth largest Chinese brewer, after the purchase of 6 per cent of shares from a US Fund. Harbin Brewery being listed on the Hong Kong Stock Exchange, Anheuser Brewery would have to bid for the remaining shares. The price paid at US$0.72/share put a total value of US$720 million for the entire company. This acquisition marked the end of a bidding war between the US giant and SABMiller, the South African brewer.

The China Beer Market in 2003

With a consumption of 24.3 billion liters of beer, China became the largest beer market by volume in the world, overtaking the US. While the consumption per capita is still modest (12 L/cap) compared to 38 L/Cap in Korea, 51L/Cap in Japan, 90L/Cap in the US and 100L/cap in the UK. With an average growth rate of 6 per cent a year the market is expected to reach 40 billion liters by 2012. Still with 400 producers and 700 local brands, the industry is fragmented but is consolidating rapidly through mergers and acquisitions. Tsingtao, the leading brand, acquired more than 40 local brewers from 1997 to 2004, followed by SABMiller. The competitive rivalry is intense due to several factors: first, the fragmentation of the market and the entry of many foreigners attracted by the growth and volume of the market. Second, the lack of national brand recognition and the low purchasing power of the masses of Chinese consumers who prefer cheap local brands – most foreigners have lost money in the China market. Fosters from Australia sold all breweries that it had in China. However strong players are emerging: some are local such as Tsingtao, Yanjing or Harbin, and some are multinational such as SABMiller, Interbrew and Anheuser-Busch.

The market share distribution in China in 2003 was:

Tsingtao	12%
CRE (SAB)	9.5%
Yanjing	8.5%
Harbin Brewery	4%

MINI-CASE

Anheuser-Busch in China

The Anheuser-Busch entry into China was in 1993 through a 5 per cent participation in the capital of Tsingtao brewery, the internationally renowned Chinese brewer based on the east coast and, later in February 1995, through a $140 million acquisition of an 80 per cent stake in Zhongde Brewery, a large brewery in Wuhan, in Hubei province, eastern China. The company produced its global brand "Budweiser" in Wuhan and engaged a massive advertising campaign to build the name as a premium brand all over China. The results were not as expected due to the fragmented nature of the market, the severe competitive rivalry in the crowded premium segments and the difficult logistical problems in transportation, warehousing and distribution. The market share of Anheuser-Busch in China in 2003 was around 1 per cent.

Harbin Brewery

Listed on the Hong Kong Stock Exchange, Harbin Brewery was in 2004 the fourth largest brewer in China with a market share of 4 per cent It was implanted primarily in the north-eastern part of China where beer consumption per capita was 36 liters, twice the national average. In its home city, Harbin, it held 76 per cent of the market and 43 per cent in the Heilongjiang province. After its listing in 2002, 41 per cent of its shares were in the hands of the public, the remaining part being shared by Harbin municipality (29.1 per cent) and an Irish Investment Fund (29.4 per cent). For Anheuser-Busch an acquisition of Harbin would give an opportunity to gain scale and geographical expansion in a high consuming region. The main financial indicators in Hong Kong dollars (HKD) millions for Harbin were the following:

	2002	2003	2004
Net assets	1600	1900	2050
Long-term liabilities	800	850	860
Shareholder's equity	800	1050	1190
Free cash flow	16	-4	106
Number of shares (million)			1000
Share price (April 2004)			3.20 HKD
Exchange rate 1US$			7.80

SABMiller

SAB, a South African company became the third largest global brewer after its acquisition of Miller in the USA. SAB, through a minority joint venture with China Resource Enterprise, developed a very successful China strategy based on an initial concentration in the north-eastern province of Liaoning (Dalian and Shenyang), the use of local brand names and a positioning of 'quality beer at an affordable price' contrasting with the premium brand strategy adopted by other foreigners. SAB was the only foreign company making a profit

MINI-CASE

in the Chinese beer market and its strategy was to expand nationally through acquisitions. Harbin Brewery would be a natural extension of SAB's strong presence in the north-eastern part of China.

The battle for Harbin

The battle started when in June 2003 the Irish fund sold its 29.4 per cent share to SABMiller for US$86.77 million. All observers thought that SABMiller was going to complete its move and acquire the remaining 29 per cent. But in March Harbin municipal government sold its 29.1 per cent share to a Hong Kong Fund. Two months later the 29.1 per cent share was sold to Anheuser-Busch for US$139 million. That left the two prospective buyers each with 29 per cent, a non-controlling position. Then a bidding war started. On May 24 SABMiller made an offer of HKD4.30 (US$0.48) a share for the remaining part, putting the total value of Harbin at US$475 million. One week later Anheuser-Busch proposed HKD5.58 (US$0.72), putting the total value at US$720 million. SABMiller retreated from the bid. (See below for financial information on Anheuser-Busch)

2004	US$ million
Net sales	14,900
Net income	2240
Free cash flow	1850
Debt equity ratio	3.1
Capital expenditures	1089

Source: Anheuser-Busch Annual Report 2004

Questions:

1) What is the value of Harbin Brewery?
2) How do you compare the value with the price paid by Anheuser-Busch?
3) Why was Anheuser-Busch willing to pay the proposed price?
4) What issues do you anticipate during the post-acquisition phase?

Source: Financial data reconstituted from Zhigang Tao (2004)

Summary and key points

1 Cross-border M&As:

- Are motivated by three factors:
  - *Consolidation* (achieving economies of scale)
  - *Global reach* and competencies acquisition
  - Options in *technologies*
- Value creation is short-term and long-term:
  - *Short-term*

    - Tax shield benefits
    - Asset disposals
    - Financial engineering
  - *Long-term*
    - Pooling and sharing resources and assets
    - Enlarged markets (in terms of geography or products)
    - Transfer of competencies (including technologies and best practices)
- Types of economic valuations for mergers and acquisitions include:
  - *Asset-based valuation:* uses replacement price
  - *Market-based valuation:* uses direct market information
  - *Cash flow-based valuation:* discounted cash flows method
- In the cash flow analysis:
  - *Stand-alone* value: is the future cash flow of the merged or acquired firm if the company continued its activities without the merger
  - *Synergies value:* is the future value of the added value brought in short-term and long-term by the merger of the two companies
  - *Premium:* the premium amount is less than or equal to the synergies value
- The success of an M&A depends on the quality of:
  - *Pre-acquisition* processes
  - *Post-acquisition* processes.

2 The pre-acquisition process consists of three steps:

- Determination of *value creation*
- *Target* selection
- *Due diligence* and *valuation*:
  - Due diligence and valuation are difficult in international M&As, particularly in emerging markets, owing to the problem of institutional context
  - For global acquisitions in emerging markets, due diligence and valuation are more difficult:
    - Emerging markets are fraught with unreliable marketing and strategic information
    - Local accounting standards may not be compatible with international standards
    - Political/nationalistic attitudes may hamper unbiased assessment.
- There are three phases in the integration process:
  - The *integration framework* leading to an integration plan
  - The *transition management*
  - The *strategic consolidation.*

3 The post-acquisition process (i.e. the integration phase) can have the following sources of failure:

- Leadership vacuum
- Determinism (stubborn implementation of integration plan)
- Cultural mishandling
- Loss of key management talent
- Wrong synergies

- Lack of:
  - Strategic direction
  - Integration plan
  - Communication
  - Operational focus
  - Buy-in
- There are three phases in the integration process:
  - The *integration framework* leading to an integration plan
  - The *transition management*
  - The *strategic consolidation.*

4 The three modes of integration within the contingent framework are:

- *Preservation* mode
  - Used when there is high need for organizational autonomy but low need for operational interdependencies
  - The integration process involves keeping the businesses separate, stimulating business development and accumulating learning.
- *Absorption* mode
  - Used when there is a low need for organizational autonomy but a high need for operational interdependencies
  - The integration process involves consolidating and rationalizing quickly, recognizing complementarities, adopting best practices and instilling a dominant culture.
- *Symbiotic* mode
  - Used when there is high need for organizational autonomy but low need for operational interdependencies
  - The integration process commences with a preservation mode but subsequently develops a common culture and implements progressively the necessary interdependencies while preserving autonomy.

5 Transition management is concerned with seven issues:

- Appointment of an executive team and interface management
- Instilling a new sense of purpose
- Focusing on concrete operational results
- Development of mutual understanding and respect
- Introduction of measurement tools to measure and control progress
- Creation of a winning spiral
- Demonstration of credibility.

6 The strategic consolidation process:

- For *mergers*: Involves creating and finalizing a new organizational structure
- For *acquisitions*: Is concerned with providing the acquired company with a strategic identity and ensuring that it has a specific role in the overall regional or global strategy of the acquirer
  - A practice of 'fair process' is important in order to gain loyalty and commitment of managers of the acquired company.

Learning assignments

1 The chapter describes six examples of cross-border mergers: can you identify the source of value creation in each case?
2 What are the problems in conducting due diligence in a global context?
3 What determines the bargaining range of a negotiation?
4 What are the critical issues in the post-acquisition transition phase?
5 In what circumstances is the symbiotic mode of integration appropriate?
6 What are the most frequent sources of failure in M&As?

Key words

- Absorption mode of integration
- Due diligence
- 'Fair process'
- Integration process
- Interface management
- Post-acquisition process
- Pre-acquisition process
- Preservation mode of integration
- Stand-alone value
- Symbiotic mode of integration
- Synergies value
- Valuation

Web resources

<http://banker.thomsonib.com/>
Provides statistics on M&As.

<http://www.bain.com/publications/capability-insights/mergers-and-acquisitions.aspx>
Bain & Company.

<http://www.bcg.com/expertise_impact/publications/default.aspx>
BCG Consulting.

Visit the companion website at **http://www.palgrave.com/business/lasserre3e** for a multitude of weblinks and resources, self-test questions for revision and a searchable glossary.

Notes

1 Purshe (1996) pp. 110–19; Ernst and Steinhubl (1999) pp. 49–57.
2 Khou and Spar (1994).
3 A series of studies by consulting firms Mercer, McKinsey and Bain & Co. show a rate of unsuccessful acquisitions ranging from 50 per cent to 75 per cent. These aggregate figures do not differentiate between domestic and international acquisitions.
4 Kitching (1973).

5 Bleeke *et al.* (1990) pp. 46–55.

6 The following literature covers both domestic and cross-border acquisition processes: Haspeslagh and Jemison (1991); Von Krogh, Sinatra and Singh (1994); Mitchell and Holmes (1996); Habeck, Kröger and Träm (2000).

7 Eccles, Lanes and Wilson (1999) pp. 136–46; Hawawini and Viallet (1999) ch. 12.

8 Eccles, Lanes and Wilson (1999).

9 Financial theory would argue that markets implicitly use the cash-flow method by discounting the flow of future dividends to determine a price: this is the efficient markets theory.

10 Lessard (1996).

11 Davidson and de la Torre (1989) pp. 296–318.

12 Smith (2000) pp. 45–50.

13 Chan and Mauborgne (1997) pp. 65–75.

References and further reading

Books and articles

Ashkenas, Ronald, Lawrence DeMonaco and Suzanne C. Francis, 'Making the Deal Real: How GE Capital Integrates Acquisitions', *Harvard Business Review*, January–February 1998, pp. 165–78.

Bleeke, Joel, James Isono, David Ernst and Douglas Weinberg, 'Succeeding at Cross-Border M&A', *McKinsey Quarterly*, 3, 1990, pp. 46–55.

Capron, Laurence, 'The Long-Term Performance of Horizontal Acquisitions', *Strategic Management Journal*, 20(11), 1999, pp. 987–1018.

Chan, Kim and Renee Mauborgne, 'Fair Process: Managing in the Knowledge Economy', *Harvard Business Review*, July–August 1997, pp. 65–75.

Davidson, William H. and José de la Torre, *Managing the Global Corporation: Case Studies in Strategy and Management.* New York: McGraw-Hill, 1989, pp. 296–318.

DePamphilis, Donald M., *Mergers, Acquisitions and other Restructuring Activities.* Academic Press, 2010.

Eccles, Robert G., Kersten L. Lanes and Thomas C. Wilson, 'Are You Paying Too Much For That Acquisition?', *Harvard Business Review*, July–August 1999, pp. 136–46.

Ernst, David and Andrew M.J. Steinhubl, 'Petroleum: After the Megamergers', *McKinsey Quarterly*, 3, 1999, pp. 49–57.

Ghemewat, Pankaj and Fariboz Ghadar, 'The Dubious Logic of Global Megamergers', *Harvard Business Review*, July–August 2000, pp. 64–72.

Ghoshal, Sumantra and Philippe Haspeslagh, 'Electrolux: The Acquisition and Integration of Zanussi', INSEAD Case Study 09/90-123, 1991.

Habeck, Max, Fritz Kröger and Michael Träm, *After the Merger: Seven Rules for Successful Post Merger Integration.* London and Englewood Cliffs, NJ: *Financial Times*/ Prentice-Hall, 2000.

Haspeslagh, Philippe and William Jemison, *Managing Acquisitions: Creating Value Through Corporate Renewal*. New York: Free Press, 1991.

Hawawini, Gabriel and Claude Viallet, *Finance for Executives*. Cincinnati, OH: South-Western Publishing, 1999, ch. 12, pp. 379–428.

Hyde, Dana and Philippe Haspeslagh, 'The Making of the Simply Better Healthcare Company: SmithKline and Beecham: The Simply Better Way', INSEAD Case Study 03/95-4449, 1994.

Khou, Julia and Deborah Spar, 'SONY Corporation and Columbia Pictures', Harvard Business School Case 9/795/025, 1994.

Kitching, John, 'Acquisitions in Europe', *Business International*, Research Report 73–3, Geneva, 1973.

Lessard, Donald, 'Incorporating Country Risks in the Valuation of Offshore Projects', *Journal of Applied Corporate Finance*, 9(3), 1996.

Mitchell, David and Gary Holmes, *Making Acquisitions Work: Learning from Companies' Successes and Failures*. London: Economic Intelligence Unit, 1996.

Probert, Joselyn and Arnoud De Meyer, 'Francolor Pigments: A Toyo Ink Acquisition', INSEAD Case Study 05/98-4756, 1998.

Purshe, William, 'Pharmaceuticals: The Consolidation Is Not Over', *McKinsey Quarterly*, 2, 1996, pp. 110–19.

Smith, Kenneth, 'A Brand New Culture for the Merged Firm', *Mergers & Acquisitions*, June 2000, pp. 45–50.

Tao, Zhigang, *Anheuser-Busch versus SABMiller: Bidding War in China's Beer Industry*. Asia Case Research Centre and Fudan University, Case HKU411, 2004.

Viscio, Albert, John Harbison, Amy Asin and Richard Vitaro, 'Post-Merger Integration: What Makes Mergers Work?', *Strategy+Business*, Fourth Quarter, 17, 1999, pp. 26–33. Also available at <http://www.strategy-business.com>

Von Krogh, George, Alessandro Sinatra and Harbir Singh (eds.), *The Management of Corporate Acquisitions: International Perspectives*. London: Macmillan, 1994.

Journal

Mergers & Acquisitions, Thomson Financial Securities Data, USA, monthly.

chapter

6 ASSESSING COUNTRIES' ATTRACTIVENESS

Introduction

Within the overall framework of their global strategy, firms have to choose the geographical locations where they will set up operational assets. This kind of decision, known as the 'entry' decision, demands that firms take into consideration several factors:

- First, there is the need to assess the *attractiveness* of the country, either in absolute terms or relative to another country. This is generally known as **'country attractiveness analysis'**.
- Second, there is the need to decide on a *form of entry*. This is generally known as **'entry strategy'**.

In Chapter 6, we will concentrate on country attractiveness assessment, while in Chapter 7 we will discuss entry strategies.

Country attractiveness is a function of the *market and resources prospects*, the *competitive context* and the *risks of operating* in a country.

The chapter presents a framework of assessing market attractiveness as well as country risks.

Learning objectives

At the end of the chapter you will be able to:

- organize a complete assessment of market opportunities and industry structure in a country
- understand and value various types of risks involved in operating in a country
- compare different countries as investment opportunities.

Why is a country attractive?

Theoretically a country will be attractive to foreign investors if, in investing in that country, they get a return that is equal to or higher than their *risk adjusted weighted cost of capital*. In fact, the foreign investment decision is fundamentally the same as any investment decision. If we apply the concept to a business investment (as opposed to a financial portfolio investment of securities), the logic of the decision is embodied in two key questions:

- Are the market and resources prospects as well as the competitive conditions in a particular country such that given a set of competitive advantages, the business is likely to generate a return *equal to or higher than the cost of capital?*

- Are the risks of operating in this country *acceptable for the shareholders and employees?*

The fundamental question of a foreign investment thus falls into the general framework of opportunities and risks analysis, as shown in Figure 6.1.

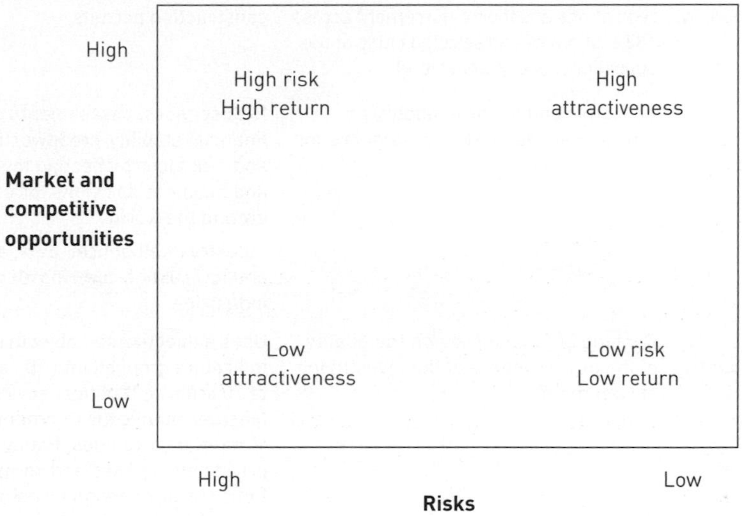

Figure 6.1 General investment framework

Although foreign investments fall into the general category of an opportunities/risks trade-off, the assessment of the international context raises some challenging issues. Many scholars, consultants and practitioners have proposed methodologies for country assessments. Table 6.1 summarizes the various approaches, giving relative rankings or scores to countries according to different economic, political and social dimensions. What we propose here is an analysis of the various dimensions that contribute to country attractiveness. These can be grouped into three broad categories:

- Market and resources opportunities
- Competitive context
- Country risks.

You must bear in mind first that market and competitive opportunities vary according to the *type of industry*, and risks affect them differently. Generalizations are thus difficult to make. Secondly, the merit of a country is first evaluated in *absolute terms* to check whether it presents minimum characteristics of opportunities and risks, and then it is generally compared with other countries having *similar features*. For instance, a company may evaluate investing in Chile and then compare Chile with Argentina. Thailand may be compared with the Philippines, Malaysia or even Indonesia, Vietnam with Cambodia, France with the United Kingdom or Germany, and India with China.

This list is a selection. You can find a guide to country analysis resources on the Internet at www.countryrisk.com

Table 6.1 A selection of models and sources of countries' assessment

Organization/publication	Type of rating	Methodology
World Bank Ease of Doing Business: Ranking and countries analysis on the regulation that makes business opening and operation more or less easy. http://www.doingbusiness.org	The Doing Business Project provides objective measures of business regulations and their enforcement across 183 economies and selected cities at the subnational and regional level.	Quantitative measure of regulations for starting a business, dealing with construction permits,
IHS Global Insight Ongoing assessment of countries and industries as well as consulting services. http://www.ihs.com/	Economic and financial analysis, forecasting and market intelligence for 204 countries	Risk services: assessments of the financial stability, creditworthiness and risk factors affecting investment and business decisions for countries around the world Industry intelligence: data, analysis, and forecasting covering all major industries
Economic Intelligence Unit Business ranking published in *Country Forecast Quarterly* report http://EIU.com	Ranking of 60 countries on the quality of the attractiveness of the investment environment	Uses subjective and objective indicators grouped into 10 categories of 70 criteria: (Political environment, Macroeconomic environment, Market opportunities, Policy toward private enterprises and competition, Policy toward foreign investment, Foreign trade and exchange control, Taxes, Financing, Labor market, Infrastructure)
ICON Group Publishes global market research and business intelligence http://www.icongrouponline.com	Cover 2,000 product categories across some 200 countries, 2,000 cities and over 16,000 companies.	Latent demand is measured by economic, demographic, urbanization, geographical and cultural factors; accessibility is measured by eight factors: Openness to trade, Openness to direct investment, Marketing and entry alternatives available, Local human resources, Local risks, Political stability, Cultural homogeneity, Demand concentration
Central Intelligence Agency The World Factbook https://www.cia.gov	The World Factbook covers 266 world entities	Provides information on the history, people, government, economy, geography, communications, transportation, military, and transnational issues
Euromonitor Global market information database http://www.euromonitor.com	Provides market sizing and forecasts for 330 consumer products across 49 countries plus marketing parameters (1000 types of data) for 209 countries over 20 years	Gives: Market size, Country data, Forecasts, Company and brand profiles, Information sources, Special industry reports
BERI SA Business Risk Service (BRS) www.beri.com	Monitors 50 countries three times a year to assess quantitatively and qualitatively political, operational and financial risks	Assessments of operating conditions, political risk, and the foreign exchange/external accounts position Computes three indices and composite score: Political Risk Index, Operational Risk, Financial Risk (R Factor), Overall Risk index.

Organization/publication	Type of rating	Methodology
World Economic Forum *Global Competitiveness Report* http://www.weforum.org/reports	Ranks 59 countries according to their competitiveness and the growth of their competitiveness Ranking is based on Porter's 'Competitive Diamond'[1]	Uses two categories of factors: • A ranking of company operation and strategy based on 15 measures of competitiveness of domestic firms • A ranking of the quality of national business environment (48 measures of infrastructure quality, demand quality, supporting industries and competitive rivalry)
IMD: *The World Competitiveness Yearbook*[2] Published annually http://www.imd.org/research/publications/wcy/index.cfm	Measures 59 countries on the basis of 331 criteria Assesses competitiveness as well as location attractiveness	Uses statistical and survey data to score 331 criteria grouped into four main criteria: Economic performance, Governement efficiency, Business efficiency, Infrastructure
Political Risk Services (PRS)[3] ICRG risk rating system http://www.prsgroup.com/	*The International Country Risk Guide (ICRG)* monitors 161 countries, rating a wide range of risks to international businesses and financial institutions.	Rating comprises 22 variables in three subcategories of risk: political, financial and economic. A separate index is created for each of the subcategories.

Market, resources and industry opportunities

When looking at a country's attractiveness, businesses need to consider its market, resources and industry opportunities, as shown in Figure 6.2.

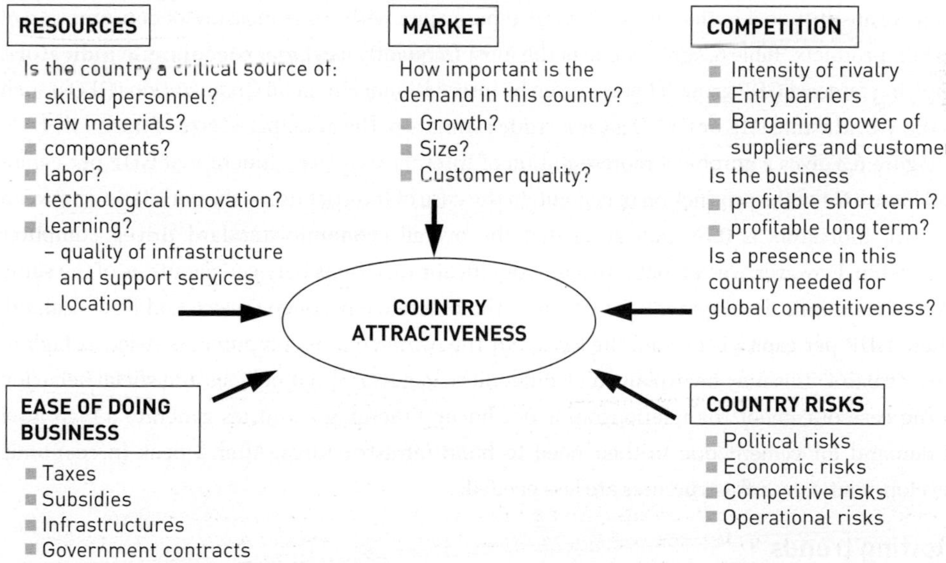

Figure 6.2 Framework for country market, resources and industry attractiveness assessment

Market opportunities assessment measures the *potential demand* in the country for the products or services of the firm:

- Market *size*
- Market *growth*
- Quality of *demand.*

Resources opportunities

- *Natural* resources
- *Human* resources
- *Infrastructure and support industries* resources.

Industry opportunities assessment measures how easy it is to compete in the country:

- The quality of the competitive climate
- The quality of the industry competitive structure
- The investment incentives granted by governments.

Appendix 6.1 (p. 204) gives a short summary of the differences between Brazil and Mexico for household expenditures.

Assessing market opportunities

The classic tools of market forecasting and analysis are presented here, in a logical sequence.

Broad assessment of the overall demand, given macroeconomic data

In many instances, this broad assessment uses some sort of correlation between macroeconomic social or institutional indicators such as GDP per capita with some measure of consumption of certain products. Table 6.2 gives some of the most frequently used **macroeconomic indicators**. Applying forecast GDP growth figures given by International Financial Organizations (IFOs) such as the World Bank, IMF or OECD gives a crude estimate of the anticipated size of the market

Figure 6.3 gives a graphical representation of Internet users as a function of GDP per capita and Figure 6.4 of the production of cement. In the case of Internet users, the correlation between the two indicators is 0.78, indicating that the overall economic standard 'drives' computer ownership. However, we can observe some significant variations between countries of the same level of economic development: for example, the difference between Greece and New Zealand, where GDP per capita is around the same but the ownership of computers is twice as high in New Zealand. This may be explained by differences in government policies and social behavior. In the case of cement the relationship is not linear. Emerging countries generate a high level of demand for cement due to their need to build infrastructures. After a peak in economic development, new infrastructures are less needed.

Plotting trends

As a first cut, the macroeconomic correlation approach may give some interesting insights into the potential size of a market. When it is used in combination with other factors such as the degree of urbanization, climatic conditions, income distribution, lifestyles and saving rates, it may give a more precise prediction. Plotting trends for comparable countries (in terms of economic conditions, economic factors, etc.) also gives a view about the potential future of demand on a per capita basis as well as in absolute value.

Table 6.2 Macro indicators used in international market assessments

• Economic	Sociological	Demographic	Institutional
• GDP size • GDP size (PPP)* • GDP per capita • GDP per capita (PPP)* • Income distribution • Disposable income • Saving rate • Exports/imports • Investment rates	• Urbanization (percentage of urban population) • Socio-economic distribution – by income groups – by regions/cities – by education level	• Population • Population growth • Age distribution	• Government spending • Infrastructure: – Power – Telecom – Internet – Roads • Education levels • Number of scientists • R&D expenditure

Note: *PPP (Purchasing Power Parity) calculations take into account differences in prices and cost of living. Generally developing countries can buy many more goods and services with one US$ than in the United States and therefore have a much higher GDP calculated with PPP than with market exchange rates.

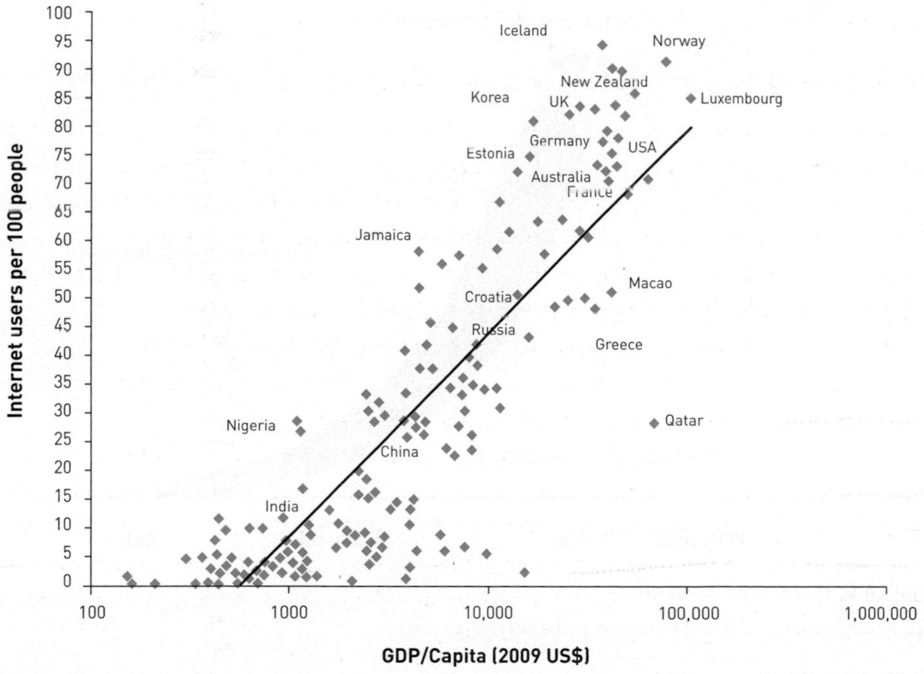

Figure 6.3 Relationship between GDP per capita and Internet users per 100 people, 2009

Source: World Bank, 2009

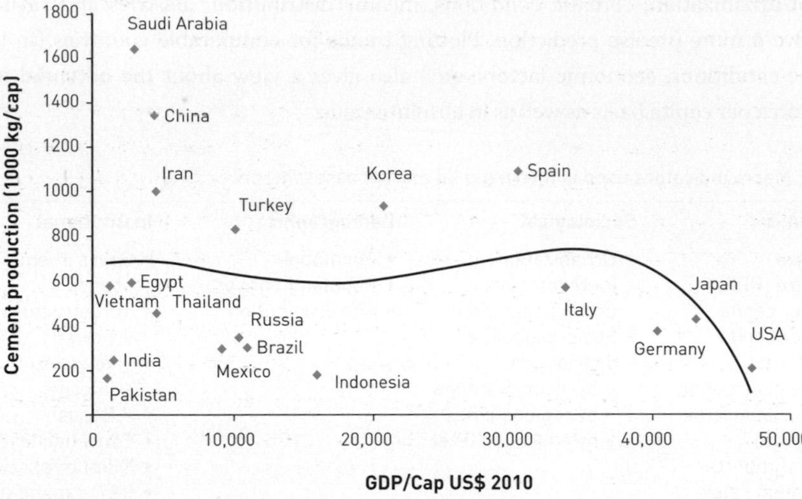

Figure 6.4 Relationship between GDP per capita and the production of cement per capita, 2010

Source: World Bank, World Development Indicators and United States Geological Survey (USGS) at <http://minerals.usgs.gov/minerals/pubs/commodity/cement/mcs-2011-cemen.pdf>

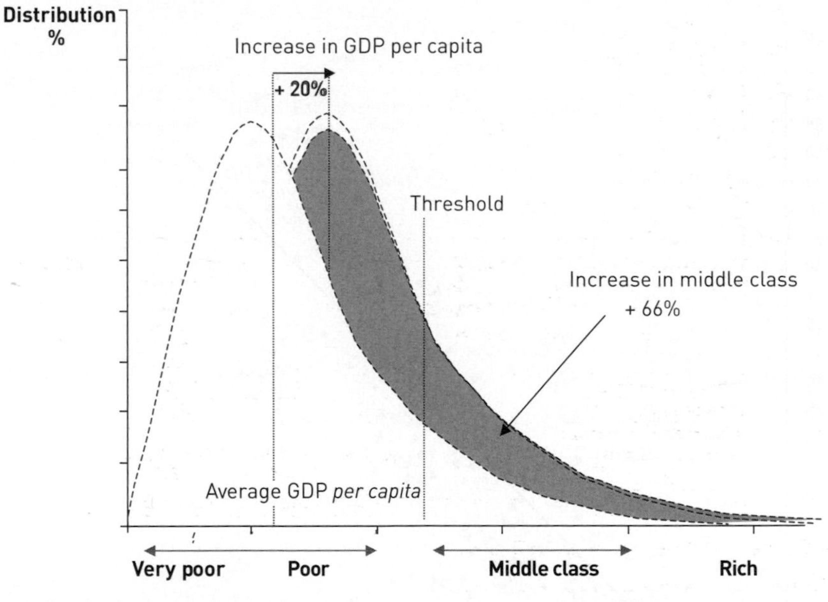

Figure 6.5 The 'middle-class effect'

Note: With an increase of 20% of GDP, the middle class increases by 66%

The middle-class effect

The demand for most mass consumer goods and their related inputs is often triggered by the presence of an affluent middle class. Emerging markets particularly experience what is known as the 'middle-class effect', illustrated in Figures 6.5 and 6.6. The middle-class effect is due to the skewed nature of the income distribution in emerging countries.

As illustrated in Figure 6.5, middle classes emerge when disposable income reaches a certain threshold. This threshold varies according to the kind of goods but it is around US$1500–2000 per household. People beyond the threshold are considered middle-class. Their number increases faster than the average income; this triggers a rapid increase in demand for branded goods and consumer durables. This phenomenon is illustrated in Figure 6.6 in the case of China. The emergence of middle classes sees an increase of demand for consumer durables and branded products higher than the average economic growth. For instance, in China between 1990 and 1995 the GNP per capita increased by 36 per cent but the demand for VCRs increased by 158 per cent and refrigerators by 79 per cent, and between 2001 and 2010 the GDP per capita multiplied by 2.32 whilst the car market multiplied by 7.5. This effect is more visible in urban centres like Shanghai, Beijing or Guangzhou, hence the huge inflow of foreign investments in those cities.

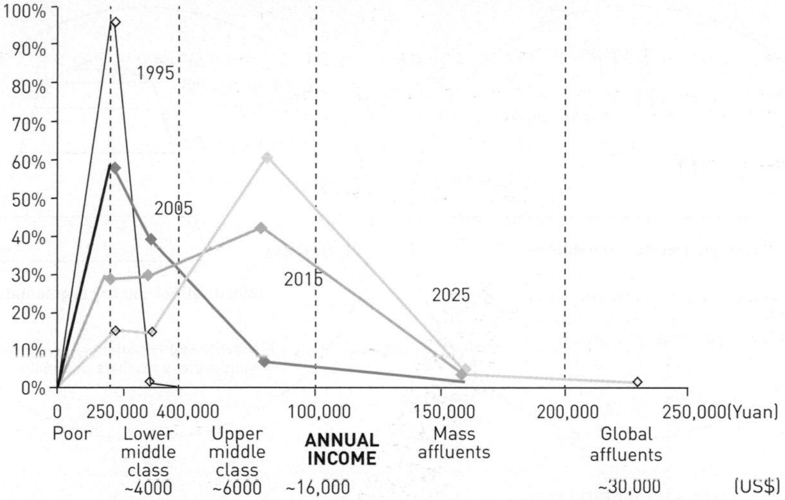

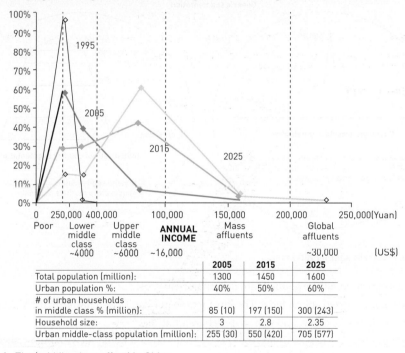

	2005	2015	2025
Total population (million):	1300	1450	1600
Urban population %:	40%	50%	60%
# of urban households in middle class % (million):	85 (10)	197 (150)	300 (243)
Household size:	3	2.8	2.35
Urban middle-class population (million):	255 (30)	550 (420)	705 (577)

Figure 6.6 The 'middle-class effect' in China

Source: Graph constructed by the author from Farrell *et al.*, 2006

Note: Between 2005 and 2015 China's middle class is likely to grow from 255 million to 550 million while the GDP is forecast to grow 2.8 times

Quality of demand

Quality of demand describes the nature and diversity of **market segmentation** prevailing in a country, and the profile of the customer value curve in each segment. Marketers and strategists generally distinguish two generic segments, 'low end' and 'high end' (Figure 6.7).

In developing countries, the main bulk of the market is a large undifferentiated, price-sensitive segment co-existing with a growing more differentiated middle-class segment. In mature, advanced economies, segmentation is more diverse in societies that are essentially middle class. However, in practice, with economic development, markets become more sophisticated than this simple dual segmentation implies.

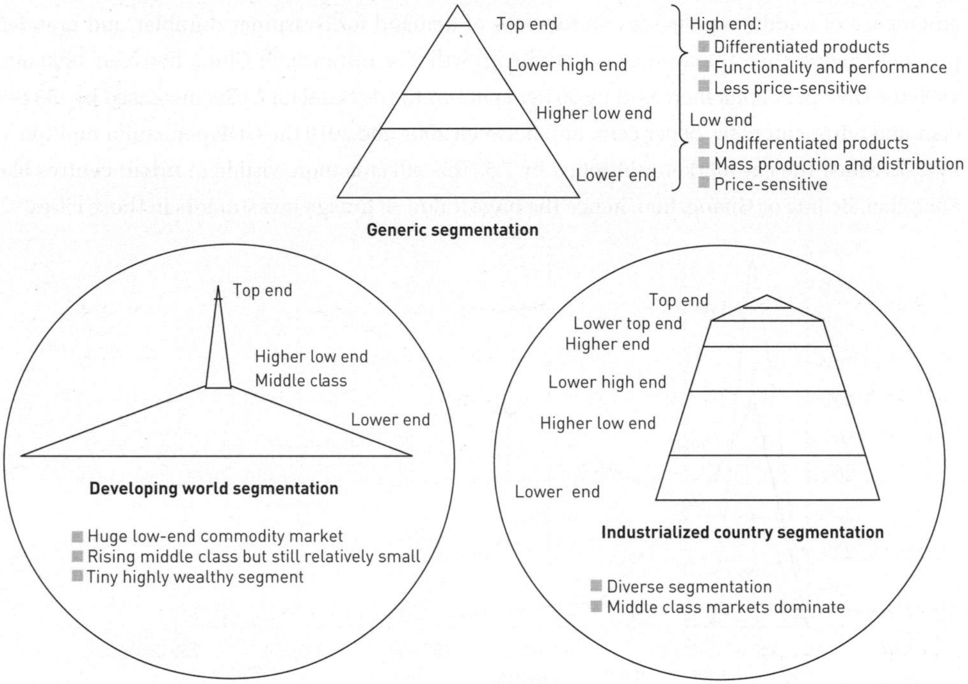

Figure 6.7 Market segmentations

Countries can generally be gouped into four major clusters:

- *developing countries*, characterized by low income per capita and low growth: Nigeria, and Bangladesh, for instance, and most sub-Saharan nations
- *emerging countries* such as China, Indonesia, Thailand and Malaysia with high growth rate and still relatively low income per capita but growing fast.
- *The Newly Industrialized Economies (NIEs)*, characterized by high growth and moderate–high wealth: Korea, Taiwan, Hong Kong, Singapore, and to a certain extent Brazil and Mexico.
- The final cluster (bottom right-hand part of the chart) consists of the relatively low-growth/high-wealth industrialized countries of North America, Europe and Japan.

The market characteristics of those clusters are described in Table 6.3.

Table 6.3 Characteristics of demand according to country life cycle clusters

Demand characteristics	Developing countries	Emerging countries	Newly industrialized economies	Industrialized countries
Growth	Low	High	High	Low
Size	Small	Small to high	Small to high	High
Segmentation	• Dominant subsistence sector • Large low-end segment	• Fast-growing middle class • Large low-end segment	• Established middle class • Increased diversity of segments	• Established middle class • Diverse and sophisticated segmentation
Customer value curve	Price	Price	Product functionality	Product functionality
	Availability	• Distribution • Emerging advertising	• Performance • Services	• Performance • Services
Distribution	Push logistics	Push logistics	• Pull • Beginning of mass	• Diversity • Mass retail important
Competition	Regulated	• Beginning of deregulation • New entrants	• Deregulated • Active • Diverse	• Deregulated • Active • Diverse

Assessing resource opportunities

The resources that attract foreign investors fall into three broad categories:

- *Natural* resources
- *Human* resources
- *Infrastructure and support industries* resources.

Natural resources

Table 6.4 gives an overview of the main resource endowment for minerals, mining, agriculture and forestry for the fifty best endowed countries in the world. Countries that do not use their production for national consumption tend to export raw materials, to promote processing by domestic companies or to invite foreign firms to invest in processing and export. Governments are very sensitive about the protection of their natural resources and very often require controls on foreign activities in this domain by negotiating production-sharing agreements as well as joint ventures. Oil and gas are probably the most globally sensitive industries, given the highly strategic nature of the commodity, the inherent risks of exploration, the capital intensity of the investments and the geographical location of the reserves. It is not by chance that the most sophisticated country risks methodologies have been developed in this industry.[4]

Table 6.4 Capital Endowment of Natural Resources (2005)

Economy	Natural capital (billion $)	Agricultural capital (billion $)	Minerals and energy capital (billion $)	Natural capital/ Capita ($)	Agricultural capital/Capita ($)	Mineral and Energy capital/ Capita ($)
China	5235	4046	1049	4013	3101	804
Russian Federation	4482	673	3469	31,317	4699	24,238
United States	4097	1991	1031	13,822	6718	3478
India	2960	2415	386	2704	2206	353
Brazil	2792	2165	433	14,978	11,615	2321
Saudi Arabia	2243	30	2003	97,012	1302	86,620
Iran, Islamic Rep.	1224	251	955	17,933	3679	13,987
Canada	1193	419	408	36,924	12,988	12,644
Indonesia	1086	671	325	4926	3042	1473
Nigeria	854	295	557	6042	2085	3940
Australia	813	340	413	39,979	16,718	20,328
Venezeula, RB	812	89	640	30,567	3341	24,090
Mexico	685	289	363	6641	2800	3525
United Arab Emirates	548	10	535	120,989	2279	118,111
Kuwait	540	2	538	213,112	876	212,013
France	524	359	4	8609	5893	71
Pakistan	523	405	73	3355	2602	467
Algeria	520	70	437	15,815	2138	13,293
Norway	509	26	461	110,162	5668	99,706
Thailand	502	280	41	7810	4360	638
Germany	471	268	44	5716	3246	535
Italy	440	282	31	7502	4819	525
Argentina	398	280	106	10,267	7220	2727
Turkey	386	349	15	5356	4838	208
United Kingdom	377	142	186	6263	2363	3085
Egypt, Arab Rep.	346	198	147	4670	2681	1989
Colombia	342	231	67	7614	5133	1488
Poland	339	208	43	8894	5462	1488
Ukraine	325	219	93	6899	4662	1970
Spain	324	274	3	7471	6318	58
Malaysia	323	45	256	12,750	1769	10,102
Chile	307	122	156	18,870	7514	9563
Vietnam	302	216	73	3630	2595	884
Ecuador	297	83	85	22,454	6289	6442

Economy	Natural capital (billion $)	Agricultural capital (billion $)	Minerals and energy capital (billion $)	Natural capital/ Capita ($)	Agricultural capital/Capita ($)	Mineral and energy capital/ Capita ($)
Philippines	288	251	12	3468	3027	139
South Africa	268	142	122	5723	3036	2595
Japan	268	245	6	2094	1920	47
Sudan	250	183	56	6911	5062	1554
New Zealand	217	123	15	52,979	29,909	3675
Netherlands	215	82	115	13,193	5050	7061
Angola	212	35	176	13,307	2175	11,052
Guatemala	210	200	4	16,691	15,898	330
Uzbekistan	200	57	140	7652	2186	5365
Oman	198	5	184	77,134	2047	71,631
Bangladesh	198	168	51	9058	6408	2353
Peru	196	139	27	1394	1188	190
Syrian Arab Republic	151	61	89	7909	3188	4657
Sweden	141	72	3	15,673	8023	366

Note: Natural Capital is the sum of agricultural, mineral and energy resources calculated as the present value of rent generated by the resources

Source: World Bank: The Changing Wealth of Nations: http://data.worldbank.org/data-catalog/wealth-of-nations

A particular type of natural resource is *geographical location* which, combined with good infrastructure and support services and industry, may give to certain countries or regions within a country the role of a 'hub' or a regional center. Singapore, located at the end of the Strait of Malacca, Hong Kong, located at the door to continental China, Brussels for the EU or Miami for Latin America have developed as hubs based on their geographical location.

Human resources

The quality and cost of labour is the cause of the migration of international investments that took place in the 1950s and 1960s. Offshore factories in South East Asia and Latin America have set up in Export-Processing Zones (EPZs) for the production and assembly of labor-intensive products. International sourcing under the form of Original Equipment Manufacturing (OEM) or straight procurement gave an opportunity for local companies in Japan in the 1950s, in Korea, Taiwan and Brazil in the 1960s, Singapore, Hong Kong and Tunisia in the 1970s, and China, Vietnam and India in the 1980s to develop manufacturing volume and competencies and establish their international presence.

In practice, two human resource elements are attractive: cost and quality. Figure 6.8 shows that there is a correlation between those two attributes (R=0.55), but you can see that countries in the upper left-hand quadrant have received the highest foreign investment per capita, indicating that the countries that have been able to combine low cost and quality have been seen as attractive for foreign investors, despite the fact that most of them have a relatively low market size (average GDP is US$200 billion/country in this quadrant as opposed to $2000 billion/country in the high-cost/high-skills quadrant and US$340 billion/country in the low-cost/low-skills one).

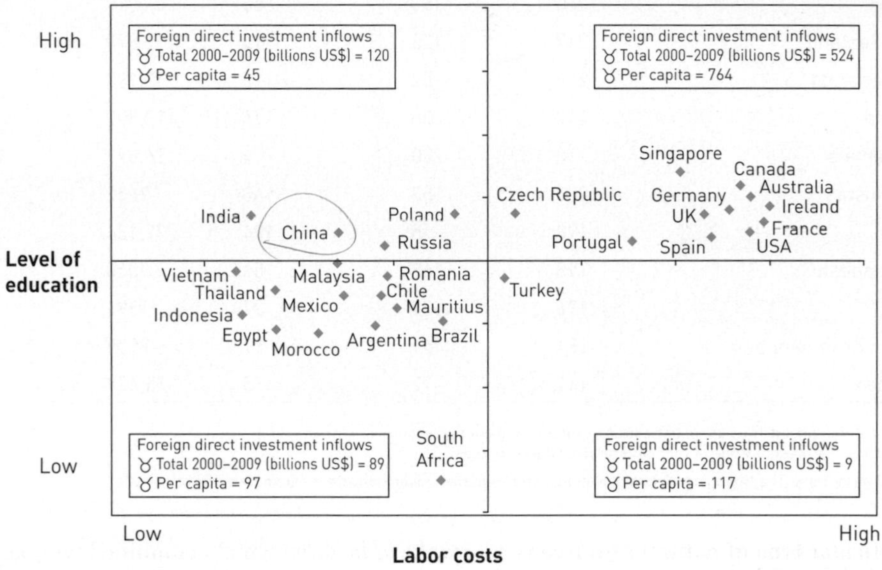

Figure 6.8 Cost of labor and level of education in service industry

Note: Scores are standardized scores of A.T. Kearney data

Source: A.T. Kearney Global Service Location Index, 2007. Copyright A.T. Kearney, 2007. Reprinted with permission

Low labor-cost countries tend to attract labor-intensive, low value-added production. Since the mid-1980s India, the Philippines and to a certain extent China have tried successfully to strengthen the production of computer software, particularly in the data capture segments. India, for instance, has focused its attractiveness on offering international companies a combination of low-labor costs but highly skilled computer software personnel.

Infrastructure and support industry resources

The third type of resource that can be of interest to foreign investors is the quality of *communication and logistics infrastructures*, as well as the availability of supporting industries and services. Figure 6.9 gives an overall ranking of countries, established by the World Economic Forum, based on the quality of their infrastructure.

Competitive context

The objective of this section is to determine the profitability potential of a presence in a country given its industry competitive context and the incentives provided by government to encourage foreign investments.

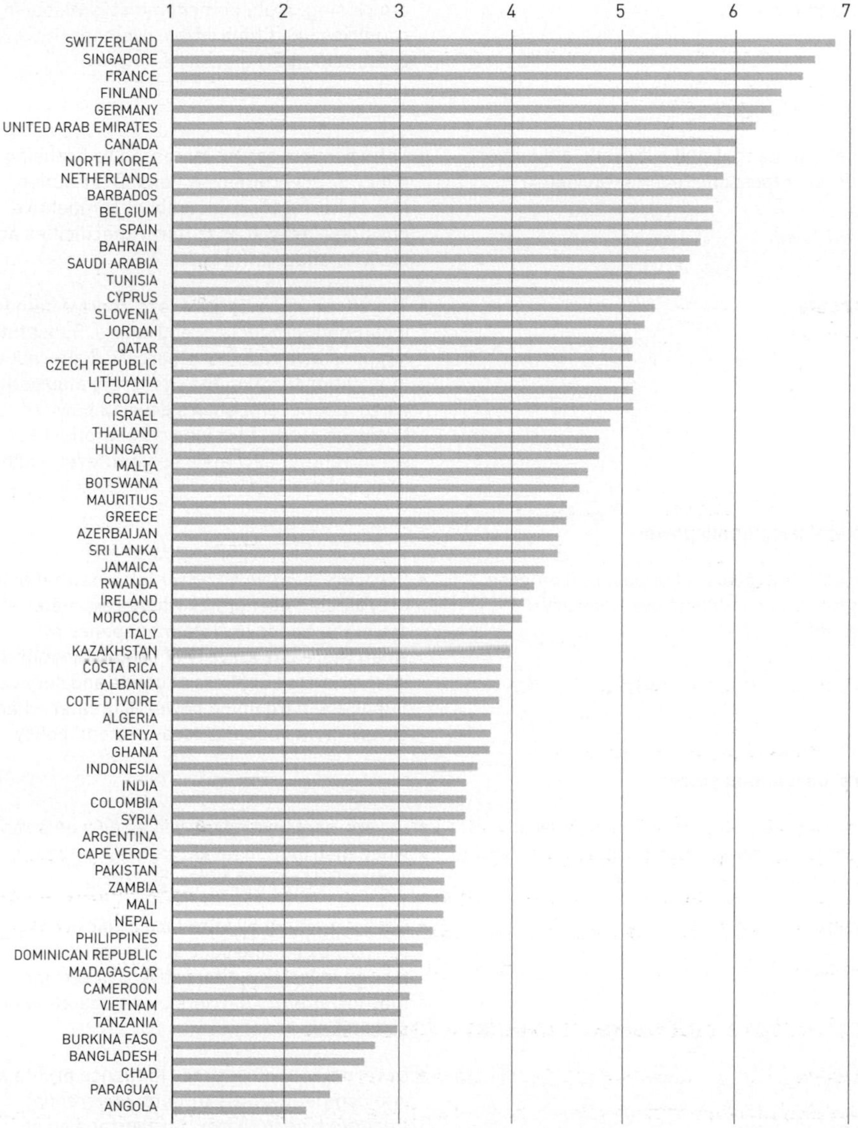

'How would you assess general infrastructure (e.g. transport, telephony and energy) in your country? 1= Extremely underdeveloped, 7= Extensive and efficient by international standard.'

Figure 6.9 Overall quality of infrastructure

Source: Global Competitiveness Report (2010–11), World Economic Forum

Table 6.5 Porter's industry analysis and international business entry

Porter's Five Forces plus one	Relevance for intenational business entry
Intensity of rivalry	
When competition is 'cut-throat' due to overcapacity and lack of differentiation of barriers to exit	• *Rivalry* increases when market growth is starting to slow down. Windows of opportunity are closing. A phenomenon that is visible in countries like China where overcapacity is present in many industries
Entry barriers	
Those elements that make it costly, difficult or sometimes impossible to enter an industry	• *Entry barriers* can be increased by licensing policy or government actions. Distribution networks, location, incumbent competitive positions, as well as cultural specificities are likely to affect entry costs.
Substitutes	• The effect of a *substitute* is to deprive demand-incumbent products of end-users. Substitution happens as a result of a perceived alternative. Internationalization may generate alternatives when global competitors develop new business models (or innovative products or services) that become a substitute for existing competitors.
Suppliers' bargaining power	
The negotiating power of suppliers to impose their price and conditions over industry's incumbents	• *Suppliers' bargaining power* is somewhat bigger in protected economies where raw materials are in the hands of state monopolies or when there is a scarcity of skilled labor or of intermediate suppliers of goods and services. Suppliers' bargaining power is greater when governments adopt a 'local content' policy.
Buyers' bargaining power	
The negotiating power of buyers to deny any price increase from industry's incumbents and to shift easily from one supplier to another	• *Buyers' bargaining powers* may also be stronger when distribution networks are tightly controlled, as in the case of Japan.
Government policies	• Governments may introduce *artificial entry barriers* by putting special constraints on foreign investors. Alternatively, governments may lower entry barriers by deregulating or subsidizing factory costs. • Government policies may influence profitability and competitiveness through *preferential treatment, price control, taxation* and so on.

Source: Based on Porter (1980)

Industry and competitive structure

Professor Michael Porter has proposed the concepts and techniques of industry analysis for strategic decision-making in his seminal book *Competitive Strategy* (1980). According to the author there are five forces that determine the *long-term profitability potential* of an industry. It is beyond the scope of this chapter to describe in detail the various forces that are presented in Porter's original work as well as in all classic textbooks on business strategy but in Table 6.5 we put in parallel Porter's five forces and their implication for international business entry. We have also added a *sixth force* under the heading of government policies.

The country 'diamond'

Professor Michael Porter (1998) has argued that countries or regions within countries (what he calls 'clusters') can build competitive advantages that make them attractive for business development in certain industries. He distinguishes four major drivers of national competitive advantage. These four drivers constitute the country or regional 'diamond':

- The *natural* endowment such as natural, human, capital, physical, technological and administrative or scientific resources.
- The quality of the *demand*: whether customers are demanding on quality, fostering the competitiveness of the firm serving them
- Vigorous *competition*: whether competitors stimulate each other
- The presence of *supporting industries*: whether there is a pool of qualified product and service suppliers that enhance the quality and competitiveness of firms operating in this country. Also whether there are clusters of successful firms in a particular industry. Examples given by Porter of successful clusters are the German printing press industry, the US patient monitoring industry, the Italian ceramic tile industry and the Japanese robotics industry.

Government incentives

In order to attract foreign investors, governments have designed and implemented a series of *incentives*: fiscal, financial, and competitive operational.[5] These incentives are summarized in Table 6.6.

Impact of incentives on foreign investor behaviour

A series of research studies on the role of incentives in foreign investment decisions has shown that their role is limited.[6] Market attractiveness, competitive conditions and resource endowments are more important than incentives, but if those conditions are comparable in several locations, incentives may play a positive role in the decision to invest in one country in particular.

Table 6.6 Major types of incentive for foreign investments

Type of incentive	*Nature of incentive*
Fiscal incentives:	
Tax reduction	• Tax holiday for a certain period • Ability to write off losses against profits after the end of the tax holiday period • Reduced tax rate • Accelerated depreciation • Reduction in social security contributions • Special deductions of taxable incomes based on certain types of activities (social, R&D, etc.) • Exemption from property taxes or other special taxes • Reduction of tax base on local content or employment levels • Income tax exemption/reduction for expatriate personnel
Imports and exports	• Exemption of import duties and value added taxes for raw material, capital equipment and parts • Exemption from export duties • Tax credits on domestic sales based on export performance
Financial incentives	• Subsidies of all kinds • 'Sweetener loans' • Guaranteed loans • Export credits • Equity participation • Risks insurance (exports, exchange rates)
Competitive incentives	• Protection against imports • Capacity regulation • Monopolistic position • Preferential purchases
Operational incentives	• Preferential rates – rents, land, power, telecoms, etc. • Assistance for market studies • Utilization of public services or government agencies for company operations • Secondment of personnel

Source: UNCTAD (1996)

Country risk analysis

The purpose of country risk analysis is to assess the probability that adverse circumstances owing to political, economic or social actions will negatively affect business performance.[7] Country risks can be grouped into four categories (see Figure 6.10):

- *Political* risks
- *Economic* risks
- *Competitive* risks
- *Operational* risks.

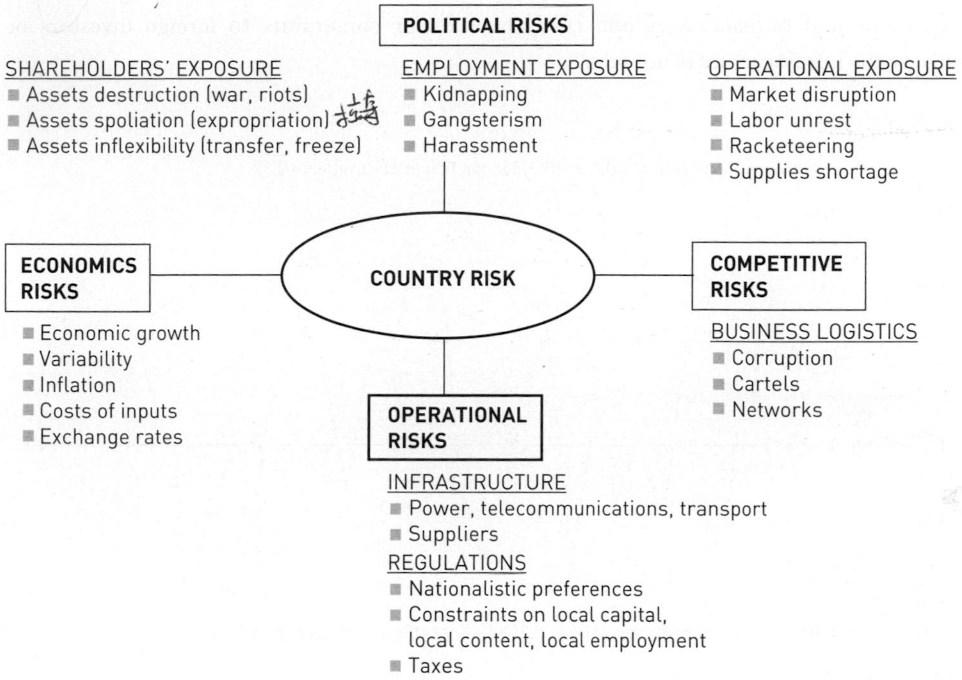

Figure 6.10 Framework for country risk analysis

- A first type of risk exposes *shareholders' value*, in terms of loss of capital or loss through the inability to repatriate dividends. This type of risk is associated with asset destruction linked to external or civil wars or riots, asset spoliation owing to expropriation or asset lock-in through funds freezing or interdiction on capital transfer.
- Another type of political risk lies in *employees' exposure* linked to gangsterism, crime and kidnapping as well as *operational exposure* linked to labor unrest, racketeering or market disruptions or supplies shortages linked to criminal activities.
- *Economic* risks expose business performance to the extent that the economic business drivers can vary and therefore put profitability at stake. As an example, Figure 6.11 shows the growth rate of Brazil as compared to Argentina from 1970 to 2009. While the two countries have a similar annual growth rate (2.9 per cent against 2.96), Argentina has more variability than Brazil (coefficient of variation of 2.19 against 0.97) and therefore *ceteris paribus* presents a higher economic risk.

Competitive risks are related to noneconomic distortion of the competitive context owing to cartels and networks as well as corrupt practices. The competitive battlefield is not even and investors who base their competitive advantage on product quality and economics are at a disadvantage.

Operational risks are those that directly affect the bottom line, either because government regulations and bureaucracies add costly taxation or constraints to foreign investors or because the infrastructure is not reliable.

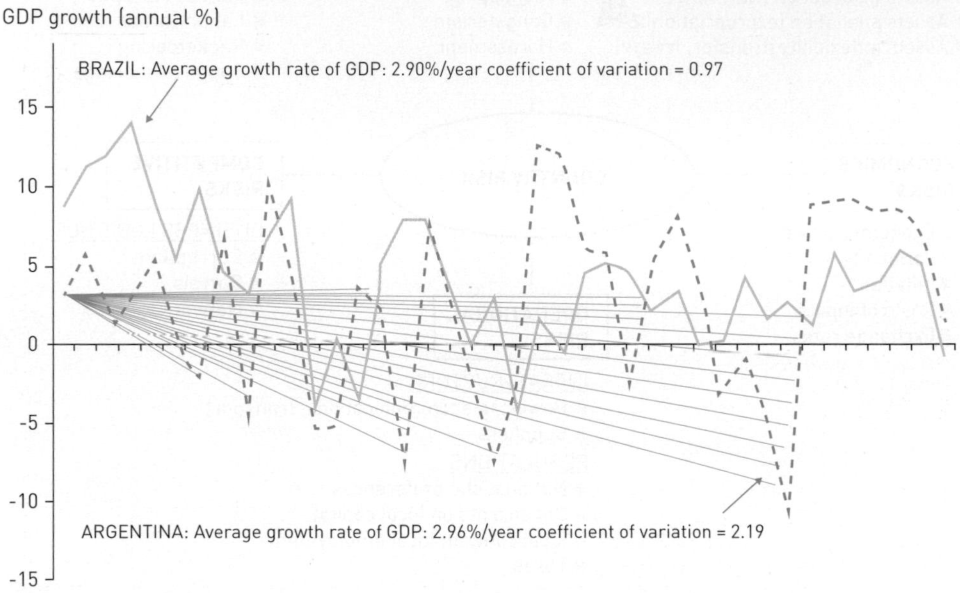

Figure 6.11 Variability of economic growth, Argentina versus Brazil, 1970–2009

Source: World Bank Economic Development Indicators. http://www.data.worldbank.org

Figure 6.12 shows how various countries score in terms of political and economical risks. Both dimensions are clearly correlated.

The impact of country risks on investment decisions is not straightforward. Whilst we can see in Figure 6.13 that foreign direct investments are more important in countries with lower level of risks, some countries like China or Brazil, although perceived as relatively risky, receive a significant amount of investment. This demonstrates that companies are likely to accept a certain level of risk if other aspects of attractiveness are present.

Putting it all together

The various factors presented in this chapter constitute the basic raw materials for assessing whether a particular country is likely to offer opportunities to conduct business safely and profitably. Such assessments first require the collection of a large amount of information and second, the capacity to *collate* information in a meaningful fashion.

Data collection

Despite the fact that various databases and consultancy firms propose statistical information and analyses, managers are often confronted with problems with the relevance, quality and accessibility of strategic and marketing intelligence specific to their industry. Macroeconomic data are too broad, and managers need to complement them by their own investigations. Various methods exist to assess country opportunities and risks.

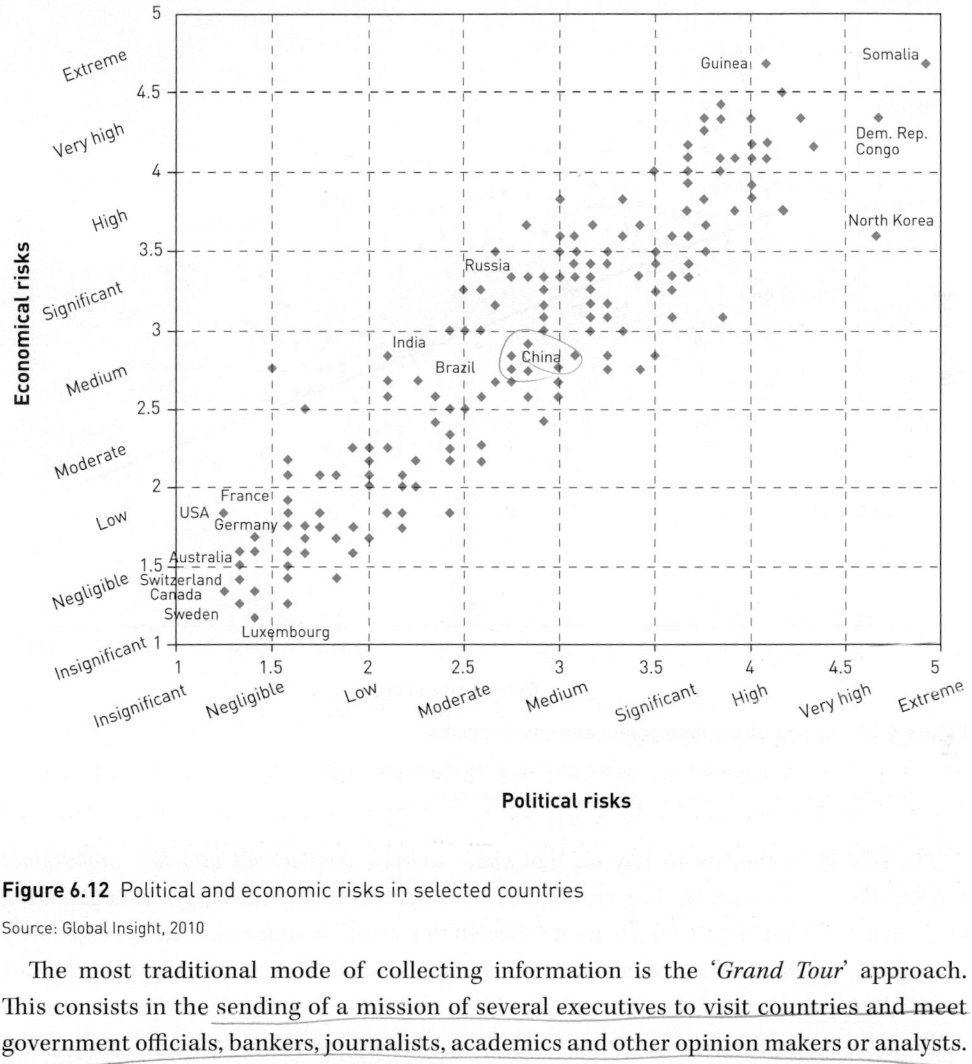

Figure 6.12 Political and economic risks in selected countries

Source: Global Insight, 2010

The most traditional mode of collecting information is the '*Grand Tour*' approach. This consists in the sending of a mission of several executives to visit countries and meet government officials, bankers, journalists, academics and other opinion makers or analysts. At the end of this exercise, managers exchange notes and prepare a report comparing the relative merits of countries. The advantage of the Grand Tour is to give a real feel of what the context is about and to focus on issues that are specific to its products or services. The disadvantages are the inherent superficiality of the exercise as well as the difficulty of *cross-validation* of information owing to time pressures. For the information to be valuable, companies need to organize several Grand Tours and to complement them with other forms of data collection and analysis. The exercise becomes quite costly, and for that reason many SMEs cannot afford it.

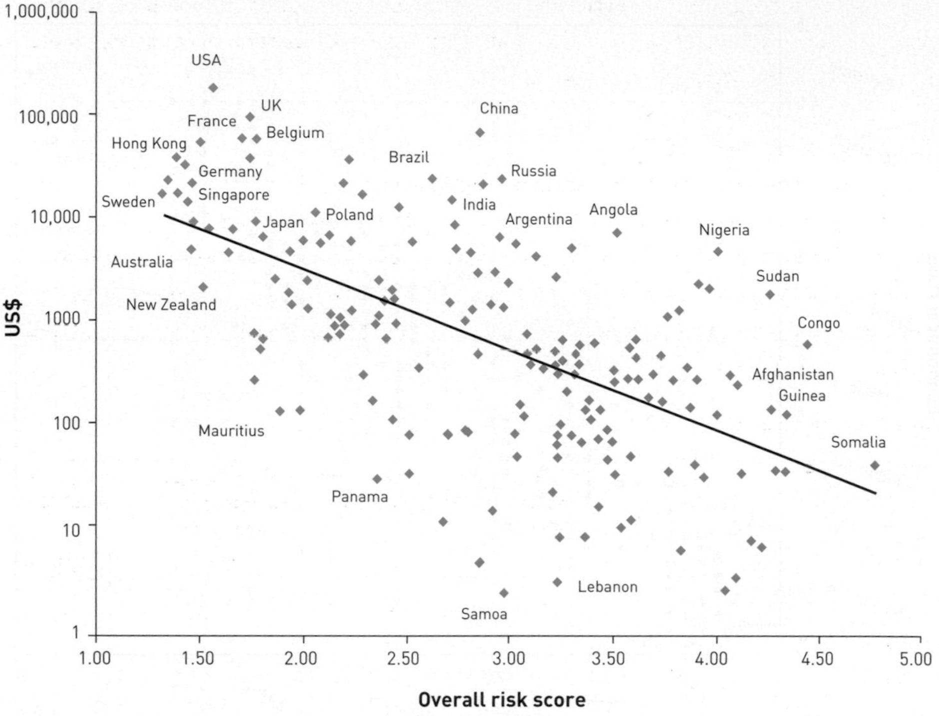

Figure 6.13: Foreign direct investment and country risks

Note: the coefficient of correlation between risk and FDI is –0.37, significant but not high

Source: UNCTAD, World Investment Report, 2010 and Global Insight, 2011

The second method is to rely on *diplomatic sources, commercial attachés, professional organizations* and *foreign banking institutions*. Although less costly, this type of data-gathering lacks specificity and depth. Information collected this way may suffer from lack of objectivity since diplomats and bankers often have a vested interest to push investments in the territories where they operate.

The third method is to call on *consultancy firms* who specialize in country risk and market analysis. The quality of the results depends upon the quality of the relationship between the *client* (the firm) and the *service provider* (the consultancy firm). It is important to ask specific questions, otherwise the firm may be flooded with masses of irrelevant data. To be fruitful, the use of a consultant needs to be preceded by a preliminary investigation made by the company either via a Grand Tour or by desktop research. The company is then in a position to calibrate the mandate given to the consultant.

Consolidating the data

As the previous paragraphs have illustrated, several parameters shape opportunities and risks. The combination of these parameters generates various *country profiles* that distinguish types of country according to the attractiveness factors of interest to foreign investors. To take the example of the Asia Pacific region, and to refer to our earlier discussion of country clusters, we can classify countries into five main groups:

- *Hubs:* Singapore and Hong Kong
- *Emerging giants:* India and China
- *Newly industrialized economies:* Taiwan, Korea, Malaysia
- *Resource-rich developing countries:* Indonesia, the Philippines, Thailand
- *Advanced countries:* Australia and Japan. Table 6.7 gives the key characteristics of those clusters. The choice of countries between clusters and within a cluster will ultimately depend on the *strategic ambition* of the global firm and the relative importance it attaches to the various factors.

Table 6.7 Cluster characteristics, Asia Pacific

	Hubs	Emerging giant economies	Newly industrialized	Resource-rich developing* countries	Advanced countries
Population	L	H	M	M/H	M/H
GDP	L	M	M	L	H
Infrastructure	H	L	H	L	H
Skills	H	L	H	L	H
Labor costs	M	L	M	L	H
Risks	L	M	L/M	H	L
Natural resources	L	M	L	H	Japan = L Australia = H

Notes: L = Low, M = Medium, H = High

* These countries share many common characteristics with the emerging giants

MINI-CASE

Fastkomfort: Assessing Countries in Eastern Europe

Fastkomfort is a *'Mittelstand'* company established in Munich, Germany in 1956. It is owned by a single shareholder. Fastkomfort manufactures auto-parts for car makers located in Europe, in particular, Volkswagen, Opel, Audi and SAAB. It has three suppliers of components, based in Italy, Slovenia and Austria. In commercial terms, Fastkomfort enjoys a relatively stable situation due to longstanding supply contracts with its buyers and its suppliers. It has only two competitors, one based in France, and the other based in Slovakia. Its competitive advantages are the sophistication and high quality of its products and its marketing based upon technology development (innovation), production (output) and reputation (customer loyalty). The weaknesses are the high labor costs in Germany.

MINI-CASE

Fastkomfort is considering three options for its factory relocation: (i) the Czech Republic, (ii) Poland and (iii) Hungary.

1. **Opportunities**

- *Wages*
  The main interest for the relocation of the factory to the Czech Republic, Poland and Hungary is to take advantage of skilled labor which is cheaper than in Germany. The following chart is based on Eurostat data:

Minimum wages	2011
(Euros per month)	
Czech Republic	319
Hungary	281
Poland	350
Germany average monthly salary for car mechanics (No national minimum wage in Germany)	Around 1900

- *EU membership, no trade or capital restrictions*
  The three economies are European Union (EU) members, any product manufactured in these countries does not face trade barriers to reach Germany and other EU markets.
- *Currency exposure*
  If the Czech Republic, Hungary and Poland were to join the Euro, that situation would mitigate the current exposure fluctuations with buyers and sellers. However, while the euro remains in crisis, there is little intention in the Czech Republic and Poland to join the Eurozone. The Czech Republic is not supposed to join the Eurozone until at least 2017 (after the end of the term of the current government in 2014 and the completion of the procedure to meet the criteria of the EU Maastricht Treaty, taking another three years). In the case of Hungary, there is also a reluctance to join the Eurozone before 2020. While the willingness to join the euro is far off, in terms of actual compliance with the criteria of the Treaty of Maastricht, the Czech Republic is closer to meeting the relevant five criteria, as shown below. However, even if they do not join the Euro, EU membership may provide an opportunity to mitigate currency exposure. There should be no restrictions on the transfer of capital and sums among EU member states. Thus, receivables from buyers and payables to suppliers may be cleared in Euros, with the need to convert into local currencies only on resulting income. The double taxation avoidance agreements signed by Germany with the Czech Republic, with Hungary and with Poland would allow the remittances of dividends to Germany to be taxed in Germany. Therefore, Fastkomfort may retain a holding in Germany while deploying manufacturing in Eastern Europe.
- *Location*
  From the suppliers in Italy up to the buyers in South Germany, the Czech Republic is the country that offers the shortest distance, hence favourable transportation costs.
  Distance from Milan (suppliers) to Munich (customers):

MINI-CASE

From Plzen, Czech Republic factory 916 km
From Budapest, Hungary factory 1479 km
From Krakow, Poland 1866 km

- *Tax and investment incentives*
  There are considerable tax and investment incentives. In the three countries, there is an income tax allowance, and job creation and training subsidies, which vary according to region and sector. In the three countries, the automotive sector is considered a priority.

2. Risks

- *Political risks*
  Given EU membership, it is unlikely that there would be major shareholders' exposure to political risks. Furthermore, the retention of national currencies, i.e., the Czech Koruna, Polish Zloty, and Hungarian Forint, gives the countries enough leeway to counter macroeconomic imbalances and avoid social discontent, which may put assets at risk and/or create operational exposure (as in Greece or Spain with the latest euro crisis). However, the Czech Republic has gone through a short period of political instability with the resignation of the government in 2009 and new parliamentary elections in May 2010. Those problems seem now to be overcome.
  Poland had a short period of political instability after the death of President Kaczynsky in an air-crash in 2009. However, the new government seems to align towards more integration with its European neighbors, which would infuse more security in national politics.
  In the case of Hungary, after a 2006 set of protests, political stability has been established. However, changes in basic laws, such as the Constitution, as well as censorship on media law, put a question mark on the predictability and certainty of the rule of law in Hungary.
- *Economic risks*
  The main economic risks are related to the performance of the EU economy, in particular Germany. The euro crisis is always a risk to the German economy.

  The Czech Republic was almost untouched by the 2008–2009 economic crisis, thanks to the solidity of its banking sector and the isolation from the Eurozone. The risk imposed by currency exposure of Czech Koruna is basically against the Euro, in particular, if the euro appreciates. However, this is unlikely to happen if Germany continues to grow.

  With respect to Poland, the economy has been continuously growing, even during the 2008–2009 financial crisis. Indeed, Poland suffered very little from it. However, there are worries that inflation may rise. As in the case of the Czech Republic, growth in Germany will ensure the avoidance of major economic turmoil, in particular with respect to currency exposure.
  Hungary was significantly affected by the 2008–2009 economic crisis because of its reliance on foreign currency loans. Hence, Hungary needed a rescue package from the IMF in order to deal with the crisis. There are still currency risks against the Euro. However, given the post-crisis austerity measures, it is likely that Hungary will maintain a prudent fiscal policy that will not trigger significant currency fluctuations.
- *Operational risks*
  There are no risks related to infrastructure. However, there may be some risk related to the bureaucratic and time-consuming nature of civil and administrative procedures

which may scare away foreign investors. Hungary is placed 51 in the 'doing business' index. In the case of the Czech Republic, the legal framework is not the best, so it is placed 64 in the doing business index.

3. **Ease of doing business**

Table 6.8 shows the 'ease of doing business' rankings from the World Bank (2011).

Table 6.8 Ease of doing business rankings for Poland, the Czech Republic and Hungary.

Economy	Ease of doing business	Starting a business	Dealing with construction	Getting electricity	Registering property	Getting credit
Poland	62	126	160	64	89	8
Czech Rep.	64	138	68	148	34	48
Hungary	51	39	55	103	43	48
Economy	**Protecting investors**	**Paying taxes**	**Trading across**	**Enforcing contracts**	**Resolving insolvency**	
Poland	46	128	46	68	87	
Czech Rep.	97	119	70	78	33	
Hungary	122	117	74	19	66	

Questions:

1) Why is Fastkomfort looking to establish a factory in Eastern Europe?

2) Which country would be the best choice for Fastkomfort? Give reasons.

Summary and key points

1 Entry decisions take into account:

- *Country attractiveness* analysis
- *Entry strategy* (to be discussed further in Chapter 7).

2 A country attractiveness assessment is based on two dimensions:

- *Market, resources and industry opportunities*
- *Country risks* (many organizations publish country assessment results based on various economic/political/social factors).

3 Market opportunities assessment measures the potential demand in the country for a firm's products or services based on:

- Market size
- Growth
- Quality of demand.

4 Demand:

- Overall demand is assessed based on a combination of:
  - *Macroeconomic correlation* approach (estimating demand based on correlation with given macroeconomic indicators)
  - Consideration of *other factors*:
    - Degree of urbanization
    - Climatic conditions
    - Income distribution
    - Lifestyles
    - Savings rates
  - *Trend analysis* with comparable countries:
    - On a per capita basis
    - On absolute value
- Demand for most mass consumer goods in emerging markets is often triggered by the 'middle-class effect':
  - The increased number of people who become middle class (i.e. reach a certain *disposable income threshold)* causes an increased demand for modern branded products
- Quality of demand:
  - *Nature and diversity* of market segmentation prevailing in a country and the profile of customers value curve in each segment
  - Low-end segment:
    - Undifferentiated products
    - Mass production and distribution
    - Price-sensitive
  - High-end segment:
    - Differentiated products
    - Functionalities and performances
    - Less price-sensitive
  - Developing world segmentation:
    - Huge low-end commodity market
    - Rising middle class but still relatively small segment
    - Tiny, highly wealthy segment
  - Industrialized country segmentation:
    - Diverse segmentation
    - Middle-class market dominates
- Demand characteristics of a country:
  - Market growth, market size, segmentation, customer value curve, distribution and competition
  - Depends on the country *life cycle cluster* that country belongs to
  - country life cycles clusters:
    - Defined based on a country's wealth and its growth rate – a country goes through a 'country life cycle' depicting the relationship between the country's wealth and its long-term growth rate

- Types of country life cycle cluster include:
- Developing countries
- Emerging countries
- Newly industrialized economies
- Industrialized countries.

5 Industry opportunities assessment determines profitability potential of a company's presence in a country given the following factors:

- Quality of industry competitive structure (including Porter's five-force Industry Analysis Framework):
  - Intensity of rivalry
  - New entrants and entry barriers:
    - High capital investments
    - Short product life cycles
    - R&D costs
    - Proprietary products
    - Industry standards
    - Economies of scale
    - Large distribution channels
    - Some closed markets
    - Fear of retaliation
    - Regulatory requirements, e.g. licences
  - Bargaining power of suppliers:
    - Scarcity or proprietary nature of supplies
    - Concentrated suppliers
    - Threat of forward integration
  - Bargaining power of buyers:
    - Low switching costs
    - Concentrated buyers
    - Threat of backward integration
  - Threat of substitutes: alternative value proposition
  - Profitability:
    - Short-term
    - Long-term
- Resource availability:
  - Natural resources:
    - Examples include raw materials and geographical location
    - Governments are protective of country's natural resources
  - Human resources: examples include low-cost labour, skilled personnel (e.g. technological skills)
  - Infrastructure and support industries resources:
    - Examples include power, telecoms, roads
    - When combined with good geographical location, provide a competitive advantage to a country to become a regional centre

- Government:
  - Investment incentives granted by governments:
    - Fiscal incentives – tax reduction, exemption of import or export duties
    - Financial incentives – subsidies
    - Competitive incentives – preferential purchases
    - Operational incentives – preferential rates for rents, land, power and telecoms
    - Incentives play only a limited role in inducing foreign investment
  - Government intervention:
    - Price controls
    - Regulatory constraints
    - Taxation.

6 There are four categories of country risk:

- *Economic* risks:
  - Economic growth
  - Variability of economic factors
  - Inflation
  - Cost of inputs
  - Exchange rates
- *Competitive* risks (noneconomic distortion of competitive context):
  - Corruption
  - Cartels
- *Operational* risks:
  - Infrastructure:
    - Power, telecoms and transport
    - Suppliers
  - Regulations:
    - National preferences
    - Constraints on local capital, local content or local employment
    - Taxes
- *Political* risks:
  - Employees' exposure:
    - Gangsterism
    - Kidnapping
  - Operational exposure:
    - Market disruption
    - Labor unrest
    - Racketeering
    - Supplies shortage
  - Shareholders' exposure (loss of capital or loss through inability to repatriate dividends):
    - Asset destruction (e.g. war or riots)
    - Asset spoliation (expropriation)
    - Asset immobility (e.g. freeze).

Web resources

<http://data.worldbank.org/country>
Countries database from the World Bank.

<http://www.doingbusiness.org/rankings>
Ease of Doing Business from the World Bank.

<http://www.unctad.org/>
UNCTAD World Investment reports.

<http://www.weforum.org/issues/global-competitiveness>
Global competitiveness ranking.

<http://www.business-insights.com/>
Provides industries and countries data.

<http://www.prsgroup.com>
Country risks reports online.

<http://www.ihs.com/products/global-insight/index.aspx>
Industries and countries information.

<http://www.oecd.org/document/49/0,2340,en_2649_34171_1901105_1_1_1_1,00.html>
Country risk classification.

<http://www.coface.com/CofacePortal/COM_en_EN/pages/home/risks_home/country_risks>
From the French export insurance company.

Visit the companion website at **http://www.palgrave.com/business/lasserre3e** for a multitude of weblinks and resources, self-test questions for revision and a searchable glossary.

Notes

1 Porter (1998).

2 *The World Competitiveness Yearbook*, IMD, 23 Ch. de Bellerive, PO Box 915, Lausanne <http://www.imd.org/research/publications/wcy/wcy_book.cfm>.

3 PRS Group <http://www.polrisk.com>.

4 See The Country Petroleum Risk Environment Index <http://www.riskworld.com>.

5 UNCTAD (1996).

6 Guisinger (1985, 1992).

7 Literature is abundant on country risk: Brewer (1985); Howell and Chaddick (1994) pp. 70–90; Rogers (1997).

References and further reading

Austin, James E., *Managing in Developing Countries: Strategic Analysis and Operating Techniques*. New York: Free Press, 1990.

Brewer, Thomas L. (ed.), *Political Risks in International Business: New Directions for Research, Management and Public Policies*. New York: Praeger, 1985.

Farrell, Diana, Ulrich A. Gerch and Elizabeth Stephensen, 'The Value of China's Emerging Middle Class', *McKinsey Quarterly*, Special Edition: Serving the New Chinese Consumer, June 2006, p. 63.

Guisinger, Stephen, 'Environment and Structural Complexity in International Business Theory', unpublished paper.

Guisinger, Stephen, *Investment Incentives and Performance Requirements*. New York: Praeger, 1985.

Guisinger, Stephen, 'Rhetoric and Reality in International Business: A Note on the Effectiveness of Incentives', *Transnational Corporations*, 1, 1992, pp. 111–23.

Guisinger, Stephen, 'From OLI to OLMA: Incorporating Higher Levels of Environmental and Structural Complexity into the Eclectic Paradigm', *International Journal of the Economics of Business*, 8(2), 2001, pp. 257–72.

Howell, Llewellyn D. and Brad Chaddick, 'Models of Political Risk for Foreign Investment and Trade: An Assessment of Three Approaches', *Columbia Journal of World Business*, Fall 1994, pp. 70–90.

James, Mini and T.M. Koller, 'Valuation in Emerging Markets', *McKinsey Quarterly*, 4, 2000.

Kearney, A.T., *Offshoring for Long-Term Advantage*. Chicago, IL: A.T. Kearney Inc., 2007. Available at <http://www.atkearney.com/images/global/pdf/GSLI_2007.pdf>

Lasserre, Philippe and Hellmut Schütte, *Strategies for Asia Pacific: Beyond the Crisis*. London: Macmillan Palgrave, 1999.

Porter, Michael, *Competitive Strategy: Techniques for Analyzing Industries and Competitors*. New York: Free Press, 1980.

Porter, Michael, *The Competitive Advantage of Nations*. New York: Free Press, 1998.

Rogers, Jerry (ed.), *Global Risk Assessments: Issues, Concepts and Applications*. Riverside, CA: Global Risk Assessment, Inc., 1997.

UNCTAD, *Incentives and Foreign Direct Investment*: United Nations Conference on Trade and Development. Geneva: United Nations Publications, 1996.

UNCTAD World Investment Reports, 1996–2011: *United Nations Conference on Trade and Development*. Geneva: United Nations Publications.

chapter

7 ENTRY STRATEGIES

Introduction

Having performed the analysis of a country's attractiveness and decided positively to enter, a company has to work out an entry strategy that consists of three choices:

- *Entry objectives* (what the company is looking for in that country)
- *Timing* of entry (when to enter)
- *Mode* of entry (what kind of operations and under which legal form).

There may be four categories of objectives: to develop the market, to access critical resources, to capture knowledge available in the country and to set up a regional or global center for coordinating various activities.

The *timing* of entry can be critical for building sustainable competitive advantage. First-movers can capture initial advantages over competitors but run a variety of risks.

The choice of a *legal structure* is contingent upon many external and internal factors. There are six legal forms of entry: wholly owned operations built from scratch, acquisitions, joint ventures, licensing or franchising, distributors' agreements or a representative office. The advantages and disadvantages of each of those forms are discussed. The chapter ends by looking at entry strategy as a 'real option', and a numerical example is examined.

Learning objectives

At the end of the chapter you will be able to:

- complete a full analysis of various entry alternatives
- assess the advantages and disadvantages of alternative entry strategies in a concrete situation
- conduct a financial analysis of alternatives.

EXAMPLE

Carrefour's entry strategy

When Carrefour, the French mass retailer, decided in the late 1980s to enter the Asia Pacific region, it analyzed the countries in the region to see whether their economic and social characteristics were favorable to the hypermarket concept. To be a sustainable retailing concept, a hypermarket requires a growing urban concentration of middle-class populations benefiting from an income per household above US$1000 per annum and an infrastructure capable of handling the heavy logistics demanded by continuous supplies. Finally, the country should have institutional and political stability. Having eliminated Japan, because of its retailing structure and its astronomic real-estate cost, Carrefour considered four countries that, at that time, corresponded to their business concept criteria: Singapore, Korea, Hong Kong and Taiwan. Taiwan was chosen because, unlike Hong Kong and Singapore, mass retailing was not yet developed and Korea was not open to foreign companies in the retailing sector. Carrefour's motivations were to capture the opportunities offered by an increasing wealthy middle class in Taiwan. It also could 'learn' how to operate in a Chinese-speaking environment and to understand Chinese consumer behavior. Such learning would be highly valuable for a further expansion in China and in South East Asia where a large middle class of overseas Chinese resided. Taiwan required foreign retailers to tie up with a local firm in joint venture agreements. Carrefour was not against a local partner because it needed to acquire contacts with government officials and suppliers as well as learn about this new environment, but the company wanted to run the operation by itself. It was fortunate to find a strong local partner, the President Group, which was willing to help but did not interfere in operations.

After a few years, Carrefour expanded to other Asian countries: Malaysia, Thailand, China, Indonesia (under the form of joint ventures) and Hong Kong, Singapore and Japan (with a wholly owned subsidiary). In all these countries Carrefour adopted different entry strategies. This short example illustrates the topic of this chapter, the multifarious aspects of entry strategies.

A company's entry strategy involves answering three questions:

- Why does the company *want to enter* the country?
- When is it *appropriate* to enter?
- *How* can it enter?

Why enter? Defining strategic objectives for a country presence

There are four major types of strategic objective, not necessarily independent of each other:

- *Market development* objectives
- *Resources access* objectives
- *Learning* objectives
- *Coordination* objectives.

Market development objectives apply to those countries offering size and growth opportunities. To a certain extent, all countries in the world offer some kind of market opportunity as a function of their population and income. Some countries, however, are more critical than others owing to their size or the quality of their customer base. Those countries are often referred as *key countries*; i.e. countries in which a presence is needed for global long-term competitiveness. China, the United States, Japan, Germany, France and the United Kingdom are often considered as key countries for that reason. Market development objectives constitute the most common entry objectives.

Resources access objectives are based on the presence of a key resource – mineral, agricultural or human – that contributes to competitive advantage. An investment in a resource-rich country will essentially be made to extract the resource by setting up the appropriate operational asset – a mine, an exploration field, a plantation, an assembly plant or a software centre.

Learning objectives are the basis of investments in countries where the industry is state-of-the-art and in which a foreign investor gains knowledge and competencies by being present, even if the long-term market prospect is not favorable. Automobile companies set up operations in Japan in the 1980s to be close to the network of car manufacturers and component suppliers and to learn about their mode of relationships. California, Washington State or Texas may similarly be considered as learning ground for the 'new economy' (see Chapter 14), while companies dealing with fashion and perfume may consider Paris or Milan as an investment site.

Coordination objectives apply to hub countries where a presence is justified for the regional coordination of activities thanks to their location and infrastructure advantages.

Table 7.1 gives a summary of the four types of objectives and the expectations of foreign investors in each category.

When to enter? First mover, follower or acquirer?

The timing of entry is contingent upon the window of opportunity as well as the type of risk the company is willing to take.

For market-based objectives, a window of opportunity is open when the demand starts to become significant and the competitive context is not yet well established. For resource-based objectives, it is opened when rights of access are available and closed when competitors have established a strong market presence or pre-empted available resources. In such cases, only acquisitions or innovation can allow entrants to open the window. The concept of a window of opportunity is not unique to international entry. It applies also to new product or service development. In the entry context, four phases can be distinguished:

- The '*premature phase*', during which a significant investment in the country would not generate enough long-term revenues because of a lack of purchasing power or the absence of demand for the product or service. This phase is characteristic of developing countries at an early stage or of a product that does not fit the demand in a particular country. Although in the United States credit card business is very active, smart card manufacturers have found it difficult to penetrate the market because of the lack of support from the banking industry. A significant investment in smart cards in the 1980s or 1990s would not have been appropriate until the window of opportunity was open. It is not suggested that no investment is required at this stage, but it should be limited to representative offices, listening posts or distribution agreements.

- The '*window phase*', during which the market takes off but the competitive landscape is not yet well established. At this stage, the choice is to take a *first-mover view* or a *follower view*. The advantages and disadvantages of being first movers have been widely discussed[1] and there is empirical evidence that to be the first to enter in a country can lead to a strong competitive advantage[2] in emerging markets. Table 7.2 lists the arguments for and against being a first mover.

Table 7.1 Entry strategy objectives

	Market	Resources	Learning	Coordination
Expectations	• Market penetration and development • Capture a share of market	• Access to natural resources • Access to skilled low-cost labor • Access to suppliers	• Understand state-of-the-art technology • Close to best practices • Learn to compete in difficult and sophisticated markets	• Set up base for global or regional development • Establish logistic centers close to financing institutions
Key Performance Indicators (KPIs)	• Growth • Market share • Gross margin	• Costs • Quality • Supply access	• Know-how • Process improvement	• Speed • Control • Synergies
Timing	• Window of opportunity • First mover versus follower	• First mover in order to pre-empt resources	• As soon as country is recognized as 'competence' center	• Three stages: – Initiation – Growth – Coordination
Types of country	• All types prioritized as a function of market potential, quality and competitive context	• Resources-rich countries	• Countries with strong technological and know-how infrastructure	• Hubs
Mode of entry	• Depending upon risks, opportunities, timing and skills • All modes of entry may apply	• Wholly owned (if allowed and if low risk) • Joint venture (if requested) • Long-term sourcing contracts	• Joint venture • R&D center • Observatory	• Representative office • Global headquarters • Regional headquarters • Logistic center • Training center • Financial center

- The '*competitive growth phase*', when various competitors have taken advantage of the window of opportunity and are jockeying for market share in a high-growth situation. New entry at this stage is hazardous and requires either massive resources or a highly differentiated competitive strategy. One way to circumvent the handicap of being a late-comer is by an acquisition or joint venture.

- The '*mature phase*'. At this stage, the competition is well established and acquisition or direct investment with an innovative product is generally the only way to enter.

Table 7.2 Advantages and disadvantages of being a first mover

Advantages	Disadvantages
• Pre-empt resources : – Distribution – Location – People – Contacts – Suppliers • Establish brands • Establish standards • Learn about customers	• Take risks: – Market immature – Product unfitted – Lack of infrastructure • Struggle for the benefit of others (do the ground work)

Entry modes: how to enter?[3]

From the point of view of a foreign investor, the typical choice on entering a country is based on a combination of two major dimensions:

- The *control* dimension: going it alone with wholly owned operations in which the foreigner has full control and ownership or entering into partnerships
- The *investment intensity* dimension: investing in assets and competencies for value adding activities or limiting operations to commercial, development and administrative activities.

Intensity of investment	Weak control	Strong control
High	■ Minority joint venture ■ Consortium ■ Minority acquisition	■ Wholly owned subsidiary with greenfield investment ■ Dominant acquisition ■ Absolute majority joint venture
Low	■ Licensing ■ Distribution ■ Franchise ■ Agent	■ Procurement office ■ Representative office ■ Marketing subsidiary ■ Technical observatory ■ Regional headquarters

Control

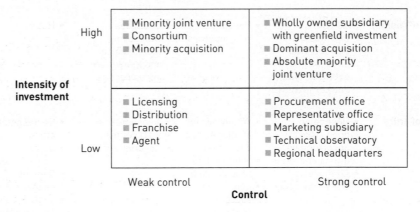

Figure 7.1 Entry modes

This leads to the various types of entry mode represented in Figure 7.1. Those choices should generally be determined by the following factors (Figure 7.2):

- The *overall attractiveness* of the market, as discussed in Chapter 6
- The *political and operational* risks involved
- The *government* requirements

- The *time pressures*
- The *internal capabilities* of the firm to enter and develop local resources, assets and competencies in order to gain and sustain competitive advantage
- The *strategic objectives* and the expected *return on investment* (ROI).

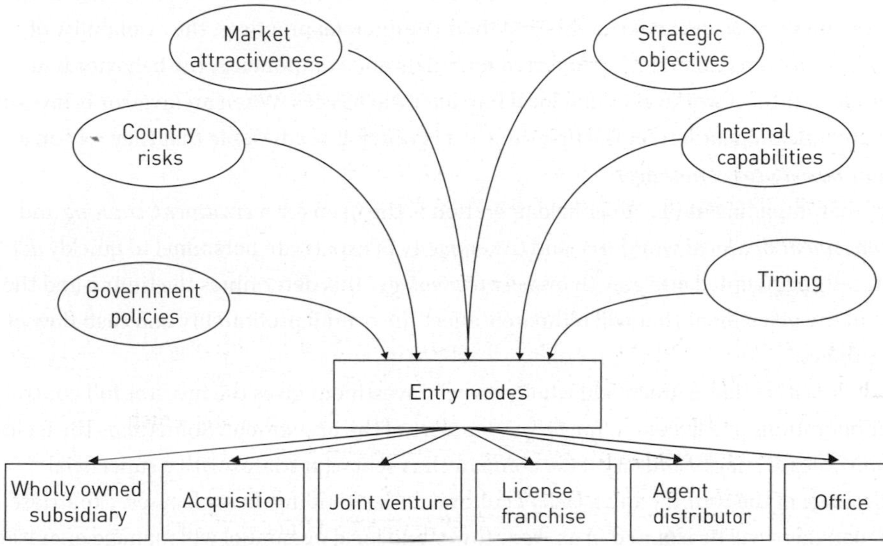

Figure 7.2 Factors influencing entry modes

The next part of the chapter is devoted to analyzing the main forms of entry along these dimensions. As far as the *joint venture mode* examined in Chapter 4 and the *acquistion mode* in Chapter 5 are concerned, the factors discussed will apply here. The analysis is summarized in Table 7.3 and in the mini case at the end of the chapter, where an example of various alternative entry modes is developed using a practical example.

Entering a country through wholly owned subsidiaries

This entry mode is the one that gives the most control over operations, but also involves the highest mobilization of resources and competencies and bears the highest risks. Creating a subsidiary in a country calls for the following requirements:

- Assuming that a proper country attractiveness and risk analysis has been done prior to the investment, you need first to familiarize yourself with the *legal, institutional, commercial* and *relational* environment. It is one thing to have analyzed the market and competition for decision-making, it is another thing to master the nitty-gritty of a full greenfield investment or an acquisition. This is the role of the *feasibility study* that analyzes the various aspects of an investment dealing with real estate, construction, project management, sourcing, recruitment, incorporation, registrations, financing, fiscal and legal matters. Feasibility studies should be supported by a full financial plan projecting future cash flow calculations and financial needs. Feasibility studies as well as project management can be contracted out to locally based consultants or engineering firms, but the overall control and responsibility fall upon the foreign investor.

- Managing a construction project in a foreign country involves a series of practical and sometimes difficult impediments, such as the norms and standards of construction, the professionalism of local contractors and their commercial practices, the availability of supplies, customs clearance of imported materials and components, the behavior and attitude of project workforces and local bureaucratic hassles. When an investor is investing in a greenfield operation for the first time in a country, it is advisable that they rely on a *locally based project manager*.
- A further impediment of a greenfield operation is the need for *recruitment, training* and *management* of a local workforce and the capacity of expatriate personnel to quickly get culturally acquainted and able to *transfer technology*. This determines the timing and the cost of the investment that will ultimately affect the overall profitability and cash flow of the project.
- On the positive side, a greenfield wholly owned investment gives the investor full control over operations and access to the *full profitability* of the investment. Sometimes the feeling of 'full control' may be illusory if the company has sent expatriates with a superficial knowledge of the country and a lack of cultural understanding. In such cases, expatriate top managers will be isolated in an ivory tower and local personnel will manage operations their own way, hiding behind apparent obedience and respect.
- On the financial front, a wholly owned investment demands that foreign investors bear the full risk of *equity and debt financing*, sometimes facilitated by export credit insurance granted by the home country government or insurance community.

Entering a country through acquisitions

Chapter 5 dealt with international acquisitions and there is no need to repeat here what was examined there. Overall, the advantage of acquisitions as an entry mode is the immediate availability of resources, assets and competencies that saves time for the foreign investor. Another advantage is the access provided to a market of resources when the competitive arena is already well occupied and the window of opportunity is closed. On the less positive side, acquisitions in foreign environments demand *cross-cultural integration skills* that may not be the prime talent of investors. Acquisitions of local firms by foreigners can also be seen in certain cases as an intrusion that bruises national pride. Finally, acquisitions are often made with high acquisition premiums that make this mode of entry more costly than other alternatives.

Table 7.3 Types of local partners for country-based joint ventures

	Suppliers	Customers/distributors	Competitors	Diversifiers	Investors	Government
Prime motive of local partner	• Secure sales of raw material • Learn about downstream technology • Pre-empt competitors • 'Control' price	• Access to product/process 'technology' • Pre-empt competitors • Control price of raw material or components	• Collusion • Technology • Product complementation • Upgrading • Market control • Best practices	• Additional source of profit • Capture new opportunities • 'Risk' spreading	• Return • Shareholder values	• National development • Technology • Employment • Political pay-off
Prime motive of foreign partner	• Secure raw material resources	• Market access • Learn about market	• Market access • Learn about market • Resources • Assets • Competencies • Market control	• Power/contacts • Flexibility • Potential target for acquisition	• Contacts • Satisfy legal requirements • Capital	• Satisfy legal requirement • Favorable preferences
Advantages	• Resources	• Distribution	• Market power	• Contacts • No or little interference • Some operational support	• Contacts • No or little interference	
Disadvantages	• Technology change • Quality • Flexibility • Pressure for vertical acquisition by partner	• Lack of overall industrial competencies • Short-term mindset of partner • Dependency • Pressure for vertical acquisition by partner	• Technology leakage • Conflicts with other products	• Thin resources from partner • Little 'learning' • Opportunism	• No 'learning' • No operational support	• Bureaucracy • Politics

Entering a country through joint ventures[4]

Local joint ventures were discussed in the previous chapter. What needs emphasizing here are the following approaches to joint ventures.

- *Partner selection:* Selecting a local partner is probably the most critical decision for a good joint venture. Multiple sources of information need to be used; track records of the partner need to be carefully scrutinized and if possible several alternatives need to be considered. Ideally, a company should select a local partner with whom it has experienced previous business dealings during which it had the possibility to appreciate the capabilities and the business practices of the local firm. *Fit analysis* as described in Chapter 4 should be done rigorously to provide some form of due diligence.
- A *joint feasibility* study has to be done jointly between the two partners as a real business plan and not considered as an administrative constraint. This joint work permits a mutual understanding of the partners before they engage themselves in the relationship. This business plan is done in parallel with the financial and legal negotiation.
- *Operational personnel* should be part of the negotiation process, at least partially, because only operational people can identify the day-to-day technical and logistical problems that may occur during the running of the business.
- Particular attention has to be given to the *selection of personnel* detached to the joint venture. Cultural, inter-personal and teaching skills should be given as much priority as technical skills.
- *Integration teams*, as described in Chapter 4, should be organized as early as possible
- *Training programs* are an important part of the technology transfer that is necessary when the joint venture is set up in an emerging country.
- Building and maintaining *trust* is an essential source of success in a joint venture. Below are the main actions and behaviors that are conducive to trust:
  - Demonstrate commitment to the joint venture, detaching the right personnel, the right technology and the appropriate financing
  - Keep personal communication running even when times are difficult and possible conflicts are arising
  - Provide advance warning of any change that you want to introduce
  - Make sure that you and your personnel are showing respect toward the other party. Cultural sense is a good ingredient of trust.
- When *ending* a joint venture make sure that a *win–win* solution is found. Even when the joint venture dissolves because of conflicts or bad results it is important to make sure that nobody loses face in the process.

Entering a country through arm's-length agreements: licensing, franchising, agents and distributors

When a direct investment is not justified, foreign companies can still be present in a particular country by contracting an agreement in the form of a license, a franchise, an agency or a distribution contract.

These contractual arrangements are made when one or more of the following characteristics are present:

- The market is *too small* for the company to justify a full investment
- The country is perceived as *too risky*
- There is already a direct investment in a nearby country and an additional one would be redundant
- The government does not allow *any other form of presence*
- The company wants to *test the market*.

Licensing agreements and franchises

Licensing agreements[5] are contractual arrangements by which a company (the *licensor*) transfers to another company (the *licensee*) its product and/or process technology with the right to exploit it commercially. The brand name of the licensor may or may not be part of the licensing agreement. The licensor receives financial compensation in the form of royalties and an up-front lump sum payment. Royalties can be calculated as a percentage of sales or as a fixed amount per unit sold. In addition to the transfer of technology, the licensor may send its engineers to help in technology transfer and functioning. It may also receive some form of technological fees. Finally, within a licensing agreement, a licensor can contractually force the licensee to buy intermediate products or components. In that case, the licensor gets the benefits and profits associated with those sales.

The benefits of licenses are the low commitment in terms of personnel and capital involved. It is an economic way to enter a market. However, the disadvantages are manifold. First, there is a risk of *technological appropriation* by the licensee, who may become a future competitor. This has been the case in the past with Framatome of France, which licensed in the technology of high-pressure nuclear reactors from Westinghouse and progressively became more advanced and more competitive than the licensor. Another risk involves *quality control.* Particularly when the license includes the brand name of the licensor, if the licensee is not quality conscious, it may ruin the name of the licensee. The main strategic disadvantage of licensing is that the licensors are very distant from the market and have no control over the company's destiny in the licensee country.

Franchises[6] are another form of indirect contractual arrangement through which the *franchiser* grants the *franchisee* the right to use its name and receive a financial compensation similar to the licensing agreement (fixed plus royalties). The franchiser generally forces the franchisee to adopt a certain number of operating policies so that it can maintain a standard level of quality associated with its brand name. Examples of international franchises can be found in the hospitality industry (Hilton, Accor), beverages (Coca-Cola bottling), fast food (McDonald's) and distribution (Benetton, Gap).

The advantages and disadvantages of franchises are very similar to those of licensing.

Local agents and distributors

The appointment of a local agent or distributor is probably the most frequent mode of entry for the thousands of SMEs who want to reach international markets. For the most established large multinational enterprises, this is also a means to reach countries that are either risky or whose size does not justify a major investment. It can also be an economic way to test markets without committing too many resources up-front. The distinction between an *agent* and a *distributor* is that the latter carries out the logistical tasks of stocking, transporting and billing, while the former is simply a salesperson and an order-taker. In emerging markets you can often find three categories of agents and distributors: domestic companies (most often medium-sized firms or large multi-business family conglomerates), government monopolies in planned economies; or large international trading companies like Jardine Matheson, the East Asiatic Company, or Diethelm or Swire in the Asia Pacific region.

The main advantage of distribution agreements is that they require a limited amount of resource from the global firm; the main disadvantages are the lack of contact with the market and the conflict of interest that can emerge when sales reach a certain level.[7] The economic reason for this conflict is caused by the fact that distributors are generally remunerated by a commission as a percentage of sales. When sales grow, the total commission may reach a point where it is bigger than the fixed costs required to set up a wholly owned marketing subsidiary. The multinational firms then try to get rid of the local distributor, as has been seen in Europe with the Japanese car makers who have progressively replaced their distributors with their own organization in major countries. Knowing this, the local distributor may be tempted to fail to push sales when it is obvious that a substitution point is approaching. Instead of fighting a lost cause, international distributors have often adopted a strategy of becoming 'partners' rather than pure distributors and raising the value added of their services to both customers and principals in order to raise 'switching costs'. However, when the country becomes a significant portion of the turnover and becomes 'key', the global firm will generally turn to another, more direct mode of entry.

Entering a country through a representative, technical or procurement office

The **representative office** is another very frequent entry mode, considered as a stepping stone or a 'beachhead'. In China, Russia, Vietnam and newly opened countries this type of entry consists of sending an expatriate manager (sometimes using a locally recruited person) to collect information, establish contacts, organize direct sales, lobby for licenses, negotiate distribution or joint venture agreements and recruit local personnel. This entry mode is frugal in resource consumption and beneficial in competencies-building, but it reaches its limit when it comes to actually running a business. It fits corporations that are selling big projects (railways systems, airport or defence contracts, turnkey plants) at the pre-bidding phase. In these cases, representative offices complement and control the local agents who are lobbying for information and access to decision-makers.

Technical offices are another form of entry. Technical offices are most relevant when the country is considered to be a source of technological innovation and a presence can give access to useful contacts and information.

Procurement or purchasing offices are most appropriate for large retailers or big commodity buyers who set up an office in order to be close to suppliers, to negotiate contracts and to control their execution. Some companies specialize in buying for third parties and are used by firms which do not want to commit resources to establishing their own office.

Entry modes seen as 'real options'

The concept of the **'real option'** has been proposed in recent business strategy literature to explain some investment decisions, including foreign investment decisions.[8] The theory of the real option is directly derived from the financial theory of options. According to the real option proponents, some investments can be assimilated to a 'call option', that is to say a preliminary investment to observe the future development of the business, and at the end of a trial period, the company has the possibility to expand or retreat. The cost of making the preliminary investment is equivalent to the price of an option. If the company sees that the foreign investment is creating future value then it can exercise its option and expand – i.e. increase its stake in a joint venture, transform a license into an acquisition or replace a distributor with a full investment. If the business does not seem to be developing, it stops the investment, sells its share in the joint venture and continues under license or as a distributor, or sells the business.

Comparing entry modes

Each mode of entry described earlier has its advantages and disadvantages. Table 7.4 summarizes the pluses and minuses of each of them based on various criteria.

Table 7.4 shows that *wholly owned approaches* and acquisitions have the most significant market impact and subsequent payout. The return on investment is high to moderate and, in our example, is close to the cost of capital. The reason is that in the case of a wholly owned investment, it takes time to build a market presence and in the case of an acquisition, the original investment requires an up-front premium. The residual value in those two cases explains most of the return, indicating that those two kinds of investments are valid from a long-term perspective and should be used only when country risks are limited. Licensing is highly profitable from a return viewpoint. This is owing to a minimal up-front investment and a constant flow of royalties, but the absolute value is small. This fits a situation of high risks and low commitment. The long-term impact of a licensing agreement is weak. Joint ventures are middle of the road and the example in the mini case below gives that strategy a higher return than both the wholly owned or acquisition modes. However, joint ventures, as mentioned earlier, do not have a brilliant performance record, showing that the theoretical value of this mode of entry is often hampered by poor implementation.

See the mini case below for details. The cash flows are the cumulative flow of investments paid by the foreign firm and the dividends or royalties received plus the terminal value at the end of the period. Net Present Value (NPV) assumes capital costs of 15 per cent.

Table 7.4 Comparing various entry modes

	Wholly owned	Acquisition	Joint venture	Licensing	Representative office	Agent/ distributor
Up-front investment, financial and managerial	High	High	Medium	Low	Low/med	Low
Speed of entry	Slow	Quick	Quick	Medium	Low	Possibly quick
Market penetration	Medium	High	Med/high	Med/low	Low	Med/low
Control of market (customer knowledge)	High	High	Medium	Nil	Low	Low/nil
Political risk exposure	High	High	Medium	Low	Low	Low
Technological leakage	Low	Low	High/med	High	Low	Low
Managerial complexity	High	High	High	Low	Medium	Low
Potential financial return	High risk High/ Medium return high payout	High risk High/Medium return High payout	Medium/High risk High/Medium return Medium payout	Low risk High return Low payout	Low risk return?	Low risk return?

Choosing an entry mode

The choice of an entry mode is a function of the factors described at the beginning of the chapter and illustrated in Figure 7.2 (p. 211). There is no ideal solution and the choice is up to each company, according to the weighting given to corporate global strategy, country risks and opportunities, capabilities, timing and government constraints. Figure 7.3 gives a mapping of possible choice as a function of some of these factors, but in the end, the final decision is a multidimensional one that resists a simplistic 3 x 3 representation.

Market attractiveness / Political investment climate	Poor	Medium	Good
High	■ Minimum financial exposure ■ Minority in joint ventures ■ Licensing	■ Wholly owned affiliate ■ Majority acquisition or joint venture	■ Maximum commitment ■ Wholly owned affiliate ■ Full acquisition
Medium	■ Limited presence ■ Distributor/agent ■ Licensing	■ Joint venture	■ High commitment ■ Wholly owned or acquisition
Low	■ Occasional exports	■ Export sales agent ■ Licensing	■ Independent distributor

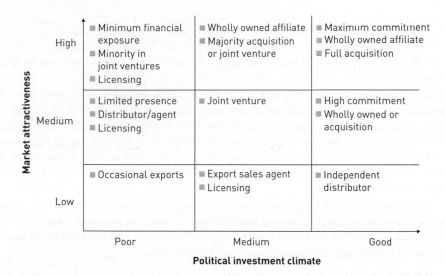

Figure 7.3 Mapping of entry modes choices

Over time, with economic growth and increased internal capabilities, foreign investors may shift from one mode to another. In China, for instance, wholly owned foreign enterprises overtook equity joint ventures in 1997.[9]

MINI-CASE

Lubricador SA

Lubricador SA is an Italian specialist chemical company with a wide range of products serving various industrial applications. The car division of the company specializes in special lubricants for brake and air-conditioning systems. In late 2011, the company sent a mission to China to analyze the market and prepare an analysis of various investment alternatives. China had become the second largest car market in the world and was on the way to full recovery after the subprime global financial crisis of 2009. The Chinese car industry was extremely competitive with local as well as international players fighting for market share. The study team had concentrated on one particular type of product: brake fluid additive. It estimated that the current domestic market of 8,000 tons a year would grow at a rate of 9 per cent a year over the decade from 2012 to 2022. The competition was made up of two domestic firms which controlled 70 per cent of the market and one Japanese joint venture which controlled 30 per cent. The study team concluded that there were four major alternatives for market entry:

- *Set up a greenfield operation and operate as a 100 per cent subsidiary.* The minimum economic capacity was 9000 tons for a total investment of US$20 million. The financing of the investment would be done entirely by the mother company and it could expect to repatriate a dividend of 100 per cent of net profit when this became positive. The subsidiary could not expect to capture more than 10 per cent of market share the first year, growing progressively 5 per cent a year and stabilizing at 30 per cent after the fifth year of operations. Export output would be around 1000 tons the first year increasing by 500 tons per year up to 3000 tons.

MINI-CASE

- The second alternative was to *buy the Japanese competitors*. The acquisition price would be US$25 million but they could expect to capture the 30 per cent market share right away. The yearly growth and export output, as compared with the first alternative, would be the same.
- A third option would be to *form a joint venture with an existing Chinese firm*. The immediate market share would be 30 per cent, rising to 50 per cent in the third year owing to the improved technology of the Italian firm. The total investment cost would be US$30 million. The financing of the joint venture would be 30 per cent equity to be shared 50/50 with the local partner and 70 per cent debts to be serviced over seven years. The maximum exports in that case would only be 2000 tons per year. All other hypotheses would remain the same.
- Finally, it was possible to conclude a *licensing agreement with a local firm* which, at best, could use and transform its existing facilities and obtain a 20 per cent market share. In such a case, Lubricador SA would have to invest US$600,000 over the next three years to transfer its technology and receive a royalty of 200 yuan/kg.

Other factors to consider were:

- *Exchange rate:* US$1 = 650 yuans (the study considered that the yuan may appreciate against the $ by 20 per cent in 2015)
- *Prices/costs:*
  Selling price (domestic) = 3500 yuans/kg
  Selling price (export) = 4.5 US$/kg
  Production costs = Declining function with cumulated volume
  $= 2500-0.025 * 10^{\text{log cum volume}}$
  Administrative/marketing costs = 1,200 million yuan, increasing to 1,600 million yuans
- *Working capital requirement* = 33 per cent of production costs
- *Tax rate on profit* = 30 per cent
- *Weighted Average Cost of Capital* (WACC) = 15 per cent
- *Domestic loans interest rate*: 10 per cent
- *Debt servicing*: 7 years

Questions:

1) What is the return for Lubricador of each option?
2) Beyond the return, what are the advantages and disadvantages of each option?
3) Which option would you select?

Summary and key points

1 Entry strategy concerns three aspects:

- Entry *objectives (why)*
- *Timing* of entry *(when)*
- *Mode* of entry *(how).*

2 Entry objectives:

- *Market development* objectives are to enter a market because of:
  - Size and growth opportunity – depends on income and population of a country
  - Criticality of countries – there are key countries in which a presence is needed for global long-term competitiveness owing to size or quality of customer base
- *Resource access* objectives – extracting key resource such as natural or human resources which contribute to competitive advantage
- *Learning* objectives – gains in knowledge/competence in countries where industry is state-of-the-art
- *Coordination* objectives – regional coordination of activities owing to favorable location and infrastructure advantages.

3 Timing of international entry – there are four phases:

- *Premature* phase:
  - Absence of demand
  - Common in developing countries at an early stage or for a product that does not fit demand in a particular country
  - Appropriate investment at this stage is the establishment of any of:
    - Representative offices
    - Listening posts
    - Distribution agreements
- *Window* phase ('Window of opportunity'):
  - Take-off of the market with relatively less competition
  - Potential strategies include:
    - Follower
    - First mover:
      - Advantages – pre-empt resources; establish brands; establish standards; learning about customers
      - Disadvantages – take risks; others can 'free ride' your ground work
- *Competitive growth* phase:
  - High market growth but competitors have received first-mover advantages
  - Potential strategies:
    - Hazardous entry but with massive resources or a highly differentiated strategy
    - Acquisition or joint venture arrangement
- *Mature* phase:
  - Well-established market
  - Potential strategies:
    - Acquisition
    - Direct investment with innovative product.

4 Mode of entry:

- Factors influencing entry mode:
  - Strategic objectives
  - Country risks (political and operational risks)

  - Opportunities
  - Company's internal capabilities
  - Time pressure
  - Government requirements
- *Types* of entry mode:
  - *Wholly owned subsidiaries:*
    - Advantages – gives most control over operations; low technological leakage
    - Disadvantages – requires the highest mobilization of resources and competencies; highest risk; high up-front investment; slow entry
  - *Acquisition*:
    - Advantages – immediate availability of resources, assets and competencies; enables access to market when window of opportunity is closed; high market penetration; high control of market; low technological leakage
    - Disadvantages – requires cross-cultural integration skills that acquiring company may not possess; some nationalities may view acquisition by foreigners unfavorably; costly, as often associated with high acquisition premiums; high political risk exposure
  - *Joint venture:*
    - Advantages – quick entry; medium to high market penetration
    - Disadvantages – medium to high technological leakage; high managerial complexity
    - Partner selection – depends on a combination of legal requirements and internal capabilities the firm possesses
    - Partners categories:
      - Sleeping
      - Complementing
      - Investor
      - 'Teaching'
      - Acquisition
    - Partners types – each has their own advantages and disadvantages:
      - Supplier
      - Customer/distributor
      - Competitor
      - Diversifier
      - Investor
      - Government
    - Partner evaluation - uses the same criteria used in assessing alliance partner: strategic fit, capability fit, cultural fit and organizational fit
    - Management:
      - Staffing – foreign managers should possess political and cultural skills; local staff should ideally be loyal to the joint venture, not to the local partner
      - Control – can be obtained through shareholding ownership or responsibility over operational functions
    - Termination renewal:
      - Termination – potential problems are the '*death valley*' issue (development of a

vicious cycle in which partners' communications are shut off) and joint venture decay (drop of mutual interest and loss of impetus for further collaboration)
      - Failures/problems – absence of strategic vision; 'believing without seeing'; failure to understand local partner's strategic logic; haste in negotiation; insufficiently prepared staff or lack of organizational support
      - Renewal – revitalize the joint venture by increasing range or broadening scope of its activities
  - *License or franchise:*
    - Advantages – economic (low commitment of personnel and capital); low political risk exposure
    - Disadvantages – risk of technological appropriation by licensee who may become future competitor; damage to brand name if licensee is not quality conscious; licensor's lack of control over license destiny in the licensee country
  - *Agent or distributor:*
    - Frequently used by SMEs for reaching international markets
    - Entry mode for reaching countries that are either risky or whose size does not justify a major investment
    - There are three categories of agent or distributor in emerging countries:
      - Multi-business family conglomerates
      - Government monopolies
      - Large international trading companies
    - Advantages:
      - Economic (low resource commitment)
      - Possible quick entry
      - Low political risk exposure
      - Low technological leakage
    - Disadvantages:
      - Lack of contact with market
      - Conflict of interest when the sales reach certain level
  - *Office* (representative office/procurement office/technical office):
    - Representative office
      - Advantages – frugal in resource consumption; beneficial in competence building; appropriate when corporations are selling big projects at the pre-bidding phase; low political risk exposure; low technological leakage
      - Disadvantages – slow entry; low market penetration; low control of market
    - Technical or procurement offices:
      - Useful when country is source of technological innovation and company presence gives access to useful contacts and information
      - Procurement offices most appropriate for large retailers or big commodity buyers who want to be close to suppliers and control contract execution
- *Choice* of entry mode – dependent on weighting a company assigned to various factors influencing entry modes
- A 'real option' (a call option)

- Price of option is the cost of making the preliminary investment
- Choices from real option are:
  - Expand investment if foreign investment is creating future value
  - Terminate investment if foreign investment does not seem to develop.

Learning assignments

1. What are the relative advantages/disadvantages of setting up a wholly owned subsidiary instead of a joint venture?
2. What is a 'window of opportunity'?
3. Under which conditions does being a first mover give sustainable competitive advantage?
4. What are the major problems associated with licensing?
5. What potential problems does a foreign investor experience in an industrial joint venture with an ex-local agent or distributor?
6. Why do joint ventures often fail?

Key words

- Entry modes
- First mover
- Franchise
- Joint venture
- Licensing
- Real option
- Representative offices
- Wholly owned operations
- Window of opportunity

Web resources

<http://www.unctad.org/>
See various publications from UNCTAD.

Visit the companion website at **http://www.palgrave.com/business/lasserre3e** for a multitude of weblinks and resources, self-test questions for revision and a searchable glossary.

Notes

1. Lieberman and Montgomery (1988).
2. Luo and Peng (1998).
3. On entry mode, see: Anderson and Gatignon (1986); Kim and Hwang (1992).
4. Beamish and Bank (1987).
5. See Contractor (1981); Beamish (1996).

6 Gompers and Connely (1997).
7 Arnold (2000).
8 Kogut and Kulatilaka (1994); Luermann (1997); Williamson (1999).
9 Vanhonacker (1997).

References and further reading

Adarkar, Ashwin, Asif Adil, David Ernst and Paresh Vaish, 'Emerging Market Alliances: Must They Be Win–Lose?', *McKinsey Quarterly*, 4, 1997, pp. 120–37.

Anderson, Erin and Hubert Gatignon, 'Modes of Foreign Entry: A Transaction Costs Analysis and Propositions', *Journal of International Business Studies*, 17(3), 1986, pp. 1–26.

Arnold, David, 'Seven Rules of International Distribution', *Harvard Business Review*, November–December 2000, pp. 131–7.

Beamish, Paul, 'Note on International Licensing', Richard Ivey School of Business, University of Western Ontario, Note 9A96G008, 1996.

Beamish, Paul and John Bank, 'Equity Joint Ventures and the Theory of the Multinational Enterprise', *Journal of International Business Studies*, 18(3), 1987, pp. 1–16.

Cavusgil, S. Tamer and Pervez N. Ghauri, *Doing Business in Developing Countries: Entry and Negotiation Strategies*. London: Routledge, 1991.

Contractor, Farok, *International Technology Licensing: Compensation, Costs and Negotiation*. Lexington, MA: D.C. Heath, 1981.

Gompers, Paul and Catherine Connely, 'A Note on Franchising', Harvard Business School, Note 9-297-108, 1997.

Kim, Chan and Peter Hwang, 'Global Strategies and Multinational Entry Mode Choice', *Journal of International Business Studies*, 23(1), 1992, pp. 29–53.

Kogut, Bruce, 'The Stability of Joint Ventures: Reciprocity and Competitive Rivalry', *Journal of Industrial Economics*, 38(2), 1989, pp. 183–98.

Kogut, Bruce and Nalin Kulatilaka, 'Options Thinking and Platform Investments: Investing in Opportunity', *California Management Review*, Winter 1994, pp. 52–71.

Lieberman, Marvin and David Montgomery, 'First Mover Advantages', *Strategic Management Journal*, 9, 1988, pp. 41–58.

Luermann, Timothy, 'Investment Opportunities as Real Options: Getting Started on the Numbers', *Harvard Business Review*, July–August 1997, pp. 51–67.

Luo, Yadong and Mike Peng, 'First Mover Advantages in Investing in Transitional Economies', *Thunderbird International Business Review*, 40, 1998, pp. 141–63.

Miller, Robert, Jack D. Glen, Frederick Jasperen and Yannis Karmokolias, International Joint Ventures in Developing Countries: Happy Marriages? *International Finance Corporation, Discussion Paper*, 29, 1996.

Rigman, Tom, 'Window of Opportunity: Timing and Entry Strategies', *Industrial Management and Data Systems*, 96(5), 1996.

Root, Franklin, *Entry Strategies for International Markets*. San Francisco: Jossey-Bass, 1994.

Vanhonacker, Wilfried, 'Entering China: An Unconventional Approach, *Harvard Business Review*, March–April 1997, pp. 130–41.

Williamson, Peter J., 'Strategy as Options on the Future', *Sloan Management Review*, Spring 1999, pp. 117–26.

Williamson, Peter J. and Hu Qionghua, *Managing the Global Frontier: Strategies for Developing Markets*. London: Pitman. 1994.

part

II MANAGING GLOBALLY

Part II, Managing Globally, considers the various *managerial issues* in the various business functions.

Chapter 8 **Global marketing** | Chapter 8 starts by discussing the theory of customers' convergence and then analyzes the practical approach to global marketing in the various elements of the marketing mix: branding, pricing, global account management, global solution selling and global distribution.

Chapter 9 **Global operations** | Chapter 9 deals with the localization of operational facilities, the various roles of manufacturing plants in a global network, global procurement and the management of the supply chain. It then discusses the various phases of project management as well as the role of the Internet in the globalization of operations.

Chapter 10 **Global innovation** | Chapter 10 deals with the management of research and development (R&D) in global companies as well as knowledge management, transfer of best practices and the issues of technology transfer and protection of intellectual property rights (IPR).

Chapter 11 **Cross-cultural management** | Chapter 11 discusses the impact of cultural differences on the management of cross-cultural teams, on international negotiations and on business practices. It begins with a presentation of different streams of research showing international differences in business cultures and economic organizations. The last part of the chapter deals with international negotiations.

Chapter 12 **Global human resource management** | Chapter 12 addresses the practical managerial aspects of human resources in global firms. Beside the classic problems of expatriation, it looks at the means of developing local talent in the various countries in which the firms operate and creating a real global organizational culture.

Chapter 13 **Global financial management** | Chapter 13 addresses some of the most current issues that global corporations face in managing their financial resources. The first section deals with the risks associated with foreign exchange fluctuations and the hedging techniques used to cover those risks. The second part looks at project financing. The third part discusses the source of global financing; both equity and debts. Finally trade financing is described in a fourth part. The chapter ends with an expanded example.

chapter

8 GLOBAL MARKETING

Introduction

In 1983 Theodore Levitt, in a far-sighted article, predicted the 'globalization of markets'. His arguments were based on the *convergence of consumer needs and behaviors* that would erase national differences and would lead to the standardization of marketing policies.

In Chapter 1 it was shown that since 1980, globalization had definitely gained ground and that many companies had designed, launched, promoted, priced and sometimes distributed products and services globally. Brands such as Coca-Cola, SONY, Intel, Kodak or Windows are known in nearly all cities on the planet. In early 2000 Unilever, one of the oldest and multinational corporations, announced that it would reduce the number of its brands from 1600 to 400. The TV cable channel CNN maintains that it reaches viewers all over the globe. The *International Herald Tribune*, a joint publication of the *New York Times* and the *Washington Herald Tribune*, based in Paris, is simultaneously printed in 11 cities and distributed in 164 countries. This chapter discusses the practical implications of globalization for marketing, as well as its limitations. It starts by examining the validity of the theory of customer convergence and then looks at the practical approach to global marketing in the various elements of the marketing mix.

Learning objectives

At the end of the chapter you will be able to:

- understand customer behavior divergence and convergence across countries
- understand differences in segmentation
- design a product policy toward standardization or adaptation
- decide whether the company will push global or local brands
- decide whether the company should have a global pricing policy
- design an appropriate global distribution system
- develop a global account and global solution selling policy.

Customer behavior, convergence and global segmentation

The prime task of any marketing manager is to understand customers' needs, embodied in customer value curves. Customer needs are driven by a series of factors, as summarized in Table 8.1.

It can be seen from Table 8.1 that several factors shaping needs are linked to *culture and geography*. For instance, Schütte (1998) has argued that Asian customers have a different hierarchy of needs and consequently exhibit value curves that differ from Western ones[1] (Figure 8.1) and Parker (2000) shows that bioclimatic conditions change customer preferences.

Beside Levitt, Kenichi Ohmae and George Yip are defenders of global convergence, arguing that an increasing percentage of the population, at least in the market-led economies, share the same tastes and needs for larger quantities of products and services. Ohmae has proposed the term '*Californization*' to describe this convergence.

There is no conclusive evidence of full convergence for consumer goods except in the case of a few products or services that are highly publicized (portable computers, mobile phones, luxury goods). However, in business-to-business sectors convergence is gaining ground, since purchasing motives are essentially technical and economic. Each industry market can be divided into different broad segments, as illustrated in Figure 8.2.

Table 8.1 Customer needs and value curves

Factors shaping customer needs	
Consumer markets	***Business-to-business markets***
• Income	• Industry type
• Psychology	• Usage
• Social habits	• Cost/benefit
• Social status	• Technological requirements
• Climatic conditions	• Time availability
• Time availability	
Typical customer value curve elements	
• Product/service functionalities (comfort, design, appeal, etc.)	• Product/service functionalities
• Product/service quality	• Product/service performances
• Image	• Reputation
• Price	• Relationships
• Availability	• Price and associated costs
• Convenience	• Associated services
• Associated services	• Financing
• Financing	• Network effects
• Network effects	

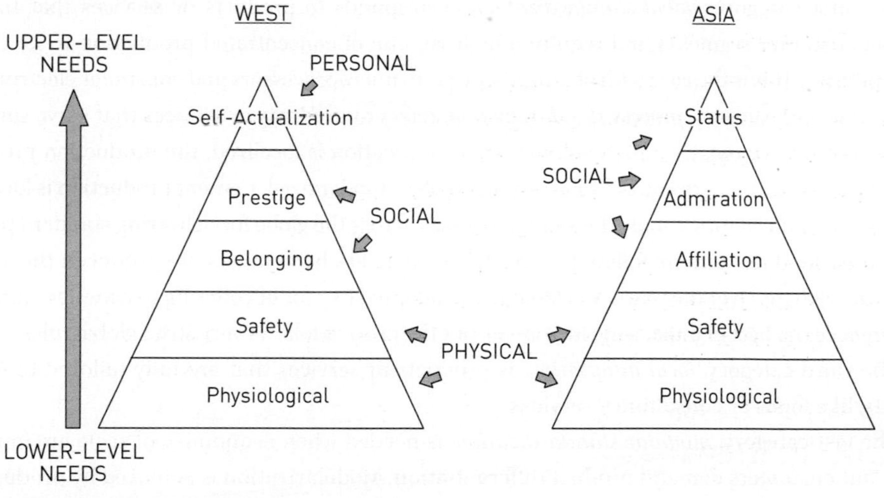

Figure 8.1 Western versus Asian hierarchy of needs

Source: Schütte (1998)

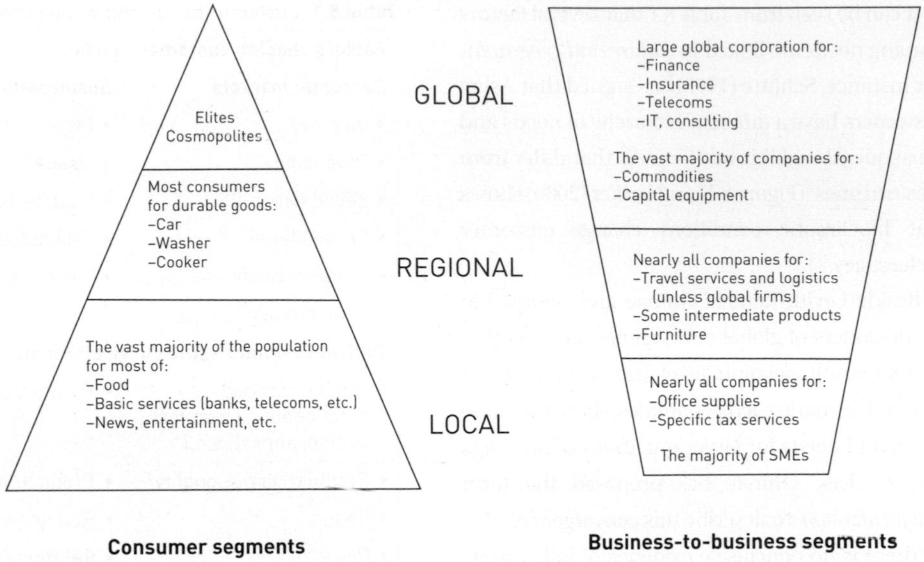

Figure 8.2 Customer segmentation

Product standardization

The standardization of products and services is a function of two main factors. First, *customer value curves*: the more similar are customer needs across the world, the more the product can be standardized. Second, the minimum economic size of production: the higher the volume required, the more standardization. Figure 8.3 shows four categories of product and the importance to them of those two factors.

The first category, *global standardization*, corresponds to products or services that target global customer segments and require a high volume of concentrated production to be cost-competitive. This is the case with chemicals, aircraft, microprocessors and consumer electronics.

The second category, *process standardization*, refers to products or services that serve similar needs but do not require a high volume. Their production is localized, the production process standardized and, as a result, the final product is also standardized. Cement production is local in production and factories apply the same processes across the globe for delivering standard products. Fast-food restaurants follow this model: McDonald's hamburgers are produced the same way everywhere. Over the years, McDonald's has adapted its product offering to cater for national differences (no beef in India, wine in France), but the process follows very strict global rules.

The third category, *local adaptation*, is products or services that are fully tailored to local needs, like foods or consultancy services.

The last category, *modular standardization*, is needed when economies of scale are important but customers demand product differentiation. Modularization is achieved by producing standard components in global factories and differentiating the product at the assembly stage. This is the case with automobiles or computers, such as Dell or ACER.

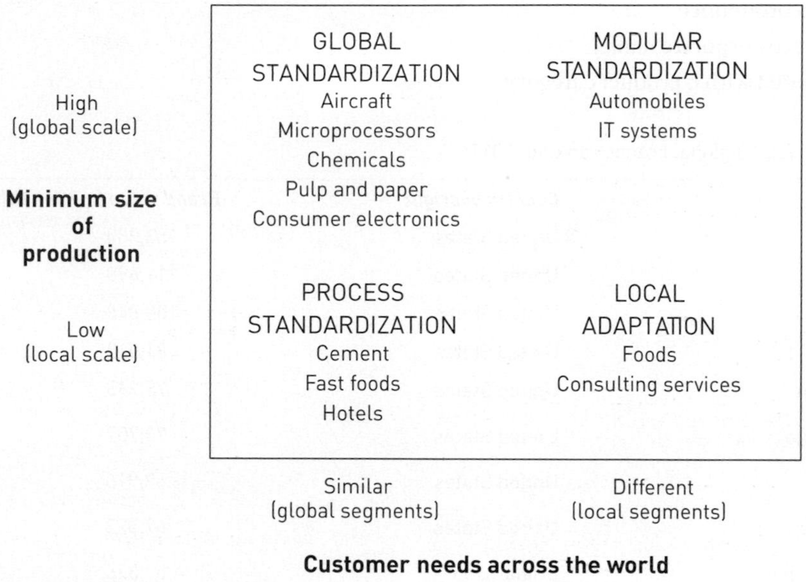

Figure 8.3 Global product standardization types

Global branding[2]

A brand is *global* when the product or service it represents is marketed across the world under its name. The most famous global brands are listed in Table 8.2.

Global brands may be the name of individual products or services (Pampers) or the name of the corporation that produces them (SONY, VISA, Coca-Cola). In the latter case, the brand is the symbol of *corporate identity* and it is encapsulated into a logo that is present in all documents of the firm, and associated with individual products or services even if those have an individual trademark. Global branding is a combination of both types: global firms develop a corporate name that will apply to all subsidiaries in the world and they also try to limit the individual product names and market products under a global name. For instance, Intel is the corporate brand and Pentium is the trademark of a family of microprocessors; Nestlé is the corporate name and Nescafé or Perrier are global names of individual products. The same would apply to Microsoft and Windows, Explorer or Office. It does not mean that all products of a global firm will make use of the same name, either corporate or product. Coca-Cola, Heineken or Electrolux use the corporate name for some of their products (global products or services) and market products locally under a local or regional name (Table 8.3).

According to Professor John Quelch, the common features of global brands are:

- Strong in their home market
- Consistent in product positioning
- Present geographically in a balanced way across regions
- Address similar consumer needs worldwide

- Easy to pronounce
- Similar to corporate name
- Associated with a product category

Table 8.2 Top 10 global brands ranking (2011)

Brand	*Country of origin*	*Brand value (million US$)*
Apple	United States	153,285
Google	United States	111,498
IBM	United States	100,849
McDonald's	United States	81,018
Microsoft	United States	78,243
Coca-Cola	United States	73,752
AT&T	United States	69,916
Marlboro	United States	67,522
China Mobile	China	57,326
GE	United States	50,318

Source: BrandZ Top 2011: BrandZ Top Most Valuable Global Brands www.millwardbrown.com © Millward Brown. Reprinted with permission

Table 8.3 Examples of corporations using global and local brands

Global corporate	*Global brand*	*Local/regional brand name*
Coca-Cola	Coke	• Beverly (herbal soft drink, Italy) • Lilt (citrus soft drink, Ireland) • Mezzo (mineral water, Germany) • Splash (citrus soft drink, Germany, Spain)
Electrolux	Electrolux	• Husquvarna (Sweden) • Electro Helios (Greece) • Eureka (United States) • Arthur Martin (France) • Zappas (Belgium, Italy, Norway, France) • Zanussi (Italy) • AEG (Germany) • Volta (Sweden) • Faure (France) • Rex (Italy) • Flymo (United Kingdom) • McCulloch (United States)
Heineken	Heineken Amstel Murphy	80 local brands among which are: • Tiger (Asia Pacific) • Bintang (Indonesia) • 33 Export (France) • Moretti (Austria) • Cruzcampo (Spain) • Zywieck (Poland)

The two last attributes are no longer valid, and as mentioned earlier many global brands are dissociated from the corporate name (Nestlé and Nescafé, Unilever and Lipton Tea) and many global names are used in many product categories (SONY, ABB).

For Hankinson and Cowking (1996), global brands can be categorized in a 2 x 2 matrix according to the degree of consistency in brand positioning (whether they convey the same message to the same segments across the world) and according to the standardization of the products or services they represent. (See Figure 8.4.) Volvo is an example of a brand representing a standardized product with different country segmentation, Nescafé has the same brand positioning with products adapted to customer tastes. McDonald's started initially with a standardized product and the same positioning across the world but has been obliged to adapt products to local conditions.

This classification shows that the meaning of global branding can be quite diverse and obliges companies to define a 'global branding' strategy by which they articulate what they are striving at in implementing it.

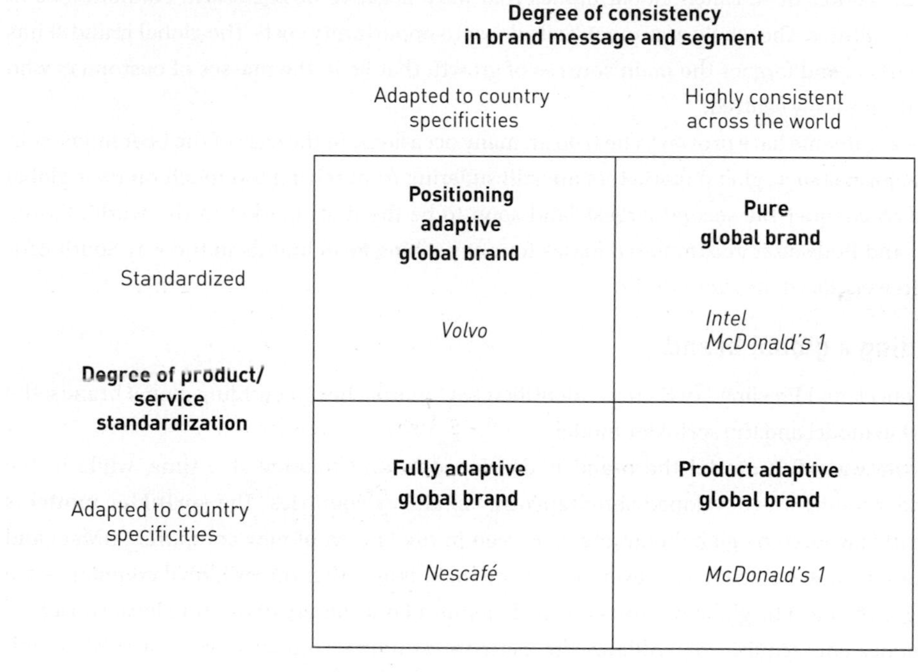

Degree of consistency in brand message and segment
Adapted to country specificities
Highly consistent across the world
Positioning adaptive global brand
Volvo
Pure global brand
Intel
McDonald's 1
Standardized
Degree of product/ service standardization
Adapted to country specificities
Fully adaptive global brand
Nescafé
Product adaptive global brand
McDonald's 1

Figure 8.4 Global brand positioning

Source: Adapted from Hankinson and Cowking (1996)

Advantages of global branding

There are three main advantages of global branding – strategic, economic and organizational.

From a *strategic* point of view, it is likely to reinforce market power thanks to a concentration of marketing effort on a single name, as well as the ability to benefit from a spillover effect from country to country. It also saves time in launching new products because, if the product is under the umbrella of a global name, it facilitates customer awareness and benefits from a more efficient promotion roll-out.

From an *economic* point of view, global branding brings savings in external communication with customers (advertising, promotion, direct selling), as well as internal costs, since it reduces inventories, product administration and accounting, as well as training and internal communication costs.

Finally, from an *organizational* point of view, it reinforces corporate identity, and facilitates transfer of personnel and best practices across the organization.

Disadvantages of global branding

The detractors of global brands argue that they ignore national differences in terms of culture, customer behavior and stages of economic development, and lead to over-standardization and heavy corporate headquarters centralization, stifling entrepreneurship. There are abundant anecdotes of so-called global names that have negative or aggressive connotations in certain cultures. The whole argument boils down to opportunity costs, the global brand skims the markets and forgoes the main sources of growth that lie in the masses of customers who are still culturally centred.

The arguments have proven to be true on many occasions. In the case of the beer industry in China, for instance, global marketers are still suffering from relying too much on their global brand to conquer the second largest (and soon to be the first) market in the world. Foster, Asahi and Budweiser accumulated losses for not pushing local brands in the way South African Brewery has done successfully.[3]

Building a global brand

Riesenbeck and Freeling (1991) have identified two approaches to building global brands: the waterfall model and the sprinkler model.

In the **waterfall model** the brand is developed in one country at a time, while in the sprinkler model it is developed simultaneously in all key countries. The **sprinkler model** is currently favoured by global marketers, as seen in the launch of new computers (iMac) and software (Windows 2000). However, one of the main issues that major global companies are facing is the need to 'globalize' under a single name a large variety of existing local subsidiaries' names and acquisitions. Allianz, the German insurance company, was confronted with multiple subsidiaries' names after their acquisitions of the French Assurances Générales de France, the US Fireman's Fund and the UK's Cornhill,[4] and had to cope with the difficulties of adopting Allianz as a global corporate brand.

Advertising

The issue of conveying the brand's image to the public is related to global branding. This is the task of advertising:

- Should the company use a *single* advertising agency for the world or local agencies?
- Should the *advertising* content be the same or differentiated?

The trend today for global companies is to deal with a single agency across the world. This trend leads the industry to consolidate and globalize (Table 8.4). There are four main advantages of working with a single agency:[5]

- *Simplicity* in relationships
- Easy *control*
- *Buying power* over global media and global supports (brochures, promotional material)
- *Economies of scale* in production.

Table 8.4 Major global advertising agencies, 2010

Company	Short profile
Dentsu http://www.dentsu.com Japan	Present in 25 countries. The Dentsu global network includes the Publicis group and DY and R. Revenues in 2010: 1800 billion Yen (US$21.5 billion)
WPP http://www.wpp.com UK	2400 offices all over the world. Young and Rubicam, Ogilvy are part of the group. Revenues in 2010: £9.3 billion
McCann Erickson http://www. mccannworldgroup.com USA	Part of the Interpublic Group: Present in 125 countries. Inter Republic Group Revenues 2010: US$6.5 billion
Havas http://www.havas.com France	World presence through EuroRSCG: 233 offices in 75 countries. Revenues 2010: €1.6 billion
Omnicom http://www. omnicomgroup.com USA	Present in 100 countries through its three leading agencies: BBDO, DDB and TBWA. Revenues in 2010: US$27.5 billion

Source: Websites of above-mentioned companies

Concerning content, global firms are careful not to offend local cultures and adapt their advertisements while retaining the same message. In 2000, the advertisement of a French perfume in Europe represented a naked young lady. In the United States the same lady was dressed. Benetton and Swatch are the 'avant-garde' of global advertising, using the same content and message everywhere, sometimes with unfortunate results.[6]

Global pricing

Global pricing consists of setting a *consistent pricing policy* across borders. The only differences in prices are due to taxation or regulatory reasons. Swatch watches are sold at a price that varies little around the equivalent of US$40.

There are three main advantages to global pricing:

- It avoids *arbitrage*. When countries are not isolated geographically and when there are no barriers to trade, consumers can shop at the lowest-priced place. In the 1980s, French car dealers were buying French cars in Belgium, where prices were lower, to resell them. The price differences were due in part to differences in taxes (VAT) but also to policies of the car manufacturers who priced differently depending upon the country's competitive climate. With the development of the EU and the arrival of the Euro, prices tend to converge.

- It protects the *brand integrity*. Customers who discover that the same product they buy in one country is sold at a discount in another may question the reason why it is so and may attribute it to an overall lower quality.
- It facilitates the servicing of *global customers*.

The disadvantages are that global pricing does not account for differences in customer utility curves and leads to *sub-optimization*. (See box opposite)

In practice, global pricing can be implemented in one or several of the following cases:

- When the product or service is targeted at customers who have *similar profiles* and share the same or similar value curve, the so-called 'global segments'. In the case of consumer goods we find luxury goods (Dom Perignon, Louis Vuitton, Gucci, etc.), fashion items (Swatch, Benneton, Esprit, etc.), personal computers and software (iMac, IBM, Microsoft Office, etc.). In the case of B2B marketing it applies to products or services sold to subsidiaries of multinational companies (global accounts)
- When the product or service is sold under a strong '*global brand*'
- When there are strong possibilities of *arbitrage*
- When the company deploys a *multi-brand policy* of global and local products and wants to differentiate clearly the global brand from the rest
- When the product or service has *standardized* functionalities, qualities and features.

Global account management

Global accounts are customers that have a presence in many countries and require products or services delivered according to the terms of a centrally coordinated buying agreement. Global account management is the organizational process by which global accounts are served. Global accounts are primarily used in the following industries:

- *Financial services:* catering for the varied financial needs of the subsidiaries of multinational companies. Citibank, for instance, created the World Corporate Group in 1974 in order to serve the cross-border financial needs of 450 major companies (see the example below for a description of Citibank's global account management).[7]
- *Advertising:* developing and implementing campaigns worldwide. Saatchi and Saatchi initiated the concept of global supermarkets in the late 1970s.
- *Telecoms equipment manufacturers:* catering for the equipment and associated services needs of globalizing telecom operators. Ericsson set up a global account management organization in 1994 serving 30 clients located in 10 home countries such as AT&T, Cable and Wireless, Vodafone, Telstra, Nynex and BT.[8]

SUB-OPTIMIZATION

Suppose that for a particular product the customer's utility curve generates a *demand function*:

In country *A*: volume sold (V_A)=204–6xPrice (P_A)
In country *B*: volume sold (V_B)=160–4xPrice (P_B)

The *cost* function of the product is
Total cost (*C*) = 600+ 10V (10 is the variable cost of the product)

The *total revenue* function is: total sales (*S*)=*P* x *V*
Then the profit is: profit (R)=R–C=P x V–C

In the case of country *A*
Profit is $R_A = -6P_A^2 + 264P_A - 2640$
Profit is maximized when $264 - 12P_A = 0$ or $P_A = 264/12 = 22$

In the case of country *B*
Profit is $R_B = -4P_B^2 + 200P_B - 2{,}200$
Profit is maximized when $200 - 8P_B = 0$ or $P_B = 200/8 = 25$

It can be seen that profit is maximized when prices are differentiated and not global.
The maximum profit is 564 when prices are set at 22 in Country A and 25 in Country B.
If you adopt a global pricing, the profit will be lower:

- If price is 22, profit is 548
- If price is 23, profit is 542
- If price is 24, profit is 536
- If price is 25, profit is 510
- If price is 23, profit is 542
- If price is 24, profit is 536
- If price is 25, profit is 510.

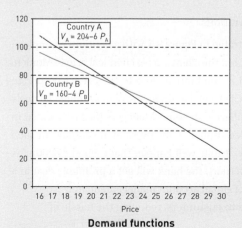

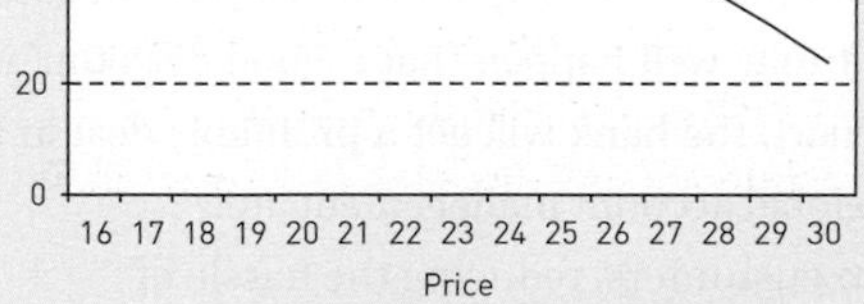

Demand functions

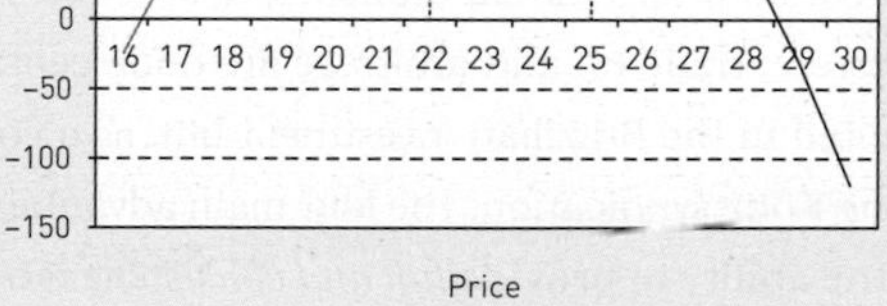

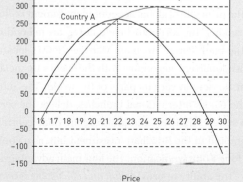

Profit functions

EXAMPLE

Citibank Global Account Management

Citibank installed a World Corporate Group (WCG) within its corporate finance division in 1974 with a portfolio of 450 global accounts. The WCG had its own staff of several hundred Parent Account Managers (PAMs) and Subsidiaries' Account Managers (SAMs). Each year the PAMs negotiated with the client a Global Account Plan to be implemented locally. Revenues were calculated per account and a complex system of reallocation to the local branches was put in place. Citibank increased its market share in global finances thanks to this system. However, the WCG was dismantled in 1981 because it was creating a 'dual' structure in the local subsidiaries. It was reinstated in 1985, but then WCG had only a coordinating role in a matrix format, with the PAMs and SAMs reporting both to the branches and to WCG. The number of global accounts was around 300 by the end of the 1990s. WCG customers were US, European, and Asian firms, with 6000 subsidiaries.

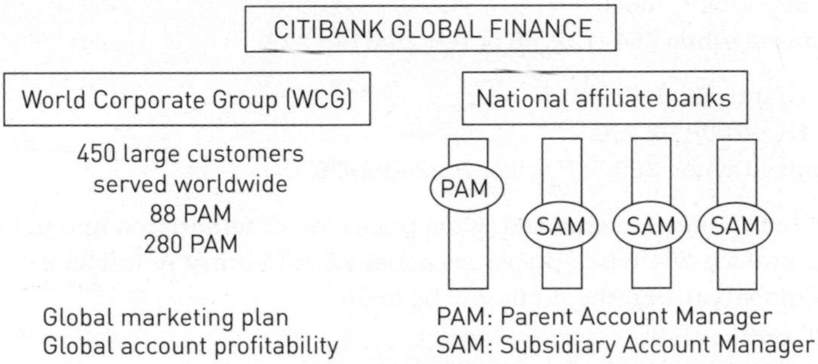

- *Telecoms services operators:* providing seamless communication data and voice services; Global One, BT, Cable and Wireless, AT&T all had organized global accounts in the 1990s.
- *Computer equipment manufacturers or software companies:* providing IT equipment and services. Hewlett Packard (HP) led the way, followed by IBM for global IT delivery. Cap Gemini, EDS and Oracle in the service sectors have set up account management.
- *Accounting firms:* PricewaterhouseCoopers, etc.
- *Aerospace manufacturers:* to support airline operations.

The principle of global account management is illustrated in Figure 8.5, with a fictitious example in banking. The corporate headquarters are in London, but the client is a big chemical firm in Munich. The bank Parent Account Manager (PAM), located at the branch close to the client's corporate headquarters, negotiates with the client's financial CFO a global financing plan for financial deals or services in various parts of the world. The Subsidiaries' Account Managers (SAMs), located in the bank's international branches, deliver the services under terms negotiated centrally. In such a system, trade-off and arbitrage are done centrally: it may well happen that a 'good discount' is granted in the Brazilian investment but, as a counterpart, the bank will get a profitable deal in a Hong Kong syndication. The four main advantages of global account management are:

- The ability to provide *full and consistent services* to customers, reducing the hassle of negotiating deal after deal
- A *lower overall cost* for the customer, partly owing to volume purchases

- The ability for customers to *optimize their procurement strategy* (in the case of banking, their financing strategy)
- For the product and service provider, it *increases overall sales and optimizes profitability.*

In the implementation of a global account management system, three main issues arise:

- Customer subsidiaries may be reluctant to accept global procurement. Local operations may find that it is cheaper or better to source locally.
- Supplier subsidiaries may be reluctant to abandon potential sources of local income for the benefit of the global account.
- A complex internal accounting system may be required for reallocating income among subsidiaries.

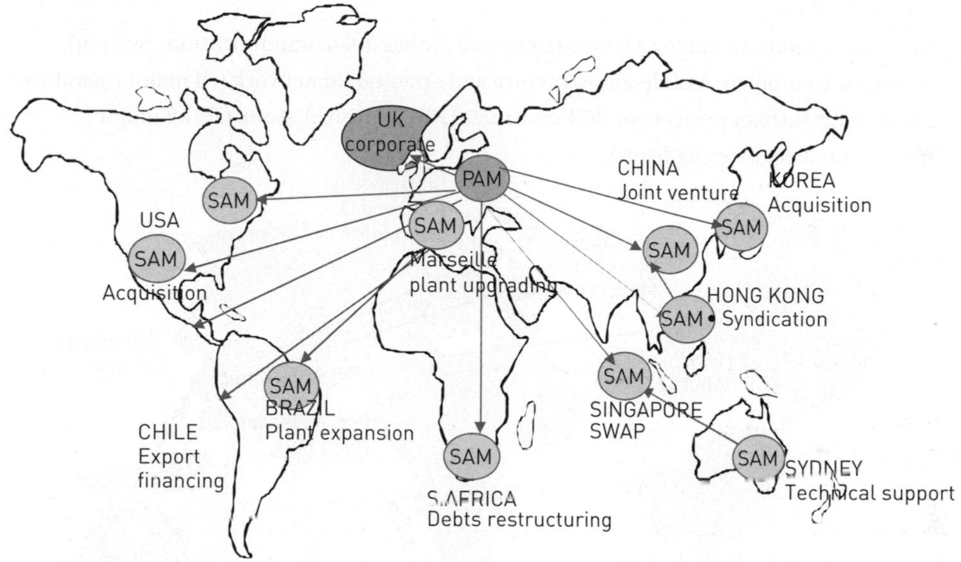

Figure 8.5 A financial global account management network servicing a leading European manufacturer

Source: Author's own creation based on information in Malnight (1995)

Global account systems have proven to be beneficial to companies that have been the first to implement them in their industries, setting the standards for others. In the sectors mentioned earlier the question is not whether to implement it, but how to do it properly.[9]

Global solution selling

Global solution selling is a mirror image of global account management. It consists of mobilizing the resources and competencies of several subsidiaries across the world in order to offer a valuable solution to a client located in a particular country (Figure 8.6). The company, a large power generation corporation headquartered in Europe, has to make an international bid for a turnkey project in Tianjin, China. The offer has to be complete and requires not only the sale of equipment but also the training of personnel and the management of the plant during five years under a Build Operate Transfer (BOT) contract. In order to give the best solution at the best price, the company has to mobilize the expertise of its US, French, German and Australian subsidiaries. The lead officer, who is in charge of preparing the bid, is located in Hong Kong; he is also in charge of negotiating the financing of the deal with a global consortium of banks with branches in Hong Kong.

This type of global solution selling is frequent in industries such as:

- *Banking:* to mount a complex financing package (all major global banks)
- *Consultancy:* to offer a complete business solution including strategy, IT, organization and change management (Accenture, McKinsey, BCG, etc.)
- *Information technology:* to offer a complete seamless IT solution (IBM, HP, EDS, Cap Gemini, SAP, etc.)
- *Telecom operators:* to bid for a UMTS (Universal Mobile Telecommunications System) license, or a complete mobile infrastructure and operational network (all major operators)
- *Engineering:* turnkey projects or BOT contracts (ABB, Enron, Alstom, GE, all major international engineering firms).

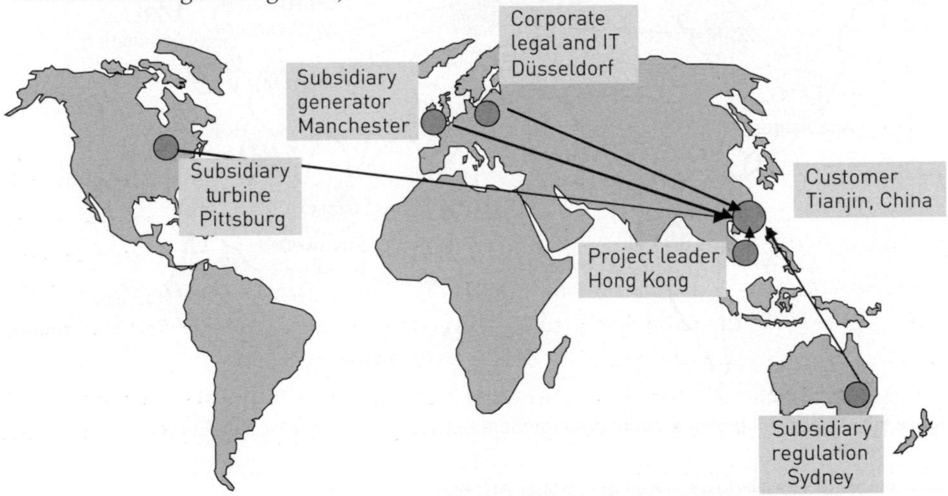

Figure 8.6 Global solution selling: an international bid for a power plant in China

The issues are quite similar to those in global account management. Global solution selling draws on resources, experience and expertise of the international business units. What matters is the speed and the coherence of the solution package, as well as the leadership of the solution selling team. It requires the cooperation of local subsidiaries and an appropriate mechanism to divide the revenues among them. There is a temptation for the local business units to 'charge' for their respective contributions; if this happens, the overall proposal will be uncompetitive and therefore needs a central global leader who decides on the overall price/content of the solution. Another issue is the allocation of resources to global projects when those resources may be more fruitfully allocated to domestic projects for which the local subsidiary would obtain full credit. Figure 8.7 describes graphically the capabilities needed to implement a global solution selling system.

CAPABILITIES

- Ability to understand customers' problems
- Ability to interpret customers' problems and to design 'solutions'
- Ability to formulate solution package
- Ability to cultivate relationships and support
- Ability to transfer solutions to customers' subsidiaries across the world

- Ability to provide consistent services across the world
- Ability to identify internal and external resources and competencies
- Ability to mobilize resources
- Ability to coordinate the use of resources
- Ability to maintain cost and price at competitive levels

Figure 8.7 Capabilities required for global solution selling

Global sales and distribution

Sales and distribution are probably the marketing mix elements that are the most difficult to standardize globally. There are many reasons:

- Language
- Social codes in supplier/buyer relationships
- Negotiation cultures
- Spatial dispersion of customers
- Local regulations
- Existing distribution structures.

However, the ability to sell and distribute globally, as against the need to localize the sales forces and the distribution channels, will depend upon the frequency of purchase and the dispersion of customers (Figure 8.8). The more a product or service is sold to a limited number of customers and where sales are infrequent, as for instance selling aircraft to airlines, the less the need for a local sales force. Salespersons located at corporate or regional headquarters can handle negotiations with the help of a local agent or representative.

At the other extreme, frequent purchases to a numerous, widely spread customer base calls for a local sales force and distribution either through a subsidiary or through a local or international distribution company.

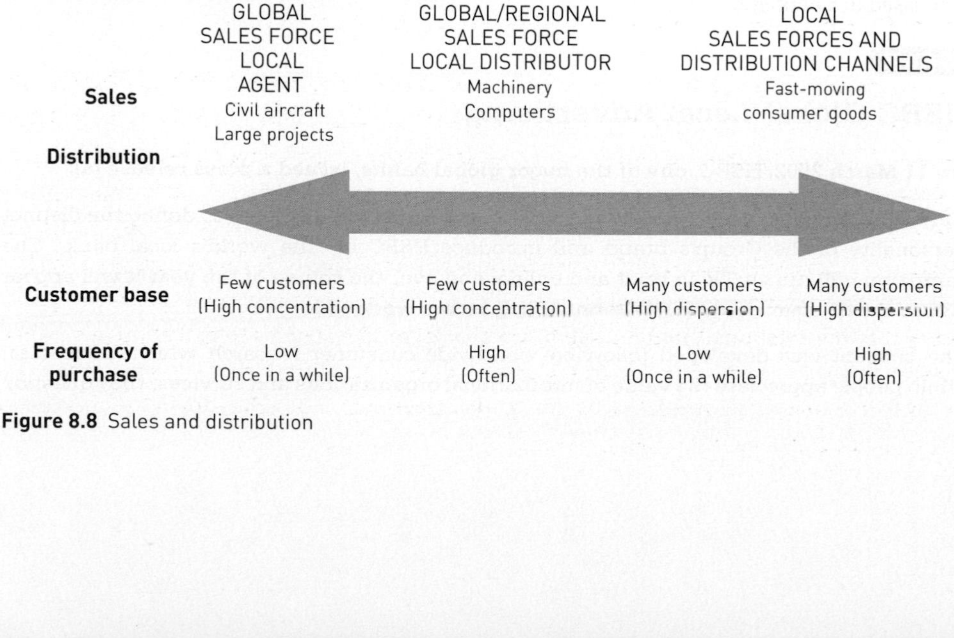

Figure 8.8 Sales and distribution

Global marketing positioning

Global marketing can take several forms. For each element of the marketing mix a trade-off has to be made between a fully-fledged standard global approach and a complete local adaptation. The combination of choices leads to a variety of marketing strategies and policies, as illustrated in Figure 8.9. The final choice, as seen in this chapter, is a function of many parameters:

- Customers' needs and value curve
- Customers' dispersion
- Frequency of purchase
- Importance of solution selling and account for globally dispersed customers
- Economies of scale.

	Global	Local usage Global product	Global usage Local product	Local
Product	Similar	Similar	Different	Different
Message	Similar	Different	Similar	Different
Customer group	Similar	Different	Similar	Different
Usage	Similar	Different	Similar	Different
Distribution	Similar	Different	Similar	Different
Brand	Similar	Different	Similar	Different
Price	Similar	Different	Similar	Different
Examples	***Swatch***	***Tiger Balm***	***Danone***	***Coca-Cola*** ***Unilever*** ***Local brands***

Figure 8.9: Various global marketing positions

Source: Author's own research

The ultimate choice will have to be made with regard to the global strategic positioning issues discussed in Chapter 2.

MINI-CASE

HSBC Global/Local Advertising

On 11 March 2002, HSBC, one of the major global banks, issued a press release (a):

HSBC has launched a new worldwide advertising campaign designed to define the distinct personality of the Group's brand and introduce HSBC as 'the world's local bank'. The campaign will run on TV, in print and online, and over the course of the year it will appear across the 81 countries and territories HSBC serves worldwide.

The concept was developed following worldwide consumer research which found that, while people appreciate the value of international organizations and services, they question

MINI-CASE

the prevailing 'one size fits all' global model. Consumers want to be treated as individuals, and to feel that companies care about them, recognize their needs and understand what makes their community unique.

Underpinning the advertising is HSBC's philosophy that the world is a rich and diverse place in which cultures and people should be treated with respect. Around the world, the Group has built its businesses locally, and HSBC's 31 million customers can be confident that the service they receive has a world of experience behind it.

HSBC's advertisements will demonstrate the importance of local knowledge by exploring distinctive national customs and practices. Carrying the strapline 'the world's local bank' the advertising will show that anyone who banks with HSBC can benefit from services and advice from a company with international experience, delivered by people sensitive to the customs and needs of their community.

In 2011 on the company's website the following statement could be read (b):

The new business strategy for the Group, unveiled in May 2011 by the CEO Stuart Gulliver, is now reflected in the latest work in our advertising campaign. The emphasis is to build our brand further by reflecting on the future forces that will shape our world and commerce, many of which are clearly visible today.

Questions:

1) What are the major changes that you perceive?
2) How do you interpret the change?

Sources: a) http://www.hsbc.com/1/2/newsroom/news/2002/new-campaign-for-the-worlds-local-bank
(b) http://www.hsbc.com/1/2/about/advertising

Summary and key points

1 Convergence of customer needs:

- No conclusive evidence of convergence of all consumer goods but gaining ground in B2B sector
- Different global product standardization types available for various types of customer needs:
  - *Similar* customer needs (global segment):
    - Global standardization, if high minimum size of production
    - Process standardization, if low minimum size of production
  - *Different* customer needs (local segment):
    - Modular standardization, if high minimum size of production
    - Local adaptation, if low minimum size of production
- Customer value curves:
  - Embody customer needs
  - Potential elements include:
    - Price
    - Product/service functionalities

  - Product/service quality
  - Image
  - Availability
  - Convenience
  - Associated services
  - Network effect.

2 Global branding:

- *Definition:* a global firm develops a corporate name that will apply to all subsidiaries while trying to limit individual product names and market products under a global name
- *Advantages:*
  - Reinforces market power through high concentration of marketing effort on a single name
  - Cost savings in external communication with customers – advertising, promotion, direct selling
  - Reinforces corporate identity
- *Disadvantages*:
  - ignores national differences and hence major sources of growth
- *Global brand*:
  - Definition: when the product or service it represents is marketed across the world under its name
  - Includes the following features:
    - Strong in home market
    - Consistent in product positioning
    - Present geographically in balanced way across regions
    - Addresses similar consumer needs worldwide
    - Easy to pronounce
  - Positioning of global brand depends on:
    - Degree of consistency in brand message and segment
    - Degree of product/service standardization
  - Building of global brand:
    - Waterfall model: develops brand one country at a time
    - Sprinkler model: develops brand simultaneously in all key countries.

3 Advertising:

- A single advertising agency is commonly used; advantages include:
  - Simplicity in relationships
  - Easy control
  - Economies of scale in production
  - Buyer power over global media and global support.

4 Global pricing:

- Involves setting consistent pricing policy across borders
- *Useful:*

  - When product/service is targeted at 'global segments' (customers with similar value curve)
  - When product/service is sold under strong 'global brand'
  - When there are strong possibilities of arbitrage
  - When company implements a multi-brand policy of global and local products
  - When product/service is standardized.
- *Advantages:*
  - Avoids arbitrage (when customers shop in the lowest-priced country)
  - Protects brand integrity
  - Facilitates servicing of global customers.
- *Disadvantages* are sub-optimization owing to a lack of consideration for differences in customers' utility curve.

5 Global account management:

- The organizational process which serves global accounts (customers present in many countries and requiring products/services as specified in a central buying agreement)
- *Advantages:*
  - For the customer.
    - Low overall cost partly owing to volume purchase
    - Ability to optimize procurement strategy
  - For the seller:
    - Increases overall sales and optimizes profitability
    - Reduces transaction cost (deal negotiation cost) and enhances ability to provide full and consistent services to customers
- *Disadvantages:*
    - Customers' subsidiaries reluctant to accept global procurement
    - Suppliers' subsidiaries reluctant to abandon potential source of local income
    - Complex internal accounting system required to reallocate income among subsidiaries.

6 Global solution selling:

- Involves mobilizing resources and competencies of several *worldwide subsidiaries* to offer a valuable solution to a client in a specific country
- *Key issues:*
  - Speed of solution delivery
  - Leadership of solution selling team
  - Revenue distribution among parties involved
  - Optimization of resource allocation.

7 Global sales and distribution:

- Very *difficult to standardize*:
  - Languages
  - Social codes in supplier/buyer relationships
  - Negotiation cultures

  - Spatial dispersion of customers
  - Local regulations
  - Existing distribution structures
- Determinants of need for *local sales force* are:
  - Frequency of purchase
  - Extent of customer dispersion.

8 Global marketing positioning:

- Choice of *marketing mix* depends on:
  - Company's global strategic positioning
  - Customers' needs and value curve
  - Customers' dispersion
  - Frequency of purchase
  - Importance of solution selling and account for globally dispersed customers
  - Economies of scale.

Learning assignments

1. What are the benefits of global standardization?
2. Can you identify 10 'global' products?
3. In Table 8.2, (p. 232) most of the top global brands are from the United States. Why do you think this is?
4. Why has Unilever announced that it is reducing its brands from 1600 to 400? What are the risks of so doing?
5. What potential problems will a marketer encounter in having a 'global' advertising campaign?
6. What are the benefits of using a single advertising agency?
7. Why can global pricing lead to sub-optimization?
8. What is the difference between global account management and global solution selling?
9. What are the typical problems associated with global account management?

Key words

- Advertising agency
- Arbitrage
- 'Californization'
- Convergence
- Customer value curve
- Global accounts
- Global solution selling
- Hierarchy of needs
- Marketing positioning
- Modularization
- Segmentation
- Sprinkler model
- Sub-optimization
- Waterfall model

Web resources

<http://www.euromonitor.com/>
Market research.

<http://www.datamonitor.com/>
Market research.

<http://www.ihs.com/products/global-insight/index.aspx>
Industries and countries information.

<http://www.accenture.com/us-en/Pages/insight-accenture-customer-satisfaction-survey-2010-summary.aspx>
Annual survey from Accenture.

Visit the companion website at **http://www.palgrave.com/business/lasserre3e** for a multitude of weblinks and resources, self-test questions for revision and a searchable glossary.

Notes

1 Schütte (1998).
2 This section is partly based on Riesenbeck and Freeling (1991) and Quelch (1999).
3 Williamson (1999).
4 Tribewalla (2001).
5 Quelch (1999), p. 11.
6 Pinson and Tribewalla (2001).
7 Malnight (1995).
8 Dragonetti and Noda (1999).
9 David, Birkinshaw and Toulan (2001).

References and further reading

Books and articles

Aaker, David A. and Erich Joachimsthaler, 'The Lure of Global Branding', *Harvard Business Review*, November–December 1999, pp. 137–44.

Barth, Karen, Nancy J. Karch, Kathleen McLaughlin and Christiana Smith Shi, 'Global Retailing: Tempting trouble?', *The McKinsey Quarterly*, Number 1, 1996, pp. 117–25.

David, Arnold, Julian Birkinshaw and Omar Toulan, 'Can Selling be Globalized?: *The Pitfalls of Global Account Management', California Management Review,* 44(1), 2001, pp. 8–20.

David, Arnold, 'Seven Rules of International Distribution', *Harvard Business Review*, November–December 2000, pp. 131–7.

Dragonetti, Nicolas and Tomo Noda, 'Building a Customer Oriented Networked Organisation: Ericsson's Global Account Management Programme', *INSEAD*, Case Study 11, 1999-4857, 1999.

Hankinson, Graham and Philippa Cowking, *The Reality of Global Brands*. London: McGrawHill, 1996.

Levitt, Theodore, 'The Globalization of Markets', *Harvard Business Review*, May–June, 1983, pp. 92–101.

Malnight, Thomas, 'Citibank: Global Customer Management', Harvard Business School and Wharton School Case Study 9-395-142, 1995.

Narayandas, Das, John Quelch and Gordon Schwartz, 'Prepare Your Company for Global Pricing', *Sloan Management Review*, Fall 2000, pp. 61–70.

Ohmae, Kenichi, *Triad Power*. New York: Free Press, 1985, 1995.

Parker, Philip, Physioeconomics. Cambridge, MA: MIT Press, 2000.

Pinson, Christian and Vikas Tribewalla, 'Benetton', *INSEAD* Case Study, 2001.

Quelch, John, 'Global Branding: Taking Stock', *Business Strategy Review*, 10(1)1999, pp. 1–14.

Riesenbeck, Hajo and Anthony Freeling, 'How Global Are Global Brands?', *McKinsey Quarterly*, 4, 1991, pp. 3–17.

Schütte, Hellmut, *Asian Consumer Behavior*. London, Macmillan, 1998.

Schütte, Hellmut and Diane Ciarlante, *Consumer Behaviour in Asia*. Paris/London: INSEAD/Macmillan, 1998.

Tribewalla, Vikas, 'Allianz: The Power on Your Side', *INSEAD* Case Study, 2001.

Williamson, Peter J., 'China's Beer War', *INSEAD Euro Asia Centre Case Study*, 05/98-4755, 1999.

Yip, George, *Total Global Strategy*. Englewood Cliffs, NJ: Prentice-Hall, 1994.

Journals

International Journal of Advertising (Quarterly), NTC Publications, United Kingdom: <http://www.warc.com>

Journal of Global Marketing (Quarterly), Haworth, United States: <http://www.haworthpress.com>

Journal of International Consumer Marketing (Quarterly), Haworth, United States: <http://www.haworthpress.com>

International Marketing Review (Quarterly), MCB University, United Kingdom: <http://www.emeraldinsight.com>

Journal of International Marketing (Quarterly), American Marketing Association, United States: <http://ciber.bus.msu.edu/jim/>

chapter

9 GLOBAL OPERATIONS

Introduction

The internationalization of value chains is a salient and controversial feature of globalization. This phenomenon, known as '*offshoring*' creates a global operational network of *integrated production and service centers* deployed across the world (Figure 9.1). Global operational management is concerned with the management of such a network. At the beginning of the chapter different types of offshoring will be discussed. Then various issues of managing global value chains will be discussed. The first issue is to decide where to set up the operational productive and logistical facilities such as factories, services and distribution centers. This kind of decision is known as the *location decision*: it requires a multiple-criteria analysis taking into account regional resources and risk characteristics as well as customer proximity. Second, each element of the network has to be attributed a specific role and *the network has to be managed*. This chapter presents different categorizations of global manufacturing networks. Third, the *procurement function,* including the recent development of electronic purchasing through Electronic Data Interchanges (EDIs) or through the Internet, is considered, as well as the role of the Internet in the management of global networks. The fourth domain of operational management is concerned with the managerial issues associated with the physical flow of goods known as '*logistics*'. The chapter continues with the analysis of the managerial issues associated with the handling of large-scale international infrastructure projects. Finally the impact of the Internet on global management will be addressed.

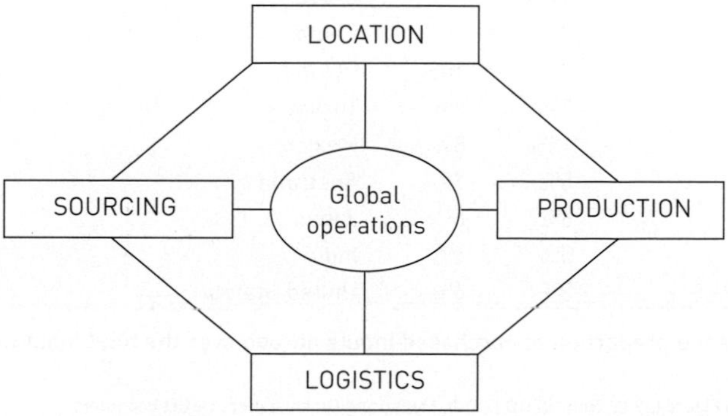

Figure 9.1 The global operations network

Table 9.1 Index of offshoring in 2005

Offshoring of manufacturing by country			Offshoring of services by country		
	1995	2005		1995	2005
Hungary	27%	36%	Luxembourg	47%	59%
Estonia	29%	32%	Ireland	33%	44%
Slovenia	–	31%	Denmark	8%	23%
Slovak Republic	15%	29%	Netherlands	11%	16%
Czech Republic	17%	26%	Estonia	15%	16%
OECD	**21%**	**26%**	Belgium	12%	15%
Mexico	–	25%	Norway	13%	14%
Belgium	21%	20%	Hungary	12%	14%
Austria	19%	20%	Sweden	9%	14%
Ireland	32%	18%	Slovak Republic	14%	13%
Portugal	16%	17%	Austria	9%	13%
Sweden	18%	17%	Greece	3%	12%
Finland	13%	17%	Indonesia	10%	11%
Canada	18%	16%	Finland	10%	10%
Poland	9%	16%	Chile	7%	10%
Denmark	16%	16%	Slovenia	–	9%
Greece	16%	15%	Korea	6%	8%
Netherlands	19%	14%	Germany	5%	8%
Germany	11%	14%	Czech Republic	10%	8%
Korea	14%	13%	Canada	10%	7%
Indonesia	14%	13%	Israel	10%	–
Norway	15%	13%	Spain	5%	7%
France	12%	12%	Russian Federation	6%	–
Spain	12%	12%	Italy	6%	7%
Israel	11%	–	United Kingdom	6%	6%
Turkey	11%	11%	France	4%	5%
Chile	14%	11%	South Africa	3%	5%
United Kingdom	13%	11%	Portugal	6%	5%
Italy	11%	11%	New Zealand	5%	–
Russian Federation	11%	–	**OECD**	**4%**	**4%**
New Zealand	11%	–	Brazil	3%	5%
China	8%	10%	China	1%	5%
South Africa	7%	10%	Poland	4%	4%
Australia	9%	9%	Turkey	4%	4%
Luxembourg	15%	8%	Mexico	–	3%
United States	5%	7%	Australia	4%	2%
India	6%	6%	Japan	2%	2%
Brazil	5%	6%	India	4%	1%
Japan	3%	6%	United States	0%	1%

This index is built as the proportion of purchased inputs abroad over the total input used by industries in a given country.

Source: Figure L.7.1. and Figure L.7.2., from OECD (2010), Measuring Globalization: OECD Economic Globalization Indicators 2010, OECD Publishing, <http://dx.doi.org/10.1787/9789264084360-en>

Learning objectives

At the end of the chapter you will be able to:

- understand the various factors contributing to the location decision
- explain the different roles of international factories and service centers, and their evolution
- evaluate the advantages and disadvantages of centralized versus decentralized purchasing
- understand the role played by the Internet in the management of global operations
- discuss the functions of a global logistics system
- set out the various phases in international infrastructure projects and their management design.

The globalization of value chains: offshore production and outsourcing

Over the past 30 years globalization of markets and competition has induced companies to internationalize their value chain. Manufacturing as well as service sites have been set-up offshore.[1] Table 9.1 gives an index of offshoring and outsourcing by country in 2005 prepared by OECD. This index shows that in the OECD countries offshoring has increased during the decade from 1995 to 2005.

Offshoring can take place internally by the setting up of factories or services in international locations (*offshore production*) or by the outsourcing of activities to external suppliers (*offshore outsourcing*). It can be motivated by the desire to take advantage of a local market (*market localization*) or by the search for resources and cost advantages that enhance *global competitiveness*. These four forms of offshoring are represented in Figure 9.2.

Offshoring objectives	**Offshoring modes:** *Offshore production*	**Offshoring modes:** *Offshore outsourcing*
For market	**Local for local production** *Production of goods or services internal to the company in internationally dispersed sites for serving local markets*	**Local for local outsourcing** *Sourcing of goods or services with external local domestic suppliers serving local operations*
For global competitveness	**Local for global production** *Production of goods or services internal to the company in internationally dispersed sites for serving local markets*	**Local for global outsourcing** *Sourcing of goods or services with external international suppliers serving global operations*

Figure 9.2: Forms of offshoring

Table 9.2 Criteria for facilities' location

COSTS	LABOR COST	• Remuneration level • Skill level • Skill availability • Productivity • Social regulations • Flexibility • Unionization
	OPERATIONAL COSTS	• Raw material costs • Telecommunications • Energy, water, transport • Property, rent • Logistics • Services • Financial costs • Environmental costs • Expatriate cost of living
	TAXATION	• Tariffs • Indirect taxes • Income taxes
	INCENTIVES	• Subsidies • Tax relief
PROXIMITY	CUSTOMER PROXIMITY	• Ability to offer fast delivery • Ability to offer fast servicing • Ability to customize
	SUPPLIER PROXIMITY	• Availability of raw materials • Quality of raw materials • Reliability of supplies
	LOGISTICS	• Import/export facilities
ENVIRONMENT	PROFESSIONAL	• Financial institutions • Legal and consultancy services • Training services
	INTELLECTUAL	• Libraries • Information • Universities
	QUALITY OF LIFE	• Government regulation • Freedom of movement • Climate • Housing • Presence of international schools • Crime
LEARNING	LEARNING FROM SUPPLIERS	• Quality of international and domestic suppliers • Supplier innovation
	LEARNING FROM CUSTOMERS	• Variety of segmentation • Variety of customer demands • Customer sophistication
	LEARNING FROM COMPETITORS	• Variety of competitors
	LEARNING FROM INSTITUTIONS	• Innovation context due to universities, technical and design centers

Sources: Haigh (1990), Ernst and Young (1992), Ferdows (1997), De Meyer and Vereecke (1994)

Although offshoring for market is accepted politically and socially in the home countries of the investing firms, the second form of offshoring for global competitiveness is not. When a company invests in a country in search of low wage costs and closes a factory or a service center in a high wage country it '*de-localizes*' and that creates a loss of jobs that in turn generates demand for sanctions and protectionism.

Over the years a particular offshore center may see its mission evolving. For instance, in 1970 Hewlett Packard chose Singapore to build a factory to produce components. Four years later it made a complete product – a hand-held calculator. In the following years more and more products were transferred there, still designed in the USA, but gradually by the mid-80s it had started to redesign products and introduce new products, and in the mid-90s it developed a new product: the Deskjet SOS.

Hewlett Packard exemplifies the topic of this chapter dealing with the four major decision dimensions of global operations as represented in Figure 9.1:

- *Location*: where to put facilities?
- *Production*: what to produce (manufacturing and services) and where?
- *Sourcing*: from whom to buy, what and how?
- *Logistics*: how to manage the flow of goods and information?

Selecting operational sites

The first type of decision in the management of a global operations network consists of selecting countries and regions in which to set up *operational facilities.* Table 9.2 presents the various criteria usually utilized to choose a location for facilities such as a plant, a back office, a distribution facility, or a service center.

Such choice is contingent upon the kind of facilities and their role in the network. Procurement offices will be located in places where resources and suppliers are available, while distribution centers will be located close to dense markets. Rotterdam in Europe, Singapore or Hong Kong in Asia play a major role as distribution and logistics centers in their respective regions because of their nodal geographical position and their world-class infrastructure. Bangalore or Manila will be chosen in the field of computer software because of their skilled and low-cost programmers, while Shenzhen in China or Batam in Indonesia are locations for labor-intensive processing.

Global manufacturing networks

Ferdows's strategic roles model

Based on extensive longitudinal research, Kasra Ferdows (1997) proposed a model of classification for manufacturing centers in a global network leading to the definition of various **strategic roles**. This classification is based on two main variables:

- The *primary strategic reason* for setting up a plant in a particular country. Ferdows identifies three main reasons:

  - To access low-cost production
  - To access skills and know-how
  - To access markets.
- The *competencies of the plant,* in terms of the various tasks that a given site is capable of doing:
  - The ability to *assume responsibility* for production
  - The ability to *maintain technical processes* (maintenance responsibility)
  - The ability to *purchase locally* (sourcing/logistic responsibility)
  - The ability to *make process improvements*
  - The ability to *develop suppliers*
  - The ability to *develop processes*
  - The ability to *make product improvement recommendations*
  - The ability to *develop products* (product development responsibility)
  - The ability to *supply global markets*
  - The ability to *become a global hub* for product and process knowledge.

Based on those two main dimensions, Ferdows identifies six types of global plants in a network (Figure 9.3):

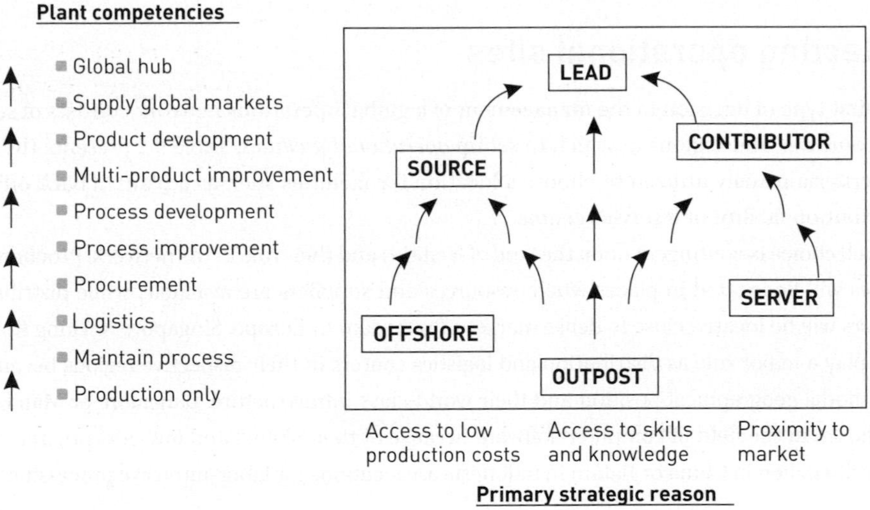

Figure 9.3 Strategic roles of international factories and their evolution

Source: Reprinted with permission from 'Making the Most of Foreign Factories' by Kasra Ferdows. *Harvard Business Review*, March 1997

- The offshore factory
- The source factory
- The server factory
- The contributor factory

- The outpost factory
- The lead factory.

Each of these has a precise role, defined below.

Table 9.3 Strategic roles of global factories

Type	Role	Example
Offshore factory	• Its role is to produce low-cost items to be re-exported either for sales or to be reworked and integrated with other components. • The factory works on design coming from other locations. • The tasks are limited to production of goods according to imported planning and control methods and maintenance of the process. • Raw materials and components are shipped to the factory. The logistics are handled outside the factory responsibility.	• Located in low-cost factor countries with limited skills and infrastructures • Special Economic Zone in China • Offshore factories in Vietnam
Source factory	• Its role is mainly to produce low-cost items, but the factory has larger responsibilities for procurement, production planning, process modifications, redesign and logistics.	• Countries with low-cost factors but with skilled labor and infrastructures • Malaysia • Singapore in the 1980s
Server factory	• Its primary role is to produce products or components for local or regional markets. • Relatively autonomous in the network for production planning and modification, but dependent on technology and critical components inputs.	• Countries with high import substitution policies • India
Contributor factory	• Its role is to produce for local or regional market but with a wider range of responsibilities in term of local sourcing, product redesign, and process modification.	• Countries with big markets and good infrastructures and technical skills • Brazil • Shanghai
Outpost factory	• The primary role is to be close to competition and key suppliers and to learn about technological development.	• Countries with dominant players • Japan • Silicon valley (for non US firms)
Lead factory	• This type of factory designs and produces products for the entire global network. It is responsible for the whole value chain of a product category.	• Countries with technological resources, good infrastructure and skills • Singapore in the 1990s

Source: Reprinted with permission from 'Making the Most of Foreign Factories' by Kasra Ferdows. Harvard Business Review, March 1997

According to Ferdows, the role of international factories may evolve as shown in Figure 9.3; the possible evolution paths are illustrated with arrows. Overall, the combination of the various types of factories constitutes a *global manufacturing network* in which all production centers are to some extent interrelated. The architecture of the network and the shifting roles of factories evolve according to new opportunities and competitive pressures. Ferdows advocates the design of what he calls a 'robust' network that evolves without resorting to drastic measures, such as plant closures or abrupt shifts of production from one country to another.

De Meyer and Vereecke's network architecture model

De Meyer and Vereecke (1995), in addition to the traditional roles of foreign factories as supply bases, emphasize the role of plants as *information and knowledge creators.* They define four main categories of plants in a network:

- *Isolated plants*, concentrating on the production of products for specific geographical markets and which do not communicate greatly with others. Those plants are installed in import-substitution countries that require local production for their domestic markets.
- *Blueprint plants*, receiving a lot of innovation but not creating any. They produce goods according to blueprints received from elsewhere. Those plants could be located in low-cost countries or Export Processing Zones (EPZs) that manufacture components or goods based on designs developed in other centers.
- *Host plant*, network players here are the well-established factories serving large markets that have developed a high degree of competency in state-of-the-art manufacturing technology but are not at the forefront of innovation.
- *Innovator plant*, network players here play a central role in product and process adaptation and innovation and are the source of inspiration for other factories.

Global services networks

The internationalization of services can take many forms, represented in Figure 9.4.

One of the key distinctions in respect of services, as opposed to manufacturing, is the relative importance of the *front-office* compared to *back-office* activities.[2]

In **front-office** activities, *consumption and production are concomitant*: in an airplane the traveler consumes the travel at the same time as its production, in a retail store the consumer consumes the act of buying at the same time that the act of selling is performed. In back offices, goods or support to services (software, insurance policies, bank transfer processing) can be performed separately from their consumption; goods or services support can be stockpiled. In global services, back-office activities can be classified in a similar way to manufacturing plants.

- Offshore centers perform *isolated acts* of *production*: computer entry performed in Guandong, for instance
- Source centers produce with a certain degree of *autonomy* for supporting local markets: catering facilities, distribution centers
- Contributor centers may have a *regional* role: maintenance centers, regional warehousing, dispatch centers

- Outpost centers: *market intelligence*
- Lead centers: *design function.*

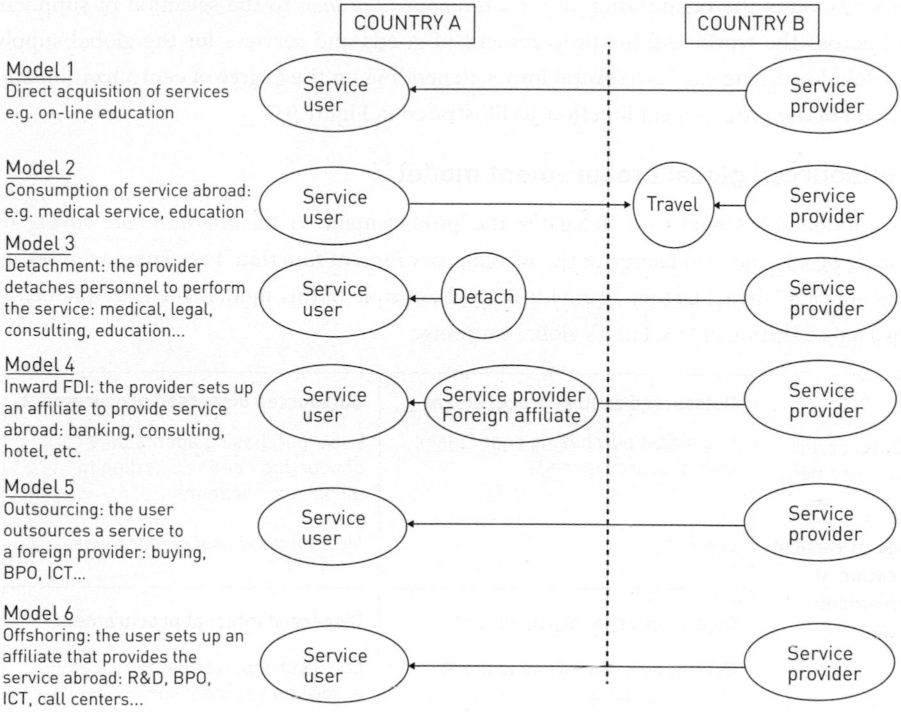

Figure 9.4 Different models of internationalization of services
Based on Chart 2 from Lindner, Cave, Deloumeaux and Magdeleine (2001)

Front-office operations are those that are in immediate contact with the customer and need to be close to the market. There are two main types of front office:

- The *physical* front office: banking branch, retail store, restaurant, repair center, hotel
- The *remote* front office: call center, reservation office, e-commerce center.

Front-office activities, because of their high degree of interaction with customers, demand a particular attention to language, customs and social codes. Adaptations require localization of facilities and personnel. For instance, medical, educational or legal as well as home hospitality or consultancy services will deploy facilities, either directly or through alliances, in order to perform the interface with their customers (models 2, 3, 4). Some online services can be performed with only contact via the Internet (e-learning for instance, model 1 in Figure 9.4).

By contrast, many back-office activities can be centralized in global or regional centers localized in places selected according to their cost-benefit characteristics. For instance, India has been the center of business process outsourcing (BPO) and IT back-office functions (models 5 and 6).

Global sourcing

Global sourcing is the organization of a *coordinated approach* to the selection of suppliers located across the world and the procurement of goods and services for the global supply chain. Global sourcing can take several forms, depending on the degree of centralization and integration of the procurement function, as illustrated in Figure 9.5.

The outsourced global procurement model

In this model, the global firm delegates the procurement to an *international buying* or *purchasing agent* who is in charge of the whole procurement function. Li & Fung, who set up the concept of a 'virtual factory',[3] provide a good example of this model. The example below provides a description of Li & Fung's global sourcing.

Degree of vertical integration of procurement function / Degree of centralization of procurement decisions	Centralized procurement	Decentralized procurement
Outsourced procurement	**Outsourced central procurement** One global purchasing agent takes care of sourcing needs *Li & Fung*	**Outsourced dispersed procurement** Local purchasing agents take care of sourcing needs according to global specifications *Most multinational corporations*
Internal procurement	**Central internal procurement** Central purchasing department sources globally *Major airlines*	**Dispersed internal procurement** Local subsidiaries source locally according to global specifications *McDonald's, Carrefour*

Figure 9.5 Different global sourcing designs

EXAMPLE

Li & Fung's 'virtual factory' concept

Founded in Guangzhou, Li & Fung began as a traditional exporter of Chinese porcelain. Today, this family-owned group has 42 offices in 20 countries, employing 2500 employees in Asia, Europe and Africa. It deals with a network of more than 3000 manufacturers for textiles, toys, sporting goods and furniture. Its main customers are major retail chains in the United States and Europe. The company participates in the design and engineering of products with its customers, selects suppliers, deals with quality control, final assembly and testing as well as logistics issues. A product like a parka, for instance, will be made of various components manufactured in different international locations: Korea (the shell), Taiwan (the lining), Japan (the zip), Hong Kong (the elastic, studs, toggles and string) and China (the filler and final assembly).

The internal central purchasing model

In this model, a central department with its own offices located in the major sourcing countries centralizes the purchase of key components, raw materials or products. The purchasing division will act exactly the same way as an *independent purchasing agent,* dealing with the whole supply chain from a request for quotations, to negotiation, orders, quality control, reception, expedition, logistics and payment. Nike, for instance, operates a central 'virtual' enterprise from its headquarters in Oregon. The product is designed centrally and then sourced from different factories in Korea, Japan, Taiwan, Indonesia and the United States.

The distributed procurement model

In this model, each production center in charge of a product or component takes care of its own procurement, based on *centrally defined product specifications.* This model applies particularly when there is a local content requirement imposed by a country or when a subsidiary has the complete responsibility for a product. It is not unusual for global companies to encourage their major suppliers to localize factories near their own plants, a process known as *piggybacking.*

Electronic sourcing (EDI and e-procurement)

The development of digital IT has enhanced the ability for companies to source globally. Proprietary software, known as **Electronic Data Interchange (EDI)** links corporations to their suppliers, making possible the exchange of information and the automatic ordering and tracking of orders. The Internet, thanks to its connectivity and language compatibility, has given birth to **electronic marketplaces** (e-marketplaces) that complement and to some extent replace traditional EDI. There are three main types of procurement marketplace and various forms of contracting method:

- The *horizontal marketplaces* (aggregators), that specialize in one category of product or service for all types of industry. An example is SciQuest <http://www.sciquest.com>, a marketplace for scientific products used mainly by pharmaceutical, chemical, biotechnology and educational organizations as well as R&D laboratories across several industries.
- The *vertical marketplaces,* that specialize in one type of industry offering a one-stop shop for a large variety of products and services for a particular industry sector. There are numerous examples of e-procurement sites ranging from food to energy and chemicals. VerticalNet <http://www.verticalnet.com> organizes marketplaces for 58 industries.
- The *exchanges,* that organize spot markets among a large number of suppliers and buyers for certain types of commodities like steel <http://www.e-steel.com> or chemicals <http://www.chemnet.com>.
- Transactions can be one-to-one transactions or made in the form of reverse auctions. The example below discusses an auction organized by Free-markets Online <http://www.freemarkets.com>, a reverse auction market-maker for more than 100 buyers and 11,100 suppliers from 64 countries.

- In theory, electronic procurement enhances the capability to organize global procurement because it gives the opportunity to reach a larger number of suppliers than in more traditional methods. It allows the company to also maintain valuable interaction between suppliers and buyers. These reach capabilities are at the roots of B2B marketplaces where global sourcing can develop. However, companies need to invest in integrated software called Enterprises Resources Planning (ERP) that is offered by companies such as SAP <http://www.sap.com> or Oracle <http://www.oracle.com>.

EXAMPLE

E-Procurement and reverse auctions[4]

Reverse auctions online is a process by which potential buyers of goods or services invite potential sellers to bid online in a given time frame. The initiator of reverse auctions was Freemarkets Online, which organized e-procurement for industrial companies using a proprietary competitive bidding software. Freemarkets Online has been sold to Ariba. The process of reverse auction works in the way shown in the following diagram:

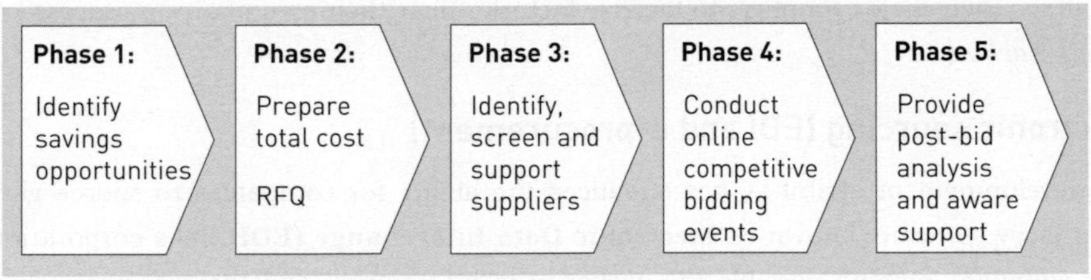

The actual auction takes place in real time and can achieve 30–40 per cent savings, as illustrated in the following bidding example.

(*x*) RFQ = Request For Qualification

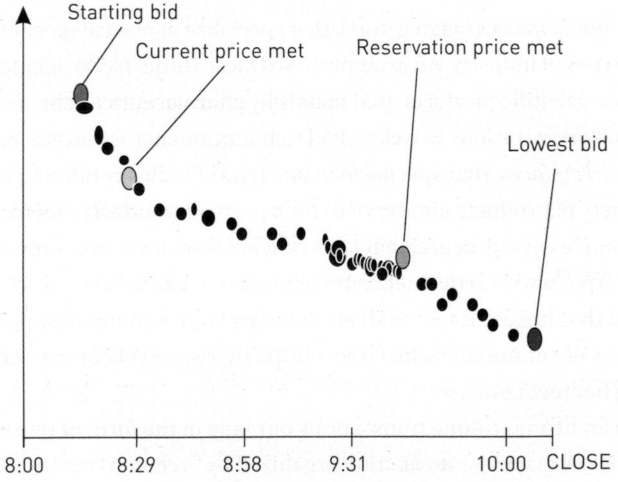

Bidding profile for reverse auction

E-procurement does not eliminate the need for the physical movement of goods. That requires good logistics as well as attention to all the vagaries of international trade such as import barriers, quotas or duties.

Global logistics

The interconnection of a network of specialized suppliers and production centers scattered across the world requires *timely, secure and 'lean' logistics.* Logistics are made up of three major functions:

- An *allocation* function
- A *distribution* function
- A *transportation* function.

The allocation function consists of deciding which *products,* in which *quantity,* and *when/where* they are going to be sent. This type of decision depends upon five major parameters:

- The *demand* for the product or component in a particular place
- The degree of *specialization* of the production or procurement unit
- The *capacity* of production or procurement unit
- The level of *acceptable inventories*
- The estimated *transportation time.*

Michelin

EXAMPLE

Michelin, in 1995, controlled a global network of 67 factories worldwide (22 in France, 20 in other European countries, 19 in North America, four in Asia and two in South America).[5] Figure 9.6 shows the European flow of products. The production planning is done at the central level and each factory is specialized in the production of certain categories of goods in order to benefit from economies of scale. The logistic function is in charge of dispatching around 2000 different product categories to several thousand dealers for the replacement tires (RT) market and several dozen car assembly factories across Europe for the original equipment market (OEM).

The central element of the system is the *forecasting function* performed at the level of countries; a central allocation demand function then uses algorithms to specify which products go where and when. The specialization of factories is such that no country is self-sufficient. Goods are sent either directly to vehicle assemblers for OEMs or to distribution centers that organize the grouping/separation of goods to be allocated either directly to large-volume dealers or indirectly to independent distributors for low-volume dealers.

The distribution function consists of selecting the various *channels* to be used in the chain. Michelin uses three major types of center:

- The factory warehouse – organizes grouping and supply of distribution centers and handling of large orders

- The distribution center – in charge of proximity storage and supply to dealers
- The advanced inventory – is dedicated to the OEMs and can be located in a factory or on a carrier site located near the customer's sites.

Customers

Original equipment: car makers
Replacement: large dealers, small dealers

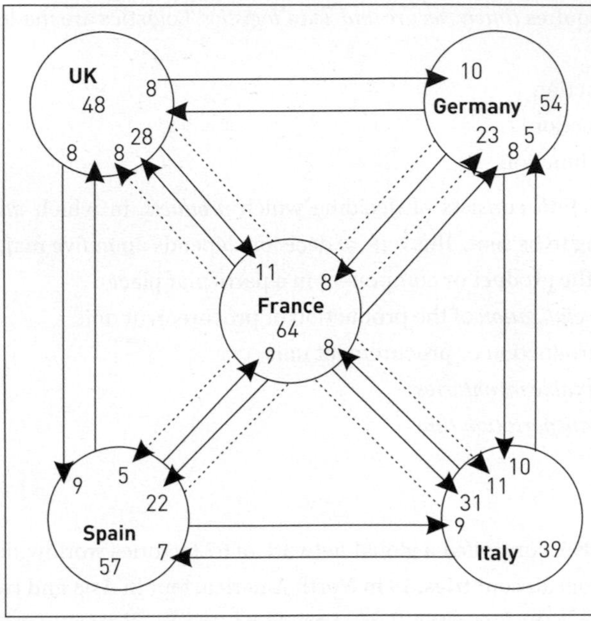

2000 Tire products
Private cars, vans, motorcycles, trucks, agricultural

Figure 9.6 Michelin's European flow of products

Note: Figure 9.6 shows the percentage of local consumption coming from different countries. Spain produces 57 per cent of its consumption and gets 9 per cent from the United Kingdom, 5 per cent from Germany, 22 per cent from France and 7 per cent from Italy.

Source: Dornier (1997)

The transportation function handles the *physical flow.* Michelin uses three modes of transport:

- Its own *fleet*
- *Rented* trucking services
- *Messenger* services.

It distinguishes two delivery modes: the proximity zone that handles two deliveries a day and a shipment zone that handles delivery once a day.

Another example of a cross-border logistic network is given in Figure 9.7, showing how Airbus Industries organizes the flow of aircraft components leading to final assembly in either Hamburg or Toulouse.

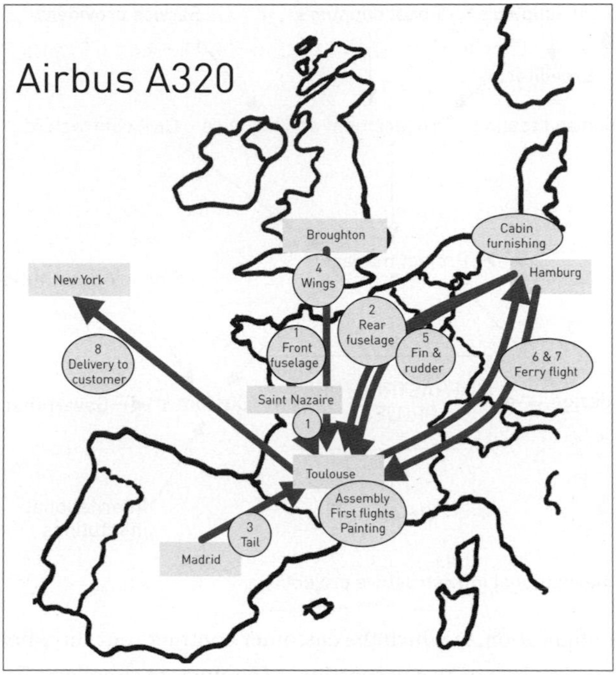

Figure 9.7 Airbus logistics

The global management of infrastructure projects

Large infrastructure projects such as airports, power plants, petrochemical plants, pulp and paper mills, railway systems, bridges, toll roads, real estate developments, etc. are a particular category of global operation. These projects involve various players, as described in Figure 9.8. The various phases of international project management are described in Table 9.4. There are many configurations of project management, but they can be grouped into three main categories:

- The *direct project management* configuration, in which the customer fulfills the role of project manager. For instance, when the Republic of Singapore decided to build a mass-transportation system, it created a special organization, the Mass Railways Transit (MRT), in charge of managing the project up to completion. The customer could call upon engineering firms to supervize the work and actually manage the project, but the engineering project team acts on behalf of the customer and is financially responsible only for the amount of its fees.

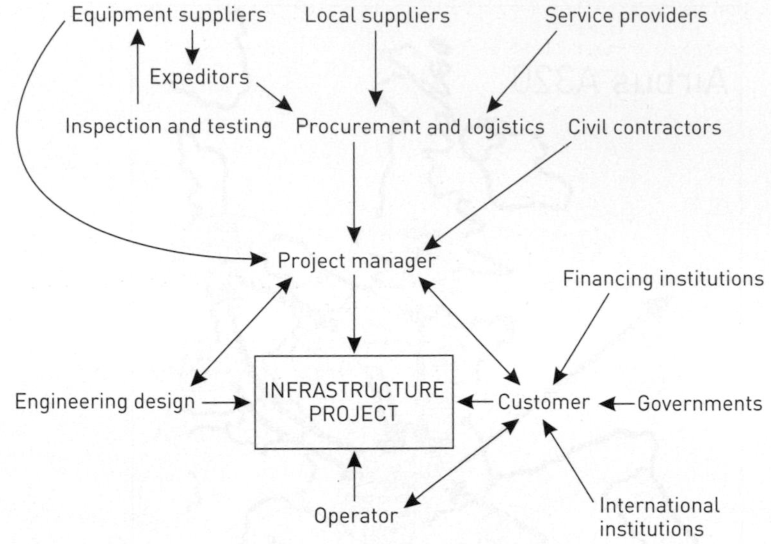

Figure 9.8 Players in an international infrastructure project

- The *turnkey project* configuration, in which the customer contracts out the whole project to a specialized engineering firm or to a consortium of equipment suppliers. The project manager takes care of completion at a fixed price and delivery time and hands over the project to the customer after the start-up phase. The project manager is financially responsible for the whole amount of the contract.
- The *Build, Operate and Transfer* (*BOT*) configuration and its derivatives, where the project manager is not only in charge of the construction, but also of the operation. At the end of a given period, the infrastructure is handed over to the customer. The project manager is responsible for the output and is paid on the basis of a predetermined price per unit of output ($ per kilowatt/hour, $ per toll fee, $ per cubic meter of water, etc.). There are three main derivatives:
  - BOO (Build, Operate and Own), the project manager keeps ownership
  - BOOT (Build, Own, Operate and Transfer), the project manager has full ownership of the infrastructure during the period of operation
  - ROT (Refurbish, Operate and Transfer), similar to BOT but involving refurbishment of old installations.

More and more infrastructure projects are now made on the basis of BOT contracts in emerging countries. BOT projects have an intrinsic risk that can be analyzed as a 'hostage risk'.[6] Before the completion of the project, the customer is willing to accept favourable conditions because she/he needs the infrastructure. Once the infrastructure is set up, the supplier has no more bargaining power and its investment is sunk in the project. Customers may argue that contracted fees for the supply of the final output are too high. This *hostage* problem has been described by Wells and Gleason (1995) and is well illustrated by the Enron Power plant at Dabhol in the state of Maharashtra in India, (see the example below).

Table 9.4 Phases in international infrastructure projects

Phases	*Content*
Pre-feasibility	• Project concept • Need/market assessment • Strategic plan • Approach international financial institutions • Approach engineering consultants and major industrial specialists • Get overall financial envelope
Feasibility	• Assign consultant for feasibility study • Get broad project characteristics, leading to cash flows and computation of financial returns • Get financing • Choose project organization • Select engineering firm
Basic engineering	• Define basic technical parameters • Infrastructure blueprints • Project decomposition into various technical areas (civil engineering, electrical, chemical, power generation, IT, regulation, etc.)
Detailed engineering/ tendering	• Prepare documents for tendering • Tenders, negotiation/selection of equipment and contracting suppliers • All detailed parameters in each project part defined
Expediting/ site construction	• Preparation of construction site • Civil engineering and construction (piling, infrastructure – roads, ports, pipelines, transmission, power, building contractors) • Reception of equipment • Erection/assembly of machinery • Layout of pipes, electrical cables, water, etc. • Final assembly
Training	• Recruitment of personnel • On-the-job training at suppliers' sites • Mock-up training
Start-up	• First operations
Operation	• Verification of technical parameters • Reception by client • Managing the operation

EXAMPLE

Enron in India: the Dabhol Power Plant[7]

The Dabhol Power Company (DPC) is a consortium of Enron Power, Bechtel Enterprises and General Electric, led by Enron. In 1995, DPC signed a contract with the Maharashtra State Electricity Board for the construction and operation of a 625 megawatt power plant costing US$922 million. According to the contract, the state committed to buy the output at a level of tariff structure that would provide DPC with a 25.22 per cent return on investment. During the same year, general elections brought to power a different state government which cancelled the project invoking a lack of transparency and too high a tariff. After negotiations, the project, was re-designed and finally accepted with different terms. The first phase of the project was completed and the financing of a second phase was closed in 1999. However, by April 2001 Enron was threatening to withdraw from India because the local utility was not complying with its obligations. Following Enron's financial debacle, the Dabhol Power Plant went up for sale in early 2002.

Internet and global operations

The combination of broadband capabilities, connectivity, standard languages (html, xml), wireless communication and portability have given birth to the digital age and its most pervasive manifestation: the Internet. The Internet is a global network connecting millions of computers across the world, exchanging data, opinions, information and news using a common architecture, the Internet Protocol (IP). In essence, the Internet is a global tool since it has abolished physical distance for the transmission of data, images and sounds and it has standardized the transmission protocol as well as the machine software, making it possible for any computer in the world to be part of the network and to 'talk' to other computers. Figures show that e-commerce reached around US$13 trillion in 2006. The usage of the Internet is spreading all over the world (see Table 9.5). The Internet is at the root of the so-called 'new economy' that flourished from 1995 to 2000 but that experienced a slump during the year 2001. According to McKinsey Research Institute, ' ... the Internet is, and will remain over coming decades, one of the biggest drivers of global economic growth.'[8]

Table 9.5 Global use of the Internet

World regions	Population (2011 est.)	Internet users Dec. 31, 2000	Internet users Latest data	Penetration (% population)	Growth 2000–2011	Users % of table
Africa	1,037,524,058	4,514,400	**118,609,620**	11.40%	2,527.4%	5.70%
Asia	3,879,740,877	114,304,000	**922,329,554**	23.80%	706.90%	44.00%
Europe	816,426,346	105,096,093	**476,213,935**	58.30%	353.10%	22.70%
Middle East	216,258,843	3,284,800	**68,553,666**	31.70%	1,987.0%	3.30%
North America	347,394,870	106,096,800	**272,066,000**	78.30%	151.70%	13.00%
Latin America/ Caribbean	597,283,165	18,068,919	**215,939,400**	36.20%	1,037.4%	10.30%
Oceania/ Australia	35,426,995	7,620,480	**21,293,830**	60.10%	179.40%	1.00%
World total	**6,930,055,154**	**360,985,492**	**2,095,006,005**	**30.20%**	**480.40%**	**100.00%**

Source: <http://www.internetworldstats.com>

The players

As with many innovations, the Internet was originally created in the 1960s out of the *Advanced Research Projects Agency (ARPA)* in the USA. It became a really widespread tool in the late 1990s and grew at a tremendous pace during the first decade of 2000. The Internet is mainly known for its main application, the *World Wide Web*, or the '*Web*'. Today the web technology has evolved into what is commonly known as '*Web2*', which allows for intercommunication among Internet users. The Internet is no longer a passive tool but a real exchange platform.

The Web space is divided broadly into two categories:

- the *individual users' space*, who are persons or organizations that use the web for e-mailing, surfing the web to get information, to download documents or videos, to play games, to listen to music , watch movies, chat on social networks like Facebook, Twitter, and possibly buy goods and services
- The *commercial space or e-business*, consisting of three major categories of players:
  - The traditional companies of the so-called 'old economy' also called **'bricks and mortar'**, that offer physically produced products and services with 'real' assets. These companies use the net for selling, buying, partnering and internal management through their Internet (open to the general public) or intranet (secured site internal to the company) websites or extranet (secured websites external to the company)
  - The 'pure plays' or the **'dotcom companies'** that have been created to enable web transactions and whose products and services essentially organize transactions, serve as e-commerce intermediaries and provide software platforms. Among those players you can find:
    - The **e-commerce** companies selling or organizing sales to customers (B2C: Business-to-Consumers), trade among companies (B2B: Business-to-Business) or among customers (C2C: Customers-to-Customers). Well-known examples are Amazon.com (B2C retailer), eBay (C2C auctioneer), E-Trade (B2C investment), Autobyline (B2C car dealership), Ariba (B2B procurement).
    - The **intermediaries** providing tools for transactions: e-payment, security, domain names, search engines, etc.(eg *Paypal* for payment, *Skype* for telephony)
    - The **search engines** or **browsers** such as Google or Yahoo!
    - The **social networks** such as Facebook, Twitter, LinkedIn.
    - Short product life cycles
  - The companies providing physical products or services to the two previous types of players:
    - Internet Service Providers (ISPs) providing access to the Web: AOL, Orange, most of the traditional telecom operators
    - Traditional software vendors and application service providers (ASPS), selling or supporting software: Oracle, SAP, IBM
    - Web hosting and maintenance: Exodus Communication, acquired in 2002 by Cable and Wireless, a UK global telecommunication operator
    - Consulting firms advising companies about Internet applications and development: Accenture, Gartner, Forrester
    - Content providers: Reuters, Time Warner, media companies
    - Equipment providers: CISCO, Nortel, Alcatel-Lucent, Huawei.

Figure 9.9 gives a pictorial representation of the Internet space.

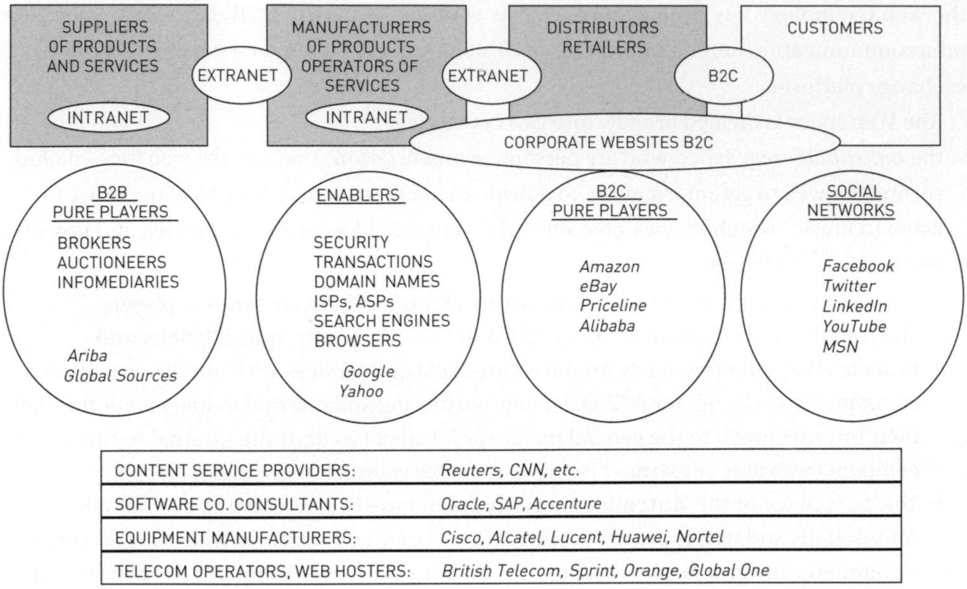

Figure 9.9 Players in the Internet space

Types of e-transaction for businesses

When we look at business-related transactions on the Web, we can distinguish three types:

- *Commercial transactions external to the firm*: e-commerce (selling), e-procurement (buying)
- *External relational transactions* other than buying and selling: e-partnering (coordinating, information-sharing, R&D with partners)
- *Internal relations*: e-management (planning and control, database sharing, recruiting, training, administration), information collection, knowledge management.

The contribution of the Internet to globalization

The Internet is, by design, a *global network*. It can be seen as an additional driver to globalization, but not a revolutionary one. As discussed in Chapter 1, globalization has been enhanced and fostered by political, technological, sociological and competitive factors. The additional contribution that the Internet brings to the globalization trends is the enhanced capability to decouple physical activities from the information exchange needed to support them. Evans and Wurster (2000) have argued that the Internet breaks the traditional **reach versus richness** trade-off. (see the box below) and, as a consequence, fosters the ability of companies to organize transactions and transfer data beyond national boundaries in real time. The Internet is a *facilitator to globalization*.

REACH VERSUS RICHNESS TRADE-OFF

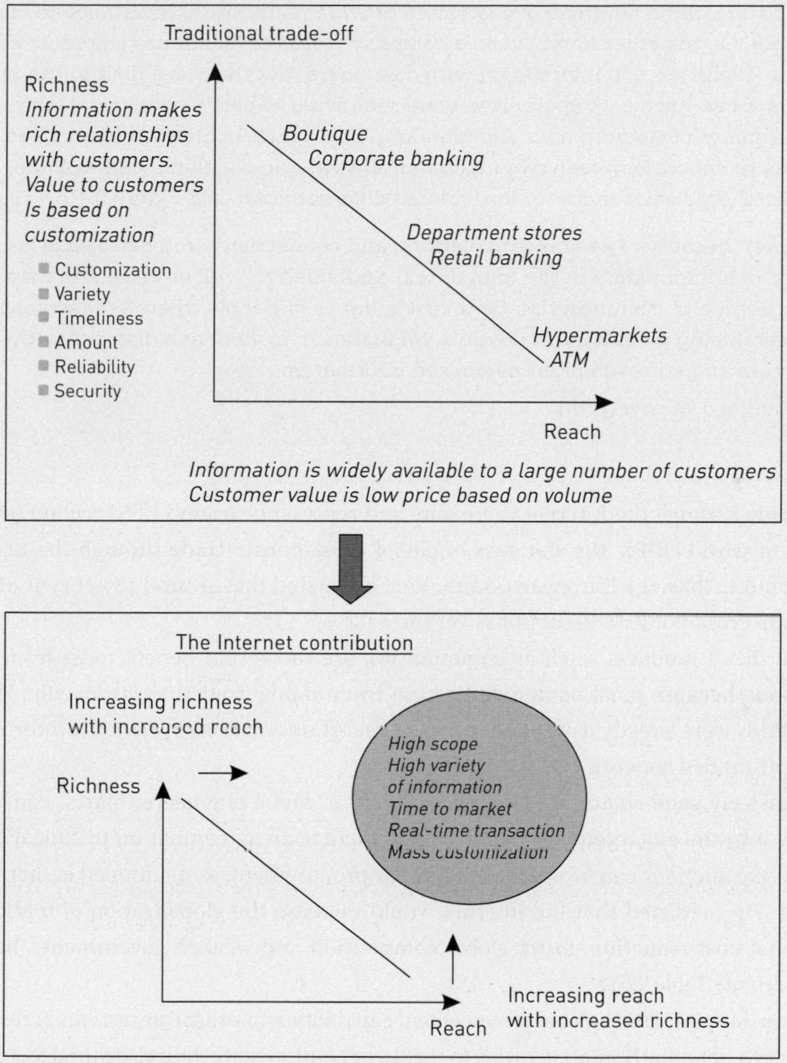

Figure 9.10 Reach versus richness trade-off

Evans and Wurster argue that, traditionally, economic activities are constrained by the difficulty of simultaneously achieving intense exchange of information (richness) with a large number of people (reach). Economic entities have therefore to choose between *mimic* (reach) and *quality* of relationships (richness). If a company wants to increase its volume and reach a larger number of people, it has to reduce the amount of information it exchanges with the customer and therefore standardize its product and customer interactions. Hypermarkets

REACH VERSUS RICHNESS TRADE-OFF cont.

that can handle large numbers of customers provide no (or little) assistance to customers, for example. On the other hand, when a company wants to customize a product or service, it needs to exchange rich information with customers, but there is a limit to the number of customers it can handle. A specialized boutique giving expert advice to customers cannot handle as many customers as a supermarket. This reach/richness trade-off has induced companies to choose between two fundamental strategic positions: high-volume, low-cost *standardized products/services* or low-volume *differentiation* (see Figure 9.10).

The Internet, because of its standard platform and connectivity, and because of its ability to carry very rich information in the form of text and video as well as voice and data, permits a certain degree of customization for a vast number of people, therefore increasing reach without sacrificing richness. It is possible, for instance, to work at a distance with suppliers or customers and still exchange customized information.

Source: Evans and Wurster (2000).

Global trade through the Internet is growing and represents around US$8 trillion (around 13 per cent of world GDP). The statistics of global cross-border trade through the net are not available but in 2006 the European Commission estimated that around 13 per cent of Internet users made cross-border transactions over the net.[9]

Standardized products, such as commodities, are those that benefit most from Internet transactions because most commodities have traditionally traded electronically. Traders in commodities were already used to anonymous, real-time transactions and the Internet adds a convenient unified network.

Progressively semi-customized products, such as metal-engineered parts, can also find their way into the e-marketplace because once there is an agreement on technical specifications, reverse auctions can be organized for their procurement, as mentioned earlier.

George Yip predicted that the Internet would increase the globalization of markets, reinforce global cost reduction, foster global competition and weaken governments' barriers to open trade (see Table 9.6).

However, in spite of their global enhancement capabilities, Internet transactions across borders are subject to potential limitation owing to regulatory and socio-technical/cultural factors:

- *Cross-border regulatory restrictions,* such as customs duties and VAT taxes still apply to the physical transfer of goods bought on the net
- *Local legislation,* as, for instance, the insistence of certain governments to restrict the access to certain websites: a well-publicized example was provided by the experience of Yahoo! with the French anti-racist legislation (see the example below)
- *Socio-technical and cultural factors,* such as the propensity of customers to accept online payment, attitude towards electronic trade versus direct face-to-face relationships which may hamper/foster the development of e-business.

Table 9.6 Effects of the Internet on globalization

Market globalization	• Increases global commonality in customer needs and tastes (facilitates customized standardization and strengthens appeal of global brands: Barbie online) • Enables global customers and global channels (facilitates global sourcing) • Supports global marketing (enhances global brands and standardizes search) • Makes global products more rapidly visible
Cost reduction	• Exploits differences in country costs and facilitates competition from low-cost small-scale companies from emerging markets • Enhances global sourcing • Speeds up global logistics • Reduces product development costs
Fosters global competition	• Makes competitive comparisons easier • Increases the number of potential global suppliers by reverse auctions • Puts new rivals in the global competitive arena
Weakens government barriers to open trade	• Makes it easier for customers to by-pass customs and tax levies • Puts pressure on government to harmonize standards and policies • Gives customers more incentives to lobby their governments to align with more customers • Friendly regulations

Source: Yip (2000)

EXAMPLE

Yahoo! and anti-racist legislation in France

In November 2000, a French court ruled that Yahoo! should block French users from viewing and buying Nazi memorabilia on its American auction site, in accordance with French anti-racist regulation. The implication of the judgment was that Yahoo!'s parent company in the United States, and not just the French subsidiary, should make sure that access to Nazi objects auctions should be banned to French citizens. Yahoo! counter-attacked by asking the US court to declare that this decision could not be enforced in the United States because it violates the First Amendment of the American constitution and that US citizens were not obliged to follow French rules outside France. A US district court followed this argument, and decided that Yahoo! was not bound by the French judgment. Two French human rights groups appealed the decision. This series of events generated a polemic about the right of governments to regulate a 'global' medium such as the Internet. Some analysts saw the French decision as a dangerous one for the future of the web, others argued that the Internet had to follow local rules.

As Jack Goldsmith, a Professor of Law at the University of Chicago, wrote in the *Financial Times* commenting on the Yahoo!–French court dispute: 'Confusion begins with the metaphor of the Internet as a "borderless medium". It is no more a borderless medium than the telephone, the telegraph, postal service, facsimile or smoke signal. All of these media facilitate transactions by someone in "real space" in one nation with someone in "real space" in another nation. When French citizens are on the receiving end of an offshore communication that their government deems harmful, France has every right to take steps within its territory to check and redress the harm.'

Sources: Press reports. Jack Goldsmith in *Financial Times*, 27 November 2000.

As Companies such as Yahoo!, Amazon.com or eBay have discovered, globalizing their business is not so different than for traditional 'bricks and mortar' companies. It implies the development of local alliances, acquisitions and an adaptation of the product offering to local conditions (see the boxed text below).

HOW DO INTERNET COMPANIES GLOBALIZE?

Internet companies, known as 'dotcoms', follow a classic pattern of international expansion in order to get a global reach. They invest in countries and set up subsidiaries, acquire local players or enter into strategic alliances. Most of the overseas investment for dotcom firms are in the creation of sales offices. Some may set up software development centers in India. Yahoo! is present in 35 countries, eBay in 24, Ariba in 22 and Google in 21.

The Internet and global firms

Overall, the Internet was seen during the heady days of the 'new economy' in 1999 and 2000 as a new business paradigm allowing firms to completely revolutionize the way they designed and implemented strategies.[10] This was fueled by the hyperinflation of stock valuations, when any dotcom newcomer could challenge the market value of well-established centenarian 'bricks and mortar' players. The later burst of the market bubble showed that traditional business strategy models are still valid, even in virtual space.[11]

For global or globalizing firms, the Internet provides a tool to manage internal and external linkages, to run business processes more efficiently, enhancing their cross-border **management capabilities**, including:

- Real-time communication over all locations with various media: video, text and data
- Ability to get customer interactions, requests and feedback and to consolidate customer data
- Ability to serve as a platform for a global knowledge management system
- Ability to reach new sets of suppliers through electronic global procurement
- Ability to identify and communicate with customers in low-density locations.

In order to do this they need to develop several types of **web-enabling capabilities**:

- Partnering capabilities:
  - The ability to form partnerships and to activate them in real time
  - The ability to share information with partners so that the transaction can be executed automatically
  - The ability to make deals instantaneously.
- A *'no secret' management system*: in order to make decisions quickly, the various internal processes of the company have to share information (in fact, automatically) horizontally
- *Decision-making*: an ability to make important decisions, such as pricing, at increased speed and, on some occasions in real time, implying a very strong decentralization of authority

- *Feedback*: to collect and consolidate feedback from customers, interpret it, disseminate it and adapt the responses to local conditions
- *IT*: to develop an IT platform and telecoms network that can work in a seamless way.

Web2

The term Web2, introduced in 1999, describes an evolution of the Internet toward full interactivity among web users who can share information under audio, text, video format, talk to each other, share programs and store data (*cloud computing*). According to a McKinsey research report: 'Web 2.0 technologies can be a powerful lure for an organization; their interactivity promises to bring more employees into daily contact at lower cost. When used effectively, they also may encourage participation in projects and idea sharing, thus deepening a company's pool of knowledge. They may bring greater scope and scale to organizations as well, strengthening bonds with customers and improving communications with suppliers and outside partners'.[12]

Among the major benefits that the survey revealed are faster access to knowledge, a reduction in communication costs and an increasing effectiveness of marketing. All of those benefits obviously apply to global management for which communication and knowledge management across borders are an important feature of their competitive capabilities.

Internal implications

In order to participate in the web economy, firms are not only cataloguing their products on the web and organizing 'clicking' sales, as currently done on most of the B2C Internet sites, but have to completely rethink their managerial systems, structures and cultures. Table 9.7 summarizes these internal implications.

Table 9.7 Organizational requirements for e-business

Internal requirements	*Consequences*
Transparency	• Integrity and consistency of information • Clear data and procedures
Sharing culture	• Horizontal as well as vertical exchange of information • External partners have access to databases • No 'silos'
Process integration	• All management processes are compatible with each other to facilitate information flow
Pooled coordination	• Ability to have different departments working together instantaneously instead of sequentially • Ability to bundle different parameters in real time • Sequential coordination too time-consuming
Real-time commitment	• Ability to make decisions quickly • No time for hierarchical checking
Horizontal processes	• Hierarchical communications and decision processes inefficient

Those organizational attributes may sometime conflict with local cultures. The challenge for the global firm is to overcome these cultural differences among their employees, suppliers, customers and partners to make web transactions effective.

MINI-CASE

eBay and Skype: Failed Synergies in the Internet Space

In November 2009 eBay (USA) announced that it would sell Skype, the Luxembourg based Internet phone company that it acquired in September 2005.

eBay and Skype

eBay was founded in 1995, in California, under the name of Auctionweb. eBay is one of the success stories of the Internet era. By 2011 it claims to have nearly 100 million users in 37 countries. As a web-based marketplace, the eBay business model is based on the connection of individual buyers and sellers of a large variety of products ranging from collectibles to real estate (only in some countries). eBay offers buyers and sellers an online auction platform through which sellers put their products for sale with a reservation price and potential buyers bid for the products during a limited time-span. Revenues come from a registration fee charged to the seller and a percentage on the actual transaction.

It has also increased its business model by the acquisition in 2002 of PayPal, the Internet secure payment company.

In 2005 the company had 180 million users and total revenues of US$4.5 billion and a net profit of US$1 billion. By 2009 the total revenues were US$8.7 billion for a net profit of US$2.4 billion. Around 53 per cent of total revenue is generated outside the USA.

Skype was created in 2003 by two entrepreneurs from Denmark and Sweden. The company was later registered in Luxembourg. The Skype business model is to offer free peer-to-peer phone conversation through the net. If the two correspondents are Skype users and linked to the Internet their conversation is free of charge. When the conversation is between a Skype user on the Internet and a fixed or mobile telephone, the caller pays a small fee that is lower than the normal telephone charge. This fee provides the revenues to Skype. In 2005 Skype's revenues were US$62 million with 60 million users from all over the 224 countries or territories of the world.

Acquisition of Skype by eBay

In September 2005 eBay acquired Skype for US$2.6 billion (half in cash and half in stocks). This move was the first acquisition made by eBay outside its traditional e-market and e-payment business and was motivated by two expected benefits:

- A synergistic effect thanks to which eBay's buyers and sellers could communicate directly by voice and video Internet telephony at no cost. This would foster the development of eBay in transactions where direct contact is important, such as with cars and real estate. This would generate additional revenue for eBay
- An expansion of eBay's international presence in Scandinavia, Eastern Europe and Asia where its presence was weaker than Skype's.

MINI-CASE

At the time of the acquisition Skype was not profitable. In 2006 it had a loss of US$27 million but eBay forecasted an increase in Skype revenue to US$200 million and a return to profit by 2008. Revenue has increased, amounting to US$600 million by 2009 and it was profitable as early as 2007. In 2008 Skype's profit was above US$100 million. But eBay was unsuccessful in making Skype produce more cash. The expected synergies did not really materialize and the profit generated was at first small compared to eBay's and essentially a stand-alone profit.

Way out

The decision was made in November 2009 to sell the business to a group of private investors for US$2.75 billion.

In October 2011 Microsoft announced that it would buy Skype for US$8.5 billion.

Questions:

1) How do you explain the failure with Skype?
2) Do you think the fact that the acquisition was international contributed to the problems?
3) Will Microsoft benefit from Skype?

Sources: eBay and Skype various annual reports; 'Did eBay Make a Profit on Skype or Not', Wall Street Journal, 1 September 2009; 'eBay to Acquire Skype', Skype Press Release, London, 12 September 2005. Available at <http://about.skype.com/2005/09/ebay_to_acquire_skype.html>

Summary and key points

1 Global operations:

- Defined as an integrated network of facilities located across the world performing the functions of procurement, production, distribution and servicing of products for customers.
- Four major decision dimensions:
  - Location
  - Production
  - Sourcing
  - Logistics.

2 Offshoring and Outsourcing

- Offshoring: production in an international locality. Two types of offshoring:
  - Local for local: production for the local market
  - Local for global: production for the global network
- Outsourcing: buying products or services internationally. Two types of outsourcing:
  - Local for local: sourcing for the local market
  - Local for global: sourcing for the global network.

3 Choice of location:

- *Criteria for location* include:
  - Costs
  - Proximity
  - Environment
  - Learning
- *Ultimate choice* depends on:
  - Kind of facilities
  - Role of facilities in the network.

4 Global production networks:

- Set of integrated production centers deployed across the world
- Two kinds of global production networks:
  - Global manufacturing networks
  - Global service networks
  - Global manufacturing networks:
- *Classifications*:
  - 'Network architecture model' based on the role of plants as information and knowledge creators
    - Four main types of plants:
      - Isolated – concentrate on production of products for specific geographical markets; do not communicate much with others; installed in import-substitution countries that require local production for their domestic markets
      - Blueprint – receive (but not create) a lot of innovation; produce goods according to blueprint received from elsewhere; located in low-cost countries or EPZs
      - Host plant network player – well-established factories serving large markets that have developed a high degree of competence in state-of-the-art manufacturing technology; not at the forefront of innovation
      - Innovator plant network player – play central role in product and process adaptation and innovation; source of inspiration for other factories
  - 'Strategic roles model' classified according to strategic role based on two main variables:
    - Primary strategic reason for setting up plant in a particular country, including accessing:
      - Low-cost production
      - Skills and know-how
      - Markets
    - Competencies of plant - tasks a given site is capable of doing:
      - Assume responsibility for production
      - Maintain technical processes
      - Purchase locally
      - Make process improvements
      - Develop suppliers
      - Develop processes
      - Make product improvement recommendations

    - Develop products
    - Supply global markets and become global hub for product and process knowledge
- Types of *global plants in a network*:
  - *Offshore factory*
    Produces low-cost items to be re-exported either for sales or to be reworked and integrated with other components
  - *Source factory*
    Produces low-cost items but factory has larger responsibilities for procurement, production, planning, process modifications, re-design and logistics
  - *Server factory*
    Produces products or components for local or regional markets, relatively autonomous in the network for production, planning and modification, but dependent on technology and critical components' input
  - *Contributor factory*
    Produces for local or regional market but with wider range of responsibilities in local sourcing, product re-design and process modification
  - *Outpost factory*
    Close to competition and key suppliers to learn about technological development
  - *Lead factory*
    Factory design and producing products for the entire global network, responsible for the whole value chain of a product category
- Evolutionary path of a global plant:
  - An outpost factory evolves to become a lead factory either directly or indirectly through becoming first a source factory or contributor factory
  - An offshore factory evolves to a source factory and possibly becomes a lead factory in the long term
  - A server factory evolves to a contributor factory and possibly becomes a lead factory in the long term
  - involves change of plant competencies.

5 Global services network:

- In the *back offices*, goods or support to services can be performed separately from their consumption - goods or services can be stocked.
- Global services can be *classified* as:
  - Offshore centers: Perform isolated act of production
  - Source centers: Produce with certain degree of autonomy for supporting local markets – catering facility, distribution centers
  - Contributor centers: May have regional role
  - Outpost centers: Market intelligence
  - Lead center: Design center
- *Front-office* operations:
  - In immediate contact with customers and need to be closed to the market
  - Physical front office and remote front office
  - Require special attention to language, customs and social code adaptation.

6 Global sourcing:

- A *co-ordinated approach* to the selection of suppliers located across the world and the procurement of goods and services to be filled in the global supply chain
- Various forms depending upon the degree of *centralization* and degree of *vertical integration* of the procurement function:
  - *Outsourced global procurement model*
    The firm delegates the procurement to an international buying or purchasing agent responsible for the whole procurement function
  - *Internal central purchasing model*
    A central department with its own offices located in the major sourcing countries centralizes the purchase; the purchasing division acts like an independent purchasing agent
  - *Distributed procurement model*
    Each production center in charge of a product or component takes care of its own procurement based on centrally defined product specifications; applicable when there is local content requirement or when a subsidiary has the complete responsibility for a product
- Electronic sourcing
  - *EDI* (proprietary software which links corporations to their suppliers and permits exchange of information, automatic ordering and tracking of orders)
  - *E-procurement* (procurement on the Internet):
    - Types of e-procurement sites:
      - *Horizontal marketplace* (*aggregators*) specializes in one category of product/service for all types of industries
      - *Vertical marketplace* specializes in one type of industry offering a one-stop shop for a large variety of products/services.
      - *Exchanges* which organize spot markets between a large quantity of suppliers and a large number of buyers for certain types of commodities.
    - Transactions can be one-to-one or made through reverse auctions
    - Provides reach and rich capabilities, opportunity to reach a larger number of suppliers than more traditional methods
    - Does not eliminate the need for the physical movement of goods.

7 Global logistics:

- *Allocation* function:
  - Which products, what quantity, when and where
  - Five major parameters
    - Demand for the product
    - Degree of specialization
    - Capacity of production
    - Level of acceptable inventories
    - Estimated transportation time
- *Distribution* function:
  - Selection of channels to be used in the chain

  - Three major types of centers:
    - Factory warehouse: organizes grouping and supply of distribution centers and handling of large orders
    - Distribution centers: responsible for proximity storage/supply to dealers
    - Advanced inventory: dedicated to OEM that can be located in a factory
- *Transportation* function:
  - Handles physical flow
  - Three modes of transport:
    - Own fleet
    - Rented trucking services
    - Messenger services
  - Two delivery modes:
    - Proximity zone (two deliveries a day)
    - Shipment zone (one delivery a day).

8 International infrastructure projects:

- Various players – project managers, civil contractors, service providers, local suppliers, customers, government, financing institutions, operator and international institutions
- Phases:
  - Pre-feasibility
  - Feasibility
  - Basic engineering
  - Detailed engineering/tendering
  - Expediting/site construction
  - Training
  - Start-up
  - Operation
- Configuration of project management:
  - Direct project management:
    - Customer fulfills role of project manager
    - If engineering firm supervises and manages the work, engineering project team is financially responsible for the amount of its fees
  - Turnkey project:
    - Customer contracts whole project to specialized engineering firm or to consortium of equipment suppliers
    - Project manager:
      - Is responsible for completion at fixed price and delivery time
      - Hands over project to customer after the start-up phase
  - BOT (build, operate and transfer):
    - Has 'hostage risk', i.e. once infrastructure is set up, supplier has no bargaining power
    - Project manager:
      - Is in charge of construction and operation
      - Is responsible for output
      - Is paid on basis of a pre-determined price per unit of output

    - BOT variants include:
        - *BOO* (build, operate and own): project manager keeps ownership
        - *ROT* (refurbish, operate and transfer): similar to BOT but refurbishing old installations.

9 The Internet is a global network connecting millions of computers across the world.

- Internet players:
  - Traditional companies 'old economy' or 'bricks and mortar'
  - 'Pure plays' or 'dotcom companies':
    - E-commerce companies
    - Intermediaries
    - Portals and browsers
  - Traditional companies providing physical products/services
- Transactions:
  - *Commercial transactions external to the firms*: e-commerce (selling), e-procurement (buying)
  - *External relational transactions* other than buying and selling: e-partnering (co-ordinating, information-sharing, R&D with partners, etc.)
  - *Internal relations*: e-management (planning and control, database-sharing, recruiting, training, administration, etc.).
- The Internet constitutes an additional driver to globalization thanks to its reach and richness capabilities:
  - *Reach* is the ability to access a large number of people in real time owing to a standard platform and connectivity
  - *Richness* is the ability to carry a high level of information in the form of text, video and voice
- Standardized and semi-customized products benefit most from Internet transactions.
- The Internet:
  - Increases globalization of markets
  - Increases global costs reduction
  - Fosters global competition
  - Weakens governments' barriers to open trade
- Limitations to the globalization of the Internet:
  - Cross-border regulatory restrictions
  - Local legislation
  - Socio-technical/cultural factors
- Provides a management tool that enhances global cross-border management capabilities:
  - Partnering capabilities
  - A 'no secret' management system
  - Ability to make important decisions in 'real time'
  - Ability to collect and consolidate feedback from customers
  - Ability to develop an IT platform and telecoms network that can work in a seamless way
  - Ability to rethink completely managerial systems, structures and cultures
- Cultural differences can restrain Internet capabilities: the challenge for the global firm is

to overcome those cultural differences among their employees, suppliers, customers and partners to make Web transaction effective.

Learning assignments

1 Compare Singapore and Malaysia as a possible location for: (i) a PC assembly plant, (ii) a wafer factory, (iii) a regional maintenance center, (iv) a customer training center for international customers, (v) a chemical processing plant.
2 According to Ferdows (1997), what are the differences between a 'contributor' factory and an 'outpost' factory?
3 What are the new roles that De Meyer and Vereecke (1995) assign to 'foreign' factories?
4 What differentiates global manufacturing of goods from global production of services?
5 What is a vertical electronic marketplace?
6 Surf the Internet and find: one horizontal e-procurement site, one vertical e-procurement site, and one exchange (different from the examples given in the text).
7 What are the three major functions of global logistics?
8 For the point of view of an infrastructure, compare the relative advantages and disadvantages of turnkey projects, direct project management and BOT.
9 What is the 'hostage' problem in BOT contracts?

Key words

- Back office
- BOT
- Distribution function
- Electronic Data Interchange (EDI)
- Electronic marketplaces
- Front office
- Location
- Logistics
- Network architecture
- Plant competencies
- Procurement
- Strategic role
- Turnkey project

Web resources

<http://www.deloitte.com/view/en_GX/global/industries/manufacturing/a1a52c646d069210VgnVCM200000bb42f00aRCRD.htm>
Global manufacturing index published by Deloitte Consulting.

<http://www.gartner.com/technology/home.jsp>
IT data information.

<http://www.forrester.com/rb/research/>
Technology research.

Visit the companion website at **http://www.palgrave.com/business/lasserre3e** for a multitude of weblinks and resources, self-test questions for revision and a searchable glossary.

Notes

1 Milberg and Winkler (2009) and OECD (2007).
2 Teboul (1991).
3 St George and Knoop (1998).
4 Rangan (1998).
5 This example is from Dornier (1997), reproduced in Ernst, Kawelis, Dornier and Fender (1998).
6 Wells (1995).
7 Wells *et al.* (1996).
8 Pélissié du Rausas *et al.* (2011).
9 European Commission Staff Paper (2009).
10 McKinsey (2009).
11 Coltman *et al.* (2001); Porter (2001); Subramanian and Adner (2001).
12 McKinsey (2009).

References and further reading

Books and articles

Bartmess, Andrew and Keith Cerny, 'Seeding Plants for a Global Harvest', *The McKinsey Quarterly,* 2, 1993, pp. 107–32.

Coltman, Tim, Timothy Devinney, Alopi Latukefu and David Midgley, 'Revolution, Evolution, or Hype?', *California Management Review*, 44(1), 2001, pp. 57–86.

De Meyer, Arnoud and A. Vereecke, 'Strategies for International Manufacturing', INSEAD Working Paper, 94/25, 1994.

Dornier, Philippe Pierre, 'Michelin', ESSEC Case Study, 1997.

European Commission, 'Report on cross-border e-commerce in the EU', Commission Staff Working Document, 283, Brussels, 2009.

Ernst, Ricardo, Pavos Kawelis, Philippe-Pierre Dornier and Michel Fender, *Global Operations and Logistics: Text and Cases.* New York, NY: John Wiley, 1998.

Ernst & Young, 'Region of the New Europe: A Comparative Assessment of Key Factors in Choosing Location', *Report,* 1992.

Evans, Philip and Thomas Wurster, *Blown to Bits.* Boston, MA: Harvard Business School Press, 2000.

Ferdows, Kasra, 'Making the Most of Foreign Factories', *Harvard Business Review,* March–April 1997, pp. 73–88.

Haigh, Ronald, 'Selecting a US Plant Location: The Management Decision Process in Foreign Companies', *Columbia Journal of World Business,* 3, Fall 1990.

Kiss, A. and W. Danis, 'Country institutional context, social networks, and new venture internationalization speed', *European Management Journal,* 26(6), 2008, pp. 388–399.

Kotabe, Masaaki, 'Efficiency vs Effectiveness Orientation of Global Sourcing Strategy: A Comparison of US and Japanese Multinational Companies', *The Academy of Management Executive,* November 1998, pp. 107–19.

Lindner, Andreas, Bill Cave, Lydia Deloumeaux and Joscelyn Magdeleine, *Trade in Goods and Services: Statistical Trends and Measurement Challenges,* Statistics Brief, October 2001, No.1, <www.oecd.org/std/statisticsbrief>

McKinsey Global Survey results, 'How Companies Are Benefiting from Web 2.0', *McKinsey Quarterly,* September 2009, pp. 1–9.

Milberg, William and Deborah Winkler, *Globalization, Offshoring and Economic Insecurity in Industrialized Countries,* DESA working paper, n°87, United Nations, New York, November 2009.

OECD, *Offshoring and Employment: Trends and Impacts.* Paris: OECD 2007.

Pélissié du Rausas, Matthieu, James Manyika, Eric Hazan, Jacques Bughin, Michael Chui and Rémi Said, 'Internet Matters: The Net's Sweeping Impact on Growth, Jobs, and Prosperity', *McKinsey Global Institute,* McKinsey & Company, May 2011, available at <http://www.mckinsey.com/Insights/MGI>

Porter, Michael, 'Strategy and the Internet', *Harvard Business Review,* March–April 2001, pp. 63–78.

Rangan, Kasturi, 'FreeMarketsOnline', Harvard Business School Case Study 9-598-109, 1998.

Sasi V. and P. Arenius, 'International new ventures and social networks: Advantage or liability?', *European Management Journal,* 26(6), 2008, pp. 400–411.

Skype, 'eBay to Acquire Skype', Skype Press Release, September 12 2005, available at <http://about.skype.com/2005/09/ebay_to_acquire_skype.html>

Social Media Landscape, 2011, available at <http://www.fredcavazza.net/2010/12/14/social-media-landscape-2011>

St George, Anthony and Carin-Isabel Knoop, 'Li & Fung: Beyond Filling in the Mosaic, 1995–1998', Harvard Business School Case Study 9-398-092, 1998.

Subramanian, Rangan and Ron Adner, 'Profits and the Internet: Seven Misconceptions', *MIT Sloan Management Review,* Summer 2001, pp. 44–53.

Teboul, James, *Managing Quality Dynamics.* Englewood Cliffs, NJ: Prentice-Hall, 1991.

Wells, Louis T. and Eric S. Gleason, 'Is Foreign Infrastructure Investment Still Risky?', *Harvard Business Review,* September–October 1995, pp. 44–55.

Wells, Louis T., Anu Bhasin, Mihir Desai and Sarayu Srinivasan, 'Enron Development Corporation: The Dabhol Power Project in Maharashtra, India' (A), (B) and (C), Harvard Business School Case Studies 9-797-085, 9-595-101, 1996.

Journals

International Journal of Operations & Production Management, MCB University, United Kingdom: <http://www.emeraldinsight.com/ijopm.htm>

International Journal of Physical Distribution and Logistics Management, MCB University, United Kingdom: <http://www.napm.org/Pubs/journal.scm/>

Journal of Supply Chain Management (Quarterly), *Institute for Supply Management,* United States: <http://www.napm.org/Pubs/journal.scm/>

chapter

10 GLOBAL INNOVATION

Introduction

The ability to create and quickly diffuse new products and processes is one of the main benefits of global management, as noted in Chapters 1 and 3. This chapter will look at the evolution of the management of innovation within multinational and global companies. It starts with a presentation and criticism of the classic model known as the *international product life cycle*, then examines the classic trade-off between centralized and distributed R&D using the case of Nestlé as an example. The issues involved in international transfer of technology will then be discussed and the chapter will end by presenting a recent model of knowledge management and transfer of best practices within global firms and examining the problems of intellectual property rights.

Learning objectives

At the end of the chapter you will be able to:

- understand the logic and the limitations of the international product life cycle
- appreciate the different designs of global R&D networks
- recognize the different management issues in the global management of R&D
- discuss the issues of the international transfer of technology
- understand knowledge management
- explain the recent development towards 'metanational' management of global knowledge creation
- recognize the issues in the international protection of intellectual property.

The international product life cycle model

In the 1960s, Raymond Vernon proposed the theory of the *International Product Life Cycle* (1966) to explain how product innovation and production could migrate from the country of origin of the innovative firm to other country subsidiaries (Figure 10.1).

The international product life cycle theory was built on observation of the TV set industry in the 1950s and 1960s. As shown in Figure 10.1, the theory identifies three stages in the international development of products and processes. In stage 1, *new products and processes* are designed in the laboratories of firms located in the innovative country. In the 1950s in the TV set industry, the innovative country was the United States. RCA, Zenith, General Electric and Motorola were the innovators and, at this stage, the products were designed in the United States for the US market. Some production was exported, mainly to Europe. In stage two, (1960s) some production was moved to industrialized countries such as Europe and Japan, either under the form of *local subsidiaries* of the innovative firms or through *technology transfer* to local firms (Matsushita, SONY, Thomson, etc.). Some adaptations to fit local needs were made to the products. Finally, in stage three, *emerging developing countries* (Korea, China) took the lead in the production of TV sets, because of cost advantages and market potential.

Stage One INNOVATION	Stage Two FOREIGN PRODUCTION	Stage Three TRANSFER
Innovative firms create new products and processes in their country of origin: an advanced industrialized country	Second-tier country subsidiaries receive products/processes from innovators and produce for local markets	Developing country subsidiaries receive products/processes from innovators and produce for local markets and global markets at low cost

Figure 10.1 The international product life cycle

Source: Adapted from Vernon (1966)

Criticism of the international product life cycle

In spite of its simplicity and appeal, the theory failed to explain the globalization of innovation that took place after the 1960s. Despite the fact that R&D resources are predominantly concentrated in developed, industrialized countries, there is no longer a major difference between the United States, Japan and Europe (see Table 10.1)

Today, a large variety of products are developed globally for world markets and launched at almost the same time in the key countries of America, Europe and Asia Pacific. The migration of R&D and production centers does not necessarily follow the sequential evolution predicted by the theory. Many research centers are set up where scientific and marketing resources are available, and global companies use global R&D networks to develop world products, as the following example illustrates.

Table 10.1 R&D capabilities

Country	R and D expenditures (% of GDP)		Number of researchers		High technology exports (million US$)		Patents applications	
	2000	2005/9	2000	2005/9	2000	2005/9	2000	2005/9
India	0.77%	0.80%**	112,971	149,892*	1569	10,143	8503	28,940**
China	0.90%	1.44%***	692,698	1,411,000***	40,837	348,295	51,906	314,513
Japan	3.04%	3.44%***	648,411	71,2062***	127,376	99,210	419,543	348,592
USA	2.74%	2.71%***	1,264,372	1,392,000**	196,698	141,519	295,895	456,154
European Union	1.80%	1.85%***	1,102,045	1,459,151***	385,186	515,167	165,513	130,278

Source: *World Bank World Development Indicators* (2011). For the period 2000/2009 data with * are for 2005, ** for 2006, *** for 2007.

Global R&D networks

In a 2006 survey done jointly by Booz Allen Hamilton and INSEAD[1] on a sample of 186 major global firms it was found that the number of foreign R&D centers located outside the home country of the parent company rose to 66 per cent in 2005 compared to 45 per cent in 1975 with a recent increase of sites located in India and China. The activities of those centers are predominantly engaged in development in order to either customize products to local markets or to concentrate on specific development while the home country centers do the core technology research. The main motivation to set up a center in a particular country is the proximity to local markets and the availability of skilled personnel. It was also found that a few companies (33 per cent) manage their research on projects involving the collaboration of multiple sites, preferring to allocate specific stand-alone projects to those centers.

EXAMPLE

Some global networks[2]

Nestlé

Nestlé is the second largest food company in the world. Its portfolio encompasses a large array of products including leading brands such as Nescafé. A Swiss multinational, Nestlé was one of the first to expand its operations worldwide. With R&D expenditure at 1.6 per cent of sales in 2005, Nestlé invests about 1.9 billion Swiss Francs on R&D a year, the largest amount in the entire food industry. Over 5000 people in total work in R&D for Nestlé, in the 28 food and beverage research, development and technology centers worldwide; there are also 320 application groups which adapt product ideas to local markets.

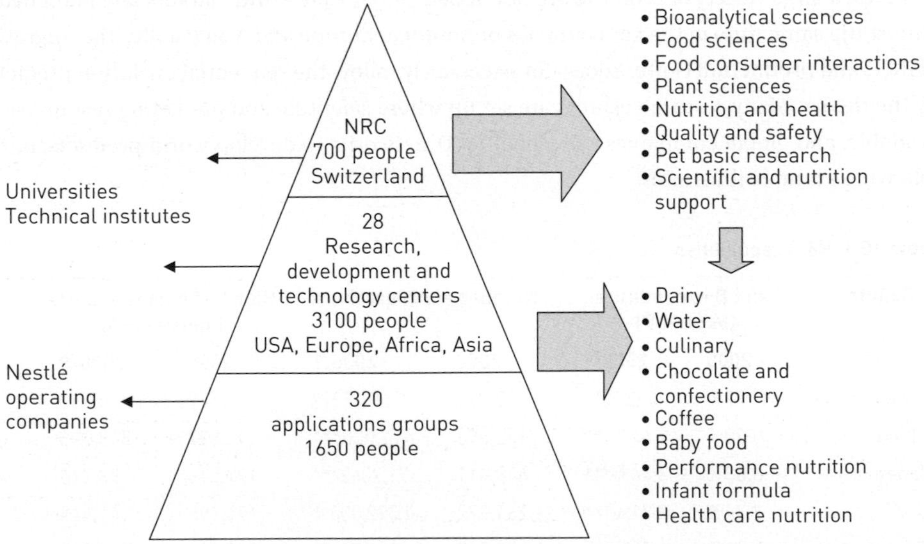

Figure 10.2 Nestlé global R&D architecture

Source: Data sourced from the Nestlé website; www.nestle.com. Retrieved October 2010.

The keystone of Nestlé global architecture is the Nestlé Research Center (NRC) opened in 1987 near Lausanne, which employs 700 people. The NRC creates the scientific knowledge base for Nestlé. It accumulates know-how in support of all sectors of activity and is the hub for all Nestlé's R&D network. Its scientists work in close and constant collaboration with teams from Food and Beverage Research, Development and Technology Centers worldwide both within the Nestlé group and with key universities around the world. The NRC is structured in eight scientific research departments, organized according to the disciplines needed for research on nutrition, food science and food safety and quality: BioAnalytical Science, Food Science, Food/Consumer Interaction, Plant Science, Nutrition and Health, Quality and Safety, Pet Basic Research and Scientific and Nutrition Support.

This system is shown in Figure 10.2. We shall now discuss the benefits and constraints of global R&D, before explaining the different organizational designs for the management of the R&D network.

ST Microelectronic

ST Microelectronic is a semiconductor supplier. Originally resulting from the merger of French and Italian companies, the company concentrates on system-on-a-chip solutions. ST Microelectronic uses knowledge from various local divisions and partners scattered around the world. Figure 10.3 gives an illustration of the mobilization of global resources for hard disk drive technology.

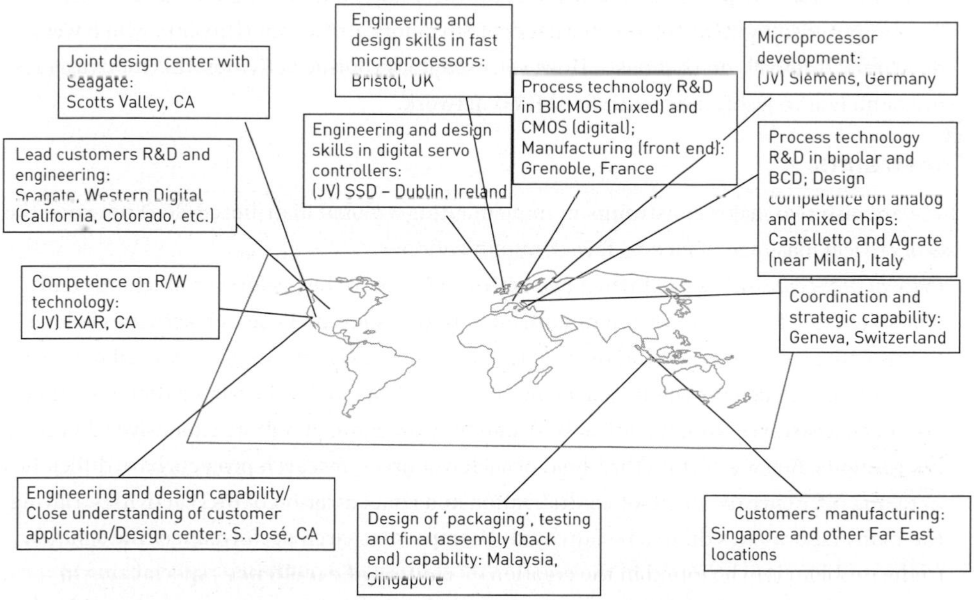

Figure 10.3 Global resources leveraging for HDD technology at ST Microelectronic

Source: Reprinted with permission from *From Global to Metanational: How Companies Win in the Knowledge Economy* by Yves L. Doz, Jose Santos, and Peter J. Williamson. Harvard Business Press, 2001.

Globalization of R&D: benefits and constraints

As illustrated in the Nestlé example, a global R&D network involves a decentralized, distributed approach to the management of innovation.

Benefits

There are four main potential benefits of decentralized as opposed to centrally managed R&D:[3]

- *Proximity to market* – the ability of a global firm to adapt or to create products fitting local customers' specificities.
- *Access to geographical clusters of knowledge creation and development* – universities, suppliers, researchers, start-up firms, venture capitalists; Michael Porter (1998) has illustrated the concept of technological centers as clusters of excellence such as Insulin in Denmark
- *Learning* – the ability of a global firm to leverage local knowledge across subsidiaries and to cross-fertilize this knowledge within a global network; De Meyer (1992) pinpointed the importance of 'learning' in international R&D:
- Learning about different markets, different problem-solving methods, different sources of technological progress, different cultures, different competitors, and rapid diffusion of that learning throughout the organization, is definitely enhanced by creating an international network of laboratories.
- *Access to low-cost and good-quality scientists and engineers* – some empirical evidence for this motivation is apparent when we look at the development of Bangalore as a center for computer software or the science parks of Singapore, or Taiwan (Hinshu), which were developed originally on that basis. However, except for routine activities, this motivation is not sufficient to justify a decentralized R&D network.

Constraints

There are also two major constraints in implementing a global distributed R&D network: the loss of critical mass and of face-to-face communication:

- *Critical mass constraints* exist when one activity, in order to be performed efficiently and effectively, needs to mobilize a minimum amount of resources. Research activities belong to this category – scientists and technologists are not lonely inventors; they need to benefit from the complementarities of colleagues in their field as well as in related domains. They also need assistance from technical staff, and they use more and more expensive laboratory instruments. Below a certain threshold of such resources, research projects have difficulties in taking off, hence the need for centralization and concentration of R&D activities. Having too many laboratories dilutes resources and hampers research performance. The solution to the problem is to be found in the creation of '**centers of excellence**', specializing in one type of technological development, where scientific resources are concentrated for that particular type of research. Paradoxically, centers of excellence may solve the critical-mass problem, but do not particularly favour internationalization of research activities concentrated in one location.

- *Communication constraints* are due to the overwhelming evidence that innovative activities require face-to-face informal communication.[4] **Innovation** is based on a combination of well-defined methodological procedures as well as ill-defined, tacit, intuitive intellectual processes, personal encounters and conversations among researchers. Geographical distance, despite all information and communication technologies such as videoconferencing, is less conducive to inductive, intuitive and ill-defined discoveries. These communication constraints militate in favour of *co-located research*, where research projects are self-contained within a single geographical location in order to minimize communication between units and maximize it within units.

In total, the benefits of a distributed network of innovative centers outweigh the costs as more and more global companies develop a decentralization of R&D networks.

Design of global R&D networks

Research centers in a global network belong to four main types:[5]

- *Research laboratories,* in charge of long projects dealing with new technologies or scientific discoveries that are not necessarily related to a particular product. Those laboratories are global by nature, and are most often, but not always, located near the corporate center
- *Development laboratories,* in charge of projects whose objective is to lead to a product or process innovation
- *Supporting/adaptive units,* that provide product or process adaptation according to local contexts
- *Scanning units,* whose mandate is to monitor technological development and contribute to the knowledge platform of the company.

The way these units are set up and organized depends upon the global evolution of the firm over time, which usually follows the pattern shown in Figure 10.4.

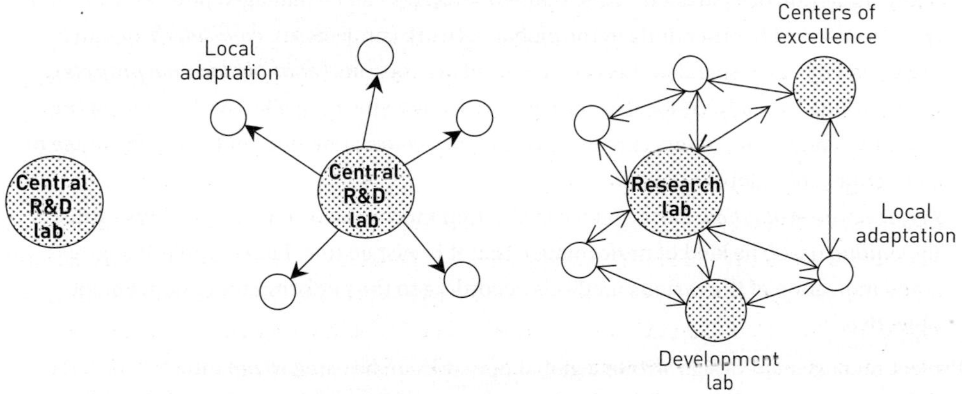

Figure 10.4 Evolution over time of global R&D activities

When the company is past the stage of central R&D activities, local laboratories are set up in order to provide local products or processes adaptation. In the third stage, centers of excellence that can specialize in basic research or certain products or process applications are established in innovative resource-rich countries. A **networked organization** is established to organize the exchange of ideas, technologies, people and information. Nestlé, as described earlier, has reached this stage.

Management of global R&D networks

The management of global R&D or innovative networks requires adaptation in structure, systems, and people/culture.

Structure

The structural aspects of R&D management relate to size, specialization, project organization and performance evaluation:

- *Size*: Research demands *communication* and *flexibility*. Large-size organizations are unfit to provide a proper innovative environment. In their research, Pearce and Singh (1992) found that 50 per cent of international laboratories employed fewer than 50 people and 80 per cent fewer than 200 people. In the case of Nestlé, the size of laboratories was between 20 and 200 employees. When a research site employs a larger number of scientists and technicians, it is usually divided into smaller, self-contained specialized units.
- *Specialization:* Specialization can be *discipline-centered* or *product-/process-centered.* The first case applies more to upstream research, while the second fits more with development work where multi-disciplinary teams work on the many facets of product design, utilization, marketability and production.
- *Project organization:* The most common arrangement for R&D is the project management structure, in which a *project leader* is responsible for the planning, budgeting, control and completion of a particular development. Projects can be managed purely locally and then transferred to other units in the global network (projects are *co-located*), or can be organized by interdependent tasks distributed across units (*multiple-location projects*). As mentioned already, co-located projects are likely to be more effective because of the communication constraints examined earlier, but co-location does not take advantage of the richness of a global network.
- *Performance evaluation:* Performance evaluation mechanisms may take various forms, depending upon the kind of performance that it is wished to enhance. Table 10.2 gives some indication of the various methods according to the performance enhancement objective.

Project management design within a global network can be categorized into:

- *Self-contained co-located independent projects,* in which one research unit in the network is responsible for the complete design and development of a product/process. In this case, the communication flow between engineers, technicians, marketers and manufacturers is entirely limited to the research unit located on one site in the network. On completion of the project, the product or process is transferred to other units. In the case of an engine manufacture, for example, a particular unit would be responsible for the whole design of a certain type of engine.

- *Integrated distributed projects,* in which several research centers take responsibility for one different inter-related element in the design and creation of the product/process. One center will take care of the combustion chamber of an engine, while another will design the regulation. In such a case, inter-unit communication is maximized since researchers will have to exchange a lot of information to make the different parts fit together.
- *Parallel distributed projects,* in which a project is still divided between several units but in such a way that inter-unit communication is limited to only a few parameters. In the case of the engine, one unit would be responsible for the combustion chamber including the regulation, while another would take charge of the compressor system. There would still be some interdependencies to manage, but fewer than in the previous case.

Table 10.2 Performance evaluation criteria

Performance	Measurement
Scientific innovation	• Number of patents • Number of publications in research journals
Commercialization	• Time to market
Profitability	• Research unit as profit center
Cost	• Budgeting targets
Collaboration	• Organization of conferences and internal seminars • Internal presentation of papers • Number of publications listed on the intranet

Hewlett Packard (HP)

EXAMPLE

An example of the distinction between the various project types is provided by the case of Hewlett Packard's development of a portable printer in Vancouver and Singapore.[6] HP wanted to develop a new printer (code name Alex) based on inkjet technology by splitting the work between Vancouver and Singapore. Vancouver was responsible for the product design and marketing while Singapore was in charge of the electronics parts design, sourcing, manufacturing design, tooling and testing. The project was designed as an integrated distributed one, demanding a large number of interactions between the two units. The project could not be completed in time and was dropped. The Singapore unit later obtained permission from headquarters to develop a printer for the Japanese market, adopting a self-contained co-located approach. This attempt was not successful either, because the unit did not benefit from the experience gained in inkjet printer design and marketing in Vancouver. Several years later, similar product developments were divided differently. Singapore was put in charge of printer engines (a self-contained key component) while Vancouver took on the ergonomic and functional design, a parallel-distributed project. The results were successful because each team could work separately with a minimum of interactions and at the same time maximize their respective skills. The overall project organization was based on the co-location principle, as illustrated in Figure 10.5.

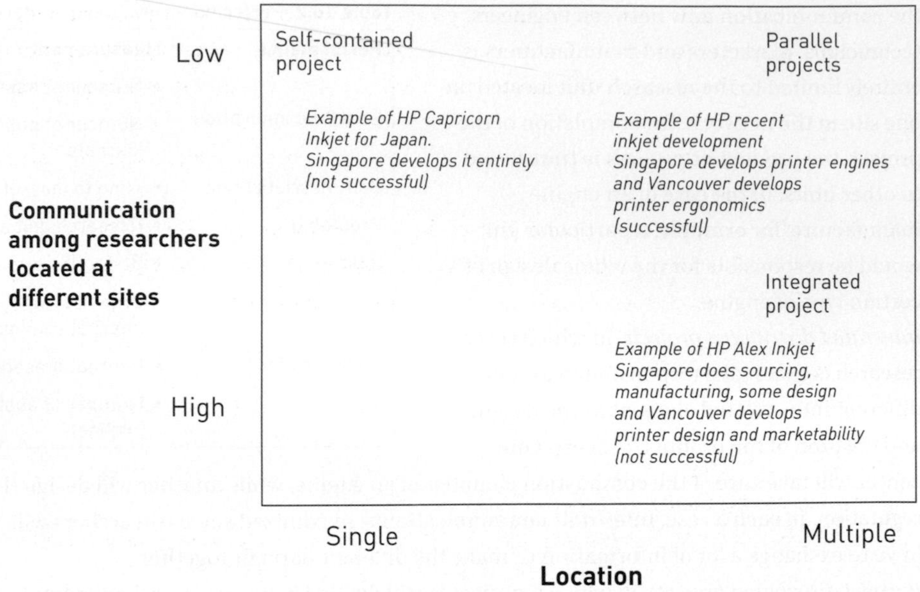

Figure 10.5 Global R&D projects

Systems

The effective management of a global R&D network calls for the implementation of systems and processes for *planning and control* and *knowledge documentation and dissemination*:

- *Planning and control systems* consist of the orderly definition of research projects and their distribution across units, the allocation of resources to the projects and the control of resources utilization alongside the monitoring of project achievements. Project definition and attribution is generally done by a global central unit like that described for Nestlé above (NRC), on the basis of the overall project management philosophy described earlier. Project proposals are initiated either by the research units within the framework of their mandate or decided centrally and then delegated by the central coordination unit. Global product managers can initiate projects based on the assessment of market needs. An important consideration in the budgeting of research projects is to give research centers some 'free budgets', consisting of unallocated resources that can be used at the discretion of the unit head for contingencies or for the exploration of new unplanned investigations.

The degree of *standardization* of the planning system is a function of the nature of the research project. More fundamentally, advanced research programmes are given a 'budgeting envelope' without asking for too detailed a justification, while more applied, business-specific projects may require cash-flow forecasts similar to any strategic investment.

Planning processes are not only useful for resource allocation but also as a *communication* mechanism. Planning can be linked with scientific conferences, during which various laboratories present their projects before the actual planning and budgeting exercise begins.[7]

Controls are exercised through *internal reporting*, measuring progress against technical and commercial milestones.

- *Knowledge diffusion and documentation* Knowledge management is not limited to R&D, and the next section of the chapter considers this in more detail. For global R&D, knowledge diffusion and documentation are based on seven main mechanisms:
  - People rotation
  - Conferencing
  - Databases
  - Publications
  - Personal networking
  - Electronic knowledge management platforms
  - Research has shown that global companies tend to use a portfolio of mechanisms usually coordinated by a central staff office.[8]

People and culture

There are four people-related practices particularly conducive to global R&D:[9]

- *Temporary assignments* as a way for researchers to be familiar with the work of other laboratories and sometimes to be assigned to a marketing team. Training programs, regular travel and conferences allow inter-personal exchanges and the inculcation of socialization and an 'open' culture of sharing.
- *Creation of 'gatekeeper' roles* in each laboratory, where the task is to translate the work from other laboratories into the language of his/her own laboratory.
- *Creation of a small central staff* whose role is to ensure a proper diffusion of information and research results.
- *Promoting openness and sharing* as important corporate values.

International transfer of technology

Every process of globalization implies some process of technology transfer. During the 1960s and 1970s, international technology transfer was considered a critical issue because of the emergence of newly independent countries that aspired to industrialize[10] and demanded an appropriate and complete transfer of technologies from multinational corporations. With the increased liberalization of economies, this topic has lost its geopolitical connotations but still remains a managerial issue when dealing with the developing or emerging world.

Table 10.3 gives a classification of the various forms of technology that can be transferred.

Table 10.3 Classification of technology

	Physical	*Informational*
Product technology	• Blueprints • Formulation • Pictures, design • Models • Samples • Lab equipment • Databases	• Product development methodologies • Research heuristics • Creative methods • Testing methods • Data mining research protocols
Process technology	• Plant layouts • Equipment • Process charts • Process handbooks	• Process control • Quality insurance • Maintenance processes • Logistics and supply chain
Management technology	• Handbooks • Flow charts • Manuals • IT equipment • Accounting documents • Planning templates	• Marketing management • Financial management • Strategic planning • Human Resources Management • (HRM) • Project management

Technology transfer takes place under five main *organizational and contractual* forms:

- Licensing agreements
- Projects (turnkey projects, BOT, etc.)
- Technical agreements with joint venture companies or local subsidiaries
- Joint projects
- Sales of equipment.

The typical issues in technology transfer are *appropriateness and completeness.* Technology transfer is *appropriate* if it fits with the local context. The classic trade-off is between modern, state-of-the-art technology that requires a solid infrastructure of human capital as well as support industries and a more modest, less advanced technology that can be assimilated locally. Global companies have often been blamed for transferring old and obsolete technology in order to protect their competitive advantage, but on the other hand many cases of expensive, advanced technology, the 'white elephants', have also been criticized as resource-wasting. When Volkswagen set up the first Western factory of modern cars (the Santana) in China in the early 1980s, it would have been difficult to transfer the new models manufactured and sold in Europe at the time. The state of the roads, the network of available suppliers, the volume involved and the skill level could not have permitted the assimilation of such complex, advanced manufacturing systems. But, over time, the progressive improvement of local conditions made the transfer of modern technology feasible. SHAIC, the Chinese partner of Volkswagen, later entered a joint venture with General Motors to produce a more advanced model than the Santana with a more sophisticated production technology.

A technology transfer is *complete* when the recipient of technology is able to perform by itself the product of the transfer. This raises the issue of the transfer of *informational technology.* The knowledge embodied in those elements is often non-explicit and calls for a 'coaching approach' to the transfer, instead of just shipping equipment or organizing a standard lecture.[11] Developing countries often regret that global companies restrict their transfer to physical content and limit information transfer to a strict minimum in order to maintain their future bargaining power. Although this interpretation is often too extreme, it is frequently true that engineers in global firms are not fully prepared to cope with the considerations of education and patience that a proper transfer implies.

Global knowledge management

Knowledge is the ability to understand and give meaning to facts and information. In the corporate world, knowledge applies not only to techniques and physical sciences, but all aspects of corporate behaviour. **Knowledge management** consists of the ability for a firm to create, combine and share knowledge among its members. Global R&D management is only one sub-set of knowledge-based strategies. Beyond the strict management of R&D, the strengths of global companies are their capability to create, combine and share knowledge across borders. According to the Japanese social scientists Nonaka and Takeuchi (1995), knowledge can be created and shared at the individual, group and organizational level. They distinguish between **explicit knowledge** (i.e. knowledge that can be codified and explained verbally, in writing or with symbolic language) and **tacit knowledge** (that cannot be codified and that can be transferred only by imitation or observation, by 'teaching'). They distinguish four types of knowledge conversion:

- *Socialization,* the process of sharing tacit knowledge through social interaction, apprenticeship and observation
- *Externalization,* the process of articulating tacit knowledge into explicit concepts through metaphors, pictures and theoretical formulations
- *Combination,* the process of combining different elements of explicit knowledge into written, codified formats
- *Internalization,* the process of transforming explicit knowledge into tacit knowledge; when knowledge is internalized it becomes part of the way of doing things and its explicitness may be lost.

According to Nonaka and Takeuchi, these four processes form a *knowledge spiral* of organizational knowledge creation from individuals to groups and then to whole organizations.

For global companies, knowledge management creates both opportunities and constraints (Table 10.4).

Table 10.4 Opportunities and constraints for knowledge management in global companies

Opportunities	Constraints
Diversity of contexts	• Languages
Variety of experiences	• Differences of cultures and mindsets
Economies of scope in knowledge creation	• 'Not invented here' reactions
Economies of speed by not 'reinventing the wheel'	• Unwillingness and lack of motivation to share knowledge • Incentive systems reinforcing local performance and not rewarding 'global' citizenship • 'Siloed', nationalistic perspectives • Lack of trust between units

Transfer of best practices

Global companies build management processes in order to overcome the constraints and take advantage of the opportunities of knowledge management. One such process is the 'transfer of best practices', which has been documented by Szulanski (1996). Transfer of best practices consists in the *systematization of exchange of internal practices* developed in one unit and considered as 'superior' to other units. 'Practices' are the use of knowledge applied to all kinds of managerial activities – the running of a customer service center, the management of a product launch, the training of salespersons or the control of accounts receivable. Szulanski found that three major factors can hamper transferring practices, what he calls *internal stickiness*:

- *Causal ambiguity* between the various elements of the practices that make it difficult to model precisely causes and effects relationships. Causal ambiguity exists when tacit knowledge is at the core of the functioning of the practice.
- *Lack of absorptive capacity* by the recipient unit which is not capable of interpreting the knowledge transfer and applying it. Here again, tacitness may constitute a barrier to knowledge transfer when the recipient unit has not got the internal resources to 'crack' the implicit, non-verbal elements of the practices.
- *Arduous relationships* that exist when tacit knowledge requires multiple interactions between individuals, particularly when geographical and cultural distance are present.
- Szulanski's work challenges the classic views about knowledge transfer, as indicated in Table 10.5, and focuses the attention on the predominant sources of stickiness, which are closely related to the amount of tacitness involved in knowledge.

The metanational corporation

Doz, dos Santos and Williamson (2001) have developed the concept of the 'Metanational Corporation' that puts knowledge transfer at the center of a mode of managing global companies, beyond the classical organizational models described in Chapter 3. The metanational corporation is capable of forgetting the concept of knowledge transfer and substituting the capability of knowledge 'melding' (a neologism comprising *melting* and *welding*). Melding knowledge implies that the tacit elements of knowledge are effectively *assimilated* and *put into practice.*

The metanational model is built on the interaction of two factors: the *location* factor (the place where knowledge is created, shared and *melded)* and the *context* factor (the intellectual foundations underlying knowledge creation such as language, mental mapping, codes, implicit rules, etc.). The basic argument is that useful knowledge is frequently tacit and that tacitness is embedded in a particular context. Tacit knowledge-creation, sharing and melding requires *co-location*: the ability for people involved to benefit from frequent interactions, random encounters ('corridor' or the 'coffee shop' interactions). This is precisely the reason why co-location is so important in the case of R&D projects. In global companies, locations between units can be distant and contexts very diverse (multiplicity of language, education, social codes, etc.). The key problem of a global company is then to take advantage of the *diver-*

sity and at the same time resolve the *co-location* imperative. The various forms of knowledge creation, sharing and melding are represented in Figure 10.6.

- In the C&C (Co-location and Co-setting) model, knowledge is entirely co-located, with people sharing the same intellectual context transferred to other business units. This is the classic use of *centers of excellence*, in which one particular business unit is the creator of knowledge that becomes the 'best practice' to be transferred. This eliminates the problem of tacitness at the level of knowledge-creation but not at the level of transfer. The issue of stickiness is still present.

Context of knowledge creation, sharing and 'melding'	Location: Same	Location: Distant
Diverse	**C&D** Co-location and Diverse setting *The 'Babel Tower'* *Knowledge creation, sharing and 'melding' in one place with the participation of managers detached from dispersed business units* *The secondment practice*	**D&D** Diversion and Diverse setting *The virtual team* *Knowledge creation, sharing and 'melding' in several places with the ability for the company to create the conditions for effective sharing of tacit knowledge*
Same	**C&C** Co-location and Co-setting *Classic co-location teams* *Knowledge creation, sharing and 'melding' in one place and possibly transferred later* *The guiding principle of 'center of excellence'*	**D&C** Diversion and Co-setting *The Diaspora team* *Virtual co-location* *Knowledge creation, sharing and 'melding' in several places but with expatriate managers coming from the same 'intellectual' mold.* *Classic role of expatriate managers*

Location

Figure 10.6 Knowledge creation, sharing and 'melding' in global firms

Source: Reprinted with permission from *From Global to Metanational: How Companies Win in the Knowledge Economy* by Yves L. Doz, José dos Santos, and Peter J. Williamson. Harvard Business Press, 2001.

Table 10.5 Tools and approaches used for knowledge management in the metanational corporation

• Business units and team leaders trained and experienced in *D&D practices*
• *Socialization* before teamwork implying 'non-productive' social interfaces
• *Transitional encounters* (conferences, seminars, workshops, etc.) with loose agenda to allow tacit knowledge to be shared
• Teams made aware of contexts through visits, education
• Strong, accessible, open, user-friendly knowledge management platforms (electronic libraries, case studies, chat rooms, etc.)
• Deadlines for project completion
• Yellow pages (who is who for what?)

- In the D&C (Dispersion and Co-setting) model, knowledge is created at different locations under the leadership of 'expatriates' who share the same intellectual and contextual background. They understand one another across cultures and they are able at the same time to adapt knowledge to local conditions and to share it, since the stickiness is reduced thanks to the common cultural background. This was the classic practice of multinational firms relying on a talented and mobile expatriate group. The problem of this approach is the difficulty of taking advantage of the contextual diversity of country units and may lead either to an inflexible application of 'central' recipes or a complete acculturation of the expatriate managers – the 'going native' syndrome.
- The C&D (Co-location and Diverse settings) model tries to take advantage of a *physical co-location* of managers coming from various parts of the world and working on a common project. This is the idea behind 'impatriation' practices. This can lead to 'Tower of Babel' consequences because of a lack of a common contextual background among participants and the lack of explicit management of the cultural differences.
- Finally the D&D (Disperse and Diverse) model, the model of the 'metanational' corporation, is the one in which the creation, sharing and melding of knowledge in a dispersed and diverse world is explicitly managed. Table 10.5 lists the major organizational tools used for managing a D&D environment.

Global knowledge and the protection of intellectual property rights

The protection of **intellectual property rights** (IPR) is a source of concern and sometimes an impediment to practicing true global knowledge management. Global firms are often confronted with imitation, reverse engineering and trademark copies. Table 10.6 gives a list of the various forms of intellectual properties and their infringement.

Protection against infringement of IPR can involve the measures summarized in Table 10.7.

Table 10.6 Intellectual property rights and their infringement

IPR	*Infringement*
Patents	Reverse engineering Straight copy • Drugs, chemicals, mechanical and electronics products, auto parts
Trademarks	Straight copy Imitation (with minor change) • All branded products
Copyrights	Rights of creators • Texts, software, video, movies, training packages
Industrial designs	Original concept and design • Fashion, auto parts, electronics, appliances
Trade secrets	Employee poaching, espionage • Client lists, marketing and strategic plans, financial information, industrial and management processes
Genetic codes	Copy, employee poaching • Bio-engineering

Source: United Nations (1993)

Table 10.7 Protection of intellectual property rights

Parties involved	*Protection methods*
Employees	• Restrict disclosure of IP to selected employees • Require key employees to sign individual secrecy agreements • Establish a strict catalog of level of confidentiality • Keep IP in secure location • Educate employees on the rationale and the consequences of infringement • Regularly interview employees • Prepare handbook listing items to be protected, and what to do in case of leakage suspicion; give recommendations about best practices
Suppliers	• Non-disclosure agreements • Establish rules about what can and cannot be disclosed
Joint venture partners	• Be specific in the joint venture contract • Use 'black box' approach when technically feasible • Screen partners' employees
Legal issues	• Lobby governments • Use diplomatic channels to support actions • Engage in legal action as soon as possible, even if legal context is unfavorable

MINI-CASE

Global Giants' R&D Networks

R&D at Siemens

Siemens is a global electronics and electrical engineering corporation, operating in energy, healthcare, infrastructure and industrial solutions sectors. Founded in Germany, the company has activities in nearly 200 regions, with 336,000 employees working at 1640 locations around the globe, including 176 R&D facilities. Its turnover in 2010 was €75 billion.

Innovation is at the core of its success. According to Peter Losgher, president and chief executive: *'We closely align R&D activities with business strategy, hold key patents and have a strong position in both established and emerging technologies. Our goal is to be a trendsetter in all of our businesses.'*[12]

In 2010, Siemens invested approximately €3.8 billion in research and development (5.1 per cent of sales), of which around €1000 million was devoted to developing green technologies. In 2011 Siemens generated 8600 inventions thanks to its 27,800 researchers and developers worldwide.

The R&D network is organized at the corporate level and within divisions and business units.

Corporate level R&D[13]

The research and development at corporate level is managed within Corporate Research and Technology (CTT), the Corporate Development Center (CDC) and the Corporate Intellectual Property and Functions (CT IT).

MINI-CASE

CTT employs 1770 people with a budget of around €280 million, who work on key technologies that are strategically important and can be applied across sectors. One of the key functions is the corporate Technology Strategic Marketing that identifies future technologies using a methodology called 'Pictures of the Future' and informs the sectors about their potential future. They also use Global Account Managers to collect technology requirements from the various Siemens industry sectors and communicate that information to the CTT researchers. CTT researchers are organized in clusters, grouping experts in domains such as Materials, Electric and Energy, Process and Production, Software Security and Systems.

- There are 13 Corporate Research and Technology centers across the world:
- Berlin (Germany): 85 researchers
- Munich (Germany): largest corporate location with 958
- Erlangen (Germany): 379 researchers
- Vienna (Austria): 80 researchers
- Moscow (Russia): 30 researchers
- St Petersburg (Russia): 30 researchers
- Princeton (USA): 369 researchers
- Berkeley (USA): 12 researchers
- Bangalore (India): established in 2004, today with 105 employees
- Singapore: 6 researchers working on water technology
- Beijing (China): established in 1998, with 140 researchers
- Shanghai (China): 64 researchers
- Tokyo (Japan): 8 researchers

The sites in China and India work on SMART technologies (low-cost innovations suitable for emerging economies).

The Corporate Development Center (CDC) employs 3160 software developers who develop software for new products and services. Locations for these activities are in Europe, Indian and China.

The Corporate Intellectual Property and Functions (CT IT) with 500 specialists in 19 locations around the world are in charge of registering and safeguarding intellectual property rights. In 2010 the CT IT registered 8800 innovations and 4300 patents.

Another feature of the Siemens R&D system is to maintain strategic partnerships with leading research institutions such as the Technical University of Denmark (DTU), the Technische Universität München, the RWTH Aachen University, the Technische Universität Berlin, MIT and UC Berkeley in the US, as well as Tongji University and Tsinghua University in China. This is done both by the corporate centers and divisional development units.

Lastly Siemens has initiated the Strategic Technology Accelerator (STA) that organizes the spin-off of new ventures out of the Siemens organization and supports these new ventures financially, legally and organizationally.

MINI-CASE

The divisional R&D

Divisional R&D centers are distributed regionally and provide local product development for the benefit of Business Units.

R&D at BASF[14]

BASF is a global chemical company founded in Germany. It sales were €63.9 billion in 2010. 109,000 employees work in six business segments: Chemicals, Plastics, Performance products, Functional solutions, Agriculture solutions and Oil and Gas. It operates 385 production sites.

9600 employees work in 70 R&D centers worldwide with a budget in 2010 of €1.5 billion.

- The distribution of R&D sites is:
- Europe: 33 sites and 7500 employees
- Americas: 25 sites with 1550 employees
- Asia Pacific: 8 sites and 550 employees.

BASF focuses on the five growth clusters: energy management, raw material change, nanotechnology, plant biotechnology, as well as industrial or 'white' biotechnology.

In addition to this direct effort, BASF has created two subsidiaries:

BASF Venture Capital GmbH is a venture capital company that invests in start-up companies and venture capital funds worldwide. It also support innovative start-ups, both financially and with expert know-how from the BASF Group.

BASF Future Business GmbH whose goal is to tap into new business fields for BASF. Special areas of innovation include solving issues in the fields of energy management, electronics, health and the environment.

BASF has developed a management approach called *Verbund* that integrates manufacturing and research. Production plants at large sites are closely interlinked and in addition, the by-products of one plant can be used as the starting materials of another. BASF considers that Verbund is the foundation of its competitiveness in all regions.

There are six *Verbund* sites and some 385 production sites. The six *Verbund* sites are in:

- Ludwigshafen (Germany): The world's largest integrated chemical complex, the location of BASF Group's technology platforms and competence centers
- Antwerp (Netherlands): The second largest site
- Nanjing (China): a 50:50 joint venture between BASF and China Petroleum & Chemical Company (SINOPEC)
- Kuantan (Malaysia)
- Freeport (USA)
- Geismar (USA)

Questions:

1) How does the global management of R&D at Siemens and BASF compare?
2) What are the potential benefits of the *Verbund* concept?

Summary and key points

1 International product life cycle:

- How product innovations and production *migrated* from country of origin of innovative firms to other country subsidiaries
- *Stages*:
  - Stage 1: innovation – *innovative country product life cycle*:
    Innovative firms create new products and processes in their country of origin
  - Stage 2: foreign production – *second-tier country product life cycle*
    Second-tier country subsidiaries receive products/process from innovators and produce for local markets
  - Stage 3: transfer – *developing country product life cycle*
    Developing countries subsidiaries receive products/processes from innovators and produce for local markets and global markets at low cost
- Criticisms
  - Cannot explain the globalization of innovation that occurred after the 1960s
  - Migration of R&D and production centers does not necessarily follow sequential evolution described by the international product life cycle.

2 Global R&D network:

- *Management* of global R&D network needs to adapt structure, systems and people/culture:
  - Structure
    - Large-size organization not conducive to communication and flexibility required in research
    - Specialization
      - *Discipline-centered* (applies more to upstream research) or
      - *Product/process-centered* (applies more to development work requiring multi-disciplinary teams)
    - Project organization:
      - Can be managed locally (co-location project)
      - Loses benefits arising from richness of a global network
      - Organized by interdependent tasks distributed across units (multiple-location projects)
      - There are three forms of project management design: self-contained co-located independent projects; one research unit in the network responsible for complete design and manufacture of a product/process; communication flow within the research unit at one site
      - Integrated distributed projects: different research centers take responsibility for one different inter-related element in design and creation of the product/process; maximum inter-unit communication
      - Parallel distributed projects: project divided between several units, as in integrated distributed projects; inter-unit communication is limited to only a few parameters; fewer interdependencies among units

        - Performance evaluation: scientific innovation; commercialization; profitability; cost; collaboration
  - Systems
    - Planning and control
      - Allocation of resources (including budgeting)
      - Control of resource utilization
      - Monitoring of project achievements
    - Knowledge diffusion and documentation:
      - People rotation
      - Conferencing
      - Databases
      - Publications
      - Personal networking
      - Electronic knowledge management platforms
  - *People and culture* – favorable factors:
    - Temporary assignments
    - 'Gatekeepers' in each laboratory
    - Small central staff
    - Openness
- *Nestlé*:
  - Central coordination (not management) of research programmes and efforts including:
    - Central planning of technical conferences and personnel transfer
    - Regular 'trialogues' between researchers, marketers and manufacturers to enhance the symbioses
    - Visits to local research centers
  - Central monitoring of progress reports sent by local research companies
  - Decentralized R&D activities in local centers (local research companies):
    - Run as profit center
    - Located near manufacturing center
    - Performing development work on products, processes and systems
    - Involved in research planning and budgeting
    - Linked with local universities and technical institutes
  - Corporate research strategy to prevent duplication of efforts
- *Benefits*:
  - Proximity to market (adapt or create products fitting local requirements)
  - Access to geographical clusters of knowledge creation and development
  - Learning
- *Constraints*:
  - Critical-mass constraint where a minimum amount of resources is required for an activity to be performed efficiently and effectively
  - Communication constraint is partly based on ill-defined, tacit, intuitive intellectual processes, personal encounters and conversations among researchers
- Types of *research centers*:

- *Research laboratories*: long projects and new technologies/scientific discoveries
- *Development laboratories*: product/process innovation
- *Supporting/adaptive units*: providing product/process adaptation according to local contexts
- *Scanning units*: monitoring technological development and contributing to the knowledge platform of the company
- *Evolution*:
- First stage is central R&D lab
- Second stage is the set-up of local laboratories to provide local products or processes adaptation
- Third stage is the establishment of centers of excellence specializing in basic research or process applications in innovative resource-rich countries.

3 International technology transfer:

- Types of *technology*
  - Product
  - Process
  - Management
- Forms of *technology transfer*
  - Physical
  - Informational
- *Key issues*
  - Appropriateness
    - Appropriate if fits with local context
    - Trade-off between state-of-the-art technology requiring a solid infrastructure of human capital against less advanced technology that can be assimilated locally
  - Completeness
    - Complete if recipient of technology is able to perform by itself the product of the transfer
    - Non-explicit knowledge often requires a 'coaching' approach for technology which is informational.

4 Global knowledge management system:

- *Definition*:
  - Knowledge is the ability to decipher and give a meaning to facts and information
  - Knowledge management is the ability of a company to create, combine and share knowledge among its members
- Conversion of knowledge forms a *knowledge spiral* of organizational knowledge creation:
  - *Socialization*: process of sharing tacit knowledge through social interactions/ apprenticeship
  - *Externalization*: process of articulating tacit knowledge into explicit concepts
  - *Combination*: process of combining different elements of explicit knowledge into codified formats
  - *Internalization*: process of transforming explicit knowledge into tacit knowledge – when

knowledge is internalized, it becomes part of the way of doing things

- *Opportunities* for knowledge management:
  - Diversity of contexts
  - Variety of experiences
  - Economies of scope in knowledge creation
  - Economies of speed by not reinventing the wheel
- *Constraints*:
  - Languages
  - Differences of cultures and mindsets
  - 'Not invented here' reactions
  - Unwillingness and lack of motivation to share knowledge
  - Incentive system reinforcing local performances and not rewarding 'global' citizenship
  - Nationalistic perspectives
  - Lack of trust between units
- *Transfer* of best practices made less effective by:
  - Casual ambiguity (difficult to have a precise model of cause and effect relationship, especially for tacit knowledge)
  - Lack of capacity for absorption
  - Arduous relationships (tacit knowledge transfer requires multiple interactions between individuals)
- Useful *tools/approaches*:
  - Trained business units/team leaders
  - Socialization
  - Transitional encounters
  - Teams trained on contexts
  - Strong, accessible, open, user-friendly knowledge management platforms
  - Deadlines
  - Yellow pages
- *Knowledge creation, sharing* and '*melding*':
  - Dependent on location and context
  - Models
    - C&C model (Co-location and Co-setting)
      - Center of excellence in which one particular business unit creates knowledge and becomes a 'best practice' to be transferred
      - Benefits include elimination of the tacitness problem
      - Problem of stickiness still persists
    - D&C model (Dispersion and Co-setting)
      - Expatriate managers who share intellectual and contextual background adapt knowledge to local conditions
      - Benefit of reducing stickiness
      - Problem of contextual diversity of the country causing 'going native' syndrome or 'central recipes'
    - C&D model (Co-location and Diverse setting)

    - Benefits of 'impatriation' practices
    - Problem of 'Towers of Babel' owing to lack of common contextual background of participants and lack of explicit management of cultural differences
  - D&D model (Dispersion and Diverse setting) – major organizational tools:
    - Trained and experienced management and staff
    - Socialization
    - Transitional encounters
    - Increased awareness of contexts through education
    - Strong, open, user-friendly knowledge management platforms
    - Deadlines for project
    - Yellow pages.

5 Intellectual property rights (IPR):

- *Types*:
  - Patents
  - Trademarks
  - Copyrights
  - Industrial design
  - Trade secrets
  - Genetic codes
- *Infringement*: common for all types of intellectual property rights
- *Protection*: methods can involve any of the following:
  - Employees
  - Suppliers
  - Joint venture partners
  - Legal sanctions.

Learning assignments

1. Why is the international product life cycle model no longer appropriate to explain global innovation?
2. What are the constraints on implementing a distributed R&D network?
3. What are the appropriate HRM practices conducive to global R&D?
4. When is technology transfer complete?
5. Give two examples of 'explicit' knowledge and 'tacit' knowledge in a business context of your choice.
6. What are the major challenges that the 'metanational' model of knowledge creation, sharing and 'melding' tries to address?
7. How can research performance be measured?
8. How can you protect intellectual property rights (IPR) in a global firm?

Key words

- Best practices
- Center of excellence
- Co-location
- Combination
- Explicit knowledge
- Externalization
- Innovation
- Intellectual property
- Internal stickiness
- Knowledge management
- Metanational
- Networked organization
- Socialization
- Tacit knowledge
- Technology transfer

Web resources

<http://www.nsf.gov/statistics/seind06/c4/c4s6.htm>
National Sciences Foundation.

Visit the companion website at **http://www.palgrave.com/business/lasserre3e** for a multitude of weblinks and resources, self-test questions for revision and a searchable glossary.

Notes

1 Doz and Wilson (2006).
2 The Nestlé example is based on publications available on its website, and the ST Microelectronic example is from Doz *et al.* (2001).
3 These categories are based on De Meyer (1992) and Wortmann (1990) pp. 175–84.
4 Allen (1977).
5 This taxonomy is inspired by Pearce and Singh (1992) and Chiesa (2000) pp. 341–59.
6 Thill and Leonard-Barton (1994).
7 De Meyer (1991) pp. 49–58.
8 De Meyer (1991).
9 De Meyer (1992).
10 Seurat (1979); Amsalem (1983).
11 Lasserre (1995).
12 <http://www.siemens.com/about/en/values-vision-strategy/values.htm>
13 Source: Global Research at Siemens. From <http://www.ct.siemens.com>
14 <http://www.basf.com/group/research/index>

References and further reading

Books and articles

Allen, T.J., *Managing the Flow of Technology.* Cambridge, MA: MIT Press, 1977.

Amsalem, Michel, *Technology Choice in Developing Countries.* Cambridge, MA: MIT Press, 1983.

Augier, Mie and David J. Teece, 'Dynamic Capabilities and Multinational Enterprise: Penrosean Insights and Omissions', *Management International Review*, 47(2), 2007, pp. 175–192.

Boutellier, Roman, Olivier Gassmann, Maximilian von Zedtwitz, *Managing Global Innovation: Uncovering the Secrets of Future Competitiveness.* Berlin: Springer, 2009.

Bowonder, B., Anirudha Dambal, Shambhu Kumar and Abhay Shirodkar, 'Innovation Strategies for Creating Competitive Advantage', *Research Technology Management*, 53(3), May/June 2010, pp. 19–32.

Chesbrough, H., *Open Innovation: The New Imperative for Creating and Profiting from Technology.* Boston, MA: Harvard Business School Press, 2003.

Chiesa, Vittorio, 'Human Resource Management Issues in Global R&D Organizations: A Case Study', *Journal of Engineering and Technology Management,* 13, 1996, pp. 189–202.

Chiesa, Vittorio, 'Global R&D Project Management and Organization: A Taxonomy', *Journal of Product Innovation Management,* 17, 2000.

De Meyer, Arnoud, 'Tech Talk: How Managers are Stimulating Global R&D Communication', *Sloan Management Review,* 49, 1991.

De Meyer, Arnoud, 'Management of International R&D Operations', Chapter 8 in O. Granstrand, S. Spölander and L. Häkanson (eds), *Technology Management and International Business.* New York: John Wiley, 1992.

De Meyer, Arnoud, 'Nestlé SA', INSEAD Case Study 07/91-093, 1993.

Doz, Yves, José dos Santos and Peter J. Williamson, *The Metanational Corporation.* Boston, MA: Harvard Business School Press, 2001.

Doz, Yves and Keeley Wilson, *Innovation: Is Global the Way Forward?.* INSEAD and Booz Allen Hamilton, 2006.

Huston, Larry and Nabil Sakkab, 'Inside Procter & Gamble's New Model for Innovation', *Harvard Business Review*, March 2006, pp. 58–66.

JiataoLi and Deborah R. Yue, 'Managing Global Research and Development in China: Pattern of R&D Configuration and Evolution', *Technology Analysis and Strategic Management,* Vol. 17(3), 2005, pp. 317–37.

Kim, Soonhee and Hyangsoo Lee, 'Factors affecting employee knowledge acquisition and application capabilities', *Asia-Pacific Journal of Business Administration*, 2(2), 2010, pp. 133–152.

Kuemmerle, Walter, 'Building Effective R&D Capabilities Abroad', *Harvard Business Review,* March–April 1997, pp. 61–70.

Kumar, Nirmalya and Phanish Puranam, *India inside: the Emerging Innovation Challenge to the West.* Boston, MA: Harvard Business School Press, 2012.

Lasserre, Philippe, 'Training: Key to Technology Transfer', *Long Range Planning,* 15(4), 1995.

Li, Jiatao and Zhenzen Xie, 'Global R&D Strategies in an Emerging Economy: The Development And Protection Of Technological Competencies'. *European Management Review*, 2011, Vol. 8 Issue 3, pp.153–164.

Nonaka, Ikujiro and Hirotaka Takeuchi, *The Knowledge Creating Country: How Japanese Companies Create the Dynamics of Innovation.* Oxford: Oxford University Press, 1995.

Pearce, Robert D. and Satwinder Singh, *Globalizing Research and Development.* Basingstoke: Palgrave Macmillan, 1992.

Porter, Michael, *The Competitive Advantage of Nations.* New York: Free Press, 1998.

Rossi, Carla, 'Online consumer communities, collaborative learning and innovation', *Measuring Business Excellence*, 15(3), 2011, pp. 46–62.

Seurat, Sylvère, *Technology Transfer: A Realistic Approach.* Houston, TX: Gutt Publishing Co., 1979.

Shengliang, Robert *et al.*, 'A Guide to Intellectual Property Rights in South East Asia and China', *Business Horizon*, 39(6) November–December, 1996.

Slone, Robert et al., 'Managing Global R&D Networks', *Research Technology Management*, Nov/Dec 2011, Vol. 54 Issue 6, pp. 59–61.

Szulanski, Gabriel, 'Exploring Internal Stickiness: Impediments to the Transfer of Best Practices within the Firm', *Strategic Management Journal*, 17, Special Issue, 1996, pp. 27–43.

Terwiesch, Christian and Yi Xu, 'Innovation Contests, Open Innovation, and Multiagent Problem Solving', *Management Science*, 54(9), September 2008, pp. 1529–1543.

Thill, George and Dorothy Leonard-Barton, 'Hewlett-Packard: Singapore', *Harvard Business School Case*, 9-694-035, 1994.

United Nations, *Intellectual Property Right and Direct Foreign Investment.* New York: United Nations, 1993.

Van Tulder, Rob *et al*, *Private Sector R&D: Global View, Locomotive Project*, Copenhagen: Erasmus University/ Interlace-Invent, 2007.

Vernon, Raymond, 'International Investment and International Trade in the Product Life Cycle', *Quarterly Journal of Economics*, 29(2), 1966, pp. 190–207.

Von Zedtwitz, Maximilian, Olivier Gasman and Roman Boutellier, 'Organizing Global R&D: Challenges and Dilemmas', *Journal of International Management*, 10 (2004), pp. 21–49.

Whelan, Eoin, Salvatore Pariso, Jasper de Valk and Rick Aalbers, 'Creating Employee Networks That Deliver Open Innovation', *MIT Sloan Management Review*, 53(1), Fall 2011, pp. 37–44.

Wortmann, M., 'Multinationals and the Internationalization of R&D', *Research Policy*, 19(2), 1990.

Journals

Research and Development (monthly), Cahners, United States.

R&D Magazine, Battelle Institute: <http://www.rdmag.com>

chapter

11 CROSS-CULTURAL MANAGEMENT

Introduction

Chapters 8–10 have studied the managerial issues of designing and running the three key operational functions of innovation, production and marketing in a global context. In Chapters 11–13 we will look at how globalization affects the management of the two key resources of corporations: *human resources and financial resources.* Before addressing the global human resource management (HRM) problems, we need to explore the underlying complexity that arises in human relations as a result of international cultural differences.

This chapter presents the results of academic research that has studied cultural differences. We will then look at the impact of cultural differences on the management of *cross-cultural teams,* on *international negotiations* and on *business practices.*

Learning objectives

At the end of the chapter you will be able to:

- understand the meaning of culture and the various layers of culture
- identify the key characteristics of international cultural differences
- appreciate the different management issues associated with cultural differences
- explain the managerial issues associated with cross-cultural teams
- recognize how cultural differences affect international negotiations
- identify the key characteristics of an economic culture
- be aware of differences in ways of conducting business across cultures.

Failures in cross-cultural interaction

Global corporations are by nature organizations that *interact* with customers, employees, partners and suppliers from different national cultures, giving rise to the anecdotal gaffes well documented by David Ricks in his book, *Blunders in International Business* (1993). Beneath the surface of these 'travelers' tales' lies one of the main challenges that global firms have to confront. Do the various players in the global ecosystem give the same meaning to the same concepts, behaviors or attitudes? Do employees around the world get the same message when policies are enacted, memos exchanged or rewards distributed? Do customers of the same age, urbanization and wealth value similar product or service attributes? Do employees in multinational teams share similar assumptions and causal relationships about decision parameters? When a contract, a business venture or a loan is being negotiated, do the parties understand each other's 'silent language'? These are the questions that all global companies have to address in their cross-cultural management competencies.

The different facets of culture

There is no universal definition of culture. Schneider and Barsoux (1997) identify 164 different definitions made by anthropologists. More relevant broad definitions of culture include 'a shared pattern of behavior' (Margaret Mead, 1953), 'system of shared meaning or understanding' (Claude Levi-Strauss, 1971; Clifford Geertz, 1983) or 'a set of basic assumptions, shared solutions to universal problems ... handed down from one generation to another' (Edward Schein, 1985). All these definitions have in common the concept that culture is *'shared'*, and imply an implicit decoding of an underlying pattern of *cause and effect relationships,* whether cognitive (meaning, assumptions), attitudinal/emotional (behavior) or decisional (solutions). Schein adds the dimension of *generational transmission,* which implies a certain degree of stickiness of culture over time.

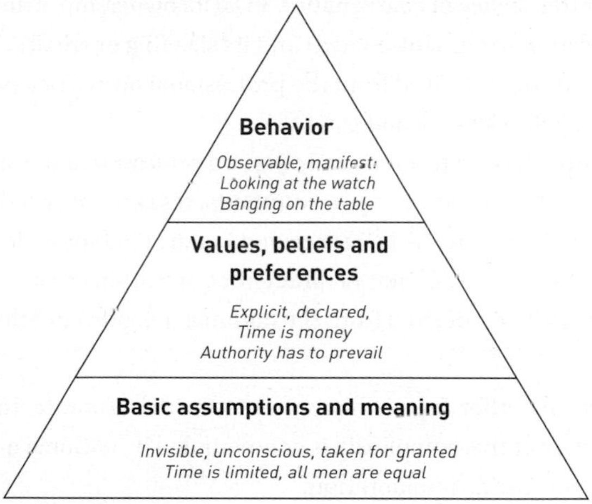

Figure 11.1 The three layers of culture

Source: André Laurent (1986)

Instead of a definition, some scholars have attempted to describe the *content* of culture. Figure 11.1 shows three major layers of culture: Basic assumptions and meaning; values, beliefs and preferences; and behavior. In ascending order, basic assumptions are the least visible and probably the most entrenched, since they deal with ingrained models of understanding, meanings and causal relationships that have been shaped by history and transmitted through the educational process to children, pupils and students. Religious faith and assumptions about human nature belong to this category. Basic assumptions are difficult to change in adults. Values, beliefs and preferences are the explicit expression of assumptions incorporated into a set of *codes* or *norms* that provide some sort of ethical and normative governance mechanisms for social groups. Values can be changed to some extent by new information and confrontation with new situations. A manager whose assumption about human nature is that men or women are fundamentally greedy, for example, will probably believe that only materialistic rewards will motivate employees. She/he may change this belief when exposed to situations where people sacrifice financial reward for others' benefit.

Behavior is the most visible part of the iceberg. It is manifested in action and can be modified through education as well as through some forms of 'conditioning'. Behavioral change does not imply a modification of beliefs or assumptions. An autocratic leader may be told to change her/his style of leading a meeting although she/he still believes that employees 'have to be told' (belief) based on the assumption that human beings are fundamentally divided into 'born leaders' and 'passive followers'. In such a case, behavioral change will be superficial.

In the management field that, by nature, is concerned with economic achievement of social groups (companies), culture will be manifest in four key dimensions:

- **Corporate culture:** the accumulated assumptions, values, beliefs and behavioral norms resulting from the history of the company (good and bad experiences), its existing and past leadership imprint (the legacy of charismatic CEOs) its ownership structure (family-owned, publicly listed, private, government-owned) and its size (big or small).
- **Industry culture:** any rules derived from the professional norms of a particular industry: heavy manufacturing, services, oil and gas, etc.
- **Professional culture:** derived from the training and professional norms/constraints of different functions within corporations: accountants, researchers, production personnel, sales and marketing people, etc. As Lawrence and Lorsh (1969) have described, professional orientation introduces a large amount of differentiation within organizations.
- **National or ethnic culture:** derived from the national, religious or ethnic origin of citizens or social groups.

Global companies, as any other firms, are confronted with corporate, industrial and professional cultural diversity, but this complexity is compounded by national and ethnic differences stemming from their worldwide implantation.

National cultural differences

The systematic analysis of national cultural differences in a business management context is the result of four main streams of research:

- *Ethnological research*: 'silent language' differences (Edward and Mildred Reed Hall, 1990)
- *Managerial values and assumptions*: work-related values differences (Geert Hofstede, 1980); value orientation differences (Fons Trompenaars, 1993; Hampton-Turner and Trompenaars, 2000); management assumptions differences (André Laurent, 1986)
- *Countries clusters*: the grouping of nations according to similarities of cultural traits (Ronen and Shenkar, 1985; Huntington, 1997)

- *Economic culture differences*: how business systems are organized and business interactions are governed (Albert, 1991; Berger and Dore, 1996; Whitley, 1999; Redding, 2001).

'Silent language' differences

According to Hall (1960), cultures differ in the way they communicate through non-verbal means or **'silent language'**. Six 'silent languages' can be identified: *time, space, material goods, friendships, agreements* and *context.* [1]

- Cultures differ according to their perception of **time**. Time can be seen as *sequential and scarce,* as in the case of Germanic culture, leading to the quest for preciseness, punctuality and deadline-keeping. Some cultures see time as *fluid, circular and abundant,* as in Arabic countries, where people will be less punctual and not really disturbed by delays and postponements.
- Differences in the perception of **space** relates to the concept of *social distance* that measures not only the length of physical proximity in social interaction but also of emotional intimacy. In high social distance cultures, people will tend to avoid physical and emotional proximity – a typical British trait – while in low social distance cultures – such as Latin countries – people will see no objection to physical contact and the sharing of emotions.
- The language of **material goods** is linked to the importance attached to financial wealth as a sign of status – a materialistic trait of Americans – as opposed to other status signifiers such as family, education or seniority.
- **Friendship** is built and maintained quite differently. In some societies, friends can be made rapidly, but at the expense of superficiality, and the friendship may not last long. The 'silent language' of this sort of friendship may shock people coming from societies where friendships are not so quickly built but last longer.
- The 'silent language' of **agreement** quite often opposes Western cultures to Eastern ones. In Western societies, most agreements or disagreements are explicitly stated and documented in writing. In Eastern cultures, verbal and sometime ambiguous agreements are accepted. In Indonesia, for instance, it is often difficult for a business partner to say a straight 'no', but a 'maybe' may in fact have the same negative connotation.
- The 'silent language' of **context** relates to the importance given to the person rather than the content in a communication. In high context societies – mostly Asian, South American or Latin – the important part of an interaction is the person (with *whom)* and the emphasis given to the setting, the ambiance and ceremonials. In low context societies – Anglo-Saxon, Nordic or Germanic – the *what* dominates the communication, hence the importance attached to written documents and technical specifications.

Managerial values and assumptions

Hofstede's work-related values differences

Hofstede's research is probably some of the most frequently quoted in international management literature, on account of the vast amount of data collected by the author. Hofstede's original (1980) survey was made with 116,000 employees at IBM worldwide. He asked questions related to their preferences in management styles and work values and related the answers to national origin; he found that national cultures differed according to four main dimensions: *power distance, individualism, uncertainty avoidance* and *masculinity*:

- **Power distance** is the extent to which people in certain societies accept *inequality in power distribution* or, on the contrary, have a somewhat *egalitarian view* of power distribution. High power distance societies will accept hierarchical control and respect authority – as, for instance, in Malaysia – while egalitarian societies will have a more democratic view of social control with no particular reverence for high-ranking functions – as, for instance, in Denmark.
- **Individualism** characterizes a culture in which individuals look after their own or immediate relative interests. This is the case in most Western cultures. This will translate into individual *assertiveness and initiative* in business contexts. Collectivist cultures, on the other hand, will put group interests above individuals: *consensus and harmony* will be preferred to assertiveness. East Asian cultures commonly put society ahead of the individual.
- **Uncertainty avoidance** is typical of societies where ambiguity and unpredictability is not accepted, and there is a continual search to codify, plan and regulate the environment (Japan, Spain). At the opposite end of the scale, there are social groups where tolerance and risk-taking is accepted and rewarded (United States, Sweden).
- **Masculinity** refers to the high value given to assertive, competitive behavior. Femininity, on the other hand, refers to societies where quality of life, non-aggressive behavior, interpersonal relations and concern for the weak are dominant values.

Table 11.1 Trompenaars' six value orientations

Value orientation	*Description*	*Examples*
Universalism vs Particularism	• Rule-based behavior; general application • Circumstance, relation-based behavior; specific application	• Nordic countries • South East Asia, China, African countries
Individualism vs Communitarism	• Individual rights are supreme; Individual performances are valued • Group's rights are supreme; harmony and cohesion are valued	• Western countries • Asian countries
Specificity vs Diffusion	• Objective, analytical, reductionist reasoning • Holistic, synthetic reasoning	• Germany, France • Middle East, Asia
Achieved status vs Ascribed status	• Status and respect achieved by 'doing' • Status and respect achieved by 'being'	• United States • Malaysia, China
Inner direction vs Outer direction	• Knowledge of 'right' and 'wrong' lies inside the individual ('guilt' culture) • Knowledge of 'right' and 'wrong' comes from society ('shame' culture)	• Protestant countries • Confucian societies
Sequential time vs Synchronous time	• Time is an arrow, is consumed in one direction • Time is a circle	• Western • Arabic, African, Asian countries

Sources: Trompenaars (1993); Hampden-Turner and Trompenaars (2000)

The 40 countries of Hofstede's original study were clustered around those four dimensions. It appears that Asian, Latin American and Arab countries are high on power distance and low on individualism while Anglo-Saxon and Nordic countries are the reverse. South European countries like Italy, Spain or France are high on power distance and high on individualism. For the dimensions related to masculinity and uncertainty avoidance the contrast is less regionally based since, for instance, in Asia Japan is very high on masculinity and uncertainty avoidance while India, Indonesia or Singapore would be relatively low on those two dimensions.

Trompenaars' value orientation differences

The cultural differentiation proposed by Trompenaars (1993), also based on survey data, identifies six value orientations that differentiate cultures and impact on the way countries conceive organizations (see Table 11.1). Trompenaars found significant differences in national groups; most Asian cultures, for instance, differ from Western cultures in all dimensions.

Laurent's management assumption differences

André Laurent (1986) asked precise questions related to organizational and managerial issues of international managers of various nationalities attending executive seminars over 25 years. He found a systematic pattern of national differences:

- Most managers seems to be more motivated by *obtaining power than by achieving objectives* (Latin European nationals – Italian, French, Spanish – agree with this statement, while Danes, Swedes and Norwegians disagree)
- It is important for managers to have at hand *precise answers to most of the questions that a subordinate may raise about their work* (Asian and Latin nationals strongly support this statement, while Anglo-Saxon and Nordic cultures do not)
- In order to have efficient working relationships, it is often necessary to *bypass the hierarchical lines* (Nordics and Anglo-Saxons agree while the Chinese, Italians, Spanish and Indonesians strongly disagree)
- An organization structure in which subordinates have *two direct bosses should be avoided at all costs* (Chinese, Italians, French and Indonesians reject this organizational mode, while Americans or Swedes accept the idea of working for two bosses)
- The main reason for having a hierarchical structure is so that everybody knows *who has authority over whom* (the Chinese, French, Japanese and Indonesians agree while Americans, Swedes or the British disagree).

Laurent's results consistently show that basic managerial and organizational assumptions concerning power, structure, clarity of roles and hierarchy are still deeply embedded in national cultures. These differences in assumptions pose a challenge to global firms that need to organize, lead and motivate people of diverse cultural heritage. Laurent even found that 'cultural differences in managerial assumptions were not reduced as a result of working for the same multinational companies', thus rejecting the idea that national cultures converge thanks to corporate cultures.

Country clusters

The clustering approach consists of grouping countries according to their degree of geographical, linguistic, religious, historical and social proximity. One example of country clusters is given in Figure 11.2.

Another type of clustering was developed by Huntington (1997), who grouped countries in what he called 'civilizations' based on language, religion, values, beliefs, and institutional and social structures. He identified eight modern 'civilizations':

- **Sinic:** the societies of China and Chinese communities as well as Vietnam and Korea; Confucianism is a major cultural trait of this 'civilization'
- **Japanese:** a distinctive civilization identified with one country

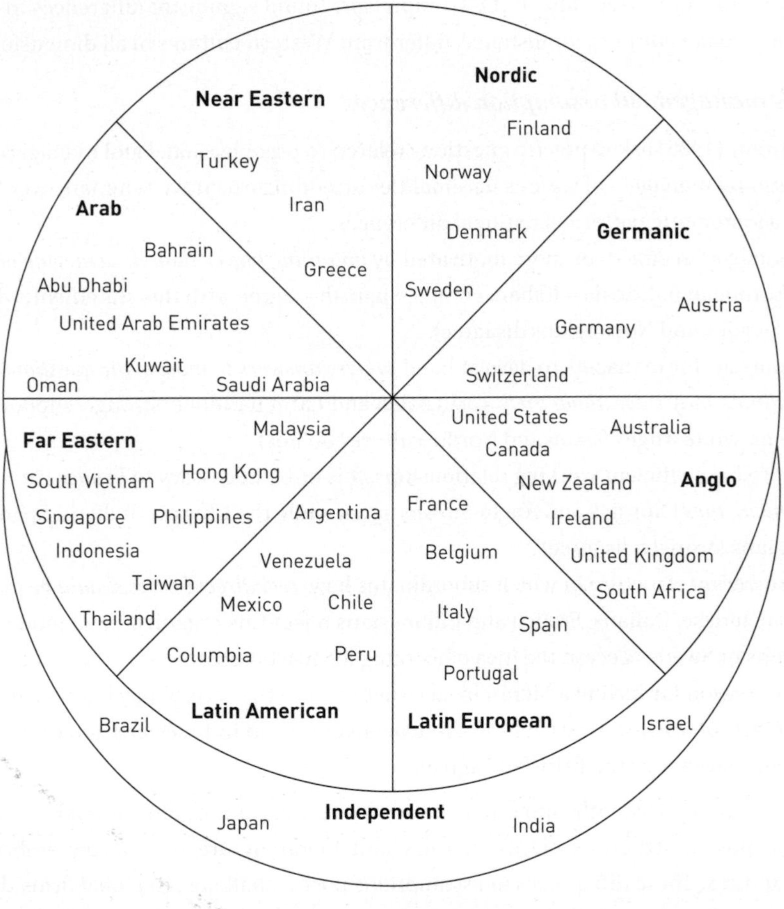

Figure 11.2 Country clusters

Source: Reproduced with the permission of ACADEMY OF MANAGEMENT (NY) via Copyright Clearance Center from Country clusters, p. 449 from Ronen, S. and O. Shenkar, 'Clustering Countries on Attitudinal Dimensions: A Review and Synthesis', *Academy of Management Review*, 10(3), 1985, pp. 435-54.

- **Hindu:** essentially India, Bangladesh and Sri Lanka
- **Islamic:** encompasses most of the Middle East and North Africa as well as Indonesia and part of Malaysia
- **Orthodox:** Central and Eastern Europe
- **Latin American:** Central and South America
- **African:** from Central to South Africa
- **Western:** North America, Western Europe and Australia.

Huntington's grouping has more to do with *geopolitics* than with management; he asserts that more and more conflicts in the world will be due to clashes of 'civilizations'.

Economic cultures

Cultures have a pervasive effect on social, economic and political institutions and on competitive behavior. In the early nineteenth century, Max Weber, a German sociologist, explained differences in competitive and business behavior between Latin European countries and Northern and Anglo countries as caused by the influence of religions. In Northern Europe, Protestantism encouraged *individual achievement* leading to free enterprises and favoring the emergence of modern 'capitalism', while Catholicism in Spain, and to a certain extent in France, induced *state control*. Several scholars have identified various forms of *business* systems,[2] *economic cultures*[3] or *forms of capitalism*[4] that explain international variations in institutional governance and competitive behaviors. Gordon Redding (2001) explains these differences according to the interaction of three sets of parameters (Table 11.2):

- The *culture* set that constitutes the foundation of social values, composed of three components:
  - *Rationale*, which describes the way societies set objectives and the importance they attach to formal systems and processes in setting objectives
  - *Authority*, which describes how societies set rules for vertical order (where the legitimate source of power is)
  - *Identity*, which describes the rules of horizontal order (what makes citizens stick together)
- The *institutional fabric* that represents the organization, development and allocation of resources, made up of three components:
  - The *financial capital*, its formation and allocation
  - The *human capital*, how human skills are developed
  - The *social capital*, the way trust is created among economic agents
- The business system that presides over the way economic activities are governed, made up of:
  - The *ownership system*, who are the primary owners of enterprises?
  - The *networking system*, how do companies and business agents relate to each other?
  - The *management system*, how are employees induced to cooperate?

Table 11.2 Differences in economic cultures

	Anglo/American	*German and Nordic European*	*French and Latin European*	*Japan*	*Korea*	*Overseas Chinese*
Rationale						
The societal ends are agreed as well as the means of pursuing them	• Material success • Democratic process • Rational system • Rules-led competition	• Community • Democratic • Consensus-led cooperation	• Democratic • Negotiation-led conflict resolution	• Employ people • Democratic • Consensus-led national	• Autocratic • National • Militaristic	• Autocratic • Familistic
Authority						
The ground rules for vertical order Origin of power	• Constitution • Law decentralization	• Law decentralization	• State • Law centralization	• State • Corporations • Decentralization	• State • Corporations • Centralization	• Family centralization
Identity						
The ground rules for horizontal order (What makes society stick together)	• Individual rights contracts • Heterogeneity (microcultures)	• Social welfare • Homogeneity	• Social welfare • Cultural identity • Heterogeneity (microcultures)	• National belonging • Cultural identity • Homogeneity	• Nationalism • Cultural identity • Homogeneity	• Clans • Ethnic bonding
Capital						
How financial capital is found and channeled	• Financial markets • Low gearing	• Banks • Medium gearing	• State and market • Medium gearing	• Banks • High gearing	• State • High gearing	• Family • High gearing

Table 11.2 Differences in economic cultures

	Anglo/American	*German and Nordic European*	*French and Latin European*	*Japan*	*Korea*	*Overseas Chinese*
Human capital						
How human skills are developed	• Academic performance-led	• Academic and apprenticeship	• Academic elitist	• Academic plus on-the-job elitist	• Academic elitist	• Academic plus on-the-job elitist
Social capital						
How trust is created	• High-trust contracts • Legal institutions	• High-trust contracts	• Low-trust • Negotiation	• High trust within groups	• High trust within groups, low outside	• High trust within family, low outside
Ownership						
Who owns enterprises	• Shareholders	• Banks, employees • Shareholders	• State, shareholders	• Banks • Cross-shareholding	• Business groups • Cross-shareholding	• Family groups
Networking						
How economic agents relate to each other (the rules of business transactions)	• Contracts	• Contracts • Some elitist relationships	• Elitist relationships • State interventionism	• Elitist relationships	• Personal relationships • State intervention	• Personal relationships
Managing						
How employees are induced to cooperate in the firm	• System-led • Motivation • Performance measures	• Hierarchical • Technical competence	• Hierarchical bureaucracy • Negotiation	• Corporate identity • Corporate loyalty	• Hierarchical • Corporate loyalty	• Hierarchical • Family loyalty

Sources: Albert (1991); Berger and Dore (1996); Whitley (1999); Trompenaars (2000); Hampton-Turner and Trompenaars (2000).

The impact of cultures on global management

The effects of cultural differences on the management of global companies are pervasive: there is no aspect of corporate life that is not impacted by culture. Six aspects of corporate life are particularly strongly influenced by cultural differences:

- Marketing and customer communications (see Chapter 8)
- Human resources (see Chapter 12)
- Partnerships, M&As (see Chapters 4 and 5)
- Multicultural teams
- Negotiations
- Business practices.

Marketing and partnership/acquisition have already been dealt with and Chapter 12 will consider human resources. This chapter focuses on teamwork, negotiations and business contexts.

Cross-cultural teams

In most activities, global firms make use of teamwork – committees, task forces, cross-functional teams, etc. Many departments at corporate, regional or subsidiary levels are staffed by managers of different nationalities and cultures (see Table 11.3).

Given the variety of cultural heritage, communication and decision-making processes can be blunted by *cultural noise*: multicultural teams can perform either significantly worse or better than monocultural firms. The performance of multicultural groups is a function of three factors:[5]

- Multiplicity of perspectives, experiences and viewpoints increases the *richness of information*
- Possible *loss of cohesion* owing to miscommunication, misunderstanding and stereotyping
- The ability of team leaders to combine the variety of perspectives and achieve group *synergy*.

Table 11.3 Types of multicultural team

Business development	Members of different nationalities working on development/ launch of new products
Regional headquarters	Different functions occupied by different nationals for regional coordination
Corporate headquarters	Permanent or temporary assignment of executives and staff of different nationalities having global responsibilities
Joint ventures and alliances	Managers and employees assigned from different partners, or an employees' pool
Task forces	Multifunctional, multinational teams in charge of a particular project

Source: Schneider and Barsoux (1997), reproduced with permission of Pearson Education Ltd

The relative impact of those three factors can lead to polarized performance. In an interesting study made with German and American staffed work teams, two researchers found that

German rational, analytical approaches to problem-solving combined with the action-oriented, free-wheeling, innovative approaches of American members contributed to high performance. However, performances were poor when the team leader was not able to introduce team-building procedures that facilitated information-sharing and group reflection of cultural assumptions.[6]

Negotiation

International operations require managers to be involved in a large variety of negotiations: contracts with suppliers, agents, distributors, licensees, joint venture partners, government authorities, trade unions and employees. The difference between those negotiations and domestic ones is the cultural background of the parties involved.

Negotiation framework

A very simple model of negotiation is provided in Figure 11.3. All negotiations can be assimilated to a buyer–seller search for settling a transaction: an export contract or a project, an acquisition of a company or part of it, a licensing contract or a joint venture agreement. In all cases the seller has explicitly (and sometime implicitly) a reservation price which is the price at which the seller is ready to walk away because there is a better alternative at this price.[7]

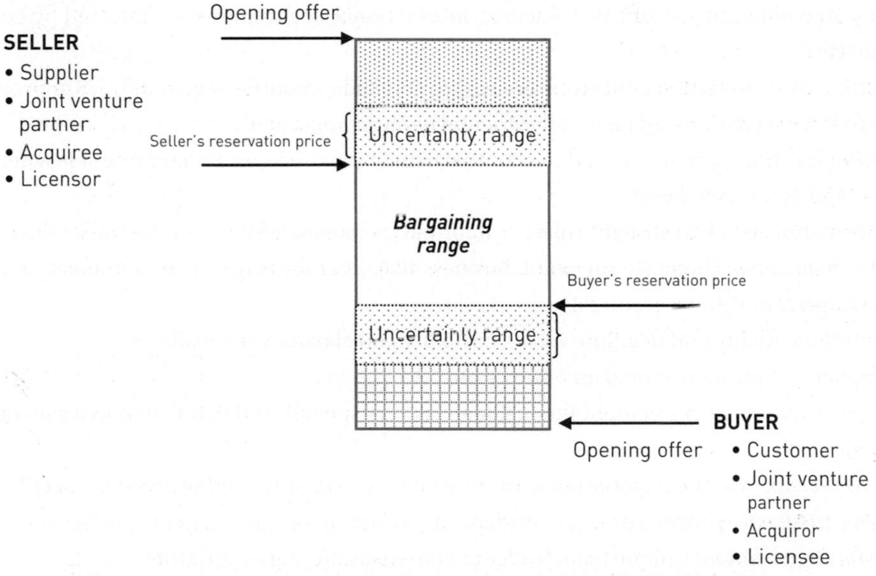

Figure 11.3 Framework for negotiation with reference to international contracts

For the buyer the situation is symmetrically similar. Generally the reservation price will be modified by an uncertainty factor because forecasts of the potential benefits or costs are always affected by risks. The opening offer in the negotiation will generally much higher than the seller's reservation price and lower than the buyer's reservation price. The negotiation will be assimilated to a '*ritual*', through which the negotiators will possibly end up finding an agreement in what is called the bargaining range in Figure 11.3. If the seller is a better negotiator the price may end up close to the buyer reservation price and vice versa if the buyer is better. But at the end, provided the agreement is within the bargaining range, a *win–win* situation is reached where both parties benefit.

Negotiation process

Negotiation '*rituals*' generally follow a sequential six-stage chronology:

- **Pre-negotiation:** each party prepares its negotiation strategy
- **Climate-setting:** introduction of negotiators, greetings, physical context
- **Presenting:** agenda-setting, opening statements
- **Mid-point bargaining:** substantive debate, request for clarification, search for common ground, trial 'concessions'
- **Closure:** Binding concessions offered, search for agreements, final drafting/signing
- **Post-negotiation:** ratification of agreements by corporate headquarters, or government bodies.

Cultural aspect of negotiating

There can be a large amount of cultural diversity in approaches and behaviors during these stages. According to Jeswald W. Salacuse,[8] international negotiations are affected by culture in ten ways:

- *Goal:* is the negotiation conceived as a way to conclude a contract (generally US approach) or to build a relationship (generally Oriental or Latin approach)?
- *Attitude:* is the approach to lead to a mutual benefit (win–win) or to have one side winning over the other (*win–lose*)?
- *Style:* Formal (stick to straight rules) or informal (personal, friendly, off the track talks)
- *Communication:* Direct (to the point, business-like, clear messages) versus indirect (implicit messages, ambiguous gestures)
- *Time:* Punctuality and deadline versus flexibility and elasticity of deadlines
- *Emotions:* Showing personal emotion or not
- *Form of agreement:* Agreement is considered as very specific and detailed or as a general framework.
- *Flow process:* Will the negotiation start from general principles and proceed to specific items (*deductive process*) or is it considered as collection of specific items (*inductive*)
- *Team Organization:* Unique team leader or consensus among negotiators
- *Risk taking:* do negotiators accept ambiguity and are they willing to find new approaches and to share information or, on the contrary, do they try to avoid giving away too much and departing from a well-known negotiation platform?

Another factor not mentioned in this list is the different approach used for *influencing the behavior* of the other party: whether negotiators use a *direct* approach (either threatening, persuading or demonstrating, or an indirect one (calling for sympathy, referring to personal stakes).[9]

Figure 11.4 gives a pictorial representation of those negotiation cultural traits with some indication of which type of culture leans to one side or the other while Table 11.4, using different criteria, summarizes the key differences between American and Japanese negotiation approaches. However, it should be noted that with the increased globalization of firms, multicultural teams are engaged more and more in negotiation, making cultural stereotypes less and less relevant. It may well be that a British firm will send a negotiating team led by a French divisional head, an Irish lawyer, a Singaporian controller and a Brazilian engineer. Which negotiation culture will prevail remains to be seen!

Examples of cultures following this style			Negotiation attributes			Examples of cultures following this style
US, UK, French	*Contract*	⇐	GOAL	⇒	*Relationship*	Asian, Arabic
US, German	*Win-Lose*	⇐	ATTITUDE	⇒	*Win-Win*	Japanese
Asian	*Formal*	⇐	STYLE	⇒	*Informal*	US
Western Europe, North America	*Direct*	⇐	COMMUNICATION	⇒	*Indirect*	Asian, Arabic
US, Germany	*Strict*	⇐	TIME	⇒	*Flexible*	Arabic, Chinese, Latin
Japan	*Hidden*	⇐	EMOTIONS	⇒	*Expressed*	Latin
US	*Specific*	⇐	FORM OF AGREEMENT	⇒	*General*	Japanese
French	*Deductive*	⇐	FLOW PROCESS	⇒	*Inductive*	Asian
Chinese	*One Leader*	⇐	TEAM ORGANIZATION	⇒	*Consensus*	Japanese
US, French	*Risk Taking*	⇐	RISK TAKING	⇒	*Risk Averse*	Japanese
US, German	*Direct*	⇐	INFLUENCING	⇒	*Indirect*	Asian, Arabic

Figure 11.4 Negotiation attributes and cultural differences

Source: Adapted from Salacuse (2003) and Brett (2001)

Recommendations in international negotiations

Negotiation styles have different impacts on outcomes, and managers engaged in international negotiations should be aware that a certain number of precautions and recommendations must be made in order to minimize failure owing to cultural hang-ups. The following checklist is a useful list of recommendations.[10]

- Understand your own cultural 'lens', using a list of negotiation parameters as in Figure 11.4 and Table 11.4.
- Understand the other party's cultural 'lens', using a similar checklist. An example of typical attitudes of Chinese negotiators is provided in Table 11.5.
- List negotiation items likely to be affected by cultural differences and anticipate counterparts' responses.
- Assess potential responses and list those that are likely to fit and those that are likely to conflict.
- Try to disentangle 'cultural' divergences from 'business' divergences in order to be ready to adjust behavior and avoid being trapped in 'cultural' clashes.

Table 11.4 Impact of culture on negotiating behavior: a comparison of US and Japanese responses

Negotiation parameters	***Typical American response***	***Typical Japanese response***
Basic approach to business in general	Transactional; profit oriented; detail-conscious; legalistic	Structured; strategic; starting from trust
Central purpose of negotiation	Reaching agreement on a contract	Launching a long-term relationship
Selection criteria for negotiator(s)	Verbally articulate generalists; technical competence; 'rational abilities'	Rank; position; 'social competence'
Appropriate **number of negotiators**	Few	Many: in order to demonstrate seriousness and for functional coverage, including learning
Appropriate **role(s) of lawyers(s)**	Key participant: leader, contract advisor, and/or draftsperson	None: seen as adversarial trouble-makers
Attitude toward **decision-making process**, and appropriate degree of delegation of authority to negotiators	Top-down decision-making; very high degree of delegation of authority	Consensual, middle-up decision-making (*ringi seido*); little or no authority delegated to negotiators
Appropriate **tone** for negotiation and communication	Direct; informal; familiar; egalitarian; candid	Highly indirect; highly formal; hierarchical; reserved
Negotiators' interest in **personal feelings** and values of counterparts	Little or none; irrelevant or improper; logic more important than emotions; issues more important than personalities	Acute; personal rapport essential to establish trust (*ningen kankei*)
Appropriateness of **socializing** with counterparts	Inappropriate; unacceptable; risks conflict of interest and loss of personal control	Highly appropriate; and traditional behavior; also, ritualized gift-giving
Attitude toward **time** during negotiations	Acutely time-conscious; 'time is money'; impatient	Patience is the key
Attitude toward **silence** during negotiations	Strongly averse; uncomfortable; 'fill the void'	Essential: for decorum and for non-verbal communication and empathy (*haragei*)
Reaction to **cross-cultural** signals	Unaware; or consider it unimportant	Aware of indifference
Attitude toward **sequential bargaining** and negotiating progress	Strongly attracted to both	Unimportant
Attitude toward **sharing information**	Open; willing	Collect it avidly, but do not give it out
Attitude toward **closure**	Essential for a successful negotiation; results oriented, not process oriented	Not necessary or even important; take the long view
Form of the contract	Long; detailed; covering all foreseeable contingencies	Prefer very short; and limited to general principles and affirmations
Commitment to the contract	Totally binding	Weak; the relationship is what counts, not the document; and inevitable changing conditions will necessitate later amendments

Source: Sunshine (1990)

Table 11.5 Chinese business negotiating styles

• Large team, vague authority, presence of technical people, often with incompetent interpreter
• Exploit 'agreed principles'
• Play 'home court'
• Buy best technology but show no appreciation for monetary value of knowledge
• Masking interests
• Price-sensitive
• Stalling, delay and indecision
• Hierarchical
• Non-legalistic approach (rely on 'relationships')
• Play competitors off against each other
• 'Sweet and sour' approach
• Attritional negotiation
• 'Shaming' technique (point out mistakes by the other party)
• Exploiting vulnerabilities
• Taking surprise actions
• Showing anger
• 'Friendship means obligation'
• Double standards
• 'The richer partner bears the heavier burden'
• Mixed feelings toward foreigners
• Re-negotiate issue thought concluded

Source: Fang (1997). With the permission of Tony Fang, author of *Chinese Business Negotiating Style* (Thousand Oaks: Sage Publications)

Business practices

Business practices refers to the day-to-day interactions that managers experience in their dealings with customers, suppliers, partners and government officials. Beside the negotiation styles described earlier, three categories of practice are impacted by cultural differences – etiquette, relations and competition:

- *Business etiquette* represents the set of rituals that take place when people communicate in business dealings. It includes the way people address each other, speak, dress, eat, stand, sit, gesticulate, pose and deal with time
- *Relations* involve the way business transactions are established, whether personal relationships or legal/technical matters are the prime ingredient of transactions
- *Competition* indicates how competitive advantages are obtained. In some countries, competition will be perceived and practised as a fair game in which products, services and performances are compared and the winner ultimately decided. In other countries, other criteria such as ethnic belonging, family connections or political considerations can determine the winner.

Table 11.6 shows examples of such practices.

Table 11.6 Business practice differences

Practices		*Examples*
Etiquette		
Addressing	How to name the other person	• In Malaysia, nobility titles are the proper form of address (*Encik*, *Tan*, etc.) • In France, people are addressed by their title (*Monsieur le Directeur*) • In the United States, the first name is normal • In Japan, the exchange of business cards is critical
Gesturing	How to position yourself and how to use body language	• Showing the soles of the feet offends Arabs • Left-hand shaking is not proper in Muslim countries • Finger-pointing is considered as highly threatening and impolite in Asia
Dressing	Dress code	• Malaysian businessmen use jacket and tie while in Singapore a long-sleeved shirt is normal business attire
Eating	Importance of meals in business dealing	• French business transactions usually take place at a lunch or dinner table
	Behavior at the table	• Chinese banquets and sometimes drinking punctuate deals
Timing	How to control time	• Signs of impatience are considered improper in many cultures • Lengthy preliminaries are usual in the Middle East
Talking	Importance of verbal communication	• Silent pauses are the norm in China or Japan
Relations		
Engaging	Importance given to establishing personal relationships in business	• Most Asian countries favor the personalization of contacts before engaging in business transactions
Contracting	Importance given to overall agreements on principles versus details	• Legal contracting is the norm in the United States while broad-brush agreements are considered satisfactory in Japan
Competing		
Advantages	Product technology versus connections as a source of competitive advantage	• In China, connections (*guanxi*) are still a very important factor in competitive advantage
Supplying	Preferences given to friends and families in supply contracts	• In Asia the notion of 'extended families' implies that preferential treatment will be given to families/ friends for supply contracts

MINI-CASE

Working Across Cultures: The Engineering Consultants' Clashes

In mid-2005 Gunawan Wiboto (Gunawan), an ethnic Chinese Indonesian entrepreneur and founder of the Ramayana Group decided to build a steel mill incorporated in a new company: PT HanumanSteel. His team began the search for an experienced consultant to develop the engineering for the project. The company approached several consultancy firms reputed for their engineering services. The difficulty, as they quickly discovered, was finding a consultant who believed they could do it their way and be successful.

The required services fell into four stages: basic design, detailed engineering, procurement and construction. Representatives from four selected reputable international consultants submitted their proposals. On 3 January 2006, the John Smith Engineering Consultant Corp., headquartered in Melbourne, was awarded the contract for the basic design development phase.

John Smith and the basic design development phase

The John Smith team began to work quickly and efficiently. According to Gunawan's Chief Engineer, *'The rapport was excellent. They treated us as personal guests, and we did the same when they came to Surabaya'*.

The first ripples of disturbance appeared when a team of specialists from John Smith travelled to Indonesia for an on-the-spot investigation. As long as matters related to engineering work, the relationship between the two firms remained good. It was the financial side, and specifically the construction budget and the overall cost of the project that caused the first actual rifts to appear. When HanumanSteel looked at Smith's costing, they found they were 'way out – they were engineers, not commercial people'. If the design side went well, the commercial side proved far more contentious; the relationship finally foundered over budget disagreements concerning the three remaining phases. Smith's estimated cost for the procurement and the construction of the mill was US$100 million. HanumanSteel estimated it at US$50 million. Smith's schedule for completion of the project was 36 months; HanumanSteel's was 18 months.

At this stage, Gunawan concluded that his interests were no longer being served, and as the basic design phase of the project was coming to an end he decided that for the next phases, he would opt for a different consultant.

A failed attempt: Lars Corp

Gunawan and his chief engineer visited Stockholm to sound out Lars Corp, a Swedish firm that had already worked for the preliminary blueprint of the project. Lars was selected for the others phases: detailed engineering, procurement and construction. At the end of November 1985, draft contract in hand, HanumanSteel negotiators went to Stockholm to finalize the agreement. Negotiations were difficult since Lars was adopting a very legalistic approach. But finally an agreement was reached and Gunawan flew to Stockholm to celebrate and sign the contract. A celebration dinner was held. The next morning, Gunawan discovered that the Lars president had left for the US. However, before leaving he had drawn

MINI-CASE

up a letter of understanding, signed it and sent it to the hotel. Inserted in this document, Gunawan found a clause concerning performance guarantees that was '*totally against the spirit of everything we had discussed*'. The clause, which had not been previously seen or discussed by the HanumanSteel people, had 'turned a fixed price contract into an open contract'. Other clauses, already agreed, had also been changed. To Gunawan, the message was clear; it indicated a lack of trust in himself and his company. Utterly frustrated by this development, Gunawan refused to sign the document and flew directly to Pittsburgh to meet Tom Brown, a shortlisted US consultant.

Another try: Tom Brown

Shortly after Gunawan's visit to Brown, a meeting was held between staff of the two companies. On the HanumanSteel side, anxiety centered on the juxtaposition of low costs and high quality as well as achieving the right balance. The director of engineering at Brown's was 'a polished, very polite and persuasive gentleman'. He and the HanumanSteel team discussed the project in Pittsburgh for two weeks, aided by visits from Gunawan and the Brown director's boss. Between them, they covered all the ground, deciding who should do what; what should be HanumanSteel's responsibility and what Brown's; what they should do jointly. Shortly after, Brown's president, Tom Brown, accompanied by the man who would be in charge of the project, flew to Surabaya to sign a letter of understanding. In February 1986, a cross-cultural seminar organized by HanumanSteel's two European consultants took place in Pittsburgh, attended by people from HanumanSteel and Brown's. The practical outcome, it was hoped, would be to resolve some of the problems before they arose and forge a team spirit.

Despite these efforts, a feeling of unease began to surface on the HanumanSteel side during the early meetings preparing for the supplier negotiations. HanumanSteel found that Brown was '*building in safety after safety, which gave us serious doubts about the eventual cost of the project*'. The breaking point came over a much more important issue. Brown's had agreed to give HanumanSteel two almost unconditional bank bonds which they could cash if the project failed, but they appeared to have second thoughts about the bank bond, and their failure to issue it turned into a serious problem. HanumanSteel then withdrew their team and sent Brown's a letter noting that '*under the circumstances, we feel we cannot work together. Thank you very much*'.

Gunawan had learnt his most important lesson: '*even when you have everything in a written contract, it doesn't mean you will get it*'. These problems had been exacerbated by the cultural gulf between the two sides. Gunawan's entrepreneurial approach and determination to keep his budget adjusted for local conditions, coupled with the Indonesian preference for keeping their financial plans flexible and in shades of grey, was diametrically opposed to the European and North American desire to play safe and have everything set in concrete down to the finest detail, with every possible guarantee and every contingency allowed for. As HanumanSteel eventually discovered, what they were asking for was outside the experience of the conservative Western consultants. It created a clash of two very different cultures.

MINI-CASE

Questions:

1) How do you assess the situation?
2) Do you think Gunawan is unreasonable?
3) Do you think the Western consultants did not understand the Indonesian context and culture?
4) How much of the clash came from cultural differences as opposed to commercial ones?

Source: Based on author's own work

Summary and key points

1 Cross-cultural management:

- *Potential issues*:
  - Are concepts, behaviors or attitudes interpreted differently by different nationalities?
  - Do policies, memos and rewards convey the same message to employees all over the world?
  - Do worldwide employees share similar assumptions about decision parameters?
  - Do parties involved in the negotiation understand the counter-party's 'silent language'?
- Culture can potentially encompass:
  - *Layers of culture*
    - Assumptions and meaning
    - Values, beliefs and preferences
    - Behavior
  - *Dimensions of culture*
    - Corporate culture – assumptions, values, beliefs and behavioral norms resulting from company history, ownership structure and size
    - Industry culture – rules of trade of a particular industry
    - Professional culture – derived from training and professional norm/constraints of different functions within corporations
    - National/ethnic culture – derived from belonging to certain national, religious or ethnic origins.

2 National culture:

- Research on *national culture differences*:
  - *Ethnological research* ('silent language' differences):
    - Perception of time
    - Perception of space
    - Language of material goods
    - Friendship
    - Agreement
    - Context
  - *Managerial values and assumptions*:

  - Work-related values differences – four main dimensions of difference in national cultures:
    - *Power distance* (acceptance of hierarchical control and respect for authority)
    - *Individualism*
    - *Uncertainty avoidance* (tolerance towards ambiguity)
    - *Masculinity* (value given to assertive and competitive behavior)
  - Value orientation differences – six orientations can differentiate cultures:
    - *Rule-based* versus *relation-based* behavior
    - *Individualism* versus *communitarism*
    - *Objective analytical reasoning* versus *holistic/synthetic reasoning*
    - Status and respect achieved by *doing* versus *being*
    - Knowledge of 'right' or 'wrong' arises from *within* versus from *society*
    - *Sequential* time versus *synchronous* time
  - Management assumptions differences – cultural heritage, i.e. national cultures have basic managerial and organizational assumptions on:
    - Power
    - Structure
    - Clarity of roles
    - Hierarchy
- *Country clusters*
  - National grouping according to cultural traits proximity
  - 'Civilizations'
- *Economic culture*
  - These are six main economic cultures:
    - Anglo/American
    - German/Nordic European
    - French/Latin European
    - Japanese
    - Korean
    - Overseas Chinese
  - Economic cultures vary according to three sets of parameters:
    - Culture – rationality; authority; identity
    - Institutional fabric – financial capital; human capital; social capital
    - Business system – ownership system; networking system; management system.

3 Impact of culture on management:

Multicultural teams:

- Types:
  - Business development
  - Regional headquarters
  - Corporate headquarters
  - Joint ventures and alliances
  - Task forces
- Performance depends on:

    - 'Rich information' resulting from multiplicity of perspectives, experiences and viewpoints
    - Possible loss of cohesion
    - Ability for team leaders to achieve group synergy
  - *Negotiations*:
  - There are commonly six stages:
    - Pre-negotiation
    - Climate-setting
    - Presenting
    - Mid-point bargaining
    - Closure
    - Post-negotiation
  - Impact of culture on negotiations:
    - Basic approach to business
    - Central purpose of negotiation
    - Selection criteria for negotiators
    - Appropriate number of negotiators
    - Appropriate role of lawyers
    - Attitude toward decision-making process
    - Appropriate degree of delegation of authority to negotiators
    - Appropriate tone for negotiation/communication
    - Negotiators' interest in personal feelings and counterparts' values
    - Appropriateness of socializing with counterparts
    - Attitude toward time
    - Reaction to cross-cultural signals
    - Attitude toward sequential bargaining/negotiation process
    - Attitude toward information-sharing
    - Attitude toward closure
    - Form of contract
    - Commitment to contract
  - Checklist for negotiators:
    - Understand the 'cultural' lens of
      - Your own position
      - Counterpart's position
    - List negotiation items which:
      - Risk being affected by cultural differences and anticipate counterparts' responses
      - Are caused by mere 'business divergence' instead of 'cultural divergence'
      - Are potential fits or conflicts with counterpart
- *Business practices*:
  - Negotiation style
  - Business etiquette
  - Relation practices:
    - Engaging (emphasis on relationship establishment)

  - Contracting (emphasis on overall agreement)
- Competition practices:
  - Advantages (product's technology versus connections)
  - Supply (give preference to friends/relatives).

Learning assignments

1. What types of cultural difference can business managers experience? Give examples.
2. What is the 'silent language' of negotiation?
3. A lower-level manager discovers that their boss is making a wrong decision that could affect the company negatively. According to Hofstede's cultural mapping, how would you expect this manager to behave if they were: (a) an Indonesian? (b) an Australian?
4. What consequences can you draw from Laurent's management assumptions differences for the organization of a subsidiary in China?
5. What cultural issues can you anticipate when a partnership is planned between a UK listed e-company and a Korean family conglomerate?
6. How would you recommend an American manager to plan a negotiation with a Japanese counterpart?
7. What 'cultural misbehavior' of misunderstanding have you experienced personally, or have you heard of? How could it have been avoided?

Key words

- Business etiquette
- Corporate culture
- Cultural heritage
- Economic cultures
- Individualism
- Industry culture
- National/ethnic culture
- Power distance
- Professional culture
- 'Silent language'
- Uncertainty avoidance

Web resources

<http://www.mckinseyquarterly.com>
McKinsey Quarterly – Teams.

Visit the companion website at **http://www.palgrave.com/business/lasserre3e** for a multitude of weblinks and resources, self-test questions for revision and a searchable glossary.

Notes

1. Hall (1960), pp. 87–96.
2. Whitley (1992).

3 Berger (1986).
4 Berger and Dore (1996).
5 Adler (1997).
6 Stumpf and Zeutchel (2001), pp. 175–94.
7 Negotiation theorists call this point the BATNA: Best Alternative to a Negotiated Agreement. See Raiffa (1982) as well as Fisher and Ury (1991).
8 Salacuse (2003), pp. 1–6.
9 Brett (2001).
10 This list is taken from Sunshine (1990), pp. 77–81.

References and further reading

Books and articles

Adler, Nancy, *International Dimension of Organizational Behavior*. Cincinnati, OH: South Western College Publishing, 1997.

Albert, Michel, *Capitalisme contre Capitalisme*. Paris: Seuil, 1991.

Berger, Peter, *The Capitalist Revolution*. New York: Basic Books, 1986.

Berger, Suzanne and Ronald Dore (eds), *National Diversity and Global Capitalism*. Ithaca, NY: Cornell University Press, 1996.

Brake, Terence, Danielle Medina and Thomas Walker, *Doing Business Internationally: Guide to Cross-Cultural Success*. New York: McGraw-Hill, 1994.

Brett, Jeanne M, *Negotiating Globally*. San Francisco, CA: Jossey-Bass, 2001.

Chu, Chi-Ning, *The Asian Mind Game: Unlocking the Hidden Agenda of the Asian Business Culture: A Westerner's Survival Manual*. New York, NY: Rawson Associates, 1991.

Fang, Tony, *Chinese Business Negotiation Style: A Socio-Cultural Approach*. Linköping University, 1997, p. 44.

Ferguson, Shelagh, 'A global culture of cool? Generation Y and their perception of coolness', *Young Consumers*, 12(3), 2011, pp. 265–275.

Fisher, Roger and William Ury, *Getting to Yes*. New York, NY: Penguin Books, 1991.

Gahuri, Pervez and Jean Claude Usunier, *International Business Negotiations*. Oxford: Pergamon Press, 1971.

Geertz, Clifford, *The Interpretation of Culture*. New York: Basic Books, 1983.

Hall, Edward, 'The Silent Language in Overseas Business', *Harvard Business Review*, May–June 1960.

Hall, Edward and Mildred Reed Hall, *Understanding Cultural Differences*. Yarmouth, ME: Intercultural Press, 1990.

Hampton-Turner, Charles and Fons Trompenaars, *Building Cross-Cultural Competence*. Chichester: John Wiley, 2000.

Hofstede, Geert, *Culture's Consequences: International Differences in Work-related Values*. Beverley Hills, CA: Sage, 1980.

Huntington, Samuel P., *The Clash of Civilizations and the Remaking of World Order*. London: Simon & Schuster, 1997.

Inglehart, Ronald and Beth Rubin, 'Modernization. Cultural Change and the Persistence of Traditional Values', *American Sociological Review*, 65(1), 2000, pp. 19–51.

Jackson, Terence, *Cross-Cultural Management*. London: Butterworth-Heinemann, 1995.

Kremenyuk, Victor, *International Negotiation Analysis: Approaches*, Issues. San Francisco, CA: Jossey-Bass, 1996.

Laurent, André, 'The Cross-Cultural Puzzle of Global Human Resource Management', *Human Resources Management*, 25(1), 1986, pp. 91–102.

Lawrence, Paul R. and W. Jay Lorsch, *Organization and Environment*. New York: Irwin, 1969.

Levi-Strauss, Claude, *L'Homme Nu*. Paris: Plon, 1971.

Mead, Margaret, *Coming of Age in Samoa*. New York: Modern Library, 1953.

Raiffa, Howard, *The Art and Science of Negotiation*. Cambridge, MA: The Belknap Press of Harvard University Press, 1982.

Redding, Gordon, *The Spirit of Chinese Capitalism*. Berlin: De Gruyter, 1990.

Redding, Gordon, (ed.) *International Cultural Differences*. Brookfield, VT: Dartmouth College, International Library of Management, 1995.

Redding, Gordon, 'Convergence or Divergence at the Millennium', INSEAD Euro Asia Center, Working Paper, 70, 2001.

Ricks, David A., *Blunders in International Business*. Malden, MA: Blackwell Business, 1993.

Riescher, Johann, Mary K. Evans-Kasala, Rose Sherman and Adolfo Gorriaran, *Management Across Time: A Study Of Generational Workforce Groups (Baby Boomer And Generation X) And Leadership*. Minneapolis, MN: Capella University, 2009.

Ronen, S. and O. Shenkar, 'Clustering Countries on Attitudinal Dimensions: A Review and Synthesis', *Academy of Management Review*, 10(3), 1985, pp. 435–54.

Salacuse, Jeswald, *The Global Negotiator: Making, Managing, and Mending Deals around the World in the Twenty-First Century*. Basingstoke: Palgrave Macmillan, 2003.

Schein, Edward, *Organizational Culture and Leadership*. San Francisco, CA: Jossey-Bass, 1985.

Schneider, Susan C. and Jean-Louis Barsoux, *Managing Across Cultures*. London: Prentice-Hall, 1997; numerous references in this chapter are drawn from this book.

Stumpf, Siegfried and Ulrich Zeutchel, 'Synergy Effects in Multinational Work Groups: What We Know and What We Don't Know', in Mark Mendenhall, Torsten Kühlman and Günter Stahl (eds), *Developing Global Business Leaders*. Westport, CT: Quorum Books, 2001, pp. 175–94.

Sunshine, Russel B., *Negotiating for International Development*. International Development Law Institute. Dordrecht: Martinus Nijhoff, 1990.

Trompenaars, Fons, *Riding the Waves of Cultural Differences: Understanding Cultural Differences in Business*. London: Nicholas Brearley, 1993.

Whitley, Richard D., *Business Systems in East Asia: Firms, Markets and Societies*. London: Sage, 1992.

Whitley, Richard D., *Divergent Capitalisms*. Oxford: Oxford University Press, 1999.

Journals

Cross-Cultural Research (Quarterly), United Kingdom, Sage: <http://www.sagepub.co.uk/>

Intercultural Management Quarterly, Washington: <http://www.american.edu/sis/imi/imq.cfm>

International Journal of Cross-Cultural Management, United Kingdom, Sage.

Society for Intercultural Education and Research (Bimonthly), United Kingdom, Elsevier: <http://www.sciencedirect.com/science/journal/01471767>

chapter

12 GLOBAL HUMAN RESOURCE MANAGEMENT

Introduction

The success of global strategies relies on the *quality of the people* who are in charge of its implementation. This chapter addresses four kinds of managerial issues that a global strategy imposes on human resources:

- First, there is a need to adopt a worldwide policy of *international movement of personnel*, differentiating in the pool of managers those who will follow a 'global' career from those who will follow a 'local' career. This is the *assignment* issue.
- Second, there is a need to *manage the career* of the global managers. This is the *expatriates* management issue.
- Third, there is a need to *recruit and motivate local personnel*. This is the *localization* issue.
- Finally, there is the need to develop *skills* fitted to the requirements of global management. This is the *global skill development* issue.

These issues constitute the structure of this chapter (see Figure 12.1).

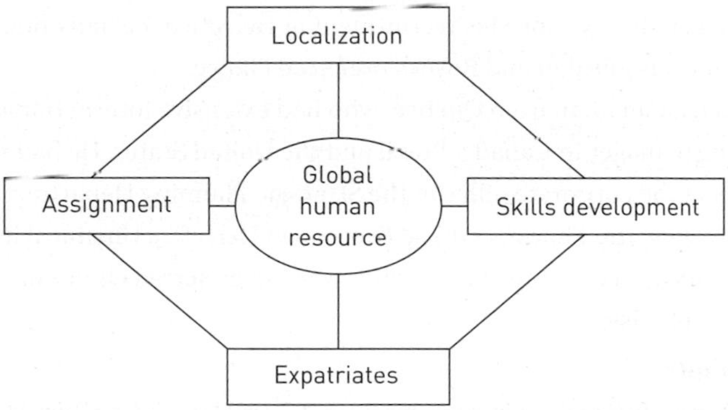

Figure 12.1 Global human resource issues

Learning objectives

At the end of the chapter you will be able to:

- appreciate the trade-offs in establishing a policy of reliance on expatriate global managers versus local ones
- understand the causes of success and failure of an expatriate policy

- contribute to the definition of an expatriate policy
- contribute to plans for developing local management
- participate in the design of global training programmes.

EXAMPLE

Appointing a divisional manager in France[1]

Helvetica Chemical was a Swiss-based multinational company engaged in pharmaceuticals, agrochemicals, dyestuffs and industrial chemicals. It operated in more than 60 countries and was organized as a matrix of product and country divisions. The corporate headquarters in Basel was staffed with global central function services establishing and supervising policies in research, IT, legal, personnel and finance. In each country there was a group company managing director responsible for the total activities of local divisional units, and for the overall financial results of the country. Each divisional general manager had dual reporting: to the group company managing director (country head) and to the global division director in Basel responsible for the worldwide performance of the product line. The case describes how a staffing decision can raise a general global strategic issue.

In France, the group company managing director, Lucien Boyer, was about to retire and the corporate headquarters designated Pierre Jourdan, general manager of the French Pharmaceutical Division, to replace him. Jourdan's promotion opened the position of the Pharmaceutical Division in France, and the issue was to appoint a replacement for him. Two potential candidates had been identified.

- *Philippe Dupont*, a French national, with a doctoral degree in pharmacy from Toulouse University, had been recruited two years previously from a competitor as marketing manager. He had had his entire career in France and had in-depth experience of the French pharmaceutical industry. Since his recruitment at Helvetica, he had obtained excellent results. Dupont was Jourdan and Boyer's preferred choice.
- *Michel Garnier*, a Canadian from Quebec, who had extensive international experience as a marketing manager in Canada, Brazil and the United States. He had spent two years in Basel at the corporate office in the Strategic Planning Department, and was currently managing the Pharmaceutical Division of Helvetica Chemical in Morocco, where he obtained excellent results. Garnier was the preferred choice of the Basel Global Pharmaceutical Division.

Whom to appoint?

Answers to the question provoked very emotional attitudes and heated debates. For some, it was obvious that Dupont was the best choice, given his knowledge of the French market, his experience and the support of the French management structure. For some others, Garnier should be appointed, because he would bring a global perspective that could enrich the French subsidiary and position Helvetica Chemical as a true global player capable of transcending national barriers. After the first instinctive reactions, it became obvious that the appointment decision was more than a pure personnel management issue, it was really a *global strategic issue.* In practice, both choices were valid, but each conveys a fundamentally different message to employees, competitors and customers. If this kind of issue systematically results in the same kind of decision, it will 'drive' the strategy of the company in a particular dimension.

Dupont was the perfect choice for a strategic orientation based on *local responsiveness.* His French education and experience with the market made him a perfect choice for the French subsidiary. No doubt, he would perform well, and Jourdan would be happy to supervise a colleague with whom he could share the same 'culture'.

Garnier brought a 'global' perspective and his appointment would be an opening into the walled city of a national subsidiary. His international experience would give him the capability to transcend national cultures and to enhance a global corporate mindset. From an operational point of view, he would bring different methods and approaches to the French subsidiary.

The final choice depends upon the strategic orientation that Helvetica Chemicals wants to give to its global operation. If, from a competitive viewpoint, there is little advantage to be gained in adopting cross-border integration, and the prime objective is to let local subsidiaries focus on their own market, the choice of Dupont is the most effective. If, on the contrary, it becomes strategically important to adopt a worldwide coordinated strategy, then it is time to implement a global human resource management (HRM) approach that fits with this objective and Garnier would be the recruit of choice.

This example illustrates the four kinds of issue presented in Figure 12.1: assignment of personnel, expatriate management, localization and skills development.

Assignment of personnel: the global human resource wheel

In terms of personnel, a global company can be represented as a wheel, as in Figure 12.2.

At the center is the corporate headquarters, where the Board of Directors and the key executives are located alongside the corporate staff. In many companies, the global business divisions are also located near the corporate headquarters, although this is not always the case.

The main wheel is made up of the countries in which the company operates. Countries are staffed with three categories of personnel:

- **Local managers and staff**, recruited at subsidiary level (the unshaded part of Figure 12.2). Their career is essentially within the local companies.
- **Global managers** (the middle circle in Figure 12.2). Their career is made up of successive appointments in different countries. Managers in this category are considered as 'expatriates', although this terminology is progressively disappearing, to be replaced by the denomination of 'international' or 'global' managers.
- **Temporary assignees** (the arrow in Figure 12.2). These are referred as 'detached' personnel.

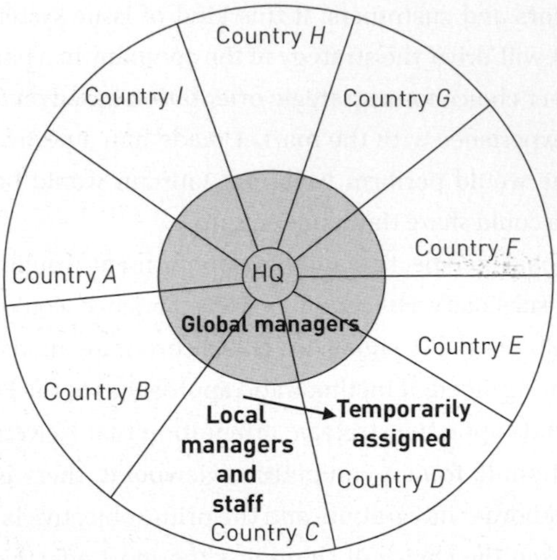

Figure 12.2 The global human resource wheel

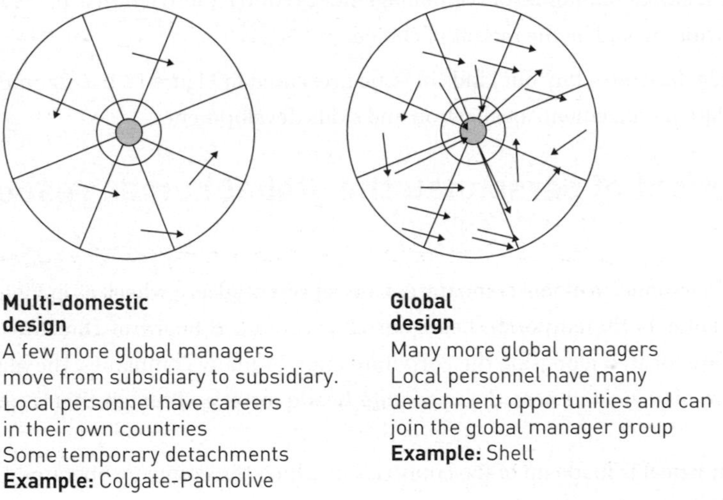

Multi-domestic design
A few more global managers move from subsidiary to subsidiary.
Local personnel have careers in their own countries
Some temporary detachments
Example: Colgate-Palmolive
Global design
Many more global managers
Local personnel have many detachment opportunities and can join the global manager group
Example: Shell

Figure 12.3 Human resource wheels

The profile of the human resource wheel is not the same in a company that has adopted a global strategic position as in a company that operates in a multi-domestic mode. Figure 12.3 shows the difference between the two models. In a multi-domestic organization global managers are relatively few and mostly from a dominant nationality. They move from place to place, generally in a top position. Local personnel progress in their own subsidiary, although they may be seconded occasionally to other subsidiaries for technical support or learning purposes. A global organization will see a larger number of multicultural, global managers moving around. Those global managers will integrate local personnel aspiring to a global career, and temporary assignments of local personnel to other subsidiaries and to headquarters will be more frequent. Cross-cultural teams generate frequent travel. Colgate-Palmolive is an example of the first model. The company in the mid-1990s had 170 managers that were part of the 'expatriate managers' group, 40 per cent of them being Americans out of a total workforce of 35,000 people. By contrast, Shell employed 6000 expatriates from some 70 different nationalities out of a total of 100,000 employees.

Expatriate management

Expatriate personnel ('expatriates' are people living and working in a non-native country) are often grouped into two categories: parent-country nationals (PCN), whose national origin is the same as that of the corporate headquarters and third-country nationals (TCN). An increased number of TCN over PCN indicates that firms are moving from a traditional international management mode toward a global one (Figure 12.4). American and European multinational firms employ a relatively larger number of TCN than Japanese or Korean corporations.

Traditional international staffing The 'expatriate' model	Global staffing The 'global/international personnel' model
• Recruitment essentially from the headquarters home country (PCN) • 'Expatriate' compensation package • Local recruits stay local • Strong 'corporate style' spreads to the subsidiaries • 'Foreign office' type of career: expatriate personnel move from country to country • Performance appraisal based on local performance	• Recruitment from all over the world (TCN+PCN) • More and more local contracts instead of expatriate packages • Possibilities for locals to become global managers • A lot of job rotation • A lot of international management development programs • Performance appraisals include local plus 'global' or 'regional' achievements

Figure 12.4 The changing nature of international staffing

Success and failure of expatriation

Numerous studies have shown that expatriate personnel are confronted with a set of challenges, summarized in Figure 12.5. Rosalie Tung (1987, 1998) found that the main causes of failure among US expatriate managers were:

- Inability of the manager to adapt
- Inability of the manager's partner to adapt
- Family-related problems
- Manager's personality or emotional immaturity
- Manager's inability to cope with responsibility
- Manager's lack of technical competence
- Manager's lack of motivation

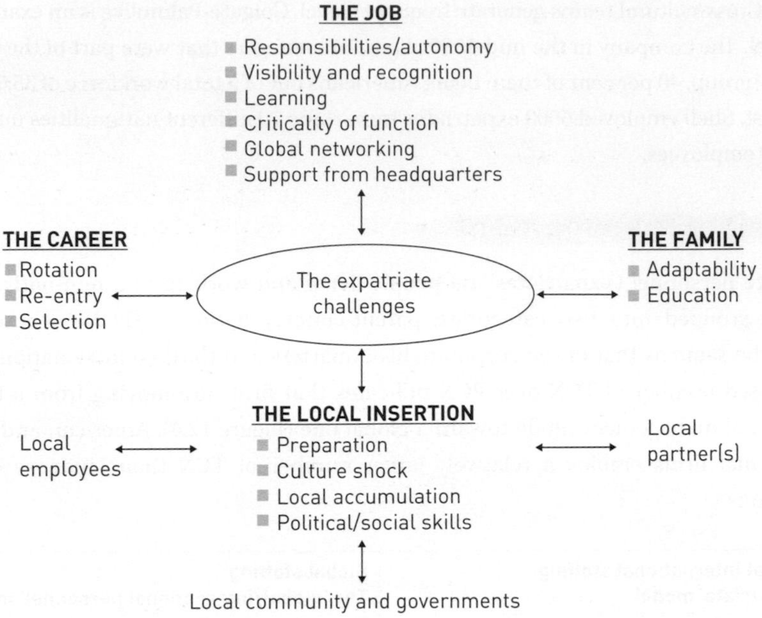

Figure 12.5 The expatriate challenges

Other studies have shown that the recognition of cross-border assignments by colleagues at corporate headquarters and the support and understanding given to expatriate personnel by the corporate center are crucial for the success of expatriation.[2] The research done on the topic all shows that extreme expatriate failure, as measured by the *recall rate* (i.e. the proportion of assigned personnel who fail to complete their predetermined contract) is relatively low (around 5 per cent). However, there are situations in which the assignments are less than satisfactory for both the firm and the individual manager.

Acculturation

Acculturation is the process by which group members from one culture adapt to the culture of a different group.[3] Acculturation can take four different attitudes - the 'four Fs' described in Figure 12.6.

- The **flight** attitude is adopted when a person wants to preserve their own cultural identity and, when confronted with a new environment, prefers to isolate him/herself.
- The **fight** attitude bears some similarity with the previous one except that instead of retreating and isolating him/herself, the person criticizes the host environment, a militant expatriate claiming the superiority of their own culture.

Both the flyers and the fighters avoid socializing with the local community and prefer to live in 'expatriate ghettos'. For the global corporation, these types of personnel lack the flexibility to adapt to local conditions: they may be good at defending the global aspect of business strategies but poor at local responsiveness.

- The **fit** attitude describes people who are capable of immersing themselves in the local culture and, at the same time, preserving their own culture. They look for contacts with locals, get interested in host-country customs, arts and culture. They have a balanced perspective between global and local competitive requirements: they are 'cosmopolitans'.
- The **follow** attitude indicates a willingness to embrace local culture and assimilate yourself to the host environment. The assimilated expatriate progressively loses contact with the global headquarters and has difficulty in balancing global and local requirements.

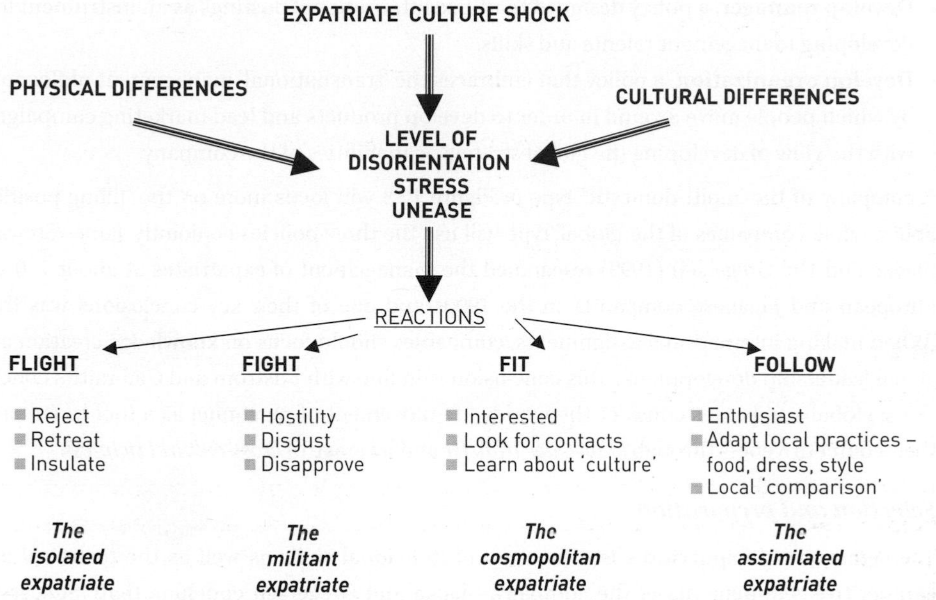

Figure 12.6 Expatriates' acculturation: the 'four Fs'

The expatriate and the company

For the company, the cost of expatriate personnel kicks in at around two to three times the equivalent position in the 'home' country (see the box on p. 345 and Figure 12.7 for cost elements). It is therefore necessary that global firms put in place a coherent set of policies and practices that optimizes the benefits of expatriation for both the company and the individuals. Such a policy has six major components:

- Strategic vision
- Selection and preparation
- Compensation
- Tenure
- Support
- Career follow-up.

Strategic vision

A **strategic vision** places expatriate assignments within the framework of the company's global strategy. Assignment policies vary according to the global positioning and management style of the company. Edstrom and Galbraith (1977) identified three modes of transfer policies:

- **Filling position**, the classic policy of expatriation for key managers and technical support transfer.
- **Develop manager**, a policy designed to utilize international postings as an instrument for developing management talents and skills.
- **Develop organization**, a policy that embraces the 'transnational' management philosophy by which people move around in order to develop products and lead marketing campaigns with the view of developing the global strategic capabilities of the company.

A company of the 'multi-domestic' type in Figure 12.3 will focus more on the 'filling position' policy, while companies of the 'global' type will use the three policies conjointly. James Steward Blacke and Hal Gregersen (1999) researched the management of expatriates at about 750 US, European and Japanese companies in the 1990s and one of their key conclusions was that: 'When making international assignments, companies should focus on knowledge creation and global leadership development'. This conclusion is in line with Edstrom and Galbraith's conclusions: global companies consider the worldwide movement of personnel as a tool to enhance their competitiveness through *knowledge transfer* and leverage of *cross-cultural richness.*

Selection and preparation

The **selection of expatriates** is a function of individual skills as well as the technical and competitive requirements of the company. Blacke and Gregersen conclude that: 'Successful companies assign overseas posts to people whose technical skills are matched or exceeded by their cross-cultural abilities'.[4]

Expatriates' skills are primarily *socio-cultural.* Figure 12.7 shows the ranking of skills that managers in Asia Pacific consider to be conducive to success.

Another study conducted by Günter Stahl with German managers (2001) revealed that seven factors were critical to success in international work assignments:

- **Tolerance of ambiguity:** the ability to function effectively in a foreign environment where expatriates experience ambiguity, complexity and uncertainty
- **Behavioral flexibility:** the capacity to vary your behavior according to the immediate requirements of the situation and the demands of the foreign culture
- **Goal orientation:** the ability and desire to achieve your task goals despite barriers, opposition and discouragement
- **Sociability and interest in other people:** a willingness to establish and maintain meaningful social relationships, combined with a genuine interest in people
- **Empathy:** the capacity to accurately sense other peoples' thoughts, feelings and motives, and to respond to them appropriately

- **Ability to be non-judgemental:** the willingness to critically re-examine your own values and beliefs, and to avoid judging other people by your own norms
- **Meta-communication skills:** the capacity to clarify culturally different perceptions and to 'guide' the intercultural communication process.

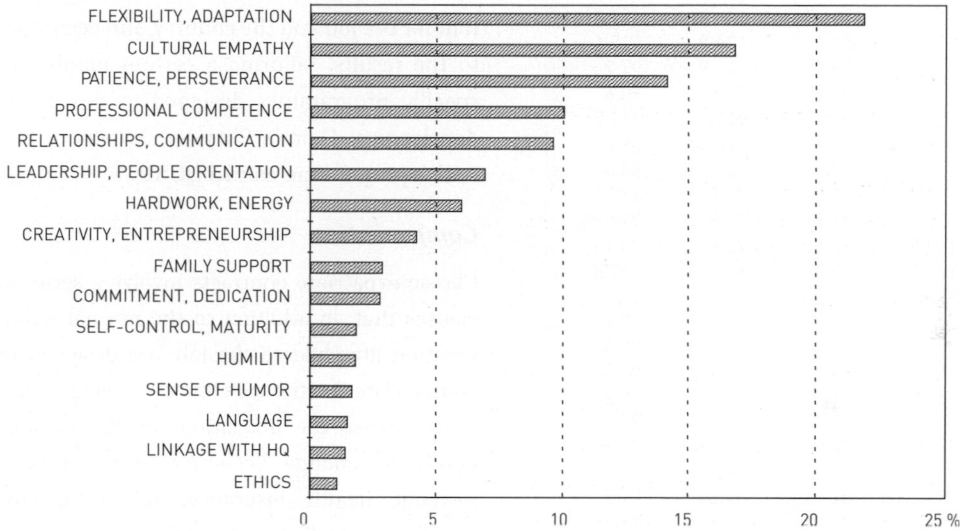

Figure 12.7 The primary ingredients of individual managerial behavior required for success in expatriate assignments in Asia

Note: The percentage indicates a ranking of the frequencies of responses to the question: 'What do you consider to be the three most important factors for success?'

Source: Lasserre *et al.* (1997)

The preparation of assignments involves several steps. First, and most importantly, international assignments must be part of a *career plan,* and the objectives of the assignment have to be clearly defined. If the assignment is only for 'filling a post', it is probably a one-shot event and the expatriate will be much more concerned about her/his future after the expatriation (a classic 're-entry problem') than by the intricacy of the foreign environment. She/he, and the family, needs to be informed about and prepared for the specific differences in living conditions and culture, but the primary concern is the 're-entry'. If the assignment is a step in an 'international' career, the person should have a 'mapping' of their future career development path. Specific learning about the foreign environment is necessary but, over the years and cumulated assignments, this aspect becomes relatively less important since the international manager 'learns to learn'.

The second and obvious step is the *cultural and logistical preparation* for the employee and the family. Numerous organizations provide cultural training,[5] and most companies subscribe to them, and provide a pre-assignment trip for the expatriate and their family in order to obtain first-hand experience of living conditions. Some companies use short-term assignments or 'missions' of several weeks to immerse the future expatriate into the real working conditions.

City	Price levels		Wage level	
	New York = 100		New York = 100	
	Excluding rents	Including rents	Gross	Net
Oslo	139.1	108.9	116.9	104.8
Zurich	135	105.5	144.1	149.1
Geneva	133.1	106.5	138.8	133.8
Copenhagen	118.4	89.4	134.8	100.4
Stockholm	117.5	88.5	101.9	97.2
Tokyo	112.6	94.2	80.8	90.6
Sydney	107.7	89.1	111.3	117.9
Helsinki	103.5	81.5	87.4	89.5
Toronto	102.8	82.1	85.4	88.4
Singapore	102.4	88.3	35.8	41.7
Vienna	102	75.2	77.9	79.9
Paris	100.9	82.8	73.6	75.1
Luxembourg	100.1	77.1	95.5	107.8
London	99.8	82.5	79.6	84.7
Munich	99.7	75	94.5	83.2
Montreal	99.4	77.6	84.2	88.5
Frankfurt	98	76.3	90.6	82.5
Sao Paolo	96.5	74.5	39	45.2
Dublin	95.7	78.8	83	97.3
Brussels	93.3	74.5	90.2	82.1
Rome	92.8	74.4	52.8	49.8
Dubai	89.7	82.7	41.5	57.2
Istanbul	89.5	71	27.9	28.9
Amsterdam	88.2	68.4	82.7	74.2
Madrid	88.1	72.7	58.3	66.6
Tel Aviv	87.6	66.5	46.8	53.6
Seoul	84.5	68.4	42.5	45.2
Hong Kong	82.3	76.5	35.2	44.3
Athens	80.1	60.1	46.9	48
Lisbon	79.9	62.4	47.7	52
Moscow	76.5	69.4	36	42.2
Johannesburg	73.9	69.4	39	40.5
Taipei	73.2	57.3	37.4	44.9
Bangkok	72.4	50.5	13.7	17.9
Warsaw	71.5	54.5	28	27.8
Budapest	70.9	54.5	23.6	20.4
Shanghai	69.6	53.8	17.8	21
Ljubljana	69.3	51.9	45.4	37.5
Jakarta	68.9	53.8	8.7	10.5
Beijing	62.3	46.2	14.7	16.3
Mexico	58.6	44.3	9.8	15
Kuala Lumpur	52.9	36.5	18.1	21
Buenos Aires	52.4	38.5	16.7	19.1
Cairo	50.5	35.6	11.6	12.6
Delhi	49	36	9.5	11.4
Manila	45.3	33.1	7.4	8.7
Mumbai	40.2	32.5	6.9	8.4

Figure 12.8 Indices of cost of living and wage level in the world (base 100 in New York)

Source: Union des Banques Suisses: Prices and Earnings Around the Globe (2011)

Note: The left-hand column under Price levels is the cost of a basket of goods and services and the right-hand column includes the rent of an average three-bedroomed unfurnished apartment.

Assessment centers are the third and probably the least used step in assignment preparation. This consists of measuring the future expatriate's skills alongside certain predetermined dimensions that are considered important for the job and the country, and according to the results, tailoring a certain number of specific programmes designed to repair any deficiencies. DaimlerChrysler Aerospace ran such a programme named QUICK.[6]

Compensation

Classic expatriate contracts involve a series of clauses that, in addition to the normal remuneration attached to the job, are designed to compensate for the difference in living conditions, prices, the obligation for the person/family to change accommodation, pension systems, health insurance, schooling, cost of living as well as any additional economic impacts of the assignment on the family. Generally, a 'hardship' allowance is also granted in the case of countries that have a significant deficit in security, infrastructure or social/political context. The box opposite shows two types of typical expatriate packages. Figure 12.8 compares the cost of living in various cities of the world as well as the wage level. An expatriate in Tokyo whose salary is based on Brussels living standards could expect to have the living-standard component of their salary adjusted by +21 per cent (112.6/93.3) if the rent is paid by the company. In most cases, housing and children's education are paid for by the company.

TYPICAL EXPATRIATE PACKAGES

There are two major types of package:

Home based package: Employees receive a compensation that is equivalent to what they would have received in their home country. In this case the adjustments are mentioned clearly in addition to the base salary. The legal contractual relationship stays in the home country.

Local based package: Employees receive compensation in line with the compensation of equivalent jobs in the host country with some adjustment. In that case the adjustments are incorporated in the base salary (for instance the salary would be increased to take into account the cost of living difference without being mentioned separately). The legal contractual relationship is in the host country; the legal contract with the home organization is suspended during the assignment tenure.

The packages may take into consideration the following adjustments:

Accommodation: Allowance to rent a house or apartment in the host country considering the local real estate market.

Car: In addition to a company car the expatriate family can be bought a car by the company or a fixed allowance can be added to the compensation.

Education: Allowance to cover tuition fees in international schools or local schools accepting foreign students. That also may apply to universities.

Compensation for home residential expenses: Compensation for rental fees in the home country when the expatriate keeps its rental agreement.

Cost of living adjustment: Additional compensation to cover for the differences in cost of goods and services in the host country. Generally applied in one direction: if the cost of living is higher in the host country the allowance is granted but if the cost of living is lower there is no negative allowance. The issue for cost of living allowance is the evaluation of the host country's costs: whether it is considered that the expatriate lives like a local person (buys goods at local markets for instance) or lives as in his/her home country (shops in expensive supermarkets).

Cultural and language training: Payment of tuition fees for language training and cultural training.

Hardship Allowance: Allowance given to compensate for living in countries considered as dangerous or subject to hard living situations such as climatic conditions or remote locations.

Health protection: The company covers for health insurance and repatriation expenses in case of serious health problems, accidents or urgent or sophisticated treatments.

Installation: Payment of costs of moving and installing, decorating the local accommodation.

Local employees: Payment of salary for servants, gardener, driver, nurses.

Pre assignment visit: One or two trips organized and paid by the company for the family to visit the future host country.

Retirement: Pension plans are kept at a similar level to those in the home country. For instance, benefit based retirement plans may be replaced by the equivalent capital based allowance or vice versa.

Spouse assistance: A job may be provided locally to the spouse or the company may help the spouse to find a local job.

Taxes: Several solutions may apply: a) the company pays the local taxes in full; b) the company pays the local taxes but calculates what should be the normal tax rate in the home country and adjusts for the difference either positively or negatively.

Trips for vacation: The company pays for the family trip to the home country for vacations at a pre-determined frequency for a given airline class. In case of harsh environments, vacation trips may be paid to the family at regular intervals.

Sources: *U.S. Expatriate Handbook: Guide to Living & Working Abroad*. West Virginia University (2007), <http://www.globalassignment.com>; *Making Choices: The Expatriate Package*. RH Expat (2010) <http://rhexpat.com/EX01_03_UK.php>; Expatica Communications B.V. (2010), <http://www.expatica.com>; author's own research.

Tenure

The length of expatriate assignments in a given country is a function of four key factors:

- The time needed to learn the *rules of business in the country* and to build the *relationships* with the various parties (customers, employees, government officials, partners, etc.) with whom the person needs to interact
- The importance of personal relationships in the job and the required *continuity* of the task (the task of building a new business requires more time than, for instance, setting up a factory)
- The *contextual hardship* of the country (difficult living conditions)
- The company's policy with regard to *career development*.

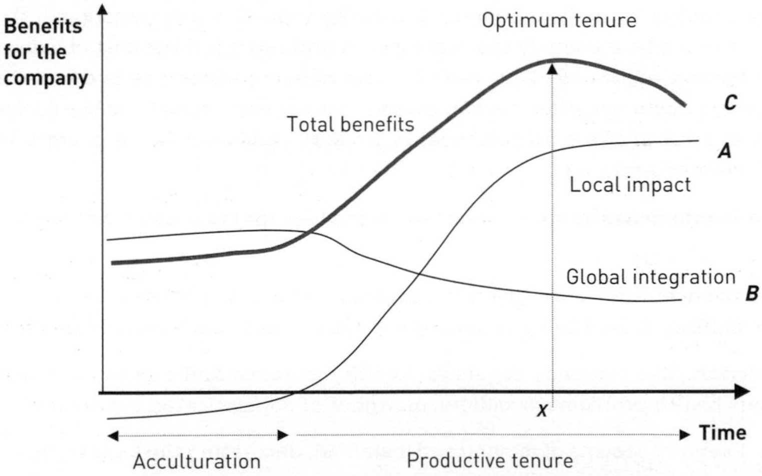

Figure 12.9 Expatriate tenure

Given that in most cases acculturation – that is, the process of getting acquainted with the other culture – takes between three and 12 months, and that a managerial job requires at least two years to show meaningful results, a 'normal' expatriate assignment should last at least three years for non-technical jobs. The classic trade-off for determining an optimal tenure is shown in Figure 12.9. The *local impact* of the expatriate, in terms of business results, is represented by curve *A*: it is a logistic function with a negative contribution during the learning period (acculturation). It progresses rapidly and then peaks when the person is in full control of the job.

Curve *B* in Figure 12.9 represents the *benefits of integration* – i.e. being in tune with the overall culture of the company, its core values and competencies that are shared across the world. Over time, if the expatriate becomes rooted in the local specificities, the risk is high that she/he will lose the *global spirit* and become *localized*. The combination of the *A* and *B* curves is given by curve *C*, showing an optimum benefit for the company at time *X* that would theoretically be when the assignment finishes. As indicated earlier, several factors affect the shape of the curves: if the acculturation is difficult and the relationships with customers are important, curve *A* moves to the right, making the optimum assignment period much longer.

Support

The overwhelming empirical evidence coming from the studies on expatriation shows that success is very closely correlated with the support and understanding coming from the mother company from which the person is detached. Support can take numerous forms, but it is the *psychological contact* – the feeling that you are not 'forgotten' or 'marginalized' – that matters the most. Some companies have put in place a process of **'mentoring'** by which a manager at 'headquarters' is in charge of regular communication with an expatriate about personnel/career issues. Companies' internal newspapers should devote a large part of their editorial content to talking about events in world subsidiaries. Visits of key executives should not only include 'business' meetings but also internal dialogues with the detached personnel. In broad terms, expatriate personnel should have the feeling that their assignment is important for the company. Figure 12.10 shows the various practices that provide support to expatriation.

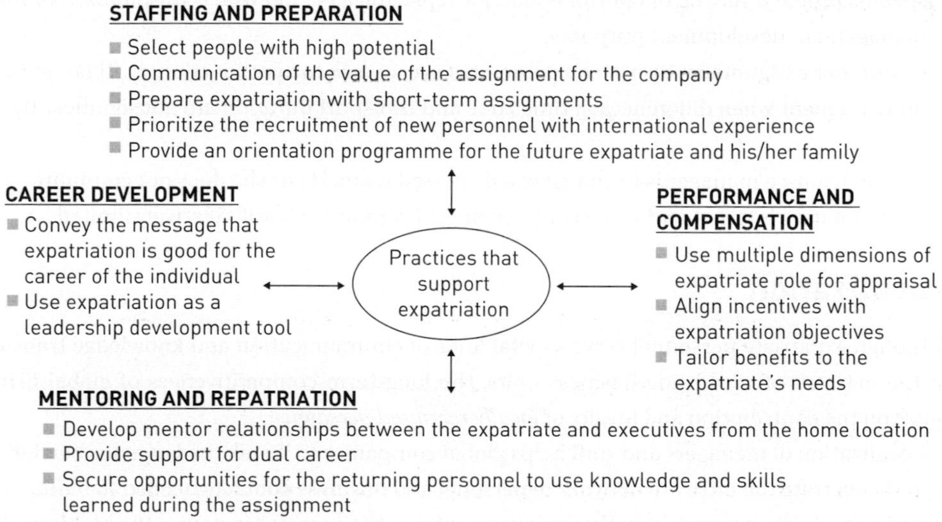
STAFFING AND PREPARATION
Select people with high potential
Communication of the value of the assignment for the company
Prepare expatriation with short-term assignments
Prioritize the recruitment of new personnel with international experience
Provide an orientation programme for the future expatriate and his/her family
CAREER DEVELOPMENT
Convey the message that expatriation is good for the career of the individual
Use expatriation as a leadership development tool
Practices that support expatriation
PERFORMANCE AND COMPENSATION
Use multiple dimensions of expatriate role for appraisal
Align incentives with expatriation objectives
Tailor benefits to the expatriate's needs
MENTORING AND REPATRIATION
Develop mentor relationships between the expatriate and executives from the home location
Provide support for dual career
Secure opportunities for the returning personnel to use knowledge and skills learned during the assignment

Figure 12.10 Human resources practices supporting expatriation

Adapted from Evans, Pucik, Barsoux (2011)

Career follow-up

Traditionally, the career follow-up issue has been known as the *repatriation* problem. At the end of the assignment, the expatriate is concerned about finding a job at the mother company corresponding to his/her skills and performances. The repatriation problem assumes that the person was going to return to the 'home country'. This is the case for temporarily assigned personnel but is less and less true in the global management context described in Figure 12.3 as the 'global design', where international managers move from position to position in the worldwide corporate network. Both 'returning home' or 'going elsewhere', however, require from the company a *proactive international career management process.* In the research conducted by Steward Blacke and Gregersen (1999), it was found that 25 per cent of professionals returning from overseas assignments then left the company because of a lack of job opportunities. The accumulated experience lost by such attrition is considerable. Companies such as Monsanto prepare the return or the next assignment at least six months before the end of the current assignment: it involves the expatriate, the human resources management and the line manager to whom the person reports. The returnee indicates his/her preferences, the line managers and the HR department scan the potential job openings during the coming year as well as the returnee's skills and knowledge. They propose several alternatives, generally including additional training for preparation for the next job.

Alternative forms to expatriation

Despite the fact that long-term assignments are still used extensively by global firms[7]. there is also an increased practice of other forms of international assignments. These are:[8]

- Short-term assignments: more than a business trip and less than a year. This is used for specific problem solving or control issues, for replacing a person who is hospitalized or for management development purposes.
- Commuter assignment: the person commutes every week to another country. This can be quite frequent when differences in time zone and transport duration are not significantly high.
- Virtual teams: a manager is in charge of a dispersed team. He or she does not commute often but uses Internet and video conferencing. This practice is still relatively limited.

Localization

Although expatriate personnel serve as vital links of communication and knowledge transfer in the network of worldwide business units, the long-term competitiveness of global firms relies on the contribution and loyalty of *locally recruited personnel*:

- Localization of managers and staff helps global companies to 'break the language barrier' and penetrate the intricate network of personal and business contacts needed to build and consolidate a presence in the various countries. In China, for instance, the building of relationships (*guanxi*) is still recognized as a major requirement for conducting a business venture.[9] While expatriate managers may be able to build good contacts at senior levels, local managers can gain access to critical relationships, particularly among the medium- and low-level echelons of government and company hierarchies.

- Modern business development also demands a large quantity of talent that the pool of international managers cannot satisfy. A fast-moving consumer goods (FMCG) company found that, in order to maintain leadership in China, it had over a period of five years to recruit 2500 sales people.[10]
- Localization also reduces expatriate costs.
- Localization is part of an overall global HR strategy, the aim of which is to attract talent everywhere in the world where the company operates, making the motto 'think globally, act locally' a reality.
- In some case, localization is perceived by the authorities of emerging nations as a demonstration of the foreign enterprise's commitment to the country. Although in some cases government officials prefer to deal with high-ranking senior expatriates because of their greater decision-making power, they appreciate that below the very top jobs, foreign enterprises will be progressively managed by local nationals. Localization is therefore an important way of developing beneficial goodwill for future expansion.

The main managerial issues in localization are in recruitment, retention and career management and performance evaluation, reward practices and cultural differences.

Recruitment, retention and career management

In some countries, foreign firms are perceived favorably by the job market, but not in some others. Japan and Korea have traditionally been places where graduates from leading universities and institutions have had a marked preference for domestic firms. As a consequence, the market for foreign firms' employees has been narrow and foreign firms have suffered a competitive disadvantage in recruitment. In fast-growing emerging countries like China, the demand for skilled personnel far outpaced the supply, creating an unhealthy bidding process, and a high turnover rate. The global companies' ability to enhance local recruitment depends on three main factors:

- The *image of the company*: firms with well-known branded products are more favorably placed than unknown ones. The latter have to promote themselves by making presentations at universities, giving scholarships, contributing to good causes and engaging in public relations, such as the sponsoring of sporting events or academic contests at schools and universities.
- The *career prospects and the training opportunities*. Firms that have a reputation of procuring good development opportunities will be in a better position to recruit.
- A good understanding of *local qualifications and of the education system*. Not all countries have the same technical and higher-education system. A simplistic projection of the US undergraduate/graduate system may miss opportunities to get the best graduates in Germany, France or Japan. In Germany or Japan, enterprises compensate for the highly

theoretical academic orientation of the school system by organizing some sort of on-the-job training. In France, the best graduate schools are not part of the university system at all.

Financial incentives have to be in line with normal practices – it is illusory to think that over-bidding on salaries will ultimately produce a higher retention rate.

The loyalty of local personnel to a global firm will be based more on career prospects and a subjective assessment of 'fair treatment' than on pure financial compensation. *Fair treatment* is the perception that local employees have an equal treatment with expatriates at a comparable level, and that their career prospects are not limited by a *glass ceiling*. 'Fair treatment' thus implies:

- The ability for local personnel to be able to join the group of 'global managers' if they have the competence and the desire
- Equal opportunities for development (training and career)
- Compensation based on the principle of 'equal job, equal pay' (expatriates' packages on housing/schooling being excluded from the comparison)
- Comparable involvement of local personnel and expatriates in information-sharing, meetings and decision-making sessions. Local personnel should not get the feeling that they are being excluded from important matters.

Performance evaluation, reward practices and cultural differences

The main difficulty in implementing global HRM practices is the need to align performance evaluation and reward processes with cultural differences. A global firm would prefer a standardized approach that fosters the diffusion of a common corporate culture and values as well as facilitating cross-border transfer of personnel. On the other hand, because of cultural differences, standard processes may not have the desired unifying impact and their implementation can be ineffective. In Asia, for instance, the most pronounced cultural divergences are found in four domains:

- *Giving and receiving feedback*. Most Western performance evaluation processes are based on the assumption that objective, open feedback between supervisors and employees is used. Oriental cultures have difficulty in accepting these assumptions. These are 'high context' cultures (Hofstede), meaning that it is difficult to untangle what performance is due to the individual and what is due to the situation. In addition, feedback is considered as unidirectional: employees do not challenge their boss. Therefore, any 'unjust' judgement will be taken but not openly discussed, and may generate covert dissident behavior, although the supervisor may think that the judgement has been 'accepted'.
- *Individual versus group performance*. As mentioned in previous chapters, most non-Western cultures place a higher importance on group belonging and assimilation than on individualism. Too great a focus on individual performance may encourage feelings of unfair favoritism, and ultimately induce group resistance or sabotage of management policies.
- *System-led versus personalized evaluation processes*. In the Asia Pacific region, loyalty is often to a person or a group (clan) rather than to an organization. Neutral, mechanical

systems based on numerical ranking and statistical distribution are not well understood. People prefer to be appreciated/evaluated by their supervisor through a holistic rather than an analytic approach.
- *Social impact of rewards or sanctions (importance of face saving).* Reward and sanction not only affect individuals in their private life but also affect their standing in their community, hence the importance of face saving: ascribing blame in front of colleagues is considered unacceptable.

The dilemma is obvious: how can a company manage globally and still take into account the many cultural specificities of the countries in which it operates? There is no single answer to this, but the example of leading global firms such as Hewlett Packard, IBM, Unilever, ABB or Shell indicates that the progressive reinforcement of a strong corporate culture through education and career management gradually fosters a worldwide acceptance of common practices.

An example of localization within an overall framework is given below, ABB in China.

EXAMPLE

ABB's localization programme in China in the late 1990s

Asea Brown Boveri (ABB) had 15 joint ventures and eight representative offices in China in early 1997, and employed a total of 80 expatriate managers. The company reckoned that by the year 2000 it would have 25 joint ventures, and if nothing changed, its number of expatriate managers would then balloon to 250! If, on average, an expatriate manager cost an additional US$200,000–300,000 per year on top of his normal salary, 250 expatriate managers would increase the compensation bill by more than US$50 million per year.

The company set up a 'localization of management committee' with the intention of locally staffing its middle-management positions within three years and its top management positions within five years. To show the company's commitment to the goal, its vice-president of Human Resources for China sat on the committee as chairman. The committee, among other things, had the key task of identifying high-potential candidates among its China operations, and ensuring that these high-potential candidates possessed the necessary training and good communication with the operating units. More importantly, the company explicitly required its expatriate managers to set targets of localization in their operations. Although ABB understood that expatriate managers were under pressure to meet short-term business goals, top management thought that the development of local managers was a long-term strategic concern and should be given priority. The expatriate managers were thus assessed not just on their business performance, but also on their ability to develop local managers. ABB believed that management must continuously scout for, identify and keep track of internal talent. High potential staff at ABB were identified through a performance appraisal system. Then they were prepared for higher positions or greater responsibility by providing them with the necessary training and promoting them to more challenging positions as early as possible. Upper-level managers were also instructed to support and coach newly promoted managers. The company reported potential local managers to its corporate headquarters in Zurich.

Although most companies embraced the goal of localization of managers and tried to implement it, ABB went one step further by systematically collecting and reporting data to monitor local performance. Its HR department in the Beijing holding company had to provide management with a monthly report which detailed the development of HR in the company, such as the training and promotion of local staff, and also positions available in the company. It also had to complete a monthly international expatriate assignment form, explaining to its regional headquarters why certain positions were filled by expatriates rather than by local Chinese. This reporting system provided feedback on how well the company was implementing its goal, and also served as a reminder of the pace and urgency of the localization programme.

ABB achieved some tangible success with this programme. At its China holding company in early 1997, there were three local Chinese divisional managers (compared with none a year earlier), five local Chinese departmental managers and 20 local Chinese segmental managers. At its joint ventures, the company in 1997 had nearly 100 local Chinese divisional managers, departmental managers and section managers. By the year 2000, it had only 70 expatriate managers instead of the protected 250.

Source: Lasserre and Ching (1997)

Skills development

Global managers' skills are a combination of the *organizational roles* they have to fulfill and some key *individual characteristics.*

Roles

Bartlett and Ghoshal (1992) have identified three main global managers' roles:[11]

- Business managers operate in global business units and 'further global scale efficiency and competitiveness'. Their task 'requires not only the perspectives to recognize opportunities and risks across national and functional boundaries but also the skills to coordinate activities and link capabilities across those barriers'. Their skills are a combination of *strategic thinking, organizational design, resource allocation* and *coordination.*
- Country managers operate in local subsidiaries. Their role is to meet local customer needs, to defend their market position and to satisfy local government requirements. Their skills are a combination of *entrepreneurship, competitive and market intelligence collection* and *local resource acquisition.*
- Functional managers sit at *corporate or regional headquarters.* Their primary role is to be an *organizer* and *coordinate worldwide learning.* They make sure that technologies and best practices are transferred across businesses and countries. 'Using informational networks, they create channels of communicating specialized information and repositories for specialized knowledge.'

During their career, global managers will normally experience all three roles in different locations and businesses. In case of conflict, it helps to create an attitude of mutual understanding and conflict resolution if you know that during your own career path, you are likely to be in the position of the other party at some time.

Individual skills

The set of managers' individual skills most frequently cited in research involves eight facets:[12]

- *Professional*: strong mastery of business knowledge in the relevant field (marketing, technology, finance, operations)
- *Cultural*: ability to respect and deal with cultural difference and avoid stereotyping
- *Negotiating*: ability to balance conflicting objectives with internal and external parties
- *Relational*: ability to relate easily with other people and show empathy
- *Leadership*: ability to set objectives, organize and motivate subordinates
- *Intellectual*: ability to balance global objectives with local realities
- *Courage* and *determination*
- *Flexibility* in moving from one role to another.

The box below shows how Percy Barnevick, the former CEO of ABB, described the characteristics he expected from global managers in his company.

CHARACTERISTICS OF GLOBAL MANAGERS

- Tough-skinned
- Fast on their feet
- Good technical and commercial backgrounds
- Ability to lead
- Open minds: respect for other ways of doing things
- Patience
- Stamina
- Humility
- Respect for other cultures
- Work experience in two or three countries
- Incisive
- Ability to sort out the debris of cultural excuses
- Generous
- People developers

Source: Kets de Vries (1994).

Developing skills through job rotation and training

Global skill development, known also as 'global leaders development', mixes career management with formal training, facilitating skills acquisition as well as coaching in the various global roles that managers are likely to play during their careers. Figure 12.11 shows how a global oil company has orchestrated the development of its international managers.

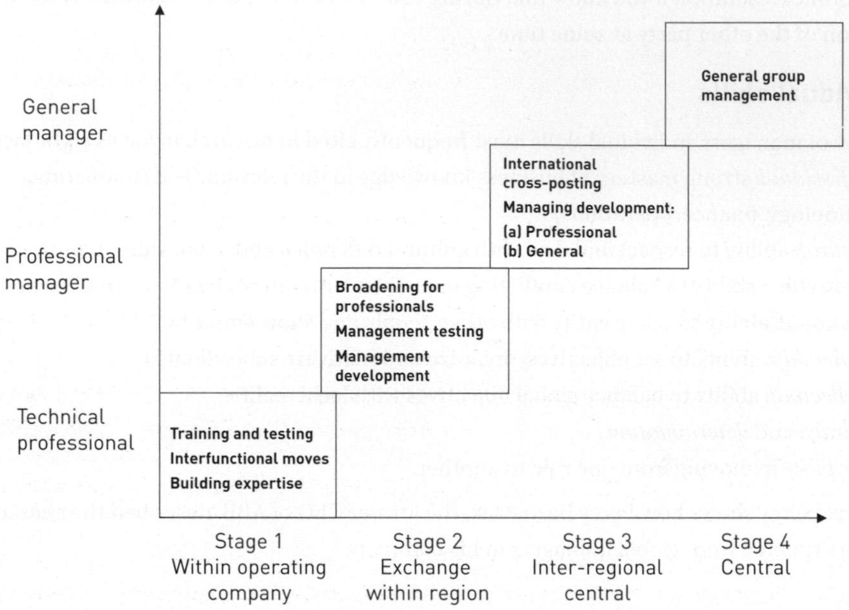

Figure 12.11 Global management development in a global oil company

In management seminars at various levels, global firms make sure that a mix of country managers, global managers and functional managers of various nationalities participate, favoring the expansion of a 'networking culture'.

MINI-CASE

Global Managers

José Azular

José Azular, 35, and Brian Hopper, 34, graduated in 2002 from Caltech (California Institute of Technology) where they obtained a Master of Sciences in Electrical Engineering. José, a native from Argentina, joined Central Electrica SA, the local subsidiary of Centerlec, a Texan based multinational specializing in construction, operation and maintenance of electrical power plants. Since his recruitment José climbed the ladder of management positions and was appointed chief engineer in the Transformer Division in Cordoba in October 2010 with a monthly salary of 12,000 ARS (Argentina Peso; 1 US$ = 4.26 ARS) plus a possible bonus of around 20 per cent at the end of the year. He was very happy with his promotion.

In December 2010 he met Brian at the company's headquarters. Brian told him that he was just appointed chief engineer in Buenos Aires with basically similar responsibilities to his own. They celebrated their encounter in a local pub and during their conversation, José found out that Brian's salary was a tax-free US$90,000 per year plus potential bonus plus a contribution to his accommodation of around 5000 ARS per month.

MINI-CASE

Questions:

1) If you were José, what would you think? What would you do?
2) What are the arguments that José will hear if he complains to the HR director?
3) Can this type of situation be resolved?

Joseph Laval

In May 2011 Joseph Laval became the newly appointed managing director of the French–Thai joint venture company Siammobile. Siammobile was a mobile telephony provider. The personnel in the joint venture were made up of people transferred from the local partner, a traditional telephone firm plus recruits from the local workforce. Joseph reported to the French parent Gallicom regional headquarters in Singapore.

Gallicom implemented a global human resource management system. One part of the system was to evaluate performance of personnel on a 1 to 5 scale (1= Low performer, 5= Outstanding performer). On that basis, bonuses were attributed and for low performers some painful lay-off decisions had to be made. By November 2011 Joseph had to review the performances of the various departments.

One case that came to Joseph's attention was Sarawong, a senior client's relationship manager who was one of the transferred personnel from the local partner to the joint-venture 3 years ago. Sarawong was a very devoted person to the company; his colleagues appreciated him for his kindness. In his early 50s he was a senior person in the company. Over the years he had always had good evaluations from his previous company. In Siammobile his rating was always 4 (High performer). This was satisfactory for him since his character was not to be an aggressive money making manager. In practice his performances were not really so good. Joseph was surprised to see that his predecessor granted a 4 to Sarawong. He decided to give him a 3 (average performer) even if he thought that a 2 would be more appropriate.

Sarawong when he received his evaluation was devastated. How could he keep face in the office with his colleagues? What did he do wrong?

He asked for a meeting with Joseph who rationally explained to him that the results of his departments were not on a par with others and that the company policy was very clear.

Joseph, as a senior person, talked to Michel Journaux, the previous managing director of Siammobile and who was now the head of Gallicom Singapore regional office with which he had good relationships.

Questions:

1) What do you think of the situation?
2) What would you do if you were Journaux?

Adapted with permission from Henri Claude de Bettignies: 'Evaluation', INSEAD Euro Asia Center, Case Study, 1996

Summary and key points

1 There are four main issues in global HRM:

- *Global human resource wheel*: personnel management and proportion of global/ local managers
- *Expatriate management*: career management of global managers
- *Localization*: need to recruit and motivate local personnel
- *Global skill development*: need to develop skills appropriate for global management.

2 There are two types of managers in global firms:

- *Global managers*: career evolves by successive cross-border appointments
- *Local managers*: career evolves within a country subsidiary.

3 Global human resource wheel (see table below).

	Multi-domestic design	*Global design*
Number of global managers	Small	Large
Proportion of local personnel	High	Low
Proportion of temporary detachments	Relatively less	Relatively more
Can local personnel join the global manager group?	No	Yes

4 Expatriate management

- There are two types of *nationals*:
  - Third-country nationals (TCN)
  - Parent-country nationals (PCN)
- Expatriate *challenges* – four main aspects:
  - *Job*
    - Inability of manager to adapt
    - Inability of manager's partner/family to adapt
  - Local integration
    - Preparation
    - Culture shock
    - Political/social skills
    - Local acculturation
  - *Family*
    - Adaptation
    - Education
  - *Career*
    - Selection
    - Rotation
    - Re-entry
- Expatriate *failure*:
  - Measured by *recall rate* (proportion of assigned personnel who fail to complete their predetermined contract)

- Main causes:
  - Inability of manager to adapt
  - Inability of manager's partner/family to adapt
  - Family-related problems
  - Manager's personality or emotional immaturity
  - Manager's inability to cope with responsibility
  - Manager's lack of technical competence
  - Manager's lack of motivation
- Reasons for expatriation *success*:
  - Recognition of cross-border assignments by corporate headquarters
  - Corporate support/understanding given to expatriate personnel
- Four expatriate *attitudes* (four 'Fs'):
  - *Flight*: expatriates preserve own cultural identities, isolate themselves and avoid socializing with local community
  - *Fight*: expatriates criticize host countries, claim superiority of their own cultures and avoid socializing with locals
  - *Follow*: expatriates willing to embrace local culture and assimilate, gradually lose connection with global headquarters
  - *Fit*: cosmopolitans who can immerse themselves into the local culture and simultaneously preserve their own cultures
- Expatriate *policy*:
  - *Strategic – transfer policies* can:
    - Fill position
    - Develop manager
    - Develop organization
  - *Selection and preparation*:
    - *Choice* of expatriates: identifying people with: tolerance for ambiguity; behavioral flexibility; goal orientation; sociability and interest in other people; empathy; ability to be non-judgemental; meta-communication skills
    - *Preparation* of expatriates: clearly communicated career plan to avoid re-entry problems; cultural and logistical preparation for the employee/family (e.g. pre-assignment trips); assessment centers to provide tailored training after comparing current with required skills.
  - *Compensation*: additional compensation for the difference in living conditions, prices and burden on family (e.g. hardship allowance)
  - *Tenure*:
    - *Duration*: company policy or function of time needed to learn business rules and build effective business relationships, depending on 'contextual hardship' of the country
    - Optimal tenure length is determined by the combined effect of the expatriates' local impact on business results (which *increases* over time) and the benefits of global integration (which *decreases* over time)
  - *Support*: mentoring, communication and assurance that the staff are not 'forgotten'
  - *Career follow-up*: proactive international career management process to ensure staff have a desirable job after the overseas posting and to avoid 'repatriation problems'.

5 Localization:

- Importance of localization:
  - Can build/maintain personal and business contacts without the potential problems caused by language barriers
  - Local staff better qualified for business development which requires local sensitivity/knowledge
  - Reduces expensive expatriate costs
  - Allows a company to reap the benefits of implementing a 'think globally, act locally' policy
  - Shows commitment to the country, which can be of concern to local government and/or people
- *Concerns*:
  - *Recruitment*: scarcity of local talent favors local instead of international firms
  - *Retention*: loyalty of local staff may be hard to secure and companies can encourage loyalty through good career prospects and 'fair treatment' instead of financial compensation
  - *Career management*: local staff need career management and equal opportunity to become 'global managers' with an absence of a 'glass ceiling' for local staff
  - *Performance evaluation/cultural difference*: dilemma of implementing a standardized approach while taking cultural differences into account
  - *Reward practices*: awareness of importance of rewards on private lives and social standing.

6 Global skill development:

- Three main roles of global managers:
  - *Business* managers operate in global business units:
    - Possess ability to coordinate activities and link capabilities
    - Role is to increase global-scale efficiency/competitiveness
  - *Country* managers who operate in local subsidiaries:
    - Possess skills of entrepreneurship, capacity to build local resources and collect competitive intelligence
    - Role is to meet local customer needs, defend market position and satisfy local government requirements
  - *Functional* managers who operate at corporate or regional headquarters:
    - Have informational networks
    - Role is to organize/coordinate worldwide learning and transfer technologies and best practices
- Global skills
  - *For individual*:
    - Professional
    - Cultural
    - Negotiating
    - Relational

    - Leadership
    - Intellectual
    - Courage and determination
    - Flexibility
  - *Skill development*:
    - Job rotation
    - Ongoing training.

Learning assignments

1. What are the relative advantages and disadvantages of having a high proportion of global managers to local ones?
2. What are the main difficulties that expatriate managers are confronted with when assigned to an emerging country?
3. What are the main problems of short expatriate assignments?
4. One of the main problems global firms are confronted with in countries such as China is the turnover of local managers. How can this be prevented?
5. What are the benefits of mentoring an expatriate?
6. More and more Western countries' expatriation packages are disappearing and are being replaced by local contracts. Why? What are the advantages and disadvantages?
7. What are the benefits and problems of applying a standardized performance evaluation system across the world?
8. What will be the key content of a management program designed to train managers to become 'country managers'?

Key words

- Acculturation
- Career plan
- Compensation
- Expatriates
- Global leaders development
- Global managers
- Local managers
- Mentoring
- Missions
- Retention
- Roles
- Skills
- Tenure

Web resources

<http://www.ipma-hr.org/>
A link to the International Personnel Management Association.

<http://www.expatriates.com/>
Community website created for and by expatriates.

<http://www.internations.org/>
International online network for people who live and work abroad.

Visit the companion website at **http://www.palgrave.com/business/lasserre3e** for a multitude of weblinks and resources, self-test questions for revision and a searchable glossary.

Notes

1 This case study is adapted from Doz (1999); the names of the company and of participants have been changed as the adaptation here is not a precise replication of the original case.
2 Lasserre *et al.* (1997).
3 This definition is from F. Rieger and D. Wong-Rieger, 'The Application of Acculturation Theory to Structuring and Strategy Formulation in International Firms', a research paper quoted in Tung (1998, pp. 125–44).
4 Blacke and Gregersen (1999), p. 4.
5 Rottenberg (1999).
6 Stahl (2001), pp. 206–7.
7 Brookfield Global Relocation Services (2011).
8 Collins, Scullion and Morley (2011), pp. 221–5.
9 Davies *et al.* (1995), pp.207–14.
10 Hsieh, Lavoie and Samek (1999a), pp. 93-101).
11 Bartlett and Ghoshal (1992), pp. 124–32; the skills quoted are from this article.
12 Adler and Bartholomew (1992), pp. 52–65; Mendenhall (2001), pp. 1–17.

References and further reading

Books and articles

Adler, Nancy and Susan Bartholomew, 'Managing Globally Competent People', *The Academy of Management Executive*, 6, 1992.

Bartlett, Christopher and Sumantra Ghoshal, 'What is a Global Manager?', *Harvard Business Review*, September–October 1992.

Blacke, J. Steward and Hal Gregersen, 'The Right Way to Manage Expatriates', *Harvard Business Review*, March–April 1999.

Budhwar, Pawan, Randall Schuler and Paul Sparrow, *International Human Resource Management*. London, UK: Sage, 2009.

Brookfield Global Relocation Services, 'Global Relocation Trends', 2011 Report.

Chalkiti, Kalotina and Marianna Sigala, 'Staff turnover in the Greek tourism industry: A comparison between insular and peninsular regions', *International Journal of Contemporary Hospitality Management*, 22(3), 2010, pp. 335–359.

Collins, David G., Hugh Scullion and Michael Morley, 'Changing Pattern of Global Staffing: Challenges to the Conventional Expatriate Assignment and Emerging Alternatives', in Günter K. Stahl, Mark E. Mendenhall and Gary R. Oddou (eds.), *Reading and Cases in International Human Resource Management and Organizational Behavior*. Abingdon, UK: Routledge, 2011.

Davies, H., T.K.P Leung, S.T.K. Luk, and Y.H. Wong, 'The Benefit of Guanxi: The Value of Relationships in Developing the Chinese Market', *Industrial Marketing Management*, 24, 1995.

Dowling, Peter J. Marion Festing, Allen D. Engle and Stefan Gröschl, *International Human Resource Management: a Canadian perspective*. Scarborough, ON: Nelson Books, 2009.

Doz, Yves L., 'Ciba-Geigy Management Development', INSEAD Case Study, no. 11/1999-1153, 1999.

Edstrom, A. and J. Galbraith, 'Transfer of Managers as a Coordination and Control Strategy in Multinational Organizations', *Administrative Science Quarterly*, June 1977.

Evans, Paul, Vladimir Pucik and Jean-Louis Barsoux, *The Global Challenge: Frameworks for International Human Resources Management*. New York: McGraw-Hill, 2011.

Harzing, Anne-Wil and Joris Van Ruysseveldt, *International Human Resource Management*. Sage, 2004.

Hofstede, Geert, Culture's Consequences: *International Differences in Work-Related Values*. Beverly Hills, CA: Sage, 1980.

Hsieh, Tsun-yan, Johanne Lavoie and Robert A.P. Samek, 'Think Global, Hire Local', *McKinsey Quarterly*, 4, 1999a.

Hsieh, Tsun-yan, Johanne Lavoie and Robert A.P. Samek, 'Are You Taking Your Expatriate Talent Seriously?', *McKinsey Quarterly*, 3, 1999b, pp. 71-83.

Kets de Vries, Manfred, 'Percy Barnevick and ABB', INSEAD Case Study 05/94-4308, 1994.

Lasserre, Philippe and Poy-Seng Ching, 'Human Resource Management in China and the Localization Challenge', *Journal of Asian Business*, 13(4), 1997, pp. 85–99.

Lasserre, Philippe, Lyman Porter, Gordon Redding and Pamela Steward, *Managing International Assignments in Asia: Individual and Organizational Challenge*. Boston, MA: The International Consortium for Executive Education, 1997.

Mendenhall, Mark E., 'New Perspectives on Expatriate Adjustment and Its Relationship to Global Leadership Development', in M. Mendenhall, T. Mailman and Günter Stahl, (eds), *Developing Global Leaders*. Westport, CT: Quorum Books, 2001.

Parsons, Andrew J., 'Nestlé: The Visions of Local Managers', *McKinsey Quarterly*, 2, 1996, pp. 5–29.

Quelch, John A. and Helen Bloom, 'The Return of the Country Manager', *McKinsey Quarterly*, 2, 1996, pp. 31–43.

Rieger, F. and D. Wong-Rieger, 'The Application of Acculturation Theory to Structuring and Strategy Formulation in International Firms', quoted in Rosalie Tung, 'American Expatriates: From Neophytes to Cosmopolitans', *Journal of World Business*, 33(2), 1998, pp. 125–44.

Rosenweig, Philip M., 'Colgate-Palmolive: Managing International Careers', Harvard Business School Case Study 9-394-184, 1994.

Rottenberg, Stephanie, 'Prepare for the Overseas Trip', *Harvard Management Update*. Boston, MA: Harvard Business School Publishing, U9904C, 1999.

Stahl, Günter, 'Using Assessment Centers as Tools for Global Leadership Development: An Exploratory Study', in M. Mendenhall, T. Kuhlman and Günter Stahl (eds), *Developing Global Leaders*. Westport, CT: Quorum Books, 2001, pp. 198–201.

Stahl Günter K., Mark E. Mendenhall and Gary R. Oddou, R. *Readings and Cases in International Human Resource Management and Organizational Behavior*. Abingdon, UK: Routledge, 2011.

Sutari, Vesa and Christelle Tornikoski, 'The Challenge of Expatriate Compensation: The Sources of Satisfaction and Dissatisfaction Among Expatriates', *International Journal of Human Resource Management*, 12, 2001, pp. 389–94.

Tung, Rosalie, 'Expatriate Assignments: Enhancing Success and Minimizing Failure', *The Academy of Management Executive*, 1, 1987, pp. 117–25.

Tung, Rosalie, 'American Expatriates: From Neophytes to Cosmopolitans', *Journal of World Business*, 33(2), 1998a.

Tung, Rosalie, *The New Expatriates: Managing Human Resources Abroad*. Cambridge, MA: Ballinger, 1988.

Wagner, Gabriele and Uwe Vormbusch, 'Informal networks as "global microstructures": the case of German expatriates in Russia', *Critical Perspectives on International Business*, 6(4), (2010), pp. 216–236.

Journal

International Journal of Human Resource Management, Routledge, United Kingdom: <http://www.tandf.co.uk/journals/titles/09585192.asp/>

chapter

13 GLOBAL FINANCIAL MANAGEMENT

Introduction

The world of global finance has been evolving quite dramatically since 1980. Alongside traditional financing instruments like international promissory notes that existed in the Middle Ages, a vast array of facilities has been opened to firms operating across borders, ranging from hedging techniques to cross-border listing and swaps. Firms operating globally face several challenges related to the management of their cash flows, the cost of their capital and their exposure to risks. The domain of international finance is vast, and cannot be fully analyzed within this chapter; a list of specialized references is given on p. 398. We shall address some key issues in global financial management, but the discussion will be limited to managerial issues and will avoid the technical examples that more specialized books often provide.[1]

Four central global financial management issues are discussed in this chapter (and see Figure 13.1):

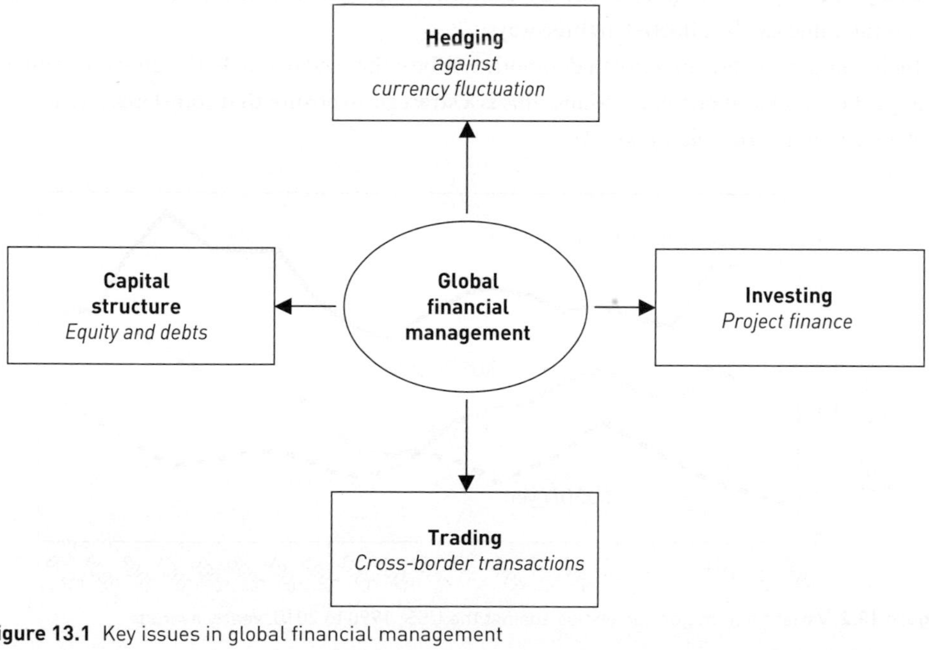

Figure 13.1 Key issues in global financial management

- **Currency risk:** exposure and hedging: how to protect against currency fluctuation
- **Project finance:** how to evaluate international investments, and how to finance them
- **Capital structure:** how to take advantage of global financial market to raise equity and deal with debt
- **Trade finance:** the traditional instruments of financing exports/imports of goods.

Learning objectives

At the end of the chapter you will be able to:

- understand the nature of the risks generated by currency fluctuations
- explain the hedging techniques available to manage currency fluctuations
- compute the cash flow of an international project and assess its economic return using either the Adjusted Present Value (APV) method or the Cost of Capital Adjustment (CCA) method
- recognize the benefits of cross-listing
- appreciate the benefits and pitfalls of raising debt internationally
- describe the mechanics and know-how of the various instruments of trade finance for global companies.

Hedging against currency fluctuations

The most prevalent feature of international finance is that *currencies fluctuate in value against each other.* Figure 13.2 shows the fluctuation of four major global currencies: the US dollar, the euro, the yen and the pound sterling.

Companies operating globally are by definition exposed to currency fluctuations. Their economic value can be affected in three ways:

- Their competitive advantage can deteriorate or be enhanced owing to the direct or indirect impact of change in currency values. This is a strategic exposure that translates into a change in *future cash flow potential.*

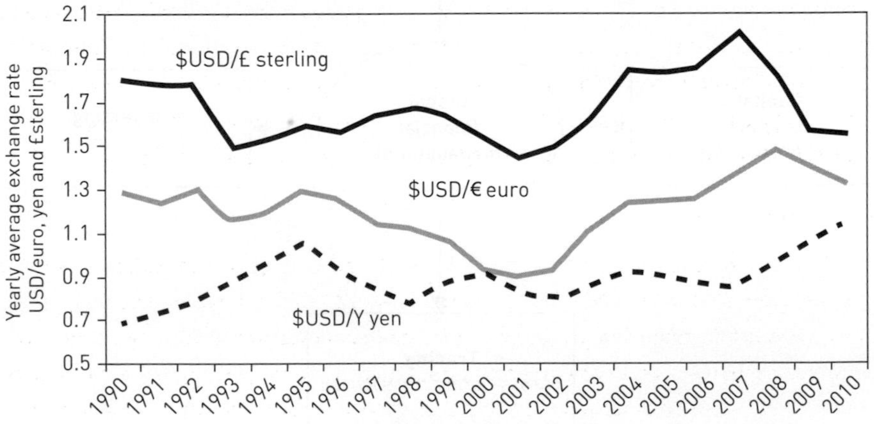

Figure 13.2 Variation of major currencies against the US$, 1990 to 2010, yearly average

Source: www.oanda.com

- The short-term cash flow resulting from existing financial or commercial commitments can be affected positively or negatively. This is a **transaction exposure**.
- The reported valuation of assets and liabilities of global firms is also affected by currency variations that in turn may affect the market perception and ultimately the market value of firms. This is the **translation exposure**.

Strategic exposure

Currency fluctuations may have a direct and indirect effect on companies' competitive advantages by increasing their costs to an uncompetitive level or by giving competitors with weakened currencies a sudden competitive edge. This type of exposure is most significant in products or services that serve price-sensitive customers, which is the case for most commodities. But even in differentiated products or services, like aero-engines or cars, a sharp increase in a country's currency value may lead to strategic disadvantage. In early 2001, Nissan was considering exiting from manufacturing its new small car in England because of the high value of the pound sterling. The group felt at a strategic disadvantage in maintaining manufacturing facilities in the country. Global firms are better positioned than domestic players to deal with strategic exposure because of their diversified market portfolio. They can also relocate production facilities, although it implies a lot of flexibility in resources transfer for effective implementation, and this may affect their reputation as responsible citizens in the countries from which they exit. In practice, it is difficult to take drastic action of this type without being certain of the *structural weakness* of a currency, which can be difficult to predict, as Figure 13.2 shows.

Hedging against this type of exposure is a matter of strategic product and geographic *positioning* and *global deployment of productive assets*:

- Hedging with strategic product positioning consists of developing products (or services) for price-insensitive market segments though *differentiation*
- Hedging with geographical positioning consists of *balancing sales and production* within exchange zones; a pure global company whose revenues and productive assets were evenly distributed across the dollar zone, the euro zone and the yen zone would be sheltered, to a large degree, against the damaging competitive consequences of currency variations
- Global deployment of productive assets would consist of *sourcing* either in-house or from external suppliers in low-cost countries like China that, despite its strong currency position, is still a low-cost manufacturing base for a large number of products.

Transaction exposure

Transaction exposure is the risk that currency fluctuations imposes on existing contractual engagements and that may result in unexpected losses. This occurs when a company borrows in a given currency to finance a productive asset that generates revenues in another currency. This also occurs when a company operating in a given country has signed a sales or supply contract that will be billed and paid in the future in a different currency. The positive or negative variation of the exchange rate will induce transaction gains or transaction losses. Obviously, transaction losses can damage company wealth while transaction gains give a speculative profit. Confronted with the probability of such gains or losses, the company can take two positions – a *speculative* attitude, betting on the probability that there will be a transaction gain, or a *hedging* perspective, making sure as soon as the contract is signed that the company will receive/pay a certain amount in its own currency whatever the exchange rate variation. There are several *hedging techniques* that can be used to guard against currency variation. The most frequent ones are: forward contracts, future contracts, swap contracts and options. Other techniques such as *leading and lagging* or *netting* can also be used but they are not considered as 'hedging' in the sense that there is still a certain degree of uncertainty. Appendix 13.1 (p. 379) gives a full numerical example of the main hedging techniques with a practical example of a US champagne importer.

Hedging techniques

- **Forward contracts** consist of buying at a fixed future date a fixed quantity of a given currency at a fixed exchange rate (the *forward rate*). A European importer of Japanese goods will buy forward yen in order to be certain of paying his Japanese supplier at a known exchange rate. The same European who exports to the United States will sell the US dollars he will receive as payment at a fixed exchange rate. An alternative method that produces exactly the same results is for the exporter to borrow euros, transform them into yen for the amount needed at the prevailing known rate of exchange on the day of the order. The yen are placed in a yen money market account and, at the date of the settlement, are used to pay the Japanese supplier; the interest gained is used to pay the interest due on the euro borrowing. The company will have to bear only the interest differential between the yen and the euros, which is exactly how the forward rate is calculated. In the case of the exporter to the United States, the company will borrow dollars and transform them into euros, put the euros in a money market account and, when it receives the money from the customer, use the dollars to pay back the loan; the interest gained on the euros pays the interest on the dollar loan. Forward contracts are the most common hedging techniques used by corporations.
- **Future contracts** are similar to forward contracts but they are standard financial instruments traded in *futures markets* such as London, Chicago or Singapore. They have a given size and a given expiry date.
- **Options** are contracts in which you buy the right to sell *(put option)* or buy (*call option*) a currency at a given exchange rate *(the strike price)* at the end of a maturity period. If at the end of the period the spot rate of the currency varies unfavorably, you will not exercise your right. This option has a price (the *option premium*):
- **Currency swaps** contracts are contracts intermediated by a swap bank that matches long-terms loans issued by two companies in their respective currency zones for use in the other company currency zone. Company *X* borrows in currency *A* to be used in country *B* with loan repayment generated in currency *B,* while company *Y* borrows in currency *B* to be used in country *A* with loan repayment generated in currency *A*. The two companies can swap their loan. Assuming a perfect symmetry of the two loans, which the swap bank

can arrange, there is a perfect hedging for companies *X* and *Y*. The swap contracts are good hedging techniques for long -term currency exposures.

Non-hedging techniques

Two other common forms of reducing transaction exposures are *leading and lagging* or *netting*:

- **Leading and lagging** is a technique by which you can collect receivables early (leading) if they are nominated in 'soft' currencies and delay collection *(lagging)* of receivables nominated in 'hard' currencies. Similarly, you would try to delay (lagging) payment of payables nominated in 'soft' currencies and accelerate payment of payables nominated in 'hard' currencies.
- **Netting** is a technique used by treasurers of global firms that have centralized cash management for subsidiaries that trade with each other. Only the *net cash balance* resulting from the forecast inter-trade movement in their respective currencies is actually transformed and hedged into the currency that has a creditor position. If a German factory is planning to sell 1 million euros of components to a Singaporean company and the Singaporean factory is expected to sell 3 million Singapore dollars of finished products, the German factory will actually hedge Singapore $650,000, which represents the net position at the rate of S$1.54 per euro at the time of the plan. This reduces the amount of currency exposed and the hedging costs. There are actually two different netting systems: *bilateral* netting (netting between pairs of subsidiaries) and *multilateral* netting (netting of all transactions and transfer of the net to a central centre).

Translation exposure

This type of exposure reflects the effects that change in currency values have on the financial statements of global firms, and therefore on their *profits* and *book valuation.* There are several techniques used to adjust income statements and balance sheets for currency fluctuations. The two main methods are the *monetary/non-monetary* method and the *current* method. An example of these methods is presented in Appendix 13.2 (p. 386). In practice, this type of exposure has relevance only to the extent that the economic source of value creation and valuation, the *cash flow,* is affected by the difference in reported translations. This may be the case concerning the tax consequences of currency fluctuation. Accounting standards require that translation exposure be reported, but market valuation is affected only to the extent to which reporting translation exposure reveals the strategic and transaction risks to which the firm is exposed.

Project finance

International project finance deals with the *valuation* and the *financing* of productive investments (different from financial portfolio investments) in different countries from that of the investor. In a global firm, there can be a multitude of configurations of international investments. A Swiss-based pharmaceutical firm may use a French subsidiary to implement a project in China jointly with a German subsidiary because it may relate to a product in which the French subsidiary has global responsibilities and for which the German engineering subsidiary has competences in building plants. Project finance may concern greenfield wholly owned investments, acquisitions or joint ventures. The two key issues in project finance are: How to value them? How to finance them?

Project valuation

As in any economic valuation, the value of an investment for an investor is equal to the value of *future cash flows discounted with the weighted average cost of capital minus the discounted value of debts.* The only complexities that an international investment generates are the strategic and transaction currency exposures and the country risks. As far as currency fluctuations are concerned, hedging techniques can possibly transform uncertainties into certainty in cash flow valuation, but what about country risks and currency risks when hedging is not available? There are two fundamental approaches for taking this type of risk into consideration: adjusting the cash flows or adjusting the cost of capital:

- *Cash flow adjustment*, also known as **adjusted present value (APV)**, is a technique in which
  - specific downside adverse risks are identified
  - their impact on the cash flow is calculated
  - probability of their occurrence is determined
  - cash flows are adjusted using the probabilistic distribution
  - cash flows are translated into the investor's currency using Purchasing Power Parity (PPP) differences as a proxy for currency fluctuations
  - cash flows are discounted using the investor's cost of capital.

Appendix 13.2 (p. 386) gives a simplified example of this method, considered the most appropriate by financial theorists.

- *Cost of capital adjustments* is applied to the cost of capital by introducing a premium risk to the cost of equity. Professor Donald Lessard from MIT (1996) argues that adjusting the risk premium by introducing a 'country beta' to the cost of capital is more appropriate in the case of investments in emerging countries when risks are not diversifiable.

Project financing

There are two sources of project financing:

- *Generic financing* provided by the corporation that uses its global equity and debt financing capabilities
- *Specific equity or debt financing* provided by various financial institutions.

Specific **equity project financing** is usually provided for projects in emerging countries by development banks. Equity for projects in industrialized market economies is financed through normal market mechanisms; either public (stock exchange), private (venture capital) or directly by the corporation using its global financing capabilities. The major development banks that provide equity financing are listed in Appendix 13.3 (p. 390).

Debt project financing is provided by banking institutions, development banks, government aid, or suppliers' credits. When provided by banks or suppliers' credits, debt financing is backed by *credit risk insurance.* When projects are structured as joint ventures, financing can also come from local institutions and governments.

Global capital structure

The major financing issue for a global company is to decide where to generate equity and debt financing, and in what proportion. The overall objective is to minimize the cost of capital in order to enhance the *value-creation capabilities* of the company. When the cost of capital of a company decreases, the value of the company increases. Finance theory tells us that the cost of capital, both equity and debt, is a function of macroeconomic factors as well as the systematic risk (non-diversifiable) incurred by the company. Finance theory makes a distinction between *unsystematic* risks (that can be diversified) and *systematic* risks (that cannot be diversified). Unsystematic risks can be reduced by diversification; a global firm reduces its unsystematic risks by having a portfolio of investments across countries, but cannot avoid the inherent risks of investing in a particular country owing to the political and economic situation of that country (systematic risks). Since in a global economy different countries have different macroeconomic outlooks and different risk profiles, and different institutions to manage them, you can expect the cost of capital to be different from country to country, giving an opportunity to optimize your portfolio of financial sources in order to minimize cost. This creates the possibility of **cross-listing** and international bond issues.

Table 13.1 Summary statistics of monthly returns for some stock markets, 1999–2010, correlation coefficients

	USA Dow Jones	*Australia AORD*	*Japan Nikkei*	*France CAC 40*	*Germany DAX*	*UK FTSE*	*Brazil BVSP*	*Mexico IPC*	*Hong Kong Hang Seng*	*Singapore STI*	*China SSEC*	*Korea KOSPI*
Dow Jones	1											
AORD	**0.800**											
Nikkei	0.274	0.087										
CAC40	0.676	0.384	0.627									
DAX	**0.782**	0.628	0.446	**0.789**								
FTSE	0.658	0.388	**0.719**	**0.818**	**0.861**							
BVSP	0.585	**0.829**	-0.213	0.061	0.562	0.207						
IPC	0.611	**0.845**	-0.211	0.057	0.561	0.215	**0.984**					
Hang Seng	**0.749**	**0.852**	0.103	0.355	**0.758**	0.478	0.900	**0.882**				
STI	**0.818**	**0.906**	0.156	0.388	**0.737**	0.504	**0.872**	**0.882**	**0.958**			
SSEC	0.611	**0.706**	0.212	0.268	0.656	0.480	**0.720**	0.696	**0.827**	**0.759**		
KOSPI	0.677	**0.859**	-0.128	0.124	0.586	0.280	**0.950**	**0.964**	**0.904**	**0.918**	0.690	1

Source: Yahoo Finances. Based on Market Indices – http://www.Finance.Yahoo.com/ Market Statistics.
Correlation coefficients in bold are the ones above 0.70 showing a rather strong co-variance above 50%.

In a pure global world in which free trade and free movement of capital, persons and goods as well as market-based institutions prevailed, such international portfolio optimization would not exist: there would be one single capital market. The capital markets would be *integrated* and raising money in the United States, in Europe or Japan would cost the same. But since the world is not fully global, at least in the early twenty-first century, capital markets are still different in their structure, costs and risks, and are *fragmented.* Fragmentation can be observed in two ways. First, you can compare the cost of capital between countries. Academic researchers have found that the cost of capital has historically differed but has tended to converge, at least in the industrialized world (see below). Correlations between returns on various stock markets show some high positive correlations among industrialized markets (see Table 13.1), except in Japan which shows nearly zero correlation with the rest of the world. Emerging markets tend to correlate among themselves.

ACADEMIC RESEARCH ON INTERNATIONAL DIFFERENCES IN THE COST OF CAPITAL

- McCauley and Zimmer found that there were different costs of capital between Japan, Germany, the United States and the United Kingdom for the period between 1978 and 1992.
- A study by René Stulz found that the effect of globalization on the decrease in cost of capital is significant but small. For globalization to reduce the cost of capital, the shareholder base has to become truly global.

Source: McCauley and Zimmer (1994); Stulz (1999).

Cross-listing

Cross-listing occurs when a firm lists its equity shares on one or more foreign stock exchanges besides its home-country exchange. There are many reasons for a company to cross-list. Four proposed benefits are:

- Cross-listing allows a company to reach a *wider investor base,* which can potentially boost demand and hence liquidity for the company shares. Increased demand for a company's stock may increase the share price, which can lower a company's cost of capital.
- Cross-listing creates a *secondary market* for the company's shares and establishes recognition of the company in a new capital market, thus paving the way for the firm to source new equity or debt capital from local investors as demands dictate.
- Cross-listing has the secondary effect of *projecting the company's name and its products* in the foreign country where it is listed.
- By widening the investor base through cross-listing, there is a potential benefit of protection from a *hostile takeover* of the firm.

Cross-listing also raises some concerns. The company incurs costs in order to comply with the disclosure and listing requirements required by the foreign exchange and regulatory authorities. Secondly, volatility of the stock in one stock market can affect the volatility of the same stock selling in another stock market. Cross-listing also provides an easy means for foreign investors to purchase a company's stock, which can potentially lead to a foreign investor challenging the domestic control of the company. Table 13.2 summarizes country distribution of listed companies for various stock exchanges.

Table 13.2 Country distribution of domestic and foreign listed companies for various stock exchanges, 2010

Source: World Federation of Exchanges, Annual Report & Statistics 2010.

Country exchange	Total	Domestic companies	Foreign companies	Percentage foreign/total
USA - NYSE	2238	1787	451	20%
USA - Nasdaq	2778	2480	298	11%
Mexico - IPC	427	130	297	70%
Brazil - Bovespa	381	373	8	2.1%
Australia - ASE	1999	1913	86	4.3%
Hong Kong Stock Exchange	1413	1396	17	1.2%
Korea	1798	1781	17	0.9%
India - Mumbai Stock Exchange	5034	5034	0	0%
Japan - Tokyo Stock Exchange	2293	2281	12	0.5%
Singapore Stock Exchange	778	461	317	41%
Europe - Euronext	1135	983	152	13%
Germany - Deutsche Borse	765	690	75	10%
London Stock Exchange	2966	2362	604	20%
Spanish Stock Exchange	3345	3310	35	1%
Swiss Stock Exchange	296	246	50	17%
Ireland - Irish Stock Exchange	228	227	1	0.4%
Luxembourg Stock Exchange	290	30	260	90%
Israel - Tel Aviv	613	596	17	2.8%
Poland - Warsaw	584	569	17	2.9%
Austria - Wien	110	89	21	19%

International bond market

The international bond market is another way in which multinationals can source new debt capital. When markets are imperfect, international financing can lower the firm's cost of capital – for instance, eurobond financing is usually cheaper than domestic bond financing.

- The international bond market consists of *foreign bonds and eurobonds,* which compete with domestic bonds for funding
- A *foreign bond issue* is offered by a foreign borrower and the foreign bond issue is denominated in the local currency of the buyer of the bonds
- A *eurobond issue* is denominated in a foreign currency to the buyer, a German borrower issues a dollar-denominated bond to investors in the United Kingdom, for instance
- A *global bond issue* is an offering by a single borrower to investors in North America, Europe and Asia.

Table 13.3 is a summary of various types of bond instrument.

Table 13.3 Types of international bond

Types of bond	*Brief description*	*Payoff at maturity*
Straight fixed rate	Fixed annual coupon payment as a percentage of face value of the bond	Currency of issue
Floating-rate note	Coupon payments which are indexed to some reference, such as three-month US dollar LIBOR*	Currency of issue
Convertible bond	Allows investors to exchange bond for a predetermined number of equity shares of the issuer	Currency of issue or conversion to equity shares
Bonds with equity warrants	Straight fixed-rate bonds with an additional call option that allows bondholder to purchase equity shares under specified conditions	Currency of issue
Zero-coupon bond	Sold at discount from face value No coupon payments over its life	Currency of issue
Dual-currency bond	Straight fixed-rate bonds issued and paid coupon in one currency but repay principal in another currency	Dual currency
Composite currency bond	Denominated in currency basket instead of single currency	Composite currency of issue

* LIBOR = London Inter-Bank Offered Rate

Benefits of raising debt globally

Global bond offerings widen the borrower's opportunities for financing at reduced cost, because with increased liquidity in global bonds, investors are willing to accept lower yields. With an increased pool of investors, global bonds also promote sources of financing.

Concerns of raising debt globally

A company may need to satisfy additional security regulations (for example, information disclosure) required by overseas regulatory bodies.

International bond market credit ratings

Moody's Investors Service and Standard & Poor's (S&P) provide *credit ratings* on various types of international bonds. Bond issues are classified into categories based upon the creditworthiness of the borrower. Potential bond ratings include investment grade, speculative grade or a grade which indicates a default risk.

Ratings providers assess the company's default probability based on current information and details of debt obligation. The ratings reflect only creditworthiness (not exchange rate uncertainty) and they are the result of an analysis of three factors:

- Likelihood of default and compliance with timely payment of interest and principal repayment
- Nature and provision of debt obligation

- Protection afforded by, and relative position of, obligation in the event of bankruptcy, reorganization or other arrangement under the laws of bankruptcy and other laws affecting creditors' rights.

There is a disproportionate percentage of international bonds which have high credit ratings when compared to domestic bonds. This can be explained by the fact that the eurobond market is accessible only to firms that have good credit ratings and reputation.

Trade finance

In addition to the classic financial facilities that exporters and importers can obtain in their respective countries from their banks, financing international trade can take three forms:

- *Documentary credit* that benefits the exporters of goods
- *Credit facilities* offered to importers and exporters by export credit agencies that also mitigate the risks of exporters.
- *Counter-trade* deals that ease the cash outflow of exporters.

Documentary credit

For exporters of goods, the most traditional method of trade finance is the documentary credit represented in Figure 13.3. The principle is that an importer of goods mandates his bank to issue a letter of credit that guarantees the exporter that they will be paid on reception of shipping documents, establishing proof that the goods have actually been delivered to the transport company. The exporter can ask the importer's bank, through his own bank, to accept a *time draft* for the amount of the contract by issuing a *Bank Acceptance* (B/A). The exporter can discount this acceptance. Figure 13.3 gives a step-by-step simplified view of this process. There is a large variety of terms regulating the transactions and delineating the respective responsibilities of the exporters and the importers. Those terms, known as *Incoterms,* are defined by the International Chambers of Commerce (ICC) based in Paris.

Export credit agencies

Exporters, and sometimes importers, of goods can benefit from credits granted through export credit agencies such as the Eximbank (Export-Import Bank) backed by the Federal Credit Insurance Association (FCIA) in the United States, the ECGD (Export Credits Guarantee Department) in the United Kingdom or the Compagnie Française du Commerce Exterieur (COFACE) in France.

These agencies will either provide credits directly or facilitate the granting of credits from banks or from the exporter's bank to importers by covering political risks and commercial risks up to a certain percentage of the contract.

In addition, these institutions may grant facilities to exporters to obtain *pre-financing* of their exports in contracts of long duration.

Appendix 13.4 (p. 394) has a list of export credit agencies in different OECD member countries.

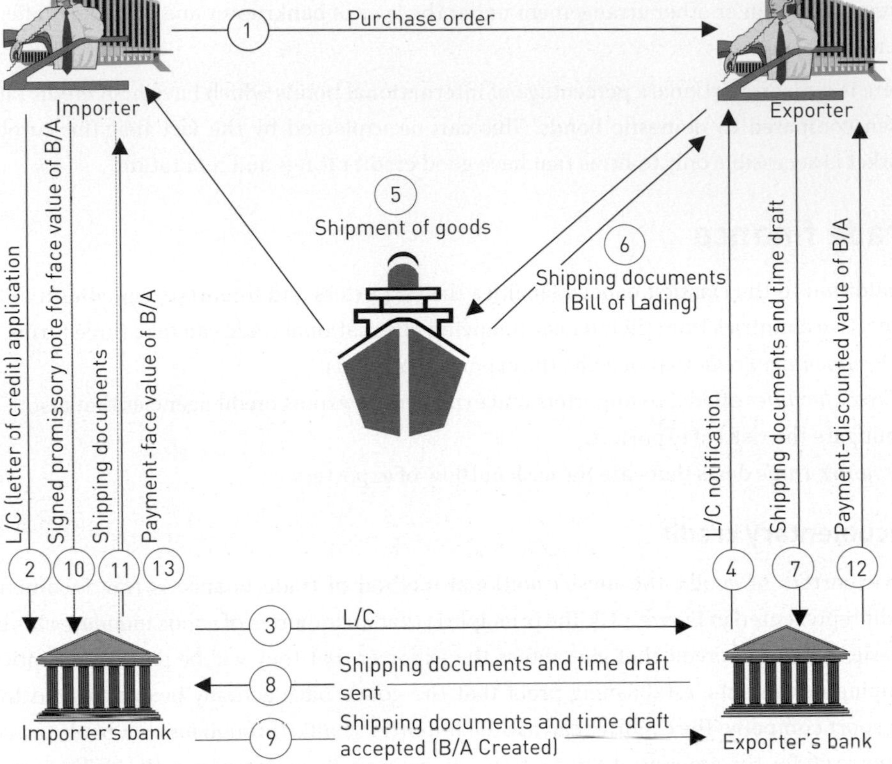

Figure 13.3 Documentary credit in international trade
Note: B/A=Bank acceptance.

Counter-trade

Counter-trade is another way of financing international transactions. It eases the pain for importers who have to find cash in hard currencies to pay for their imports. The principle of counter-trade is that the buyer pays the total or part of the contract in products or services. Counter-trade can take three main forms:[2]

- *Barter* trade, the most direct form of counter-trade. The exporter is paid in products coming from the importer's country.
- *Buy-back* contracts, in which the supplier of equipment agrees to buy part of the output of the exporter's facilities. In this case, there is cash outlay on both sides but the importer recoups his investment from the cash generated by the sales of products. A variant of buy-back is known as *counter-purchase* contracts, in which the products sold to the exporters come from a third party.
- *Bilateral clearing agreements,* which exist at government level when two governments agree to trade and the debit and credit of the trade are registered in an account whose balance is cleared at the end of an agreed period. In some cases, the balance can be 'sold' to a third

party that can use it for purchasing goods in the debtor's country. This last arrangement is known as *switch trade*.

Counter-trade agreements mostly involve developing countries that are short of hard currency. They were common practice at the time of the state-planned economies in communist countries until the early 1990s, and have tended to decrease in importance with the liberalization of markets.

MINI-CASE

Aguaciudad in the Philippines

Aguaciudad SA is a Spanish public company involved in water treatment projects.

In November 2009 it was involved in negotiation with the municipality of Manila in the Philippines.

Following the negotiations a proposed contract was submitted. The terms of the contract are summarized below:

- Aguaciudad will build a waste water treatment plant for 500,000 cubic meters/day capacity serving 2 million people via a joint venture company created with the Manila Water Authority (10%), a private local conglomerate, the San José Conglomerate (30 per cent), in which Aguaciudad holds 60 per cent of the capital. The joint venture operates as a concessionaire of the project under the form of a BOT contract.
- The capital cost is estimated at US$200 million of imported equipment and services + 8 billion pesos of local costs (rate of exchange is .02 $ to the peso)
- The financing of the project is:
  - Shareholders: US$100 million
  - IFC: 10-year US$90 million loan at 8 per cent interest repayable in 6 installments after the fourth year
  - Export credit from Spain: 8-year loan of US$100 million, with interest at 5 per cent refundable after year 2
  - Asian Development Bank: local currency 10-year loan of 3 billion pesos at 10 per cent, interest repayable straight after 10 years
- The contributions of shareholders to the joint venture are the following:
  - Aguaciudad: 60 million cash
  - Manila Water Authority: the capitalization intangible assets of the license to operate (US$1 million) plus 9 million cash
  - San José Conglomerate: 30 million
- The cost of operations and maintenance without depreciation and financing is estimated at 14 million US$/year plus 340 million pesos
- It has been agreed that the joint venture will charge the water at 27 pesos/m^3.

Questions:

1) What are the risks in this project for Aguaciudad?
2) What do you think of the financing of the project?
3) Aguaciudad shareholders request a 15 per cent return in risky environments Will they approve the project?

Summary and key points

1 There are four key issues in global financial management:

- *Currency risk*: exposure and hedging against currency fluctuations
- *Project finance*: how to evaluate international investments and how to finance them
- *Capital markets*: how to take advantage of global financial market to raise equity and handle debts
- *Trade finance*: financing exports/imports of goods and services.

2 Currency fluctuations and hedging:

- Currency fluctuations can affect the economic value of companies that operate globally in three ways:
  - *Strategic exposure*:
    - Change in competitive advantage of a company in terms of future cash flow owing to increased/decreased costs arising from changes in currency values
    - Global firms better positioned to deal with strategic exposures because of their diversified market portfolio and abilities to relocate production facilities
    - Hedging techniques include:
      - Hedging with *strategic product positioning*: developing products/services for price-insensitive markets through differentiation
      - Hedging with *geographical positioning*: balancing sales and production assets within exchange zones
      - *Sourcing in low-cost countries*, e.g. countries with relatively low wages despite having strong currencies
  - *Transaction exposure*:
    - Positive or negative changes in short-term cash flows owing to existing financial or commercial commitments
    - Hedging techniques include:
      - *Forward contracts*: buying at a fixed future date a fixed quantity of a given currency at a fixed exchange rate (the forward rate); most common hedging technique used by corporations
      - *Future contracts*: similar to forward contracts but standard financial instruments traded in recognized futures markets
      - *Options*: contracts allowing you to sell (put option) or buy (sell option) a currency at a given exchange rate (the strike price) at the end of the maturity period
      - *Currency swaps*: when one company borrows in currency *X* but repays in currency *Y* and another company borrows in currency *Y* but repays in currency *X*; the two companies can swap their loans through a bank
    - Non-hedging techniques:
      - *Leading and lagging*:
        - » For payments, a company would try to collect receivables early (leading) if they are nominated in 'soft' currencies and delay (lagging) the collection of receivables nominated in 'hard' currencies

    - » For receipts, a company would try to pay early (leading) if they are nominated in hard currencies and delay (lagging) payments nominated in 'soft' currencies
  - *Netting*:
    - » Allows treasurers of global firms which have centralized cash management to hedge net cash position for any currency that has a creditor position
    - » Types of netting system – *bilateral netting*, netting between pairs of subsidiaries; multilateral netting, netting of all transactions and transfer of the net to a central account
- – *Translation exposure*:
  - Currency movement affects valuation of assets/liabilities of global companies and this can affect market perception and hence market value of the firm
  - There are two main methods of adjusting financial statements for currency fluctuations:
    - *Monetary/non-monetary* method: monetary assets are translated at the exchange rate prevailing on the date of the balance sheet; non-monetary assets are translated at the historic rate, i.e. the rate prevailing at the date they were entered in the balance sheet
    - *Current* method: all balance sheet assets/liabilities are translated at the exchange rate on the balance sheet date; the income statement accounts can be translated either at the exchange rate at the date when the revenues and expenses are incurred or at the average exchange rate of the period; translation gains or losses are reported in a separate equity account of the parent company's balance sheet.

3 Project finance – international project finance deals with the valuation and financing of productive investments in countries that are not the investor's countries:

- *Project valuation* – two approaches are available to take into account country risks and currency risks which are not diversifiable:
  - – *Cash flow adjustments* (Adjusted Present Value, APV) involves the following four steps:
    - Specific downside risks are identified, their impact on the cash flow is calculated and the probability of their occurrence is determined
    - Cash flows are adjusted using probabilistic distribution
    - Cash flows are then translated into the investor's currency using Purchasing Power Parity (PPP) differences as a proxy for currency fluctuations
    - Cash flows are discounted using the investor's cost of capital.
  - – *Cost of capital adjustments* (CCA) which introduces a premium risk to the cost of equity; adjusting the risk premium by introducing a 'country beta' to the cost of capital is argued to be more appropriate in case of investments in emerging countries where risks are not diversifiable
- *Specific project financing*:
  - – *Equity project financing*:
    - For *developing countries*, equity project finance is usually provided by development banks
    - For *industrialized market economies*, equity project finance is usually provided by development banks

  - *Debt project financing* – provided by banking institutions, development banks, government aid or supplier credits; when provided by banks or supplier credits, debt financing is backed by credit risk insurance.

4 Global capital structure:

- Capital markets can be either integrated or fragmented:
  - *Integrated* capital markets mean that raising money in any country comes at the same cost
  - *Fragmented* capital markets mean that capital markets still differ in their structure, costs and risk:
    - Fragmentation can be observed in:
      - Correlation between the movements of a country's stock exchange against an index of all stock exchanges in the world (the world index); this measures the relative riskiness of different stock markets (like a country stock market 'beta')
      - Difference in cost of capital (debts and equity) in different countries
    - With the different macroeconomic outlooks of different countries and different risk profiles, cost of capital can differ in different countries, which allows companies to benefit through:
      - Cross-listing
      - International bond issues
- *Cross-listing*
  - Advantages include:
    - Reaching wider investor base which can boost demand and liquidity of company shares
    - Creating a secondary market for the company's shares and establishing name recognition in a new capital market
    - Projecting the company's name and products in the foreign country where it is listed
    - Potential benefit of protection from hostile takeover with a widened investor base
  - Disadvantages include:
    - Costs incurred in compliance with disclosure/listing requirements of foreign exchange
    - Volatility of the stock in one stock market can affect volatility of the stock in another
    - Foreign investors can easily purchase a company's stock and challenge the domestic control of the company
- International bond issues
  - Benefits:
    - Means of financing at lower cost
    - Promotes diversified investor base
    - Dual currency bond assists parent company to finance its overseas subsidiaries' operation – the parent company can pay off the periodic coupon payment at local currency of the parent company but principal repayment by foreign subsidiaries is in foreign currency
  - Potential disadvantages – company may need to satisfy additional security regulations (for example, information disclosure) required by overseas regulatory bodies.

5 Trade finance:

- *Documentary credit*: an importer of goods mandates their bank to issue a letter of credit that guarantees that the exporter will be paid at reception of shipping documents establishing the proof that goods have been actually been delivered to the transport company
- Credit facilities offered by *export credit agencies* to importers and exporters
- Counter-trade deals that ease the cash outflow of exporters; in counter-trade, the buyer pays the total or part of the contract in products or services mostly used by developing countries that are short of hard currency:
  - *Barter trade*: exporter is paid in products coming from the importer's country
  - *Buy-backs*: supplier of equipment agrees to buy part of the output of the exporter's facilities; a variant of buy-back is counter-purchase contracts in which the products sold to the exporters come from a third party
  - *Bilateral clearing agreements*: governmental level when two governments agree to trade and the debit and credit of the trade is registered in an account whose balance is cleared at the end of the agreed period.

Appendix 13.1 Hedging exposure to currency risk: a case study[3]

We will assume that a US wine distributor has just signed a contract with a French company for the delivery of 400 cases of champagne. The contract calls for the payment of 100,000 euros (EUR or €) when delivery takes place in three months. As soon as the contract is signed, the distributor is exposed to exchange rate risk because the dollar cost of the champagne will not be known until dollars are exchanged for €100,000 at the exchange rate that will prevail in three months. We will say that the distributor's contractual, or transaction, exposure is €100,000.

Exposure

Each time our US distributor places an order for champagne from France, he enters a contract to deliver euros to the French champagne exporter and is immediately exposed to foreign exchange risk. If the distributor's business is to sell French champagne, his exposure to foreign exchange risk is not limited to the *outstanding* contracts with his French suppliers. Future purchases of champagne will generate continuous exposure to the volatility of the US dollar–euro exchange rate. This exposure to future exchange rate changes is an example of an operating exposure.

Importers (or exporters) of goods and services are not the only firms subject to operating exposure. A firm that has only domestic operations can also be exposed to changes in exchange rates. Consider a US distributor of champagne made in the United States. If the value of the euro decreases relative to the US dollar (you get more euros for a dollar), the US distributor of the French-produced champagne can keep the same margin by selling his champagne at a lower price and, in the process, take market share from the distributor of US-made champagne. A similar situation occurs when domestic firms that buy, produce and sell domestic goods are faced with competition from abroad. For example, in the early 1980s, US car manufacturers lost market share to Japanese competitors when the US dollar appreciated against the Japanese yen.

Transaction exposure

Our US distributor of French champagne has a contractual exposure of €100,000, which will remain outstanding for the next three months. As the EUR/USD exchange rate varies during that period of time, the dollar value of the €100,000 will change. There are many ways the distributor can hedge this exchange rate risk, that is, protect himself against currency fluctuations. He can choose among the many hedging techniques commonly used to reduce or eliminate the exchange rate risk associated with the purchase of raw materials, the sale of goods, the purchase of assets, or the issuance of debt when they are denominated in a foreign currency. These techniques use instruments available in the financial markets, such as forward, futures and option contracts.

Hedging with forward contracts

The **forward hedge**, which is the hedging technique most widely used by corporations, can completely eliminate the exchange rate risk associated with foreign transactions. The distributor can arrange a forward hedge simply by entering into a forward contract with a bank to buy from that bank €100,000 with US dollars in three months. In other words, the distributor can fix *today* the rate at which he will buy €100,000 from the bank in three months. The bank will most likely require the importer to establish a **foreign exchange line of credit** to guarantee his ability to deliver US dollars in three months.

What is the *net* result of the two transactions, the purchase of champagne and the purchase of euros forward? If today's three-month *forward rate* is EUR/USD 0.80, the distributor will have to pay the bank $125,000 (€100,000 divided by 0.80) in three months to get the €100,000. Regardless of how the EUR/USD exchange rate changes between the purchase date and the delivery date, the dollar value of the purchase will not change. It will remain equal to $125,000. The exchange rate risk has been eliminated. By entering into a forward contract, the distributor has 'locked in' an exchange rate of EUR/USD 0.80. Note that this rate is the *forward rate* quoted today and *not* the spot rate, which may be higher or lower than the forward rate.

What would happen if the cases of champagne are not delivered on the agreed-upon date and, consequently, the €100,000 payment to the French exporter is delayed? The distributor would still have to buy the €100,000 from his bank for $125,000 at the date fixed by the forward contract. He would then have the choice of keeping the €100,000 until the champagne is delivered or exchanging them for US dollars at the prevailing spot rate. If the distributor exchanges the euros, he will need €100,000 to pay the French exporter when the champagne is delivered and will again be exposed to exchange rate risk. However, he can hedge this risk as before by entering into a new €100,000 forward contract with the bank. This strategy is known as **rolling over the forward contract**. An alternative to a rollover would be for the distributor to enter a **forward window contract** at the beginning. This contract is the same as a standard forward contract except that the transaction does not have to be settled on a fixed date. It can be settled on any day during an agreed-upon period of time known as the *window*. The importer would have to pay an additional fee for this flexibility, but it may be cheaper than rolling over the original contract.

What if the distributor wants to get out of the forward contract before its expiration date? In this situation, he would have to *sell* €100,000 forward by entering a forward contract that has the same expiration date as the first contract. The cash settlement for both contracts will take place at their common expiration date. The distributor would gain or lose depending on whether the forward rate on the second contract is lower or higher than the rate on the first contract (EUR/USD 0.80). For example, suppose the forward rate on the second contract is EUR/USD 0.78. He will receive $128,205 from this contract (€100,000 divided by EUR/USD 0.78) and will pay $125,000 on the first contract. His gain will be $3,205 ($128,205 less $125,000). If the forward rate of the second contract is EUR/USD 0.82, he will lose $3,049, the difference between the $121,951 from the sale of euros (€100,000 divided by EUR/USD 0.82) and the $125,000 on the first contract.

Hedging with futures contracts

If our champagne distributor wants to use currency futures contracts to hedge his exposure to euros, he will have to buy three-month futures contracts worth €100,000. Because currency futures contracts and forward contracts are similar instruments, the futures hedge should have the same overall effect as the forward hedge. However, there will be some differences.

First, the other party in the futures contract is not a bank, but is instead the clearing corporation. The distributor, through his broker, will have to *buy* euros futures and then *sell* them later. If, in the meantime, the euro appreciates (or depreciates) relative to the US dollar, the distributor will make a profit (or loss) from his futures trade. But, if the euro appreciates (or depreciates) relative to the dollar, he will also have to disburse more (or fewer) dollars to buy, in the spot market, the €100,000 needed to pay his supplier. The profit (or loss) made in the futures market will compensate for the increase (or decrease) in the amount of dollars needed to buy the €100,000 in the spot market.

Second, because the size and the maturity of the futures contracts are standardized, it is not always possible to *perfectly* hedge transaction exposure using a futures contract. For example, if the distributor decides to buy euros futures contracts at the Chicago Mercantile Exchange (CME), he will have to buy contracts with a unit size of €125,000. If he buys one contract for €125,000, he will 'overhedge' his exposure by €25,000. Moreover, the distributor will have to decide on the maturity date of the futures contract. The only four expiration dates for a futures contract are the last Wednesday of March, June, September and December. Suppose the champagne supplier wants to be paid by the end of May? The distributor will buy June futures contracts because their expiration date is closest to the end of May. Then he will *sell* the futures contracts at the end of May. However, he will still be exposed to exchange rate risk because he cannot know at the time the contract is bought what the price of the June futures contracts will be at the end of May. Suppose the supplier agrees to wait until 1 July to be paid and the distributor chooses to hedge with June futures? In this case, the distributor will be exposed to the USD/EUR exchange rate volatility between the last Wednesday of June (when the June futures contracts expire) and 1 July.

Finally, the distributor will have to place a margin with a broker. Also, the daily marking to market may trigger margin calls if the USD/EUR futures exchange rate goes down. In this situation, the distributor would have to make additional cash payments until the futures contracts expire.

To summarize, a futures hedge has some disadvantages that are not present in a forward hedge. A futures hedge is more complicated, it does not completely eliminate exchange rate risk, and it requires intermediary cash payments. These drawbacks are particularly significant for our distributor of champagne who may rightly prefer to hedge his contractual exposure with forward contracts. However, there are features of the futures market which, in some circumstances, cause corporations to hedge with futures rather than with forward contracts. For example, a small firm without any established reputation or a firm that does not enjoy a high credit standing may find it convenient to use futures contracts because no credit check is required before trading in the futures market.

Hedging with option contracts

Suppose our distributor hedges his exposure to the euros by buying euros forward at EUR/USD 0.80. Regardless of whether the euro appreciates or depreciates during the hedging period, the US dollar cost of the champagne will be $125,000 (€100,000 divided by EUR/USD0.80). If the euro appreciates, the hedge will have accomplished its purpose, that is, it will have protected the distributor against an increase in the value of the euro. But if the euro depreciates, the distributor would have been better off if he had not hedged with forwards because he would then have benefited from the decrease in the value of the euro. Indeed, it is always the case that a forward hedge protects a firm from unfavorable exchange rate movements but prevents it from benefiting from favorable changes in the exchange rate. Does a hedging technique exist that insulates the distributor from an appreciation of the euro but allows him to benefit from its depreciation? The answer is yes and the technique is the currency option hedge.

The currency option hedge

If our distributor of champagne decides to hedge his euro exposure with options, he will buy a three-month euro *call* option. This will give him the right to buy euros at a predetermined exchange rate (the exercise rate). He is not obligated to exercise the option, and he will not do so if the exchange rate is unfavorable. For example, if the spot rate of the euro in three months is lower than the exercise rate of the option, the distributor will not exercise his option and, instead, will buy the needed euros in the spot market. On the other hand, if the spot rate is higher than the exercise rate, he will exercise his option to get the euros at a lower rate. The option hedge provides a flexibility that is absent in a forward or futures hedge. However, this flexibility comes with a price, which is the price of the option.

To illustrate, suppose the distributor can buy from his bank a three-month European call option at 0.04 dollars per euro, with an exercise rate of $1.25 per euro. This means (1) the distributor must now pay the bank 0.04 dollars per euro, or $4,000 for €100,000 ($0.04 multiplied by 100,000 euros) and (2) in three months, the distributor can buy 100,000 euros from the bank at $1.25 per euro for a total of $125,000 ($1.25 multiplied by 100,000 euros).

Whether or not the distributor will exercise the option in three-months depends on the USD/EURO spot exchange rate prevailing at that time. Table 13.A1 examines four cases corresponding to the following exchange rates in three months: EUR/USD 0.77, 0.78, 0.80 and 0.82.

Table 13.A1: Comparison of currency option costs for four exchange rates

Spot rate in three month's time		Exercise rate	Will the option be exercised?	Dollar amount paid for 100,000s	Cost of option	Total cost
EUR/USD	USD/EUR	USD/EUR				
0.77	1.3	1.25	Yes	$125,000	$4,000	$129,000
0.79	1.27	1.25	Yes	$125,000	$4,000	$129,000
0.8	**1.25**	**1.25**	**No**	**$125,000**	**$4,000**	**$129,000**
0.82	1.22	1.25	No	$121,951	$4,000	$125,951

If the exchange rate is EUR/USD 0.77 (USD/EUR 1.30), the distributor will exercise his option because he will be able to buy at $1.25 what is worth $1.30. He will get the €100,000 for $125,000 ($1.25 multiplied by €100,000) from the bank (the seller of the option) and pay his supplier of champagne. However, the option costs $ 4,000, so the total cost of the champagne will be $129,000 ($125,000 plus $4,000). If the exchange rate is EURO/USD 0.79 (USD/EUR 1.27), he will also exercise his option and the total cost of the champagne will remain at $129,000. If the exchange rate is EUR/USD 0.80 (USD/EUR 1.25), that is, if it is equal to the exercise rate, there is no longer any incentive for the distributor to exercise the option because he can get the €100,000 in the spot market at the same exchange rate. For any USD/EUR exchange rate higher than the exercise rate of $1.25 per euro (or for any EUR/USD exchange rate *lower* than EUR/USD 0.80), the distributor will exercise his option and the total cost of the champagne will be $129,000.

If the exchange rate is EURO/USD 0.82 (USD/EUR 1.22), the distributor will not exercise his option to buy at $1.25 what is worth only $1.22. He will buy the €100,000 in the spot market at EUR/USD 0.82 for a total cost of $121,951 (€100,000 divided by EUR/USD 0.82) and pay his supplier. However, because he paid $4,000 for the option, the total cost of the champagne will be $125,951 ($121,951 plus $4,000). For any USD/EUR spot rate lower than the exercise rate of $1.25 euro (or for any EUR/USD exchange rate higher than EUR/USD 0.80), the distributor will let the option expire without exercising it and exchange dollars for euros at the spot rate. And the lower the USD/EUR exchange rate, the lower the dollar cost of the champagne.

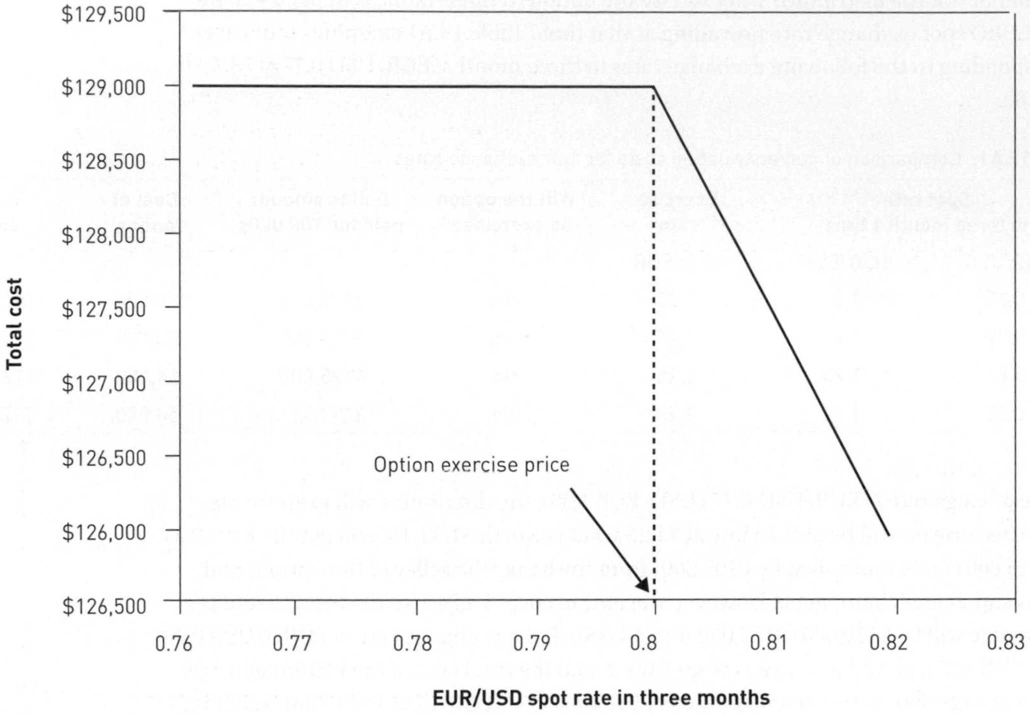

Figure 13.A1 The option hedge for the US champagne distributor.

Contractual exposure: €100,000 to be paid in three months' time
3-month call option price: USD/EUR 0.04
Exercise price: $1.25 per euro or EUR/USD 0.80

Figure 13.A1 shows the net result of the option hedge for the distributor for a wide range of spot rates in three months. The hedge accomplishes the dual goal of (1) protecting the distributor from an appreciation of the euro by setting an upper limit to the dollar amount he will have to pay for the champagne ($129,000), and (2) allowing him to benefit from a depreciation of the euro. If the euro rises above the exercise rate (the EUR/USD rate drops below 0.80), the distributor will exercise his right to buy euros at that rate; thus he limits the dollar cost of the €100,000 to $129,000, the amount he will pay the bank ($125,000) when exercising the option plus the cost of the option ($4,000). However if the euro falls below the exercise rate (the EUR/USD rate rises above 0.80), the distributor will not exercise his option. The dollar cost of the €100,000 will be equal to €100,000 multiplied by the spot rate in three months plus the $4,000 cost of the option.

Which hedging technique to choose?

Before deciding which technique to use in hedging a currency exposure created by a particular transaction, a manager must first decide if a hedge is needed at all. A hedge is not needed if another business unit belonging to the firm has a currency exposure that is the opposite of the one created by the transaction. However, a business unit manager is not usually informed of the size and timing of the currency exposure of other business units. This is the reason why large firms engaging in foreign trade have a centralized foreign currency management group that constantly monitors the firm's *net exposure* on a currency-by-currency basis and makes the required hedging decisions. Having all the business units' currency exposures consolidated and managed by a central unit prevents the multiplication of unnecessary and costly hedges.

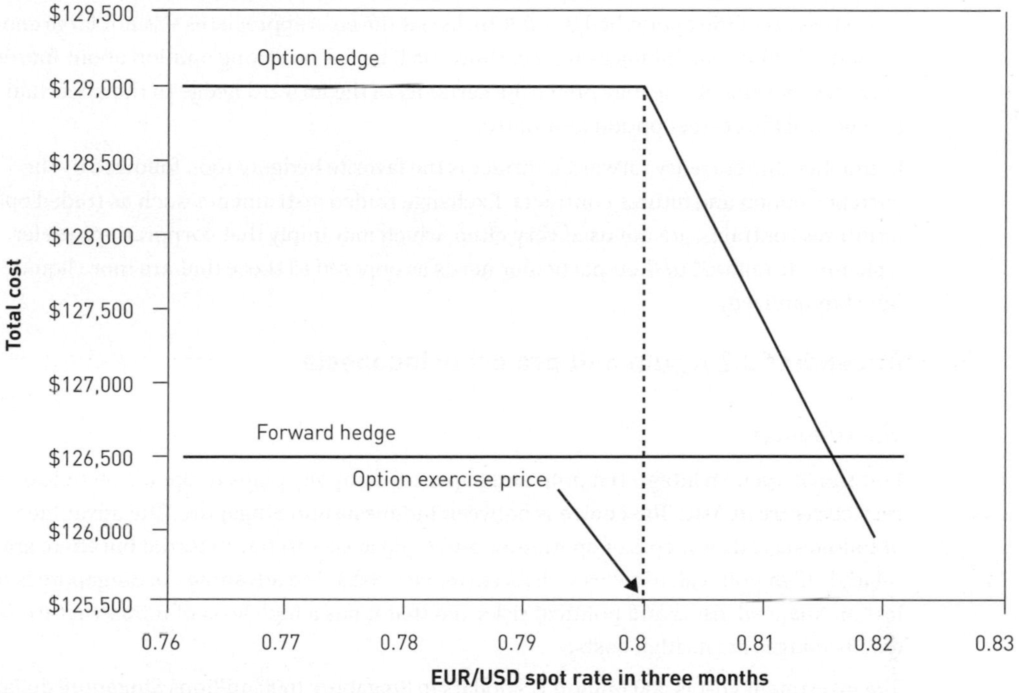

Figure 13.A2 The forward and option hedges for the US champagne distributor

Contractual exposure: €100,000 to be paid in three months' time
3-month forward rate: EUR/USD 0.80; 3-month call option price: USD/EUR 0.04
Exercise price: $1.25 per euro or EUR/USD 0.80

Currency risk exposure can be further reduced using a procedure known as **leading and lagging**. This process consists of timing the cash inflows and outflows from the different foreign business units to minimize the firm's *overall* exposure to exchange rate risk. For example, if a US company has to make a payment in Japanese yen, it can ask its Japanese subsidiary – assuming it has one – for an early payment of the same amount of yen on any of the subsidiary's outstanding debt to the parent company. This procedure is known as *leading*. If the parent is owed money denominated in yen, it can delay the payment of some of its debt to the subsidiary until that money is received. This procedure is called *lagging*.

What hedging technique should our champagne distributor use? We have shown that a forward hedge is preferable to a futures hedge for eliminating his €100,000 exposure. What about an option hedge? Figure 13.A2 shows the net dollar cost of the €100,000 when using either the forward hedge or the option hedge for different spot rates in three months. The difference in the outcomes of the two hedging techniques is clear. With a forward hedge, the net cost is $80,000 regardless of the prevailing spot rate in three months. Furthermore, the distributor knows that cost when he enters the contract. With an option hedge, the net cost depends on the spot rate in three months, with the cost limited to $83,000. Thus, the choice depends on the distributor's opinion of future changes in the USD/EUR spot rate. If he strongly believes the euro will depreciate in the following three months, he may consider that the extra cost of the option hedge – if it turns out the euro appreciates – is not large enough to dissuade him from taking a chance. However, if he has no strong opinion about future currency movements, he may prefer the certainty of the forward hedge to the uncertain outcome of the costlier option alternative.

In practice, the currency forward contract is the favorite hedging tool, followed by the currency option and futures contracts. Exchange traded instruments, such as traded options or futures contracts, are not used very often, which may imply that corporations prefer instruments tailored to their particular needs as opposed to those that are more liquid, but standardized.

Appendix 13.2 A pulp mill project in Indonesia

The situation

LouisianaPaper, an integrated pulp and paper US company plans to open a technical service centre in Asia. The choice is between Indonesia and Singapore. The advantage of Indonesia is its low cost of operations and rapid access to raw material but there are relativly high political, fiscal as well as currencies risks. The advantage of Singapore is to be low on financial, fiscal and political risks and that it has a high level of infrastructure. The disadvantages are its high costs.

The investment cost is 400 Million US dollars in Singapore (600 millions Singapore dollars at the prevailing exchange rate of 1USD= 1.5 SGD) and 367 million USD in Indonesia (3300 Indonesian rupiah at the prevailing rate of 1USD = 9000 IDR).

The cash flows of the projects are the following:

	Singapore project	Indonesia project	Singapore project	Indonesia project
	SGD millions	IDR billions	USD at the prevailing exchange rate	
Investment costs	-600	-3150	-400	-350
Cash flow yr 1	128	990	85	110
Cash flow yr 2	135	1170	90	130
Cash flow yr 3	150	1350	100	150
Cash flow yr 4	180	1800	120	200
Cash flow yr 5	210	2160	140	240
Cash flow yr 6	270	2700	180	300
Cash flow yr 7	330	2880	220	320
Terminal value yr 7	600	3600	400	400

Figure 13.A3 Projected cash flows for LouisianaPaper project

The inflation rate is 1% in Singapore, 4% in the US and 8% in Indonesia.

The LouisianaPaper's Weighted Average Cost of Capital (WACC) in the US is 10%.

There is a 10% chance that a major terrorist event may occur in Indonesia over the period. If that is the case, 50% of the cash flow will disappear. There is also a 20% chance over the period that the government will impose a special tax that would decrease the cash flow by 10%.

Project evaluation and comparison

- Baseline project: value at prevailing exchange rate and without risks in Indonesia
  - NPV at 10% = 361 USD In Singapore and 705 USD in Indonesia.
- Value after taking into consideration the exchange rate fluctuation.

In order to evaluate the possible exchange rate fluctuation, you can use the inflation differential. This technique, based on the purchasing power parity, assumes that if prices increase faster or slower in one country than in another country, the exchange rate will vary according to the following formula:

- Spot rate X/Y at time n = Spot rate at time n-1 * 1+Inflation in country X/1+ inflation in country Y
- In the case of Singapore: Spot SGD/USD= 1.01/1.04= 0.9711
- In the case of Indonesia: Spot IDR/USD= 1.08/1.04= 1.0384

Therefore the new cash flow in USD becomes:

	Singapore project SGD millions	Indonesia project billions IDR	Rate of SGD	Rate of IDR	Singapore project millions USD	Indonesia project millions USD
Investment costs	-600	-3150	1.500	9.000	-400	-350
Cash flow yr 1	128	990	1.457	9.346	88	106
Cash flow yr 2	135	1170	1.415	9.706	95	121
Cash flow yr 3	150	1350	1.374	10.079	109	134
Cash flow yr 4	180	1800	1.334	10.467	135	172
Cash flow yr 5	210	2160	1.296	10.869	162	199
Cash flow yr 6	270	2700	1.258	11.287	215	239
Cash flow yr 7	330	2880	1.222	11.721	270	246
Terminal value yr 7	600	3600	1.187	12.172	506	296
			NPV 10%		**$480.68**	**$533.18**

Figure 13.A4 The Indonesia project is still more attractive in spite of higher inflation

- Value after taking into consideration the country risks

Two methods:

- *Adjusting the cost of capital*

  This method is simple but requires to introduce a risk premium into the Weighted Average Cost of Capital (WACC) of LouisianaPaper. The simplest way would be to add to the base WACC a premium calculated on the sovereign risk of Singapore and Indonesia compared with the USA. According to Moody, the risk premium on Singapore is 0.6% and 6.5% for Indonesia.

  The discount factor for the Singapore project becomes 10.6% and for Indonesia 16.5%.

  The NPV under this calculation is

  – 454 million US$ for the Singapore project

  – 315 million US$ for Indonesian project

  This method often used in practice has some theoretical flaws since sovereign risks are related to government finances and not to specific project risks.

  It is preferable, although more complex, to use the Adjusted Present Value method based on a probabilistic risk assessment.

- *Adjusting the cash flows*

  Given the 10% risk of major terrorist attack and a 20% risk of additional taxes the Indonesia project cash flow becomes as shown in Figure 13A.5.

  The Indonesian project NPV goes down just below the Singaporean project, which is free of political and tax risks.

  Various risks hypotheses in Indonesia can be simulated, giving the Indonesian project cash flows according to various probabilities of risks (Figure 13A.6).

CALCULATING EXPECTED EXCHANGE RATES USING THE PPP RELATION

The Purchasing Power Parity (PPP) relation says that exchange rates should adjust so that the same basket of goods will cost the same in different countries. It is based on the following premise: if the price of goods increases faster in one country than in another because the inflation rate is higher in the first country than in the second, then the exchange rate between the two countries should move to offset the difference in inflation rates and, consequently, the difference in prices. More formally, according to the PPP relation:

$$\text{Expected future spot rate} = \text{current spot rate} \times \frac{1 + \text{Expected inflation rate in the home country}}{1 + \text{Expected inflation rate in the foreign country}}$$

If $S^0_{h/f}$ is the current spot rate and $E(S^1_{h/f})$ is the expected future spot rate in one year, both expressed in units of the home currency per unit of the foreign currency, and if $E(i_h)$ and $E(i_f)$ are the expected inflation rates for next year at home and in the foreign country, respectively, then:

$$E(S^1_{h/f}) = S^0_{h/f} \times \frac{1+E(i_h)}{1+E(i_f)}$$

Equation 13.A1

The Indonesian project is better than the Singaporean one if there is no terrorist attack or if there is only 10% of chance of terrorist attack with no tax increase.

Indonesia project cash flow after exchange rate variations and political and tax risks (M US$)	
Investment costs	-350
Cash flow yr 1	99
Cash flow yr 2	112
Cash flow yr 3	125
Cash flow yr 4	160
Cash flow yr 5	185
Cash flow yr 6	222
Cash flow yr 7	229
Terminal value yr 7	275
NPV 10% WACC	**$473.59**

Figure 13.A5 The Indonesian project NPV goes down just below the Singaporean project, which is free of political and tax risks

Probabilities of taxation	Probabilities of terrorist Attack			
	0%	10%	20%	30%
0%	533	491	448	405
10%	525	480	440	397
20%	516	474	431	388
30%	508	465	423	380
40%	499	457	414	371
50%	491	448	405	363

Figure 13.A6 The Indonesian project is better than the Singaporean one if there is no terrorist attack or if there is only a 10% chance of terrorist attack with no tax increase

Appendix 13.3 Development banks providing project equity financing

Name of development bank	*Details of funding available*
Asian development bank (ADB) <http://www.adb.org>	ADB's traditional modes of financing include equity investments. Equity may include preferred stock, convertible loans, and other forms of mezzanine financing. *Eligibility for ADB assistance* To be eligible for ADB assistance, the proposed investment should be in the private sector of a Developing Member Country (DMC) and owned by local or foreign private sector entities. An enterprise owned jointly by private interests and the government of the DMC may be eligible for ADB assistance, provided the majority of its equity is privately owned and it is controlled by private investors. *Sale of ADB equity investment* ADB intends to divest its shareholdings at a fair market price once the objective of its investment is considered achieved. In general, ADB will prefer to sell its shares to nationals of the host country to broaden local ownership and further develop local capital markets.
CDC Capital Partners (formerly Commonwealth Development Cooperation (CDC)) <http://www.cdcgroup.com/>	CDC Capital Partners provides equity capital to businesses in the emerging markets, especially poorer countries. As a medium- to long-term investor which ultimately aims to realize its investments in consultation with its partners, the following constitute key elements of CDC Capital Partners' investment policy: • It seeks to establish a partnership with sponsors to acquire, expand or restructure a business • It invests primarily in equity or equity-related finance and can arrange the provision of debt finance

Name of development bank	*Details of funding available*
CDC Capital Partners *continued*	• It may co-sponsor and invest during the due diligence or bid stage of a potential business • It looks to invest from US$0.5million to US$60 million in any one investment. CDC Capital Partners is on track to become a Public Private Partnership (PPP) – essentially a joint venture between UK government and the private sector in order to mobilize greater investment into emerging markets.
Agence Française de Développement (AFD) <http://www.afd.fr/lang/en/home>	Private sector financing is provided by Proparco, a member of the European economic interest group EDFI, which unites the 12 European financial institutions that finance the private sector. Proparco invests in enterprises in the form of equity, medium- and long-term loans, including subordinate loans, and guarantees. In the overseas departments and territories, it engages only in long-term investments The investments may involve financing of projects promoted by start-up companies, development programmes, privatization or restructuring. Proparco also executes specific financing provided by the International Finance Corporation (IFC) and the European Investment Bank (EIB). The group also invests long-term in the overseas departments through two vehicles: • A regional development corporation, the Société de Développement Economique de la Réunion (Sodere) makes equity or quasi-equity investments in SMEs • Proparco can make equity investments (shares and participating loans) in companies of a certain size. Proparco's investments are always minority shareholdings. They are intended for transfer to other shareholders, or sale on the financial market in the case of negotiable securities, after an average period of six years when the company has reached a sustainable level of maturity. That is why, when the investment is made, the project's internal rate of return must be at least 15 per cent in order to ensure a reasonable return on the capital invested and thus facilitate the liquidity of the shares held.
European Bank for Reconstruction and Development (EBRD) <http:// www.ebrd.com/>	The EBRD exists to foster the transition towards open market oriented economies and to promote private and entrepreneurial initiative in the countries of Central and Eastern Europe (CEE) and the Commonwealth of Independent States (CIS) committed to applying the principles of market economics. EBRD provides project-specific direct financing for private sector activities, restructuring and privatization, or financing of infrastructure that supports these activities. *EBRD projects:* Each project is assessed according to the appropriate country strategy and certain guidelines apply for any EBRD project: • The EBRD funds up to 35 per cent of the total project cost for a greenfield project or 35 per cent of the long-term capitalization of an established company • Significant equity contributions from other investors are required, in particular from industrial sponsors in the case of greenfield projects or new joint ventures, where special technical and management skills are needed; in such cases, industrial sponsors are expected to have a majority shareholding or adequate operational control • Typical private sector projects are based on no more than two-thirds debt financing and at least one-third equity

Name of development bank	*Details of funding available*
European Bank for Reconstruction and Development *continued*	• Additional funding by other co-financiers is typically required • Equity from sponsors need not be exclusively in cash but can be in the form of equipment, plant machinery, etc. As a guideline, the standard minimum involvement for the bank is €5 million, though this may be reduced if the project has fundamental benefits for the country.
	Equity finance
	In order to support privatization and restructuring of medium-sized enterprises, the EBRD uses a number of equity financing instruments known collectively as 'early-stage equity' funds. Two such instruments developed by the EBRD are Special Restructuring Programmes (SRPs) and Post-Privatization Funds (PPFs). While most of the SRPs and PPFs are in the 'start-up' phase, several of the funds moved into the 'investment phase' in 1997. PPFs are designed to provide equity and management assistance, mainly to formerly state-owned firms that have been wholly or partially privatized by mass privatization or individual auction schemes. These funds seek minority stakes in enterprises, with the fund manager taking a proactive role in developing the company through board representation and support for the enterprise's management. SRPs, in contrast, target enterprises requiring more comprehensive restructuring support before being viable for access to market-based financing on acceptable commercial terms.
	Equity finance for SME (also called 'equity window')
	EBRD has established links with a variety of financial intermediaries to provide financing for projects that are too small to be funded directly. This allows the bank to support SMEs. Equity finance will be available to SMEs through privately managed investment funds in the region. The EU and the EBRD have each contributed €25 million to the equity window, which will invest in private equity funds focused on SMEs. The size of the fund is expected to range between €10 and €15 million on average, and maximum financing per investee will be restricted to €1 million for a minority stake. To take account of the higher risks and costs involved in managing equity funds for SMEs, the EU contribution may be structured to provide appropriate incentives, such as an operating cost subsidy. This is intended to overcome the private sector's reticence about SME investment. Otherwise, SME funds will be structured on a case-by-case basis in line with business practice for private equity funds as well as local market conditions.
	Eligibility criteria and investment policy of SME funds
	All accession countries are eligible for the establishment of an SME fund. These funds could cover a region within one country, or a whole country when this is deemed manageable. The bank will seek to share the resources of the equity window evenly among accession countries.

Name of development bank	***Details of funding available***
European Bank for Reconstruction and Development *continued*	Investment funds committed in their investment policy to focusing on SMEs, according to the EU definition of SMEs, will be eligible for equity funding. Other requirements for investment under the SME funds are that: • The target SMEs should be incorporated and operate in an accession country • Only private, unlisted enterprises are eligible, regardless of ownership (domestic, foreign or joint venture) • The maximum size of investment is capped at €1 million. SME funds will be allowed to use the full range of equity and quasi-equity instruments. SME funds will, as a matter of policy, hold minority positions in their investee companies, with a minimum stake of 10 per cent and a maximum of 49 per cent. The average shareholding is expected to be between 25 and 49 per cent. The fund managers will secure rights enabling them to exercise appropriate corporate governance over the SME portfolio.
International Finance Corporation (IFC) <http://www.ifc.org>	IFC (an affiliate of the World Bank) provides equity finance for private companies operating in emerging economies. It provides equity investments based on project needs and anticipated returns. IFC is never the largest single shareholder and is considered a passive investor. Its equity investment is usually maintained for 8–15 years and it is considered a long-term investor. IFC also provides a full range of quasi-equity finance, including convertible debentures, subordinated loans, loans with warrants and other instruments. These products are provided, whenever necessary, to ensure that a project is soundly funded. In order to receive funding, a project must meet IFC's investment guideline: • the project must be in the private sector • it must be technically sound • it must have a good prospect of being profitable • it must benefit the local economy • it must be environmentally sound (i.e. meet the IFC's stringent environmental standards). IFC financing is generally limited to no more than 25 per cent of project cost. IFC also provides equity financing to commercial financial institutions which lend to local businesses for working capital, trade finance, project finance, venture capital and equipment leasing.
Japan International Cooperation Agency (JICA) <http://www.jica.go.jp/english/index.html	The development cooperation program is intended to contribute to autonomous economic development in developing countries by providing financial and technical support on a governmental basis for development projects implemented by Japanese private companies in these countries. Of the various types of development project implemented by Japanese private companies in developing countries, this cooperation program is concerned primarily with projects that contribute to social development and the development of agriculture, forestry, mining and industry. Having assessed the public benefits, technical and economic risks, profitability and experimental features of a project, the funds required for implementation are made available under long-term, low-interest conditions.

Name of development bank	*Details of funding available*
	Investment and financing.
	Financing is provided over the long term and at low rates of interest to: • Japanese corporations implementing development projects in developing countries, and • Japanese corporations which finance local corporations implementing development projects. Projects eligible for financing and investment are: • Projects involving the provision and upgrading of related facilities are intended to deal with situations where development projects have already received loans, guarantees of obligations or financing from other government bodies.
	Experimental projects
	An experimental project is a type of development project that cannot be realized unless combined with technical improvements and development. Experimental projects include cultivation of crops, livestock breeding, forestation, development of unused timber resources, excavation, screening and refining of non-ferrous minerals such as limestone, rock phosphate and rock salt, and construction of low-cost housing.
United States Agency for International Development (USAID) <http://gopher.info.usaid.gov/>	USAID works to support long-term and equitable economic growth and advance US foreign policy objectives by supporting: • Economic growth and agricultural development; • Global health; and • Conflict prevention and developmental relief. USAID typically works in countries committed to achieving sustainable development but which lack the technical skills or resources necessary to implement policies and programmes that will accomplish these results. It provides assistance in four regions of the world: sub-Saharan Africa; Asia and the Near East; Latin America and the Caribbean; and Europe and Eurasia. An example of the USAID Equity Finance Program is the Trans-Balkan SME Equity Finance Program. This provides equity and quasi-equity financing in combination with active business assistance and trade linkages to SMEs in the former Yugoslavia and neighbouring Balkan states. Investments generally range between $100,000 and $500,000 per transaction.

Appendix 13.4 Official export credit agencies for OECD member countries

Country	Agency	Abbreviation
Australia	Export Finance and Insurance Corporation	EFIC
Austria	Oesterreichische Kontrollbank AG	OeKB
Belgium	Office National du Ducroire/Nationale Delcrederedienst	ONDD
Canada	Export Development Corporation	EDC
Czech Republic	Export Guarantees Development Corporation	EGAP
	Czech Export Bank	CEB
Denmark	Eksport Kredit Fonden	EKF

Country	Site	Abbreviation
Finland	Finnvera Oyj	Finnvera
	FIDE Ltd.	FIDE
France	Compagnie Française d'Assurance pour le Commerce Extérieur	COFACE
	Direction des Relations Economiques Extérieures (Ministère de l'Economie)	DREE
	Coface Scrl	SCRL
Germany	Hermes Kreditversicherungs-AG	HERMES
	Gerling Credit Insurance Group	GCIG
Greece	Export Credit Insurance Organization	ECIO
Hungary	Magyar Exporthitel Biztositó Rt.	MEHIB
Italy	Sezione Speciale per l'Assicurazione del Credito all'Esportazione	SACE
Japan	Export-Import Insurance Department	EID/MITI
	Japan Bank for International Cooperation	JBIC
Korea	Korea Export Insurance Corporation	KEIC
	The Export-Import Bank of Korea	Korea Eximbank
Mexico	Banco National de Comercio Exterior, SNC	Bancomext
Netherlands	Nederlandsche Credietverzekering Maatschappij NV	NCM
Norway	The Norwegian Guarantee Institute for Export Credits	GIEK
Poland	Korporacja Ubezpieczén Kredytów	KUKE
Portugal	Companhia de Seguro de Créditos, SA	COSEC
Spain	Compañía Española de Seguros de Crédito a la Exportación, S.A.	CESCE
	Compañía Española de Seguros y Reaseguros de Crédito y Caucíon, SA	CESCC
	Secretaría de Estado de Comercio (Ministerio de Economía)	SEC
Sweden	Exportkreditnämnden	EKN
Switzerland	Export Risk Guarantee	ERG
United Kingdom	Export Credits Guarantee Department	ECGD
United States	Export–Import Bank of the United States	Exim Bank
Hong Kong	Hong Kong Export Credit Insurance Corporation	HKEC
India	Export–Import Bank of India	Eximbankindia
Indonesia	Asuransi Ekspo Indonesia	ASEI
	PT Bank Ekspor Indonesia (Persero)	BEI
Israel	Israel Foreign Risks Insurance Corporation Ltd	IFTRIC
	Israel Discount Bank	Discount Bank
Italy	Societa Italiana Assicurazione Credit SpA	EULER-SIAC
Malaysia	Malaysia Export Credit Insurance Berhad	MECIB
New Zealand	EXGO	EXGO
Oman	Export Credit Guarantee Agency, Oman Development Bank	ECGA

Country	Site	Abbreviation
Singapore	ECICS Credit Insurance Ltd	ECICS
Slovenia	Slovene Export Corporation, Inc.	SEC
South Africa	Credit Guarantee Insurance Corporation of Africa	CGIC
Sri Lanka	Export Credit Insurance Corporation	SLECIC
United Kingdom	EULER Trade Indemnity plc	EULER
United States	Overseas Private Investment Corporation	OPIC

International organizations	
Organization	***Abbreviation***
Asian Development Bank	ADB
Asia Pacific Economic Cooperation	APEC
European Union	EU
European Bank for Reconstruction and Development	EBRD
European Investment Bank	EIB
Inter-American Development Bank	IADB
International Monetary Fund	IMF
Multilateral Investment Guarantee Agency	MIGA
United Nations	UN
World Bank	WB
Banks for International Settlements	BIS

Source: <http://www.oecd.org/countrylist/0,3349,en_2649_34169_1783635_1_1_1_1,00.html>

Learning assignments

1 What are the three types of risk that a global company is exposed to as a consequence of currency fluctuations?

2 On 14 January 2002 it was announced that the US carrier Jetblue would buy 10 Airbus 320 for US$500 million. The planes were to be delivered over four years (two in 2002, two in 2003, three in 2004 and 2005). Airbus incurs 70 per cent of its cost in euros. What can Airbus Industries do to cover its currency fluctuation risks?

3 Why are most major British global companies in favour of joining the eurozone?

4 What are the benefits and problems for a Japanese firm being listed on the New York Stock Exchange?

5 Why is the Adjusted Present Value (APV) method preferred to the Cost of Capital Adjustment (CCA) method in valuing international projects?

6 How can a company deal with strategic exposure?

7 What is a letter of credit?

8 Why are correlation coefficients between stock market returns so high (Table 13.1)?
9 What type of global financial management tools would a global firm have used to counteract the adverse impacts of the 1997 Asian Crisis?
10 The central finance function is one of the central corporate functions of a conglomerate. Do you foresee a trend towards the formation of a global swapping bank account? What are the pros and cons of implementing such a financial tool?
11 Can companies take advantage of favorable exchange or tax rates and make purchases in different currencies/countries?
12 Name six commodity products which have forward and futures trades. Can you think of a commodity product not related to natural resources which has forward and futures trades?
13 When a global company originates from a country which may not have a sound financial system (e.g. Korea), should its overseas offices/subsidiaries hedge their local currencies against the currency of the head office or hedge it against a foreign currency (e.g. US$), which is less prone to attack from international finance companies (IFCs)?
14 Why do you think the Japanese stock market, in Table 13.1, was not correlated to other markets?

Key words

- Adjusted Present Value country risk (APV)
- Cost of Capital Adjustment (CCA)
- Country stock market beta
- Cross-listing
- Currency swaps
- Documentary credit
- Export credit agencies
- Forward contracts
- Future contracts
- Hedging
- Leading and lagging
- Netting
- Options
- Project valuation
- Strategic exposure
- Transaction exposure
- Translation exposure

Web resources

<http://www.euromoney.com>
Global financial information.

<http://www.imf.org/external/index.htm>
IMF website.

<http://www.euroweek.com/Default.aspx>
Euroweek provides information on the global capital markets spanning Asia, the Middle East, Europe, Africa and the Americas.

Visit the companion website at **http://www.palgrave.com/business/lasserre3e** for a multitude of weblinks and resources, self-test questions for revision and a searchable glossary.

Notes

1 See Eun and Resnick (2001); Hawawini and Viallet (2011).

2 See Hennart (1989), pp. 243–70.

3 This example is reproduced with permission from chapter 13 in Hawawini and Viallet (1999).

References and further reading

Ammer, J. and Jianpoing Mei, 'Strategic Returns to International Diversification', *European Financial Management*, 1(1), 1996.

Bailey, Warren, Peter Y. Chung and Jun-koo Kang, 'Foreign Ownership Restrictions and Equity Price Premiums: What Drives the Demand for Cross-Border Investments?', *Journal of Financial and Quantitative Analysis*, 34(4), 1999, pp. 489–511.

Eun, Cheol S. and Bruce G. Resnick, *International Finance Management*, 2nd edn. New York, NY: McGraw-Hill, 2001.

Giddy, Ian, *Global Financial Markets.* Lexington, MA: D.C. Heath, 1994.

Hawawini, Gabriel and Claude Viallet, *Finance for Executives: Managing for Value Creation.* Cincinnati, OH: South Western Publishing, 1999, 2011.

Hennart, Jean-François, 'Some Empirical Dimensions of Counter Trade', *Journal of International Business Studies,* 21(4), 1989.

International Finance Corporation, *Project Finance in Developing Countries: Lessons from Experience*, 7, 2001.

Lessard, Donald, 'Incorporating Country Risks in the Valuation of Offshore Projects', *Journal of Applied Corporate Finance*, 9(3), 1996.

McCauley, Robert and Steven Zimmer, 'Exchange Rates and International Differences in the Cost of Capital', in Y. Amihud and R. Levich (eds) *Exchange Rates and Corporate Performance.* Burr Ridge, NY: Irwin, 1994.

Sarkissian, Sergei and Michael J. Schill, 'The Overseas Listing Decision: New Evidence of Proximity Preference', Working Paper Series, McGill University and University of Virginia, 2000.

Solnik, Bruno, *International Investments.* Reading, MA: Addison-Wesley, 1996.

Stulz, René M., 'Globalization of Equity Markets and the Cost of Capital', NYSE Working Paper, 99-02, February 1999.

part

III BROAD ISSUES IN GLOBALIZATION

Part III, Broad Issues in Globalization, is particularly concerned with some recent technological and social developments that affect global firms as well as the challenges of the future.

Chapter 14 Emerging global players | Chapter 14 describes the main characteristics of emerging countries, their development paths, and their attractiveness as markets and as offshore operational bases as well as their competitiveness and the role of their global champions.

Chapter 15 The social responsibility of the global firm | Chapter 15 describes the environmental and social issues associated with globalization and the work of global firms: corruption, environment protection, child labor and human rights being among the topics covered.

Chapter 16 Global trends | Finally, Chapter 16 reviews some of the salient trends that can be anticipated in the future and that may affect the development of global firms. The chapter ends by presenting some future scenarios as well as some future global organizational designs.

chapter

14 EMERGING GLOBAL PLAYERS

Introduction

In its 2010 report on global development, the Organisation for Economic Co-operation and Development (OECD) stated: 'Over the past decade, a group of emerging and developing economies has been leading the way in terms of growth and development, shifting the world's economic centre of gravity'. At the micro level, companies like Lenovo or Haier from China, Ranbaxy or Infosys from India, Embraer from Brazil, Gazprom from Russia, SAB from South Africa or Petronas from Malaysia have joined the league of global players traditionally occupied by Western or Japanese multinationals. In the *Financial Times* FT Global list in 2011, there totalled 62 firms from emerging counties while there were only 15 in the 2006 report, and the first on the list was Petrochina. The growing importance of emerging countries companies and markets in the world is today one of the key characteristics of the global business environment. This chapter will describe the main characteristics of emerging countries, their development paths, and their attractiveness as markets and as offshore operational bases, as well as their competitiveness and the role of their global champions. Strategies dealing with emerging countries will also be discussed.

Learning objectives

At the end of the chapter you will be able to:

- understand the characteristics of emerging countries
- identify the market and outsourcing opportunities they offer to global firms
- define the components of business strategies specially designed for emerging countries
- describe the strategic development of competitors coming from emerging countries.

Emerging countries and their development

There is no clear definition of an 'emerging country'. The phrase is often used to describe countries that exhibit:

- a high economic growth
- an increasing development of a middle class
- a high degree of infrastructure investments
- the opening of their market to international trade and investment.

For global firms, emerging countries are source of opportunities, but their business and institutional environments are still significantly different to those in OECD countries.

Three types of emerging country that fulfill those characteristics can be distinguished:

- The emerging giants: Brazil, Russia, India, China, South Africa (BRICS).[1] During the first decade of the twenty-first century, the BRICs are considered as the most powerful representatives of the emerging world; their profile is detailed in Appendix 14.1.
- The Eastern European ex-communist countries, also called the 'transition economies'. Most of those have now joined the European Union and are rapidly moving toward a standard of living comparable to Western countries.
- The industrializing countries of Latin America, Asia or Africa that do not belong to the first group, such as Chile or Malaysia. In this category we find companies that have achieved the status of global champion despite the fact that their economies are still considered as 'developing'.

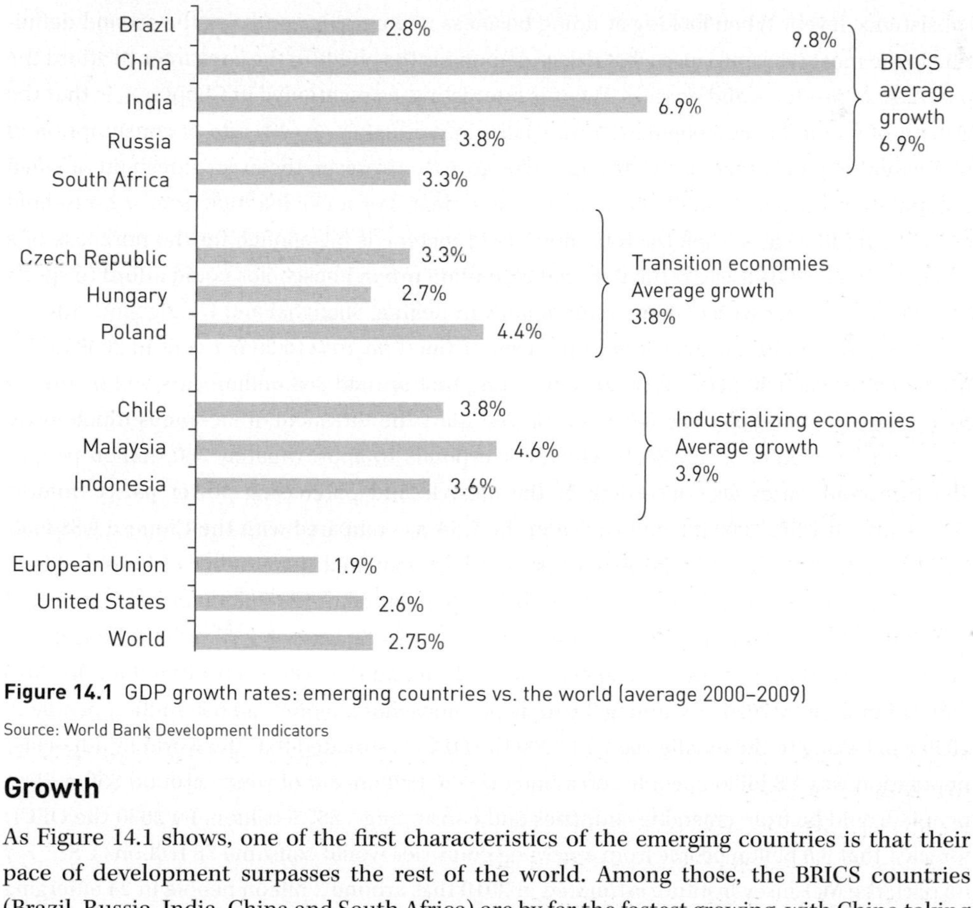

Figure 14.1 GDP growth rates: emerging countries vs. the world (average 2000–2009)

Source: World Bank Development Indicators

Growth

As Figure 14.1 shows, one of the first characteristics of the emerging countries is that their pace of development surpasses the rest of the world. Among those, the BRICS countries (Brazil, Russia, India, China and South Africa) are by far the fastest growing, with China taking the lead. China GDP in dollar terms overtook Japan as the second world economy in 2010.

In 2003, researchers at Goldman Sachs posited that the overall total incremental demand of the then four BRIC countries (Brazil, Russia, India and China) will be *four* times larger by the year 2050 than that of the G6 countries (US, Japan, Germany, UK, France and Italy), at around US$4500 billion versus US$1100 billion.

The incremental demand is due to three factors: a rapidly growing urban middle class, an investment in infrastructure and a drive to conquer international markets.

Middle class

As indicated in Chapter 6, the middle-class effect is a key characteristic of emerging countries. The concept of middle class, although widely used by economists and sociologists, is very vague. The definition of the Swedish middle class, for instance, would differ considerably from the one in Indonesia. The middle class definition can be a purely statistical one (the population that occupies the center on the distribution of income) or it can be a purchasing power one (the population that can afford to purchase goods and services beyond the traditional subsistence level). When looking at doing business in emerging countries the second definition is the most relevant, since what drives demand is the ability of the consumer to afford the purchase of products and services. What is interesting, as mentioned in Chapter 6, is that the growth of a middle-class population translates into a higher growth rate of consumption of non-essential goods than of the average GDP growth. However, the exact threshold of when a population becomes middle class is not very clear. For a car manufacturer a household becomes middle class when the total household income is big enough for the purchase of a car. In China in 2004 it was estimated that 38 million urban households could afford to spend $12,000 to buy a car with cash or credit, mainly in Beijing, Shanghai and Guangzhou. The car ownership rate in urban areas was 12 per cent at the time, rose to 28 per cent in 2009 and is predicted to reach 50 per cent in 2015, meaning that around 360 million cars will be on the road.[2] For a mass retailer like Carrefour or Wal-Mart the threshold of income is much lower and can be evaluated at US$3600, which corresponds to approximately 360 million people. The threshold varies also according to the lifestyle and purchasing power parity: middle class starts at US$25,000 income/capita in the USA as compared with the Chinese US$3600. On that basis the McKinsey Research Institute has estimated the number of households in the middle and upper class in the Chinese urban population at 120 million in 2005, projected to become 454 million in 2015.[3] Euromonitor estimates that around 75 million households in China earned more than US$10,000 a year in 2010 and this will reach 140 million by 2015 and 218 million by 2020.[4] Assuming 3 people per household, more than 650 million people in 2020 will belong to the middle class. In 2009 the OECD estimated that the world middle-class population was 1.8 billion people consuming US$20 trillion, out of which around 850 million people would be from emerging countries and consuming US$7.5 trillion. By 2030 the OECD forecast that 3.8 billion people from emerging countries would consume 38 trillions US$.[5] For its part, the McKinsey institute estimated in 2010 that around 2 billion people in 24 emerging countries are middle class and consume US$6.9 trillion per year, a figure that is expected to rise to US$20 trillion by 2020.[6]

Middle-class population, because of its ability to consume goods and services beyond subsistence level, drives demand in consumer goods both durable and fast moving as well as raw materials, components and intermediate products and associated services.

Investment

The second driver of incremental demand is the investments in infrastructure. The ration of growth capital formation over GDP representing investments in road, housing, telecommunications, transportation, energy etc. in those countries is above the average of industrialized countries (Figure 14.2). In its 2008 World Investment Report, the United Nations Conference on Trade and Development (UNCTAD) has stressed the importance of the need for infrastructure in the developing world and the opportunities that are offered to international as well as local firms to contribute to the investment in those much needed infrastructure projects.[7] Just for Asia, McKinsey has estimated that the investment needs in energy, telecom, transport and water amount to US$8.1 trillion between 2010 and 2020.[8] Infrastructure projects because of their contribution to demand of equipment, raw materials, services and labor have a multiplier effect on income and ultimately demand.[9]

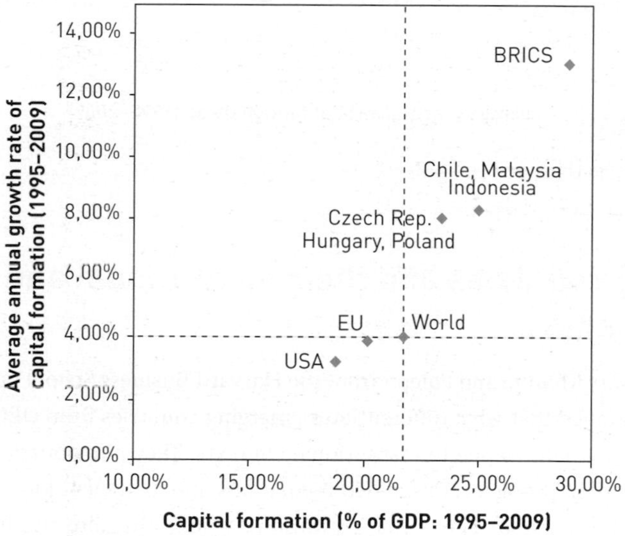

Figure 14.2 Capital formation

Source: World Bank Development Indicators

Opening of markets to international trade and investments

Finally, the third leg of economic development in emerging countries is the opening of their economy to international trade and investment. Over the past two decades, emerging countries have seen a significant increase in their inflow of Foreign Direct Investment (FDI) as well as their participation in international trade (Figure 14.3). Overall international trade is still dominated by industrialized countries but the weight of emerging countries grows very fast. In 2000 the four BRICs countries' share of world trade was 6 per cent; by 2009 it had risen to 12 per cent while their stock of FDI rose from 8 per cent to 11 per cent during the same period. This, together with the two others drivers of growth, contribute to give to the emerging economies a definite attractiveness for global as well as for local firms.

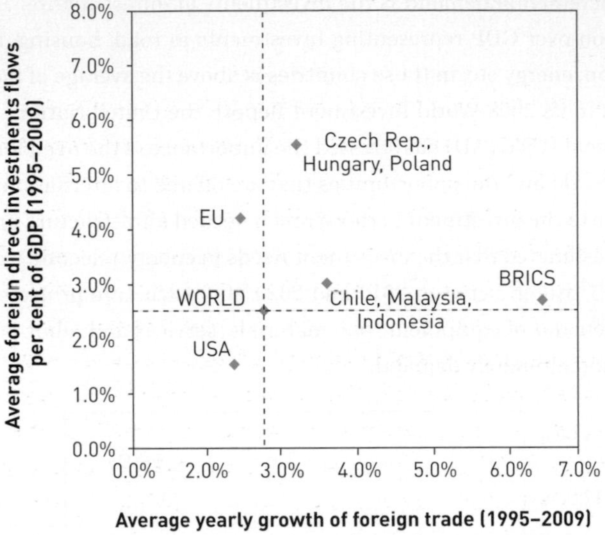

Figure 14.3 Foreign trade and investments

Source: World Bank Development Indicators

Emerging countries and their institutional and business environments

In 1997 Professors Khanna and Palepu from the Harvard Business School published an article in which they argued that what differentiates emerging countries from OECD countries are a number of market failures due to institutional contexts. They pinpointed three such market failures: information problems, misguided regulations and inefficient judicial systems.[10] They later redefined those market failures as 'institutional voids'[11] that directly affect business. They developed a set of questions that companies need to address in order to identify the institutional context related to the political and social system, the openness of government and administration, the product markets, the labor and capital markets.

The overall conclusion is that first companies need to understand the differences, need to adapt their strategies accordingly, but also need to be aware of rapid evolution within those contexts.

Emerging countries and global firms

For global firms the growth and opening of emerging countries has far-reaching consequences for market development as well as for sourcing and localization of productive capacities. Also, emerging countries have created strong firms that raise a competitive challenge to the traditional global firms in their local as well as global markets.

Market opportunities

As mentioned earlier, the emerging middle-class market generates strong demand for fast-moving consumer goods as well as consumer durables, which in turn creates demand for the supply of intermediate products and natural resources along the value chain. However, emerging countries also have a large base of non-middle-class people, what C.K Prahalad called the 'bottom of the pyramid'.[12] According to Prahalad, in emerging countries the largest proportion of the population located at the lower end of the income spectrum are willing to consume goods that are of good quality but obviously cheaper and less sophisticated. This population, contrary to conventional wisdom, is brand conscious and to the extent that their future is to one day become middle class, multinational firms need to capture these market opportunities. This implies that in emerging countries, global firms are advised to adopt a two-pronged strategy: one for the middle class, that looks like, with the relevant adaptation, their traditional approach, and one for the bottom of the pyramid that differs quite a lot from the tradition. Table 14.1 shows the difference between those two approaches.

Table 14.1 Difference between traditional middle-class strategies and bottom of the pyramid strategies

Traditional middle class	Bottom of the pyramid
• Value pricing based on differentiation and segmentation	• Find new price-performances relationships leading to quality at low prices
• Product obsolescence and renewal	• Products built to last
• Products, services, functionalities and packaging are adaptation of industrialized markets	• Products, services, functionalities and packaging are 'reinvented' to fit local conditions
• Advertising on mass TV and media supports	• Communication and advertising rely less on mass advertising and more on educational campaigns using government programs and nongovernmental organizations
• Products designed on 'regular' environments	• Products designed on 'hostile' environments
• Urban areas focus	• Rural focus
• Transfer of technology	• Hybrid technology: combination of advanced and adaptation
• Use of skilled resources	• Deskill the work process
• Build supply chains similar to industrialized world	• Adapt supply chains to local conditions

Sources: Adapted from Prahalad (2005) and Dawar and Chattopadhyay (2002)

At the opposite end of the spectrum, firms making luxury goods find the emerging markets very attractive due to the appearance of a class of 'nouveaux riches' who built their fortune by taking advantage of the benefits of deregulation, economic growth and to a certain extent 'wild capitalism'. A firm like LVMH from France has seen its revenues from emerging countries go from 2 billion euros in 2004 to 5 billion in 2009. Emerging markets account for 30 per cent of the firm's total revenues. Similar trends are observed in companies like Mercedes, BMW, Gucci or Swiss jewelry watches.

Altogether emerging markets see dynamism in the three major segments of the market: upper high end for 'nouveaux riches', middle class and bottom of the pyramid (Figure 14.4), each of them having its own characteristics and each of them offering opportunities to local and international firms that approach them with the appropriate strategy.

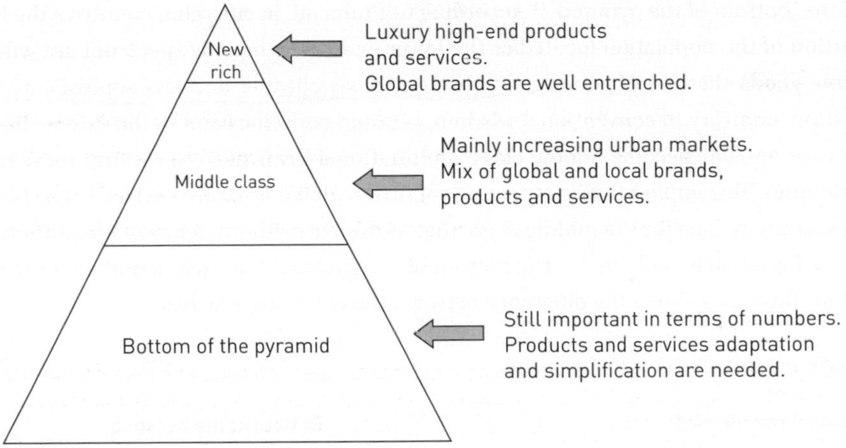

Figure 14.4 The three segments in emerging markets

Strategies for emerging markets

Beyond the classic steps in strategic analysis and formulation that require companies to perform a proper assessment of environments, markets and competition, emerging countries require three decisions to be made: 1) what product/service redesign and adaptation are needed for the selected segments; 2) what level of localization of strategic capabilities is appropriate; 3) is strategic partnership with local firms appropriate?

- *Decide on the kind of product/service redesign and adaptation needed for the selected segment.* As seen earlier there are three types of market segment, each of them with a high level of growth opportunities. Global firms will have to decide whether they want to concentrate on one segment or several segments. This applies particularly to entering and designing products and services for the bottom of the pyramid segment. This approach implies a simplification of products' characteristics. Below are three examples of companies having made the choice to adopt a dual strategy, one for the middle segment and one for the bottom of the pyramid segment.

Multi-segment approach in emerging countries

Saurer

In 2003, Volkman, the German subsidiary of the Swiss company Saurer, was a global leader in textile twisting machines. In China the company had achieved dominance in the high-end market but was not present in the low-end market that represented 70 per cent of the demand. The low-end market was dominated by Chinese competitors that sold machines at half of Volkman's price. The company had to make a decision about whether to develop a simple and low-cost machine. The decision was difficult since it was not part of the engineering culture of the company. Eventually, after the mobilization of a team of young Chinese and German engineers they put on the market a machine that sold at a competitive price with a much simpler performance although of superior quality than competitors. This move proved very successful not only in China but in other emerging countries.

Unilever Brazil

In 1996, while Unilever was the dominant player in the detergent market in Brazil, it developed and marketed 'Ala', a type of detergent that targeted the needs of low-income customers in the North East of the country. This detergent was positioned as a hand washing detergent with a perfume giving the sensation of cleanliness at a cost affordable to the low-income population.

General Electric

In 2010, General Electric in India launched the Mac 400, a portable electrocardiograph equipped with a small printer and with rechargeable batteries that doctors can transport easily and operate in remote villages. This machine was priced at a third of that of conventional machines.

Sources: Saurere: The China Challenge, 2006, IMD case n° 5—0688; Unilever Brazil: Marketing Strategies for Low-Income Customers, 2004, Insead case 04/2004-5188; GE Healthcare: Innovating for Emerging Markets, 2011, Insead Case 311-048-1

- *Decide on the localization of strategic capabilities.*
  According to a study published in 2006, more than 50 per cent of US global firms and 40 per cent of Europeans were planning to enter or expand their sourcing in China before the end of the decade and 36 per cent of US global firms and 27 per cent of Europeans were planning to enter or expand their manufacturing in China before the end of the decade.[13] The phenomenon of purchasing products in emerging countries (offsourcing) and of relocation of manufacturing operations (offshoring) is not new but it has increased considerably since the 1990s. The traditional offshoring and offsourcing were based on low costs and were essentially directed to manufacturing and the procurement of parts, components and OEM products. For instance Wal-Mart was buying for around US$13 billion of Chinese products in 2004 and Carrefour 1.6 billion. Nowadays offshoring and offsourcing encompass all elements of the value chain: R and D, manufacturing and services. Although the cost advantage of buying and producing in emerging countries can be significant and on average be 50 per

cent of the costs of producing in the US or in Europe, global firms find other advantages of doing so: higher flexibility and speed, better responsiveness to change in environments, higher service orientation. Figure 14.5 gives a pictorial representation of the advantages and disadvantages of offshoring and offsourcing in the various elements of the value chain.

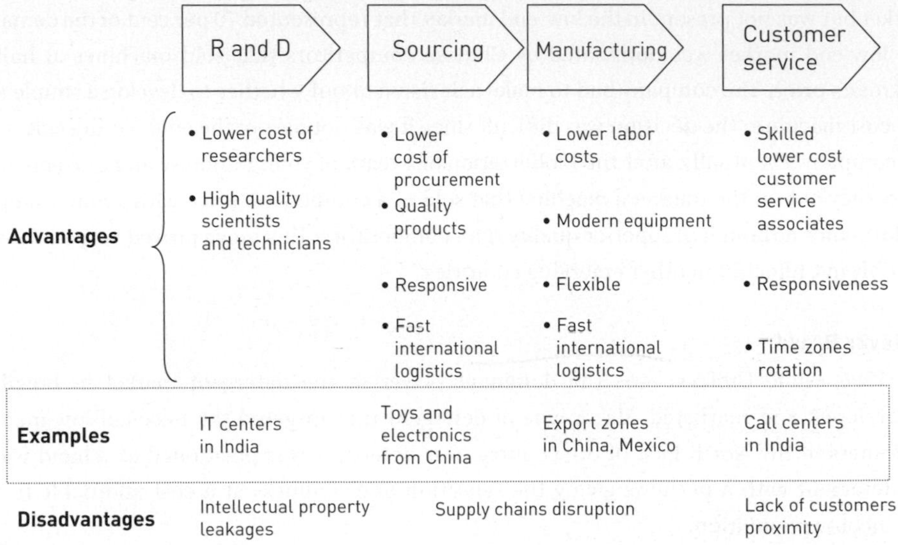

Figure 14.5 Advantages and disadvantages of offshoring and offsourcing in the various elements of the value chain

- *Decide whether to engage in strategic partnership with local firms.*
  The governments of emerging markets are very keen to see local firms engaging in joint ventures with global firms, even if they not force them to do so. In return global firms may benefit from engaging in such partnerships provided that they do a proper job of planning and implementation (as discussed in Chapter 4).

Emerging competitors

Until the 1970s, corporations from the emerging world were viewed as exploiters of cheap labor or imitators of outdated technologies. This perception started to change in the 1970s *vis-à-vis* Japanese corporations, Korean, Brazilian and Taiwanese firms and more recently those from China, India and also Russia. Today the traditional competitive trajectory of those firms is described in Figure 14.6. From a competitive point of view we can observe that multinational firms traditionally concentrate their efforts on the differentiated segment of the markets deploying their competitive advantages based on technology and marketing competences. Emerging markets champions adopt a two-step approach:

- In their protected home markets they concentrate on the lower end segments, benefiting from a low cost base, from imported technology and from their knowledge of the local environment. They succeed in building volume in a market largely ignored by multinational firms
- In the international markets they start first importing low priced products through OEM and

distributors brands and progressively build their own distribution network and later on their foreign presence via acquisitions.

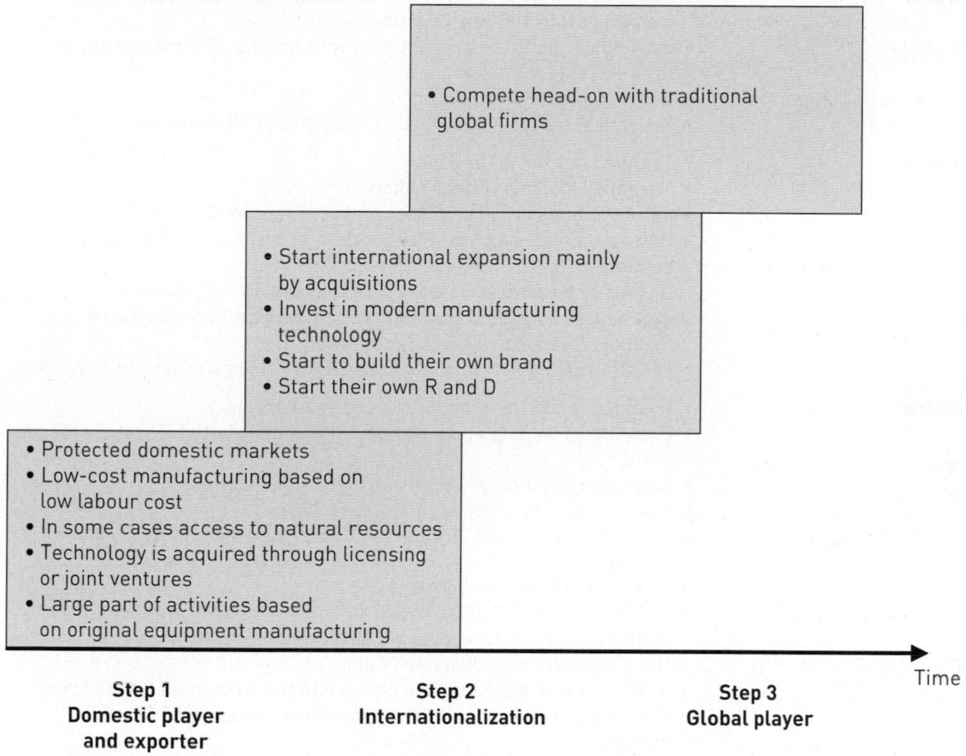
• Compete head-on with traditional global firms
• Start international expansion mainly by acquisitions
• Invest in modern manufacturing technology
• Start to build their own brand
• Start their own R and D
• Protected domestic markets
• Low-cost manufacturing based on low labour cost
• In some cases access to natural resources
• Technology is acquired through licensing or joint ventures
• Large part of activities based on original equipment manufacturing
Time
Step 1
Domestic player and exporter
Step 2
Internationalization
Step 3
Global player

Figure 14.6 The strategic development of emerging markets champions

The competitive dynamic is illustrated in Figure 14.7, while Table 14.2 gives the profile of a selected sample of corporate champions from emerging countries.

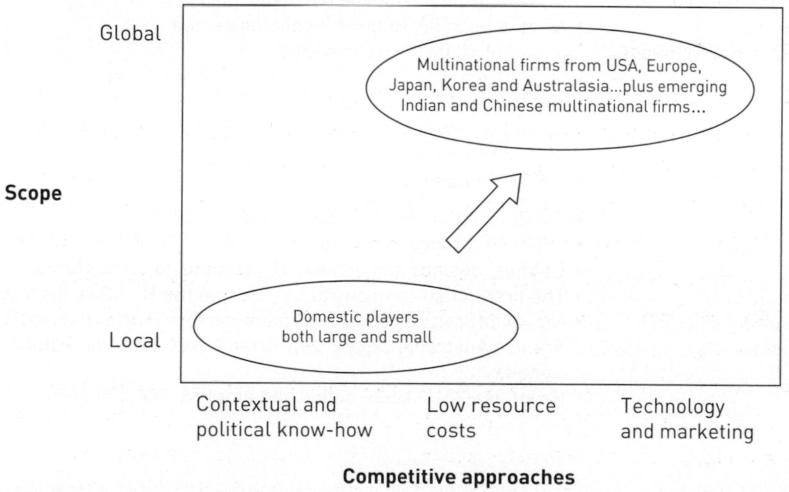
Global
Multinational firms from USA, Europe, Japan, Korea and Australasia...plus emerging Indian and Chinese multinational firms...
Scope
Domestic players both large and small
Local
Contextual and political know-how
Low resource costs
Technology and marketing
Competitive approaches

Figure 14.7 Competitive dynamic of emerging countries champions

Table 14.2 Some examples of emerging countries global champions

China Lenovo Personal computers, servers	• Founded in 1984 in Beijing, (China Academy of Sciences), Listed in KH in 1994 as 'Legend' • Dominated the PC Market in China with around 27% market share • Acquired IBM PC division in 2005 • No. 2 PC maker in the world • Revenues: US$16 billion in 2010. Operates in 60 countries.
China Haier Home appliances, IT	• Founded in 1984 in Qingdao • Revenues in 2010: US$5.6 billion • Sells products in 160 countries and produces in 13 countries • Haier announced its 4th strategic development stage of global brand buiding: *'Guided by business philosophy of CEO Zhang Ruimin, Haier has experienced success in the three historic periods, noted as Brand Building, Diversification and Globalization.'* • By 2011 ranked no.1 in appliances brands in the world by Euromonitor.
China TCL Multimedia, Telecommunication	• Founded in 1981 to produce telephone handsets • Early 1990s went to audio equipment and distributed TV sets produced in HK • Started production on TV sets in 1996 in Shenzen • Became no.1 TV producer in China in 2003 • Expanded production in Vietnam, Philippines, Indonesia, Thailand, Russia • Acquired Scheider in Germany • In 2004 created TTE (TCL Thomson Enterprise with Thomson Multimedia) (TCL owns 67% of the venture) • No. 1 worldwide producer of TV sets • In 2005 fully acquired mobile phone handsets business from Alcatel • Employs 50,000 people in 80 corporations including 18 R and D centers • Revenues were US$8.3 billion in 2010.
China Huawei Telecommunication networks products and solutions	• Started in 1988: digital fixed switch • In 1997: Launched GSM equipment • Established joint R&D labs with Texas Instruments, Motorola, IBM, Intel, Agere Systems, Sun Microsystems, Altera, Qualcomm, Infineon and Microsoft • As of June 2006, Huawei Technologies had a total of 10 joint research labs • In 2000, established R&D centers in Silicon Valley and Dallas, United States • Cisco Systems alleged that Huawei Technologies had infringed some of Cisco's technology patents. Litigation resolved • US$27 billion revenue in 2010.
India Infosys Consulting and IT services	• Established in 1981 by 7 people with US$250 • 1987: First office in the USA • Defines, designs and delivers IT solutions to global firms • The first Indian company to be listed on the NY stock exchange • Has 64 offices and 65 development centers in the USA, India, China, France, Australia, Japan, Switzerland, Netherlands, Poland and Canada • Revenues 2010: US$6 billion and employs 144,000 people.

India Ranbaxy Pharmaceuticals	• Created in 1961, Ranbaxy Laboratories Limited, India's largest pharmaceutical company, is an integrated, research based, international pharmaceutical company. It is ranked amongst the top ten generic companies worldwide. The company has manufacturing operations in 8 countries with a ground presence in 49 countries and its products are available in over 125 countries. Ranbaxy went public in 1973 • Revenues in 2010: US$1.9 billion with 13,000 employees.
India Tata Group Conglomerate	• The Tata Group is one of India's oldest business conglomerates The group's businesses are spread over seven business sectors: Engineering, Chemicals, Materials, Energy, Consumer Products, IT, Communication. It comprises 96 companies operating in six continents. Its sales amounted to US$21.9 billion in 2005 and it employs 202,712 people.
South Africa SABMiller Beer	• SABMiller is one of the world's leading brewers with brewing interests or major distribution agreements in over 75 countries spread across five continents with 70,000 employees. SABMiller owns over 200 brands around the world • Revenues in 2011: US$28.3 billion.
Mexico Cemex Cement	• Founded in 1906, CEMEX has grown from a small local player into a top global building solutions company. Today the company is strategically positioned in the Americas, Europe, Africa, the Middle East, and Asia. It operates in more than 50 countries • Revenues in 2010 totalled US$14.07 billion. It employs 46,500 people worldwide.
Malaysia Petronas Oil and Gas	• Petronas, founded in 1974, is an integrated government-controlled company involved in exploration, production and distribution of oil and gas, petrochemicals, logistics, maritime, and engineering. Originally a domestic player, in 2011 it is a global firm engaged in Myanmar, Turkemenistan, Indonesia, Iraq, Sudan, Uzbekistan, Mozambique, Vietnam, Ethiopia, Congo, Australia, Egypt, Cuba, East Timor, Philippines, Pakistan Its revenues for the year to March 2011 were US$76 billion.
Brazil Embraer	• Founded in 1969, Embraer is a manufacturer of commercial and executive jets as well as defence systems. Embraer has operating units in Brazil, China, USA, France, Portugal and Singapore • Revenues in 2010: US$5.4 billion. It employs 17,200 people.

MINI-CASE 1

PANELSOL Ltd

PANELSOL Ltd is a medium-sized British-German company headquartered in Gibraltar. Its principal manufacturing is in Spain and its research and development center is in Germany. PANELSOL has developed in the photovoltaic segment with a broad customer base ranging from households (distribution through a series of distribution networks), industry and state (government and regional) projects within Europe.

PANELSOL is conscious that the European market has attained a certain maturity. Government and local incentives have been reduced in the last couple of years and competition is quite tough. PANELSOL would like to find new markets for its products and also to improve the

MINI-CASE 1

efficiency of the energy conversion of its solar panels. It judges that an important research and development effort would enable it to develop new generation photovoltaic cells which, in the long run, would have greater energy conversion coefficients and ultimately be cheaper to produce. Its ambition would be to set up a production facility in an emerging country for reaching the local market and to export some elements for its European operations. It would also like to open an R and D center to complement the German laboratory.

PANELSOL strategists have carried out some risk analysis to present to the board, shown in Table 14.3:

Table 14.3 Analysis for possible PANELSOL expansion

	Countries			
	Brazil	**Russia**	**India**	**China**
Solar market				
Solar market potential	Medium high	Medium	High	Very high
Substitute	Many (biofuel, oil)	Many (gas & oil)	Not much	Medium (coal)
Political risks				
Shareholder's exposure	Medium	Medium	Low	Medium
Employer's exposure	Medium	Low	Medium	Medium
Operational exposure	High/Medium	High/Medium	High/Medium	Medium
Economic risks				
Growth	Medium	Medium	High	Very high
Variability	Medium	High	Medium	Low
Inflation	High	Medium	Medium	Medium
Government incentives	High	Low	High	Medium
Solar exposure	Low	High	Low	Medium
Cost of inputs	High	High	Medium	Medium
Exchange risks	Medium	Medium	Medium	Low
Operational risks				
Infrastructure power	Medium	Medium	Medium	Medium
Infrastructure suppliers	Low	Medium	Low	Medium
Administrative complexity	Low	Medium	Low	Medium
Enforcing contracts	Medium	Low	Low	Medium
Competitive risks				
Import protection	Medium	Medium	High	Medium/High
Corruption	High	High	High	High
Networks	Medium	High	Medium	High
Existing competitors	Medium	Low	Low	High

Questions:

Based on the data provided plus your own research:

1) Which country would you select?
2) How do you enter that country?

Source: From a paper written by Pascal Lupton for the course on emerging countries at the University of Geneva, 2011. Reproduced with permission of the author.

MINI-CASE 2

BYD (Build Your Dream)

Founded in 1995 by Mr Wang Chuanfu in Shenzhen in Southern China, BYD (Build Your Dream) is today the largest supplier of rechargeable batteries in the world and has diversified into electronic components, car making and solar energy. Today it has operations primarily in China, India, Hungary and Brazil and employs more than 180,000 people. Its turnover in 2010 was 46 billion RMB (US$6.8 billion).

Mr Wang Chuanfu was a chemist and researcher at Beijing Non-Ferrous Metal Research Institute. He was assigned to be the general manager of a government-owned battery factory. After he read that Japan was going to stop the production of the NiCd1 battery due to environmental concerns, Wang quit his job and founded Shenzhen BYD Battery Company Limited with 2.5 million yuan borrowed from his cousin. It had 20 employees at the start.

When BYD started out by making rechargeable batteries for tools such as electric drills, Wang and his engineers built their own production line, thanks to which cheap labor costs replaced expensive machinery, giving BYD a competitive advantage on price. In 2000 it was qualified as a Li-ion battery supplier for Motorola and in 2002 for Nokia. BYD had to compete not only with traditional Japanese battery makers but more and more with local newcomers who tried to copy BYD's production system.

With increased competition, Wang diversified into mobile phone components such as LCD screens, keypads and modules. Those electronic manufacturing activities became the second leg in the BYD corporate portfolio. In 2008 this division bought the Sino MOS semiconductor, which became a significant part of BYD activities.

However, the major strategic move came on 22 January, 2003 when BYD purchased Xi'an Tsinchuan Auto Co. and entered the auto industry. Immediately Wang replicated in the car industry its method of production based on cheap labor-intensive methods rather than expensive automation. But BYD also had to build an R and D capability and Wang went to top universities and hired thousands of new mechanics and engineering graduates. By the end of 2009, BYD had more than 12,000 engineers working in basic research and development functions. Wang said that he was blessed with engineers who work hard for only 3600 yuan a month. He also engaged in reverse engineering practices, dismantling competitors' products in order to understand and possibly replicate some components. Another practice derived from the battery business was to vertically integrate and manufacture most of the part internally. Wang bought a mold-making factory in Beijing and another in Japan.

The first car produced by the company, the BYD F3, was very much like a Toyota AYGO. In order to fight against possible legal suits, BYD had hired 200 legal people.

In 2007, Warren Buffett's Berkshire Hathaway bought 10 per cent of BYD shares for US$230 million.

By 2008 Wang announced the launch of a hybrid model and a full electric car for 2009.

By 2009 the F3 became a success with 290,000 cars sold and Wang announced his intention to become the No. 1 car maker in China by 2015 and the world's best car maker in 2025.

In the electric car business Wang claimed a competitive advantage in electric car batteries with its lithium-ion ferrous phosphate (LFP) technology.

MINI-CASE 2

However the year 2010 was marked by a decline in profit due to distribution problems.

In 2011 BYD and Daimler signed a memorandum of understanding and announced they will jointly launch electric cars under a new brand in China in 2013 through Shenzhen BYD Daimler New Technology Co. Ltd., a joint venture with a capital of 600 million RMB, combining Daimler's proprietary technologies in vehicle structure and safety areas with BYD's auto battery.

In 2008, BYD signed an agreement with the local government of Shangluo, Shannxi to build a solar power battery plant and announced that it was going to build 5000 MW per year of solar photovoltaic cell manufacturing capacity at a cost of 22.5 billion RMB by 2015. This was considerably more than Suntech Power Holdings Co. Ltd, a major Chinese player in this market, whose current capacity is about 100 MW per year.

The launch of the first pure electric vehicle was announced in January 2010.

In October 2011 BYD opened its North American Headquarters in Los Angeles.

Questions:

1) How do you analyze the success of BYD?
2) Given what you know about the global car industry, do you think that BYD is going to realize its dream to become the number 1 global player? What elements are in its favor?
3) What elements against?

Source: Anna Wang, 'BYD, Build Your Dream', paper, 2010

Summary and key points

1 'Emerging countries' describes countries that exhibit:

- a high economic growth
- an increasing development of a middle class
- a high degree of infrastructure investment
- an opening of their market to international trade and investment.

2 Three types of emerging country fulfill those characteristics:

- The emerging giants, Brazil, Russia, India, China, South Africa (BRICS)
- The Eastern European ex-communist countries, called the 'transition economies'
- The industrializing countries of Latin America, Asia or Africa that do not belong to the first two categories.

3 Economic growth is driven by:

- a rapidly growing urban middle class
- an investment in infrastructure and
- a drive to conquer international markets.

4 The major differences between emerging countries and OECD countries are a number of market failures due to institutional contexts.

5 Global firms benefit from emerging countries for:

- market development
- for sourcing and localization of productive capacities.

6 Emerging countries have a large base of non-middle-class people at the 'bottom of the pyramid'.

7 Strategies for emerging countries consist of deciding:

- the kind of products/services redesign and adaptation needed according to the selected segments
- the localization of strategic capabilities
- whether to engage in strategic partnership with local firms.

8 Emerging countries champions:

- Concentrate on the lower end segments in their protected home markets
- Succeed in building volume in a market largely ignored by multinational firms
- In the international markets they start first importing low-priced products through OEM and distributor brands
- progressively build their own distribution network and later on their foreign presence via acquisitions.

Appendix 14.1 A profile of the BRICS (2009)

	Russia	Brazil	China	India	South Africa
Area (thousand sq km)	16376.87	8459.42	9327.48	2973.19	1214.47
Demography					
Population (million)	141.85	193.73	1331.46	1155.35	49.32
Rural population (% of total population)	27.18	13.96	56.00	70.18	38.78
Population growth (annual 2000–2009 %)	−0.31	1.21	0.61	1.45	1.39
Urban population (%)	72.82	86.04	44.00	29.82	61.22
Life expectancy at birth, total (years)	68.86	72.64	73.31	64.05	51.62
Birth rate, crude (per 1,000 people)	12.40	15.63	11.99	22.45	21.73

	Russia	Brazil	China	India	South Africa
Economic data					
GDP (US$2009)	1232	1594	4985	1377	285
GDP, PPP (billion $ 2009)	2686	2008	9091	3808	507
GDP growth (annual average 2000–2009 %)	5.47	3.29	10.28	7.21	3.63
GDP per capita (current US$)	8.684	8.230	3.744	1.192	5.786
GDP per capita, PPP (Current international $)	18,932	10,367	6.828	3.296	10,278
Adjusted savings: net national savings (% of GNI)	11.39	3.15	42.91	25.22	1.63
Inflation, consumer prices (average 2000–2009 %)	14.0	6.9	1.8	5.5	6.1
Unemployment, total (% of total labor force)	8.16	8.28	4.30	4.29	23.80
Foreign direct investment, net inflows (BoP, current US$)	36.75	25.95	78.19	34.58	5.35
Foreign direct investment, net inflows (% of GDP)	2.98	1.63	1.57	2.51	1.88
Agriculture, value added (% of GDP)	5.00	7.00	11.00	18.00	3.00
Services, etc., value added (% of GDP)	62.00	66.00	42.00	55.00	65.00
General government final consumption expenditure (% of GDP)	20.13	21.81	13.04	11.99	20.98
Household final consumption expenditure, etc. (% of GDP)	53.78	61.74	34.88	55.97	60.45
Gross capital formation (% of GDP)	18.73	16.51	47.66	36.48	19.43
Exports of goods and services (% of GDP)	27.73	11.12	26.74	19.58	27.29
Imports of goods and services (% of GDP)	20.37	11.18	22.33	24.02	28.15
	100.00	100.00	100.00	100.00	100.00
Ease of doing business indicators					
Lead time to import, median case (days)	2.88	3.88	2.56	5.31	3.25
Logistics performance index: ability to track and trace consignments (1 = low to 5 = high)	2.60	3.42	3.55	3.14	3.73
Average time to clear exports through customs	4.58	15.89	6.64	15.00	4.00
Infrastructure					
Fixed broadband Internet subscribers (per 100 people)	9.09	7.51	7.78	0.67	0.98
Internet users (per 100 people)	42.09	39.20	28.84	5.31	8.96
Mobile cellular subscriptions (per 100 people)	162.50	89.79	56.10	45.45	94.15
Telephone lines (per 100 people)	31.58	21.42	23.56	3.21	8.76
Quality of port infrastructure, WEF (1 = extremely underdeveloped to 7 = well developed and efficient by international standards)	3.55	2.65	4.28	3.47	4.66

	Russia	Brazil	China	India	South Africa
Government and society					
Government type	Federal republic	Federal republic	Centralized communist	Federal republic	
Religions	Orthodox 15% Muslim 15%	Catholic 73,6% Protestant 14%	Taoist 4% Buddhist 4% Christian 4% Muslim 1–2%	Hindu 80% Muslim 14%	Christian 85%
Armed forces personnel (1000s)	1495	713	2945	2626	77
Military expenditure % of GDP)	4.33	1.64	2.01	2.69	1.44
Governance indicators (from –2.5 to 2.5)					
Voice and accountability	–0.95	0.51	–1.65	0.47	0.56
Political stability and absence of terrorism	–0.72	0.29	–0.44	–1.19	0.02
Government effectiveness	–0.28	0.08	0.12	-0.01	0.51
Regulatory quality	–0.46	0.18	–0.20	–0.28	0.42
Rule of law	–0.77	–0.18	–.35	0.05	0.06
Control of corruption	–1.12	–0.07	–0.53	–0.33	0.10

Source: Data from World Bank Development Indicators

Note: These indicators combine the views of a large number of enterprises, citizens and expert survey respondents in industrial and developing countries

Learning assignments

1 What are the differences between an emerging country and a developing country?
2 Why is a growing middle class contributing to growth?
3 What benefits do emerging markets champions get from OEM contracts?
4 What are the threats coming from emerging markets champions to Western global firms?

Key words

- BRICS
- Emerging countries champions
- Emerging country
- Institutional voids
- Middle class
- Bottom of the pyramid
- OEM
- Offshoring
- Offsourcing

Web resources

<http://www.securities.com/>
Business information on emerging markets.

<http://www.worldbank.org/>
World Bank website.

<http://www.unctad.org/>
UNCTAD website.

<http://www.emergingmarkets.com/>
List of websites devoted to emerging markets.

Visit the companion website at **http://www.palgrave.com/business/lasserre3e** for a multitude of weblinks and resources, self-test questions for revision and a searchable glossary.

Notes

1 Wilson and Purushothaman (2003).
2 Estimate from Credit Suisse.
3 Farrell, Gersh and Stepehenson (2006), pp. 60–69.
4 Euromonitor International (2010).
5 Karas (2009).
6 Court and Narasimhan (2010), pp. 1–6.
7 UNCTAD (2008).
8 Tahilyani, Tamhane and Tan (2011).
9 Ifzal and Pernia (2003).
10 Khanna and Palepu (1997), pp. 41–51.
11 Khanna, Palepu and Sinha (1997), pp. 2–16.
12 Prahalad (2005).
13 Deloitte Research (2006).

References and further reading

A.T. Kearney, 'The Rise of Emerging Markets in Mergers and Acquisitions', Report 2008, available at <http://www.atkearney.com/images/global/pdf/Emerging_Markets_MandA.pdf>

Besouri, Christopher P., 'A Grassroots Approach to Emerging Market Consumers', *McKinsey Quarterly*, 4, 2006, p. 61–71.

Boston Consulting Group Reports (available at <http://www.BCG.com/>)
-'The 2009 BCG New Global Challengers', January 2009.
-'The 2009 Multilatinas', September 2009.
-'The African Challengers', May 2010.
-'Winning in Emerging Markets Cities', September 2010.
-'The Internet's New Billion', September 2010.

Court, David and Laxman Narasimhan, 'Capturing the World's Emerging Middle Class', *McKinsey Quarterly*, July 2010, pp1–6.

Dawar, Niraj and Amitava Chattopadhyay, 'Rethinking Marketing Programs for Emerging Markets', *Long Range Planning*, 35, (2002), pp. 457–74.

Deloitte Research, *Unlocking the Value of Globalization: A Deloitte Research Global Manufacturing Study*. New York and London: Deloitte, 2006.

Euromonitor International, 'Consumer Lifestyle China', December 2010.

Farrell, Diana , Ulrich Gersh and Elizabeth Stephenson , 'The Value of China's Emerging Middle Class', *McKinsey Quarterly*, 2006 Special Edition.

Gupta, Anil K. and Haiyan Wang, *Getting China and India Right*. Hoboken, NJ: Jossey-Bass, John Wiley & Sons, 2009.

Ifzal, Ali and Ernesto M. Pernia, 'Infrastructure and Poverty Reduction – What is the Connection?', ERDB Policy Brief Series, No. 13, Asian Development Bank, Manila, January 2003.

Karas, Homis, 'The Emerging Middle Class in Developing Countries', OECD Development Centre, Working Paper 285, OECD, Paris, 2009.

Khanna, Tarun and Krishna Palepu, 'Why Focused Strategies May Be Wrong for Emerging Markets', *Harvard Business Review*, July–August, 1997.

Khanna, Tarun, Krishna Palepu and Jayant Sinha, 'Strategies that Fit Emerging Markets', *Harvard Business Review*, June 2005.

Prahalad, C.K, *The Fortune at the Bottom of the Pyramid*. Upper Saddle River, NJ: Wharton School Publishing, 2005.

Redding, Gordon and Michael A. Witt, *The Future of Chinese Capitalism: Choices and Chances*. Oxford: Oxford University Press, 2007.

Shankar, Satish, Charles Ormiston, Nicolas Bloch, Robert Scahus and Vijay Vishwanath, 'How to Win in Emerging Markets', *Sloan Management Review*, Spring 2008, pp. 19–23.

Tahilyani, Naveen, Toshan Tamhane and Jessica Tan, 'Asia's $1 Trillion Infrastructure Opportunity', *McKinsey Quarterly*, March 2011.

UNCTAD, 'Transnational Corporations and the Infrastructure Challenge', World Investment Report 2008, New York and Geneva: UNCTAD, 2008.

Wilson, Dominic and Roopa Purushothaman, *Dreaming with BRICs: the Path to 2050*. Goldman Sachs, Global Economic paper 99, 1 October 2003.

Zoubir, Y. and F.S Lhabitant, *Doing Business in Emerging Europe*. Basingstoke: Palgrave Macmillan, 2003.

chapter

15 THE SOCIAL RESPONSIBILITY OF THE GLOBAL FIRM

Introduction

Globalization has had, and still has, deep social, political and environmental consequences. The effects of globalization on society and general welfare are often challenged on the grounds that globalization tends to widen the gap between the rich and the poor and encourages, supports or generates practices that are detrimental to the well-being of the world population, particularly in developing countries. Global companies, as the agents of globalization, are the front-line targets of critics who blame them for misconduct in a vast array of domains, ranging from global warming, pollution, corruption, and encroachment on human rights, child labor and poor citizenship. This chapter tries to address some of the issues that global companies face in dealing with the societies in which they operate, with a particular emphasis on the kind of 'ethical' dilemma that firms and global managers have to confront in their worldwide operations. Most of these ethical and societal issues are not limited to global enterprises: a purely domestic firm can be confronted with corruption or environmental pollution; this chapter does not pretend to give an exhaustive coverage of business ethics in general, it concentrates only on those related to global operations. Figure 15.1 shows the four main categories of social and ethical issues facing global companies.

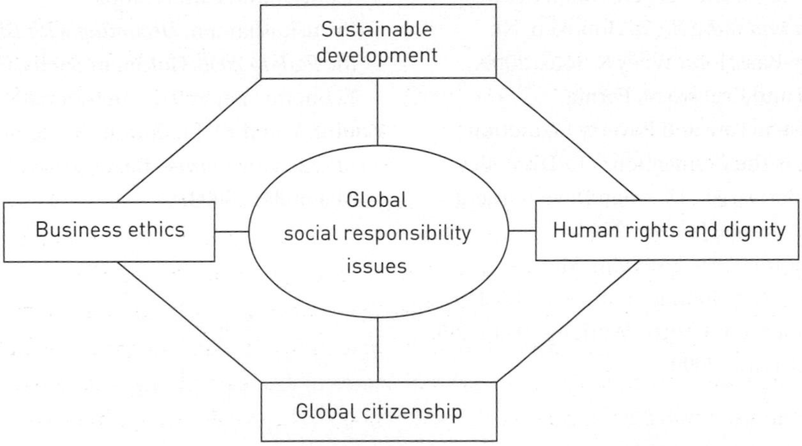

Figure 15.1 Social responsibility issues and the global firm

Learning objectives

At the end of the chapter you will be able to:

- understand the domain of corporate social responsibility
- describe the causes and effects of corruption in business and the role that a global company can play in fighting corruption
- participate in the formulation of environmentally friendly policies
- appreciate the social responsibility of global firms in maintaining appropriate practices with regard to child labor, human rights and labor conditions
- explain the many aspects of global citizenship
- understand the role of codes of conduct and of global nongovernment organizations (NGOs).

Corporate social responsibility

Corporate social responsibility has been defined as 'the obligations of firms to society or more specifically to those affected by corporate policies and practices'.[1] Corporate social responsibility is not new and for a long time dealing with social issues was left to the conscience of individuals, to religious sermons[2] or to legislators. But since the 1960s a series of events (see p. 422) generated a vast global public opinion movement that puts in question the role of multinational corporations (MNCs) with respect to the environment and social matters and pushed corporations to enforce policies and communicate about their practices with regard to their responsibilities in those domains, hence the development of social reporting. Today environmental, ethical and social issues are considered at the top of the list of corporate concerns and it engages a multiplicity of organizations that interact and form an 'ethical web' as described in Figure 15.2.

An ongoing debate

In 1970, Milton Friedman wrote an article in the *New York Times* entitled: 'The social responsibility of business is to increase its profits'[3] in which he claims, first, that only individuals can have responsibilities and, second, that it is not the responsibility of business executives to spend shareholders' money on tasks that are elected legislators' duties. This extreme line of thinking has been strongly challenged on philosophical grounds as well as practical ones: today it is admitted that '*the debate is no longer whether to make substantial commitments to corporate social responsibility but how*'.[4] For some, being responsible is a hypocritical application of self-interest: '*doing well by doing good*'. Given the negative commercial consequences that can be attached to misconduct, self-enlightened companies are better off by taking care in their practices and communication of significant issues such as environmental protection, the fight against corruption or the protection of human rights. Although corporate social responsibility seems well accepted now, there are still some companies that deny the responsibility of corporations in certain issues such as global warming or the free licensing of medical treatment for AIDs in the developing world. Hypocritical behavior is also experienced by managers who '*feel strong organizational pressure to do things that they believe are sleazy, unethical and sometimes illegal*',[5] despite the fact that officially their company claims to be socially responsible. With the increasing globalization of the world and the variety of ethical conducts as well as the increasing global issues such as climate change or terrorism, multinational firms are forced willingly or unwillingly to confront their responsibility in those areas listed in Figure 15.1

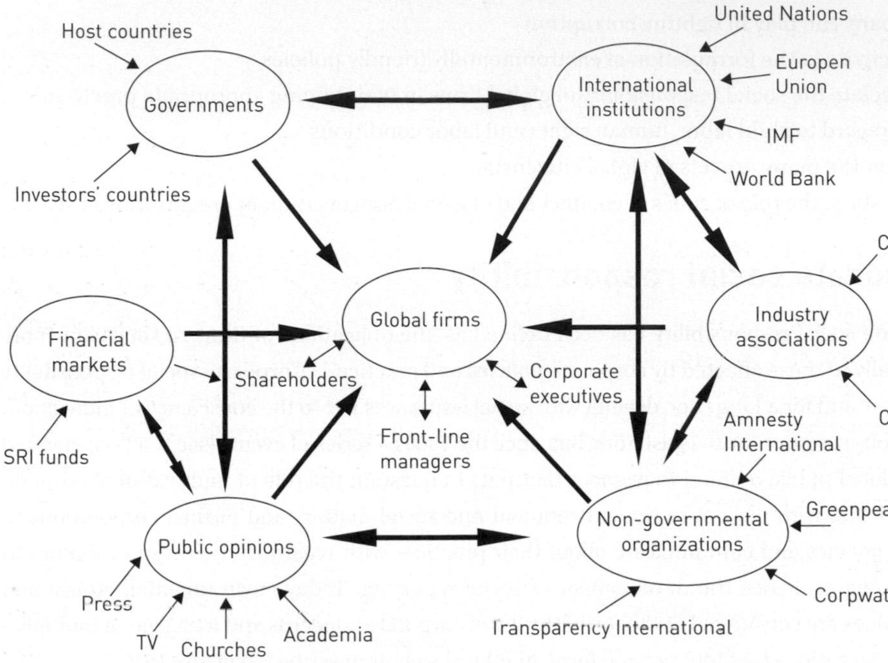

Figure 15.2 The global ethical web

Note: The list of organizations is not exhaustive

WHAT SPARKED THE CORPORATE RESPONSIBILITY MOVEMENT?

In February 1976, a Lockheed executive revealed that the company had paid bribes to Japanese government officials in order to sell its aircraft. The ensuing scandal accelerated the enactment of America's Foreign Corrupt Practices Act of 1977.

In 1984, a gas leak at a pesticide plant of Union Carbide in Bhopal, India, killed more than 2000 people.

In 1988, the Asian-American Free Labor Association (AAFLA, a branch of the AFL-CIO trade union) found that Nike, the sporting goods company, used contractors in Indonesia who were breaking Indonesian labor laws and paying workers below-subsistence wages.

In 1995, environmentalists from Greenpeace occupied a Brent Spar oil rig in the North Sea to prevent Shell going through with their original plan to dump the rig in the water. This triggered a complete re-evaluation of the company's policies and practices that led to the yearly Shell Report on sustainable development.

Global companies and business ethics

Business ethics has been defined as '*the critical, structured examination of how people and institutions should behave in the world of commerce*'.[6] It encompasses issues of conflict of interests, financial and accounting integrity, corruption and bribery, ethical advertising, bioethics and employee privacy. Those issues are not specific to international business but the differences in legislation, cultures and practices make the implementation of ethical behavior more subject to what is known as 'ethical dilemma'.[7] Ethical dilemma describes moral conflicts that occur when a morally right choice may generate a bad outcome or when a morally wrong choice may result in a good outcome. For instance, terminating the contract to a supplier who employs children is an example of making a morally right choice but may result in a bad outcome, the loss of income to poor families. Paying a bribe to buy back the freedom of prostitutes is a morally wrong choice that may result in a good outcome. It has been argued that despite a strong temptation to postpone or shelve those difficult decisions, the resolution of ethical dilemmas is the responsibility of business managers who need to be guided by the key principle of transparency. According to Sir Adrian Cadbury, '*actions are unethical if they don't stand scrutinity*'.[8] The remainder of this section will be devoted to one of the most predominant and worrying ethical issues in global business: the practice and effects of corruption and bribery.

Corruption and bribery

According to the World Bank Institute, more than US$1 trillion is paid in bribes each year, 3.3 per cent of the world GDP or the equivalent of the size of the Canadian economy. In certain countries this may represent as much as 20 per cent of GDP. The same stream of research '*shows that countries that tackle corruption and improve their rule of law can increase their national incomes by as much as four times in the long term, and child mortality can fall as much as 75 percent*'.[9] Corruption is therefore considered as one of the main global business issues.

Corruption can be simply defined as '*the abuse of entrusted power for private gain*'.[10] This definition applies to public officials as well as employees of private companies who receive a personal benefit (a *bribe*) in the form of a cash or non-cash advantage (such as a car, family travel or the employment of a relative) and, in return, give a preferential advantage to the donor. Transparency International (TI), a nongovernmental organization (NGO, see below) regularly publishes two indices: the Corruption Perception Index (CPI) and the Bribe Payers' Index (BPI). The CPI is a score that relates to the perceptions of corruption in different countries as seen by business, academics and risk analysts. It represents a compilation of different surveys. The BPI ranks the leading exporting countries in terms of the degree to which their companies are perceived to be paying bribes abroad. This index is based on extensive interviews done by Gallup International Association with senior executives, bankers, lawyers and accountants.

Table 15.1 gives the 2011 CPI and BPI.

The Chairman of Transparency International, at the launch of the results of the 2001 index, declared: '*There is no end in sight to the misuse of power by those in public office and corruption levels are perceived to be as high as ever in both developed and developing worlds*'.[11]

The industries in which corruption is most acute are: public works contracts and construction, arms and defense, power (including petroleum and energy), mining, telecoms, aerospace and banking. Although the practice of corruption is not limited to global enterprises, their visibility and power give them a particular responsibility to, as well as a great impact on, the societies in which they operate.

Table 15.1 Corruption indices

Corruption Perceptions Index (CPI) 2011			**Bribe Payers' Index (BPI) 2011**		
(measures perceived levels of public sector corruption) From 0 = highly corrupt to 10 = highly clean) Out of 183 countries			(evaluates the likelihood of foreign bribery) (From 0 = high level of bribery to 10 = low level) Out of 28 countries		
Low corruption			*Low propensity to bribe*		
1	New Zealand	9.5	1	Netherlands	8.8
2	Denmark	9.4	1	Switzerland	8.8
2	Finland	9.4	3	Belgium	8.7
4	Sweden	9.3	4	Germany	8.6
5	Singapore	9.2	4	Japan	8.6
6	Norway	9.0	6	Australia	8.5
7	Netherlands	8.9	6	Canada	8.5
8	Australia	8.8	8	Singapore	8.3
9	Switzerland	8.8	9	United Kingdom	8.3
10	Canada	8.7	10	United States	8.1
			11	France	8.0
High corruption			*High propensity to bribe*		
172	Equatorial Guinea	1.9	19	India	7.5
172	Venezuela	1.9	19	Turkey	7.5
175	Haiti	1.8	22	Saudi Arabia	7.4
175	Iraq	1.8	23	Argentina	7.3
177	Sudan	1.6	23	United Arab Emirates	7.3
177	Turkmenistan	1.6	25	Indonesia	7.1
177	Uzbekistan	1.6	26	Mexico	7.0
180	Afghanistan	1.5	27	China	6.5
180	Myanmar	1.5	28	Russia	6.1
182	Korea (North)	1.0			
182	Somalia	1.0			

Source: Transparency International: <http://www.transparency.org>. The 2011 **Corruption Perceptions Index (CPI)** measures the perceived levels of public sector corruption in 183 countries around the world and the 2011 **Bribe Payers' Index (BPI)** evaluates the supply side of corruption: the likelihood of firms from the world's industrialized countries to bribe abroad.

There is vigorous debate about the exact limits of corruption (When does it start?), its origin (Why?), its real effect (Is corruption having a negative effect?) and its practice (How is corruption activated?).

When gifts become bribes, where does corruption start?

It is current practice in some countries to offer gifts as recognition of friendship and relationships.[12] The boundary between a bribe and a gift is frequently ambiguous, but the common rule would be to consider as a gift a present offered openly whose content can be disclosed in the person's professional and social environment. Gifts can also be offered to communities (school sponsoring, donation to communities, etc.), the rule still being that it must be openly offered. Beyond the frontiers of transparency, the land of bribery begins.

In the United States the Foreign Practice Act of 1977 that exposes American executives to criminal sanctions strictly forbids bribery. Such legislation does not exist in other countries, although the Convention on Combating Bribery on Foreign Public Officials in International Business Transactions adopted by the OECD on 21 November, 1997 has been ratified by nearly 30 countries. This convention prohibits the use of bribes, states that criminal sanctions should be applied to the persons engaged in bribery, and recommends that tax deductibility of bribes should not be permitted.[13] The OECD convention, however, has a lower dissuasive power than the American Foreign Practice Act.

Causes and effects of corruption

The causes of corruption are diverse,[14] and belong to five main categories:

- *Administrative resource allocation*: when transparent market mechanisms are substituted by administrative authorization and distribution. Price controls, multiple exchange rates, subsidies and administrative authorizations granted without competitive bidding are mechanisms that induce corruption.
- *Lack of institutional checks and balances and information*: absent or powerless public audit, single source of power without right of appeal, cowed legal system.
- *Insufficient funding of public services*: leading to low remuneration of public officials relative to private sector, lack of proper financing of political parties or under-supply of public goods for hospitals, transport and schools.
- *Social and cultural factors*: such as a societal division along ethnic and linguistic lines leading to nepotism.
- *Natural resources*: abundant natural resources are also an incentive for bribery.[15] This is more prevalent in developing countries; as Figure 15.3 shows, there is a positive correlation between GDP per capita and the CPI. Countries that formerly had a planned economy score lower on the scale.

Several studies converge to demonstrate the adverse effects of corruption on the economy.[16] The effects are both direct and indirect.

Direct effects

We can list three in particular:

- It *discourages domestic and foreign indirect investment* because of the additional cost burden on projects: it amounts to another *hidden tax.* If India could reduce its corruption level to Singapore's level, the effect on foreign investment would be the same as a reduction of the corporate tax rate by 22 per cent.[17] Corruption thus hampers economic growth.
- It *skews public capital expenditure* in favor of new equipment as opposed to maintenance and operational expenditures. It also discriminates against educational and health expenditure, which are less amenable to bribery.
- It *reduces the productivity of public investments* and reduces the *collection of taxes.*

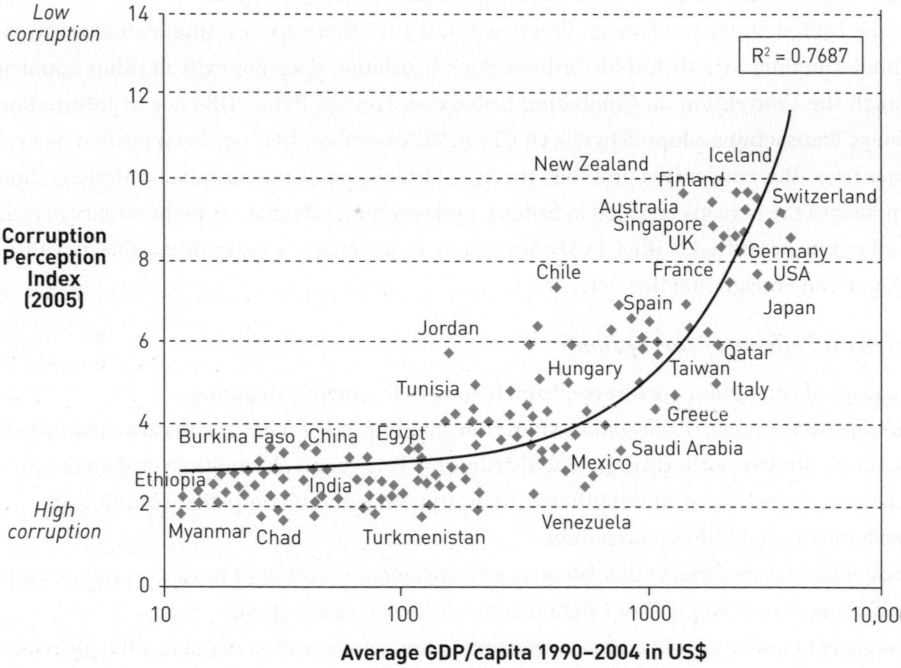

Figure 15.3 Corruption and development

Source: World Bank, World Development for the growth rate and Transparency International for the Corruption Perception Index, http://www.transparency.org

Indirect effects

The most common:

- *Reduction in work productivity as a result of demotivation*
- *Dislocation of social fabric*
- *Loss of integrity inside the bribe-giving companies: employees may feel authorized to benefit from corrupt practices for themselves*
- *Corruption money is often linked to criminal and terrorist activities*

Although some economists have argued that corruption facilitates transactions in inefficient markets and therefore is a form of '*grease, speeding the wheels of commerce*',[18] the negative effects are overwhelmingly dominant.

The practice of corruption and the role of global companies

Many companies, despite the damaging, economic and social effects, engage in bribery to obtain contracts. Companies coming from countries that are themselves 'immune' from corrupt practices bribe officials or executives from other countries. This paradoxical behavior[19] is attributed to competitive necessities ('If I don't my competitor will and my shareholders and employees will lose out') as well as cultural justifications ('In Rome do as the Romans do'). Performance and rewards systems that focus entirely on economic achievements also induce local managers to engage in corrupt practices in order to 'make the figures', even in corporations that officially assert a global code of ethics. As a result, many global firms implicitly put their managers in a schizophrenic position.[20] The distribution of bribes is often delegated to a third party such as an agent or a joint venture partner.

In the late 1990s some firms, as well as private and public international institutions, created platforms to fight against corruption and introduce practical codes of conduct within global firms. In addition to the OECD Convention on Combating Bribery of Foreign Public Officials in International Business Transactions, and the US Foreign Practice Act mentioned earlier, the most prominent private and nongovernment organization is Transparency International.[21]

Transparency International (TI) is an international NGO based in London organized in national chapters in 77 countries. The stated mission is 'to curb corruption by mobilizing a global coalition to promote and strengthen international and national integrity systems'. Its activities consist of distributing information about corrupt practices and ways to fight against them. It has launched an annual awards program to honour individuals and organizations around the globe that are making a difference in ending corruption. The goal is to give greater recognition to the efforts of journalists, civil society workers, activists, government and corporate whistleblowers who work to investigate and unmask corruption, often at great personal risk. The Integrity Awards also seek to encourage those whose example provides leadership in the global anti-corruption effort. It publishes the CPI and the BPI as well as a Global Corruption Report. It gives free access to a Corruption On-Line Research and Information System and its national chapters implement a large variety of activities to inform about and fight against corruption. In a recent book (Pope, 2000), TI draws 32 lessons that constitute a source of inspiration and guide for action. Table 15.2 gives a checklist of the most common measures that governments and companies can take to fight corruption.

Other anti-corruption initiatives

Other organizations have issued guidelines and regulations to prevent corrupt practices. Among them:

- The UN **General Assembly** in 1996 adopted a *Declaration against Corruption and Bribery*

- The **International Chambers of Commerce** in 1977 issued the *Rules of Conduct on Bribery.*
- The **World Bank** in 1995 issued *procurement guidelines* in order to prevent corruption in projects financed by the bank.
- The **Council of Europe** in 1994 created a Multidisciplinary Group on Corruption and in 1997 issued the *Guiding Principles for the Fight against Corruption* and in 1999 a *Criminal Law Convention on Corruption.*
- **The Caux Round Table**. Founded in 1986, the Caux Round Table is a network of senior business leaders from both the industrialized and developing nations who recognize that business must take a leadership role in developing a more fair, free and transparent society, leading to greater world prosperity and sustainability of resources.

Despite all this effort, there is still a long way to go before bribery disappears, but global firms and global executives are under increasing public scrutiny and the most progressive firms have made considerable progress in the implementation of ethical behavior.

Table 15.2 A checklist of anti-corruption measures

For the public sector • Issue and implement anti-corruption legislation • Adopt human resource policies for public officials based on transparency for recruitment, fair remuneration and adequate education • Establish an enforceable code of conduct for public employees • Set up transparent, open and fair public procurement procedures • Simplify regulations and procedures and limit or suppress administrative authorizations in the hand of single officials • Set up a system of transparent reporting and control • Do not allow tax reduction for non-transparent money transfer (List based on the United Nations Convention Against Corruption)
For the private sector • Disclose publicly and make widely known its endorsement of the Anti-Corruption Measures • Establish a clearly articulated written policy prohibiting any of the firm's employees from paying or receiving bribes and 'kickbacks' • Implement the policy with due care and take appropriate disciplinary action against any employee discovered to have made payments in violation of the policy • Provide training for employees to carry out the policy, and provide continuing support, such as helplines, to assist employees to act in compliance with the firm's policy • Record all transactions fully and fairly, in accordance with clearly stated record-keeping procedures and accounting controls, and conduct internal audits to assure that all payments made are proper • Report annually on the firm's bribery and corruption policy, along with a description of the firm's experiences implementing and enforcing the policy • Have the annual report audited either by an independent financial auditor or an independent social auditor, or both • Require all agents of the firm to affirm that they have neither made nor will make any improper payments in any business venture or contract to which the firm is a party • Require all suppliers of the firm to affirm that they have neither made nor will make any improper payments in any business venture or contract to which the firm is a party • Establish a monitoring and auditing system to detect any improper payments made by the firm's employees and agents • Report publicly any solicitations for payments whenever such reporting will not lead to harsh reprisals of material consequences to the company or its employees (or report privately to a monitoring organization, such as Transparency International or a social auditor) • Establish a system to allow any employee or agent of the firm to report any improper payment without fear of retribution for their disclosures (List established by the Caux Round Table Global Dialogue in September 2000 in Singapore)

Global companies and sustainable development

The concept of sustainable development was first introduced by the World Commission on Environment and Development, in what is known as the 'Bruntland Report'[22] and was defined as '*development that meets the needs of the present without compromising the ability of future generations to meet their own needs*'. According to the World Business Council for Sustainable Development, '*development means the building of societies in which people are able to enjoy security, good health, decent housing, clean water and modern power supplies*'. To be sustainable the development demands a respectful, careful and possibly renewable utilization of natural resources as well as the protection of the ecological system. Sustainable development is the subject of global meetings attended by political leaders discussing the kind of measures that can be taken to preserve the planet. The first of such meetings was held in Rio de Janeiro in 1992, which stated a declaration of principles in 27 recommendations.[23]

The main environmental issues are listed in Table 15.3.

All companies are concerned with sustainability but some industries bear a larger responsibility in dealing with sustainable development. These are to be found in the extractive and energy industries (oil, mining, forestry), biotechnology and agro business (genetically modified organisms), chemical, pulp and paper. Multinational and global firms in those sectors plus others are permanently challenged on the grounds that they are contributing to the degradation of the environment. The most common issues that multinational corporations are confronted with are:

- Global warming and CO_2 emissions
- Control of suppliers
- Eco-friendly capital investments
- Waste disposal in the developing world
- Effects on monocultures, deforestation and intensive agriculture.

Global warming and CO_2 emissions

One of the most prominent environmental issues is the increasing warming of the planet due to greenhouse effects resulting from the emission of CO_2. Global emissions of CO_2 were 23,900 million tonnes in 1996, four times the level of 1950 and mainly from industrialized countries (Figure 15.4). Without proper control of the 'greenhouse effect', the emission of CO_2 and other gases threatens to raise the average temperature of the globe, inducing a rise in sea-levels and other natural disasters (Figure 15.5). Industries are the major producers of CO_2 and without proper control the whole ecology of the planet may be disrupted. CO_2 emissions are due to natural as well as human induced industrial development causes. The long-term effects of global warming are potentially dramatic in terms of human health, natural disasters, farming and human settlements.

There is a scientific and political controversy on the exact role that industries play in this phenomenon but the magnitude of the potential consequences are such that following a United Nations assessment on climatic change published in 1990, 154 nations signed in 1992 a United Nations Framework Convention on Climate Change in Rio de Janeiro, inciting members to adopt policies to reverse the trend. This led to the Tokyo Protocol in 1997 that provided binding commitment for industrialized countries to reduce their yearly emission of greenhouse gases (GHG) by 5 per cent between 2008 and 2020.[24] Since then yearly regular meetings called 'Conference of the Parties' have taken place in various part of the world. In 2009, big hopes were put on the Copenhagen meeting where ambitious goals were set but unfortunately no agreement could be found. By the end of 2011, 191 countries had signed and ratified the protocol, with the notable exception of the USA and Canada. The USA have not ratified the protocol on the basis that it would hamper economic development without the scientific evidence that it will really help the issue. As a consequence of the ratification of the treaty by many industrialized countries, companies in those countries are committed to implementing actions leading to reduction of CO_2 emissions.

Table 15.3 List of environmental issues linked to industrial and agricultural activities

Industry	Possible negative effects
Agriculture and plantation	• Ecosystem conversion to agriculture or forest • Fragmenting habitats • Introduction of non-native species • Pollution of ecosystems through farm chemical run-off • Genetic homogenization through monoculture use • Erosion, siltation, etc.
Fisheries	• Destruction of habitats through damaging fishing practices • Potential over-fishing of target species or by-catch species • Introduction of non-native species • Pollution of marine and freshwater ecosystems through effluent discharge, excessive nutrient and chemical loading (aquaculture), noise
Natural forests	• Habitat loss or fragmentation through forest clearing and infrastructure construction • Pollution of forest ecosystems through effluents and noise • Erosion and associated effects • Colonization of natural areas facilitated through infrastructure and access provision
Oil production	• Pollution of ecosystems through spills • Destruction of ecosystems through infrastructure construction • Pollution of ecosystems through extraction (e.g. effluents, noise, etc.) • Emission of greenhouse gases
Mining	• Pollution through leaching etc. • Habitat destruction through infrastructure construction • Pollution of ecosystems linked to use of inputs in extraction (e.g. effluents, noise, etc.)
Transport and related infrastructure	• Facilitating access to fragile ecosystems, fragmenting habitats, pollution • Use of land for transport infrastructure • Water pollution and over-use destroying habitats and ecosystems • Pollution associated with transport use, including greenhouse gas and air pollution emissions
Industry and distribution	• Pollution of ecosystems • Loss of habitat through infrastructure development • Emission of greenhouse gases • Waste disposal (electronic components, batteries, etc.) • Packaging
Energy production	• Emission of greenhouse gases • Destruction of ecosystems through infrastructure construction • Disposal of radioactive waste

Source: *OECD Environmental Outlook*, OECD: Paris, 2001

One initiative that is conducive to the reduction of CO_2 is carbon trading through regulated market mechanisms. The most utilized market mechanisms are the *cap-and-trade*. *Cap-and-trade* are schemes by which a regulatory body sets a limit (a cap) on the amount of CO_2 that companies are allowed to emit. Companies that emit more than their cap have to purchase, at a price credits from a company that is below the cap. Carbon credits can be traded in Exchanges such as the European Union Emission Trading System (EU ETS) that was launched in 2005[25] (see box below).

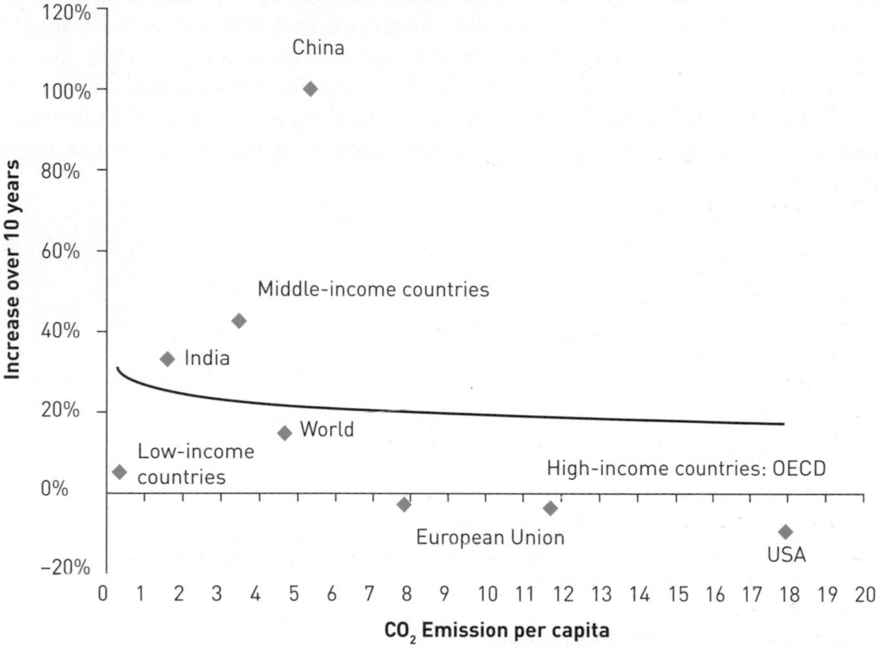

Figure 15.4 Industrial CO_2 emissions, 1998, metric tons per capita

Source: World Bank <http://data.worldbank.org/indicator/EN.ATM.CO2E.PC>

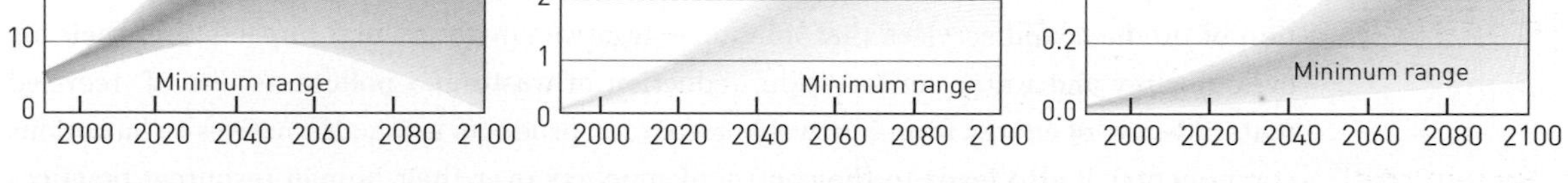

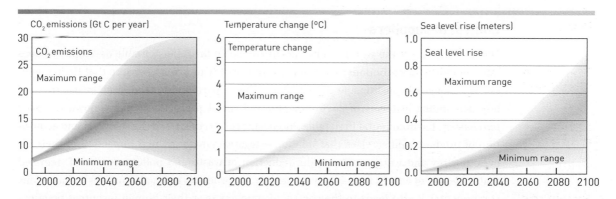

Figure 15.5 CO_2, temperature and sea level projections

Source: Intergovernmental Panel on Climate Change (2001) reproduced in *United Nation Framework Convention on Climate Change: The First Ten Years*, Bonn, Germany, Climate Change Secretariat, 2004, UNFCC, 2004 p. 22

THE EU EMISSIONS TRADING SCHEME (EU ETS)

The EU Emissions Trading Scheme (EU ETS) is a cap-and-trade system in which participation is mandatory for businesses in the following sectors: energy production (combustion, refinery, coke ovens), ferrous metal production , cement and lime, ceramics and bricks, glass, pulp and paper. In 2012 aviation will be added. Under the scheme individual industrial sites are granted an allowance (EUA allowance) that gives the right to emit a certain level of CO_2 (one ton of CO_2 equals one allowance). Companies that emit below the level of their allowances can sell their excess allowances at a market price (see Figure 15.6). Companies that emit more than their allowance can buy extra allowance on the market. Allowances are granted for each individual plant, via a National Allocation Plan in each EU member state and approved by the commission. Around 12,000 companies across Europe are participating in this scheme.

Figure 15.6 Spot prices for CO_2 (EUA in euros)

Source: Bloomberg: <http://www.bloomsberg.com/quote/EUETSSY1:IND>

Control of suppliers

Outsourcing across the world is a key feature of global firms. Sustainable development does not stop at the firms' boundaries. It is the responsibility of firms to ensure that their suppliers are engaged in sustainable development. This is particularly true in countries that are less demanding in terms of environmental and social protection. Often known as '*green purchasing*', Environmental Preferable Purchasing (EPP) consists of the selection and acquisition of products and services that minimize negative environmental impacts over their life cycle (energy and water conservation, reduction of waste and pollutants, use of recycled materials, use of energy from renewable resources, products using alternatives to hazardous components). It also leads to the control of suppliers over their human resources practices prohibiting forced labor, child labor and discriminatory employment.

Green purchasing is adding sustainable issues to the classic price/performance criteria used in the evaluation of suppliers. It implies that an audit and control of the respect for those criteria are exercised by the buyer. It also requires appropriate training of suppliers for adoption of good practice in sustainable development.[26]

Eco-friendly capital investments

Factories and facilities built for domestic and global expansion should be designed with a low environmental impact. Figure 15.7 represents in diagrammatic format all the elements that need to be taken into consideration when planning an industrial investment.

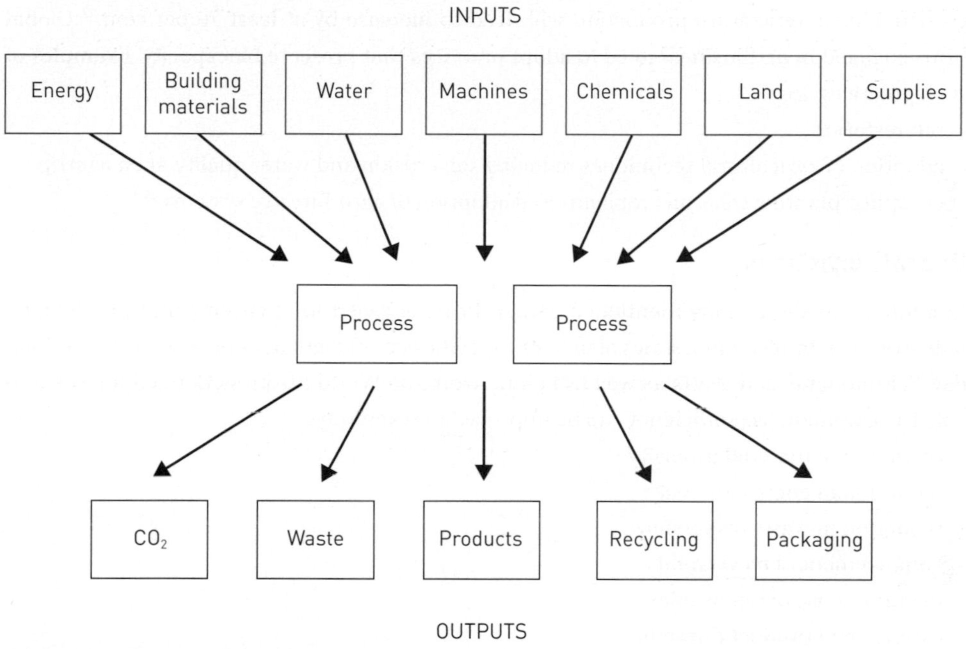

Figure 15.7 Eco-investment components

In the developing world of Asia, Africa and Latin America careful attention has to be given to:

- the potential disruption to the eco-system: deforestation, water requirements
- the potential disruption to the social and cultural environment
- the appropriateness of the technology transfer with regard to the existing environment and capabilities.

Waste disposal in the developing world

Because of their lack of financial resources and their quest for international currencies, many developing countries are keen to accept waste that is not tolerated in the developed world. This concerns particularly the dismantling of electronics equipment, vessels, machineries, computers and nuclear residues that contain a lot of hazardous materials.

Effects on monocultures, deforestation and intensive agriculture

Agro-based industries, forestry and pulp and paper are particularly concerned with sustainability issues. The main sustainable problems associated with these industries are:

- soil erosion due to intensive agriculture
- loss of rain forest due to deforestation
- reduction of bio-diversity
- depletion of water resources
- disruption of traditional farming.

However, it is estimated by the Food and Agriculture Organization that due to population growth, global agriculture production will need to increase by at least 70 per cent.[27] Global firms engaged in agribusiness need to adopt practices that preserve biocapacity. Examples of such practices are:

- reforestation
- adoption of agricultural techniques reducing soil erosion and water quality, such as strip cropping, planting trees on croplands and adoption of agro-forestry systems.[28]

Overall practices

In addition to the actions mentioned earlier, firms engaged in environmental problematic industries can implement a series of industry specific eco-efficient actions. According to Holliday, Schmidheiny and Watts as well as Lehni[29] from the World Business Council for Sustainable Development, eco-efficiency can be improved in seven ways:

- reduction in material intensity
- reduction in energy intensity
- reduction in waste dispersion
- enhancement of recyclability
- maximum use of renewables
- extension of product durabilit
- increase of service intensity.

Global corporations and human dignity

Global executives are often confronted with the issue of procuring components, materials or services in countries that do not respect normal labor practices. The most significant are the utilization of school-aged children as workers, the lack of respect for acceptable working hours and working conditions, forced labor, the exploitation of legal and illegal immigrants or the obstruction or elimination of trade unions. Other issues are linked to the activities of global companies in countries where human rights are not protected and abuses such as forced labor, arbitrary detention of trade unionists and political opponents, repression against ethnic or religious minorities. In such cases multinational companies are accused of collaborating with the government or of indirectly benefiting from those practices (see the examples opposite).

Child labor is the most publicized and the one that provokes a typical ethical dilemma (see the examples below). In a thought-provoking article, Martha Nichols (1993) explained the dilemma as the choice between respecting a code of ethics and canceling an order to a supplier employing young children, and therefore accepting the consequences of depriving their families of much needed income and putting the children back on the street, or accepting the order knowing that children are working to fulfill it.[30] According to UNICEF an estimated 246 million children are engaged in child labor. Of those, almost three-quarters (171 million) work in hazardous situations or conditions, such as working in mines, working with chemicals and pesticides in agriculture or working with dangerous machinery. They are everywhere but invisible, toiling as domestic servants in homes, laboring behind the walls of workshops, hidden from view in plantations. Some of them are trafficked (1.2 million), forced into debt bondage or other forms of slavery (5.7 million), into prostitution and pornography (1.8 million), into participating in armed conflict (0.3 million) or other illicit activities (0.6 million).[31] The main domain in which multinational companies can be indirectly involved in child labor is in procurement to companies that use children as a labor force. Mass retailing companies such as Wal-Mart or Carrefour with their billion-dollar purchases of goods in the developing world are often confronted with that issue.

EXAMPLES

Child labor and the global firm

Soccer balls[32]

By the mid-1990s, Sialkot, located in the Punjab province of Pakistan, was the center for the production of customized, high-quality sporting goods and surgical equipment: 25,000 jobs were involved in these activities. Soccer ball production and the export of 35 million balls accounted for US$45 million in 1995. Since the stitching of soccer balls is labor-intensive, children were used to perform this task. In Pakistan, it was estimated that 3.6 million children were employed as laborers; one-third earning wages, the remainder being engaged as family helpers for agricultural tasks.

In the mid-1990s, child labor cases were brought to public attention via television reports and news magazines. This drew attention to soccer ball production. Reebok, a leading sporting goods global firm, implemented its own policy in order to abolish child labor. Reebok's policy was (1) to buy finished goods from a child-labor-free factory where stitching is brought out of the home, (2) to set up a monitoring program or (3) to start an educational program. David Husselby, Programme Director of Save the Children Fund's UK office went to Sialkot and served as a catalyst to facilitate dialogue between the industry and the International Labor Organization (ILO). This resulted in a Sialkot Partnership to End Child Labor that induced an agreement with the Sporting Goods Manufacturers' Association in Atlanta in 1997. The Atlanta Agreement stated that:

- Stitching centers were to be established which would bring the work out of households
- Workers would be systematically registered in order to check ages
- Alternative educational programs would be created for children
- Rewards, warnings and penalties were set up to encourage vendors who did not use child labor

- Members of the World Federation of Sporting Goods would favor vendors who did not use child labor.

The program was a success from the point of view of child labor in the soccer ball industry but it had some indirect negative effect such as the fact that by taking the work out of households, Punjabi women could not work in the factory for religious reasons. Other industries, like carpet or brick making, were still employing children and some of the children that went out of stitching, a relatively flexible job, moved to more hazardous work.

Nike[33]

In 1988, the Asian-American Free Labor Association (AAFLA, a branch of the AFL-CIO trade union) found that Nike, the sporting goods company, used contractors in Indonesia who were breaking Indonesian labor laws and paying workers below-subsistence wages. The author of the AAFLA report, denouncing those practices, initiated a public campaign that reached the media. Nike's reaction was to deny any responsibility. During the 1990s, the name of Nike was consistently mentioned as a company using contractors who exploited workers in Indonesia or used children in Pakistan. By 1996–97 the anti-Nike campaign had large visibility in the media and on American campuses where students organized protests. Nike adopted a defensive approach, hiring Ernst & Young to audit their foreign operations as well as asking Andrew Young, an African American, ex-mayor of Atlanta to produce a report. Those attempts were criticized on methodological grounds. In May 1998 Phil Knight, Nike's CEO, admitted that '*Nike products have become synonymous with slave wages, forced overtime and arbitrary abuse*'. He announced a series of reforms: raising the minimum age of workers to 18 for shoes and 16 for apparel, adopting clean air standards based on the US standards in all factories, expanding the monitoring program, expanding educational programs for workers and making micro loans available to workers. Nike worked to bring apparel manufacturers to join the Apparel Industry Partnership task force created by President Clinton in order to reach an agreement on labor standards to be accepted by all competitors.

Sources: Crawford, Cadot and Traça (1999); Burns and Spar (2000)

With regard to **human rights**, global corporations are often confronted with their direct or indirect complicity in all sorts of abuses. This happens when global firms operate in countries whose political regimes use methods of enforcement that do not respect the principles of the Universal Declaration of Human Rights (UDHR) as adopted by the United Nations. This includes arbitrary detention, execution of political dissidents, non-respect of legal procedures for trials of opponents, deportation of population, use of military force for civilian unrest, rape or torture by security forces or by factions in civil wars, and so on. Global firms can be involved directly when human rights abuses are committed, to protect their operations, or indirectly when their activities contribute to maintaining political regimes involved in human rights abuse. The examples below give a sample of some cases of global firms that have been criticized for being associated with human rights abuses.

EXAMPLE

Global firms and human rights: an example

Oil companies in Myanmar[34]

Unocal and its partner, Total of France, built in 1998 a natural gas pipeline (the Yadana project) from the Andaman Sea through the rainforests of southern Burma into Thailand. This represents the country's largest foreign investment, with commercial exploitation starting in 2000. The pipeline has become the target of intense lobbying by international human rights groups. Groups that oppose Unocal's investment in Myanmar filed lawsuits against Unocal in the USA and Total in France in order to link this investment with forced labor and human rights abuse committed by the Burmese military. Both Unical and Total settled the case by indemnifying people who were subjected to military forced labor without admitting to any participation in this.

According to Amnesty International Secretary General Pierre Sane (2000), there are five reasons why business should care about human rights.

- 'The first one is the moral argument. We do not need to convince managers and boardrooms that the amputation of children's limbs in Sierra Leone in order to terrorize a population and win a war is wrong, or that the gang rape of women by Serb soldiers in Kosovo is evil, or that the killing of civilians in East Timor or Chechnya is to be condemned. These acts are wrong, insidious. They have been prohibited internationally'.
- 'The second argument is the legitimacy of human rights. They have been codified in treaties ratified by governments. Peoples the world over are struggling to hold their governments accountable for the implementation of international law. Believe me, if a free ballot was upheld globally today, overwhelmingly people will say they want their human rights, all their human rights'.
- 'The third argument is that it is in the interest of business to see human rights protected. The rule of law protects investments by guaranteeing political stability. An educated and healthy population increases economic productivity. A company tarnished by controversies around human rights violations can see its reputation destroyed and its profitability threatened'.
- 'Fourthly, companies and, more specifically, Multinational Corporations, have secured for themselves freedoms to operate which have given them enormous power to affect the lives of people but with power comes responsibility'.
- 'Finally, the Universal Declaration of Human Rights (UDHR) calls upon all organs of society to protect and promote human rights. The ILO conventions protect the rights of the workers. Other conventions place direct responsibility on companies to act in accordance with international human rights law'.

Amnesty International proposes a checklist of conduct principles for global firms to adopt (see Table 15.4).

Table 15.4 Human rights principles for companies: a checklist[35]

Company policy on human rights All companies should adopt an explicit company policy on human rights that includes public support for the Universal Declaration of Human Rights (UDHR). Companies should establish procedures to ensure that all operations are examined for their potential impact on human rights, and safeguards to ensure that company staff are never complicit in human rights abuses. The company policy should enable discussion with the authorities at local, provincial and national levels of specific cases of human rights violations and the need for safeguards to protect human rights. It should enable the establishment of programs for the effective human rights education and training of all employees within the company and encourage collective action in business associations to promote respect for international human rights standards.
Security All companies should ensure that any security arrangements protect human rights and are consistent with international standards for law enforcement. Any security personnel employed or contracted should be adequately trained. Procedures should be consistent with the United Nations (UN) Basic Principles on the Use of Force and Firearms by Law Enforcement Officials and the UN Code of Conduct for Law Enforcement Officials. They should include measures to prevent excessive force, as well as torture or cruel, inhuman or degrading treatment. Companies should develop clear rules for calling in or contracting with state security forces and for not hiring security personnel who have been responsible for serious human rights violations. Any complaint about security procedures or personnel should be promptly and independently investigated. Companies which supply military security or police products or services should take stringent steps to prevent those products and services from being misused to commit human rights violations.
Community engagement All companies should take reasonable steps to ensure that their operations do not have a negative impact on the enjoyment of human rights by the communities in which they operate. This should include a willingness to meet with community leaders and voluntary organizations to discuss the role of the company within the broader community. Companies should work cooperatively with organizations which promote human rights.
Freedom from discrimination All companies should ensure that their policies and practices prevent discrimination based on ethnic origin, sex, colour, language, national or social origin, economic status, religion, political or other conscientiously held beliefs, birth or other status. This should include recruitment, promotion; and remuneration, working conditions, customer relations and the practices of contractors, suppliers and partners. It should include measures to deal with sexual or racial harassment, and to prohibit national, racial or religious hatred.
Freedom from slavery All companies should ensure that their policies and practices prohibit the use of chattel slaves, forced labor, bonded child laborers or coerced prison labor. This should include ensuring that suppliers, partners or contractors do not use such labor.
Health and safety All companies should ensure that their policies and practices provide for safe and healthy working conditions and products. The company should not engage in or support the use of corporal punishment, mental or physical coercion, or verbal abuse.
Freedom of association and the right to collective bargaining All companies should ensure that all employees are able to exercise their rights to freedom of expression, peaceful assembly and association, as well as a fair means of collective bargaining without discrimination, including the right to form trade unions and to strike. Companies have a responsibility to ensure such rights for their employees even if such rights are not protected in a particular country's national law. Companies should take steps to ensure that suppliers, partners or contractors do not infringe such rights.
Fair working conditions All companies should ensure just and favorable conditions of work, reasonable job security and air and adequate remuneration and benefits. This should include provision for an adequate standard of living for employees and their families. Companies should take steps to ensure that suppliers, partners or contractors do not infringe such rights.
Child labor Companies shall not engage in or support the use of child labor as defined by applicable national laws and relevant international standards.

Monitoring human rights
All companies should establish mechanisms to monitor effectively all their operations' compliance with codes of conduct and international human rights standards. Such mechanisms must be credible and all reports must periodically be independently verifiable in a similar way to the auditing of accounts or the quality of products and services. Other stakeholders such as members of local communities in which the company operates and voluntary organizations should have an opportunity to contribute in order to ensure transparency and credibility.

Sources:

United Nations Universal Declaration of Human Rights (UDHR), Preamble Organization for Economic Cooperation and Development (OECD), Guidelines for Multinational Enterprises.

UN Code of Conduct for Law Enforcement Officials, UDHR Articles 3, 5 and 9.

UP Basic Principles on the Use of Force and Firearms by Law Enforcement Officials.

Principles Governing Conventional Arms Transfers of the Organization for Security Cooperation in Europe.

UDHR Articles 21 and 26, International Labour Organization (ILO), *Tripartite Declaration of Principles Concerning Multinational Enterprises and Social Policy*

UDHR Article 2, ILO Conventions 100, 111 and 165.

UDHR Article 4, ILO Convention 29, 105 and 138.

UDHR Article 3, ILO Convention 155.

UDHR Articles 20, and 23, ILO Conventions 87, 98 and 135.

UDHR Articles 23 and 24, ILO Convention including 95 and 131 (on wages), 14 and 4006 (on weekly rest) and 132 (on holidays with pay).

ILO Conventions 138,146.

Reproduced from Human Right Principles for Companies, AI index number ACT 70/001/1998, with permission of Amnesty International Publications <http://www.amnesty.org>

Global corporations and global citizenship

Corporate social responsibility is not limited to restrictive practices relating to corruption, environment protection or human dignity: those are the 'Don'ts' of global management behavior. There are more positive aspects of doing business internationally: the 'Dos' that encompass the contributions to economic, social, technological and human development in the country in which global firms operate. This is what is called 'global citizenship'. There is no accepted definition of global citizenship but according to Hewlett Packard, which has appointed a senior vice president for Corporate Affairs and Global Citizenship, it represents a commitment to '*Conducting business with uncompromising integrity, to engage with a variety of external stakeholders—from local communities, to the United Nations, to provide resources to improve access to technology and educational opportunities, to develop products and services that are environmentally sustainable, to protect the privacy of our customers, partners and employees*'. As can be seen, three out of the five commitments are on the proactive, positive side of conducting business. Below are the kind of actions that can be exhibited in those three categories:

- Dialogue and engagement with local stakeholders and communities:
  - Participate actively in community development under the form of grants, social, cultural and sporting events
  - Dialogue with schools and universities by offering research funds, individual grants and opportunities for internships.
  - Offer educational opportunities
  - Participate in local chamber of commerce and contribute to dialogue with authorities in debate concerning ecological, technical or economical issues

  - Sponsor medical campaigns
  - Facilitate the ad hoc detachment of 'in house experts' to local councils, schools and community institutions.
- Provide resources to improve access to technology and educational opportunities:
  - Donation of computers to schools, institutions
  - Donation of machinery that fosters rural development
  - Engage in training campaigns on development programs such as Internet usage, irrigation, preventive medicine
- Develop products and services that are environmentally sustainable:
  - Use of biodegradable packaging
  - Favor renewable energy when possible

The examples below demonstrate these actions.

Some examples of global citizenship

EXAMPLES

AMD and the project 50x15

50x15 is a project to empower 50 per cent of the world's population with basic Internet access by the year 2015. As part of this project, AMD and four other companies are funding a non-profit-making organization called One Laptop Per Child. The laptops are planned to sell at US$100 and are powered with a wind-up crank, have very low power consumption and will let children interact with each other while learning.

HP and i-community

On 21 February, 2002, HP signed a three-year alliance with the government of Andhra Pradesh to develop an HP i-community in Kuppam, India. The announcement was that the company would be investing over $1 million for the pilot project. An i-community is 1) a community where ICT is strategically deployed for sustainable socio-economic development and 2) an experimental platform for testing and developing emerging market solutions and business models.

Bayer in Mozambique

Bayer has signed a two-year agreement with the Roman Catholic Community of Sant'Egidio, a charitable organization, concerning the supply of diagnostic systems and services. The project aims to enable targeted therapy for HIV-infected patients in Mozambique and other African countries. The shipments will first be made to Mozambique, where local authorities and volunteers are working to establish nationwide care and therapy programs for HIV patients. In addition to the diagnostic systems, Bayer HealthCare will offer scientific and technical cooperation, as well as training courses and workshops for specialist personnel.

Carrefour in Bolivia

In 2003, Carrefour signed up a line of organic quinoa grown in Bolivia that meets fair-trade standards. In 2004, 400,000 packets were distributed in French stores. In cooperation with the Point d'Appui NGO, a medical clinic for the Tres Cruces communities and the surrounding area was inaugurated in September 2004. Carrefour is helping fund it with €0.10 on the sale of each packet.

DaimlerChrysler in Argentina

Manos Unidos ("Joined Hands") is the name of a project in La Plata set up by the Catholic Church with financial support from DaimlerChrysler. Women from the poorer neighborhoods are given 'micro-credits' and advice on starting up small businesses. Just three years after the program was launched, things are looking very positive: most of the businesses are running successfully and, in many cases, no longer require loans.

Sources: The HP example comes from Sara Foryt and Daniel Traca, *Bridging the Digital Divide (A), HP's e-inclusion*, INSEAD case study, 2003

Integrating social responsibility policies into business strategies

Confronted with such criticisms, some firms have developed policies and practices designed to integrate social responsibility issues into their business strategies. Forest Reinhart at the Harvard Business School (1999) found that those strategies were based on three inter-related developments:

- Design and implementation of **information systems**, both internal and external, in order to understand the environmental impact of products over their entire life cycle as well as the concerns and expectations of customers, employees, environmentalists, international institutions and governments. Such information is complemented by proactive communication such as the yearly publication of the *Shell Report: People, Planet and Profit*, in which the company documents the actions that it has taken to meet its economic, environmental and social responsibility.[36] The UN Global Compact has developed a Communication on Progress model for companies to follow for social reporting implementation (see appendix 15.2). In parallel, 250 companies participate in the Business for Social Responsibility, a non-profit-making corporate membership organization that has developed a Global Reporting Initiative that proposes a series of indicators to measure and disclose their performance in social responsibility.[37] Those indicators are compatible with the Global Compact guidelines.
- Design and implementation of incentives systems devoted to fostering sustainable development performances, such as tying bonuses to good environmental practice.
- Contribution to **institutions**, such as the Global Compact (see Table 15.5) and the World CSR, which groups different organizations such as the Business Impact, The Center for Corporate Citizenship at Babson College, The Prince of Wales Business Leader Forum (PWBLF), CSR Europe and Business Impact, Global Sullivan Principles. Appendix 15.3 gives a list of organizations that are active in promoting corporate social responsibility.

Table 15.5 Global Compact and the Ten Principles

At the World Economic Forum, Davos, on 31 January 1999, UN Secretary-General Kofi A. Annan challenged world business leaders to 'embrace and enact' the Global Compact, both in their individual corporate practices and by supporting appropriate public policies. These principles cover topics in human rights, labor and environment. The Global compact is now a network of organizations and corporations that adhere to the Ten Principles.

The Global Compact's Ten Principles in the areas of human rights, labor, the environment and anti-corruption enjoy universal consensus and are derived from:

- The Universal Declaration of Human Rights
- The International Labour Organization's Declaration on Fundamental Principles and Rights at Work
- The Rio Declaration on Environment and Development
- The United Nations Convention Against Corruption

The Global Compact asks companies to embrace, support and enact, within their sphere of influence, a set of core values in the areas of human rights, labor standards, the environment and anti-corruption:

Human rights

- *Principle 1:* Businesses should support and respect the protection of internationally proclaimed human rights; and
- *Principle 2:* make sure that they are not complicit in human rights abuses.

Labor standards

- *Principle 3:* Businesses should uphold the freedom of association and the effective recognition of the right to collective bargaining;
- *Principle 4:* the elimination of all forms of forced and compulsory labor;
- *Principle 5:* the effective abolition of child labor; and
- *Principle 6:* the elimination of discrimination in respect of employment and occupation.

Environment

- *Principle 7:* Businesses should support a precautionary approach to environmental challenges;
- *Principle 8:* undertake initiatives to promote greater environmental responsibility; and
- *Principle 9:* encourage the development and diffusion of environmentally friendly technologies.

Anti-corruption

- *Principle 10:* Businesses should work against all forms of corruption, including extortion and bribery.

Companies, academic institutions, business associations and public institutions from all regions of the world have pledged support to the Global Compact and are implementing the Ten Principles.

Codes of conduct

As mentioned earlier, many public and private organizations have tried to provide guidelines to companies under the form of codes of conduct.

There are 5 types of code of conduct:[38]

- **Company codes**
  Codes that are adopted unilaterally by companies such as Levi Strauss , Marks and Spencer, Starbucks, HP, Adidas, 3M and Reuters.
- **Trade association codes**
  These are adopted by a group of firms in a particular industry. Like company codes, they tend to be a unilateral measure adopted by the firms. They may be adopted by associations of firms based in developed countries, as in the case of the British Toy and Hobby Association

code, or by developing country firms, such as the Bangladesh Garments Manufacturers and Exporters Association (BGMEA) code and the Kenya Flower Council code.

- **Multi-stakeholder codes**
  These are adopted as a result of negotiations between several stakeholders, including firms or their industry representatives, NGOs and/or trade unions. Governments may also be involved in the development of such codes. The UK's Ethical Trade Initiative Base Code is an example of such a multi-stakeholder approach.
- **Model codes**
  These are designed to provide a benchmark of what a particular organization regards as good practice in terms of codes of conduct. They are not generally applied in practice, but intended as a model which companies or trade associations could follow. These have been proposed both by trade unions as, for example, the ICFTU's Basic Code of Conduct covering labor practices, and by NGOs such as Amnesty International.
- **Intergovernmental codes**
  These are negotiated at an international level and are agreed by national governments. They date back to the 1970s when both the OECD's Guidelines for Multinational Enterprises and the ILO's Tripartite Declaration of Principles Concerning Multinational Enterprises were adopted.

Appendix 15.2 gives a list of those codes associated with the organization that provides them. The first and most prominent is the OECD Guidelines for Multinational Enterprises.[39] The guidelines are recommendations addressed by governments to multinational enterprises operating in or from adhering countries (the 30 OECD member countries plus nine non-member countries: Argentina, Brazil, Chile, Estonia, Israel, Latvia, Lithuania, Romania and Slovenia). They provide voluntary principles and standards for responsible business conduct, in a variety of areas including employment and industrial relations, human rights, environment, information disclosure, competition, taxation, and science and technology. The guidelines were first published in 1976 and have been regularly reviewed since then. The latest revision was done in 2000. These guidelines serve as a template for others' initiatives.

Codes of conduct are important instruments of communication, education and reporting for the firms that are genuinely willing to accept their social responsibility. Codes of conduct, however, have been criticized on the grounds that 'codes are little more than general statements of business ethics with no indication of the way in which they are to be implemented'.[40]

Social responsibility and global firms: an on-going challenge

We have described the most salient issues concerning the social responsibilities of global firms. The list is not exhaustive and every day new cases appear; firms are often taken off guard and have to try to react and adjust their policies. Some adopt a very defensive attitude, but soon realize that it does not work. A multiple dialogue between governments, NGOs, international institutions, the media and public opinion and industry associations has been going on since the 1990s and will progressively align corporate strategies and human dignity.

The 'ethical dimension' has now reached the financial markets with the development of Socially Responsible Investing (SRI) in which investors select companies that are considered as socially responsible.[41] However, as the case of corruption demonstrates, improvement is slow and regressive behavior can still be exhibited, such as the refusal by the US government, on behalf of American industrialists, to sign the 1997 Kyoto Treaty on the reduction of carbon dioxide emissions. New ethical debates arise daily, as in the cases of bio-ethics, genetically modified (GM) organisms or the right of pharmaceutical companies to limit the development of alternative HIV drugs in developing countries. More and more, global firms are being held accountable for impacts that were traditionally the domain of government and this looks likely to be one of the most challenging issues for the future.

EXAMPLE

Jack Cumberland

Jack Cumberland was the managing director of IndoMedia, a leading advertising agency in Indonesia in South East Asia. IndoMedia was formed as a joint venture between EuroMedia from the UK and a local entrepreneur. Jack, born in Scotland in 1975, joined Procter & Gamble as a junior brand manager after graduating from London University Business School in 1992. Six years later he was recruited by EuroMedia. He was assigned to a client group in London for five years, then moved to Spain for four years and finally was named managing director of IndoMedia.

IndoMedia had a good reputation in Indonesia as a very creative agency and well connected to the media. It also had a reputation of being reliable in a country where media rates could be discounted up to 60 per cent from the 'official' rate. Most agencies charged the 'official' rate to their clients and pocketed the discount for themselves. IndoMedia charged only a 20 per cent commission on top of the discounted rate, giving it a competitive advantage over competitors despite the fact that its art work was more expensive. For printing jobs, quotations were requested from at least three competitors in order to obtain the best price.

A few months after his nomination, Jack was approached by Eddy, a representative of a big printing company in Indonesia. Eddy was very upset because he saw the volume of his business with IndoMedia was declining although his job was of the highest price/quality relationship. He mentioned that IndoMedia's manager in charge of buying print jobs, Omar, was asking that the quotation include 'not only the usual 10 per cent, but then 15 per cent and recently 25 per cent to be paid as soon as the printer receives the money from the agency'.

Jack asked Eddy if he was ready to maintain his accusations in front of Omar. The answer was immediate: 'No way. It would kill my business.'

Later Jack talked to Andreas, the finance director, a man of experience and wisdom. He became angrier as he was talking. Andreas was smiling and finally when Jack stopped talking, he told him: 'Have you realized that you work in Indoland?'

Adapted from Schütte (1986), with permission

MINI-CASE

Shell and Cosan

In June 2011 Shell and Cosan announced the start of operations at Raízen, a 50/50 joint venture with Royal Dutch Shell to produce ethanol, sugar and electricity from sugar cane, as well as to distribute and market fuels. Raízen started with 40,000 employees, and is among the five largest companies in terms of revenue in Brazil, with a market value estimated at US$ 12 billion, and produce and sell over 2 billion liters of fuel a year. Shell indicates that turning sugar cane into ethanol offers a number of environmental benefits over other biofuel production processes. As it grows, sugar cane generally absorbs CO_2 at a greater rate than other biofuel crops such as soy.

Shell in a press release indicated that 'Ethanol made from Brazilian sugar cane produces around 70 per cent less CO_2 than petrol and by-products from turning sugar cane into ethanol are recycled as organic fertilizer. Plant waste, called bagasse, is burned to produce power for the processing mills and surplus energy is supplied to the national grid'.[42]

But critics of ethanol also pinpoint its harmful effects on the environment and society. According to the Transnational Institute:[43] 'Sugar cane is grown as a monocrop, predominantly in southern and central Brazil as well as in parts of Asia and Africa. It relies on heavy quantities of inputs, particularly fertilizer. Harvesting is often done by hand, and working conditions are notoriously harsh. A number of studies in Brazil have shown that demand for land for sugar cane is leading to the conversion of grasslands and wooded savannah for crops, releasing stored carbon dioxide, and displacing previous users like cattle farmers who move into tropical forests. Sugar cane also has devastating effects on biodiversity – with the Cerrado savannah of Central Brazil, where sugar cane is grown, being one of the world's most biodiverse and also most threatened habitats. Sugar cane expansion is also affecting Brazil's Atlantic Forest, and indirectly the Amazon, as cattle farmers move into the forest in the search for new pasture.

'Sugar cane expansion is leading to land conflicts, as rural communities are forced off land to make way for the plantations. Small-scale farming has become unviable in the plantation areas and many small farmers feel they have no financial choice but to sell up. Sugar plantations are displacing small farms, food crops and subsistence food systems – leading to food shortages and price rises.'

Questions:

1) As a socially responsible Shell shareholder, what is your view on the issue?
2) Shell has been criticized over environmental concerns and human rights in Africa, Europe and USA. What can an energy company do to answer criticisms?

Summary and key points

1 There are four main categories of social and ethical issues facing global companies:

- Business ethics
- Sustainable development

- Human rights and dignity
- Global citizenship

The challenge ahead is how global companies handle an increasing responsibility for social issues that were traditionally the domain of governments.

2 Corporate social responsibility is the obligations of firms to society or more specifically to those affected by corporate policies and practices.

3 Business ethics encompasses issues of conflict of interests, financial and accounting integrity, corruption and bribery, ethical advertising, bioethics and employee privacy.

4 Corruption:

- *Definition*: Corruption can be defined as the abuse of public office for private gain; a gift can be offered openly but a bribe cannot
- Two *indices* relate to corruption:
  - Corruption Perception Index (CPI)
  - Bribe Payers' Index (BPI)
- There are five *causes* of corruption:
  - *Administrative resource allocation*: when administrative authorization and distribution replaces transparent market mechanisms
  - *Lack of institutional checks,* balances and information
  - *Inadequate funding* of public services leading to relatively low remuneration of public servants and under-supply of public goods
  - *Social and cultural factors* leading to nepotism
  - *Abundance of natural resources* leading to discrimination in funds allocation
- *Effects* of corruption:
  - *Direct*:
    - Discourages domestic and foreign investments owing to additional cost burden on projects
    - Skews public capital expenditure in favor of new equipment instead of operating existing equipment
    - Reduces the productivity of public investments and reduces tax collection
  - *Indirect*:
    - Decreased work productivity through demotivation
    - Dislocation of social fabric
    - Loss of integrity within firms
    - Linkage with terrorism and criminal activities
- Global companies *engage in bribery* because of:
  - Need to keep up with competitors' practices
  - Cultural justifications
  - Result of an incentive system which emphasizes economic achievements
- *Anti-corruption* measures:
  - Disclose publicly and make widely known the company's endorsement of anti-corruption measures

- Establish a clearly articulated written policy prohibiting employees from paying/receiving bribes
- Implement policies with due care and take disciplinary action for any violations
- Provide training and support to employees to carry out the policy
- Maintain full and proper accounting records, subject to periodic internal audit review
- Report annually on firm's bribery and corruption policy and describe the company's experience in its enforcement; the annual report should be independently audited.
- Require all agents/suppliers to affirm that they have neither made nor will make any improper payments
- Establish a monitoring and auditing system to detect any improper payments made by firm's employees/agents
- Report publicly any solicitation for payments
- Establish a system for employees/agents to report any improper payment without fear of retribution.

5 Sustainable development is defined as 'development that meets the needs of the present without compromising the ability of future generations to meet their own needs'.

6 Main environment issues:

- Destruction of ozone layer
- Global warming
- Persistent organic pollution
- Radioactive waste
- Environmental pollution
- Deforestation
- Over-fishing

7 Global warming is linked to CO_2 emissions.

8 The Kyoto Protocol aims to reduce CO_2 emissions by 5 per cent by the year 2020.

9 Actions that improve eco-efficiency are:

- Reduction in material intensity
- Reduction in energy intensity
- Reduction in waste dispersion
- Enhancement of recyclability
- Maximum use of renewables
- Extension of product durability
- Increase of service intensity.

10 Human rights and dignity

- Global firms' involvement:
  - Direct involvement: human rights invoked by global companies to protect their operations

  - Indirect involvement: contributions to political regimes involved in human rights abuse
- Principles for global firms:
  - Formulate company policy on human rights
  - Security arrangements should protect human rights and be consistent with international standards of law enforcement
  - Be involved in community that promotes human rights
  - Company policy should not approve discrimination, slavery or child labor practices
  - Provide safe and healthy working conditions and products
  - All employees should have the freedom to associate with and right to join collective bargaining mechanisms
  - Mechanisms should be established to monitor a company's compliance with international human rights standards.

11 Global citizenship covers the following areas:

- Dialogue and engagement with local stakeholders and communities
- Provide resources to improve access to technology and educational opportunities
- Develop products and services that are environmentally sustainable
- Use biodegradable packaging
- Favor renewable energy when possible.

12 Global companies can handle their increasing responsibility for social issues that were traditionally the domain of governments by:

- Design and implementation of information systems and social reporting
- Design and implementation of incentives systems devoted to fostering sustainable development
- Contribution to public and private institutions.

Appendix 15.1 The OECD Guidelines for Multinational Enterprises

The guidelines contain ten chapters:

1) **GENERAL PRINCIPLES:** sets out general areas for good corporate behavior in the countries in which enterprises operate.
2) **DISCLOSURE:** deals with public dissemination of essential information on the activities of the enterprises.
3) **EMPLOYMENT AND INDUSTRIAL RELATIONS:** covers a number of issues, such as the rights and treatment of employees and forced and child labor.
4) **ENVIRONMENT:** recommendations on environmental management systems and the prevention of environmental damage.
5) **COMBATING BRIBERY:** provides recommendations on the avoidance of bribery and other corrupt practices.
6) **CONSUMER INTERESTS:** Recommendations to ensure respect for all consumer rights.
7) **SCIENCE AND TECHNOLOGY:** companies are encouraged to contribute to the development of local capacities through technology transfer.
8) **COMPETITION:** business competition consistent with all applicable competition laws.
9) **TAXATION:** Fulfillment of tax liabilities and cooperation with the local tax authorities.

Source: <http://www.oecd.org/dataoecd/56/36/1922428.pdf>

Appendix 15.2 Major business ethics codes

The Asian Pacific Economic Cooperation Forum
Business Code of Conduct
<http://www.apec.org>

Caux Round Table
Principles for Business:
<http://www.cauxroundtable.org/index.cfm?menuid=8>

Coalition for Environmentally Responsible Economies (CERES)
The CERES Principles
<http://www.ceres.org/ceres>

Clarkson Centre for Ethics & Board Effectiveness
The Clarkson Principles of Stakeholder Management
<http://www.valuebasedmanagement.net/methods_clarkson_principles.html>

The Ethical Trading Initiative
The Ethical Trading Initiative Base Code
<http://www.ethicaltrade.org/resources/key-eti-resources/eti-base-code>

The Fair Labor Association (FLA)
The Fair Labor Association Workplace Code of Conduct
<http://www.fairlabor.org/labor-standards>

International Confederation of Free Trade Union (ICFTU) and International Trade Secretariats (ITS)
Basic Code of Labor
<http://www.icftu.org/displaydocument.asp?Index=991209513&Language=EN&Printout=Yes>

International Labour Organization (ILO)
The ILO Declaration of Fundamental Principles and Rights at Work
<http://www.ilo.org/declaration>

Tripartite Declaration of Principles concerning Multinational Enterprises and Social Policy
<http://www.ilo.org/public/english/standards/norm/sources/mne.htm>

International Council of Chemical Associations
Responsible Care Global Charter
<http://www.responsiblecaretoolkit.com/pdfs/GLOBAL_CHARTER.pdf>

Interfaith Declaration:
A Code of Ethics on International Business for Christians, Muslims and Jews
<http://institute.jesdialogue.org/fileadmin/bizcourse/INTERFAITHDECLARATION.pdf>

Organisation for Economic Co-operation and Development (OECD)
The *OECD Guidelines For Multinational Enterprises*
<http://www.oecd.org/dataoecd/56/36/1922428.pdf>

OECD Principles of Corporate Governance
<http://www.oecd.org/dataoecd/32/18/31557724.pdf>

Social Accountability International
SA 8000 Standards
<http://www.sa-intl.org>

The Social Venture Network
SNV Standards of Corporate Social Responsibility
<http://www.svn.org/index.cfm?fuseaction=page.viewpage&pageid=538>

United Nations
The United Nations Global Compact
<http://www.un.org/Depts/ptd/global.htm>

United Nations Convention against Corruption
<http://www.unodc.org/pdf/corruption/publications_unodc_convention-e.pdf>

The United Nations Draft Human Rights Principles and Responsibilities for Transnational Corporations and Other Business Enterprises
<http://www1.umn.edu/humanrts/links/NormsApril2003.html>

Appendix 15.3 Main nongovernment organizations involved in corporate social responsibility

Amnesty International (AI) is a worldwide movement of people who campaign for internationally recognized human rights. Its mission is to undertake research and action focused on preventing and ending grave abuses of the rights to physical and mental integrity, freedom of conscience and expression, and freedom from discrimination.
<http://www.amnesty.org>

Aspen Institute
International non-profit dedicated to fostering enlightened leadership and open-minded dialogue through seminars, policy programs, conferences and leadership
<http://www.aspeninstitute.org>

GreenBiz is a program of The National Environmental Education & Training Foundation. NEETF is a 501(c)(3) non-profit organization based in Washington, DC, dedicated to advancing environmental education. It considers itself as an information resource on how to align environmental responsibility with business success. It provides news and resources to large and small businesses through a combination of websites, workshops, daily news feeds, electronic newsletters and briefing papers. Resources are free to all users.
<http://www.greenbiz.com>

Greenpeace is a non-profit organization, with a presence in 40 countries across Europe, the Americas, Asia and the Pacific. Greenpeace focuses on the most crucial worldwide threats to our planet's biodiversity and environment.
<http://www.greenpeace.org>

Human Rights Watch started in 1978 as Helsinki Watch, to monitor the compliance of Soviet bloc countries with the human rights provisions of the landmark Helsinki Accords. Composed of lawyers, journalists, academics and country experts of many nationalities who investigate and expose human rights violations and hold abusers accountable.
<http://www.hrw.org>

Oxfam International is a confederation of 12 organizations working together with over 3,000 partners in more than 100 countries to find lasting solutions to poverty, suffering and injustice.
<http://www.oxfam.org>

The Pew Center on Global Climate Change brings together business leaders, policy makers, scientists and other experts to bring a new approach to a complex and often controversial issue. Their approach is based on sound science, straight talk, and a belief that we can all work together to protect the climate while sustaining economic growth. The Pew Center on Global Climate Change was established in 1998 as a nonprofit, non-partisan and independent organization. The center's mission is to provide credible information, straight answers, and innovative solutions in the effort to address global climate change.
<http://www.pewclimate.org>

Transparency International (TI) is an international nongovernmental organization devoted to combating corruption. Through its International Secretariat in Berlin and its more than 85 independent National Chapters around the world, TI works at both international and national levels to curb the supply and demand of corrupt practices. In the international arena, TI raises awareness about the damaging effects of corruption, advocates policy reform, works towards the implementation of multilateral conventions and subsequently monitors compliance by governments, corporations and banks.
<http://www.transparency.org>

The World Business Council for Sustainable Development (WBCSD) is a coalition of 180 international companies. Its mission is to provide business leadership as a catalyst for change toward sustainable development, and to promote the role of eco-efficiency, innovation and corporate social responsibility. Its main activities are publications, conferences and projects leadership.
<http://www.wbcsd.org/home.aspx>

Learning assignments

1 What are the main causes of corruption?
2 What corrupt practices involving global firms have you heard of?
3 What dilemma may a country manager face when confronted by a request to solicit a bribe to obtain a major contract?
4 What policies should a global firm implement to prevent corrupt practices?
5 How can corporate policies be designed to contribute to global environment protection?
6 What should the country managers do if a local supplier in a developing country is employing 12-year-olds as labor force?
7 Should a global company pull out of Myanmar, a country well known for human rights abuses by the military power?
8 Draw a global ethical web for a pharmaceutical company engaged in anti-HIV drug production.

9 What are SRI funds? Select an SRI fund and track its evolution as compared to the general evolution of the stock market.

Key words

- Bribe
- Child labor
- Corporate social responsibility
- Corruption
- Environmental crisis
- Ethics
- Human rights
- Socially responsible investment (SRI)
- Transparency International

Web resources

In addition to the resources mentioned in the appendix you will find the following website useful to consult:

<http://www.corpwatch.org/>

Corpwatch's Globalization and Corporate Rule website.

Visit the companion website at **http://www.palgrave.com/business/lasserre3e** for a multitude of weblinks and resources, self-test questions for revision and a searchable glossary.

Notes

1 This definition is from Smith (2003), pp.1–25. There are many definitions of it but this one is the most comprehensive in its simplicity.

2 In 1899 Pope Leon XIII issued the *Rerum Novarum* in which he outlined to firms their duties to society and particularly to their labor force.

3 *New York Times Magazine*, 13 September, 1970.

4 Smith (2003) p. 2.

5 Badaracco and Webb (1995), p. 8.

6 Business Ethics, The Canadian Resources for Business Ethics: <http://www.businessethics.ca>, accessed 21 January 2012.

7 Donalson and Dundee (1999), pp. 45–63.

8 Cadbury (1987), pp. 69–73.

9 See <http://web.worldbank.org/wbi>.

10 The definition is from Transparency International: <http://www.transparency.org>.

11 Press release from Transparency International, Paris, 27 June 2001.

12 Fadiman (1986), pp. 4–12.

13 See the OECD website at: <http://www.oecd.org/topic/0,2686,en_2649_37447_1_1_1_1_37447,00.html>.

14 See Mauro (1997) and Tanzi (1998).

15 Leite and Weiman (1999).

16 Besides the IMF papers cited earlier, there is a series of World Bank reports showing the negative effects of corruption available at <http://econ.worldbank.org/>.

17 The calculation is from Wei (1998).

18 Kaufmann and Wei (1999).

19 Hess and Dunfee (2001).

20 Badaracco and Webb (1995).

21 <http://www.transparency.org>.

22 Bruntland (1987).

23 United Nations Conference on Environment and Development, *Rio Declaration on Environment and Development*, <http://www.unep.org/Documents.multilingual/Default.asp?DocumentID=78&ArticleID=1163>.

24 You will find a good account of the series of meetings that preceded and followed the Kyoto meeting plus some data on climate change in *United Nations Convention on Climate Change: The First Ten Years*, UNFCCC, Bonn, Germany, 2004; you can also consult the Wikipedia Free Encyclopedia at <http://en.wikipedia.org/wiki/Kyoto_Protocol>.

25 European Commission (2008).

26 Plas and Erdmenger (2000).

27 Food and Agriculture Organization, How to Feed the World 2050, <http://www.fao.org/fileadmin/templates/wsfs/docs/expert_paper/How_to_Feed_the_World_in_2050.pdf>.

28 World Business Council for Sustainable Development, *Vision 2050*, <http://www.wbcsd.org>.

29 Holliday, Schmidheiny and Watts (2002) and .Lehni (2000).

30 Nichols (1993), pp. 2–10.

31 See UNICEF at <http://www.unicef.org/protection/index_childlabor.html>. See also the Child Labor Coalition at <http://www.stopchildlabor.org/>.

32 Crawford *et al.* (1999).

33 Burns *et al.* (2000).

34 Hennebel (2006).

35 Amnesty International (1998).

36 The Shell report is available at <http://sustainabilityreport.shell.com>.

37 See <http://www.bsr.org>.

38 This classification is from Jenkins (2001).

39 These guidelines are available on the OECD website.

40 Jenkins (2001), p. 28.

41 See <www.sustainability-index.com>.

42 See <http://multivu.prnewswire.com/mnr/prne/shell/48921>.

43 See <http://www.tni.org/>.

References and further reading

Amnesty International, *Human Right Principles or Companies,* AI index number ACT 70/001/1998, Amnesty International Publications, 1 Easton Street, London, WCIX 0DJ, 1998. Available at <http://www.amnesty.org>.

Badaracco Jr., Joseph L. and Allen P. Webb, 'Business Ethics: A View From the Trenches', *California Management Review,* Vol. 37, 2, Winter 1995.

Banerjee, Neela, 'US Lawsuit Snares Exxon', *International Herald Tribune,* 22 June 2001.

Bruntland, G., *Our Common Future : The World Commission on Environment and Development.* Oxford: Oxford University Press, 1987.

Burns, Jennifer L. and Debora L. Spar, 'Hitting the Wall: Nike and International Labor Practices', Harvard Business School Case 9-700-047, 2000.

Cadbury, Sir Adrian, 'Ethical Managers Make Their Own Rules', *Harvard Business Review,* Sept–Oct 1987.

Crawford, Robert, Olivier Cadot and Daniel Traca, 'Soccer Balls: Made by Children for Children? Child Labor in Pakistan', INSEAD Case Study 12/1999-4865, 1999.

De Bettignies, Henri-Claude and François Lépineux, *Business, Globalization and the Common Good.* Frontiers of Business Ethics series, 6. New York, NY: Peter Lang, 2009.

Donalson, Thomas and Thomas W. Dundee, 'When Ethics Travel: The Promise and Perils of Global Business Ethics', *California Management Review,* Vol. 40, No. 4, Summer 1999.

Dunchin, Faye and Glenn-Marie Lange, *Our Common Future.* Oxford: Oxford University Press, 1994.

EFMD, *Globally Responsible Leadership: A Call for Engagement.* EFMD: Brussels, 2005.

European Commission, *EU Action against Climate Change.* European Community, Brussels, 2008.

Fadiman, Jeffrey A., 'A Traveller's Guide to Gifts and Bribes', *Harvard Business Review,* July–August 1986.

Hennebel, Ludovic, 'L'affaire Total-Unocal en Birmanie Jugée en Europe et aux Etats Unis', CRIDHO Working Paper, 2006/09. Available at: <http://cridho.cpdr.ucl.ac.be/documents/Working.Papers/CRIDHO.WP.2006.09.pdf>.

Hess, David and Thomas Dunfee, 'Fighting Corruption: A Principled Approach', Wharton School Working Paper, 2001.

Holliday, Charles, Stephan Schmidheiny and Philip Watts, *Walking the Talk: The Business Case for Sustainable Development.* Sheffield, UK: Greenleaf Publishing, 2002.

Jenkins, Rhys, *Corporate Codes of Conduct. Self-Regulation in a Global Economy.* United Nations Research Institute for Social Development, Technology and Society Programme Paper 2, 2001.

Kaufmann, Daniel and Shang-Jin Wei, 'Does "Grease Money" Speed up the Wheels of Commerce', *National Bureau of Economic Research,* NBER Working Paper w7093, April 1999.

Kolk, A., R. van Tulder and Carlijn Welters, 'International Codes of Conduct and Corporate Social Responsibility: Can Transnational Corporations Regulate Themselves?', *Transnational Corporations,* 8(1), 1999, pp. 143–80.

Laszlo, Christopher, *Sustainable Value: How the World's Leading Companies Are Doing Well by Doing Good.* Palo Alto, CA: Stanford University Press, 2008.

Lehni M., *Eco-efficiency: Creating More Value with Less Impact*, Geneva: World Business Council for Sustainable Development, 2000.

Leite, Carlos and Jens Weiman, 'Does Mother Nature Corrupt Natural Resources? Corruption and Economic Growth', IMF Working Paper WP/99/85, July 1999.

Mauro, Paolo, 'Why Worry About Corruption?', *Economic Issues*, 6, Washington, DC: IMF, 1997.

Nichols, Martha, 'Third-World Families at Work: Child Labor or Child Care?', *Harvard Business Review*, January–February 1993.

OECD, *No Longer Business as Usual*, Paris: OECD, 2000.

OECD, *Sustainable Development.* Paris: OECD, 2001.

Orsato, Renato J., *Sustainability Strategies: When Does It Pay To Be Green?* INSEAD Business Press series. Basingstoke: Palgrave Macmillan, 2009 .

Plas, Géraldine and Christoph Erdmenger, *Green Purchasing Good Practice Guide*, The International Council for Local Environmental Initiatives, ICLEI European Secretariat, Eschholzstrasse 86, D-79115 Freiburg, Germany, European Eco-Procurement Programme and Eco-Efficient Economy (ICLEI EPP), 2000.

Pope, Jeremy, 'Confronting Corruption: The Elements of a National Integrity System', *TI Source Book 2000.* London: Transparency International, 2000; available at the TI website as a free-of-charge download.

Reinhart, Forest L., *Down to Earth: Applying Business Principles to Environmental Management.* Boston, MA: Harvard Business School Press, 1999.

Schütte, Hellmut, 'Peter Clausen', INSEAD Case Study, 1986.

Smith, Craig, 'Corporate Social Responsibility: Whether or How?' *California Management Review*, Vol. 45, 4, Summer 2003.

Sroufe, Robert and Joseph Sarkis, *Strategic Sustainability: The State of the Art in Corporate Environmental Management Systems.* Sheffield: Greenleaf Publishing, 2007 .

Tanzi, Vito, 'Corruption Around the World: Causes, Consequences, Scope and Cure', *International Monetary Fund Staff Paper*, 559, 1998.

Van Tulder, R. and A. Kolk, 'Multinationality and Corporate Ethics: Codes of Conduct in the Sporting Goods Industry', *Journal of International Business Studies*, 32(2), 2001.

Wei, Shang-Jin, 'Corruption in Economic Development: Beneficial Grease, Minor Annoyance or Major Obstacle?', Harvard University and National Bureau of Economic Research Working Paper, 1998.

chapter

16 GLOBAL TRENDS

Introduction

As it is often heard, 'the future isn't what it used to be'. There are plenty of examples of predictions made by experts that turned out to be wrong. In 1989, Francis Fukuyama asserted that the world had entered a period that he called 'the end of history' by which, after the end of the Cold War, humanity was entering a period dominated by liberal democratic societies. The first decade of the twenty-first century has shown that this was not the case. The same can be said about globalization. Every year anti-globalization militants gather at G8, IMF or Davos meetings, in order to protest against certain aspects of globalization. Joseph Stiglitz, a 2001 Nobel Prizewinner, criticized the global economic policies of the International Monetary Fund, World Trade Organization, and World Bank in his book *Globalization and Its Discontents*.[1] The past fifteen years have seen the occurrence of four major financial crises: the Asian crisis of 1997, the dot.com burst of 2001, the subprimes crisis in 2008 and the Eurozone's overindebtedness of 2011 have shown that the road toward globalization is paved with many hurdles. At the same time, international conferences and meetings are organized by UNESCO, UN, G20 Davos and other international agencies or private initiatives to coordinate and promote multilateral programs to cope with global issues.

Throughout the previous chapters, it has been assumed that globalization is ineluctable, and most corporations are building strategies based on that assumption. The past 30 years have evolved in that direction. If we look at the future, however, the pursuit of globalization seems one likely scenario, but not the only one.

This last chapter is devoted to describing some of the most salient trends that are likely to affect firms' global strategic management. Many of the issues described are conjectural and incomplete. When we look at the future we have to identify the ideological, social, demographic, political and scientific developments that affect the world of economics and business. Some of those are already visible today; some others are hidden or are present only in the form of 'weak signals'[2] or 'black swans'.[3]

Nevertheless, several organizations have projected future scenarios: all come up with three possible images: a globalized world, a fragmented world and an intermediate world in which globalization is partially achieved.

Figure 16.1 shows how this last chapter is organized. First some of the most significant global challenges will be briefly described. Then we shall summarize the best-known scenarios. Finally, we will look at the emerging theories of *global management.*

Learning objectives

At the end of the chapter you will be able to:

- set out the arguments in favour and against globalization
- appreciate the major trends in the global economy
- contribute to the building of future scenarios.

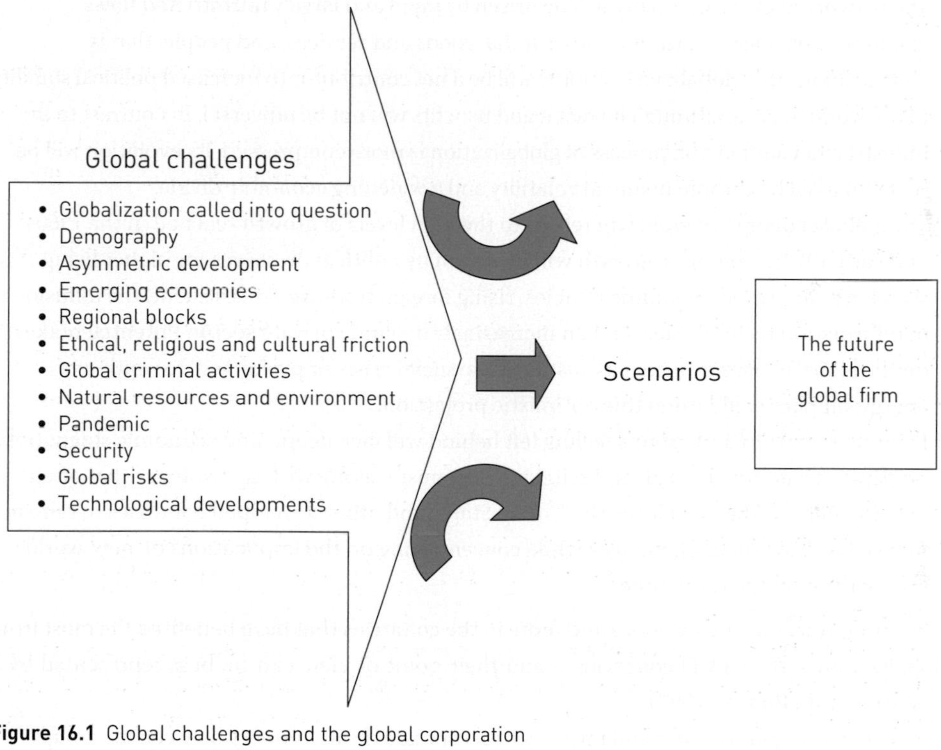

Figure 16.1 Global challenges and the global corporation

Global challenges[4]

Globalization called into question

From a historical perspective, the globalization phenomena experienced at the end of the twentieth century were not new. Some economic historians have observed that at the end of the nineteenth century the world was more 'global' than it is today. Obviously, the state of affairs was different: global powers such as Britain, France or the United States were globalized because of their colonial influence. Trade barriers were limited and people, money and goods moved easily across borders. Nationalism, epitomized by the First and Second World Wars, provoked protectionism and restriction of exchange. The postwar technological, political and economic factors described in Chapter 1 reintroduced globalization and generated new management paradigms. But at the dawn of the twenty-first century, while globalism seems to be triumphant, some dissonant voices are increasingly calling into question the concept of a borderless, free-market, monocultural world. This dialectic tension between the zealots and the dissidents dominates the background of any future scenarios.

The zealots' point of view is best represented by a quotation from a report published by the US National Intelligence Council (NIC) entitled *'Global Trends 2015: A Dialogue about the Future with Non Government Experts'*:[5]

- The networked global company will be driven by rapid and largely unrestricted flows of information, ideas, cultural values, capital, goods and services, and people: that is, globalization. This globalized economy will be a net contributor to increased political stability in the world in 2015, although its reach and benefits will not be universal. In contrast to the Industrial Revolution, the process of globalization is more compressed. Its evolution will be rocky, marked by chronic financial volatility and a widening economic divide.
- The global economy, overall, will return to the high levels of growth reached in the 1960s and early 1970s. Economic growth will be driven by political pressures for higher living standards, improved economic policies, rising foreign trade and investment, the diffusion of information technologies, and an increasingly dynamic private sector. Potential brakes on the global economy – such as sustained financial crisis or prolonged disruption of energy supplies could undo this optimistic projection.
- Regions, countries and groups feeling left behind will face deepening economic stagnation, political, ethnic, ideological, and religious extremism, along with the violence that often accompanies it. They will force the United States and other developed countries to remain focused on 'old-world' challenges while concentrating on the implications of 'new-world' technologies at the same time.

Dissenting voices are heard more and more in the countries that have benefited the most from globalization – the OECD countries – and their point of view can be best represented by a quotation from Rodrik (1997).

- First, reduced trade barriers and investment accentuate the asymmetry between the groups that can cross international borders (directly or indirectly via outsourcing, owners of capital, skilled workers, professionals) and those that cannot (semi-skilled and unskilled) can be substituted by other cheaper workers. This undermines the social fabric in the developed world.
- Second, globalization engenders conflicts within and between nations over domestic norms and the social institutions that embody these. (Pension funds, social security, values and culture...).
- Third, globalization has made it increasing difficulty for governments to provide social insurance. The welfare state is under attack.
- The question therefore is how the tension between globalization and the pressure for socialization of risks can be eased. If the lesson is not managed intelligently and creatively,

> the danger is that domestic consumers in favour of open markets will ultimately erode to the point where a generalized resurgence of protectionism becomes a serious possibility.

More radical views are obviously expressed by militant groups. Below is an extract from a talk given by Walden Bello, a representative of Corpwatch, during demonstrations in Melbourne against the World Economic Forum:[6]

What is ***deglobalization***?

I am not talking about withdrawing from the international economy. I am speaking about reorienting our economies from production for export to production for the local market;

- about drawing most of our financial resources for development from within rather than becoming dependent on foreign investment and foreign financial markets;
- about carrying out the long-postponed measures of income redistribution and land redistribution to create a vibrant internal market that would be the anchor of the economy;
- about de-emphasizing growth and maximizing equity in order to radically reduce environmental disequilibrium;
- about not leaving strategic economic decisions to the market but making them subject to democratic choice;
- about subjecting the private sector and the state to constant monitoring by civil society;
- about creating a new production and exchange complex that includes community cooperatives, private enterprises, and state enterprises, and excludes TNC [transnational corporations];
- about enshrining the principle of subsidiarity in economic life by encouraging production of goods to take place at the community and national level if it can be done so at reasonable cost in order to preserve community.

We are speaking, in short, about re-embedding the economy in society, rather than having society driven by the economy.

This anti-globalization view has been gaining support in the early twenty-first century in places and among populations that had traditionally pushed for and benefited from globalization.

Demography

In 2009 the world population was 6.9 billion, is forecasted to reach 8 billion by the year 2025 and is expected to peak at around 9 billion by 2070. As seen in Table 16.1, the increase in world population comes from the developing world of Asia, Africa and Latin America. Europe as a whole will experience a decline in population. The age pyramid in the industrialized countries of North America, Europe and Japan will shift toward aging people. Japan's population shrunk in 2005 for the first time and is expected to continue falling. Even China will experience an aging of its population due to its one-child policy as well as an increase in life expectancy. China will match the present European level of aged population in 2025 (20 per cent) and by 2050 both Europe and China will have 30 per cent of people above the age of 60 years. That will create enormous pressures on health care, social services and pensions management.

We can expect an increase in cross-border migration. According to the United Nations: '*Net migration numbers have been steadily increasing in the more developed regions and reached an all-time high of 2.6 million annually between 1990 and 2000. For the next 50 years, the average number of net migration being added to the populations in the more developed regions is projected to average about 2.2 million persons annually*'.[7]

Populations tend to concentrate more and more in urban areas. It is forecast that more than half (58 per cent) of the world population will live in urban areas by 2025, leading to the development of **megacities** of more than 10 million people: Beijing, Shanghai, Kolkata, Mumbai, Karachi, Dhaka, Jakarta, Cairo, Lagos, Mexico, São Paulo, Buenos Aires, Tokyo, New York and Los Angeles.[8]

Table 16.1 World population, from 2010 to 2100

	Population (millions)					Population aged 60 or over (%)				
	2010	2025	2050	2075	2100	2010	2025	2050	2075	2100
Africa	1022	1417	2192	2966	3574	5.5	6.4	9.8	14.7	20
Asia	4164	4730	5142	4965	4596	9.9	14.8	24.4	29.9	32.1
Europe	738	744	719	681	675	21.8	27.3	33.6	32.3	32.5
Latin America	590	679	751	738	688	10	14.9	25	32.3	34.4
North America	345	388	447	493	526	18.6	24.7	27	28.9	31.5
Oceania	37	45	55	62	66	15.3	19.1	23.5	27	30.4
World	**6896**	**8003**	**9306**	**9905**	**10,125**	**11**	**15**	**21.8**	**25.6**	**28**
China	1341	1395	1296	1086	941	12.3	20.2	33.9	36.8	34.1
India	1225	1459	1692	1692	1551	7.6	11	19.1	27.3	31.9

Source: United Nations: Department of Economics and Social Affairs <http://esa.un.org/unpd/wpp/Documentation/pdf/WPP2010_Volume-I_Comprehensive-Tables.pdf>

Asymmetric development

According to the United Nations' 2011 report on the world social situation, inequality can be assessed either between countries or regions or within countries.[9] The inequality between countries after having increased from 1990 to 2000 has slightly decreased since 2005 mainly due to the 'middle classes' of China and India (Figure 16.2). Although according to the World Bank the number of people living below the poverty level of 1.25 dollars a day has decreased from 1.9 billion in 1981 to 1.4 billion in 2005, the evolution is unequal. In East Asia, the number of people below the poverty level has decreased, but it has increased in Africa from 211 to 600 million.[10] The income inequality within countries is continuing to increase. Data reveals that income inequality rose during the period 1990–2005 in more than two-thirds of the countries for which data are available.[11]

This unequal development is a factor of instability that can generate conflict and ultimately disrupt global trade and investments.

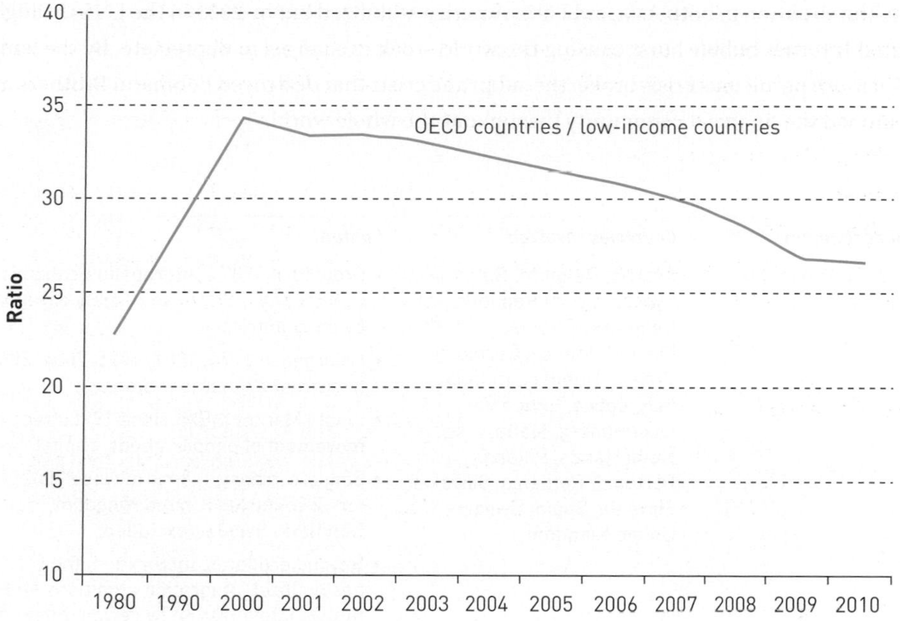

Figure 16.2 The global income gap, GDP per capita OECD/ low income, 1980–2010

Source: World Bank

Emerging economies

In Chapter 14, the characteristics of emerging countries have been described as well as their new role in the world economy. Their future impact will be felt predominantly in low skilled labor content industries where de-localization to low wage countries will continue forcing somewhat painful restructuring. Medium level technology products will also be challenged by the emerging competitors forcing companies to invest more in innovation. Another challenge raised by emerging economies is their impact on resources. China's consumption per capita of resources is much below the world average but its growth policy and its population make the overall demand very big in absolute terms. Already China is the largest consumer of steel and the second largest consumer of oil. Lester Brown, founder of the Earth Policy Institute, calculated that if Chinese consumption reaches by 2031 the existing level of US citizen consumption, China alone would demand more than the whole world's production of oil and coal, and four-fifths of the world production of meat.[12] Such development is unsustainable unless other sources of energy and new materials are found combined with different modes of production and consumption.

Financial capitalism crisis

In 1997, four major South East and North East Asian countries, Thailand, Indonesia, Korea and to a lesser extent Malaysia entered a massive depression due to highly leveraged financing and improper banking regulations. At approximately the same time Argentina entered a period of turmoil due to its inability to face high government debts. Eventually Argentine defaulted in

2001. The situation in both Asia and Latin America stabilized but by 2001 in the USA the highly inflated Internet bubble burst causing the world stock exchanges to depreciate. By the end of 2007 a more pernicious crisis broke: the subprime crisis that destroyed Lehmann Brothers and threatened the financial community throughout the whole world.

Table 16.2 Regional agreements

Region	*Regional agreement*	*Countries involved*	*Content*
Europe	EU (European Union) (ex-EEC and EC)	Austria, Belgium, Bulgaria, Cyprus, Czech Republic, Denmark, Estonia, Finland, France, Germany, Greece, Hungary, Ireland, Italy, Latvia, Lithuania, Luxembourg, Malta, Netherlands, Poland, Portugal, Romania, Slovakia, Slovenia, Spain, Sweden, United Kingdom	• Created in 1957 as European Economic Community (EEC) by the Treaty of Rome by six countries • Enlarged in 1974, 1981, 1995, 2004, 2007 to current 27 member states • Single Market (SEM) since 1992: free movement of people, goods, capital • Single currency, the euro, since 2002 for 12 countries (United Kingdom, Denmark, Sweden excluded) • Beyond economic integration, the EU has political integration ambitions still thrown into question by certain member states. By 2011 European Union faces a financial crisis.
Latin America	MERCOSUR (Mercado Común del Sur)	Argentina, Bolivia, Brazil, Chile, Paraguay, Uruguay	• Created by the Treaty of Asunción in 1991 • Aims at establishing a common market
North America	NAFTA (North American Free Trade Agreement)	Canada, Mexico, United States	• Created in 1992 • Aims at establishing a common market
South East Asia	ASEAN (Association of South East Asian Nations)	Brunei, Indonesia, Laos, Malaysia, Myanmar, Philippines, Thailand, Vietnam	• Created in 1967 • Initial objective was to promote regional stability • Progressively transformed into economic cooperation • Aims at implementing an ASEAN Free Trade Area (AFTA)
Asia-Pacific	APEC (Asia-Pacific Economic Cooperation)	21 countries from Asia, North and South America, Australia and New Zealand	• Created in 1989 • Begun as an informal dialogue group promoting open trade and practical economic cooperation • Goal is to advance Asia-Pacific economic dynamism and sense of community
North Africa	MAU (Maghreb Arab Union)	Algeria, Libya, Mauritania, Morocco, Tunisia	• Created in 1989 • Aims at establishing a common market
Southern Africa	SADC (Southern African Development Community)	Angola, Botswana, Democratic Republic of Congo, Lesotho, Malawi, Mauritius, Mozambique, Namibia, Seychelles, South Africa, Swaziland, Tanzania, Zambia, Zimbabwe	• Created 1979 and expanded in 1992 to harmonize economic development among the countries of Southern Africa

Governments all over the world have injected money into their economies in order to avoid the nightmare of the Great Depression that followed the Wall Street Crash of 1929. By doing so government debts increased up to a point where creditors realized that the Argentine scenario may happen in Greece and affect the whole of Western Europe. As the IMF points out: 'the current financial crisis has put globalization on hold, with capital flows reversing and global trade shrinking...the drivers of the recent globalization wave getting undermined, with protectionism on the rise'.[13]

Regional blocks

An alternative to globalization is regionalization. The argument put forward by Professor Alan Rugman to announce the 'end of globalization' (2000) projects that instead of a free flow of goods, services, people and capital across the world, regional 'fortresses' may emerge as the dominant form of economic structure. Table 16.2 lists the various forms of such regional agreements.

Ethnic, religious and cultural friction

An increased search for *communal identity* – religious, ethnic or linguistic – is expected to develop alongside, or against, globalization. Manifestations of such movements have been experienced in the Balkans, in Chechnya, in Mexico, in Indonesia, China, Corsica and Spain. Communities that were living alongside each other are increasingly asserting their differences, even with extreme violence as was experienced in Rwanda in the mid-1990s and in Iraq and Lebanon with the tensions between Shiites and Sunnis.

Huntington (1997) has argued forcefully that future conflicts will be primarily rooted in cultural differences, and will thus occur between different 'civilizations'.[14] The terrorist attacks of 11 September, 2001 in the United States give some credence to this thesis.

The globalization of criminal activities

Illicit criminal activities are increasingly crossing borders: drug trafficking, prostitution, smuggling, 'cybercrimes' or illegal immigration are the most frequent and increasing criminal global activities, as well as global terrorism. Transnational organized crime takes advantage of globalization to increase its power. It is estimated that US$2 trillion a year (more than 5 per cent of world GDP) consists of money resulting from illegal activities.[15] Not all comes from pure criminal actions.

Natural resources and the environment

According to a scenario developed by the US NIC (2000):

- Contemporary environmental problems will persist and in many instances grow over the next 15 years (2000–2015). Environmental issues will become mainstream issues in several countries, particularly in the developed world. The main future environmental concerns are water supply, global warming and deforestation. Those three issues are those that were mentioned as the major emerging issues according to a survey conducted by the Scientific Committee on Problems of the Environment of the International Council for Science among 200 scientists in 50 countries (UNEP, 1999).

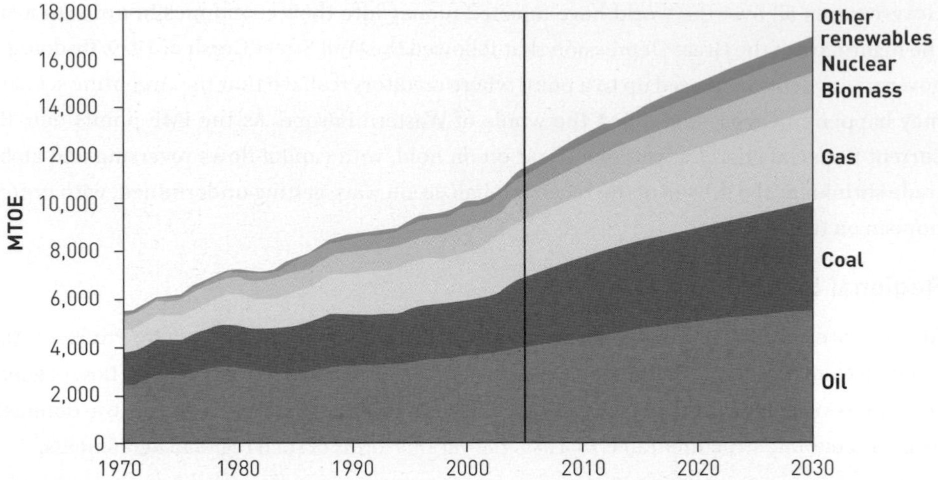

Figure 16.3 Total primary energy demand in Million Tons of Oil Equivalent (MTOE)

Source: International Energy Agency: World Energy Outlook (2006)

Energy

Demand for energy is expected to increase by 50 per cent above the 2003 level by 2030. This represents an additional investment of US$20 trillion (Figure 16.3). At present the major supply of energy comes from non-renewable sources: oil (35 per cent), coal (24 per cent), gas (21 per cent). By 2030, oil will remain the dominant source although oil reserves are likely to pass through what is known as the 'Hubbert's peak', the point at which production of oil will decline as resources are depleting. Controversies remain about the exact time of the Hubbert's peak. Renewable energies are increasing in absolute terms but remain relatively small.

Water supply

It is anticipated that 'by 2015 nearly half of the world population will live in countries with less than 1,700 cubic meters of water *per capita* per year, a water-stressed situation' (National Intelligence Council, 2000). According to the UN Environment Programme, if the trend continues this proportion will grow to two-thirds of the world's population by 2025 (UNEP, 1999). In the developed countries the price of water is likely to increase considerably, and in the developing world water disputes may degenerate into armed conflicts.

Global warming

Global emissions of CO_2 were 23,900 million tonnes in 1996, four times the level of 1950 (see Figure 15.4 in Chapter 15). Without proper control of the 'greenhouse effect', the emission of CO_2 and other gases threatens to raise the average temperature of the globe, inducing a sea-level rise and other natural disasters (see Figure 16.4). Industries are the major producers of CO_2 and without proper control the whole ecology of the planet may be disrupted.

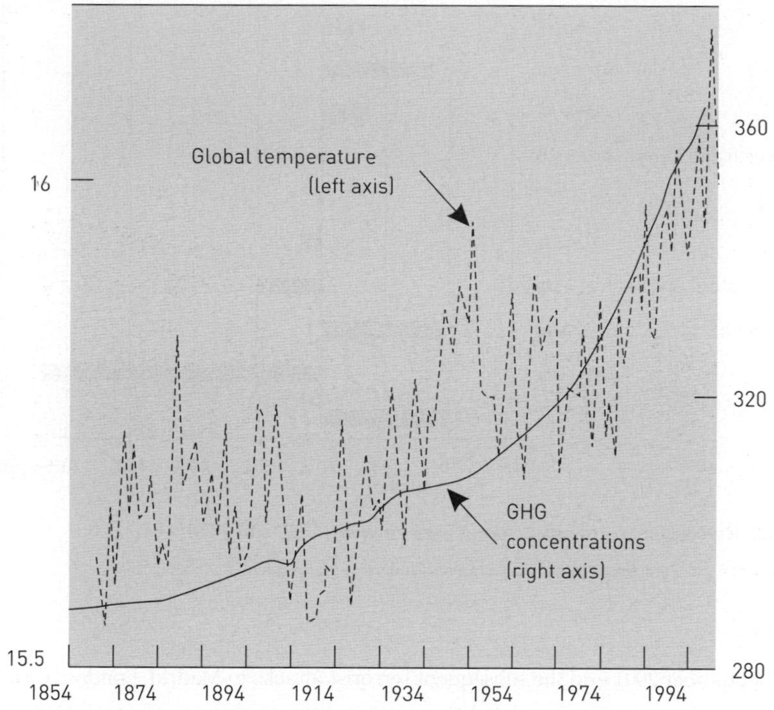

Figure 16.4 Global temperatures and concentration of greenhouse gases (GHG) 1854–1994

Source: OECD (2001)

Deforestation

The progressive cutting of forests without proper renewal creates droughts and desertification (Figure 16.5).

Marine fisheries

According to the Food and Agricultural Organization (FAO) around 75 per cent of the world's marine fishing stocks are exploited either at or above their maximum sustainable levels.[16]

Pandemic

Between 1918 and 1920 a pandemic known as the 'Spanish flu' killed 20 to 40 million people (some estimates are of 100 million). It was the worst pandemic of modern history due to the H1N1 virus transmitting from ducks to pigs and then to humans. Over the past two decades the world has experienced the outbreak of diseases that have diffused globally: AIDS and SARS notably. Since 2006 the fear of a repetition of the 'Spanish flu' with a possible transmutation of the H5N1, the agent of the 'Avian flu' has alarmed health authorities all around the world. According to the World Bank, in addition to the potential losses of life, the world GDP would decrease by 3 per cent in one year should a human pandemic of N5H1 appear.

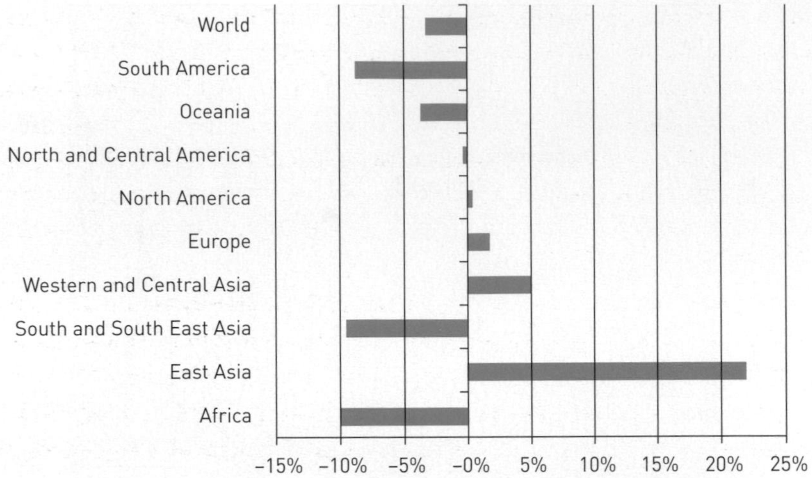

Figure 16.5 Deforestation change in forest area between 1990 and 2010

Source: Food and Agricultural Organization, United Nations <http://www.fao.org/forestry/fra/fra2010/>

Security

Since 11 September 2001 and the subsequent terrorist attacks in Madrid, London, Casablanca and Bali, security issues are affecting global transport and the movement of people. While, according to the Stockholm International Research Institute, overall the number of armed conflicts have decreased since the early 1980s, some potential major 'hot spots' can create the conditions for major wars: Middle East, North Korea, Iran and Sudan are all places where such a development may occur.

Global Risks

Table 16.3 gives a summary of the main global risks with an estimate of the probability of occurrence of those risks and their economic as well as human life impact to the international community over the next 10 years identified by a team from the World Economic Forum.[17] Some of the risks have already been mentioned earlier.

Technological developments

We will see technological developments in the following four major areas: biotechnology, materials and nanotechnology, information technology and renewable energy.

Biotechnology

Based on a better knowledge of cellular genetic codes (genomics) and the ability to manipulate genes, biotechnology is likely to develop a variety of innovations:

- *genetic profiling* based on DNA comparisons can lead to applications in diagnostics and security. DNA analysis is already used for solving criminal cases but its possibilities extend well beyond that.

- *Cloning*, even limited to crops and animals, without mentioning the ethically problematic human cloning, finds its application in agriculture or animal breeding.
- *Genetically modified organisms* are likely to be used further, extending to medical and pharmaceutical applications.
- *Biomedical engineering* will allow the production of organic or artificial tissues or organs that can be used for therapeutic purposes.

Materials and nanotechnology

New materials based on the integration of composite substances with or without electronic sensors will give rise to a new generation of applications. Some materials will be made at nano scale (1/1,000,000 mm). Examples of applications are:

- Smart textiles and clothes that can react to weather conditions
- Buildings or vehicles that can adjust to weather conditions
- Faster and smarter semiconductors
- Integrated Microsystems: Systems-on-Chips (SoC) embedding electronic and mechanical or optical components (MEMS, Micro-Electro-Mechanical Systems)
- Self-assembling materials.

Information technology

The combination of new materials and the increase in computing power as well as miniaturization and the extension of wireless communication will enable the development of:

- Pervasive information technology with computers everywhere, including homes, cars, public transport, workplace, streets, etc.
- Embedded information technology will extend its traditional areas (computers, mobile phones and other 'obvious' electronic devices) to become part of all objects used for daily living: domestic appliances, lamps, blinds, clothes, etc.
- Context awareness IT, able to use the information from the environment (location, neighbouring persons or objects, resources etc.) in order to inform the user.
- Networking: most of the progress in this area will be the development of a pervasive wireless network.

Renewable energy

Most of the expected progress in this area will come from

- the development of new sources of renewable energy both to make existing technology more efficient and cheaper (solar energy) or safer (nuclear energy), or to access new technology (hydrogen fuel cells)
- the widespread extension of hybrid or electric vehicles.

Table 16.3 Global risks

Nature of risk	Global impact	Perceived likelihood in the next ten years	Perceived negative global economic impact
ECONOMIC			
• Asset price collapse	• Reversal of economic growth • Collapse of banking system	Low	High
• Extreme commodity price volatility	• Uncertainty for investments • Hunger and malnutrition	Medium	Medium
• Extreme consumer price volatility	• Inflationary spiral • Deflationary spiral reinforcing depression	Low	Low
• Extreme energy price volatility	• Dampening economic growth • Social unrest • Financial imbalance between oil importing and oil exporting countries • Supply crunch	Medium	High
• Fiscal crisis	• High government debt to GDP ratios • European integration threatened • Cutback in innovation and education • Social unrest	Medium	High
• Global imbalance and currency volatility	• Adverse foreign exchange imbalance • Increase in protectionism • Fiscal crisis	Medium	High
• Infrastructure fragility	• Cost increase and business disruption • Environmental damage • Domino effects on other risks	Low	Low
• Liquidity/credit crunch	• Sharp recession • Reduced profitability and higher products prices	Medium	High
• Regulatory failures	• Failure of international structures (G20 …)	Medium	Medium
• Retrenchment from globalization	• Decrease in innovation and economic growth • Higher levels of poverty	Low	Medium
• Slowing of Chinese economy	• Reversal in globalization • Bursting of infrastructure projects • Socio-economic unrest	Low	Medium
GEOPOLITICAL			
• Corruption	• Increased costs • Barriers to growth • Reduced level of citizens' trust • Erosion of institutions • Increased security concerns	Low	Medium
• Fragile state	• Increasing economic disparity • Civil wars and reduced security • Migrations • Illicit trade and organized crime • Conflicts and terrorism	Medium	Medium
• Geopolitical conflicts	• Loss of human lives • Loss of resources and properties • Distrust among nations • Breakdown of global trade	Medium	High

Nature of risk	Global impact	Perceived likelihood in the next ten years	Perceived negative global economic impact
• Global governance failures	• Increase of other global risks • Reduced growth • Potential geopolitical conflicts • Reduced trust among states	High	High
• Illicit trade	• Reduced public and private sectors revenues • Corruption, organized crime and state fragility • Threatening of biodiversity	High	Low
• Organized crime	• Reduced public and private sectors revenues • Social stability and security	Medium	Medium
• Personal security	• Geopolitical conflicts • Reduced opportunities for economic and human developments • Human injuries and loss of life	Low	Low
• Terrorism	• Human injuries and loss of life • Reduced trust among people • Psychological trauma	High	Low
• Weapons of mass destruction	• Economic opportunity costs • Geopolitical conflicts • Terrorism • Power shift	Low	High
ENVIRONMENTAL			
• Air pollution	• Detrimental effect on biodiversity • Human health hazards • Healthcare costs • Loss of productivity	Medium	Low
• Biodiversity loss	• Irreversible environmental damages • Climate change • Economic losses • Migrations, psychological trauma, economic damages	High	Medium
• Climate change	• Declining crop yields, risks of starvation • Destruction of marine diversity • Economic losses • Spread of infectious diseases	High	High
• Earthquake and volcanic eruptions	• Loss of life • Displacement of people • Interruption in global logistics	Medium	Low
• Flooding	• Economic losses • Displacement, migrations • Water contamination	High	Low
• Inadequate ocean governance	• Environmental degradation • Geopolitical tensions • Wide-scale pollution	Low	Low
• Storms and cyclones	• Economic loss • Loss of life • Interruption in global logistics • Increased costs • Crop damages	High	Low

Nature of risk	Global impact	Perceived likelihood in the next ten years	Perceived negative global economic impact
SOCIETAL			
• Chronic diseases	• Increased death rate • Decrease in productivity and savings • Increased burden on human resources • Increased financial burden • Increase in mental illness and depression	Medium	Medium
• Demographic challenges	• Economic and financial burden on healthcare and pensions systems • Threats on financial solvency • Growing impoverishment of old ages • Skewing of political systems • Resentment of younger generations • Large number of unemployed youth	High	Medium
• Economic disparity	• Social fragmentation • Mistrust of the system of governance • Chronic disease and depression • Destruction of local ecosystem • Social and political unrest • Malnutrition • Migration • Commodity price volatility	High	High
• Infectious diseases	• Significant loss of life • Disruption in business activities • Burden on health systems • Public panic • Loss of productivity • Emergence of drug resistant bacterias	Medium	Low
• Migration	• Social tensions • Strain on social services • Brain drain	Medium	Medium
• Water security	• Reduced agricultural yield • Physical and economic conflicts • Spread of diseases • Migration pressure • Social and political unrest	Medium	Medium
TECHNOLOGICAL			
• Critical information infrastructure breakdown	• Disruption to government, communication, energy and financial systems	Low	Medium
• Online data and information security	• Disruption of e-commerce and communication networks • Paralysis of business and government • Breaches of privacy • Hampering of innovation and trust	Medium	Low
• Threats from new technologies	• Strong public concerns and mistrust • Impact on health and healthcare • Proliferation of court cases • Unconventional weapons proliferation	Low	Low

Source: World Economic Forum (2011)

Future scenarios

The technique of **scenario** building is used to picture potential images of the future (Wack, 1985a, 1985b). Scenarios are built upon contrasted configurations of key socio-economic and political drivers. The configurations are based on expert opinion. Two to four possible futures are pictured – most scenarios contain two or three extreme representations and a middle one, although there is some argument for developing at least four scenarios in order to avoid the middle of the road choice.[18] Appendix 16.1 gives a simplified methodology for elaborating scenarios.

The main attractiveness of scenario building is that it expands the range of possible futures beyond pure extrapolation. It obliges decision-makers to uncover the underlying drivers of change. Scenario building is not without pitfalls, however; in particular the main criticism relies on the fact that no scenarios have identified 'black swans', or unexpected events such as the terrorist attack of 11 September.

Table 16.4 summarizes some alternative scenarios set out in the following publications: *Global Trends 2025*,[19] published by the US National Security Agency, the *Millennium Project*,[20] organized by the United Nations University, the *Global Scenarios 1998–2020*, prepared by Shell Corporation[21] and *Which World?* prepared by Allen Hammond, a director of Strategic Analysis at the World Resources Institute (1998). The example below gives a detailed description of the Millennium Project.

Table 16.4 Four global scenarios

Name of project and origin	*Scenarios*	*Brief description*
Global Trends 2025 (National Intelligence Council, 2000)	**A world without the West**	The new powers supplant the West as leaders of the world and develop the capacity to be global players.
Four alternative scenarios	**October surprise**	Global inattention to climate change leads to unexpected impacts. Potential major dislocations could threaten both developed and developing countries.
	BRIC's bust-up	China sparks a clash with India for resource supply. Increased potential for conflicts in a multipolar world.
	Politics is not always local	A new world emerges in which nation states gave away power to multinational and transnational entities.
Global Exploratory Scenarios, 2005 State of the Future (Glen and Gordon, 2005)	**Cybertopia**	The explosive growth of Internet-accelerated globalization in all forms.
		Explosive growth in international activity.
Four alternative scenarios		Developing countries make remarkable progress. Government involvement is low, communications are vibrant, security is high.
	The rich get richer	While the poorer countries in Africa and Asia run into a plethora of problems, the richer countries experience a period of robust GNP growth.
		Government involvement is low, communications are vibrant, security is low.
		Globalization goes on.

Name of project and origin	*Scenarios*	*Brief description*
Global Exploratory Scenarios, 2005 State of the Future *continued*	**A passive mean world**	Isolation prevails, government involvement is high, communications are stagnant, security is high. Population growth outpaces job growth in most regions, and the concomitant unemployment and under-employment produces pressure on economic systems and fosters political unrest.
	Trading places	Loss of Western industrial leadership in key sectors, growing Asian economic and political power, and structural economic problems in the United States set the US economy on a downward slope. Government involvement is low, communications are vibrant, security is low. Globalization goes on.
Shell Energy Scenarios to 2050 (Shell Oil, 1998)	**Scramble**	Immediate pressures to achieve energy security draw attention of governments to supply side levers resulting in nationalistic resource scramble. Actions to address climate change are given secondary priorities. The energy system is characterized by discontinuities.
	Blueprints	Actions to manage energy use are driven by a combination of concern about supply but also environmental interests and the opportunities to transform the energy system. Alliances to drive better economies and lifestyles are initiated by coalitions across countries. New policies encourage the adoption of new technologies and innovation.
The World in 2025 (European Commission 2009) Trends	**The Asian century**	61 per cent of the world population will be in Asia. China will become the second economic power. Asia will be the main destination of business R and D.
	Poverty and mobility	International migration will develop. A third of the world population is undernourished but obesity increases in developed countries. Global health is improving but new risks are emerging.
	Increased scarcity of natural resources and vulnerability of the planet	Relative balance of the strategic energy importance of Russia, Middle East and the Caucasus. More than 50 per cent of the major ore reserves are located in poor countries.
	Tensions	Tension between the current methods of production, consumption and the future availability of non-renewable resources. Tensions between a general and simultaneous process of increasing economic interdependence and differentiation. Accelerated urbanization and cultural distance.

The Millennium Project

The Millennium Project, founded in 1996 with the United Nation University, the Smithsonian Institution, Futures Group International and the American Council for the United Nation University, is an independent nonprofit global participatory futures research think tank of futurists, scholars, business planners and policy-makers who work for international organizations, governments, corporations, NGOs, and universities. Its mission is to improve the thinking about the future and make that thinking available through a variety of media. Since 1996, about 2500 futurists, scholars, decision-makers and business planners from over 50 countries have contributed their views to the Millennium Project research. Every year it publishes 'State of the Future'. 15 global challenges have been identified:

The 15 Global Challenges

- How can sustainable development be achieved for all while addressing global climate change?
- How can everyone have sufficient clean water without conflict?
- How can population growth and resources be brought into balance?
- How can genuine democracy emerge from authoritarian regimes?
- How can policy-making be made more sensitive to global long-term perspectives?
- How can the global convergence of information and communications technologies work for everyone?
- How can ethical market economies be encouraged to help reduce the gap between rich and poor?
- How can the threat of new and re-emerging diseases and immune micro-organisms be reduced?
- How can the capacity to decide be improved as the nature of work and institutions change?
- How can shared values and new security strategies reduce ethnic conflicts, terrorism and the use of weapons of mass destruction?
- How can the changing status of women help improve the human condition?
- How can transnational organized crime networks be stopped from becoming more powerful and sophisticated global enterprises?
- How can growing energy demands be met safely and efficiently?
- How can scientific and technological breakthroughs be accelerated to improve the human condition?
- How can ethical considerations become more routinely incorporated into global decisions?

In its 2011 edition of 'State of the Future' the project has identified 28 variables that contribute positively or negatively to the global challenges.

Global State of the Future in 2011 – The World Score Card

Positive developments	Negative developments	Uncertain developments
• Improved water source • Improved literacy rate • Improved school enrollment • Decrease in poverty headcount • Drop in population growth • Increase in physician per 1000 people • Increase in Internet users • Decrease in infant mortality • Increase in women in parliaments • Increase of GDP per unit of energy use • Decrease in number of major armed conflicts • Decrease in undernourishment • Decrease in prevalence of HIV • Decrease in countries having or thought to have nuclear weapons • Decrease in total debt service in low- and mid-income countries • Increase of R and D expenditures	• Increase in CO_2 emissions • Increase in surface temperature anomalies • Decrease in people voting in elections • Increase in level of corruption • Increase in number of people killed in terrorist attacks • Increase in number of refugees	• Unemployment • Non-fossil fuel consumption • Population in countries that are free • Percentage of forest land

Source: 2011 State of the Future, The Millenium Project, Washington, D.C.

The future of global corporations

Academic and consulting research on the future roles, capabilities and organization of global firms is all based on the fundamental assumption that globalization is progressing and that global firms are the main vectors of that 'progress'. The main focus of organizational and strategic thinkers is to imagine and craft the organization of the future as more innovative or 'revolutionary'[22] in order to lead, and adapt to, the changes brought by global competition. We can identify two major models or 'blueprints' for the future global firm: the **individualized corporation** model and the **metanational** model.

The individualized corporation

'The individualized corporation' is a terminology suggested by Ghoshal and Bartlett (1997). Based on the example of some leading global firms such as Canon, ABB or 3M, the authors argue that the future organizational form is best described by a *portfolio of three key processes*, embodied into a *new organizational model* in which *new management competencies and roles* are redefined:

- The *key processes* are: the renewal process, the integration process and the entrepreneurial process (Figure 16.6).
- The *new organizational model* is based on a network of relationships as opposed to the traditional hierarchical structure (Figure 16.7)

- The *new management roles* are: the operating entrepreneurial role of front-line managers, the management-developer of senior and middle-level managers and the top-level institutional builder of top leaders (Table 16.5).

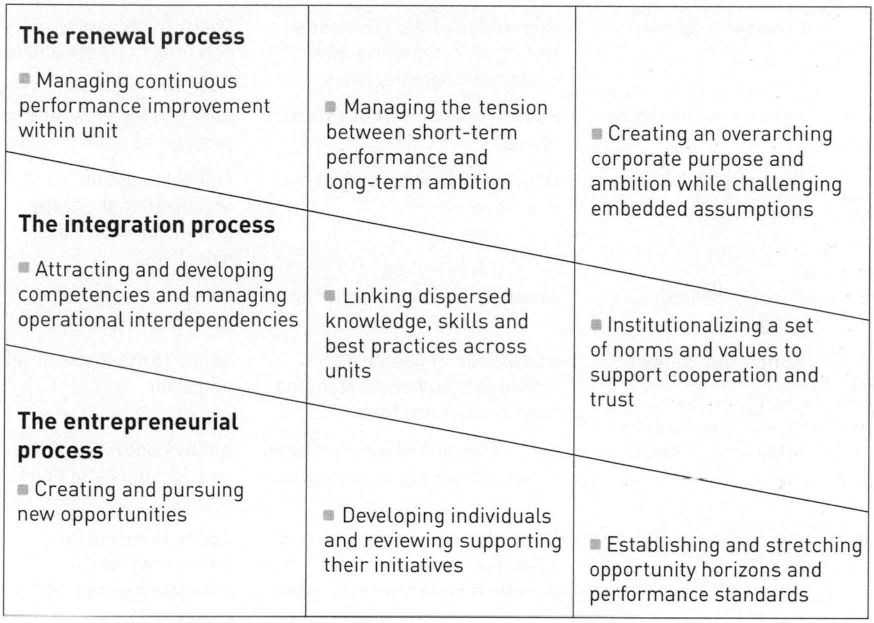
The renewal process
Managing continuous performance improvement within unit
Managing the tension between short-term performance and long-term ambition
Creating an overarching corporate purpose and ambition while challenging embedded assumptions
The integration process
Attracting and developing competencies and managing operational interdependencies
Linking dispersed knowledge, skills and best practices across units
Institutionalizing a set of norms and values to support cooperation and trust
The entrepreneurial process
Creating and pursuing new opportunities
Developing individuals and reviewing supporting their initiatives
Establishing and stretching opportunity horizons and performance standards

Figure 16.6 Portfolio of processes

Source: Ghoshal and Bartlett (1997), p. 201

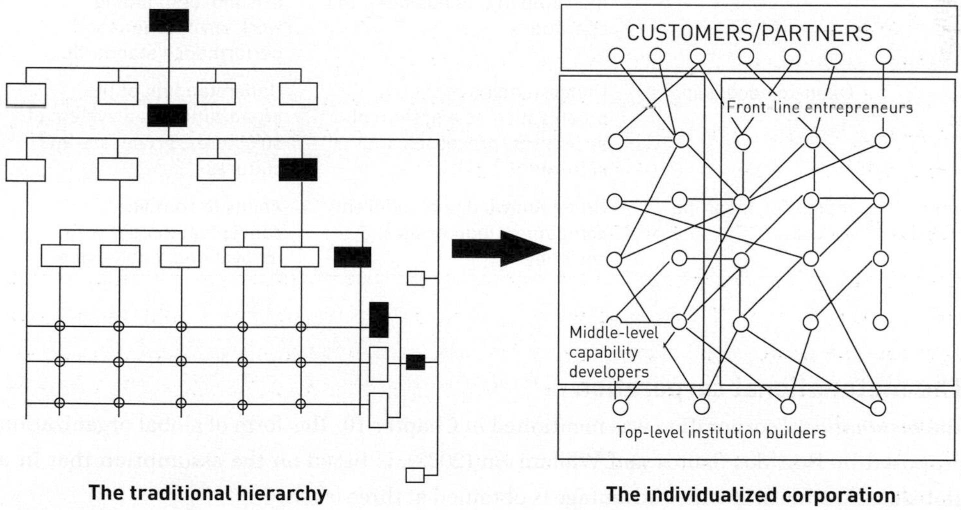
CUSTOMERS/PARTNERS
Front line entrepreneurs
Middle-level capability developers
Top-level institution builders
The traditional hierarchy
The individualized corporation

Figure 16.7 A new organizational model

Source: Ghoshal and Bartlett (1997), p. 205

Table 16.5 Management competencies for new roles

Role/tasks	*Traits*	*Knowledge/experience*	*Skills/attitudes*
Operating entrepreneurial	*Results-oriented competitor*	*Detailed operating knowledge*	*Focuses energy on opportunities*
Creating and pursuing opportunities	Creative, intuitive	Knowledge of the business's technical, competitive and customer characteristics	Ability to recognize potential markets and make commitments
Attracting and utilizing scarce skills and resources	Persuasive, engaging	Knowledge of internal/external resources	Ability to motivate and drive people
Managing continuous performance improvement	Competitive, persistent	Detailed understanding of the business	Ability to sustain organizational energy around demanding objectives
Management-developers	*People-oriented integrator*	*Broad organizational experience*	*Focuses energy on opportunities*
Reviewing, developing, supporting individuals and their initiatives	Supportive, patient	Knowledge of people as individuals and understanding how to influence them	Ability to delegate, develop, empower
Linking dispersed knowledge/skills	Integrative, flexible	Understanding of interpersonal dynamics among diverse groups	Ability to develop relationships and build teams
Managing short-term and long-term pressures	Perceptive, demanding	Understanding of means–ends relationships linking short-term priorities and long-term goals	Ability to reconcile differences while maintaining creative tensions
Top-level institutional builders	*Institution visionary*	*Understanding company in its context*	*Understanding company in its context*
Challenging assumptions while setting stretching opportunities/horizons	Challenging, stretching	Grounded understanding of the company, its business and operations	Ability to create an existing, demanding work environment and performance standards
Building a context of cooperation and trust	Open-minded, fair	Understanding of the organization as a system of structures, processes and cultures	Understanding of the organization as a system of structures, processes and cultures
Creating an overarching, sense of corporate purpose and ambition	Insightful, inspiring	Broad knowledge of different companies, industries and societies	Ability to combine conceptual insight with motivational challenges

Source: Ghoshal and Bartlett (1997), pp. 221–22

The metanational corporation

The *metanational* corporation was mentioned in Chapter 10. This form of global organization proposed by Doz, dos Santos and Williamson (2002), is based on the assumption that in a globalized world competitive advantage is obtained at three levels:

- The ability to *identify* and access new competencies, innovative technologies and lead market knowledge

- The speed and the effectiveness with which companies can connect scattered pieces of knowledge and use them to create *innovative products and services*
- The ability to optimize the efficiency of global sales, distribution, marketing and supply chains to *leverage those products, services and process innovations* across global markets rapidly and cost-effectively.

The traditional global firms were 'projectors', meaning that the source of their competitive advantage was to be found in their home countries, and their globalization was to *project those advantages* internationally. The metanational corporation is a 'prospector', meaning that the source of their competitive advantage is to be able to prospect, tap and leverage knowledge *scattered across the world* in a speedy and efficient manner. Although the authors have not yet identified fully fledged companies that correspond to the characteristics of their model, they found that companies like Nokia, the Finnish leader in mobile phones, or ST Microelectronics, a European microprocessor firm, are examples of metanationals in the making. The metanational firm has a dispersed internal and external network of design, production and customer relationship centers, each of which contributes to knowledge-creation and leverage. The concept of a 'center' or 'home headquarters' disappears in this type of organization – it is a *pure global firm within a global world.*

Both models are based on the form of a networked organization that implies the coordinated combined effort of 'unbundled' business units (Hagel and Singer, 1999), some of them being 'internal' to a corporation (subsidiaries), some external (partners, suppliers, distributors), some in between (joint ventures, strategic alliances). The concept of the networked organization is not new but it gained momentum during the 1980s and 1990s because of the restructuring of firms, the forming of global strategic alliances and the development of IT.

MINI-CASE

The Pandemic Threat

The Minister of Health of Pulau Vicente, a South Pacific island, was concerned about a potential pandemic flu carried by wild animals. He asked a group of health and economic experts to form a team in order to evaluate the potential economic and social consequences of a pandemic irruption in the island under various contrasted scenarios.

The team gathered first in order to establish a plan of action. They determined that their study would be divided into four phases:

1. List first the elements to be assessed in order to build a scenario:
   a) The impacted issues: what does the minister wants to assess in terms of economic and social consequences and define a measurable variable of those issues (dependent variables)
   b) the most important driving forces either external or internal, direct or indirect that can possibly influence the selected issues in the future (independent or intermediate variables).
2. For each driving force select its possible state of affair (variables): either the variable is a number: for example, growth rate or the variable is expressed as a range of high to

MINI-CASE

low, frequent, and infrequent; in both cases no more than three discrete values for each variable (the two extreme and a middle range). They planned to use a kind of Delphi technique (asking a group of experts to hypothesize on a given situation interactively and qualitatively).

3, Build a model in which the relationship between variables is represented and calculate the potential outcome.

4. Analyze each of the projected outcomes and reduce it to a small number of plausible and contrasted stories under the form of 'scenarios'. This is considered as the most creative part of the exercise, where two or three alternative futures have to be extracted from the data and described within a narrative.

Having adopted this methodology they financed a series of research studies in order to collect data. Below are the results of their data collection.

a) According to the sanitary authorities the anticipated flu could affect the population with various intensities. Assuming that the virus could be transmitted to humans a possible one-tenth of the population could develop the flu up to a maximum of one-third.

b) Some experts say that there is no vaccine available but others think that a vaccine could be developed with an efficacy of 30 to 70 per cent.

c) The infected population if not vaccinated or with a failed vaccination could receive a classic treatment to develop self-defense mechanisms (antibodies) but unfortunately around 2 to 3 per cent would die.

d) Statistical data is shown in Table 16.6:

Table 16.6 Data relating to Pulau Vicente

Population (millions)	27
Working population	40%
GDP (US$ billion)	195
Total hours worked/year	2500
Total hours worked/week	48
GDP per employee (US$)	18,000
GDP per worked hour (US$)	7,2
Cost of vaccination per person (US$)	100
Cost of classical treatment per person (US$)	400
Death rate for non-vaccinated population	2%

Question:

1) What are the possible scenarios?

Summary and key points

1 The significant challenges to globalization include:

- Globalization called into question:
  - *Zealot* point of view:

    - Globalization will drive networked global company
    - Globalized economy will increase political stability but reach and benefits will not be universal
    - Globalization process will evolve with financial volatility and a widening economic divide
    - Potential brakes on global economy include sustained financial crisis or prolonged disruption of energy supplies
    - Regions, countries and groups feel left behind and will face deepening economic stagnation, political, ethnic, ideological and religious extremism
    - Developed countries will be forced to focus on 'old-world' challenges while concentrating on the implications of 'new-world' technologies
  - *Dissenting* point of view:
    - Reduced trade barriers and investment increases asymmetry between groups that can cross international borders and groups that cannot
    - Globalization stimulates conflicts within and between nations over domestic norms and social institutions embodying them
    - Globalization makes it increasingly difficult for governments to provide social insurance
    - How to ease tension between globalization and pressures for socialization to minimize the possibility of a generalized resurgence of protectionism?
  - *Radical* point of view:
    - Re-embedding the economy in society instead of having society driven by the economy:
      - Obtain financial resources for development from within instead of foreign investment
      - Implement measures of income and land redistribution
      - De-emphasize growth and maximize equity
      - Make strategic economic decisions subject to democratic choice
      - Subject private sector and state to constant monitoring by civil society
      - Create a new production/exchange complex that includes community cooperatives, private enterprises and state enterprises but exclude TNCs
      - Encourage production of goods at community/sub-national level
- Demographic trends:
  - Increase in world population will come from developing world
  - Age pyramid in industrialized countries will shift towards aging people, increasing pressures on health care, social services and pension management
  - Increase in cross-border migrations and intense urbanization will create megacities of more than 10 million people
- Asymmetric development – the unequal development of people living below a certain poverty level will generate conflicts and ultimately disrupt global trade and investment
- Emerging economies – China (the emerging giant):
  - Projected to catch up with US GDP in PPP terms by 2020
  - Has built a large industrial base with progressively modernized state-owned enterprises

  - Likely to become a global economic and political power with corporations challenging established global firms
- Regional blocks:
  - As alternative to globalization, regional blocks emerging as the dominant form of economic structure
  - Examples include EU, MERCOSUR, NAFTA, ASEAN, APEC, MAU, SADC
- Ethnic, religious and cultural friction – increased search for community identity (religious, ethnic, linguistic) which will develop against globalization, as evidenced by the Balkans area
- Global criminal activities – increasingly cross-border, e.g. drug trafficking
- Natural resource and environment:
  - Environmental issues:
    - These issues will become mainstream issues in the developed world
    - Main future concerns are water supply, global warming and deforestation
- Technological developments:
  - *Internet*: a global tool abolishing physical distance for multimedia transmission with usage spreading throughout the world; theoretically, Internet technology creates the basis for the development of global virtual marketplaces and makes borders irrelevant, in practice, governments still can control the physical flow of goods and access to websites
  - *Biotechnology*: genetic engineering will raise fundamental ethical and environmental issues.

2 There are four publications that set out possible future scenarios:

- *Global Trends 2015* (US National Security Agency):
  - Majority of the world's population benefit from globalization (inclusive globalization)
  - Majority of people do not enjoy the benefits (pernicious globalization)
  - Regional economic integration (regional competition)
  - Economic and political tension between United States and Europe, Asia generally prosperous and stable (post-polar world)
- *Millennium Project* (UN University):
  - Periods of explosive growth of Internet-accelerated globalization (Cybertopia)
  - Richer countries experience a period of robust GNP growth (the rich get richer)
  - Concomitant unemployment and under-employment produce pressure on economic system and foster political unrest (a passive mean world)
  - Loss of Western industrial leadership, growing Asian economic and political power and US economy on a downward slope (trading places)
- *Global scenarios 1998–2020* (Shell Corporation):
  - Existing institutions and organizations successfully adapt to new and evolving complexities and global corporations continuously reinvent themselves (the new game)
  - A fragmented world with changing values and unequal development (people power)
- *Which World?* (World Resources Institute):
  - Free market prevails with economic reforms, privatization and deregulation, globalization achieved with transnational corporations as core players in the world (market world)

  - Widespread social instability with rising conflict and return to protectionism (Fortress world)
  - Social, environmental, economical and political issues are harmoniously managed (transformed world).

3 Emerging theories of global management with two major company models:

- *Individualized corporation* with a portfolio of three key processes by which new management competencies and roles are defined:
  - Key processes are the entrepreneurial process, the integration process and the renewal process
  - The new organizational model is based on a network relationship instead of the traditional hierarchical structure
  - The new management roles are the operating-entrepreneurial role of front-line managers, the management-developer of senior and middle-level managers and the top-level institutional builder of top leaders
- *Metanational*
  - The networked organization implies the coordinated combined effort of 'unbundled' business units, some 'internal' to a corporation (e.g. subsidiaries), some 'external' to a corporation (e.g. partners, suppliers, distributors) and some in between (e.g. joint ventures, strategic alliances)
  - Assumes competitive advantage is obtained at three levels:
    - Ability to identify and access new competencies, innovative technologies and lead market knowledge
    - Speed and effectiveness with which companies can connect scattered pieces of knowledge and use them to create innovative products and services
    - Ability to optimize the efficiency of global sales, distribution, marketing and supply chains to leverage those products, services and processes innovations across global market rapidly and cost-effectively.

Appendix 16.1 A simplified methodology for elaborating scenarios

The proposed methodology consists of seven steps:

- Define a future 'issue'
- List underlying driving forces
- Reduce the number of forces to a manageable number
- For each force select its possible state of affairs (variables)
- Combine the variables (independent combination or causal combination)
- Analyze each of the projected outcomes and reduce it to a small number of plausible and contrasted stories under the form of 'scenarios'
- Discuss the possible consequence of each scenario for the company.

Define a future 'issue': 'What could happen in the future for ... and what are the consequences for ... ?'

At this first stage the team in charge of writing a scenario has to address three questions:

- What is the primary purpose of the project? Is it to:
  - Improve understanding of the environment?
  - Improve the quality of strategy?
  - Prepare contingent actions?
  - Assess risks?
- Who will be using the scenarios?
  - Top management?
  - Operational decision makers?
  - General internal and external communication?
- What are the expected outcomes?
  - Support strategy or specific investment decisions?
  - Raising the public profile of particular issues?
  - Improving a team's expected performance?

List underlying driving forces
The team has to identify the elements that drive the phenomenon under consideration. These can be:

- External forces (exogenous): Forces that affect directly or indirectly the phenomenon and whose origin is in the external environment:
  - Economic
  - Social
  - Technological
  - Political
  - Ecological
- Internal forces (endogenous): Forces internal to the organization, either controllable or given as constraints:
  - Costs
  - Organizational structure
  - Behavior of players

The team should come up with a list of two to a maximum of five external and internal forces.

Reduce the number of forces to a manageable number by ranking them and take only those that are seen to be the most important (based on consensus or the Delphi method). One question to address to reduce the number of forces is to see whether some of them are two different ways to describe the same phenomenon and are highly correlated (for instance inflation and price increase). Those forces are now qualified as variables.

Select a possible state of affairs for the variables, either continuous (with a numerical score) or discrete (by categories, e.g.: high, medium, low).

Combine the variables (independent combination or causal combination):

- Independent combinations are combinations when variables act independently of each other and the outcome is a combination of various states of affairs. For instance, in the decision tree in Figure 16.A1 the outcome is derived from a yes/no combination of independent variables.

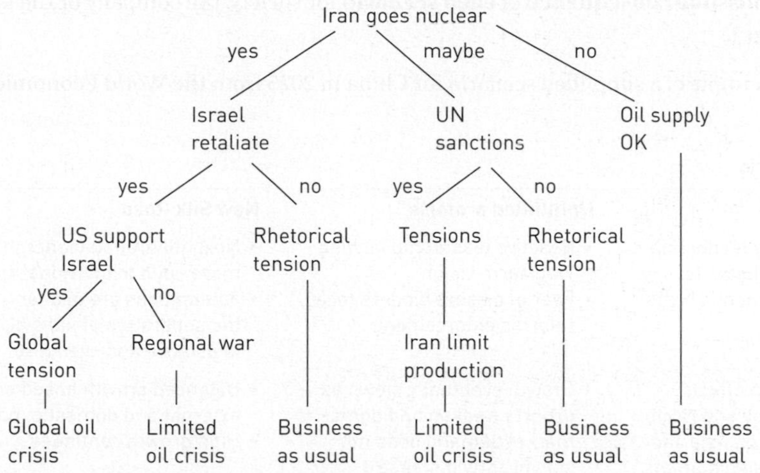

Figure 16.A1 Decision tree of independent variables

- Causal relationships are variables that influence others as, for instance, in the causal path illustrated in Figure 16.A2:

Many techniques for combining variables are available:

- Some of them highly quantitative: cross impact analysis, simulation models, mutivariable models
- Some others are less quantitative: decision trees, simple matrices and simple causal paths.

Analyze each of the projected outcomes and reduce it to a small number of plausible and contrasted stories under the form of 'scenarios'. For instance, in 2006 the World Economic Forum designed three possible scenarios for China by 2025: *Unfulfilled Promise, New Silk Road, Regional Ties* (see p. 484).

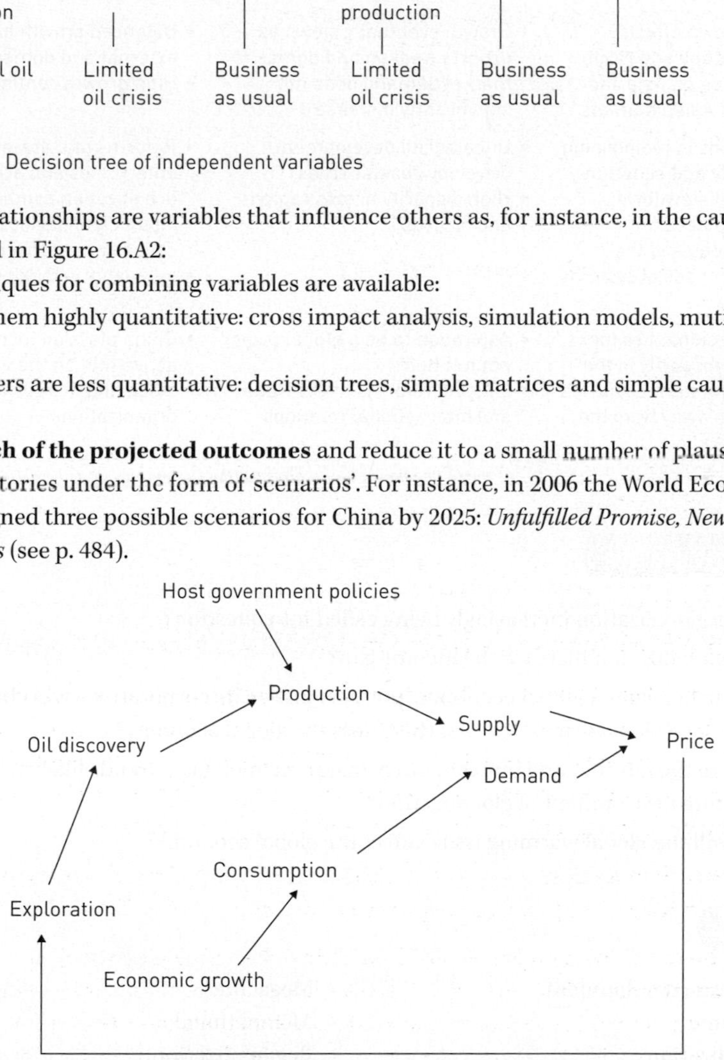

Figure 16.A2 Example of simple causal paths for price setting in the oil industry

Discuss the possible consequence of each scenario for society, the company or the issue defined in step 1.

Below is an example of a simplified scenario for China in 2025 from the World Economic Forum.

An example of an uncertain scenario

	Regional ties	Unfulfilled promise	New Silk Road
Leadership & governance	• Strong one party leadership • Strategic vision helps to weather the economic crisis	• Reactive leadership lacking long-term vision • Fear of dissent hinders local reforms enforcement	• Next generation leadership more open to individual rights • Foundations are laid for the separation of judicial, legislative and executive
Economic performance	• Global slowdown affects exports to Europe and North America. Focus on Asia and domestic and Asian markets	• Growth eventually slows as exports weaken and domestic market demand does not significantly increase	• Balanced growth based on both external and domestic markets • High growth continues
Social development	• China succeeds in maintaining social stability and cohesion despite global slowdown • Emphasis is placed on social inclusions and the development of social systems	• Unbalanced development driven by coastal areas • High disparity across regions and classes	• Reforms of state-owned enterprises and accelerated urbanization combined with an insufficient social safety net cause some concerns • Inequality is tackled in earnest by 2015
External relationships	• Successful regional ties fuel growth and prosperity in the region after Western countries shift attention away from the region	• Aspiration to be a global player not fulfilled • Lagging reforms affect trade and international relations	• China plays an increasingly active role on the world stage and in international organizations

Source: China and the World: Scenarios to 2025. Word Economic Forum: <https://members.weforum.org/pdf/Asia/China_Scen.pdf>

Learning assignments

1. Why is globalization increasingly being called into question?
2. Does globalization increase the income gap?
3. If China becomes a global economic/political power, its corporations will challenge established global firms. How will this affect the global economy?
4. Why are the Internet and biotechnology major technological trends likely to influence the future development of globalization?
5. How will the 'global warming issue' affect the global economy?

Key words

- Asymmetric development
- Cybercrime
- Deglobalization
- Global warming
- Individualized corporation
- Megacities
- Metanational
- Regionalization
- Scenarios

Web resources

<http://www.imf.org/>
The IMF website.

<http://www.oecd.org/>
The OECD website.

<http://www.unmillenniumproject.org/>
The Millennium Project website.

<https://www.cia.gov/>
The Central Intelligence Agency website.

<http://www.dni.gov/nic/NIC_2025_global_scenarios.html>
National Intelligence Council global scenarios.

Visit the companion website at **http://www.palgrave.com/business/lasserre3e** for a multitude of weblinks and resources, self-test questions for revision and a searchable glossary.

Notes

1 Stiglitz (2002).
2 Ansoff (1975), pp. 21–33.
3 Taleb (2007).
4 The term global challenge is used by the UN University, Millennium Projects published every year since 1997; the latest published edition is: Glen, Jerome Theodore Gordon, *2006: State of the Future.* Washington, DC: American Council for the United Nations University, 2006. Most of the challenges discussed in this chapter are also part of the 15 global challenges of the Millennium Project.
5 NIC (2000), p. 20.
6 Bello (2000).
7 United Nations, *World Population Prospects, the 2004 Revision Analytical Report.*
8 NIC (2000), p. 20.
9 United Nations (2011).
10 <http://web.worldbank.org/WBSITE/EXTERNAL/TOPICS/EXTPOVERTY/0,,contentMDK:22569747~pagePK:148956~piPK:216618~theSitePK:336992,00.html>, accessed 21 January 2012.
11 NIC (2000).
12 Abib Aslam (2005).
13 International Monetary Fund, 'Crisis jolts globalization process': <http://www.imf.org/external/np/exr/key/global.htm>, 2011.
14 Huntington (1997); the original article, 'The Clash of Civilizations?' (*Foreign Affairs,* Summer 1993, pp. 22–49), sparked a fierce debate about a new 'civilization paradigm',

replacing the former demarcation of the First, Second and Third Worlds. (See *Foreign Affairs,* September–October 1993, pp. 2–26, and Huntingdon's response, *Foreign Affairs,* November–December 1993, pp. 186–94.)

15 UN University, *2005: State of the Future* (see note 4).

16 World Bank, *Global Economic Prospects*, 2007, p. 146.

17 World Economic Forum, *Global Risk 2007: A Global Risk Network Report* (2007).

18 Roxburg (2009), pp. 1–9.

19 NIC (2000).

20 UN University, *State of the Future (1997–2006)* (see note 4).

21 Shell (1998).

22 Hamel (2000). The author is not centered on the issues of globalization, but the book implicitly assumes that corporations will become more and more globalized.

References and further reading

Abid Aslam, 'Planet Faces Nightmare Forecasts as Chinese Consumption Grows and Grows', *One World News*, 10 March, 2005.

Ansoff, H. I., 'Managing Strategic Surprise by Response to Weak Signals', *California Management Review*, vol. XVIII no. 2, 1975.

Bello, Walden, 'The Struggle for a Deglobalized World', Focus on the Global South, September 2000. Available at <http://www.corpwatch.org/article.php?id=322>.

Beneviste, Guy, *The Twenty-First Century Organization: Analyzing Current Trends – Imagining the Future.* San Francisco, CA: Jossey-Bass, 1994. Presents two scenarios of the organization in the twenty-first century.

Doremus, Paul N., William W. Keller, Louis W. Pauly and Simon Reich, *The Myth of the Global Corporation.* Princeton, NJ: Princeton University Press, 1998.

Economist, The, 'A Survey of Globalization', 29 September–5 October 2001.

Doz, Yves L., José dos Santos and Peter Williamson, *From Global to Metanational: How Companies Win in the Knowledge Economy.* Boston, MA: Harvard Business School Press, 2002.

Friedman, Thomas L., *The Lexus and the Olive Tree: Understanding Globalization.* New York: Farrar, Strauss & Giroux, 1999.

Ghoshal, Sumantra and Christopher A. Bartlett, *The Individualized Corporation: A Fundamental Approach to Management.* New York: HarperCollins, 1997.

Glen, Jerome Theodore Gordon, *1998 State of the Future.* Washington, DC: American Council for the United Nations University, 1999.

Hagel, John III and Marc Singer, 'Unbundling the Corporation' *Harvard Business Review* 77(2) March/April 1999, pp. 133–44.

Hamel, Gary, *Leading the Revolution.* Boston, MA: Harvard Business School Press, 2000.

Hammond, Allen, *Which World? Scenarios for the 21st Century.* Washington, DC: Island Press, Shearwater Books, 1998.

Harvey, Michael, Mirolad Novicevic and Timothy Kiessling, 'Hypercompetition and the Future of Global Management in the Twenty First Century', *Thunderbird International Business Review,* 43(5), 2001, pp. 599–616.

Heilbroner, Robert, *21st Century Capitalism.* New York: W.W. Norton, 1993. Presents five scenarios of capitalism in the twenty-first century.

Huntington, Samuel P., *The Clash of Civilizations and the Remaking of the World Order.* London: Simon & Schuster, 1997.

Institute for the Future (IFTF), *1990 Ten Year Forecast,* Corporate Associates Program, Menlo.

International Bank for Reconstruction and Development, *Global Economic Prospects, Managing the New Wave of Globalization.* Washington, DC: The World Bank, 2007.

Laszlo, Ervin, *Vision 2020: Reordering Chaos for Global Survival.* New York, NY: Gordon & Breach, 1994. Presents world environment scenario in the twenty-first century.

Maddison, Angus, 'Chinese Economic Performance in the Long-Run', *OECD Development Centre Studies,* 1998.

Mitroff, Ian I., *Business Not as Usual: Rethinking Our Individual, Corporate, and Industrial Strategies for Global Competition.* San Francisco, CA: Jossey-Bass, 1997. Presents four scenarios of US development into the twenty-first century.

National Intelligence Council (NIC), *Global Trends 2025: A Dialogue about the Future with Non Government Experts,* December 2000, p. 34. Available at <http://www.dni.gov/nic/NIC_205_project.html>.

OECD, IMF, World Bank, UN, *A Better World for All.* Paris: OECD, 2000.

OECD, *Policies to Enhance Sustainable Development.* Paris: OECD, 2001.

Rodrik, Dani, *'Has Globalization Gone Too Far?'.* Washington, DC: Institute for International Economics, 1997.

Roxburg, Charles, 'The Use and Abuse of Scenarios', *McKinsey Quarterly*, November 2009.

Rugman, Alan, *The End of Globalization: A New and Radical Analysis of Globalization and What it Means for Business.* London: Random House, 2000.

Saari, David J., *Global Corporations and Sovereign Nations: Collision or Cooperation?* Westport, CT: Quorum Books, 1999.

Sheffield, Charles, Alonso Marceto and Morton A. Kaplan (eds). *The World of 2044 – Technological Development and the Future of Society.* St. Paul, MN: Paragon House, 1994. A global economy scenario to the year 2044.

Shell, *Global Scenarios 1998–2015.* London: Shell 1998. Available at <http://www.shell.com>.

Stiglitz, Joseph E., *Globalization and Its Discontents,* New York: W.W.W. Norton & Company, National Intelligence Council, 2002.

Taleb, Nassim Nicholas, *The Black Swan: the Impact of the Highly Improbable.* London: Allen Lane, 2007.

UNEP, *Global Environment Outlook..* CARY, NC: Oxford University Press, 1999, p. 4.

United Nations Department of Economics and Social Affairs, *The Global Social Crisis: Report on the World Social Situation 2011.* New York, NY: United Nations, 2011. Available at <http://social.un.org/index/ReportontheWorldSocialSituation/2011.aspx>.

Wack, Pierre, 'Scenarios: Uncharted Waters Ahead', *Harvard Business Review,* September–October 1985a, pp. 73–89.

Wack, Pierre, 'Scenarios: Shooting the Rapids, *Harvard Business Review,* November–December 1985b, pp. 139–49.

White, James (ed.), *Global Climate Change: Linking Energy, Environment, Economy, and Equity.* New York: Plenum Press, 1992. Presents energy scenarios in the twenty-first century.

World Bank, *World Development Report 2000/2001: Attacking Poverty.* Washington, DC: World Bank, 2001.

World Economic Forum, *Global Risk 2011.* Sixth edition. Wharton School Risk Center, 2011.

GLOSSARY[1]

Absorption mode of integration
According to Jemison and Haspeslagh, absorption acquisitions take place between companies operating in similar industries and business contexts. The objective here is to achieve as rapidly as possible the necessary synergies through consolidation and rationalization of activities.

Adjusted Present Value (APV) country risk
Adjusted Present Value (APV) is a technique of discounted cash flow in which specific downside adverse risks are identified, their impact on the cash flow is calculated, a probability of their occurrence is determined, the cash flows are adjusted using the probabilistic distribution, the cash flows are translated into the investor's currency using the Purchasing Power Parity differences as a proxy for currencies fluctuation and cash flows are discounted using the investor's cost of capital.

Alliance
An alliance is the sharing of capabilities between two or several firms with the view of enhancing their competitive advantages and/or creating new business without losing their respective strategic autonomy. Alliances can take several legal forms from simple long-term contracts to equity joint ventures.

Arbitrage
Economic arbitrage exists when it is possible to buy a product in one market and simultaneously sell it in another market at a higher price. Dealers in foreign exchange often use arbitrage on foreign currencies that are not exactly quoted at the same rate of exchange on different markets. With electronic transactions it is possible to buy and sell simultaneously. Commodities traders use also arbitrage. By extension the concept is often used even if there is no simultaneity: for instance difference in taxation between countries in free trade areas may take advantage of arbitrage opportunities.

Asymmetric development
In international economics, economic development is considered as asymmetric when countries develop at considerably different rates. For instance, the gap in revenues between African and Western countries has increased over time, showing a strong asymmetry.

Back office
Refer to those activities of a firm that are not in contact with customers such as warehousing, IT, accounting or the kitchen in a restaurant.

Bargaining range
In a negotiation the difference between the buyer's and the seller's reservation prices. If the seller's reservation price is higher than the buyer's reservation price negotiation is not feasible.

Best practices
Any practice, knowledge, know-how, experience, that has been proven to be valuable or effective within one organization that may have applicability to other organizations (this definition is due to Chevron Corporation). For instance if one subsidiary of a multinational company has developed a successful way to launch a product, this may be considered as a best practice that can possibly be transferred to other subsidiaries. Professor Sulanzki has pinpointed that there are a lot of difficulties in transferring best practices between units of the same company. He calls this 'stickiness'.

Blue Ocean strategy
A term given by Professors Chan Kim and Renée Mauborgne to define innovative strategies based on redefining completely the components of a business system and creating a new market space.

Bottom of the Pyramid
According to Prahalad the 'Bottom of the Pyramid' in emerging countries is comprised of the largest proportion of the population located at the lower end of the income spectrum, who are willing to consume goods that are of good quality but lower at price level, adapted formulation and packaging.

BOT
BOT (Build Operate and Transfer) is an infrastructure construction or maintenance contract by which the project manager is not only in charge of the construction but also of the management of operations. At the end of a given period the infrastructure is handed over to the customer. The project manager is responsible for the output and is paid on the basis of a predetermined price per unit of output ($ per kilowatt/hour, $ per toll fee, $ per cubic meter of water, etc.). For instance, a Western electricity company that build or take over a power generation plant in China or a water treatment company managing the water distribution network in Jakarta. There are many derivatives of BOT:

- BOO (Build Operate and Own), the project manager keeps ownership.
- BOOT (Build Own Operate and Transfer). The project manager has full ownership of the infrastructure during the period of operation.
- ROT (Refurbish Operate and Transfer), similar to BOT but with old installations to refurbish.

Bribe
A form of direct corruption, generally a cash payment or a bank transfer to an overseas account.

Bricks and mortar
As opposed to Internet-based operations, brick and mortar operations are those that require tangible fixed assets to operate: factories, branches, stores and so on.

BRICS
Refers to Brazil, Russia, India, China and South Africa but becomes more and more a term to name emerging countries.

Browsers
A software application used to locate and display web pages. The most popular browsers are Netscape Navigator, Microsoft Internet Explorer, and most recently Mozilla Firefox. All of these are graphic browsers, which means that they can display graphics as well as text. (Definition from GreatNexus Webmaster Resources)

Business etiquette
The set of body gestures, dress code, way of expressing yourself, social behaviour and attitude that are considered as proper in a given business circle. For instance business etiquette in Japan requires a ceremonious exchange of business cards.

Business strategy
There are many definitions of business strategy. In this book we offer the following definition: A company business strategy is a set of fundamental choices, which define its long-term objectives, its value proposition to the market, how it intends to build and sustain a competitive business system and how it organizes itself.

Californization
This word has been used by Kenichi Ohmae, in his book *Triad Power* to describe the world convergence of consumers' tastes, particularly among young people.

Capabilities fit
In an alliance or an acquisition, capabilities fit assessment consists in determining whether the respective contributions of the partners in an alliance or the combination of assets, resources and competences in a merger or acquisition are supplementing or complementing each other. When performing a capabilities fit analysis you should first determine the required resources, assets and competencies needed for competitiveness of the alliance or the merged entity. Then you draw for each partner the specific contribution in each element of the value chain. Then in the last phase you determine the potential gap to be filled by joint investment and you evaluate whether the mutual contributions plus the additional investments make the future alliance effective.

Career plan
The planned evolution of a person in an organization in terms of potential future functions, job rotation and training.

Center of excellence
An organizational unit (plant, laboratory, product development center, etc.) that has developed a high quality particular expertise that can possibly be transferred to other units.

Clusters
Professor Michael Porter in his book *Competitive Advantage of Nations* uses the term 'clusters' to describe regions of the world in which some industries have developed a high level of competitiveness thanks to a supporting demand, supply and competitive context.

Coalition alliance
Coalitions are alliances in which competitors, distributors and suppliers in the same industry put together their capabilities to develop markets or to establish a common standard.

Co-location
People or organizational units physically located at the same site.

Comparative advantage
The theory of comparative advantage is commonly referred to as the 'Ricardian model'. The original description of the idea can be found in the 'Essay on the External Corn Trade' by Robert Torrens in 1815. David Ricardo formalized the idea using a compelling, yet simple, numerical example in his 1817 book entitled *On the Principles of Political Economy and Taxation*. According to the principle of comparative advantage, gains from trade follow from allowing an economy to specialize. If a country is relatively better at making wine than wool, it makes sense to put more resources into wine, and to export some of the wine to pay for imports of wool. This is even true if that country is the world's best wool producer, since the country will have more of both wool and wine than it would have without trade. A country does not have to be best at anything to gain from trade. The gains follow from specializing in those activities which, at world prices, the country is relatively better at, even though it may not have an absolute advantage in them. Because it is relative advantage that matters, it is meaningless to say a country has a comparative advantage in nothing. The term is one of the most misunderstood ideas in economics, and is often wrongly assumed to mean an absolute advantage compared with other countries. (This definition comes from the International Study Centre at <http://internationalecon.com/v1.0/ch40/40c000.html> for the first part and the World Trade Organisation website for the second part.)

Compensation
Remuneration and benefits given to a person for a given job. Refers to remuneration of employees.

Competencies
Refer to collective know-how of an organization. This know-how can be technological or managerial. Competencies can be a source of competitive advantage if the know-how is difficult to buy, replicate or imitate by competitors. Some competencies are called 'core competencies' when they are specific to a firm.

Constellations
A form of alliance with multiple partners. Doz & Hamel identified three types of constellations: networks, portfolios and webs. Alliance networks are those to which multiple partners contribute to one goal, increase reach, adopt a common standard or promote a new technology. Alliance portfolios are those in which a company enters into a partnership with multiple companies. Alliance webs are those in which multiple partners contribute and benefit interdependently.

Convergence
Theory according to which societies become more and more similar. This concept is used in international marketing to describe the fact that consumers tend to progressively behave the same way across the world.

Corporate culture
The set of values and beliefs that are shared by employees in a corporation.

Corporate strategy
In a multi-business corporation, the corporate strategy consists in defining its long-term objectives, selecting its business portfolio, allocating resources across businesses and designing its organizational structure, processes and systems.

Corruption
The definition of corruption given by Transparency International is: 'the abuse of public office for private gain'. Corruption involves a corruptor (the person who delivers the private gain) and a corrupted (the person who receives it). As compensation the corruptor expects some favor or gain from the corrupted.

Co-specializations
Co-specialization alliances are alliances in which partners combine complementing capabilities.

Cost of capital
The cost of capital is the cost at which future cash flows are discounted in order to obtain the Net Present Value (NPV) of an investment. Generally the cost of capital is calculated as the weighted average of cost of debts (interest on loans) and cost of equity (the minimum return that shareholders are expecting from their own investment).

Cost leadership
According to Professor Michael Porter, cost leadership is a strategy by which firms gain and sustain competitive advantage thanks to a lower cost position than their competitors. Generally cost leadership is linked to size: the higher the size, the higher the economies of scale and hence the lower the costs.

Country diamond
Term used by Professor Michael Porter in his book *The Competitive Advantage of Nations* to describe the four context dimensions that characterize the competitiveness of a country (or a cluster – see above). The four dimensions are:

- a context that encourages vigorous competition and encourages investment
- the presence of related and supporting industries
- demanding customers
- the quality of resources (human capital, natural resources, infrastructure, etc.).

Country life cycle
The theory according to which countries follow a development path from emerging to maturity.

Country risk analysis
Set of techniques used to assess how risky a country is. The four dimensions of country risks are: political, economic, competitive and operational.

Country stock market beta
A measure of risk developed by Professor Don Lessard comparing the volatility of a country stock market with another one.

Cross-listing
Refers to the listing of a corporation on several world stock markets.

Cultural fit
In an alliance or an acquisition, cultural fit assessment consists in determining whether the companies involved exhibit similar or dissimilar values and ways of doing business.

Cultural heritage
The values and norms that are the result of past historical experience.

Currency swaps
Technique of currency risk hedging. It consists in contracts intermediated by a swap bank that is matching long-term loans issued by two companies in their respective currency zone for use in the other company currency zone. Company X borrows in currency A to be used in country B with a loan repayment generated in currency B, while company Y borrows in currency B to be used in country A with a loan repayment generated in currency A.

Customer value curve
The set of factors that customers explicitly or implicitly consider valuable for them in a product or service. Also called 'customer utility curve'. Customer value curve can be used by firms to compare their product or service offering with that of their competitors. Customer value curves are one of the main tools used by the strategic approach designed by Professsors Kim and Mauborgne called 'Value Innovation'.

Cybercrimes
All kind of threats to property (or sometimes to human physical integrity) through the Internet. The most frequent cybercrimes are the diffusion of electronic viruses and the illegal access to databases to steal money or information.

Death valley
A frequent phenomenon encountered in joint ventures and alliances at the early stage of implementation when partners discover unexpected behavior or surprises. Death valley can degenerate into deep conflicts.

Deglobalization
A neologism used by ATTAC, an anti-globalization NGO, to recommend that countries (particularly developing countries) reorientate their production to serve local markets and not global ones.

Differentiation
How firms position themselves differently to their competitors. According to Professor Michael Porter, differentiation is a strategy by which firms gain and sustain competitive advantage thanks to superior product functionalities, superior service and superior quality that create 'barriers to imitation'.

Documentary credit
A well-established technique of trade financing. The principle is that an importer of goods mandates his bank to issue a letter of credit that guarantees the exporter that he will be paid

on receipt of the shipping documents establishing the proof that goods have been actually delivered to the transport company.

Dotcom companies
Companies operating essentially though the Internet.

Dotted-lines relationship
Term used to describe a non-hierarchical relationship between individuals or organizational units but that however need to establish some kind of mutual reporting.

Due diligence
The investigation that a potential acquirer performs in order to value a targeted asset. Originally due diligence was essentially financial. More recently it is also applied to non-financial elements such as managerial capabilities and culture.

e-Commerce
Generic term to describe commercial transactions through the Internet.

Eco-friendly capital investments
Factories and facilities designed and built with a low environment impact perspective.

Electronic Data Interchange (EDI)
The sharing of data between a supplier and a customer used to place orders and settle transactions electronically.

Electronic marketplaces
Internet-based procurement websites.

Emerging countries
Countries that exhibit: a) a high economic growth, b) an increasing development of a middle class, c) a high degree of infrastructure investment, d) an opening of their market to international trade and investment.

Emerging countries champions
Companies based in emerging countries and that can claim to be globally competitive.

Entry modes
The kind of operation that a foreign investor is setting in order to operate in a country. Entry mode describes the legal form of the operation as well as the size of the investment that the foreigner is willing to make. The main types of entry modes are: wholly owned investment, acquisition, joint venture or licensing.

Environmental crisis
An ecological disaster.

Ethics
The codes of conduct that guide a non-corrupted behavior.

Expatriates
People employed in one country with a contract originating in another country. Frequently designates managerial personnel sent by corporate headquarters to work in foreign subsidiary.

Explicit knowledge
Knowledge that can be documented precisely and therefore that can be communicated and transferred.

Export credit agencies
Government agencies that act like insurers and cover the risks associated with international trade and investments. As a result the exporter and the foreign investor can benefit from export credits.

Extractive agenda
When partners in a strategic alliance are primarily motivated to enter into an alliance in order to learn something from their partner or to obtain some resources that otherwise they would have difficulties in obtaining by themselves.

Fair process
A management practice that consists of:

- **Engagement:** Involvement of relevant people, seeking inputs and allowing them to challenge ideas
- **Explanation:** everybody involved or affected should understand why a particular decision was taken
- **Expectation:** defining clearly role and responsibilities.

According to Professors Kim and Mauborgne, fair process is needed in order to get people involved in difficult or innovative decisions.

First-mover advantages
The competitive advantages that a company gains by being the first or among the first to enter a new market. First-mover advantages can be due to the preemption of existing resources, the creation of a standard or the ability to rapidly create entry barriers for newcomers.

Fit analysis
The study of the possible compatibility between partners in an alliance or between buyers and sellers in an acquisition. There are four types of fit: strategic, capabilities, cultural and organizational.

Forward contracts
Contracts by which the contracting parties commit to buy or sell goods or a currency at a given price on a predetermined date. Foreign exchange forward contracts are a classic way to hedge against exchange rates fluctuation.

Franchise
A contract by which the owner of a brand (the franchiser) grants an individual or a company (the franchisee) the right to operate under its brand. Franchise contracts are generally granted under the condition that the franchisee respects a certain number of quality practices defined by the franchiser.

Front office
Activities that are in direct contact with customers.

Future contracts
Contracts by which the contracting parties agree to perform a transaction at an anticipated date under predetermined conditions. Forward contracts are one category of future contract but future contracts can also cover agreements that are not necessarily based on a financial transaction.

GINI ratio
Measures the extent to which the distribution of income in an economy deviates from a perfectly equalitarian distribution of income. The ratio varies from 0 for perfect equality to 1 for perfect inequality.

Global accounts
Global accounts are customers that are operating globally and for whom the suppliers negotiate and manage the delivery of goods or services in an integrated way across borders.

Global business strategy
A business strategy that defines the ways and where a company decides to compete across borders.

Global Capability Index (GCI)
An index to measure to what extent a company has globalized its assets and personnel: how assets or personnel are distributed across the world.

Global chess
The ability for a multinational company to cross-subsidize one country by another in order to compete more effectively in that country. For instance, selling at a loss in country A to oblige competitor in country B to lower its profits in country A.

Global hub
A highly centralized organization such as worldwide functional or global product structure.

Global industries
Industries in which, in order to survive, competitors need to operate in the key world markets in an integrated and coordinated way.

Global managers
Managers whose career is made up of successive appointments in different countries.

The global/multi-local mapping
Analytical and graphic tool developed to position industries and industry segments according to the relative importance of global and local forces.

Global positioning
Global positioning consists of the definition of the various value propositions for the products or services of the company, corresponding to the types of segment and country in which the company wants to compete.

Global Revenue Index (GRI)
An index measuring the distribution of sales of a company across the major regions of the world relative to the distribution of markets across the same regions.

Global solution selling
The sale of a valuable solution to a client located in a particular country that implies the mobilization of resources and competencies of several subsidiaries across the world on the part of the seller.

Global warming
Increasing warming of the planet due to greenhouse effects resulting from emission of CO_2.

Globalization
The progressive change in competitive structures from multinational (country by country) to global (worldwide).

Grand tour
The fact-finding trip of corporate executives in countries where the company is considering foreign investment with a view to assessing the countries' attractiveness.

Hedging
A technique of reducing risk by settling risky transactions at predetermined fixed terms. Used very often to manage risks resulting from currency variations.

Hierarchy of needs
A theory developed by Maslow according to which humans start by satisfying their primary needs and progressively move up to more intellectual and artistic needs when the lower levels of need are satisfied.

Hub
In the context of global business a hub is a location that serves and supports several other locations in a region. Typically in a hub services and logistical activities would be concentrated: for example Singapore or Hong Kong for Asia, Geneva, London or Brussels for Europe.

Industry analysis
The systematic analysis and forecast of demand, competitive forces and risk in an industry.

Industry culture
The norms and ways of thinking that are common to people operating in a given industry.

Innovation
The process of inventing and developing new concepts, products and services.

Integration process
The process by which various firms and activities are made to work together. Following a merger, acquisition or an alliance, the post-merger integration process organizes the way two firms work together from partial to full integration of their activities.

Intellectual property
The legal ownership of a patent, a design, a brand, an artistic or a literary production.

Internal stickiness
The difficulty for different units of an organization to exchange ideas and practices.

International division
An organizational design for managing international operations by centralizing the control of geographical subsidiaries in one division reporting to top management.

International product life cycle
The theory according to which new products are launched sequentially over time internationally from developed countries to less developed ones.

Joint venture
The legal form by which two or more companies organize their collaboration. Joint ventures can be done under the form of equity contribution or under a contractual arrangement.

Joint venture decay
The phenomenon that typically occurs in a joint venture after several years when partners have obtained what they wanted from their collaboration and no longer see the value of the joint venture.

Knowledge management
A managerial process by which companies capture and distribute internally strategic, commercial and technical information.

Leading and lagging
A technique of international cash management consisting of delaying or accelerating the payment of expenses and the receipt of income according to the strengths and weaknesses of the currencies involved.

Learning alliances
Alliances whose main purpose is for the companies involved to generate new knowledge or to learn knowledge from each other.

Licensing
A contract by which the owner of a product, a service or a process (the licensor) authorizes another party (the licensee) to manufacture the product, deliver the service or use the process for its own benefit.

Local manager
A manager recruited and operating in a country.

Logistics
The physical handling, transportation and storage of goods.

Macroeconomic indicators
Measures that indicate the economic characteristics of a country such as production, growth, income, trade and investments.

Market segmentation
The division of consumers into categories according to different criteria and different demand characteristics.

Marketing positioning
The choice by a company of the market segments in which it wants to compete and the definition of the various elements of its approach to those segments (its 'value propositions').

Matrix
An organizational design in which the line of command is shared by two or more decision-makers. In the global firm the typical matrix is either function and geography or business and geography.

Megacities
An urban area with a population of 10 million or more.

Mentoring
In global firms the human resource management process by which expatriate personnel are coached by a 'mentor' at the corporate level.

Metanational
A global firm that leverages innovation across countries.

Middle-class effect
The effect by which the size of the middle class increases more rapidly than the average growth of the economy.

Missions
Short-term international assignments.

Modularization
The technology of producing goods and services by subcomponents that can be assembled according to various configurations.

Multinational companies
Companies that operate in different countries.

National and ethnic culture
Norms and values that are characteristic of a nation or an ethnic or religious group.

Netting
An international cash management system by which only the net cash movements are transferred across borders. Netting minimizes foreign exchange risk exposure.

Network externalities
The economic benefits accrued to a product or service derived from the number of existing users of this product or from related products. Examples of network externalities are products based on technical standards such as mobile phones, video disks, IT systems or services such as auctions.

Networked organization
An organization that manages its activities though a strong exchange of information and coordination of actions between internal and external units through partnerships and alliances.

Offshoring
The production of goods and services outside the country in which a company is located. Generally offshoring takes place in low-cost countries. It is also known as 'de-localization'.

Offsourcing
The purchasing of goods and services outside the country in which a company is located. Generally offsourcing takes place in low-cost countries.

Options
The ability to make an investment with the possibility to retreat with minimum costs.

In the financial sector an option is materialized by a tradable instrument that allows the investor to exercise its full investment if the conditions are favorable or not to exercise if the conditions are not favorable. In the nonfinancial world options are called 'real options' and consist of making a minimum investment with the possibility not to continue if the conditions are not favorable.

Organizational culture
The set of values, beliefs and behavioral norms that are predominant in an organization.

Organizational fit
The ability for two organizations in an alliance, a merger or an acquisition to synchronize their structures, systems and processes.

Organizational processes
The way decisions are made and actions are controlled in an organization: Processes can be bureaucratic, mechanistic, participative, top-down, bottom-up, etc.

Organizational structure
The way the chain of command, the roles and functions are defined in an organization. For example, centralized or decentralized structures; flat or hierarchical structures; structure by functions, products, or country; or matrix structures.

Piggybacking
The practice for large multinational firms to help their smaller sub-contractors or suppliers to set operations close to their own foreign investments.

Pre-acquisition process
The process by which the decision to acquire is made, the acquisition target selected, the valuation and negotiation conducted.

Post-acquisition process
The process by which an acquisition is integrated after the deal has been signed.

Power distance
A dominant social value in a group or a society by which group members accept authority. In a high-power distance society people are obedient and respectful of leaders while in a low-power distance they can openly challenge the views of the leader.

Preservation mode of integration
A mode of post-merger integration that consists in keeping the acquired company autonomous from the acquiring company.

Procurement
The purchase of good and services.

Professional culture
The dominant values, beliefs and norms that members of a profession share. Examples are medical culture, engineering culture, accounting culture, academic culture, etc.

Project valuation
The techniques used to calculate the return or the price of a projected investment. Discounted cash flow is the most used valuation technique.

Real option
See options above.

Regionalization
The concentration of the international expansion of a company in a particular region of the world.

Representative offices
A limited form of implementation in a foreign country. In a representative office people make contacts, collect information and negotiate contracts but do not sign or implement the contracts.

Reservation price
In a negotiation the economic limit above which a buyer will not buy or below which the seller will not sell.

Scenarios
The description of possible anticipated future states of affairs.

Segmentation
The division of a market or a business into sub-components that share similar features. Examples are the division of consumers by income levels.

Silent languages
The non-verbal expression of opinions, emotions, decisions. Silent languages are important modes of expression in certain societies and for the person external to that society it becomes critical to understand the meaning of physical gestures and facial movements that express opinions, emotions and decisions.

Social network
For sociologists a social network is a group of individuals that are connected to each other. Recently websites like Facebook, Twitter or LinkedIn are platforms to connect people via the Internet.

Socialization
The process by which newcomers in a group or an organization are initiated to the norms, values and practice of the group.

Socially Responsible Investing (SRI)
Investment in companies that are respectful of the environment and human rights.

Sprinkler model
The simultaneous launch of a new product in all markets.

Stand-alone value
The value of an acquisition calculated without the potential synergies that the acquisition may bring. If the acquired company is listed on a stock market, the stand-alone value is the market value. Alternatively the stand-alone value has to be calculated by the classic valuation techniques: discounted cash flow, net assets, comparables, etc.

Strategic fit
In an alliance or an acquisition, strategic fit is where the parties engaged have compatible objectives and are committed to the success of the association.

Sub-optimization
The negative or lower economic performance resulting from one or more decisions ignoring the overall effect on a system. An instance of sub-optimization would be to adopt a global price, ignoring the adverse effect it can have in different markets that have different demand curves.

Symbiotic mode of integration
A mode of post-merger integration that consists in first keeping the acquired company autonomous from the acquiring company and progressively integrating the functions for which real synergies exist.

Synergies value
The calculation of the additional value brought in a merger, an acquisition or an alliance by the integration of the entities concerned.

Tacit knowledge
Knowledge that cannot be codified.

Technology transfer
The process by which knowledge is transferred from one individual, group or organization to another individual, group or organization. Technology can be transferred through documents when the knowledge is codified or though apprenticeship and collaboration when the knowledge is tacit.

Time incompressibility
When a capability needs as much time in order to be replicated as originally spent to create it. Time incompressibility makes imitation difficult and gives the creator of the capability a first mover advantage.

Transaction exposure
Transaction exposure is the risks that currency fluctuations impose on existing contractual engagements and that may result in unexpected losses.

Translation exposure
Translation exposure reflects the effects that changes in currency values have on the financial statements of global firms, and therefore on their profits and book valuation.

Transnational
Two meanings:

- the meaning given by the United Nations to designate multinational corporations;
- an international organizational design model described by Bartlett and Ghoshal that does not focus on organizational structure but on management processes and culture.

Turnkey project
A project in which the customer contracts out the whole project to a specialized engineering firm or to a consortium of equipment suppliers. The project manager takes care of completion at a fixed price and delivery time and hands over the project to the customer after the start-up phase. The project manager is financially responsible for the whole amount of the contract.

Value chain
The set of activities needed for the creation, production and commercialization of a product or service.

Value curve
The set of product or service attributes that customers value such as performance, quality, responsiveness, price, convenience, etc.

Value proposition
The set of product or service attributes such as performance, quality, responsiveness, price, convenience, etc. that companies propose to customers.

Values
Set of beliefs and code of conduct to which a person or an organization adheres.

Waterfall model
The sequential launch of a new product market after market.

Wholly owned operations
An organization that is controlled entirely by another organization.

Window of opportunity
The span of time at the beginning of a market opportunity when the market is not saturated and it is possible to enter without creating overcapacity.

[1] This glossary is the sole responsibility of the author

INDEX OF SUBJECTS

A

Absorption, mode of integration, 149, 161, 162
Acculturation, 298, 340–1, 346–7
Acquisition, 47
Adjusted Present Value country risk (APV), 364, 368
Advertizing, 234
Alliance, 47, 103–43
Alliance constellation, 132, 133
Alliance manager, 127
Ambition, 26, 28, 31, 33, 35, 51
Arbitrage, 8–9, 16, 20, 45
Arbitrage clause, 128
Asymmetric development, 460

B

Back office, 256
Barriers to internationalization, 53, 54
Best practices, 296, 299
Beta for risk premium, 368
Blue Ocean Strategy, 43
BOT, 264
Bottom of the pyramid, 405–6
Bribe, 422–8
BRICS, 401–4, 415
Business etiquette, 325
Business practices, 325–6
Business strategy, 27, 29

C

'Californization', 6, 229
Capabilities building, 27, 28
Capabilities fit, 108, 116, 118
Career plan, 343
Centre of excellence, 297
Child labour, 432, 435–6, 438, 442
Clusters, 182–3, 189, 195, 316–17
Coalition alliance, 112
Code of conduct, 442
Co-location, 290–1, 296–8
Comparative advantage, 31
Compensation, 339, 341, 344–6
Competencies of plant, 254
Competitive context, 187
Convergence, 228–9
Corporate culture, 119, 121, 140, 312, 315
Corporate social responsibility, 421, 439, 441
Corporate strategy, 27, 28, 50
Corruption, 412, 423–7, 439, 469, 474
Co-specializations, 107
Cost leadership, 39, 42, 43, 46
Country attractiveness, 174–7
'Country diamond', 189
Country life cycle, 183
Country risk analysis, 190–1
Cross-cultural teams, 320
Cross-listing, 369–70
Cultural fit, 108, 116, 119
Cultural heritage, 315, 332
Currency swaps, 366
Customer value curve, 229, 230, 243, 246
Cybercrime, 463

D

'Death valley', 109
Deglobalization, 459
Demography, 459
Differentiation, 43
Documentary credit, 373, 374
'Dotted-lines' relationship, 80
Due diligence, 155–7

E

Ease of doing business, 176, 177, 198, 204
e-business, 14, 267, 270, 272
Economic cultures, 317–19
Electronic Data Interchange (EDI), 259
Electronic marketplaces, 259
Emerging countries, 27, 38, 264, 368, 400–1, 461
Emerging countries champions, 410
Entry modes, 210–11, 217
Environmental problems, 421, 429–30, 463
Ethics, 423, 443
Expatriates, 337, 339–49
Explicit knowledge, 295
Export credit agencies, 373, 394
Export processing zones, 256
Externalization, 295
Extractive agenda, 117–18, 138

F

Fair process, 166
First mover, 208–9
Fit analysis, 116
Foreign Direct Investments (FDI), 5, 7, 70, 135, 194, 257, 403–4
Forward contracts, 366
Franchise, 210, 211, 215–16
Front office, 256
Functional organization, 77–9
Future contracts, 366

G

Geographical organization, 80–7

Global
  accounts, 236–9
  brand, 231–4
  business strategy, 27
  Capability Index, 35–6
  companies, 4, 9, 12
  corporate strategy, 50
  industries, 3, 4, 16
  knowledge management, 295, 298
  leaders, development of, 363
  logistics, 261–2
  managers, 337–9, 363
  manufacturing networks, 253–6
  marketing positioning, 242
  pricing, 235–6
  positioning, 32, 38, 42, 51
  Revenue Index, 67, 68–9,
  R&D networks, 286–93
  sales and distribution, 241–2
  services networks, 256–7
  solution selling, 239–41
  sourcing, 258–60
Global/multi-local mapping, 16–17
Global warming, 429–32, 464–5
Globalization, 1–18
'Grand Tour', 193

H

Hedging, 363, 364–368
Hierarchy of needs, 229
Hub, 74, 93, 96, 185, 195
Human rights, 420, 421, 434, 436–9
Hybrid organization, 91

I

Incentives, 178, 187, 189–90
Individualism, 314–15
Individualized corporation, 474–5
Industry analysis, 188–9,
Industry culture, 312
Infrastructure projects, 263–5
Innovation, 284–5, 288–9
Institutional voids, 404
Integration process, 155, 159–62
Intellectual property, 298–9
Interface management, 163
Internal stickiness, 296
International divisions, 91
International product life cycle, 284–5
Internet, 266–73

J

Joint ventures, 135–41
  decay, 139–40
  for market entry, 135

K

Key countries, 37, 207–8
Knowledge management, 295

L

Leading and lagging, 367
Learning alliances, 107, 113, 123, 130, 134
Licensing, 215
Local managers, 337, 338, 349
Localization, 337, 348–9
Location, 249, 251–3
Logistics, *see* global logistics

M

Macroeconomic indicators, 178
Market entry, 47
Market opportunities, 174, 176, 178
Market segmentation, 181–2
Marketing countries, 38
Marketing positioning, 242
Matrix, 84–6
Megacities, 460
Mentoring, 347
Metanational, 296, 476
Middle class, 180–3, 402
'Middle-class effect', 180–1
Missions, 343
Modularization, 230
Multi-business firm, 50
Multinational companies, 2, 3, 4, 7, 8, 9–12, 14, 18, 19, 52, 136

N

National/ethnic culture, 312
Negotiation, 321–5
Netting, 367
Network architecture, 256
Networked organization, 477
Niche player, 39

O

OEM, 261
Offshoring, 250–1, 257
Opportunistic agenda, 138
Options, 366
Options agenda, 117–18
Organizational culture, 71
Organizational design, 71, 75, 79–89
Organizational fit, 108, 116, 121
Organizational processes, 71
Organizational structure, 71, 79, 91–7
Outsourcing, 251, 257

P

Partner analysis, 115
Partner selection, 108, 134, 136–9
Partnership, 47, 53, 59, 105–8, 116–18
Performance evaluation, 350
Plant competencies, 254
Platform countries, 38
Political partner, 137
Positioning, 27, 28, 31–2, 37, 113, 242
Post-acquisition process, 155
Power distance, 314–15
Pre-acquisition process, 155
Preservation mode of integration, 161
Procurement, 253, 255, 258–60, 272
Product standardization, 230
Professional culture, 312
Project valuation, 368

Q

Quality of demand, 178, 181

R

Real option, 217
Recruitment, 349
Regional Headquarters, 95–7
Regionalization, 463
Representative offices, 210, 216
Resource opportunities, 183
Retention of personnel, 349–50

Risk Analysis, *see* county risk analysis
Roles of organization units, 93, 94–5, 251, 253–6
Roles of managers, 126, 352

S

Scenarios, 456–7, 458, 471–4, 481
Segmentation, 228, 230, 233
Selection, 341–2
Sharing agenda, 117–18
'Silent language', 313
Skills, 337, 340, 342–3
Sleeping partner, 136
Small and medium-sized enterprises (SMEs), 51–5
Socialization, 293, 295, 297
Sourcing countries, 38
Sprinkler model, 234
Stand-alone value, 158–9
Strategic exposure, 365
Strategic fit, 108, 116,
Strategic role (of plants), 253–4
Sub-optimization, 236–7
Symbiotic mode of integration, 161
Synergies value, 158

T

Tacit knowledge, 295–7
Technology transfer, 293–5
Tenure, 344
Transaction exposure, 365
Transfer, Adapt, Create model, 47
Transferability of capabilities, 44
Transnational, 35, 49, 67, 92
Trust, 105, 127, 137, 141–2, 214, 468, 469, 470, 475, 476
Turnkey project, 264

U

Uncertainty avoidance, 314–15

V

Valuation, 156–8
Value chain, 40–6, 52–3
Value curve, 38, 39, 229, 230, 236
Value orientation, 312, 314–15
Value proposition, 26–7, 38–9,
Venturing agenda, 117–18, 137

W

Waterfall model, 234
Wholly-owned operations, 211
Window of opportunity, 208–9, 212
Winning spiral, 154, 163, 165

INDEX OF NAMES

A

Aaker, David, 247
Ackenhusen, Mary, 101
Adil, Asif, 147, 225
Adler, Nancy, 333, 336
Akadar, Adhwin, 147, 225
Albert, Michel, 319, 333
Alexander, Marcus, 65
Allen, T.J., 307
Ammer, J., 398
Amsalem, Michel, 307
Anderson, Erin, 225
Ansoff, Igor, 486
Ariño, Africa, xlv, 147
Arnold, David, 225, 247
Ashkenas, Ronald, 172
Asin, Amy, 173
Aslam, Abid, 486
Austin, James, 203

B

Badaracco, Joseph L., 454
Baden-Fuller, Charles, 133, 148
Bailey, Warren, 398
Baker, Michael, 22
Banerjee, Neela, 454
Bank, John, 225
Barnett, Carole, 102
Barnevick, Percy, 353
Barsoux, Jean-Louis, 311, 320, 347, 361
Barth, Karen, 247
Bartholomew, Susan, 360
Bartlett, Christopher, xxxv, xl, xlv, 22, 65, 93, 101, 102, 352, 360, 475, 476, 486
Bartmess, Andrew, 282
Battacharya, Hrishi, 94
Beamish, Paul, 225
Bello, Walden, 486
Beneviste, Guy, 486
Berger, Peter, 333
Berger, Suzanne, 319, 333
Besanko, David, 65
Besouri, Christopher P., 418
Bhasin, Anu, 283
Birkinshaw, Julian, 247
Blacke, James Steward, 342, 348, 360
Bleeke, J.A., 147, 172
Bloch, Nicolas, 419
Bloom, Helen, 361
Boutellier, Roman, 309
Brake, Terence, 333
Brett, Jeanne, 323, 333
Brewer, Thomas, 203
Brown, Lester, 461
Bruntland, G., 454
Budhwar, Pawan, 360
Bughin, Jacques, 283
Burns, Jennifer, 454

C

Cadbury, Sir Adrian, 454
Cadot, Olivier, 454
Campbell, Andrew, 65
Capron, Laurence, 172
Cave, Bill, 257, 283
Cavusgil, S. Tamer, 225
Cerny, Keith, 282
Chaddick, Brad, 203
Chattopadhyay, Amitava, 405, 418
Chiesa, Vitorio, 308
Ching, Poy-Seng, 361
Chu, Chi-Ning, 333
Chui, Michael, 283
Chung, Peter Y., 398
Chwo-Ming, Yu, 102
Ciarlante, Diane, 248
Cladderton, Lisa, 102
Clyde-Smith, Deborah, 102
Coltman, Tim, 282
Connely, Catherine, 225
Contractor, Farouk, 225
Court, David, 418
Cowing, Philippa, 233, 247
Crawford, Robert, 102, 454
Cunningham, Mark, 147

D

Dah-Hsian, Seetoo, 102
Davidson, William, 65, 172
Davies, H., 361
Davis, Stanley M., 102
Dawar, Niraj, 405, 418
DeBettignies, Henri-Claude, 454
de la Torre, José, xlv, 147, 172
Deloumeaux, 257, 283
De Meyer, Arnoud, 173, 252, 256, 282, 308
DeMonaco, Lawrence, 172
Dent, Stephen M., 148
DePamphilis, Donald M., 172
Desei, Mihir, 283
Devinney, Timothy, xlv, 282
Donalson, Thomas, 454
Dore, Ronald, 319, 333
Doremus, Paul N., 65, 486
Dornier, Philippe, 282
Dowling, Peter J., 261
Doz, Yves, xxxv, xl, xlv, 65, 66, 128, 132, 148, 247, 287, 296, 297, 308, 361, 476, 486
Dragonetti, Nicolas, 247
Dranove, David, 65
Dunchin, Faye, 454
Dundee, Thomas W., 454
Dunfee, Thomas, 454
Dunning, John H., xlv

E

Eccles, Robert G., 172
Edstrom, Anders, 342, 361
Engle, Allen D., 361
Erdmenger, Christoph, 455
Ernst, David, 147, 148, 172, 225
Ernst, Ricardo, 282
Eun, Cheol, 398
Evans, Paul, 347, 361
Evans, Philip, 269, 282

F

Fadiman, Jeffrey, 454
Fang, Tony, 325, 333
Farrell, Diana, 181, 203, 419
Faulkner, David O., 65
Ferdows, Kasra, 252–5, 282
Festing, Marion, 361
Finlay, Paul, 66
Fisher, Roger, 333
Flamant, Anne-Claire, 102
Francis, Suzanne, 172
Franko, Larry, 102
Fraser, Jane N., 23
Freeling, Anthony, 234, 248
Friedheim, Cyrus F., 148
Friedman, Milton, 421
Friedman, Thomas I., 486
Frynas, Jedrzeil, 66
Fujimura, Sumie, 102

G

Galbraith, Jay, 342, 361
Gassmann, Olivier, 309
Gatignon, Hubert, 225
Gee, Francesca, 148
Geertz, Clifford, 311, 333
Geringer, J.M., 148
Gersh, Ulrich, 203, 419
Ghadar, Fariboz, 172
Ghauri, Pervez N., 225
Ghemawat, Pankaj, xlv, 66, 172
Ghoshal, Sumantra, xl, xlv, 22, 65, 93, 102, 172, 352, 360, 475, 476, 486
Ghosn, Carlos, 109, 148
Giddy, Ian, 398
Gleason, Eric, 283
Glen, Jack, 225, 471, 486
Glen, Jerome, 471, 485
Goldsmith, Jack, 271
Gomez-Casseres, Benjamin, 148
Gompers, Paul, 225
Goold, Michael, 65
Gordon, Theodore, 471, 486
Gregersen, Hal, 342, 348, 360
Gröschl, Stephan, 361
Guey-Huey, Li, 102
Guisinger, Stephen, 203
Gupta, Anil K., 419

H

Habeck, Max, 172
Hagel, John III, 486
Haig, Ronald, 282
Halevy, Tammy, 148
Hall, Edwards, 313, 333
Hamel, Gary, 66, 128, 132, 148, 486
Hammond, Allen, 471, 486
Hampden-Turner, Charles, 314, 319, 333
Hanawa, Yoshikazu, 109
Hankinson, Graham, 233, 247
Harbison, John, 173
Harrigan, Kathryn, 148
Hart, Susan, 6, 22
Harvey, Michael, 486
Harzing, Anne-Wil, 361
Haspeslagh, Philippe, 161, 172
Hawawini, Gabriel, 172, 398
Hazan, Eric, 283
Hedlund, Gunnar, xlv
Heenan, David, 66
Heilbroner, Robert, 486
Hennart, Jean-Francois, 398
Henneben, Ludovic, 454
Herbert, Louis, 148
Hess, David, 454
Hill, Charles W. L., xlv
Hitt, Michael A., xlv
Hofstede, Geert, 313, 361
Hogan, Harold, 102
Holliday, Charles, 454
Holmes, Gary, 173
Howell, Llewellyn, 203
Hsieh, Tsun-yan, 361
Humes, Samuel, 23
Huntington, Samuel, 316, 487
Husselby, David, 435
Hwang, Peter, 225
Hyde, Dana, 172

I

Ifzal, Ali, 419
Inglehart, Ronald, 333
Inkpen, Andrew, xlv, 148
Isabella, Lynn A., 127, 148
Isono, Isone, 172

J

Jackson, Terence, 333
James, Mini, 203
Jasperen, Frederick, 225
Jemison, Wiliam, 161, 172
Jenkins, Rhys, 454
Joachimsthaler, 247

K

Kamel, Mellahi, xlv
Kang, Jun-Koo, 398
Kaplan, Morton A., 487
Karas, Homis, 419
Karch, Nancy J., 247
Karmokolias, Yannis, 225
Kaufmann, Daniel, 454
Kavelis, Pavos, 282
Keller, William W., 65, 486
Kennedy, Robert E., 102
Kets De Vries, Manfred, 102, 353, 361
Khanna, Tarun, 404, 419
Khou, Julia, 173
Kiessing, Timothy, 486
Kim, Chan W., 66, 172, 225
Kitching, John, 173
Knoop, Carin-Isabel, 283
Kogut, Bruce, 148, 225
Kolk, A., 454, 455
Koller, T.M., 203
Kotabe, Masaaki, 282
Kremenyuk, Victor, 334
Krishna, L.N., 148
Kröger, Fritz, 172
Kuemmerle, Walter, 308
Kumar, Nirmalya, 308

L

Lanes, Kersten L., 172
Lange, Glenn-Marie, 454
Lasserre, Philippe, 102, 203, 308, 343, 361
Laszlo, Ervin, 454, 487
Latufeku, Alopi, 282
Laurent, André, 311, 315, 334

Lavoie, Johanne, 361
Lawrence, Paul, 334
Lawrence, Robert Z., 23
Lehni, M., 455
Leite, Carlos, 455
Leonard-Barton, Dorothy, 308
Lepineux, François, 454
Lessard, Donald, 173, 368, 398
Leung, T.K.P., 361
Levi-Strauss, Claude, 311, 334
Levitt, Theodore, 229, 247
Lhabitant, F.S., 419
Li, Jiatao, 308
Liebermann, Timothy, 225
Lindner, Andreas, 257, 283
Lloyd-Reason, Lester, 66
Lorenzoni, G., 133, 148
Lorsh, Jay, 334
Lowell, L. Bryan, 23
Luk, S.T.K., 361
Lundan, Sarianna M., xlv
Luo, Yadong, 225

M

Maddison, Angus, 487
Magdelene, Jocelyn, 257, 283
Malnight, Thomas, 102, 248
Mankin, E., 131, 148
Manyika, James, 283
Marceto, Alonso, 487
Mauborgne, Renée, 66, 172
Mauro, Paolo, 455
McCauley, Robert, 370, 398
McLaughlin, 247
Mead, Margareth, 311, 334
Medina, Danielle, 333
Mei, Jianpong, 398
Mellahi, Kamel, 66
Mendenhall, Mark, 361
Michaels, R.E., 23
Micklethwait, John, 23
Midgley, David, 282
Mikko, Kosone, 65
Milberg, William, 283
Miller, Robert, 225
Mirza, Hafiz, 23
Mitchell, David, 173
Mitroff, Ian, 487
Montgomery, Cynthia A., 102
Morrisson, Janet, xlv
Moss Kanter, Rosabeth, 141, 142, 148
Mughan, Terry, 66

N

Narasimhan, Laxman, 418
Naraynada, Das, 248
Nichols, Martha, 455
Noda, Tomo, 247
Nonaka, Ikujiro, 308
Novicevic, Mirolad, 486

O

Ohmae, Kenichi, 6, 22, 66, 229, 248
Olshaysky, R.Z., 23
Oppenheim, Jeremy, 23
Ormiston, Charles., 419
Orsato, Renato, J., 455

P

Palepu, Krishna, 404, 419
Parker, Phil, 229, 248
Parsons, Andrew J., 361
Pauly, Louis W., 65, 486
Pearce, Robert, 308
Pélissié du Rausas, Matthieu, 283
Peng, Mike W., xlv, 225
Perlmutter, Howard, 66
Pernia, Ernesto M., 419
Phanish, Puranam, 308
Pinson, Christian, 248
Plas, Géraldine, 455
Pope, Jérôme, 427, 455
Porter, Lyman, 361
Porter, Michael, 23, 39, 66, 188, 189, 203, 283, 308
Prahalad, C.K., 23, 66, 94, 102, 148, 405, 419
Probert, Joselyn, 173
Pucik, Vladimir, 102, 347, 361
Purshe, William, 173
Purushothaman, Roopa, 419

Q

Qionghua, Hu, 225
Qualls, W., 23
Quelch, John, 248, 361

R

Raiffa, Robert, 334
Ramaswamy, Kannan, xlv
Rangan, Kasturi, 283
Rangan, U., 148
Redding, Gordon, 317, 334, 361, 419
Reed Hall, Edward and Mildred, 333
Reich, R.D., 131, 148
Reich, Simon, 65, 486
Reinhart, Forest, 455
Rennie, Michael W., 66
Resnick, Burce, 398
Ricardo, David, 18, 23
Ricks, David, 310, 334
Rieger, F., 361
Rigman, Tom, 225
Risenbeck, Hajo, 234, 248
Rodrick, Dani, 487
Rogers, Jerry, 203
Ronen, S., 316, 334
Root, Franklin, 225
Rosenweig, Philip, 361
Ross, Jerry, 148
Rottenberg, Stephanie, 361
Roxburg, Charles, 487
Rubin, Beth, 333
Rugman, Alan, 18, 23, 66, 487

S

Saari, David, 487
Said, Remi, 283
Salacuse, Jeswald, 323, 334
Salle, R., 23
Samek, Robert A.P., 361
Santos, José dos, 287, 296, 297, 308, 476, 486
Sarkis, Joseph, 455
Sarkissian, Sergei, 398
Satish, Shankar, 419
Scahus, Robert, 419
Schein, Edward, 334
Schill, Michael, 398
Schmidheiny, Stephan, 454
Schneider, Susan, 311, 320, 334
Schuler, Randall, 360
Schütte, Hellmut, 102, 203, 229, 248, 455
Schwartz, Gordon, 248
Seurat, Sylvere, 308
Shaefer, Scott, 65
Shanley, Mark, 65
Sheffield, Charles, 487
Shengliang, Robert, 308
Shenkar, O., 316, 334
Shih, Stan, 102
Singer, Marc, 486
Singh, Harbir, 173

Singh, Satwinder, 308
Sinha, Jayant, 419
Slone, Robert, 308
Smith, Craig, 455
Smith, Kenneth, 173
Smith Ring, Peter, 147
Smith Shi, Christiana, 247
Solnik, Bruno, 398
Spar, Deborah, 173, 454
Sparrow, Paul, 360
Spekeman, Robert E., 127, 148
Srinivasan, Sarayu, 283
Sroufe, Robert, 455
Stahl, Günter, 342, 362
Stalk, Georges, 66
Steinhubl, Andrew, 172
Stepehenson, Elizabeth, 203, 419
St George, Anthony, 283
Stiglitz, Joseph, 456, 487
Stopford, John, 66
Stulz, René, 370, 398
Stumpf, Siegfried, 334
Subramanian, Rangan, 23, 283
Sun Tzu, 27
Sunshine, Russel, 324, 334
Sutari, Vesa, 361
Szulanski, Gabriel, 296, 308

T

Tahilyani, Naveen, 419
Takeuchi, Hirotaka, 308
Taleb, Nassim, Nicholas, 487
Tallman, Stephen, xlv
Tamhane, Toshan, 419
Tan, Jessica, 419
Tanzi, Vito, 455
Tao, Zhigang, 173
Teboul, James, 283
Thill, George, 308
Tibewrala, Vikas, 248
Tichy, Noel, 102
Tornikoski, Christelle, 361
Toulan, Omar, 247
Traca, Daniel, 436, 441, 454
Tram, Michaël, 172
Trap, Daniel, 454
Trompenaars, Fons, 314, 315, 319, 334
Tung, Rosalie, 362

U

Ury, William, 333
Usunier, Jean Claude, 333

V

Vaish, Paresh, 147, 225
Valla, J., 23
van Heck, Dick, 66
Vankonacker, Wielfried, 225
Van Ruysseveldt, Joris, 361
Van Tulder, Rob, 309, 455
Verbeke, Alain, xlv
Verdin, Paul, 66
Vereecke, André, 252, 256, 282
Vernon, Raymond, 285, 309
Viallet, Claude, 172, 398
Viscio, Albert, 173
Vishwanath, Vijay, 419
Vitaro, Richard, 173
Von Krogh, George, 173
Von Zedtwitz, Maximilian, 309

W

Wack, Pierre, 471, 487
Walker, Thomas, 333
Wang, Haiyan, 419
Wang, J.T., 102
Watts, Philip, 454
Webb, Allen P., 454
Weber, Max., 317
Wei, Shang-Jin, 454, 455
Weiman, Jens, 455
Weinberg, Douglas, 172
Wells, Louis, 66, 283
Welters, Carjin, 454
White, James, 487
Whitley, Richard, 319, 334
Willes, Pierre, 102
Williamson, Peter, 148, 225, 248, 287, 296, 297, 308, 476, 486
Wilson, Dominic, 419
Wilson, Keeley, 308
Wilson, Thomas C., 172
Winkler, Deborah, 283
Witt, Michael, 419
Wong, J.H., 361
Wong-Rieger, D., 361
Wooldridge, Adrian, 23
Wortmann, M., 309
Wurster, Thomas, 269, 282

X

Xie, Zhenzen, 308

Y

Yeung, Arthur, 102
Yip, George S., xxxiv, xl, xlv, 23, 66, 229, 248, 271
Yoshino, Michaels, Y., 102, 148
Yue, Deborah, 308

Z

Zeutchel, Ulrich, 334
Zimmer, Steven, 370, 398
Zoubir, Y., 419

INDEX OF COMPANIES AND ORGANISATIONS

3M, 85, 442

A

A.T. Kearney, 186, 203, 418
Accenture, 240, 267, 268
Acer, 39, 93, 97, 230
Adidas, 442
Advanced Research Projects Agency (ARPA), 266
AES Corporation, 67
Agence Française de Développement, 391
AGF, 234
Air France, 151
Airbus, 133, 262–3
Alcatel-Lucent, 19, 33, 267
Alibaba, 268
Allianz, 234
Alstom, 240
Amazon, 14, 267, 268, 272
AMD, 440
Amnesty International, 437, 450, 454
Amoco, 151
Anglo-American, 67
Anheuser Busch, 167
AOL, 267
Apple, 19, 79, 232
ArcelorMittal, 67, 151
Arco, 151
Ariba, 260, 267, 268, 272
Asahi, 234
Asea Brown Boveri (ABB), 233, 240, 351
Asia Pacific Economic Cooperation (APEC), 462
Asian American Free Labour Association (AAFLA), 422, 436
Asian Development Bank (ADB), 390
Aspen Institute, 450
Association Of South East Asian Nations (ASEAN), 15
Assurance Générales de France (AGF), 234
Astra Zeneca, 67
AT&T, 232, 236
Autobyline, 267
Aventis, 151

B

Bangladesh Garments Manufacturers and Exporters, 88
Barrick Gold Corporation, 67
Basf, 265, 301
Bayer, 440
Benetton, 176
Beri, 19
Bhopal, 422
Bloomberg, 432
BMW, 406
Boeing, 160
Booz-Allen Hamilton, 240, 286
Boston Consulting Group (BCG), 240, 418
Bridgestone, 151
British American Tobacco, 67
British Telecom (BT), 236, 267
Bruntland Report, 429
Business Environment Risk Index (BERI), 176
BYD, 413

C

Cable & Wireless, 236, 267
Canon, 33
Cap Gemini, 240
Carrefour, 38, 39, 46, 206, 402, 407, 440
Caux Round Table, 428
CDC Capital Partners, 390
Cemex, 67, 176, 411
Center for Corporate Citizenship, 441
Central Intelligence Agency, 232
Cisco Systems, 267
Citibank/Citicorp/Citigroup 7, 33, 84, 236, 238–9
CNN, 268
Coca Cola, 6, 231
Columbia Studio, 151
Compagnie Française du Commerce Exterieur (COFACE), 36, 374
Continental, 234
Corning, 133
Corpwatch, 422
Council of Europe, 428

D

Dabhol Power Corporation, 265
Daewoo, 106
DaimlerChrysler, 105, 151, 344, 441
Danone, 142
Datamonitor, 205
Dell, 230
Deloitte, 419
Dentsu, 235

E

eBay, 268, 272, 274–5
ECGD (Export Credit Guarantee Department), 176, 374
Economic Intelligence Unit (EIU), 240
Economist, 486
EDS, 39, 232